NEW ESSAYS ON CANADIAN THEATRE
VOLUME TEN

THEATRE AND (IM)MIGRATION

NEW ESSAYS ON CANADIAN THEATRE
VOLUME TEN

THEATRE AND (IM)MIGRATION
EDITED BY YANA MEERZON

PLAYWRIGHTS CANADA PRESS
TORONTO

LIBRARY AND ARCHIVES CANADA CATALOGUING IN PUBLICATION
Title: Theatre and (im)migration / edtied by Yana Meerzon.
Other titles: Theatre and migration
Names: Meerzon, Yana, editor.
Series: New essays on Canadian theatre ; v. 10.
Description: First edition. | Series statement: New essays on Canadian theatre ; v. 10 | Includes bibliographical references and index.
Identifiers: Canadiana 20190105615 | ISBN 9780369100016 (softcover)
Subjects: LCSH: Canadian drama—History and criticism. | LCSH: Emigration and immigration in literature. | LCSH: Immigrants in literature. | LCSH: Multiculturalism in literature. | LCSH: Nationalism in literature. | LCSH: Immigrants' writings, Canadian. | CSH: Immigrants' writings, Canadian (English) | CSH: Canadian drama (English)—History and criticism. | CSH: Canadian drama (French)—History and criticism.
Classification: LCC PS8619.I56 T44 2019 | DDC C812/.609352691—dc23

Playwrights Canada Press acknowledges that we operate on land, which, for thousands of years, has been the traditional territories of the Mississaugas of the Credit First Nation, Huron-Wendat, Anishinaabe, Métis, and Haudenosaunee peoples. Today, this meeting place is home to many Indigenous peoples from across Turtle Island and we are grateful to have the opportunity to work and play here.

We acknowledge the financial support of the Canada Council for the Arts—which last year invested $153 million to bring the arts to Canadians throughout the country—the Ontario Arts Council (OAC), Ontario Creates, and the Government of Canada for our publishing activities.

To Canadian immigrant theatremakers—
of the past, the present, and the future.

CONTENTS

GENERAL EDITOR'S PREFACE
ROBERTA BARKER

When Ric Knowles founded New Essays in Canadian Theatre in 2011, he set out to complement his previous book series for Playwrights Canada Press, Critical Perspectives on Canadian Theatre in English (CPCTE). Each volume of the CPCTE series offered a critical history of a key topic in Canadian theatre studies; most of the essays featured in these volumes were reprints of important articles in the field, though they were supplemented by newly commissioned works that brought novel perspectives to the questions at hand. With NECT, Knowles chose to foreground new work, underexplored subjects, and fresh viewpoints. As he wrote in his General Editor's Preface for *Performing Indigeneity* (2016), these volumes

> are designed to fill what I perceive to be gaps in the critical record, often . . . taking new approaches, often . . . from minoritized and under-represented perspectives, and in almost every case introducing topics that have not received book-length coverage . . . [T]hey are designed at once to follow, lead, and instantiate new and emerging developments in the field. (v)

Responding to major questions of the present as well as to silences in the past, these books strive to shape the future of the field by opening exciting new avenues of exploration for artists, students, and scholars of Canadian theatre.

The six volumes published under Knowles's editorship richly fulfill this mandate, covering in the process a wide range of topics and approaches. Some, like *Asian Canadian Theatre* (edited by Nina Lee Aquino and Knowles) and *Latina/o Canadian Theatre and Performance* (edited by Natalie Alvarez), illuminate the vibrant and important work of key communities within the Canadian theatrical ecosystem. Others, like *New Canadian Realisms* (edited by Kim Solga and myself) and *Theatres of Affect* (edited by Erin Hurley), strive to reconsider established genres and forms of theatre through new theoretical lenses. The 2015 volume, *Daniel MacIvor* (edited by Richie Wilcox), brings long overdue scholarly attention to the work of one of Canada's most beloved and innovative theatre artists. Finally, 2016's volume makes a particularly mighty contribution: *Performing Indigeneity*, edited by Yvette Nolan (Algonquin) and Knowles, is the first collection of essays on performance in Turtle Island to offer an all-Indigenous list of contributors. Many of these volumes, or the articles they feature, have been garlanded with scholarly prizes and awards: a fitting tribute to their impact on the field.

Since taking over the General Editorship of NECT in 2017, I have been continually inspired by the work of Knowles, his collaborators, and the many other brilliant scholars and artists who continue to transform our understanding of the field of Canadian theatre and performance. The editors with whom I have been fortunate enough to work have responded thoughtfully to the goals that shape the series. In the 2017 volume of NECT, *Canadian Performance Histories and Historiographies*, editor Heather Davis-Fisch and her collaborators set out to rethink the subject we have been used to calling "Canadian theatre history." The following year represented an epoch in the history of NECT, marking the first time Playwrights Canada Press has published two volumes in the NECT series within the span of one calendar year. The first 2018 volume, *Q2Q: Queer Canadian Theatre and Performance* (edited by Peter Dickinson, C.E. Gatchalian, Kathleen Oliver, and Dalbir Singh), brings together the voices of many of this country's leading makers and scholars of queer theatre and performance to explore, celebrate, debate, and redefine the ways in which LGBT2Q+ identities and perspectives have shaped theatre and performance on this land mass. The second, *Linda Griffiths* (edited by Jacqueline Petropoulos), is the first edited collection ever to focus solely on the work of one of Canada's most multi-talented, influential, and complex theatre artists. All of these volumes model Knowles's vision of NECT as a series that "takes new approaches" while foregrounding "minoritized and under-represented perspectives."

This year's volume, edited by Yana Meerzon, speaks to that vision in a particularly powerful and timely way. Though celebratory references to Canada as a "welcoming" country and a "nation of immigrants" abound, the lived reality of immigrants to this land mass is far more complex. Anti-immigrant sentiment, systemic racism, the ongoing harms perpetrated by settler colonialism against Indigenous Peoples, and the contradictions knit into official discourses of multiculturalism—among many other factors—pose deep challenges to immigrants and refugees, and indeed to the health of all communities living on this land. In the midst of these ongoing challenges, immigrant artists have had a transformative impact upon Canadian theatre and performance.

Drawing upon the insights of a large and diverse group of artists and scholars—many of whom, including the editor, identify as immigrant Canadians—*Theatre and (Im)migration* sets out to explore the depth and breadth of that impact in both historical and present-day contexts. Among the vital topics it examines are the relationships between immigration, Indigeneity, and performance; the roles those relationships have played in both the formation and the critique of the settler colonial state in Canada; the myriad performance forms and practices immigrant artists have explored in this land, both in the past and today; the diverse ways in which such forms and practices have engaged with (and often deconstructed) discourses of multiculturalism and interculturalism in various Canadian regions and contexts; and the complex alliances that have formed within and between immigrant and non-immigrant communities. The work forged by such alliances is constantly reshaping what Meerzon calls the "shimmering map" of this land and its theatre. I am deeply grateful to her and to her contributors for helping us to consider how we may live, work, and perform more responsibly on these ever-shifting terrains.

THEATRE AND (IM)MIGRATION: THE CANADIAN THEATRE OF SHIMMERING MAPS[1]

IN LIEU OF A FOREWORD

YANA MEERZON

On 22 October 2015, three days after the Liberal Party of Canada came to power, the *Globe and Mail* published an editorial entitled "Canada's Election Message to the World: Xenophobia Doesn't Play Here." The author suggested that in times of migration crises, rising xenophobic discourse, and neo-nationalism, it is essential for Europe and other countries to start taking lessons in navigating cultural diversity from Canada, the first country in the world that institutionalized principles of multiculturalism. For many Canadians, it asserted, multiculturalism is "more than just a demographic fact: it is an approach to social integration that recognizes that sometimes treating people as moral equals means allowing them to be different" (Larin). This view of Canadian multiculturalism takes its roots in Michael Ignatieff's concept "civic nationalism," which "maintains that the nation should be composed of all those—regardless of race, color, creed, gender, language, or ethnicity—who subscribe to the nation's political creed" (3–4). Such a position has definite benefits. Canadian theatre, for example, since the mid-1980s has seen a significant increase of plays, productions, and companies created and run by

---

1 An earlier version of the ideas put forward in this introduction can be found in my article "Theatre and Immigration: From the Multiculturalism Act to the Sites of Imagined Communities."

first- and second-generation immigrant artists supported by Canadian arts funding under the banner of cultural diversity. The full picture, however, is not necessarily that rosy. On one hand, the Canadian ideology of multiculturalism encourages the preservation of heritage cultures and languages; on the other, it prompts newcomers to assert their identities through their past experiences and thus risks both slowing down their integration into a new culture and jeopardizes their emotional investment in the future (Ahmed, *Strange Encounters*). Sometimes it also functions as an incentive for immigrant artists to make art for diasporic subjects only: those who share their language, cultural principles, and past histories, and who identify themselves as "hyphenated Canadians," such as Chinese-Canadians, Lebanese-Canadians, or Russian-Canadians.[2] However, theatre is a deeply communal form, and many first- and second-generation immigrant artists aspire to transgress the borders of their communities, aiming to speak both to their members and to wider multicultural urbanites.

Integration of immigrant artists into the mainstream Canadian arts scene has never been easy. Even today, artists of colour (visible minorities), artists of accent (audible minorities), and artists of hyphenated identities continue to struggle for their stories to be presented on stage and for their voices to be heard both by people in power and by general audiences. In this tendency, immigrant theatre approximates the work of post-colonial theatre, in which "the colonised subject exists in a complex representational matrix, variously situated between opposing forces [. . .] or figured in opposition to the imperial powers" (Gilbert and Tompkins 11). The artistic strategies of resistance and the performative devices of counter-discourse define post-colonial aesthetics (11). Similarly, immigrant theatre reflects, criticizes, subverts, and reimagines the social, linguistic, and ideological formations of Canadian multiculturalism. By proposing an artistic configuration of cultural diversity

---

2   The chosen style for this book—and the overall series—however, is to not use a hyphen when specifying one's background, unless it is a preference stated by the individual authors. The use of the hyphen has been studied extensively elsewhere, and is currently at the forefront of a debate stemming from a recent change in the Associated Press's style guide (see Graham).

on stage, it rehearses new scenarios of civic nationalism. This practice grows in parallel to the mainstream Canadian theatre scene, as immigrants create independent companies dedicated to the representation of cultural diversity on stage and collaborate with established theatre enterprises, including, occasionally, Indigenous theatre groups. Although highly diversified from one community to the next, Canadian immigrant theatre's political and artistic output is often characterized by a shared potential to stage and enact the phenomenon of *imagined immigrant community* analogous to *imagined theatrical nationhood* as theorized by Filewod and Hurley (Filewod, *Performing Canada*; Hurley, *National Performance*).

* * *

In his theorization of how the phenomenon of national theatre (specifically in Europe) came about, Bruce McConachie suggests that "nationhood has always depended on 'imagination,' not authenticity," with theatre—as an institute of cultural mediation—playing a major role in the formation of a nation (59). Among the five characteristics that define the formation of national theatres, he underlines the medium's ability to "address (or seek to address) a part of the national people that can legitimately represent the whole of it" (51) and the emergence of the "national actor," who stems "from the nation itself (primarily through the accident of birth) and speak[s] the national language on stage" (51), and who thus through his/her "signature characters [stands] in as the part that represent[s] the whole of the nation" (51). "Strong bourgeois patronage" serves as the third principle of national theatremaking (51). Finally, national theatre—as an ideological paradigm—reflects, serves, and constructs new audiences, "the legitimate representatives of the nation" (52). Historically, it also fostered the emergence of the new dramatic repertoire to celebrate "the language, traditions, and culture of a people," and stimulated construction of theatre buildings "prominently located in what was recognized as the national capital" (51).

The development of national theatre in Canada—or rather the development of an idea of a Canadian national theatre—faced somewhat similar objectives, challenges, and obstacles, but within a historical, social, and economic context radically different to that of European nations. The conceptualization of the Stratford Festival and the creation of the National Arts Centre in Ottawa offer revealing examples of this context (Filewod, *Performing Canada*; Jennings). As Filewod states, theatre can easily work as a mechanism for building nation through the arts. In the Canadian context, he demonstrates, "the phrase 'Canadian theatre' has always meant an imagined theatre contained within (and often inhibited by) the material theatre of the day. It is a phrase that has expressed longing for a sense of national community and which has been the site of severe contestation" (10). Filewod proposes the narrative of Canadian national theatre as a historical project seeking its own authenticity, in which "theatre and nation collapse into each other at the point of imagined authenticity: 'the real' nation is out there, the 'real' theatre is its articulation" (10).[3]

Looking at the project of Canadian national theatre from the perspective of immigration constitutes the leading objective of this volume. In 2011, Erin Hurley put forward a view of the émigré culture of Québec as a culture of simulation, imitating in its artistic output the social, linguistic, and artistic structures of the host nation. She analyzed the dramatic corpus of Marco Micone, a Québécois playwright of Italian origin, as an example of this process, arguing that he "approaches the issue of ethnic difference from this immigrant space of exiguity and in the mode of simulation" (*National Performance* 90). Through this gesture, Micone's theatre (and, by extension, any other immigrant project) "writes back to the centre of the Quebec literary institution [. . .] in a process that not only de-centres the centre but uproots it" (90). In this tendency it "evinces a feminist politic that undoes the masculinist national fantasy of self-originating" (90). Analogously, immigrant theatre today, both in English Canada and in French Québec, sets up an example of the "imagined community," marked by the cultural and cognitive synesthesia

---

3   Ideological, political, and historical differences mark the various processes that constituted the development of the national theatres of Québec and English Canada; these important differences cannot be properly addressed in the pages of these introductory remarks and deserve a separate in-depth study.

of the artists' personal experiences and inherited traditions with those of a new world. It repeatedly stages this tension between continuity and difference, so that an immigrant artist's process of making a theatre performance turns into the work of crafting a new homeland, which "transcends cultural specificity and encourages the development of an identity that is formed from living in the theatre rather than a society" (J. Turner 23).

I have argued this idea previously ("Theatre and Immigration" and "Multiculturalism, (Im)Migration, Theatre"), but this collection—work on which began in 2016, after "Theatre and Immigration," a special issue of *Theatre Research in Canada* (36.2), was published—takes the argument one step further. It proposes a new model of imagining Canadian theatrical multitude. It envisions today's theatre in Canada (including Québec) as a multidimensional, shifting, and shimmering map that reflects Canada in both synchronic and diachronic dimensions.

This image has several connotations: first, it stems from and enhances Gilles Deleuze's metaphor of the ever-evolving rhizome as it refers to Canada's geography and history, connoting the country's cultural landscape, in which its urban centres of intense theatremaking (necessary for the emergence of immigrant theatre practices) are remote from each other, and thus create a series of obstacles for theatre companies and audiences when it comes to maintaining a constant dialogue and exchange of ideas. Secondly, it suggests the diversity of immigrant voices and artistic work that have contributed (perhaps silently or even invisibly sometimes) to making Canadian theatre. Neither situated on mainstream Canadian stages nor necessarily taking place in large urban centres, these immigrant theatre enterprises and the work of individual artists have factored into the perpetual movement of becoming that we often associate with making Canadian theatre in general. In fact, the image of a shimmering map reflects the years of relentless learning that an immigrant artist spends understanding the Canadian arts-funding system, as well as the theatre politics, aesthetic tendencies, and dramaturgical tropes that make up the Canadian theatre project. In this need to constantly evolve and to start every project anew, the story of immigrant theatre is not very different from that of other emerging theatre groups who face the challenges of securing funds, seeking performance venues and partnerships, and cultivating their own audiences. Hence, similarly to these other groups, many immigrant theatre practices are continuously rising within and disappearing from Canada's professional theatre scene. There are, however, successful examples of companies that have sustained long histories of theatremaking, including the Modern Times Stage Company and Teesri Duniya Theatre.

The articles selected for this book, organized thematically in three complementary sections, speak broadly to these realities and bring the metaphor of a shimmering and shifting map to life. Before I describe this volume's conceptual road map or its layout, however, I propose a brief theoretical intervention dedicated to charting this project's terminology.

FROM STRANGER TO (IM)MIGRANT: MAPPING A TERMINOLOGICAL TERRAIN

The stranger, wrote Georg Simmel in 1908, is the reason to examine how our society works. He proposed this statement in regard to the functioning of the nineteenth-century European nation-state, made of settlers who had been living together and collectively nourishing their land, language, and cultural traditions for centuries. But what does the notion of the stranger mean in the context of a national history that is made up of immigrants who have turned into settlers, or who are in the process of becoming settlers? Especially when the racial, ethnic, and linguistic makeup of this population changes with each new wave of immigrants hitting the country's borders.

In his recent book, *Staging Strangers: Theatre and Global Ethics*, Barry Freeman has addressed these questions too. To Freeman, the stranger is someone who "can only exist [. . .] at a threshold," the position that "distinguishes stranger from the neighbor—who is nearby and may share certain values or belong to a shared community—or from the Other, who has been marked as 'outside'" (xviii). In this view, the stranger appears at the threshold of some kind of "home," "a guest hoping for hospitality" (xix), and acts as a defining factor in our understanding of "the swirling ideological currents of nationalism, multiculturalism, and globalization" that make up Canada's identity as a nation (xxii).

This figure also serves as the delineating feature in "'immigrant theatre,' in 'multicultural theatre,' and in a 'theatre of global ethics,'" as the stranger can offer a perspective "in which ethical relationships proposed between the local and global, the stage, and audience are realigning in a global context" (xxi).

This volume unfolds in a similar critical direction. However, it does not always use the stranger as its imperative metaphor or central character. Rather, it sticks to the enigmatic word *(im)migrant*: a term that takes displacement—international or within one's own country, imposed or voluntarily—as the basis for the political and artistic search that drives both the dramaturgy and the visual language of the work chosen for this volume.

The use of brackets in the word *(im)migration* is not accidental. It refers to several practical and ideological issues with which this book aims to deal. On one hand, we continue using the term *immigrant theatre artist* that I introduced in 2015 ("Theatre and Immigration" 181–82). This term links back to Immigration, Refugees and Citizenship Canada's (IRCC) definition of an immigrant as an individual eligible to be "admitted to Canada because they have relevant experience in working for himself or herself." This immigrant "must intend and be able to become self-employed in Canada in the arts or athletics" ("Glossary"). To further clarify the eligibility criteria to enter Canada as a self-employed immigrant, IRCC states,

> When applying to immigrate as a self-employed person, relevant experience means: at least two one-year periods of experience in the period from five years before the application date to the day a decision is made on the application. Experience must be in one of these areas: self-employment in cultural activities or athletics or, participating in cultural activities or athletics at the world-class level. ("Glossary")

Thus, in the legal renditions of this concept, *immigrant theatre artist* refers to someone who holds a post-secondary diploma in the performance arts, has work experience in this trade, and earns a living in professional theatre or as an educator in English and/or French in Canada.

In its practical applications, the term does not only refer to immigrant theatre artists who entered Canada as self-employed individuals. The spectrum of biographies and stories (im)migrant theatre tells exists far beyond the IRCC's narrow definition. This theatre features refugee and asylum-seeking stories; it speaks of migration on a global scale and in the diasporic context; it provides a venue for second- and third-generation immigrants to grapple with identity issues and questions of (non)belonging; and it raises issues of human rights, *dissonant acculturation* (Portes and Rumbaut),[4] and *affective citizenship* (Parati) to name a few. Thus, in its symbolic conceptualization, the term also refers to a theatremaker who is found in the position of *cultural translator* (Cronin), and whose role includes not only the efforts of social translation based upon "the (physical) translatability of human beings [that] implies their (symbolic) translatability" (71), but also the labour of "construction of dialogical self through translation" (69).

Immigrant theatre practice originates at the borders between Canada's official culture and that of immigration, and works across languages, theatrical genres, and generations. It envisions an immigrant artist as an outsider who possesses a pluralistic point of view and locates her artistic output away from Canada's notorious English/French dichotomies. This position reveals a complex subject capable of challenging the administrative structures of Canadian theatre. At the same time, it reinforces the conditions of solitude and marginality from which immigrants speak. By actively participating in constructing Canadian multiculturalism on stage—whether granting agencies, audiences, or critics acknowledge it or not (Curtis et al. 17)—these artists contribute "to the strengthening of national boundaries within Canada" (Blad and Couton 647). They often assert their identities through irony and self-distancing, freely mixing languages, traditions, and cultural referents. Their work becomes a repository of their communities' collective history and memory, helping former compatriots to overcome the traumas of the past and deal with

---

4   The terms dissonant, consonant, and selective acculturation refer to the diverse processes of assimilation as practised by first-generation immigrants and their children (Portes and Rumbaut).

the challenges of the present. In this context, the primary function immigrant theatre carries is "to create translation spaces in contemporary places of residence and work" (Cronin 69). The artistic methodologies of such translation have to "actively embrace a much expanded range of languages if such a strategy were to have any chance of succeeding" (69).

These methodologies, which have been repeatedly and continuously rehearsed and staged in Canadian theatre, also constitute five strategies or axes for critical analysis of (im)migrant theatremaking. These strategies refer to immigrant theatre artists

1) Seeking innovative linguistic means to speak about the condition of immigration and creating multilingual performances with dialogue written in English, French, or the artist's native language;

2) Constructing a dramatic repertoire focused on stories of (im) migration, with the characters and themes that make these experiences and the social and cultural worlds that correspond to fictional chronotopes (Bakhtin) and the geo-historical space-time dichotomies of migration;

3) Creating independent companies under the banner of multiculturalism and diversity[5];

---

5   A list of such companies is expansive; here I can site only several examples, including Cahoots Theatre (1986, Toronto); Modern Times Stage Company (1989, Toronto), established by Iranian-born theatre artist Soheil Parsa; Neworld Theatre, created by Camyar Chai in the 1990s, and run by Marcus Youssef since 2005 in Vancouver; MAI/Montréal, arts interculturels, which opened in the late 1990s as a research and production venue for intercultural and multidisciplinary arts in Montréal; Rahul Varma's Teesri Duniya Theatre (1981, Montréal); the MT Space, founded in 2004 by Majdi Bou-Matar; Orange Noyée, which was opened in 2011 by Mani Soleymanlou; fu-GEN Theatre Company, which is dedicated to the development of professional Asian Canadian theatre artists and run by

4) Recognizing and forming immigrant theatre's target audiences, a process that might involve a) immigrant companies playing for diaspora audiences, i.e., people who share the same language and cultural background; b) producing their work independently in English or French; and c) creating collaborations with mainstream companies, including such established enterprises as the National Arts Centre in Ottawa; Soulpepper, Tarragon, and Factory in Toronto; Théâtre d'Aujourd'hui in Montréal; and Arts Club Theatre Company in Vancouver, to name a few.

5) Seeking new aesthetics of performance-making and artistic vocabulary that include a) working within the testimonial and autobiographical genres of documentary theatre; b) creating (autobiographical) solo performances, whether movement or logos based; c) employing devices of domestic melodrama that focus on intergenerational conflicts; d) creating liminality on stage and in the audience by using the devices of movement- and sound-based theatre; e) exploring fragmented dramatic structures of non-realistic dramaturgy and memory plays; f) refocusing the Western dramatic and literary canon within the framework of Canadian immigrant experiences; g) re-enacting the past by using the techniques of performative interweaving (Fischer-Lichte); h) reimagining historical and contemporary events of migration through fictional lenses; and i) investigating potentials of immersive, interactive, durational, and technologically augmented theatre practices to stage the stories of immigrant departures and returns.

These strategies, as this volume aims to demonstrate, can force Canadian theatremakers, granting agencies, scholars, and audiences to conceptualize

---

David Yee; Puente Theatre, founded in 1988 by the Chilean-born artist Lina de Guevara in Victoria; and Co.ERASGA Dance Society, established by Alvin Tolentino, a Filipino Canadian artist, in Vancouver.

new visions of Canada and its theatre beyond the proverbial English/French solitudes. They can offer new images and models of the Canadian national theatre of the future.

Moreover, the word *(im)migration* suggests the conflated binary *immigration/migration* that implies the inherited interdependency—not opposition—these two terms carry. *Immigration*, Umberto Eco explained, is a regularized practice of individuals and (nation) states negotiating the civic status of people crossing into a new territory; *migration* is an unregulated human flow for which neither European states nor their North American counterparts are prepared (93–95). Global and irregular movement of people, "violent or pacific as it may be, is like a natural phenomenon: it happens, and no one can control it" (93). Eco wrote this statement in the wake of the new millennium, reflecting on the significance of the year 2000. He also spoke about Europe, outlining the fear of the Other as the continent's primary strategy to deal with human flow. Canada is, of course, in a very different position. Protected by its geographical location—far away from the African, Middle Eastern, and Central American territories from which most of today's migration originates—Canada does not really experience the impact of the irregular global movements that are perceived as posing a danger to the old nation-states. Canadian immigration systems operate under various legislations that were introduced and implemented in the 1970s and that have been evolving ever since. Hence, the issues of how to negotiate difference and how to live together with your neighbour have been institutionalized and regulated in this country over several decades, with the fiftieth anniversary of Pierre Trudeau's 1971 policy and commitment to the principles of multiculturalism fast approaching. This system and this policy are not without their inner contradictions and faults, including the problematic institutional implementation of their principles, as seen for instance in the work of the Canada Council for the Arts (Fatona). Still, theatre—an institute of cultural mediation in itself— has served and continues to act as one of the leading public venues to try this policy out and to challenge its shortcomings.

In his recent book, *Performing the Intercultural City*, Ric Knowles speaks of Toronto's theatre culture as an example of "the intercultural performance ecology" that reflects the working of a "multiethnic global city" in general, and that can also serve as a model to describe the multitude of its performative outputs (1). He cites the productive role of "interculturalism from below," which imagines diverse cultural groups, including the Indigenous peoples of Canada, as participating equally in this project (2). This ecosystem privileges the plurality, relationality, and simultaneity of artistic practices and political gazes over familiar *us/them* binaries and paradigms. This volume aims at painting a similar picture: in its conceptualization it tries to embrace as many of the voices, multitudes, and geographies that contribute to the shimmering map of Canadian theatre as possible. Exclusions and oversights are inevitable, as they are imposed by the historical temporality of the book and the length of a single publication. At the same time, this book capitalizes on the tradition of Canadian theatre scholarship to "take the temperature" of our collective historical moment, to better understand where we are standing today and where we might be heading tomorrow.

History, however, is a curious phenomenon, as it constantly conflates the monumental narratives of the state with the stories of its people (Foucault; Ricoeur). This conflation marks the standpoint of every artist or scholar engaged in the action of taking the historical temperature of today, and those involved in this project are no exception. The collection's dramaturgy is heavily marked by this vision of history and the nation, stemming from and reflecting back the collective and individual stories of migration of each of the book's contributors. These histories are radically different: mine, for example, is one of a happy immigrant, an unintended pun on Sara Ahmed's term (*The Promise of Happiness* 129).

I arrived in Canada on a spousal visa in the mid-nineties. I held an M.A. in theatre studies and had an excellent infrastructure of personal support in Toronto that allowed me to dedicate five years of my early stay in Canada to finessing my English-language skills and learning more about Canadian theatre. I was sheltered by the privilege of Canadian academia with prestigious scholarships, part-time teaching, and tax-free student loans. I was a happy immigrant, but I was also a curious one. The first impression that made a deciding imprint on my imagination and understanding of Canada was my first class in drama theory at the University of Toronto, in which about twenty graduate students, very different from each other in colour, origins, accents, and knowledge of theatre traditions, were sitting around a discussion table with Michael Sidnell. There I learned such concepts as feminism and post-colonialism, while my classmates were introduced to Mikhail Bakhtin's dialogicity and heteroglossia for the first time. The diversity and inclusion that I experienced in this class created for me the image of Canada. The everyday and theatrical realities of that Canada were, however, quite different. My friends—immigrant theatre actors and directors—had tremendous difficulties getting cast or acquiring jobs and artistic grants. My other friends—immigrant academics—also experienced difficulties securing university positions and getting published. But then, I was also a lucky immigrant. The full-time job that I secured at the University of Ottawa meant privilege and exception, but also it implied hard work and many sacrifices in return. The question that kept haunting me and that eventually gave birth to this project was, what exactly is this assemblage of different people that makes Canada Canada? What is this country's true national agenda and national practice? What makes it the place that many people view as an island of acceptance in a world turning increasingly xenophobic, racist, and pro-nationalist? This book is a reflection of my acknowledged privilege and an attempt to respond to these questions, as well as an effort to recreate in its pages the multiplicity of Canada that struck my imagination in my first Canadian theatre theory class.

THE ROAD MAP OF THE VOLUME

Alan Filewod's opening article, "Playing on Indigenous Land: Settlers, Immigrants, and Theatre in Fictive Canada," is essential for this conversation. It provides yet another model to think about what Canadian pluralism is and how theatre reflects and constructs it. Filewod opens his argument with the necessary acknowledgement of the critical gaps that mark the conversation about immigration and the construction of Canadian nationhood through theatre arts: the conversation that has repeatedly failed to address the trying tensions between Indigenous peoples and white settlers. To change this practice, he suggests, theatre scholars and artists need to take "a step toward the difficult work of decolonization,"[6] and thus must recognize the embedded "'trialectic' of subjectivities created by settler colonialism." Filewod bases his argument on Emma Battell Lowman and Adam J. Barker's definition of the term "trialectic," which refers to three major groups of Canadian people: "settler colonizers, Indigenous Others and exogenous Others (which includes, for example, enslaved peoples, imported labour, and marginalized migrants)" (Lowman and Barker 28). Speaking of the next steps in this work of decolonization, Filewod invites today's theatre audiences and makers to share a gesture of collective responsibility that would involve both settler Canadians and immigrant-identified Canadians, and thus lead to "productive alliances" not only with each other but also with Indigenous theatre groups.

Filewod's proposed gesture of shared responsibility as a recipe for participating in and constructing new pluralisms echoes Zygmunt Bauman's call for creative dialogue between differences. Strangers, Bauman writes, "provide a convenient [. . .] outlet for our inborn fear of the unknown, the uncertain and the unpredictable. In chasing strangers away from our homes and streets, the frightening ghost of uncertainty is, if only for a brief moment, exorcised: the horrifying monster of insecurity is burnt in effigy" (*Collateral Damage* 60). At the same time, whether "we like it or not, we the urban dwellers find ourselves in a situation that requires us to develop the skills of living with difference daily, and in all probability permanently" (Bauman, "Symptoms" 16). These practices of human pluralism not only serve as illustrations of

---

6   In this book, the term decolonizing sits beside decolonial and is used differently within the context of each article. In general, however, "decolonizing often means identifying colonial systems, structures and relationships and working to challenge those systems. Decolonizing frequently goes hand-in-hand with Indigenization and is a response to the inherent colonialism in Canada. Decolonizing practices work to transform what is important in settler society and involve long-term structural changes" (Hogan and McCracken 2016). Understood in the context of the Indigenization of Canadian post-secondary institutions, *decolonization* should not be practised as only "the token inclusion of Indigenous ceremony. Rather, it involves a paradigm shift from a culture of denial to the making of space for Indigenous political philosophies and knowledge systems as they resurge, thereby shifting cultural perceptions and power relations in real ways" (Regan 189).

Ulrich Beck's theory of the new cosmopolitanism as "global interconnectivity" between people and states (1348–49), they can also elucidate rising tensions between moving and settled populations, as well as mounting neo-nationalist, racist, and anti-migration discourses worldwide. This reality is marked by the "jarring contradiction between our *already-close-to-cosmopolitan plight* and virtual absence of a *cosmopolitan awareness*, mindset or attitude" (Bauman, "Symptoms" 18). Rising stranger-phobia creates perpetual uncertainty in the life of the settlers, because politically, economically, and socially "we are still left with the instruments designed in the past to service the conditions of autonomy" of the nation state (19). This story can be changed if present political formations radically transform, as none of them "measures up to a genuinely 'cosmopolitan' standard; all of them pair a 'we' against a 'them'" (19). The potential success of these measures depends upon humility and respect for the individuals that make this shared collectivity; but it can also lead to personal frustrations and disappointments. Displacement, exile, and immigration, as Joseph Brodsky has it, are the "ultimate lesson[s]" in humility (25). These lessons remind an exilic artist of their major ethical duty to "be lost in mankind," "to put down your vanity," and to "measure yourself not against your pen pals but against human infinity" (Brodsky 25). Literature and the arts can serve as a cure for the distracting force of progress that leads civilizations to wars, social and economic disasters, and humanitarian and environmental catastrophes (23). The function of theatre is to provide this cure: to create a perspective, retrospectively and retroactively, on the history of mankind and on its current moment, as one of history's variables.

Immigrant theatre shares this responsibility. It can help its audiences in negotiating similarities and differences. It can signpost the benefits that Canadian society can acquire by making new immigrants more welcome, and it can create "an imagined virtual community" (Imre 77). To sustain "the creation, maintenance, and self-definition of such a community, [however,] it needs to manifest links between the physically separated individuals by representing their common elements and their difference from other peoples and communities" on stage (77). In the process, it can instigate new debates about Canada as a nation and provoke a systematic "redefinition of nationhood that integrates rather than rejects cultural pluralism" through the arts (Blad and Couton 647–48). Such work can also confirm that Canadian cultural production is capable of reflecting "transnational social forms" of collective being. It can exemplify "the transformative impact of immigration on state sovereignty and national identity," with waves of migration helping "to dissolve parts of the traditional cleavages, replacing them with a looser form of postnational reality" (647). This work can empower individuals, and it can create an opportunity to recognize immigrants as a cohesive group, who despite their cultural differences share the traumatic history of migration. This volume aspires to reflect these tendencies in its carefully crafted three sections.

Part One, entitled Canadian Immigration and Theatre History Paradigms, features articles by theatre and cultural historians, theoreticians, and practitioners, offering a brief historical overview of how different movements of people, as well as multiple historical and cultural encounters, have contributed to constructing the image of Canada on its stage(s)—and continue to do so. For example, Ian McWilliams insists on a more detailed look at the performative encounters between Indigenous population and white settlers during the process of settlement on the Prairies, and at the forms of inclusion and exclusion that characterized them. Using Joseph Roach's theoretical framework, McWilliams examines how processes of effigying and surrogation can "take place through live bodies" and how certain performances of indigeneity were "viewed as acceptable within the wider historical events and ideological forces at play in the settlement of the Canadian West circa 1885–1905." Moira Day continues with this quest: she focuses on immigrant theatre practices of the mid-twentieth century, specifically in Alberta and Manitoba. Her essay examines the work of the Irish Canadian immigrant playwright John Coulter (1888–1980), including his 1950 drama Riel and its sequels, as an example of the critical distancing necessary to differentiate between nation-building tendencies in Ireland and Western Canada—both processes often marked by "dreams crushed, hopes deferred, and a perpetual sense of exile, alienation, and displacement."

Echoing the concept of the shimmering map that characterizes the history of Canada's theatre landscape, David DeGrow examines the role American

Vietnam War draft dodgers played in establishing a number of prominent theatre companies in Toronto, whereas Rebecca Margolis investigates how the work of the Yiddish diasporic theatre added to the image of Montréal in the time period that coincided with the development of the Toronto theatre scene described by DeGrow. This shimmering map, as the following essays show, has been always marked by the multiplicity and simultaneity of its many-cultural practices: a point that helped to lead to Pierre Trudeau's ideas on multiculturalism. Embracing the complexity of this ideology and its associated practices, the collection goes on to offer a critical discussion of the difference between the so-called "multicultural script" implemented in the performative dramaturgy of Toronto's cultural festivals (as outlined by Jacqueline Taucar) and Québec's policy of interculturalism, which has often fed into a toxic artistic environment for the development of immigrant theatre companies in Montréal, as shown in the analysis of Teesri Duniya Theatre offered by Rahul Varma, Sheetal Lodhia, and Jaswant Guzder. This section closes with my own look at Olivier Kemeid's work as an example of a theatre project situated between philosophy and historiography, a theme that often marks our conversations about immigration and Canada.

Part Two—broadly called Canadian Immigration and the Paradigms of Performance—studies how immigrant theatre negotiates intercultural practices of performance-making and pedagogy, and challenges the idea of (im) migration as a phenomenon of external movements. Offering a kind of survey of contemporary Canadian theatre practices whose artistic experiments transgress disciplinary boundaries of theatre performance, this section examines devices of translation and encounter as they are manifested in the language, acting pedagogy, and time/space of immigrant theatre performance. Focusing on the negotiation of differences in the rehearsal hall and on stage, the selected articles examine a number of artistic experiments that demonstrate how (im) migration as one's personal condition and as a socio-cultural point of view can help collective rethinking and reshaping of Canadian theatre today.

In the opening chapter of this section, Ric Knowles describes acting methodologies and strategies of devising as practised by the MT Space theatre company, run by Majdi Bou-Matar, who came to Canada from Lebanon in 2003. Knowles's contribution is followed by Art Babayants and Marjan Moosavi's essay on Iranian Canadian theatre, in which the authors differentiate between Iranian and Persian cultures and linguistic contexts, using as their case study *Yek Daqiqeh Sokout* (*A Moment of Silence*), a play by the prominent Iranian writer Mohammad Yaghoubi and presented at Toronto's SummerWorks Festival in 2016.

Eleanor Ty continues this discussion by focusing on the devices of resistance and innovation as presented in contemporary Asian Canadian dramaturgy and "refining the traditional form of immigrant drama." She demonstrates how David Yee's *acquiesce* and Ins Choi's *Kim's Convenience* employ the devices of magic realism and humour to "confront issues that are not usually dealt with by visible minorities, such as domestic violence and intra-ethnic conflicts." Aida Jordão brings similar questions forward by looking at Portuguese Canadian theatre and the role sex and gender stereotypes play in the community and on its stages. She uses "a feminist lens to interrogate the stereotypes and revisionist creations in the plays," as well as to examine "feminine and masculine tropes that may limit the social activities or material possibilities of female and male characters." Echoing the need to challenge cultural and gender stereotypes often used and abused in (im)migrant performance, Martha Herrera-Lasso González brings into focus the autobiographical work of Helena Martin Franco, "a tri-lingual Colombian Canadian performance artist who has been working in Montreal since 1998." This work transgresses the boundaries of traditional theatre and "expresses a recurring frustration for Latina artists who have migrated north—a feeling that their bodies, their voices, and their art are nothing more than a blank screen upon which stereotypes are constantly being projected."

Nicole Nolette examines the roles the language and personal multilingualism of an (im)migrant theatre artist can play in reshaping the ideals of nationhood within Canada. The work of Mani Soleymanlou, "an artist of Iranian descent who migrated with his family to Toronto after a short stay in France," and that of Christian Essiambre, an Acadian actor—both "immigrants to Montreal and, more generally, to Quebec"—shake the narratives of nation-building in Québec. The article not only asks, "How does one insert oneself into a milieu where/when one is an outsider?" it also proposes that language, specifically the multilingualism of (im)migrant subjects, can serve as a tool of reshaping the nation from within and hence "can be seen as equal to *joual* in its power." With this statement, Nolette brings the conversation back to Knowles's proposal that we should seek the means of practising a new interculturalism in the rehearsal hall and on stage.

In his essay closing this section, Peter Kuling positions this proposal within a wider context of digital technologies, social media, and global migration. Looking at several participatory and immersive productions that invite audiences to encounter the experience of (im)migration in a more direct fashion, he questions the political and ethical work that goes into these artistic experiments. Although performance can be a site for the effective practice of interculturalism, it can also be one whose means and ends we must question when it comes to the representation of migration, specifically by the artists whose personal stories of transcultural encounter is limited to the experience of privilege and even cultural tourism, and whose audiences are themselves far removed from the ordeals of global migration.

The concluding section of this book—Canadian Immigration in the First Person Singular and Plural—features essays based on personal statements, dialogues, and academic inquiries written by theatre practitioners and pedagogues who are themselves first-generation immigrants or refugees or who work with recent immigrants and refugees. Monica Prendergast converses with Lina de Guevara, a Chilean Canadian performer and theatre director, on the hardships and consolations of her personal journey in Canada as a professionally trained actress and founder of the community-run Puente Theatre in Victoria, BC. Natasha Martina Koechl proposes a dramaturgical report and a directorial self-reflection on her own journey as a creator of the production *Displaced*, which dramatizes the journey of migration from the perspective of a female traveller in three different contexts of Canada's history. Yasmine Kandil speaks of her personal voyage as a theatre performer who is also a refugee. Speaking as a practitioner of applied theatre, she weighs the pros and cons of working with traumatized people, the hopes such theatre work can create, and the ethical problems it can manufacture. Kirsten Sadeghi-Yekta, Taiwo Afolabi, and Anita Hallewas reflect on similar problematics within the context of their work as theatre educators and community facilitators. The volume closes with a piece written by Lisa Ndejuru, who recognizes Kigali, Rwanda (the place of her birth), and Montréal, Québec (the place of her professional habitat), as two homes that in their symbolic and emotional values stand tightly and irreversibly intertwined in the artist's mind and everyday experiences. Ndejuru's text presents an example of an academic essay that is highly marked by the author's performative expression and her personal experience as a cosmopolitan subject who is actively involved in the conversation about Canada's past, present, and future as a nation of differences and multitudes.

TO CONCLUDE . . .

Immigrant theatre, as this collection demonstrates, is made by artists who carry within themselves multi-layered performative contexts. In their work, immigration appears as a lonely process, conditioned by the circumstances of one's departure and arrival, and by the artists' willingness to negotiate the theatrical aesthetics of the new land. Creating new repertoire, forming companies, and educating audiences about immigration helps these artists further challenge the myth of Canadian nationhood and multiculturalism, defining the new Canadian *common space* through arts:

> [Canadian *Common Space* refers to the] locations in time and space where visible and religious minorities and other Canadians meet and interact; such spaces are the foundation for creating and enhancing a strong Canadian identity. They are the vehicle through which a multicultural, multi-racial, multi-religious population develops synergies that are strong enough to lead to a collective national identity. The cumulative result of shared experience is a common economic, social, and cultural demographic infrastructure, which leads to a shared sense of belonging. [. . .] Such multicultural common spaces

naturally foster an evolving and organic Canadian identity, allowing
visible and religious minorities to develop a sense of belonging to
community based on lived experiences, rather than on abstract and
often purely historical or symbolic notions of what it means to be
Canadian. (Dib et al. 162)

Theatre is one of the most desirable common spaces we share. It invites
immigrant artists and their audiences to seek dialogue amongst one another
and across their differences. In this gesture of cultural transgression, a
new theatrical community is formed, which speaks to the newly emerging discourse of Canadian *post-multiculturalism*. "The central premise of
the anti- and/or post-multiculturalism discourse is that multiculturalism
is not working [. . .] because it is segregating, rather than integrating
diverse racial, ethnic, and religious groups" (Garcea et al. 2). Instead, the
advocates of post-multiculturalism see its everyday and artistic practices as
"foster[ing] social cohesion and promot[ing] assimilation and a common
identity" (1). An immigrant theatre production can be seen as an example
of such post-multiculturalism, an instance of what Jill Dolan calls a "utopian
performative": the place where different "audiences are compelled to gather
with others, to see people perform live, hoping, perhaps, for moments of
transformation that might let them reconsider and change the world outside
the theatre, from its macro to its micro arrangements" (455). Immigrant theatre can offer just such an artistic venue, where people gather to "articulate
a common future, one that's more just and equitable, one in which we can
all participate more equally, with more chances to live fully and contribute
to the making of culture" (455).

    This practice should be studied holistically as a comprehensive and self-
contained phenomenon, not as a case of occasional presentation of cultural
diversity on stage. At the same time, building an imaginary community
through the arts can be a complicated process, "since it is often thought to
be based on a collective identity supposedly shared by most of its members.
Collective identity needs to have a (mutually formed) past. [. . .] The past

has to be (re)constructed consciously and (of course) unconsciously through the selective process of remembering and forgetting in a retrospective way" (Imre 78). In Canada,

> cultural differences are overlapping or interrelated in various ways, not only as a result of cross-cultural relations and marriages, but, also, as a result of shifts in defining cultural and racial identities. [. . .] The metaphor of the cultural mosaic may have to be replaced with other metaphors such as "cultural tapestry" or "jazz" in which a "weave" of various strands of similarities and differences produces an assortment of cultural patterns and identities. (Garcea et al. 7)

Within this context, immigrant performance can force us to recognize the syncretic nature of a theatre practice produced by immigrant artists, embodying their critical response to the official doctrine of multiculturalism and their demand to be more actively involved in building the post-multicultural Canadian common space.

This collection brings these complex issues into focus. However, it would not have come to life without the very hard work of the writers, editors, and a team of consultants who spent hours researching, writing, commenting on, and discussing these chapters. Roberta Barker, the chief editor of the series, who accepted the proposal for this work back in 2015, has been this project's guardian angel. As she spent hours working on this book, providing detailed and insightful comments, helping authors polish their arguments and finesse their style, I came to think of Roberta as the most devoted, knowledgeable, and supportive partner of this journey. Without Roberta's wise navigation and advice, this project might have lost its course. My second special "thank you" goes to the CATR 2018 conference team that accepted the working group Theatre and Migration into its program, thus providing a venue for the contributors to share their ideas in person. My particular gratitude goes to Blake Sproule, who tirelessly worked on clarifying and checking historical and contextual details of this work. Annie Gibson has been the most dedicated publisher; without Annie's support this project would not ever have lifted off the ground. Last but not least, a very special thanks goes to every writer, artist, and scholar who has either worked on this project or been mentioned in these pages. This conversation is just a beginning: like an empty seat in a theatre hall, the absence of many voices from the pages of the book only indicates how much potential and how many stories are to be yet unearthed and brought into the spotlight of future publications on theatre, immigration, and Canada.

THEORETICAL PRIMER

PLAYING ON INDIGENOUS LAND: SETTLERS, IMMIGRANTS, AND THEATRE IN FICTIVE CANADA

ALAN FILEWOD

White Canadians are sunk in deep denial.

—Lee Maracle

I. COMPLICITY

A conversation about immigration and theatre in Canada must begin with the acknowledgement that theatre is deeply complicit in the ongoing colonial project of invasion, subjugation, and extraction on Indigenous land. The development of a theatre profession and a dramatic canon in Canada has functioned as a historical mechanism for creating affect to naturalize colonialism in what Richard Saunders calls "the fictive nation" (2). Saunders, an activist journalist and founder of the Coalition to Oppose the Arms Trade, argues that "Canada is built on a vast foundation of legal fictions, cultural constructs, religious fantasies, political fabrications and literary escapisms." Canada, he states, "is a true crime fiction in the imperial genre," and "we, as characters in this literary creation called Canada, must confront the true-crime mystery into which we've been written" (3). Saunders's provocative rhetoric makes a crucial point that helps to identify the particular link between nationhood and theatre.

The lived metanarrative of nationhood may be a fiction, but it is phenomenally and physically real to its citizens and its dispossessed victims. Like other resource-extraction colonies that transformed self-government and local economic regulation into nation-states in the nineteenth century, settler Canada's narrative developed as a simulacrum, as a state without any national purpose other than extraction. In the nineteenth-century sense of what a nation is, Canada lacked the fundamental requirement of nationhood; it lacked unity, whether ethnic, linguistic, or ideological. The anxiety generated by that lack is what has been so often called a search for identity, but in fact is simply the awareness that if nations are perceived to manifest principles of historical distinction, the only real national principle underpinning the settler Canadian nation is resource extraction. In this project, immigration has always been a necessary resource, to overwhelm and remove Indigenous populations, and to import a labour force to prepare the land for extraction.

If the nation is a simulacrum, the theatre is a space of simulation that makes it feel real. Nation and theatre do the same work of creating affective experiences; in the theatre we rehearse different simulations and reconfirm (often through dissent and contestation) our sense of who we are as a community. As a social mechanism for creating and transmitting feelings, theatre has been complicit in stabilizing understandings of nation and citizenship in an always adaptive, ongoing project of imperial colonization. In working through this troubled and troubling relationship, I have found the concept of theatrical nationhood to be a useful tool to explain the ways in which nation is imagined, rehearsed, and replayed in theatre culture: imaginatively in dramatic literature and performance texts, materially in its economic and disciplinary infrastructures, and ideologically in its systems of value. In this essay, I revisit some of the keywords that constitute theatrical nationhood, but to do that I need to critique my own usage of them, and to examine what I have invested in them. That is because for most of my career I have described myself as a "Canadian Theatre historian," which I now know really meant "historian of settler theatre in fictive Canada," of theatre in the colonial project of dominance and extraction on land that has been stewarded by Indigenous peoples for millennia.

Those who, like me, are settler-descended can only undertake this work by acknowledging what it means to be complicit in that colonial project. I take that as an ethical imperative. Because theatre has been from the beginning of European invasion an instrument of conquest and dominance, complicity means that it is impossible to speak about the history and culture of settler Canada from the comfort of an assumed impartiality. *Because* I have for much of my career focused on Canadian theatre history, this means that I find myself unsettling some core assumptions.[1] Consequently, this essay is necessarily personal: in part analysis, in part memoir, and in part apologia. It is also a manifesto: if theatre can be an instrument of colonization, it can also be used to decolonize. If we who are settler-descended are to unsettle theatre culture and begin the work of redress, we need to understand how our cultural industries have functioned as nation-building mechanisms that make the fictive nation seem real and establish categories of national subjectivity, thereby enforcing a sense of otherness in immigrants who are taught that they can aspire to sharing that sense.

Like all Canadians who are neither Indigenous nor first-generation immigrants, I am descended from immigrants, but that was never a word in my family history. My ancestors, including my parents, were of English descent and thought of themselves as British subjects. "Immigrant" to my young ears meant "foreign," like the Italian craftsmen who worked in my maternal grandfather's cabinetry firm, or my father's high-school chum in Victoria, who was Japanese Canadian and interned in a camp during the war because of it. Or the Lebanese grocer around the corner from my Ottawa home when I was in high school; I never knew his name, but many years later when I was in the neighbourhood by chance, he greeted me with a big smile and said, "I haven't seen you in a while." He had seen me more than I had seen him, because I was a part of the world he had to decode in order to survive.

We spoke casually, in the postwar decades that saw new waves of immigration, of "DPs" who were "fresh off the boat." Some were friends. A Hungarian refugee who lived with my family in 1957 introduced us to paprika, and my parents ever after sprinkled it on their baked potatoes. But there was always

---

1   I use "unsettling" here discursively, as Laura Moss introduced the term in 2003 in *Is Canada Postcolonial? Unsettling Canadian Literature*, and politically, as Arthur Manuel uses it in his 2015 *Unsettling Canada: A National Wake-up Call.*

an invisible line that separated "us" from "them." The settler state inculcates a sense of belonging in its subjects so that they (we) believe in the "home and native land." And yet the veneer of that belief is thin. We are bound in an emotional allegiance to a land that was stolen and repurposed as new, so that we could believe it was our homeland and we were native to it. "O Canada, our home and native extraction colony" cannot command love, but the mystical idea of a land that is new and untouched can. That is the power behind Tom Thomson's lonely jack pine on the Georgian Bay rock and Lawren Harris's theosophical iceberg. (Significantly, in all the paintings of the Group of Seven there are few images of industrial presence, let alone despoliation. The land is ancient, unspoiled, unpopulated.) As a child at my grandparent's cottage in Georgian Bay (where I never quite figured out where Lawrence, our "Indian" handyman, actually came from), I thrilled to walk into the forest and imagine that I was the first person to ever step there—oblivious, as too many are still today, to the obvious fact that people had been stepping there for thousands of years.

This is hard to write. It is hard to write that my grandfather, who had served in the First World War, had later clerked for the Toronto Dominion Bank in Cuba and then managed the cabinetry firm his father had founded, was a warm, generous man and a complete racist. He sponsored Italian and British immigrants because their skills enhanced his business, but, he said one night over supper, jabbing the air with his fork, he wouldn't hire "nigras" (his word) because they were lazy, nor "Indians" because they were shiftless drunks. Jews, he confided, gathered dead fish from the Humber River to sell on their pushcarts.

How did this racism become so entrenched in the Canada we believed to be peaceful and tolerant? And how did theatre function to reinforce this idea of an immigrant nation that refused to see its Indigenous population and cultivated racism to differentiate categories of subjectivity? That refusal to see indigeneity was deeply entrenched. As a child I knew that there were Indigenous people, but we were schooled in the nineteenth-century lie that they were the remnants of a disappeared world. When I was ten, I went to an "Indian Days" camp at the National Museum in Ottawa (the old museum on

Metcalfe Street). There we erected teepees, learned "crafts," and handled arti-facts. We all chose our "tribe." Having recently moved to Ottawa from Halifax, I declared for Mi'kmaq. Because I could, because it was a game.

What I came to realize over the years, in stages, over decades, was that the theatre culture I loved was perniciously complicit in the colonial vio-lence of racist differentiations and genocidal erasures. The very proposition of Canadian theatre, as historical aspiration and collective practice, had as its aim the cultivation of a sense of indigeneity in settler Canadians. That is the process by which extraction colonies remake themselves as sovereign states when they are given the legislative autonomy to raise revenue through taxa-tion and tariffs and to define the terms of citizenship. Emma Battell Lowman and Adam J. Barker, in their book *Settler: Identity and Colonialism in 21st Century Canada*, make the point that

> [a]s settler collectives exercise their sovereignty, over time narratives and stories are developed that construct that particular settlement territory as "special"—particularly beautiful or productive—and Settler people come to identify themselves through residency and belonging in this special locale. They differentiate themselves from their societies of origin by intensely identifying and focusing on the aspects of their new homelands that are "unique" and also by com-mitting violent or displacing acts against Indigenous peoples who have competing claims to these unique, special place. (28)

In effect, in order for colonizers to believe in their right to the land, they need to evolve over time a narrative that proposes the nation as historically inevi-table. Lowman and Barker develop this point to the next logical conclusion:

> We articulated the end goal of the settler colonial process as a drive to settler colonial transcendence, in which the settler soci-ety is normalized and universalized alongside the elimination of Indigenous peoples. This drive is informed by the settler colonial narrative structure that starts with the land as a blank canvas, then

follows the exceptional, individualized, and ultimately triumphant struggles of Settler people to establish themselves in the new land, and concludes with the emergence of a progressive, successful, and coherent society—one which proceeds confidently into the future with little memory of how or at whose expense their society was established. (108)

That narrative is the plot of thousands of Settler Canadian[2] plays; it was as true of Charles Mair's *Tecumseh* in 1886 as it was of Theatre Passe Muraille's iconic *The Farm Show* in 1972. It brings to mind the opening scene of *Paper Wheat*, the wildly successful 1977 collective play from Saskatoon about the founding of the western grain co-operatives and the establishment of the Saskatchewan Wheat Pool. At heart it was a sentimental tribute to the immigrant settlers who broke the prairie ground and endured years of toil and deprivation, as perceived by their grandchildren's generation.[3] The play begins with pageant-like scenes of European immigrants arriving to claim homestead grants and setting out to endure epic hardships. Nowhere in the play is there even a hint of a mention of the displaced Indigenous peoples and the wars they fought to resist this invasion. The heroic narrative of European sodbusters who built prosperity through adversity requires the land to be uninhabited and unclaimed, and so the play does the same work as the colonizers: it empties the land and repopulates it.

Darcy Lindberg, a Plains Cree legal scholar, connects the dots between the genocidal homesteader myth and Gerald Stanley, the Saskatchewan farmer who shot Colten Boushie in the head and was acquitted by an all-white jury: "You can choose to remember how Canadian-state law created the mythical Wheat King from the homesteader, how this myth-making was and still is one of the more important tools of colonialism. To enable this myth, the Plains

---

2   In this paper I follow Lowman and Barker's usage of identifying settler subjectivity as Settler Canadian, but retain the small s for the categorical "settler."

3   *Paper Wheat* was the subject of a National Film Board documentary made in 1979 by Albert Kish. It can be viewed on the NFB site, nfb.ca.

Cree in the area were imagined as a constant threat to the maintenance of such prairie kingdoms." Referring to the trial, he adds, "Wheat King imagery was very much alive in Stanley's defence. While not raising a claim of self-defence, his counsel found it important to let the jury know that 'we all know that a person's yard is his castle.'"

Even by mentioning *Paper Wheat*, I come up against my own complicity once more, because I wrote a chapter about it in my first book, and not once in my research and analysis did I perceive the genocidal absence of Indigenous Peoples (*Collective Encounters* 90–111). (How that could be the case is the subtext of this essay.) *Paper Wheat* was staged less than a century after Saskatoon had been founded. That is approximately the span of a human life, and in that time the settler narrative had successfully reorganized history. It is more than disconcerting to realize, nigh on fifty years since the play was done, that when it was produced there were people alive who had been born before Riel was executed for resisting colonial invasion.

Lowman and Barker's book calls upon Canadians of non-Indigenous descent to acknowledge Settler identity as a step toward the difficult work of decolonization, "the dismantling of the spaces, systems and stories of invasion that root Settler people to nation and state, and the simultaneous restoration of Indigenous ways of knowing and being on the land" (112). In that identity, the historical distinctions of anglophone, francophone, and immigrant/allophone identities are subsumed in what Lowman and Barker call a "trialectic" of subjectivities created by settler colonialism: "These three groups are settler colonizers, Indigenous Others and exogenous Others (which includes, for example, enslaved peoples, imported labour, and marginalized migrants)" (28). They caution that "there is far more dynamism between these groups than settler colonial perceptions might suggest" (29). Immigrants find themselves interpolated in a centuries-old colonial project in which they are often disadvantaged and subjected to violence. Lowman and Barker's trialectic complicates, but does not rupture, the fundamental colonial binary of Indigenous/Settler. The trialectic of Indigenous, settler, and immigrant is one of dynamic flux, adaptation, and resistance. The three parts of the trialectic intersect, often merging in human bodies and family homes. Lowman and Barker add that

[u]nder settler colonialism, all three categories are intended to eventually collapse down into one. What that means is that ultimately,
all problematic Others will be managed out of existence. Exogenous
Others will either be disciplined to fit into the dynamics of the settler collective as a whole [. . .] or they will be excluded permanently
through legal dehumanization or actual removal from the settler
state, both of which we can witness in the ongoing and increasing
deportations of refugees. Meanwhile, Indigenous Others are not targeted for incorporation. Rather, they and their competing claims to
the land are targeted for elimination. (29–30)

The notion of Settler identity explodes the foundations of Canadian theatre, which has developed as a nation-building enterprise predicated on the
idea that there is a historically viable, if elusive, Canadian nationality rooted
in founding cultures, which can expand to embrace and absorb newcomers
from other cultural backgrounds; this leads to the 1970s and the proposal of
a nation that is framed by founding cultures in tradition but is in actuality
multicultural. To confront what is at stake in that idea and its structures, I
need to take you into the room of a recent academic workshop on Canadian
theatre history, to expose a debate about an obscure play that retains the power
to rupture conventionalized understandings of what and who Canadian theatre has historically included. The purpose of the workshop was to discuss the
proposed contents for a forthcoming collection of documents and plays from
the history of theatre in Canada before the middle of the twentieth century. It
became clear in our discussions that there were very different understandings
of what Canada means, and how it is located historically.

The text that showed this rupture was one I had heard of but had never
read; in fact, for a long time it was considered lost. Written in 1766, George
Cockings's *The Conquest of Canada* may have been, as noted by Glen Nichols,
who brought it to the workshop, the first play in English set in Canada. It is
a thumping, bombastic, heroic tragedy about the conquest of Québec that
eulogizes Wolfe, catalogues the imperial conquests of 1759, and fetishizes
British naval and military glory. It is more of a pageant than a drama, with

a thin plot and roaring battle scenes. Eighteenth-century British theatre was busy with patriotic plays that, like this, stoked popular passion: many lines in this play are there to rouse cheers and applause from the house as they transform imperial conquest into theatrical affect, so that colonial power becomes mass feeling. This was the decade that saw Britain consolidate its global power with conquests in Canada and India, and thus consolidate what came to be known as the British Empire. The patriotic frenzy whipped up in the theatre was an important tool to recruit the working-class soldiers and sailors who did the dirty work of empire.

The discussion of *The Conquest of Canada* fractured around two opposing objections. On one hand, a participant objected that the play was unacceptable for inclusion because the author was an Englishman who had lived in New England for a time and had likely never set foot in Canada, and because there is no evidence that the play was ever staged in Canada. How could a play be included in a book about Canadian theatre if it was neither written by a Canadian nor staged in Canada?

There was a time when I would have agreed with that. But I found myself arguing that the play should be included for the very reasons I objected to it. It was a toxic instrument of colonization and eradication, but it could be useful to teach if it could lead to a fundamental reorganization of the cultural foundations of our theatre and reframe the history of performance in Settler Canada. *The Conquest of Canada*, when it was played before a London audience, claimed ownership of the newly conquered territory, and the play reminds us that our modern understanding of nation derives from that claim. As colonial politics sundered the British settler lands in ensuing years, forming different states and evolving new nationalisms, this play was an instrument of the imperial colonialism that organized part of itself as a Canadian state. It leads to the proposition that a Canadian play can be defined not by citizenship, geography, theme, or style, but as any play that enables, contributes to, arises from, or resists Settler dominance.

The Conquest of Canada was the first in what would become a long history of military dramas that staged settler invasion as heroic victory while at the same time enacting hierarchy that established racialized boundaries, between settlers and Indigenous peoples, and between British and "Exogenous Others." A useful example is a play written by veterans of the colonial expeditionary force that suppressed the Métis anticolonial uprising in 1885. *The 90th on Active Service, or, Campaigning in the North-West*, written by George Broughall (with songs by numerous others who served in the unit) and staged in Winnipeg with a cast of veterans, all identified by their militia rank in the cast list, is a cheery operetta that fondly recalls the daily routines of life on the campaign. Typical of late nineteenth-century popular theatre across North America, it is viciously racist, staging Black, Chinese, and Cree caricatures that are as vile as any minstrel show. At a time when there was not yet a category of Canadian citizenship, such caricatures differentiated classes of immigrants by national and ethnic origin, naturalized some as more legitimate as others, and marked others as inferior.

II. SUBJECTS, CITIZENS, AND OTHERS

The work of colonial settlement needed a continuous supply of labour, and as immigrants came from Europe and Asia to meet that demand, the developing settler colony needed to implement systems of categorization, both legal, as we see in the development of citizenship laws, and cultural, as we see in plays like *The 90th on Active Service*. That importation was the result of active recruitment of experienced farmworkers, famously described by Clifford Sifton (who was Minister of the Interior and Chief Superintendent of Indian Affairs in the Laurier government): "I think a stalwart peasant in a sheep-skin coat, born on the soil, whose forefathers have been farmers for ten generations, with a stout wife and a half dozen children, is good quality" (16). For Sifton, East European farmers were preferable to British workers, who were infected by socialism:

> A Trades Union artisan who will not work more than eight hours a
> day and will not work that long if he can help it, will not work on a
> farm at all and has to be fed by the public when his work is slack is,
> in my judgement, quantity and very bad quantity. I am indifferent as

to whether or not he is British-born. It matters not what his nationality is; such men are not wanted in Canada, and the more of them
we get the more trouble we shall have. (16)

But how were these immigrants to be assimilated into a Canadian identity? For the millions of British settlers who poured into the Canadian colonies
in the nineteenth century there were no borders to cross; they were British in
a British territory. There was no concept of Canadian citizenship until it was
used in the Immigration Act of 1910, and even then as a descriptor rather
than a legal status. From the moment that the Canadian provinces federated to
form a national state in 1867, the question of citizenship was fraught. Existing
subjects of the crown, including the Québécois (who had never asked for that
status but had it imposed upon them) were now subject to the regulatory laws
of the new federal state, which was more than a colony but something short
of a country. The 1868 Aliens and Naturalization Act stipulated that subjects
were either "Locally Naturalized Subjects" (by British birth) or Aliens, who
could become subjects after three years of residency by swearing an oath of
allegiance to the crown.

At the end of the nineteenth century, the rate of immigration swelled,
especially into the newly conquered western territories, purchased by the
Canadian government from the Hudson's Bay Company, to whom they had
been "given" by a far-away king centuries earlier. At the turn of the century,
the population of Canada was 56.47% British and 30% French. That ratio
would diminish over time, but it was not until after the Second World War that
the British-descended population decreased to less than 50% of the national
total (43.8 in 1961) (Historical Atlas). British Canadians saw immigration
both as an economic necessity and a cultural threat, and sought ways to erect
racial barriers to ensure white supremacy and anglo dominance within it.
According to the Canadian Human Rights Commission, "Between 1894 and
1899, 154,613 immigrants came to call Canada home. . . . Between 1896 and
1907, Canada admitted 1.3 million European and American immigrants. Less
than 900 Blacks were included in that number. . . . In fact, the black population of Canada decreased from 50,000 in 1860 to 17,000 in 1911." In 1911,

Wilfrid Laurier placed a one-year moratorium on "the Negro race, which race is deemed unsuitable to the climate and requirements of Canada" (Canadian Human Rights Commission).

The most famous single episode of racial exclusion—one of many—came three years later with the arrival of the *Komagata Maru* with its shipload of Sikh migrants seeking to settle in Canada, as was their legal right as British subjects. Anticipating that eventuality, the Canadian government had created a spurious reason to exclude non-white British subjects in 1908: "The Governor in Council may, by proclamation or order wherever he considers it necessary or expedient, prohibit the landing of any specified class of immigrants or of any immigrants who have come to Canada otherwise than by continuous journey from the country of which they are natives and upon tickets purchased in that country" (Van Dyk). Because the *Komagata Maru* had come via Japan, the government refused permission for the immigrating Sikhs to land. (Another moment of complicity: when I saw Sharon Pollock's *The Komagata Maru Incident* in 1976, I had no idea that my grandfather, then still living, was part of the story, as the chief medic on the naval cruiser that barred the ship from the port.)

Prior to the Second World War, Canadian citizenship was a loose concept that applied to any British subject who was allowed to live in Canada. (It wasn't until 1947 that the legal category of Canadian citizen came into being; my parents were born British subjects who had the right to call themselves Canadian citizens, even if it was a meaningless term; on 1 January 1947, they ceased to be British subjects. My father, the son of British immigrants, never reconciled to that.) But if subjectivity and citizenship status determined the right to live in the land claimed by the Canadian settler state, it did bring with it the right to vote, which was subject to racial, gender, and property restrictions that changed over time to adjust to political priorities. The history of voting in Canada is one of strategic racism.

In the cultural anxiety over immigration that permeated Canadian settler society at the turn of the twentieth century, the first conversations and proposals of a Canadian drama (understood as the theatrical and literary expression of the uniqueness of the new settler nation) emerged as a form of racial gatekeeping. It is significant, in the context of mid-century culture, that two prominent dramatists played significant roles in the establishment of the white supremacist state. The first was Nicholas Flood Davin, an Irish immigrant (and thereby a British subject) and publisher of the *Regina Leader*. His 1876 play *The Fair Grit or The Advantages of Coalition* is a clever political satire that became part of the project of building the field of (Settler) Canadian theatre history in the 1970s when it appeared in the first volume of Anton Wagner's recuperative anthology series, *Canada's Lost Plays*. The editorial introduction noted Davin's political career and described him as a "colourful figure" but made no reference to his formative role in one of the most horrific innovations of white settler hegemony (Wagner and Plant 12). Davin was a lawyer and Conservative member of Parliament whose 1879 *Report on Industrial Schools for Indians and Half-Breeds*, based on an extensive study of American models, was the blueprint for the residential school system that would inflict unthinkable violence against Indigenous People for the next century. Davin did make the point that these schools should be "non-sectarian" and operate under direct government control, but this was to "prevent dissension among the Indians," not to save them for the church-sponsored abuse that resulted in so many thousands of dead children, lost generations, and destroyed communities (17). Five years later, Davin was involved in another gatekeeping taskforce when John A. Macdonald appointed him Secretary to the Royal Commission on Chinese Immigration. After hearings in Canada and the United States, the commission dismissed most of the lurid racist accusations levied against Chinese immigrants but recommended limited immigration and the imposition of the notorious head tax.

The government quickly implemented Davin's recommendations for a residential school system; three decades later it came under the supervision of Duncan Campbell Scott, whose government career as Deputy Superintendent of Indian Affairs from 1913 to 1932 was his day job. His real vocation was literature. He was a celebrated poet, the author of short fiction and several dramas, and a frequent contributor on literary matters to periodicals in Canada and the United States. Today we would call him a "public intellectual." His play *Pierre* premiered at Hart House Theatre in its second season in 1921, but it is significant only because Vincent Massey included it in his pioneering anthology, *Canadian Plays from Hart House Theatre*, in 1926. Massey published his anthology as evidence of an emergent Canadian dramatic tradition: "plays that are Canadian—not self-consciously Canadian because they may have been given mechanically a 'Canadian' atmosphere, nor because they may deal with Canadian history or Canadian politics—but Canadian because the dramatists are good Canadians" (vi). For Massey, a country becomes a nation when that tautology becomes real in the theatre. Scott's one-act play is a curious domestic tragedy set in a small Québec village. The plot is a paternalistic anglophone's vision of a simple and rustic Québécois family: a cold winter night, a widowed mother missing her errant son, maple sugar shared with her faithful daughter, the village priest dropping by, the prodigal son returning, the son's deceit as he steals her money and returns to his dissolute life on the road. When considered in the context of the mystic nationalism of Hart House Theatre's early seasons, the hackneyed plot of *Pierre* seems odd.[4] It may be that Scott's impulse was to write folk tragedy in the genre of John Millington Synge's *Riders to the Sea*. But it is folk culture as perceived from an upriver position of political, cultural, and racial power. No one will remember Scott for his playwriting, but no one will forget him for the determination and zeal with which he oversaw the residential schools "to get rid of the Indian problem" (McDougall). In both his work and his literary writing, Scott was a builder of walls that reinforced white settler supremacy in the ostensible cause of inclusion.

III. SETTLER, IMMIGRANT, EMIGRÉ

Dramatists had been writing plays in Settler Canada for almost two hundred years when Massey published his volume, but the emergence of a Canadian drama, in the sense of "the" drama as a synecdoche of a dramatic canon that

---

4   For information on the early repertoire of Hart House, see Vincent Massey's two volumes of *Canadian Plays from Hart House Theatre*. For a discussion of theosophical mysticism at Hart House, see Scott Duchense's "The Impossible Theatre."

manifests the nation, entailed a curated selection mechanism that included some plays and precluded others, marginalizing them as "immigrant" or "multicultural." This process can be seen in the work of three playwrights writing in western Canada in the 1920s and '30s. All three were immigrants; two of them I encountered in my research into plays written by returned soldiers about their experiences in the trenches in France. The third I encountered in my previous research into the history of radical political theatre between the world wars. Together they offer a useful example of the complexity of the emergent categories of settler identity. These three men were immigrants to western Canada in the early years of the twentieth century, but they experienced different subjectivities. One was a British subject, and thus automatically a Canadian citizen; another was a Lithuanian Jew who, although he became a naturalized subject and later a citizen, negotiated the boundaries of settler and immigrant identities; and the third was a Ukrainian political émigré who refused Settler identity. They have curious overlaps: two of them served in the Canadian army in roughly the same time and place in the First World War, and two of them lived in the same city after the war. In each case, we can see how Settler status frames theatre work and how that work consolidates subjectivity.

In 1910, a young Englishman named William Staebler Atkinson arrived in Saskatchewan to take up a homestead grant that had been previously allocated to another settler. That settler had failed to make his land clearance deadlines, so the land was again up for grabs. Atkinson also failed, and he knocked around the west taking work in building trades until war broke out in 1914. He signed up, as did many others; most of the original contingent of the Canadian Expeditionary Force were British-born, although their proportion would decrease as the war went on. Atkinson had an eventful war. After serving for half a year in the trenches, he was transferred to England because of illness; while recovering, he became an administrator in an army hospital and married a local woman. He was transferred to a recuperation hospital in Vernon, BC, in 1917, and after his discharge from the army remained there for the rest of his life. He was variously a hospital administrator, an insurance agent, and a tax accountant, but his great passion was writing plays. Between

1925 and 1943, he registered fifteen plays for copyright, some of which were produced with success. With the exception of a bleak memoir play based on his experiences in the trenches, they are light comedies, with titles that tell us all we really need to know about them, such as *Percy of the Prairie*, *Sentimental Sally*, and *Ogo Pogo, or the Sea Serpent*. His most successful plays were romantic comedies set in the fruit-growing farms of the Okanagan. He had a major theatrical breakthrough early on when the impresario and early film exhibitor J.A. Schuberg produced *So This Is Canada* for a six-week run at the Empress Theatre in Vancouver, followed by a cross-country tour (which seems to have run out of steam in Winnipeg).

So *This Is Canada* is a genial and witty farce about three ex-service-men trying to run a fruit farm in the Okanagan. They are on the verge of failure and bankruptcy, but they labour to maintain the pretense to their families back "home" in Britain that they are successful, prosperous, and married. Antics ensue when relatives arrive without warning, which triggers the familiar mechanics of farce—cross-dressing, doors slamming, disastrous coincidences, romance, and happy endings. With its cast of British characters (one of whom was played by a popular Australian comedian) and its com-fortably familiar plot, *So This Is Canada* transforms its Okanagan locale into an imperial orchard, and indeed Atkinson titled one of his follow-up plays in that genre *Little England*. Atkinson was the exemplary settler who planted his cultural history on land that had been seized from the Interior Salish people within his lifetime, and that was still contested.

If Atkinson embodied what Daniel Coleman has called "white civility," the proposition of a normalizing citizenship that privileges whiteness and British descent, Simon Jauvoish embodied the successful immigrant who lives on the margins of Settler identity. He had immigrated to Winnipeg in 1903 at the age of seven, from what is now Lithuania, in the company of his older brother, a rabbi, and his sister. Jauvoish studied medicine at the University of Manitoba, but his studies were interrupted by the First World War. He was a pacifist and an idealist, but he enlisted because he believed firmly that the war, which he ascribed to German militarism, would be the last war human-ity would ever fight. Of the approximately one thousand men named in the nominal roll of his battalion, he is the only one listed as originating from somewhere other than Britain, the colonial dominions, or the United States. Jauvoish had a brutal war in the trenches, and was wounded at Vimy Ridge; on his return he completed medical school and practised as a physician (with another spell in the army as a medical officer on the home front in the Second World War). He was active in the Jewish community, giving lectures about Spinoza to the local chapter of Young Judaea. And he wrote poetry and plays, one of which he produced in 1934. *Dawn in Heaven* is a bitter character study about a young idealist who joins the army, only to be destroyed by the brutality of the military judicial system for a casual moment of insubordination.

Jauvoish was typical of many immigrants in his time, living in the interstices of British settler identity, not quite assimilated—anti-Semitism was pervasive in immigrant communities as well as in the dominant British settler society—but not quite isolated. Winnipeg, like Montréal and Toronto, was a centre of Jewish culture and education. There had been a small Jewish population in the Red River Settlement in 1901, sixteen years after the defeat of Riel. Two years before Jauvoish arrived, there were 1,164 Jews in Winnipeg out of a total population of 45,000 (Beit Hatfutsot). In 1921, when Jauvoish was in his final year in medical school, the Jewish population numbered 14,837 out of a total of 180,000. During a time of dizzying urban growth, the Jewish population grew from approximately 6% to 12% of the population. Like the large communities of Poles and Ukrainians, the Jewish community in Winnipeg found itself marking the boundaries of white Settler identity: boundaries that were, as Jauvoish's example shows, open to class privilege. Winnipeg was a multicultural city dominated by a British settler mercantile elite, to which Jauvoish's military record and medical degree gave him access. The *Winnipeg Tribune*, when reviewing *Dawn in Heaven*, noted that the premier of Manitoba was in the audience ("War Play").

The third playwright in this example was an émigré who also came to Winnipeg, but with no intention of acquiring citizenship and certainly no intention of swearing allegiance to the crown. Andrii Babiuk had been born in Kolomyia in what is now Ukraine, but was then a territory of the Austro-Hungarian empire. He trained as a teacher in Lviv, and joined the

Austro-Hungarian army when war broke out; by the end of the war, his unit
had been absorbed into the revolutionary Red Ukrainian Galician Army.
He served as an editor and propagandist in the army, and assumed the pen
name Myroslav Irchan. In 1922 he moved to Winnipeg to undertake cultural
activism with the Ukrainian Labour-Farmer Temple Association, the primary
communist organization in the politically polarized Ukrainian community.
In his seven years in Canada, Irchan wrote ten plays, all in Ukrainian; they
were extraordinarily popular, and some were still being performed in the
1950s. The Ukrainian community, like many other immigrant communities
but more so than most, was partial to theatre as a commemorative, collective
vehicle of cultural patriotism. Orest T. Martynowych makes the point that,

> The repertoire to which Winnipeg's Ukrainian theatre-goers were
> exposed before 1924 was quite narrow and parochial. Unlike Jewish
> and Finnish immigrants, whose theatre familiarized them with the
> European classics, introduced them to mainstream North American
> culture, and examined contemporary topics such as the status of
> women and class relations in modern industrial societies, most plays
> performed by Ukrainian drama circles were fixated on the nine-
> teenth-century Ukrainian village. . . . Sentimental comedies and
> works of populist "ethnographic realism" were popular in Winnipeg
> and throughout Canada because they were written with unsophisti-
> cated rural and lower-class urban audiences in mind. (16)

Jars Balan has identified 120 plays by two dozen Ukrainian Canadian
playwrights in the first half of the century. Ten of these were by Irchan. They
are, for the most part, anti-capitalist potboilers: in *Underground Galicia* a
Polish spy infiltrates a Ukrainian communist organization and kills the woman
who risked her life to save him from the police in a staged prison escape;
in *The Miser*, Irchan transposes Molière's comedy into a story about a rich
Ukrainian patriarch in Canada whose greed almost destroys his family. His
most popular play, *Family of Brushmakers*, had more than seventy separate
productions. In total, by Balan's count, there were approximately 260 separate

productions of Irchan's plays. No other playwright at that time comes close to that number. Irchan was by far the most successful playwright in Canada in the first half of the century. Charles Roslin, in an article on Irchan in *Saturday Night*, wrote, "He addresses himself exclusively to his compatriots, lives aloof from the general life of Canada, and is unknown to the mass of Canadians. Yet he is, one may contend, the most popular and influential author in the country" (77). No one, not even Irchan himself, would consider him a Canadian playwright, and yet, in a doubled negative that speaks to the complexities of Settler culture, he is not *not* a Canadian playwright.

For Atkinson, theatre was a vector of cultural transplantation that confirmed the settler nation as an expansion of Britain; for Jauvoish, it was a place of cultural negotiation that tested the boundaries of inclusion in Settler identity; but for Irchan, it was a means to resist inclusion and to perpetuate a militant Ukrainian left-wing nationalism. What they had in common was a theatre culture that existed only in entrepreneurial or amateur ventures; there was no theatre profession as we know it today, no system of public support, and no equation of theatre and state nationhood.

IV. FICTIVE INDIGENEITY

Over the first half of the twentieth century British dominance in Settler culture came under pressure from two destabilizing forces. Immigration was of course one, as an increasing percentage of the population rubbed up against colonial attitudes and racism; the second, not unrelated, was socialism. The crack in settler dominance was most visible in 1919 when Winnipeg trade unionists called a general strike. Ten thousand war veterans paraded in the streets to pressure the government to settle it, but the federal government, fearing Bolshevik insurrection, passed repressive legislation to prevent "subversive" labour actions. To enforce that legislation, the government established the Royal Canadian Mounted Police as an anti-communist domestic security service, costumed in the regalia and romantic (to British Canadians) traditions of the former North-West Mounted Police. Three years later, representatives of various left-wing trade unions and socialist parties met in a barn in Guelph,

Ontario, to form the Communist Party of Canada as a diverse coalition of "language federations," chiefly British, Finnish, Jewish, and Ukrainian (until the Stalinist Communist International decreed that the separate divisions be abolished in favour of a unitary party in 1929). Settler culture was increasingly polarized politically, and in this struggle theatre became on one side a way of consolidating a new Settler identity that saw itself as coming into autonomous nationhood, and on the other a weapon to attack the capitalist regime.

It was in this cauldron of class and ethnic tensions that the idea of "Canadian theatre" developed and its infrastructures roughed out. The key concept in this was the idea of national theatre. Throughout the twentieth century there were various schemes to establish a theatre that would represent and enact the Canadian nation, although no one was really sure what that might be. Many of the proposals drew on the ornate governance model and rhetoric of the Dominion Drama Festival, which had been formed in 1932 to produce national competitions of amateur theatre. Many saw in its decentralized structure as a model for a possible National Theatre, but in almost every case the proposals were heavy on bureaucratic structures and light on considerations of actual artistic practice. They were also paternalistic in their cultural assumptions. In the early 1950s, for example, the Writers and Players Club of Ottawa made a bid to become the National Theatre Company, and requested that the government build a theatre to house it. They proposed that "encouragement be given to the writing and production of 'native' Canadian plays—that is drama dealing with a) the mythical legendary or 'pre-historic' Canada[,] b) the period from the earliest historic contact of white with Indian, on through the French and British regimes to the present era of Canadian nationhood" (Writers and Players Club). To consolidate the idea of Canadian settler culture as "native," they further proposed to place this pedagogical cultural nationalism in the context of European tradition, "the world classics of the stage shall be given due attention, and two months of every year shall be devoted to French-spoken drama."

The idea of a national theatre that manifests the spirit of a people derives from the ethnic nationalisms of nineteenth-century Europe that arose in the breakdown of the imperial system. They typically used as their metonym the work of a poet/playwright who wrote the nation into being, and whose work became the proof of national genius. Britain was a bit late to the game of national theatre, but when it did get there it had the advantage of an already ensconced national playwright who would be hailed (by the British) as the supreme genius of all literature and all time. But that racialist conflation of nation, literature, and ethnicity was never going to work in a settler society. National theatre schemes in Canada thus focused on instrumentality: a theatre culture would, with proper training and guidance, in time produce the literature that would prove nationhood. In his introduction to *Canadian Plays from Hart House Theatre*, Vincent Massey articulated the superimposition of theatre and nation: "Let us welcome therefore every group of men and women who come together 'to do a play', whether they use a theatre, a church, a school or a barn for their purpose. There is no finer form of communal effort than this, in which everyone, whatever his or her calling, can find a place" (vi).

Massey was in time the man called on by the Liberal government of Louis St. Laurent to chair a royal commission into culture, which in 1951 called for the introduction of public funding in the arts (as a form of Cold War cultural defence), and the creation of the Canada Council for the Arts (modelled on the British Council). Massey's protege, the journalist, novelist, and playwright Robertson Davies, wrote a brief for the commission which looked to London's Old Vic Theatre, where he had worked briefly under Tyrone Guthrie, as a model for a Canadian theatre. It drew upon the Dominion Drama Festival for a cultural federalist system in which a national theatre might function as a summit company without claiming centricity. The Massey Commission's chief legacy to the theatre was the institutional system in which it would develop: a system clearly designed to implement a model of theatrical federalism that would serve as a metonym of the national state, with an apex exemplary company and a system of regional theatres that would spawn smaller alternatives. And it follows that the *ways* in which a play is done, in its productive procedures and systems of organization, also model the logic of the nation.

This vision of a theatrical profession grounded in tradition that would channel talent up the pyramid from local efforts to a standardizing peak company became the source code for the development of a professional theatre

economy in Canada. This logic was later applied to theatre companies themselves in the Canada Council's policy of hierarchical funding, which placed
theatres in a pyramid of value and material support according to their (perceived) importance in the tradition of humanist culture. The conditions of a
hierarchical, elite, and federalist theatrical profession had been articulated and
demonstrated, but the logic of the pyramid was missing one crucial element:
the emergent theatrical company that would earn the honorific of "National
Theatre" by its uncontested "traditions, its methods of work, its individual
style, and its faithful and appreciative public" (Davies 169). The missing cat-
alyst in Canada was the absence of a leader, an artistic director who would
provide "inspiration, instruction, succour, rebuke and a focus of faith for all
who worked with him," and who would "provide the public with a figurehead
whom they could trust and admire" (167). In describing this patriarchal theatrical "messiah," Davies gestured obliquely to Tyrone Guthrie and by so doing
brought his two mentors together in a conversation that would culminate two
years later in the founding of the Stratford Festival (167).

Stratford set out to do what Davies expected of a national theatre, to
"move Canadians to tears and laughter with great plays of the past, and with
great plays of the present (including perhaps a few of their own)" (170).
For the next fifty years Stratford would adhere to its claim as the summit of
Canadian theatre professionalism, the peak of disciplinarity that was supposed to produce coherence in the theatrical system. But it failed to produce
a theatre culture that would submit to the authority of mastery and tradition.
As the Canada Council found to its dismay in the early 1970s when the new
wave of "alternative" theatremakers came knocking at the door, the Stratford
model was not what young Canadian artists wanted.

Why, at a time when Canadian settler society opened the doors to
increased immigration and began to drop racial restrictions, when public
discourse in Canadian society circulated a new kind of nationalism that was
more receptive of pluralism, and when Settler Canadians began to think of
themselves as post-colonial subjects rather than the colonizers they continued
to be, did this emergent theatre system seem so British? In part it was because
the systems of value trickled downward from Shakespeare: to do Shakespeare

you need a proper playhouse; you need trained theatre craftspeople; you need actors who can carry it off. From those assumptions unrolled an entire structure of disciplinarity that never stopped to question why we would be doing Shakespeare in the first place. Was he really the universal genius? Or was he an over-invested ethnic playwright?

In another light, Shakespeare offered immigrant settlers a pathway to becoming Canadian—that is, to merge with the Settler identity. And so it was, to give just one example, that Bruno Gerussi, the son of Italian working-class immigrants, stepped onto the Stratford stage in its second season to become one of the most acclaimed classical actors in Canadian theatre history. Sustained by Shakespeare and the power of British tradition, the colonial project claimed ownership not just of land, but of history itself, slowly ascribing to its citizens a sense of indigenous right to what it had stolen. But that sense required the dispossession and displacement of the actual Indigenous Peoples. In the theatre, we see this act of removal in the long history of racial surrogation in which white colonists used the same techniques to erase Indigenous identity as they did to suppress Black presence, using mimicry and distortion in surrogative representations.[5] We like to think of that as a nineteenth-century phenomenon, but it is still very much alive.

Shakespeare was a crucial link that offered a surrogative mechanism by which immigrants could become Canadians, and Canadians could become (or believe themselves to become) indigenous. At the same historic moment that immigrant actors like Gerussi found that to be Canadian was to perform Shakespeare in high classical style, Shakespearean actors closed the bracket of the equation by "indigenizing" Shakespeare. The notorious example is the "Eskimo *Lear*," which the Canadian Players, an offshoot of the Stratford Festival that sought to realize the Massey Report's vision of an exemplary

---

5   Joseph Roach introduced the concept of surrogation in theatre history discourse in his landmark 1996 book *Cities of the Dead: Circum-Atlantic Performance*. Whereas Roach uses the term to explore how culture renews itself through performance in material spaces, I borrowed it in my book *Performing Canada: The Nation Enacted in the Imagined Theatre* to describe how post-imperial culture expropriates indigeneity through racial mimicry, and beyond that, how colonial cultures create simulations of imperial authenticity.

national touring company, played across Canada and the United States in
1961. William Hutt played Lear in a production design that placed the play
in an Inuit setting with no involvement by or consultation with Inuit collaborators. It is a project that would, I hope, be unthinkable today; it not only
involved the most flagrant appropriation of Inuit culture, it also deliberately
distorted that culture for artistic effect.[6] David Gardner, then at an early stage
of a distinguished career as an actor, director, cultural bureaucrat, and theatre
historian, conceived of the idea of a King Lear ranting in furs in the arctic.
Gardner later recalled the origins of the production:

> I was lying in the sun, visiting with friends on an island in Georgian
> Bay, when I hit upon the idea of a Native Peoples *Lear*, either
> Amerindian or Eskimo; a non-Christian semi-oriental culture intro-
> duced to America across the Bering land-bridge and reaching back
> centuries before the coming of the Europeans, perhaps as far back as
> the stone age. I settled quite quickly on an arctic *Lear* situated on top
> of the world, Eskimo rather than Indian, because of an extra sense
> of bleak removal and heightened universality. (3)

He did not explain how the northern landscape was to his cultural eye "bleak"
and universal, but perhaps there is a clue in a remark he made to a journalist
with *Life* magazine: "We were trying to put the play back into primitive context where it belongs" ("A Deep-Freeze Lear").

Gardner and designer Herbert Whittaker (best known as the influential
drama critic for the *Globe and Mail* from 1949 to 1975) studied artifacts at

---

6   There have been subsequent productions that situate (as opposed to adapt) Shakespeare
in Indigenous contexts, such as Skylight Theatre's Haida Gwaii themed *The Tempest*, in
1987, with a cast of Stratford veterans and Indigenous performers (including Monique
Mojica, René Highway, and Billy Merasty) directed by Lewis Baumander, and the 2012 *King
Lear* directed by Peter Hinton at the National Arts Centre, with an all-Indigenous cast that
included August Schellenberg, Tantoo Cardinal, Jani Lauzon, and Monique Mojica. It can
be argued that both of these productions recruited Indigenous artists into artistic structures
that reproduced colonial relations in Settler theatre institutions under settler direction.

the Royal Ontario Museum to ensure ethnographic exactitude in the costumes and props, although Whittaker admitted some compromises: "Eskimo
women dress just like men, so I've put them in what you might call arctic tea
gowns" ("A Deep-Freeze Lear"). Gardner later claimed that the production ·
contributed in its way to cultural reconciliation, writing that "Canada's Eskimo
Lear happened at a time when Canadian theatre was just getting into gear
and Canada was openly attempting to discover its own identity, and doing
so by very belatedly honouring the art and culture of its Native Peoples" (9).

The Gardner-Hutt *Lear* was by no means the only Indigenous-themed
Shakespearean production that confused colonial extraction and "honouring," but it is important because it shows so clearly how deeply the colonial
extraction project has been rooted in theatre culture. Like the Wheat King
myth on the plains, the "Eskimo *Lear*" took place in evacuated cultural space;
its fake anthropological primitivism bore no relation to the actual lives and
culture of Inuit people. That evacuated space was not just metaphorical; it is
important to recall that only seven years earlier the Canadian government
had relocated Inuit communities from their homes, moving them a thousand
kilometres north to Ellesmere and Cornwallis islands in order to assert sovereignty over the high arctic in the Cold War.

V. MANIFESTO: DECOLONIZING THEATRE

Theatre developed in Settler Canada as a means to make colonialism feel right
and to instill fictive indigeneity, but it also developed as a means to critique,
resist, and disrupt. The irony of my own formation was that the oppositional theatre of my youth was really a generational reset of settler cultural
appropriation. The alternative theatre movement of the 1960s and '70s was a
repudiation of the British cultural tradition, perceived as residual colonialism
by Settlers who were ourselves colonizers. Much of the thrust of the movement came from immigrants, among whom American draft resistors were
particularly vocal and adept at working their way into influential positions.
I first encountered the idea that we were struggling to create "indigenous"
theatre in the early seventies in the pages of *Canadian Theatre Review*, which

was co-founded and edited by Don Rubin, himself an American immigrant. Some time later I used that same appropriative vocabulary in my first book, writing about plays like *Paper Wheat* and *The Farm Show* without seeing the genocidal source of the vision of a fictive post-colonial Canadian cultural authenticity (where everyone is white and heterosexual, and where multiculturalism means that some people have strange names and accents).

The idea of the ruthless corporate extraction colony has become a familiar trope in contemporary science fiction (think of *Avatar*), possibly because we who are settlers can never pretend that we have deep history in these lands. There is always dissonance. The theatre has been a mechanism to ease that dissonance, to make a short history seem deep, and to cultivate a sense of belonging, which becomes a sense of ownership, which reinforces the right to extract. That is how the operation of the trialectic aligns Settler identity with the work of global neo-liberal economics. But extraction colonies need labour, and immigrants need to be able to feel a sense of belonging, to "put down roots," and so the scripts of Settler identity are adaptive. In this, too, theatre has been instrumental. It has functioned as a mechanism for assimilation and for resistance, and often as both at once, because, as we discovered in the 1970s, the work of resistance can replenish the structures we contest.

In 2018, theatre in Settler Canada is still an extractive industry, mining stories for what I have called self-selected value-seeking audiences. The theatre profession is formed in cultural assumptions that are part of the apparatus by which the colonial state renews itself. It is also materially embedded in local economies; the Stratford Festival, for example, is the public sector economic pump for a city of 31,000 people. Culturally and materially, the theatre reproduces the neo-liberal state, and like that state it feeds on pluralism. It needs a constant infusion of creative energy, which it channels to replenish its fundamental structures. We see that in the sectoring of theatre work, with the chaotic pluralism of the fringe functioning as the research and development lab for the institutionalized theatre industry.

To change that, to move toward a decolonized theatre that disrupts the stratification that materially and culturally privileges "founding culture" settlers, those of us who have benefited by our identity as Settler Canadians, need to acknowledge that privilege. We need to understand the relationship of that identity to the cultural blocs it contains, and to build alliances with Indigenous activists. Lowman and Barker define decolonization as the "dismantling of the spaces, systems and stories of invasion that root settler people to nation and state" (111). That is obviously a long and difficult process. For Settler Canadians who are engaged in theatre culture, the question we face is: How do we decolonize theatre?

For those whose identity is shaped by immigration or precarious migrancy, the question has always been one of negotiating a reconciliation between the culture of origin and the promises of a new home that is multicultural in its civic life, monocultural in its hegemonic colonial formation, and bicultural in its relationship to European settler cultures and Indigeneity. Theatre has been an effective platform for that negotiation, as countless plays about generational conflict and adaptation in immigrant families have shown. Immigrant-identified Canadians may resist being defined as colonial settlers, just as Settler Canadians may resist taking responsibility for a history into which they were born, but all are positioned in the dynamic of colonialism in which identity forms in relational positions.

So, how do we work toward decolonizing theatre? Lowman and Barker point to one direction in their reference to dismantling stories: theatre developed in Settler Canada as a means (one of many) to create stories that instill fictive indigeneity. That explains the historic preoccupation with "the Canadian playwright," as expressed by early settler-nationalist writers like Massey, and by the playwrights and cultural bureaucrats who came together in 1971 under the auspices of the Canada Council to discuss why so few theatres were producing Canadian plays. In their deliberations, they "examined the working conditions of the playwright, looked at his economic prospects, discussed practical ways to enhance his professional status and improve his economic lot" (Gaspé 302). The document they produced, familiarly known as the Gaspé Manifesto, called for a quota of fifty percent Canadian plays in publicly funded theatres because "we believe there is no meaningful Canadian theatre except where our playwrights take a major role in it" (Gaspé 303). I suggest that there is a direct relationship between the metonymic, male-gendered concept of "the playwright" and the larger project of colonial extraction; "the playwright" carried the responsibility of creating the stories that would make the settler-nation real, even if they were oppositional or dissident.

The alternative that I see is one that has already proven effective in theatre work by immigrant and minoritized artists whose experience of subjectivity as settlers has been difficult because of racism, sexism, and ableism, and who have had to struggle to establish themselves in what the Canada Council used to call the theatre "ecology." They bootstrapped new artistic ventures by identifying and reaching out to audiences that needed them. Playwrights were involved in that, but so were directors, actors, designers, and craft workers. Their theatre projects were audience-driven in a way that was not the case for the white anglo theatres that continue to dominate the stratified cultural pyramid. Decolonizing theatre means dismantling that pyramid and building alliances within the trialectic. There are examples of this kind of alliance-building all across the country; the one closest to me in my home community of Kitchener-Waterloo is the MT Space, a theatre that in its ten years of operation has become a leading innovator in rethinking what theatre can do. It was founded by an immigrant from Lebanon who realized that if he was a trained theatre artist unable to find work, there must be others. Over time Majdi Bou-Matar developed the MT Space as a culturally diverse ensemble that drew on Kitchener-Waterloo's growing immigrant communities. The company's name references both its mission to create multicultural theatre and its creative method of making devised physical theatre (with a nod to Peter Brook). Along with its creative programming, the company hosts a biennial IMPACT Festival of national and international Indigenous / culturally diverse physical theatre. This may sound not unlike other immigrant-centred theatre companies, but two things stand out for me about the MT Space. The first is that it has developed to become the most acclaimed theatre in the culturally underserviced region between Toronto and Stratford; the second is that from the outset it has engaged in an active alliance with Indigenous artists, including a co-production with Gwaandak Theatre. Productive alliances between immigrant and Indigenous artists like this open a path to a means of decolonization, but they are othered by cultural politics that continue to prioritize the extraction values of the settler state. Forty minutes down the road from the MT Space, the Stratford Festival is still there. In 2016–2017, the Canada Council gave the Stratford a subsidy of $970,000. It gave the MT Space $17,800. That inequity points clearly down one road to decolonization.

PART ONE.
CANADIAN IMMIGRATION AND THEATRE HISTORY PARADIGMS

IMMIGRATION HALL AND LAST STANDS IN NORTHWEST PERFORMANCE (CA. 1885–1905)

IAN MCWILLIAMS

The appearance of the boys, dressed as they were in military uniform and equipment with rifles and bayonets . . . suggested the idea, that the red man of the west, if trained as these cadets are, might also be called upon to take up arms for king and country, if required.
—Review of the "Emmanuel College Band Concert"
in the *Prince Albert Advocate*, 3 February 1902

Her forte lies in portraying the unflinching bravery and the unquenchable hatred of the red man . . . it is with difficulty that the listener can persuade himself that she is not really possessed of the feelings she portrays.
—Review of "Miss E. Pauline Johnson, the Famous Indian Elocutionist"
in the *Prince Albert Advocate*, 25 January 1898

During the era of settlement, prairie town halls and their associated performative events contributed to foundational and ongoing negotiations of community identity in the new populations of Canada's northwest. Central to these negotiations was establishing who was *included* and who was *excluded* from the community. Most of the (im)migrants to the Canadian Prairies of this era were of European origin, many coming via Eastern Canada or the United States. These immigrants will hereafter be referred to as settlers: a term commonly used in the era of European prairie settlement, as these were immigrants who were actively (re)settling/colonizing the region. Today, "settler" (defined in brief and broad terms only) is a term often used to differentiate between the Indigenous Peoples of a region and those who come from settler/colonizer backgrounds generally. As Alan Filewod discusses in this volume's opening essay, immigrants *are* necessarily settlers. He also notes the additional stratifications of immigrant-settlers. In the Canadian West, British subjects were self-positioned at the height of privilege and power. Their position depended upon displacing Indigenous people to the lowest end of this same spectrum. Hence, local Indigenous Peoples were, with few notable exceptions, almost completely excluded from prairie town-hall performances. Indeed, settlers' senses of security or permanence depended heavily upon the literal and figurative removal of local Indigenous peoples.

Performances in early settler communities helped to establish and reinforce settlers' founding stories. The study of such performances and stories is thus key to better understanding the deep roots of the colonial founding myths upon which the story of Canadian settlement has been established. These founding myths, born out of the cult of prosperity and agreed-upon denial of the realities of Indigenous populations, entrenched colonial power structures and were vital to the negotiation of community identity in the Canadian Northwest.

The performances presented in this paper are atypical, for they involve presentations of, and performances by, Indigenous people in settler town-hall spaces in Qu'Appelle and Prince Albert of what is now Saskatchewan. I give context for these performances by considering a painting by Robert Rutherford, displayed in the Qu'Appelle Immigration Hall, which helps to introduce Joseph Roach's theories of effigying and surrogation: two processes that drive the creation of memories that erase historical storylines perceived as undesirable by the communities involved. The processes of effigying and surrogation also take place through live bodies, as will be discussed in relation to performances by E. Pauline Johnson (Tekahionwake) and students from Emmanuel College (a residential school near Prince Albert). Local reactions to these Indigenous performers, who were cast in traditional Anglo European performance forms, reflect the degree to which—and conditions under which—such performers were viewed as acceptable within the wider historical events and ideological forces at play in the settlement of the Canadian West circa 1885–1905.

Perhaps the most prominent settler-ideal of this time and place was Progress, a word that I capitalize here to reflect its use throughout the press in the Canadian West during this era. The necessity of Progress—especially when linked to boosterism, settlement, land- and resource-development, economic expansion, and the imperial exercise—was viewed as an ever-present, all-consuming, unquestionable Truth. The notion of Progress is thus a powerful force behind colonialization. Its value is reaped by settler "civilization" and its price borne by Indigenous populations. While that price is being extracted, settlers sentimentalize. Sunera Thobani's work aptly summarizes our nation's shaky foundation myths, identifying Canadian colonization as a "'phantasmogoric project' that embraces colonialism as inevitable and desirable by ambivalently positing First Nations peoples either as members of a doomed race to be mourned or as noble savages requiring 'forceful subjugation'" (58). The performances discussed herein certainly demonstrate some of the ways in which this project played out in the Prairies. They also show, however, that there was also room for more complex readings and even occasional challenging of the settler mythos in the Canadian West.

PROGRESS AND GROWTH

During the 1885–1905 era, population growth in the Prairies was astounding. Bill Waiser observes that, in the area that would become Saskatchewan, "the 1891 population (41,522) grew 127% by 1901 (91,279) and another 182% just five years later (257,763)" (9). This population boom was almost entirely a result of settlement, as "immigrants effectively swamped the First Nations population" (9). This overwhelming of the Indigenous populations—by settler populations that were mostly British, young, and male (Department of Agriculture 10–18)— bolstered myths that positioned settlers as rightful inheritors of the west, for "Canadian colonialism . . . lay grounded in one key assertion: Aboriginals did not own the land upon which they had lived, loved, and died for thousands of years" (Anderson and Robertson 43). Settlers adopted the persistent, incorrect belief that Indigenous populations were dying out (Anderson and Robertson 12). In fact, the Indigenous population did drop slightly between 1901 and 1906, but increased thereafter. This rise didn't convince the Department of Indian Affairs (as it was then called) to re-evaluate its deep-seated opinion that "Indians" were a dying race to be segregated from the rest of the population (Waiser 16). This opinion was accepted as a natural course, according to Daniel Francis: "Canadians believed firmly in Progress, and progress demanded that the inferior civilization of the Indian had to give way to the superior, White civilization. Progress had its price, and the Indian was expected to pay it" (73).

QU'APPELLE, NWT

Between 1885 and 1905, the town of Qu'Appelle was a regional hub of commerce, transportation, communication, religion, governance, and justice (Qu'Appelle Historical Society; McLennan). Prominent residents believed in the ideal of Progress; Qu'Appelle boosters hoped that their town would someday become a territorial or provincial capital (Wickenheiser; Amos). The Immigration Building (or Immigration Hall) was the social hub of this crossroad town in Canada's "new" West. Built by the federal government to house settlers temporarily, it also variously housed governmental, judicial, and religious entities. Qu'Appelle's settlers commandeered it as a theatre, dance hall, and meeting place. Imported performance traditions were almost entirely British (with offshoot traditions from North America's eastern seaboard and Central Canada). The hall hosted various performances by professional touring troupes, local amateurs, overwintering militia troops, North-West Mounted Police (NWMP) officers (whose minstrel troupe was regionally popular), and local religious and civic groups.

As the Canadian Pacific Railway's railhead, Qu'Appelle served as a transfer point for soldiers deployed in response to the 1885 North-West Resistance.[1]

---

1 The North-West Resistance has also been referred to by other names, e.g., the North-West Rebellion, Northwest Uprising, or the Second Riel Rebellion.

When those troops were recalled, the Royal Canadian Artillery B Battery over-wintered in Qu'Appelle before returning to Québec. They lived in Immigration Hall and built its first stage. By Christmas 1885, Qu'Appelle's newspaper, the *Progress*, reported on plans to start performances in the theatre, "where during the winter minstrels, farces, plays, etc., will entertain the citizens of this town . . . leading amateurs are taking part" ("Area Belle").

As the name Immigration Hall suggests, this was not a place that welcomed Indigenous people. Settler audiences expected that the region would be dominated by white, British, and Christian peoples and that this domination would only become more complete as time passed. The persistence of the disappearing or doomed "Indian" trope in settler mythology is identified by Thobani as one of the discursive tools that enables settlers to forcefully subjugate Indigenous populations (58), and immigrant-settlers in Qu'Appelle embraced such subjugation. Indeed, B Battery was part of the larger force brought into the region for that very purpose, and locals lobbied for the soldiers' permanent presence. In 1886, upon hearing that the soldiers would soon return home, a local editorial argued:

> The presence of artillery in the Northwest is a wholesome deterrent to reckless spirits among the Indians, and as the stream of immigration is now flowing into our country, they should be retained here at least for the season, to inspire confidence among such newcomers as may be timid for want of knowledge of the true state of affairs, especially after having heard of the rebellion of last year, and being perhaps somewhat apprehensive on consequence. ("Although it was Reported")

The artillery was a symbol of security guarding against the entrenched settler idea that the region was unsafe.

In fact, it was more unsafe for Indigenous communities than for settlers. Actual physical removal of local Indigenous Peoples was being carried out by the local NWMP, who were tasked with enforcing governmental orders stemming from the Indian Act (1876) and interpretations of the Pass System

(1885). The settler perception was that any Indigenous community living close to town was too close: a point typified by a report that "the mounted police stationed here have been instructed to order back to their reserves the several lodges of Indians that are located in the vicinity of town" ("The Mounted Police").

B Battery's stay in Immigration Hall did produce one of the few representations of Indigenous Peoples ever enacted therein, albeit via a temporary and purely symbolic presence. The soldiers' dramatic performances in March 1886 included the first showings of a painting by Captain R.W. Rutherford. Displayed as a drop curtain, it made a positive impression on the audience:

> The scene represents the big powwow at Battleford, of Poundmaker and his chiefs and head men before General Middleton. Most of the figures are portraits specially those of the old General, Poundmaker, and others. The grouping is quite artistic and the whole picture stands out with marvelous reality, and has brought back to those who were present the most vivid recollections. ("B. Battery Dramatic Club")

Rutherford continued to improve the work ("Garrison Theatricals"). Eventually, it found its way into the collection of the National Archives of Canada, where it remains (Rutherford). A mixture of triumph and tribute, the painting is an effigy of sorts.

Joseph Roach uses the term "effigying" to describe a performance of substitution that "fills by means of surrogation a vacancy created by the absence of an original" (36). This effigying process often fails, since the substitution cannot match the expectations established by the original (Roach 2). The process of effigying Indigenous people in Immigration Hall via Rutherford's painting, however, might have functioned differently. If such effigying commemorated and/or eulogized Indigenous people while also *celebrating* their absence, perhaps it succeeded in Qu'Appelle. The audience could read it as confirming settler founding myths, such as the notion that the previous inhabitants of the land had been physically and symbolically removed. This idea persists to this day, thanks to what Daniel Keyes identifies as "a desire to integrate into the Canadian context a pliable, nostalgic image of the 'noble native' that excludes the narrative of colonization and invasion." A painting of Indigenous people surrendering was thus acceptable in Immigration Hall, but any local First Nations person was not permitted near town. This specific exclusion does not seem to have been a concern for Rutherford and his audience of settlers and soldiers in an 1886 Northwest "barracks." The painting confirmed notions of a past surplus (i.e., more Indigenous Peoples than the settlers preferred) and of the current, hoped-for deficit of Indigenous Peoples (which would allow settlers' replacement of same). It wasn't the real thing—but then, this simulation might have been precisely what the settlers needed. After all, throughout and beyond this period local people and performers would regularly present themselves in the role of "Indians" at fancy-dress balls, in tableaux, in displayed artistic renderings, or in dramas. Settlers would also take on indigeneity as a means of adding power to dissent, as Heather Davis-Fisch notes: "In 18th and 19 century North America, settler-colonists often referenced ideas and images of Indigeneity in acts of protest [. . .] referencing aboriginal identities allowed protestors to position themselves as upholding the 'native' customs of the 'new' world in opposition to authorities enforcing laws and social practices from the 'old' world" (37). In other words, surrogated versions of Indigenous identities were not only popular among, but actually necessary to, the settlers' sense of their own roles in the region.

The only clear example of an Indigenous performer who actually performed in Immigration Hall is that of E. Pauline Johnson (Tekahionwake). Johnson was welcomed and celebrated as an "Indian" in 1898, but with several qualifying layers of identity that augmented her acceptability within the community. Johnson was of mixed English/Mohawk heritage. As Theodore Watts-Dunton described in his introduction to the 1917 edition of Johnson's *Flint and Feather*, she was "born to the late G. H. M. Johnson (Onwanonsyshon), Head Chief of the Six Nations Indians, and his wife, Emily S. Howells, a lady of pure English parentage" (par. 1). That Howells's English ancestry was described as "pure" highlights the esteem in which the biographer held such lineage. Watts-Dunton propagates settler founding myths when describing Johnson's place in Canadian posterity, opining "that

Canada will, in future times, cherish her memory more and more, for of all Canadian poets she was the most distinctly a daughter of the soil, inasmuch as she inherited the blood of the great primeval race now so rapidly vanishing, and of the greater race that has supplanted it" (par. 24). Johnson was in some ways a complicated living effigy, simultaneously celebrated and mourned as an exemplar of the presumed soon-to-be-vanished Indigenous Peoples of Canada.

As such combinations of celebration and mourning suggest, the "Indian" occupied a complex place in the settler psyche, where, Thobani argues, "although Indigenous peoples were declared as doomed to extinction for the 'sin-crime' of indigeneity, they were also simultaneously valorized as sacred in the western imagination" (39). Roach notes a similar romantic notion of "new-world" conquest, highlighting "the historic tendency of Europeans, when reminded, to recall only emotions of deep love for the peoples whose cultures they have left in flames, emotions predicated on the sublime vanity that their early departure would not have been celebrated locally as deliverance" (46). We are still living with the effects of this vanity, argues Roach, for "the stark polarity of the frontier trope of centre versus margin traps the imagination of historians as well as dramatists in a monotonously self-replicating closure, a monolithic foregone conclusion in which only the victor remains to mourn his vanquished victim" (189).

Such substitution is typical of a cultural amnesia that is required of settler societies, in which "memory is a process that depends crucially on forgetting" (Roach 2). This may be especially true of settler societies seeking to create "new" founding myths in their "new" place. According to Roach, "newness" requires a dark amnesia of sorts:

Newness enacts a kind of surrogation—in the invention of a new England or a new France out of the memories of the old—but it also conceptually erases indigenous populations, contributing to a mentality conducive to the partial implementation of the American Holocaust. While a great deal of the unspeakable violence instrumental to this creation may have been officially forgotten, circum-Atlantic

memory retains its consequences, one of which is that the unspeakable cannot be rendered forever inexpressible: the most persistent
mode of forgetting is memory imperfectly deferred. (4)

Johnson's performances and their reception in Qu'Appelle highlight how
this community received Johnson as a representation (or effigy) of a generic
Canadian "Indian."

Johnson's performances were a skilful mixture of artifice and authenticity.
She wrote and performed poetry that ranged from patriotic verses praising
Canada and the British Empire, to pieces expressing anger over the treatment
of Indigenous Peoples in the face of that empire, to works that celebrated (and
often eulogized) Indigenous Peoples across Canada. Her successes abroad
sanctioned her to the Qu'Appelle audience; the local newspaper noted she had
played major British and American cities, "all of which endorse and applaud
her" ("Miss E. Pauline Johnson," *Qu'Appelle Progress*). She was not from the
prairies, or any prairie First Nation or Indigenous group. As her audience did
not distinguish beyond her being "Indian," such specifics were unrequired.
Her first show in Qu'Appelle in 1898 was a critical and popular hit:

> Miss Johnson's entertainments consisted of recitations of her own
> compositions, and deal principally with legends of her race, the
> Indians. Her introductory remarks are always interesting and often
> humerous [sic]; though not professing to be an elocutionist, she has
> few equals, and certainly no superiors in many of her recitations.
> ("Miss Johnson's Entertainments")

The works she chose for this specific, abbreviated show in Qu'Appelle included
"Ojistoh," "Wolverine," and "The Riders of the Plain," as well as two other
selections. Her piece based on the region's naming story, "The Legend of the
Qu'Appelle Valley," was yet unfinished; Johnson planned to premiere it at her
show in Fort Qu'Appelle the following evening. That show was cancelled, however, when a doctor ordered Johnson three weeks of bedrest ("Miss Johnson's
Entertainment").

In Qu'Appelle, as so often elsewhere, Johnson presented a program wherein her appearance was as much performance art as it was elocution of her poetry. Her costume included a fringed buckskin dress and leggings, brooches, furs, and other elements:

> At her waist she carried a hunting knife and an authentic Huron scalp inherited from her great-grand-father. A red wool cloak hung from one shoulder. One sleeve was a long piece of fringed buckskin, attached at the shoulder and the wrist; the other was a drape of rabbit pelts. Johnson seems to have come up with this polyglot costume herself. She wore it during the half of her program devoted to Indian poems. For her non-Indian material, she wore a simple dinner gown. (Francis 128)

Many scholars, including myself, have accepted previous arguments that Johnson's varied costume was an inauthentic construction and, as such, a failure. Thankfully, Alexandra Kovacs is challenging such notions by

> offering an alternative to the prevailing interpretations that discredit the costume's sophistication [by] recontextualiz[ing] the parts of Johnson's dresses . . . viewing them alongside theatrical conditions within which they operated. This reconceptualizing practice analyses reviews to identify Johnson's repertoire and then addresses how these performed selections demanded a multifunctional set of costumes that could represent a plethora of both settler and Indigenous identities. ("Beyond Shame" 34)

In her article "Beyond Shame and Blame in Pauline Johnson's Performance Histories," Kovacs illustrates how Johnson's costumes can also be read as not only practically functional in terms of the demands of her performance repertoire, but also "correct" in terms of performance costuming standards of the day. Her costume pieces were more curated collection than convenient conglomeration.[2] Rather than create a unique head-to-toe culturally accurate costume for each character, she sought costume pieces that referenced one or more characters and wore them together, allowing her to switch between the plethora of identities (settler and Indigenous).

In her recitations, Johnson ranged from works of unflinching patriotic fervor (e.g., "The Riders of the Plains") to pieces highlighting the mistreatment of Indigenous People by settlers (e.g., "As Red Men Die"). In "Wolverine," Johnson speaks as though retelling an old trapper's story of his time in the Northwest, which he describes as being "Wild? You bet, 'twas wild then, an' few an' far between / The squatters' shacks, for whites was scarce as furs when things is green, / An' only reds an' 'Hudson's' men was all the folk I seen" (lines 7–9). As if answering a listener's negative comment about "Indyans," Johnson, through the character of the old trapper, corrects: "No. Them old Indyans ain't so bad, not if you treat 'em square. / Why, I lived in amongst 'em all the winters I was there, / An' I never lost a copper, an' I never lost a hair" (lines 10–12). To further make the point, "the trapper" tells the story of how the "Indyan, 'Wolverine'" saved his life courageously, while asking nothing in return. Later, Wolverine is killed by English settlers:

"They said, 'They'd had an awful scare from Injuns,' an' they swore
That savages had come around the very night before
A-brandishing their tomahawks an' painted up for war.

"'But when their plucky Englishmen had put a bit of lead
Right through the heart of one of them, an' rolled him over, dead,
The other cowards said that they had come on peace instead.

"'That they (the Whites) had lost some stores, from off their little pack,
An' that the Red they peppered dead had followed up their track,
Because he'd found the packages an' came *to give them back.*'

---

2   For a more complete, recent, and detailed exploration of Johnson's work, see also Alexandra Kovacs's "Pauline Johnson: Poet and Performer."

> "'Oh!' they said, 'they were quite sorry, but it wasn't like as if
> They had killed a decent Whiteman by mistake or in a tiff,
> It was only some old Injun dog that lay there stark an' stiff.'
>
> "I said, 'You are the meanest dogs that ever yet I seen,'
> Then I rolled the body over as it lay out on the green;
> I peered into the face—My God! 'twas poor old Wolverine." (lines 49–63)

This piece by Johnson, which significantly was among those performed at Immigration Hall, uses the character of the white trapper to contrast and critique settler founding myths that cast "Indians" as aggressors and justified settlers' violent acts.

If all the pieces Johnson performed in Qu'Appelle had made similar points about the injustices wrought upon the Northwest's Indigenous Peoples, it would be easier to identify a singular goal for Johnson and her poetry. But she also performed "The Riders of the Plains," which champions a symbol of British dominance in the Northwest, the NWMP (who were also at various times stationed in, or users of, Immigration Hall). Johnson's footnote explains the poem's inspiration: "At a dinner party in Boston the writer was asked, 'Who are the Northwest Mounted Police?' and when told that they were the pride of Canada's fighting men the questioner sneered and replied, 'Ah! Then they are only some of your British Lion's whelps. We are not afraid of them.' His companions applauded the remark" (*Canadian Born*, 29–30). Given the paramilitary nature of the NWMP, Johnson's definition of them as "fighting men" is accurate. The NWMP was a force for not only policing but subduing the Northwest. Johnson penned a patriotic response (supporting her Canadian/British allegiances) to her dinner companion over five verses, each ending with the words "they keep the peace of the people and the honor of British law." The third verse specifically alludes to the Métis resistance:

These are the fearless fighters, whose life in the open lies,
Who never fail on the prairie trail 'neath the Territorial skies,
Who have laughed in the face of the bullets and the edge of the
rebels' steel,
Who have set their ban on the lawless man with his crime beneath
their heel;
These are the men who battle the blizzards, the suns, the rains,
These are the famed that the North has named the "Riders of the
Plains,"
And theirs is the might and the meaning and the strength of the
bulldog's jaw,
While they keep the peace of the people and the honor of British law.
("The Riders of the Plains," 29–30)

This heroic ballad, recited on stage in Qu'Appelle, depicts a specific experience with the NWMP that most settler audience members would likely have appreciated more than would local First Nations, Métis, and other Indigenous Peoples.

After all, Indigenous Peoples in the region had often resisted the "British law" that Johnson's poem constructs as honourable. Beginning in the late 1890s, Chief Piapot organized and conducted spiritual ceremonies in the region against the wishes of federal authorities. Constance Backhouse offers an estimate, which remains approximate due to gaps in the archival records, "that between 1900 and 1904 there were 50 arrests and twenty convictions for dancing in contravention of the Indian Act" (*Colour-Coded* 69). The situation came to a head in 1901, when Piapot "was imprisoned for two months in a Regina prison for participating in a Give-Away Dance and encouraging six others to resist arrest" (*Colour-Coded* 68–69). Backhouse summarizes Piapot's history of arrests related to spiritual dances:

In the late 1890s, he was incarcerated for performing the piercing ceremony for approximately twenty young men at a Thirst Dance, but the official charge was apparently 'drunkenness' . . . Department

of Indian Affairs removed Piapot from his position as chief for these
transgressions . . . In protest, members of Piapot's community refused
to elect another chief until after his death. ("Extended Endnotes" 84)

Piapot and his descendants likely would have developed a starkly different
opinion than Johnson's regarding the local exemplars of "might, meaning, and
the strength of the bulldog's jaw" and how they were used to "keep the peace
of the people and the honor of British law" ("The Riders of the Plains" 27).
The NWMP, in turn, were doing their part as enforcers of the settler myth
that Indigenous Peoples were vanishing, leaving a cleared territory that was
claimable by preferred (im)migrants.

    In truth, both "Wolverine" and "The Riders of the Plains" were perform-
ances that explored how law and lawlessness were being redefined by settlers
colonizing the region. Thobani observes that "[c]laims of legality in Canada . . .
rest historically upon one elemental 'truth': Europe was lawful, Indians were
not. European powers claimed sovereignty over the Americas through the
power of their law, pronouncing as lawless, anarchic, and even despotic the
conditions of existence in the 'savage' worlds that Europe was discovering"
(39). "Wolverine" challenges this idea, casting European settlers as lawless
aggressors. In contrast, "The Riders of the Plains" praises the representatives
of the European law overtaking the Northwest. Perhaps these contrasting
views, presented via Johnson's complex array of characters and sympathies in
performance, challenged—or at least complicated—settler audiences' notions
that the West's being "won" was a wholly positive event.

    Another layer complicating Johnson's performances is their acceptance
by audiences as being somehow authentically "Indian" as well as supportive of
the romanticized notion of the "noble savage." Keyes points out how Johnson
has been read as part of a popular trend among Canadian artists of the time,
including Emily Carr, who "recoil[ed] from European modernity (characterized by colonialism, capitalism, patriarchy, etc.) to embrace 'aboriginal
modernity' as a utopian alternative" (33). It was within the context of such
cultural eddies and founding myths that the Immigration Hall performances
of Pauline Johnson were locally both anticipated and successful.

Upon her return to Immigration Hall in the fall of 1898, Johnson was hailed in Qu'Appelle as "Canada's greatest poetess" ("Everybody Talks"). Her poems and performances were praised for having "depth of feeling, purity of thought and power of expression" ("Miss E. Pauline Johnson's"). But her power of expression was taxed in this show, according to one critic, who wrote that "Miss Johnson had just returned from Prince Albert, and the trip had been so tiring that she did not appear at her best" ("Miss Johnson's Entertainment"). Such active tracking of Johnson's travels and performances throughout the region allows for us to deepen our understanding of Johnson's relationship to settler mythos and the process of surrogation by comparing the reception of her performances in Qu'Appelle to that of her appearances in Prince Albert.

PRINCE ALBERT, NWT

Like Qu'Appelle, Prince Albert was also a regional hub of settlement, trade, transportation, and religion. When governmental and judicial functions were added to the community, its place as the centre of various economic, governmental, legal, and faith groups increased its regional influence. Its Town Hall Opera House hosted events and performances akin to those in Qu'Appelle's Immigration Hall. Also, like Qu'Appelle, the population of the region surrounding and including Prince Albert was very young and very male. However, the total Indigenous population was significantly higher in the Prince Albert region than it was in Qu'Appelle (Department of Agriculture 10–14; Dominion Bureau of Statistics 324–25, 340–41).

As in Qu'Appelle, Prince Albert audiences eagerly anticipated Johnson's performances of "her unique, pathetic, dramatic, and quaintly humorous Indian stories and poems" ("Miss E. Pauline Johnson," *Prince Albert*). Specifically of interest, according to one local reviewer, was her ability to "express, both in action and in word, all the wild passions of the race from which she is sprung. Her forte lies in portraying the unflinching bravery and the unquenchable hatred of the red man . . . it is with difficulty that the listener can persuade himself that she is not really possessed of the feelings she portrays" ("Miss E. Pauline Johnson, the Famous Indian "). This observation shows the complicated position Johnson occupied in Prince Albert. For this settler audience, her identity lent credence to her performances of Indigenous characters. Here, though, the reviewer assures that any potentially violent emotions (e.g., hatred) must be artifice. Otherwise, how could an Indigenous person expressing such feelings be welcome in the Town Hall Opera House? The notion that these feelings might reflect local Indigenous Canadian's frustrations and anger—especially any born of interactions with current colonial power structures—is too threatening to consider. The reviewer presents Johnson's performances as an opportunity for the settler audience to engage in a reversed suspension of disbelief. Theatregoers are usually asked to pretend that what is portrayed on stage is real, if only within the confines of the performance; Johnson's settler audience, however, was being reminded to disbelieve the notion that she might be performing real-world frustrations and anger on stage.

Johnson's performance was "a real success" ("The Novel Entertainment"). One reviewer noted, "[T]his lady proved herself to be a capable and forceful elocutionist and portrayer of the Indian character in its various phases" ("Miss Johnson Concluded"). In this review, Johnson, one of few Indigenous performers accepted in Prince Albert, is treated as a singular representative of all aspects of "the Indian character." At the same time, the range of her material was also noted, as "each selection had its own peculiar bearing upon the humorous, the patriotic and thrilling side" ("Miss Pauline Johnson," *Prince Albert*). Throughout her career, Johnson's patriotic poems were particularly popular (Francis 136). Notably, the veracity of her patriotic expressions was not questioned, nor were her previously mentioned performances of "hatred" expressed by her Indigenous characters. This aspect of her identity—the proud British subject—was easily accepted by settler audiences.

Johnson returned to Prince Albert in 1904, touring with Walter McRaye ("Miss Pauline Johnson, the Famous Authoress and Elocutionist"). McRaye, an Irish Canadian, specialized in impressions of French Canadians based upon the writings of an English Canadian doctor, William H. Drummond. As in Qu'Appelle in 1898, much of Johnson's and McRaye's pre-show press in Prince Albert focused on their successful tour of England, especially Johnson's successes in London. She had played venues from sold-out theatres to drawing rooms for England's notable, noble, and influential people ("Great Iroquois Indian Poetess"). Perhaps such stories provided Prince Albert audiences with a sense of pride in their fellow Canadian. The Prince Albert audience likely also appreciated a show from the theatrical margins of their "new" country had been accepted in the theatrical heart of the "old" country, England.

The second half of the show was an English society sketch called "Fashionable Intelligence," which was "written especially for Miss Johnson and Mr. McRay" ("The Famous Indian Poetess"). The sketch allowed the performers to trade buckskin and *bottes sauvages* for Victorian evening dress. The range of characters and costumes presented in these shows was a continuation of what Kovacs identifies as Johnson's innovative "dual-costume recitals," which had been newsworthy nationwide for at least four years ("Beyond Shame" 41).

Despite the complexity of such representations of identity, and much to her frustration, Johnson's performances were usually read as representative of a universalized "Indian-ness." She pointed out that identifying her as "Indian" was as culturally specific a label as calling someone "European," but noted that she heard few people singled out for representing all Europeanness ("A Strong Race Opinion" 1). In Prince Albert Johnson was almost unique in being welcomed as an Indigenous performer, highlighting the degree to which her performance was read as being universally representative of "Indianness." Her acceptance, however, came with a certain level of surrogation; she performed in place of local Indigenous people, who were almost entirely absent from community performances. Moreover, Johnson represented no threat of permanence; once her performance finished, she moved on to her next venue.

LAST STAND

The insertion of real, local Indigenous bodies into settler-performance tropes, on the other hand, was not so widely accepted in Prince Albert. In 1902, the community's upper crust gathered for a performance by the students of Emmanuel College, which was at this time described as being "almost

altogether an Indian Training School" ("Emmanuel College Band Concert").
The night was eagerly anticipated; pre-press assured audiences that "the pupils
have been under training for a long time and know their exercises perfectly . . .
anyone missing this treat will be 'sorry they did it'" ("The Entertainment to
be Given"). Specifically regarding the schoolboys' cadet corps, the newspaper predicted that "the boys are all well up in their parts, and should have a
hearty reception from a good house" ("The Programmes").

The performance itself was staged under the patronage of local dignitaries.
First, female students exhibited physical skill and discipline: "The girls' marching, drilling, and dumb bell exercise, were loudly applauded and encored by
the audience—their fancy costumes looking very neat and adding much to
the effect of their graceful and active movements" ("The Programmes"). Next,
male students were called upon to exhibit their potential military prowess:

> The appearance of the boys, dressed as they were in military uniform
> and equipment with rifles and bayonets, and the execution of their
> drills in such a soldier-like manner, suggested the idea, that the red
> man of the west, if trained as these cadets are, might also be called
> upon to take up arms for king and country, is [sic] required.
>
> The tableaux, known as "The Last Stand," presented by the cadet
> corps, under a flash of red light and accompanied by the soft and sad
> tones of "Just Break the News to Mother," was very realistic, and was
> received with intense silence by the audience. ("Emmanuel College
> Band Concert")

For this scene, the anticipated "hearty response" was missing. It is possible
that the Victorian audience, who even in territorial Prince Albert would have
been well-versed in the appreciation sentimental tableaux, was simply moved
by the students' performance. Reviews of similar Town Hall Opera House performances by other groups, however, do not report similar, quiet reactions.

It is also possible that, to evoke such notable silence, the Emmanuel
College performance could have brought together an extraordinarily complex
web of meanings. As most performances in Prince Albert excluded Indigenous

people altogether, the Emmanuel College performance is a rare exception: one that supports Roach's observation that wilful amnesia is tenuous and has consequences. A perilous founding mythos breeds insecurity, as Justin Edwards notes:

> If a nation is imaginary, a precarious fabrication that is built upon questionable cultural narratives, then a nation is also haunted by the spectral figure of its own fabrication. This means that nations like Canada rely upon delusions that call attention to the fictions that exist at the heart of their national metanarratives . . . the nation is not just a socio-political fact, but also a ghost story. A way of "storying" or talking about ourselves is always haunted by the spectre of the Other. (xix)

When that dark amnesia is challenged, it unsettles the settler community. When the now-not-so-ghostly Others—upon whose absence the settlers' founding stories are built—are brought onto the town-hall stage, their presence might well produce "intense silence."

In Victorian Britain, live performances of paintings were a common "merging of the arts of painting and stage production to incarnate the age and the historical moment in a striking, living image" (Booth 14). However, no specific historical incident was identified as inspiring the Emmanuel College tableau. Then-recent British military history provides several "last stands," many of which inspired artistic reproductions. Most of these last stands are reducible to the following story: a colonial power assumes itself to be superior due to its technological advantages and its "advanced" state of nationhood and/or empire. Usually victorious armed representatives of that power are slaughtered by the "savages" over whom their technology and advancements are supposed to prevail. The soldiers unquestioningly die for their queen/country/empire in an expectedly brave and heroic manner. An event popularly known as the last stand of Major Wilson is one likely inspiration of the cadets' scene (Stewart). Wilson and thirty-four soldiers were killed by Matabele warriors near the Shangani River (in what is now Zimbabwe) in

December 1893 (Barnard and Hickman 11). According to Matabele accounts, surrounded British soldiers fired from behind a makeshift barricade of their dead horses (Creswicke 124). After exhausting their ammunition, the soldiers stood, shook hands, sang "God Save the Queen," and were killed. The event was reproduced in multiple mediums—paintings, stage, film—and was presented throughout the British Empire (Booth 15).

The familiar sentimental tradition of last-stand commemoration becomes complex in the Prince Albert performance. The cadets were, for their audience, members of what was then typified as a "savage" race themselves. The cadets' relations and ancestors had been the source of fear and fear-mongering locally for decades. If not for accidents of timing and geography that placed them within the grasp of repressive forces like the residential school system, these cadets themselves might have been cast as the attacking hordes of an actual last stand. Local settlers could either recall, or were well-versed in stories about, the events of 1885, when Prince Albert had barricaded itself out of fear that the town would be attacked—perhaps by the relations and forebears of these young cadets.

Even more recently, the town had been shaken by the nearby last stand of Almighty Voice (Kitchi-manito-waya), a Cree born in 1875 near Duck Lake (Butts and Filice). He was arrested in 1895 for—depending upon who is retelling the history—either killing a government steer or butchering a steer without permission of the Indian agent on his home One Arrow Reserve. While in custody, a guard joked that, if found guilty, Almighty Voice faced hanging. He escaped, later killing NWMP Sgt. Colin Colebrook during another attempted arrest. Approximately eighteen months later, Almighty Voice was surrounded in a poplar bluff and killed along with his brother-in-law Topean and his cousin Little Saulteaux (Nestor). Almighty Voice was perceived as such a threat to community security—and the colonial forces maintaining privilege—that the force mustered against the three young men included over sixty individuals (the entire Prince Albert NWMP barracks, twenty-five volunteers from Prince Albert, and thirty policemen from Regina) and two pieces of field artillery (a seven- and a nine-pound gun). The siege took three days ("A Small Rebellion"). Three men in the group assembled to confront Almighty Voice died. Since this group included twenty-five volunteers from Prince Albert in addition to the local NWMP detachment, it is entirely likely that members of that group—and/or their relatives—were in the audience for the Emmanuel College "last stand" performance.

Education is also a means of subjugation. Perhaps the teachers at Emmanuel College were hoping to show the successful "civilizing" of their students. But the last stand they presented seems likely to have evoked uncomfortable memories and realizations. The audience saw the symbolically armed Indigenous cadets performing in British uniforms with British drill and discipline. The cadets were learning dominant techniques and technologies that Victorians saw as the keys to defeating "savages" throughout their empire. The reviewer even observed that the performance showed how "properly" trained First Nations warriors could fight "for king and country" ("Emmanuel College Band Concert"). Could the audience also imagine these boys fighting *against* king and country? Was there menace in the ease with which the cadets adapted to British warfare? Did the event produce uncomfortable memories of Almighty Voice amongst those who might have been his besiegers? This performance may have challenged the settlers' sense of new permanence, which presumed the country had been irrevocably claimed from its previous occupants.

Imagining the possible staging of this piece further informs my reading of the resulting intense, silent audience. The review mentions no opposing forces on stage. A logical staging situates the boys in a defensive position against an *imaginary* foe, presumably requiring the armed cadets to face outward to the audience. The well-to-do settlers of Prince Albert, comfortable in their privilege and superiority, may have suddenly found themselves recast as the invading, savage hordes. Healthy, force-trained Emmanuel College students were proof against settlers' core founding myths of the "vanishing Indian" and white superiority. An evening that began as a chance for Prince Albert settlers to feel smug regarding their "civilizing" of the local "savages" might thus have been overturned.

The cadets' "Last Stand" could have been an uncomfortable, if temporary, reversal of accepted local ideology that demanded that "[p]rogress had its price, and the Indian was expected to pay it" (Francis 73). The injustice of such a debt turns Canadian-created history into a ghost story:

> The ground upon which the colonized encounters the colonizer is a haunted site where we find the recycling of a previous demand that has been inadequately dealt with . . . to be haunted is to be called upon, for the phantom presence returns to collect an unpaid debt . . . Even when the colonized figure is shut up, incarcerated, or excluded from reality . . . his or her voice returns to haunt the colonizer from the margins. (Edwards xxix)

Think, then, what power could be unleashed by the act of bringing these voices out from the margins and placing them centre stage—in direct opposition to the colonizers. Edwards continues:

> hegemonies [are] socially constructed . . . they are built on history, memory, anxiety, fear and desire . . . hegemonies mirror ghosts— both rise out of the same products of our collective imaginations and, because the politics of the national, the racial, the classed and the gendered are politics of memory and false memory, both are the politics of spectrality. (xxx)

If only for a moment during this "Last Stand" performance, a more equitable distribution of discomfort might have existed between colonized and colonizer. Think of the unease and anxiety experienced by a settler community when they are unexpectedly forced to face the false nature of their accepted founding myths in their "new" West. To succeed, such a myth required an ideological substitution for, or surrogation of, the "old" West. For the developing settler myths to attain new, self-created authenticity, the community origin story would need to acceptably account for, explain away, or remove the local Indigenous people from that vision. Though clearly designed to affirm the mythos of empire, the "Last Stand" performance by the students of Emmanuel College seems likely to have challenged the false narratives upon which such mythos depended.

UNSETTLING SETTLER MYTHS IN PERFORMANCES

As Thobani observes, transforming insiders into outsiders and vice versa via the creation of a class of new, exalted insiders requires a home with a sense of permanence. This transformation resulted in what Roach identifies as imperfectly deferred memories of previous inhabitants of the region. The most accepted forms of presence for Indigenous peoples in these sites were as effigies—through their substitution by white settlers in plays, skits, and fancy-dress balls in both Prince Albert and Qu'Appelle. Pauline Johnson, an Indigenous performer, appeared in both communities under some layers of effigy. To the settler audiences in Prince Albert and Qu'Appelle, Johnson was to some extent a representative of a generalized, Canadian "Indianness." Even her most ardent admirers praised her in blatantly racialized/racist terms, privileging her English ancestry while identifying her paternal lineage as a connection to a sentimentalized "dying" race.

Opinions regarding Johnson's place in the performance of Canadian culture are complicated. Johnson's "complex self-positioning" leaves some scholars of mixed opinions, perhaps "because Johnson's role in Canadian literary and cultural history satisfies a variety of positions related to racial identity from princess to pawn to self-professed promoter of Aboriginal culture" (Anderson and Robertson 102). In performance, she presented herself first in "Indian" costume and then in a Victorian dinner gown. Such a transformation might have fit into the dominant settler mythos, in that it "served as an effort to visually affirm her cultural evolution (and reify the central tenets of Canada's colonial dream): the transformation from Mohawk princess to patriotic Canadian" (Anderson and Robertson 104–05). That she might have been both proud Mohawk and loyal Canadian at once—as well as a skilled and savvy performer—might have been too fine a point for audiences, as well as subsequent scholars, to consider. Shaming of Johnson's performances as inauthentic can also essentially be read as an attempt to diminish, or dismiss, her as a person and performer, as Kovacs observes:

The critical shaming of Johnson's theatricality (as represented by the spectacle of her costumes) threatens her claim to her own Indigenous

nationality (a nation of which she was very proud), it is imperative
to return to the artefact of Johnson's performance history that is
most troubling—her "Indian" costume—and ask if its shaming has
distracted historians from assessing its function within a particular
theatrical context that served to embody a repertoire of several characters and personalities. ("Beyond Shame" 40)

Johnson's skilful costuming and presentation were a large part of her success.
Her performance proved very successful with white audiences, who "love[d]
these 'authentic' Indian props. They thrilled at the war whoops, the dangling
scalp, the name they could not pronounce, the poems of torture and war. She
enjoyed immense popularity" (Francis 128). Perhaps Johnson's acceptance
was a local, ideological expression of what Daniel Francis observed as a wider
Canadian motif: "Civilization had conquered the West . . . it was no longer
necessary to mobilize public opinion against the frontier's original inhabitants. Having successfully subdued the Indians, Whites now could afford to
get sentimental about them" (136).

As her reviewer in Prince Albert noted, though, Johnson's performances were also read as including hauntingly realistic depictions of "bravery
and unquenchable hatred" ("Miss E. Pauline Johnson, the Famous Indian
Elocutionist"). Audiences linked such performed feelings to indigeneity and
celebrated her for them—as long as they believed these feelings were merely
pretence. Her performances of "Indianness" were perhaps most acceptable
to settler audiences when read as nostalgic stories of the past, reinforcing the
myth that settlers were replacing a disappearing Indigenous presence. As long
as any anger over this replacement was dismissible as a flicker, rather than
a flame, the settlers could work to forget it. Such substitution and forgetting
had to happen for sites like Qu'Appelle and Prince Albert to gain the authority
begat of new permanence. Similar agreement was enacted when the settlers
in Qu'Appelle celebrated Rutherford's painting, *The Surrender of Poundmaker*.
It symbolized an affirmation of the power of the colonial government in a
community still uneasy at the artillery's return home to Eastern Canada after
its quashing of the North-West Resistance.

Settlers who still felt threatened by Indigenous populations could, and did, justify their ongoing subjection. The audience's subdued response to "The Last Stand" of the Emmanuel College cadets at the Prince Albert Town Hall Opera House suggests unease, exposing lingering tensions surrounding the veracity of the developing settler mythos. This performance appears to have created an unsettling dichotomy for the audience as the cadets filled the roles of British warriors in a last stand while, under their uniforms, still being the "savages" who were usually cast as attackers of such warriors. Insight into what may have inspired the "intense silence" with which the audience greeted the scene can be gained through thorough investigation of the cultural, local, and regional context surrounding this performance. Though the community appeared to have successfully substituted away most Indigenous participation in the town hall, the tenuous nature of their colonial ghost-story histories and phantasmological settler founding myths could still surface.

* * *

Some theatres still deploy a ghost light. Before the last crewmember leaves and the lights are extinguished, a lone bulb is placed on the stage. Superstition claims that the light keeps phantoms at bay. It dispels imagined threats in the darkness by rendering visible what is real. It also can prevent someone from wandering across a darkened stage and falling into the orchestra pit.

In Canada after the Truth and Reconciliation Commission, re-examination of settlers' founding myths is crucial. This process sets up the theoretical equivalent of a ghost light. Illuminating the colonial ghost stories underpinning current structures of power, privilege, and intolerance helps dispel untruths inherent in settler founding myths. Once exposed, remnant colonial phantoms can be dispersed, clearing the way for truth-based progress in reconciliation. Revisiting the histories of performance in sites like Qu'Appelle's Immigration Hall and Prince Albert's Town Hall Opera House offers one opportunity to begin this process.

"A NEW IRELAND IN THE NORTHWEST": SHADES OF IRISH/CANADIAN NATION, IMMIGRATION, AND THEATRE-BUILDING ON THE CANADIAN PRAIRIES

MOIRA DAY[1]

> WILLOUGHBY: *He [Riel] said there would be a new Ireland in the Northwest.*
> —John Coulter, *The Trial of Louis Riel* 12.

In 1974, Don Rubin invoked the nineteenth-century French critic Ferdinand Brunetière in reminding Canadian theatre advocates that "it is always at the exact moment of its national existence when the will of a great people is exalted within itself, that we see its dramatic art reach also the highest point of its development, and produce its masterpieces" (307). In 1990, Alan Filewod reflected that what alarmed him was how little that archaic belief in "the hegemonic idea of a nation" being "expressed in simple cultural codes" ("National Theatre" 415) had changed since the nineteenth century. Far from exalting the universal will of the people, most national theatre movements simply perpetuated "the national ideals of the governing elite" by canonizing forms of drama that upheld "the 'high' educated culture" associated with "historical arrangements of wealth and power"—while denigrating "'low' popular culture" forms and the people who practised them (Filewod, "National Theatre" 414–15).

---

1   I would like to thank my research assistant, Domini Gee, for her invaluable help in completing reference and quotation checks for this article.

Filewod specifically pinpoints the opening of Hart House Theatre in Toronto in 1919 as the beginning of a serious amateur Canadian Art Theatre movement. Positively, it attempted to wean Canadians from the crass, colonizing influence of the foreign, commercial, touring theatre largely emanating from New York. Less positively, it simply replaced one form of hegemony with another; under the literary, cultural, and political leadership of Vincent Massey, Hart House Theatre set the mode for a Canadian national theatre model that upheld traditional British Canadian literary, cultural, and power structures (410–12) as being the most definitive arbitrators of "the will of a great [Canadian] people" (Rubin 307). Nonetheless, it could be argued that even during that inaugural season at Hart House Theatre, other international streams, driven by new waves of non-British immigration, were beginning to introduce new revolutionary forces antithetical to or at least existing in lively tension with those imperial power structures and authority.

One such resistant stream was represented by the theosophist thought and practice of Roy Mitchell, the first artistic director of the theatre. In *Creative Theatre*, he argued that the divine fire kindled in all human breasts was made flesh in the living medium of theatre and dwelt among us as a redemptive force in all times, places, and peoples (118–19, 124). His theosophy allowed the theatre to transcend the British exemplum and to justify art as the universal passport that granted all immigrants full citizenship as fellow pilgrims in the expanding human, spiritual, and cultural mosaic in Canada. Long after Mitchell had left Hart House Theatre behind, his influence as a thinker, writer, and guest artist continued to inspire the educational and extension (adult education) drama movements in Western Canada. Both movements generated a number of ambitious, innovative—and flawed—attempts in 1920s–1940s Alberta and Manitoba, where levels of recent non-English immigration were high, to use drama and the other performing arts to negotiate between older British/American power structures and society on the prairies, and the new Canadian communities, especially in the rural areas where immigrants were simultaneously seen both as a necessity and as a threat to provincial prosperity.

A second resistant stream was represented by the appearance of W.B. Yeats on the Hart House stage in February 1920 to lecture on the Abbey Theatre and to draw favourable comparisons between the Irish and Canadian art theatres as nationalist movements resistant of British hegemony ("W.B. Yeats" 1). The second resistant tendency led to the Canadian movement's affinity with early-twentieth-century Irish drama and the immigrants associated with them.

Ultimately, this paper argues that, as propelled by the paradoxical Canadian tendency to mediate between its older identity as the final bastion of British North America *and* more contemporary visions of itself as an emerging post-colonial state and a peaceable kingdom of immigrants, both resistant streams ended up meeting mid-century in complex, unique, and unexpected ways in the work of Irish immigrant playwright, John Coulter (1888–1980). As an artist, Coulter appeared to be most at home in the urban centres in Central Canada that reminded him of the cosmopolitan centres in England, Ireland, and America that had shaped his earlier years and that he continued to visit frequently even after he had moved to Canada. In this respect, there is little doubt that the playwright's international credentials helped ensure both Coulter and his Irish-themed work a warm welcome in the mainstream Canadian art-theatre movement; his Irish family dramas, *The House in the Quiet Glen* and *The Drums are Out*, won best Canadian play awards at the Dominion Drama Festival in 1938 and 1950 respectively, and *The Family Portrait* appeared on the Hart House stage in 1938.

Yet, while complicit in Massey's project of creating a hegemonic national theatre, Coulter was also highly critical of older nineteenth-century concepts of nationhood where "the will of a great people" (Rubin 307) could also manifest itself in policies of imperialism, colonization, and immigration designed to destroy smaller nations. His most significant body of dramatic work written in and on Canada was set in the nineteenth-century prairie provinces, in ways that both looked back to "the troubles" of his native Ireland and forward to the complex intersections between art and immigration that many of the Western extension and education specialists were still dealing with a century later. In his groundbreaking 1950 drama *Riel*, and in the two additional Riel dramas he wrote afterward, Coulter suggests that the distance between Irish nation building and Western Canadian nation building in Riel's Northwest was not so different in terms of dreams crushed, hopes deferred, and a perpetual sense of exile, alienation, and displacement. Yet, beyond that, Coulter, who never seemed quite at home in either his native or his adopted country, also remained sensitive, in both his critical and creative writing, to the complex and troubling legacy such imperial policies of immigration, usually designed to exert stronger political and economic control over a fractious native population, often bequeathed the immigrants themselves.

COULTER AND THE NON-BRITISH BRITISH SUBJECT: MID-NINETEENTH TO MID-TWENTIETH CENTURY

As an immigrant to Canada from Ulster, Coulter was particularly aware that the twentieth-century "troubles" of Northern Ireland could be traced back to the decision by English rulers to encourage waves of Scottish and English Protestant immigration into the northern counties of Ireland some three hundred years earlier.[2] However, he was also aware of the long-term impact of that decision not only on the descendants of the colonists and colonized in Ireland,

---

2   The Normans, who conquered Britain in 1066, arrived in Ireland in 1167, and soon established a presence there in the eastern territories. However, it was not until the reign of Henry VIII (1509–47) that a more concentrated campaign to bring the entire island under English sovereignty began. By 1603, James I (1603–25) had succeeded in bringing all of Ireland, including present-day Northern Ireland, under English control. It was at this time that large numbers of Scottish and English farmers were moved into the North to displace a rebellious Irish population on the land and to ensure that the Crown would be dealing with settlers more tractable to English social, political, and economic interests. Irish uprisings during the Irish Confederate Wars (1641–53) and the Williamite War (1688–91) were brutally suppressed, leading to a long-standing national pattern of a Protestant minority, largely of English/Scottish heritage, holding land and power at the expense of a large, disempowered native Catholic population. Riel's Irish Catholic ancestors likely fled Ireland in the wake of the 1688–91 conflict. In at least one of Coulter's Irish plays, *The Red Hand of Ulster*, he identifies Oliver Cromwell, who brutally reconquered Ireland between 1649 and 1653, and oversaw up to 80% of its land confiscated and redistributed to English landholders, as the malignant spirit underlying the continuing "troubles" in contemporary Northern Ireland.

but in Canada as well. Certainly in *Riel*, Coulter makes the point, through the character of his Fenian firebrand, O'Donohue, that the nineteenth-century English Canadian establishment—including as it did an older population of largely Protestant, British-loyalist Ulstermen—was more inclined to see dangerous, subversive troublemakers than poets in the waves of "Famine" Irish Catholics that arrived in the second half of that century. Already suspect for arriving from the extremes of poverty and political radicalism in the Old World, these later Irish immigrants soon garnered fresh hostility for forging what were perceived as dangerous new alliances not only with the largely Catholic bloc of French Canada, but with Irish revolutionaries on both sides of the border (Wilson, *Irish* 3–4); as such, they were seen as sympathetic toward if not actively complicit in the violence of the Fenian raids between 1866 and 1871[3] and the associated assassination of Thomas D'Arcy McGee (1825–1868) only months after he had become one of the Fathers of Confederation.[4] Ironically, McGee, who had been forced to flee Ireland himself in 1848 because

---

3   The term "Fenian" was an adaptation of the Gaelic word for warrior (fianna). It was meant to connect the exploits of the heroic, legendary warriors of second- and third-century Ireland with the revolutionary nationalist attempts of several radical nineteenth-century fraternal movements in Ireland, America, and Canada to free Ireland from British rule. While some of the raids aimed at capturing Canada and holding it ransom in exchange for a free Ireland, other raiders, mostly Irish American, hoped that the arrival of armed "liberators" would incite an American-style revolution amongst those, Irish and otherwise, also eager to throw off the yoke of British rule north of the border. For more on the influence of the Fenian movement in Canada see David Wilson, *Thomas D'Arcy McGee* Vol. I and II and his *Irish Nationalism*.

4   Thomas D'Arcy McGee (1825–1868) was an Irish Canadian politician, poet, editor, journalist, and Catholic spokesman. Born in Carlingford, Ireland, to Roman Catholic parents, he ardently embraced the nationalist cause for independence and, after immigrating to America at age seventeen, soon became an influential advocate, mostly through his editing and writing, for the Fenian movement, urging both the independence of Ireland and the annexation of Canada to the American Republic. Between 1845–48, he returned to Ireland and became involved in the Irish Confederation and the Young Irelander Rebellion of 1848. The failure of the latter forced him to flee back to America to avoid arrest. However, by 1851, he had become disillusioned with America, republicanism, and Fenian radicalism, and became much more conservative in both his Catholicism and his politics. Immigrating

of his radical nationalist ideals, was shot by a suspected Fenian sympathizer in 1868 as "the archetypal traitor" to Ireland, "the former revolutionary who had sacrificed his principles on the altar of his ambition" to achieve power in British North America (Wilson, *McGee* Vol. II 15).

However, as Coulter was to suggest in his later Riel play, *The Crime of Louis Riel*, it was not a dynamic exclusive to nineteenth-century Irish immigrants. A similar suspicion for similar reasons met the large wave of East Europeans aggressively recruited to fill the *fin de siècle* Canadian prairie provinces with settlers. If anything, they were even more alien than the Irish, since they lacked a shared language, culture, religion, and history with the British Canadian majority. Nonetheless, outside of the unalterable issue of race, most nineteenth-century officials felt there was little that couldn't be assimilated with proper education or acculturation. "The Chinese, like the Blacks, were too different from the Anglo-Canadian norm to ever be capable of assimilation. With new clothes, proper food, and the right amount of acculturation a Ukrainian could be 'Canadianized,'" if not in this generation than the next (Hewitt 119). It was assumed that with continued patience, peace, and prosperity, there would soon be no real difference between Irish and Ukrainian Canadians as British subjects, even in art and culture.

Instead, World War I drove a deep and lasting division between British Canadians who largely embraced the war effort and many "New Canadians" who did not or could not. Under the War Measures Act between 1914 and 1920, some 8,579 Austro-Hungarian citizens and emigrants—mostly Ukrainian men, women, and children—were declared "enemy aliens" and confined to internment or work camps. While confining or monitoring "enemy aliens" was consistent with war-time American and European practice as

---

to Canada in 1857, he spent the remainder of his life urging Canadian Catholics to turn their backs on the Fenian movement, and worked with moderate Protestants to create a new country within the British Empire, one that he believed would be more capable of peaceable compromise, tolerance, and respect for diversity than the American model. While he succeeded in becoming a Father of Canadian Confederation in 1867, he was shot dead at the age of forty-two in April 1868 while returning from a late-night session at Parliament, likely by Fenian sympathizer Patrick Whelan. See Wilson, *McGee* Vol. I and II.

well, Bohdan Kordan suggests that Canada was unique not only in the dis-
proportionate number of "resident enemy aliens" it interned relative to its
population, but also in treating those interned "as captive military prisoners"; in doing so, it showed disturbingly "little consideration" for either the
immediate or long-term "consequences" of that action (56). The deep-rooted
fear and suspicion of those who were allowed to remain in the community
despite their "enemy alien" status also extended to their theatre activity. In
Vegreville, Alberta, a wave of anti-foreign sentiment climaxed in February
1919 when a Ukrainian-language play produced to raise funds for a new
memorial hall was abruptly cancelled; just as "the curtain was about to rise
on a packed opera house" constables entered and announced that, consistent
with war-time regulations, "the performance was interdicted, because public
meetings in the Ukrainian language are forbidden by law" ("Beaver Lake").
Even after local authorities had granted the group permission to proceed,
the local theatre had to withdraw its offer of space after receiving threats of
a riot and "rough-housing" if the show went on ("The *Observer*"). Clearly,
too many people agreed with the local newspaper that, the innocence of
this particular show notwithstanding, "[e]ven the pulpit and the stage may
harbor treason" and "the sooner the foreigners consent to [. . .] adopt in
their speeches and in their plays the language of the land in which they dwell,
the sooner they will be admitted to the full friendship and confidence of a
common citizenship" ("Beaver Lake"). The "foreigners," who now had even
less reason to trust their British neighbours, were for the next few decades
to retreat further into silence, their own culture, or more radical expressions
of politics, art, and drama.

By contrast, the Irish Renaissance and founding of the Abbey Theatre
had considerably raised the stock of the Irish in matters poetic, dramatic, and
theatrical. While the Fenian raids were still a part of the communal living
memory, many post–World War I Canadians now felt they shared more of a
"common citizenship" ("Beaver Lake") with Irishmen of William Butler Yeats's
stamp who mirrored so clearly their own generation's cultural aspirations to
shed their colonial status with Britain. Irish historian Thomas Mohr suggests
that even though Canadians were not consulted as part of the negotiations,

many were nonetheless aware that the Irish Free State was designed to be "a Dominion that shared key aspects of its autonomy with Canada which was often called 'the eldest Dominion'" (35); as a consequence, the response of the French- and English-language Canadian press to the declaration of the Irish Free State on 6 December 1922 was largely fraternal and encouraging (57). The perception, correct or otherwise, that the "new" Irish nation was now working out of much the same template for national aspiration and self-governance as that "eldest Dominion" certainly inclined Canadian theatre artists, more than ever, to turn to the Abbey as a preferred model for the kind of mature national theatre that Canada also needed to establish to express its own distinct vision, character, and stories. But where to find a Yeats?

In 1936, Canada finally received its own personal prophet from the Abbey; John Coulter, who was born in Belfast in 1888 to a tolerant, well-educated Protestant family, was to be arguably the only significant Canadian dramatist, author, and poet "directly influenced by the Irish Literary renaissance" (Anthony, *John Coulter* 21) that was to serve "as a model for theatrical and dramatic developments in Canada in the first three decades of the century" (Wagner, *Canada's Lost Plays, Volume Four* 22). Moving to Dublin in 1914, Coulter saw most of the plays produced at the Abbey, and in 1917 he consulted with Yeats about trying to convert the amateur Ulster Literary Theatre into a similar professional company with its own theatre building. However, a new outbreak of "the troubles" in 1920 led him to flee to London and pursue a career in journalism, editing, writing, and radio instead. In 1935 he met and fell in love with a Canadian poet and short-story writer, Olive Clare Primrose, and moved to Canada to marry her in 1936 (Anthony, *John Coulter* 19–26).

However, unlike Yeats, who confidently saw the imminent genesis of a new Abbey Theatre in the Hart House Theatre of 1920, Coulter quickly discovered that, outside the medium of radio, he was now a playwright in exile with little more than a vision of the theatre or a country he wanted to write for. In an often-quoted 1938 essay, "The Canadian Theatre and the Irish Exemplar," he commented:

It is well to say at once that I speak of the theatre in Canada as a visiting Irishman from London, England. [. . .] I confess, therefore, that
my notion of values in the theatre was powerfully and permanently
affected by years of [. . .] watching with delight and wonder while
the life I knew, the dreary secular life of Irish parlors and kitchens
and farms and pubs, was turned by the Abbey playwrights and players into parable, lovely and rich and lively dramatic parable. [. . .]
And I was naïve enough to assume that the plays of other countries
were similarly rooted, [. . .] [in] imaginative criticism, portrayal,
and interpretation of national life and character. (119)

However, even if there was as yet "no such thing as Canadians, in the sense
that there are Irish in Ireland," Coulter believed that this emergent national
type would only be discovered if "playwrights, actors and producers north
of Niagara would turn their eyes from Broadway and look around them at a
place called Canada. In the streets of Canadian towns, on the prairies, in the
lake settlements and mining villages, a hundred grand plays are waiting for
Canadians who will write them" (122).

COULTER, DRAMA EDUCATION, AND EXTENSION
WORKERS: WESTERN CANADA, 1923–1945

It is perhaps telling of Coulter's perspective as "a visiting Irishman from
London, England" that the main focus of his essay is on the need for his
adopted country to aim for the same kind of unified national character he had
experienced in Ireland; and this largely through the writing of the same kind
of sophisticated literary plays that could be produced in a theatre building with
a professional company in a large urban centre like Dublin, Belfast, or New
York. Nonetheless, as an immigrant himself he acknowledges the presence of
the wide diversity of peoples in Canada, including every kind of "European
and Asiatic nationality" ("The Canadian" 120); he also observes that even
without a native school of playwriting, the diversity of the nationwide amateur and educational theatre was nonetheless an important instrument of

social cohesion and "practical [. . .] political influence, in the sense that it interpenetrates the whole structure of Canadian society and draws together its diverse communities of race, language, vocation and religious or political creed" (120).

While their work was peripheral to his vision, Coulter nonetheless gives credit, even in passing, to the innovative extension and education drama programs of the Western provinces that were set up over the 1920s and 1930s. These programs differed substantially from those of most of their counterparts in Central and Atlantic Canada. Where continuing education divisions existed in Ontario or the Maritimes, they were usually based more closely on British models, and most arts training, if offered, came in the form of a modest number of credit or non-credit evening or summer courses given at a central location; educational drama often meant the study and occasional production of "good plays" on the school curriculum at the high-school level, an experience that could be enhanced by the decision of an extension division to augment its teaching activities by mounting or sponsoring good productions that could then be toured to schools within an acceptable radius of the centre. By contrast, the Western educational and continuing education (extension) departments and divisions—established either in the closing years of the nineteenth century or opening decades of the twentieth century—were based more strongly on populist American models specifically designed to serve the needs and realities of small, often scattered farming or agricultural communities with a larger mix of ethnic groups, and where the school, from the primary through to the high-school level, was often the main cultural as well as educational centre. In this model, the associated art and drama programming tended to be driven by the needs and resources of the communities and schools themselves, and involved considerably more personal outreach through field trips, radio broadcasts, bulletins and library materials, and on-site training workshops and short courses to help the local schools and community groups mount and perform their own productions.

In Western Canada, the educational and extension drama/music/art programs were also far more flexibly designed to deal precisely with the complex, intensely political, and volatile realities of largely non-British immigration in rural farming areas well beyond the boundaries of the larger urban centres. Unlike the mainstream art theatre movement, or even Toronto's immigrant-friendly "socially conscious and propagandist Theatre of Action" ("The Canadian" 122), which Coulter also acknowledges, the extension and education specialists went deeply into the rural areas and focused their programming more closely on the grassroots there; they were faster to celebrate folk art and drama forms, and to work within festival, fair, or concert formats more open to exposing a larger, more diverse range of music, art, dance, and theatre selections at significant community gatherings. And they were very acutely aware of the difficult and contradictory politics of social and cultural celebration, inclusion, and assimilation that went with those activities.

The trauma of the war and the internment, and the growing appeal of Marxist alternatives after the Russian Revolution, continued to reverberate beyond 1919. According to Hewitt, by the late 1920s it was estimated that some 80% to 90% of the Communist Party in Canada was composed of Ukrainians, Finns, and Jews (113). The onset of the Depression and further social and economic loss again fed an increase in political radicalization as well as various forms of social disintegration, disillusionment, and distress. It was no coincidence that Alberta, Manitoba, and British Columbia all developed strong arts- or drama-specialist extension/education positions over the 1920s and 1930s, or that all three positions were held by immigrants themselves: Esther Thompson in Manitoba (1923–1940), Elizabeth Haynes in Alberta (1932–37), and Llewellyn Bullock Webster in British Columbia (1936–1946).

Most of these field workers attempted to dialogue with "the Other." But these were dialogues rife with internal inconsistencies and contradictions. At their most enlightened, extension and education specialists practised as well as preached the philosophy that immigrants were fully welcome additions to the expanding mosaic of human, artistic, and cultural richness in Canada. There were the attempts of a local Alberta school inspector to draw local Hutterite colonies, in recognition of the richness of their musical and song traditions, into an inter-colony festival of their own that could possibly be integrated into the main festival system ("Position" 3). There was Esther Thompson's statement about how her work could awaken the anglo majority of Manitoba

to the cultural richness of their German, Norwegian, and Galician neighbours. Noting their "intense desire to preserve their native arts," Thompson
was reported as seeing a real value in creating outreach programs that built
on "their dramatic and musical talent, their handicrafts, their sense of color,
their dancing and folk songs" (Speechly 27). Nor were the benefits one way.
Arguing for the establishment of folk song and folk-dancing festivals as well,
Thompson, in 1929, insisted that the arts activities of New Canadians represented not a threat, but a "cultural wealth, in our midst, of which people are
not aware," and that the "[Women's] Institute, which has as neighbours people
from Ukrainia, Germany, Iceland, Denmark and Holland, has an opportunity
denied to those living in an all English-speaking community" to experience
"an artistic wealth similar to that of paintings, music, literature and other
forms of art" (Thompson 3). Haynes certainly seemed to share very similar
views to Thompson's when she commented in a 1935 Toronto lecture that
Alberta Extension's rural program had been especially successful in "preserving and using the dramatic heritage of her people from Ukrainia, Denmark,
Scandinavia, China and other nations" in promoting an intercultural mosaic
in Alberta ("Mrs").

   In practice, Haynes likely followed E.A. Corbett, who as Extension head
attempted to negotiate a middle ground between the preservation and assimilation of ethnic identity. On one hand, he was open to the idea of building
up a library of Ukrainian-language literature as part of the Extension library
(Wallace). At the same time, he was to recollect that he had first really appreciated "the potential educational value" of the festival movement, and drama
specifically, while adjudicating the winner of the high-school section at the
1931 Vegreville festival—"a young Ukrainian lad of sixteen, with ragged
sweater and patched trousers, who electrified all of us with his rendition of
Mark Antony's speech from *Julius Caesar*" (Corbett 90). But what he meant
by this "educational value" remains ambiguous. The Reverend George D.
Armstrong, in responding in his weekly column to a series of plays prepared
with Elizabeth Haynes's help at the local high school, noted that activities like
play production could also be an active instrument in designing a progressive new society in the West that forged the existing elements into something

new: "Rarely have we seen such a blending of varied races, creeds and classes in the fellowship of a common enterprise[;] and mutual understanding, co-operation and friendliness cannot fail to produce 'a more abundant life' in the new day that is at the dawn" (4).

It has to be noted that a number of school inspectors, observing that many of these "New Canadian" children came from a rich European cultural background, also continually mentioned the usefulness of games, art, music, and drama in bridging the language barrier and motivating children to learn and communicate in English:

> If you teach in the north of the province and have any number of Ukrainians among your pupils, you will discover, if you have not already done so, that they are particularly good at dramatic expression. They are ready to act without being self-conscious and of course, dramatization of stories is a very good vehicle for the teaching of spoken English, since they have something in their minds to say, plus some of the words in which to say it—both very necessary to setting the little non-English pupil on his way to really talking. ("Classroom" 27–28)

Corbett likely meant "educational value" mostly in Armstrong's sense of using the arts to forge a new fellowship of "mutual understanding, co-operation and friendliness" among "varied races, creeds and classes" (4). Nonetheless, it has to be stated that many of these arts strategies were also used to subtly enforce the Department of Education's "speak-English-only" policies in the school-ground and classroom, and were aimed at weaning New Canadian children away from the "dangerous" cultural, linguistic, and political practices of their suspect, foreign-born parents. Like many other liberal educators, Corbett saw no contradiction between celebrating, in Thompson's words, "the cultural wealth, in our midst" (3) and acknowledging the power of educational drama to create bonds of social harmony, co-operation, and cohesion among the most divergent communities brought together in the school system, while also implicitly supporting policies that placed the onus for the necessary change, compromise, and accommodation largely on the shoulders of the newcomers.

Beyond the carefully nuanced contradictions were the outright explosions, when a different drama or art form was interpreted by the British Canadian establishment—sometimes correctly—as a denial or betrayal by aliens of the "full friendship and confidence of a common citizenship" as the elite understood it ("Beaver Lake"). While the French Canadians were seen as particularly obstinate in their refusal to assimilate, East Europeans were seen as especially dangerous forces intent on using any means at their fingertips, including theatre, to subvert and destroy the social, political, and cultural system that most British Canadians embraced. The most obvious example of that had been the banning of the 1919 Ukrainian production in Vegreville in connection with World War I hostility against "alien enemies." But it was a fear that continued to be very current during the rise of communist sympathies and workers' movements and theatres over the 1920s and 1930s, and the rapid rise of fascist regimes.

Corbett and Thompson's later attempts at establishing a folk school in 1938 at the Pas in Manitoba under the auspices of the Canadian Association for Adult Education floundered in the face of an "unbridgeable chasm of suspicion between the foreign groups and those of English-Canadian origin" (Corbett 156). Many of the province's British Canadian elite clearly had no interest in letting Eastern European upstarts corrupt their theatre—let alone their society or politics—with dangerous, subversive influences. Confronted by a pernicious whisper campaign that the project was "a communist set-up" (156) and that the instructors, one of whom was rumoured to be Jewish, spent a suspicious amount of time "with the foreigners," the school lasted for only three years (Corbett 157). Manitoba's brave attempt to next create a unique bilingual drama extension program in 1941—the first and only one of its kind in the Western provinces—lasted barely five years. Less than two years in, the English Canadian specialist, Edith Sinclair, resigned because of what she considered irreconcilable differences not only with her French counterpart, René Dussault, but also with the head of the division, Watson Thomson, whom she accused of corrupting the unit with his radical socialist agendas. Two years later, Thomson also left under a cloud, paving the way for the unit to be quietly dismantled as part of a general post–World War II restructuring of the university (M. Day 5–12).

COULTER AND RIEL: WESTERN CANADA 1869–1885

By 1945, the year the Manitoba division closed, John Coulter, "the visiting Irishman from London," was still in Canada, but increasingly frustrated with his own inability to translate his native eloquence and revolutionary passion into an authentic dramatic voice for his adopted country. Even if his dream of an Abbey Theatre of the North seemed slightly less quixotic in the postwar climate than it had in 1938, Coulter felt that, at almost fifty, he had immigrated too late in life to master the cadences and rhythms of contemporary Canadian speech required to create convincing dialogue on stage (*In My Day* 260). In an interview with Canadian critic Nathan Cohen, Coulter was asked: "But you want to write about the life you know, the life you care about, that's a life that dates back, that really relates to Ireland, and that's the theatre that wants you. So why stay in Canada?" Coulter responded, "Because I have something to say and I want to say it here. But it is a grinding and intolerable thing" (Anthony, *John Coulter* 149).

When Coulter had brightly suggested in 1938 that all an aspiring Canadian playwright had to do was to turn his or her eyes to "the streets of Canadian towns, on the prairies," to find "a hundred grand plays" waiting to be written, he likely had not imagined that that playwright would be him ("The Canadian" 122). Yet, when inspirational lightning finally struck Coulter in his early sixties, and he at last found the archetypal Canadian hero who "rides the political conscience of the nation [. . .] and is manifestly on his way to becoming the tragic hero at the heart of the Canadian myth" (Anthony, *John Coulter* 61–62), he discovered him not in the great urban and cultural centres of the playwright's own experience, but in the small, remote towns and settlements of the Canadian prairies where many of the education and extension drama specialists were at work. However, Coulter found his hero not in the prairie landscape of the present, but in a key moment in the past that crystallized many of the playwright's own concerns about how the past actions of imperial forces, whether in Ireland or Canada, could have enormous repercussions on the "structure of [. . .] society" in the present ("The Canadian" 120). It was also a key historic moment that touched on Coulter's own experiences as an immigrant, and resonated with his awareness of how the historic policies of strategic destruction, displacement, assimilation, resettlement, and immigration that tended to go with the process of nation or empire building could cast a long shadow over that nation's ongoing struggles in the present to draw "together its diverse communities of race, language, vocation and religious or political creed" (120).

In 1869, Louis Riel (1844–1885)[5] had reportedly told a British reporter that if his readers wanted to know why the Red River had declared a provisional government in Manitoba to negotiate terms with Canada, he should tell them "'our great thought is to resist being made Irishmen of'"(Anthony, *John Coulter* 61). When the playwright approached the librarian at the University of Toronto library about doing research on the subject, and was told, "'What!

---

5   Born in the Red River Settlement, in present-day Manitoba in 1844, to devout Catholic parents dominantly of Franco Chipewyan stock, Riel first trained for the priesthood, then for law in central Canada, before returning to the Red River in 1868. There, his intelligence, charisma, education, and strong roots in the Métis community led him to becoming the leader of the Red River Settlement's resistance to Canada's unilateral attempt to purchase and annex Rupert's Land from the Hudson's Bay company in 1869. As president of the provisional government, Riel succeeded in unifying the racially, linguistically, and ethnically diverse elements of the local community long enough to negotiate a bill of rights and the entry of Manitoba into Confederation as a province in summer 1870. However, his execution of a fanatic young Orangeman, Thomas Scott, in March 1870 in retaliation for several attempts on the part of Scott and other dissidents to subvert or overthrow the provisional government, was a fatal error that left Riel fleeing to the States in advance of a military expedition / "errand of peace" led by Colonel Wolseley. In 1884, a delegation of Métis from Saskatchewan approached Riel, now married and settled with a family in Montana, to return to Canada to present their grievances and negotiate on their behalf with the federal government. When the petitions went ignored, Riel declared a second provisional government in March 1885, this time committed to creating a new nation through armed force, in potential alliance with Indigenous allies. Despite several initial victories under the military leadership of Gabriel Dumont, Riel's forces were decisively defeated at Batoche in May 1885, and Riel surrendered to government forces. His subsequent trial, conviction, and execution for treason in November 1885, despite multiple petitions for clemency on mental health and political grounds, bitterly divided French and English Canada, and attracted strong international controversy as well (Thomas).

Louis Riel! You don't seriously mean to tell me you mean to stir up trouble again about that—that infamous scoundrel!'" Coulter noted with satisfaction that "I needed no more incentive than this to go ahead!" (*In My Day* 261).

Of course, Coulter was not the first playwright in Canada to make a connection between Métis, French Canadian, and Irish national aspirations. In his 1886 drama, *Riel: Tragedie en Quatre Actes*, written only a year after Riel's hanging for treason, Québec writer Elzear Paquin used Riel's compatriots in the Northwest Uprising, Gabriel Dumont and Michel Dumas, to explicitly draw parallels not only between the British crushing of the French Catholic nation of New France in 1760 and the similar British destruction of what Québec viewed as the French Catholic Métis nations of Manitoba and Saskatchewan, but also between the British treatment of these nations and its response to the largely Catholic nation of Ireland:

> **DUMONT:** Misfortune to those who frighten the British nation which believes itself to be the superior race.

> **DUMAS:** But which is not ashamed of persecuting, oppressing and tyrannizing weaker nations like Ireland, for example! (253)

However, in excavating Riel again for audiences in mid-twentieth century English Canada, Coulter not only had to peel away multiple layers of "bitter partisan propaganda" passing as "history" on the English Canadian side (Coulter, *In My Day* 261), but also Paquin's romanticized alternative "history" of Riel as "the great Patriot martyr" (Paquin 206). Coulter's personal experience of a post-revolution twentieth-century Ireland had left him more conflicted than Paquin about the high human cost of even justifiable resistances and revolutions—and the frailties of the "heroes" serving them. Coulter could have been speaking of some of the characters in his Irish plays, *The Drums Are Out* (1948) and *God's Ulsterman* (1971), when he commented that he saw much in Riel of the "patriotic, God-obsessed paranoid with a touch of political genius" who could easily have become just one more quickly forgotten "irascible, discontented, religious and political fanatic" (*In My Day*,

261). Instead, by uniquely catching the historical tide of the time and moment with the intensity of his passion and sense of mission, Riel had become for Coulter that ruling "dark and haunting symbol nagging our political conscience" (Anthony, *John Coulter* 61). That he remained a "dark and haunting symbol" for Coulter as a playwright can be indicated by the fact that he ultimately wrote three Riel plays, *Riel* (1950), *The Trial of Louis Riel* (1968), and *The Crime of Louis Riel* (1968), covering the rise and fall of Riel's provisional government in Manitoba to Canadian forces over 1869–70, his flight to the States and return to Saskatchewan to lead a second uprising over 1884–85, and finally his trial for treason and his hanging in 1885.

However, for Coulter, the 1950 *Riel* remained *the* Riel play, possibly because it represented the most compelling synchronicity between his Irish and his Canadian political conscience. Part one, in particular, would have had strong echoes for a 1950 Ontario audience of the nineteenth constitutional debate between D'Arcy McGee and the American Fenians—though one with a grimly ironic twist. Significantly, Coulter puts the line, "We won't let Canada do to us what England did to Ireland" (3) not in Riel's mouth but in that of his Fenian lieutenant, O'Donohue, a character based on Riel's actual treasurer for his Manitoba provisional government, William Bernard O'Donohue (1843–1878). O'Donohue's quixotic attempt to tear down the Union Jack at the provisional government headquarters with the promise that the "Fenian Irish would come across the border and help us [. . .] to kick the English out and keep out Canada and fly our own [green-and-white] flag—fleur-de-lis and shamrock . . . " (Coulter, *Riel* 23) eerily foreshadows the historical character's later actions, as described by historian George Stanley. Fleeing to the States after the fall of the provisional government, O'Donohue returned almost immediately in 1871 as co-leader of the last (extremely brief) Fenian invasion of Canada; as Coulter's Riel had scathingly predicted, O'Donohue's dream of establishing a Republic of Rupert's Land in Manitoba through armed force essentially amounted to grown men playing "at schoolboy nonsense" (Coulter, *Riel* 24).

While Riel may agree that O'Donohue has designed a "much prettier" flag than the Union Jack, Riel's insistence that his "one little drop of Limerick

Irish blood"[6] does not make him "lose [his] senses" enough to tear down and spit on the British flag situates him philosophically as Coulter's D'Arcy McGee in opposition to O'Donohue's Irish American Fenian (Coulter, *Riel* 25). Riel's stance that "we in the North-west are loyal subjects of her Majesty" is partially driven by practicality: given the fact there are only seven hundred people in the Northwest, he wants to ensure that "three million British will have the honour of protecting us when we cannot protect ourselves [. . .] even if the would-be grabber is Canada—or the U.S.A." (24–26). Ideologically, though, he puts a great deal of trust in Canada, again as "the eldest Dominion" (Mohr 35), being able to see in the Northwest's request to enter Confederation as a province, a close reflection of Canada's own aspiration as a nation to evolve slowly and peaceably toward a form of self-government respectful of differing religions and politics, and of "the lives and property of all races and creeds" under British protection (Coulter, *Riel* 54).

Again, Canadians aware of the connection between their own national aspirations and those of the Irish Free State in 1922 may have felt that in Riel's initial stance, Coulter was again simply acknowledging those same synchronicities in a way that, once more, reflected well on his adopted country. However, by 1950, as reflected in his play *The Drums Are Out*, Coulter was intensely aware of how little the Irish Free State had actually achieved in creating a sustainable model of Irish nationhood acceptable to either the south (Ireland ceased to be a dominion in 1937 and officially became a republic in 1949) or the north, where the factionalism and sectarian violence that had plagued Coulter's youth

---

6   Riel was descended from a Limerick-born father, and possibly even mother, who had at least one son who immigrated to Canada in the late seventeenth or early eighteenth century. Tina Farrow speculates that this ancestor may have been the Jack Reilly (b. 1640s) who was among the forces supporting the Catholic Stuart king, James II, against William of Orange. Unfortunately, the Jacobites lost at the Battle of the Boyne in 1690, and Reilly had to flee to France with other Irish loyalists in 1691; here, he apparently assumed the name Jean Riel. Farrow suggests that there is evidence that he (or more likely his son) travelled to Canada with the army of Louis XIV to fight in the French–English wars there, and finally settled in Québec under the name Jean-Baptiste Riel d'Ireland (Farrell). One of his descendants, Jean-Baptiste Riel dit L'Irelande (1785–1868), who married Marguerite Boucher (c. 1790–1892), a Métis woman in Saskatchewan, was the grandfather of Louis Riel.

was, if anything, worsening. If Riel is devastatingly accurate about the political naïveté of O'Donohue's proto-IRA revolutionary solution in this context, O'Donohue is devastatingly accurate about Riel's political naïveté in thinking that a McGee-style constitutional arrangement will work for the Northwest. He denounces Riel as "a fool" if he believes that the British commander, Colonel Wolseley, will follow the directions of either Ottawa or London to simply keep the peace and supervise a smooth transition of power from Riel's provisional government to Governor Archibald (53). On the frontiers, "thousands of miles away" from the big centres, commanders and soldiers alike do what they want to do "and square it after with—instructions" (53). Moreover, in executing fanatic Orangeman Thomas Scott, Riel has already introduced the sectarian violence of the old Ireland into his "new Ireland in the Northwest" (Coulter, *Trial* 12), and with so many of Wolseley's forces composed of Ulster Orangemen out for blood, Wolseley could not enforce the peace and "stop his Orangemen even if he wanted to" (Coulter, *Riel* 54).

Coulter seems to suggest that the failure of Canada to allow Riel to follow McGee's path in becoming a "Father of Confederation" for Manitoba is the fatal turning point that starts the Métis leader down O'Donohue's path toward revolution and an increasingly delusional perception of himself, driven by his increasing religiosity and megalomania, as the "noble patriot, betrayed! The tragic man!" (54). In Part Two of the play, set fourteen years later in Saskatchewan, Riel completes his transformation from the constitutional monarchist of Manitoba to the failed revolutionary of Saskatchewan whose vision and passion, even in being crushed, nonetheless leave an indelible mark on the oppressor. Once again though, polemics that may have been more open to interpretation for audiences in Coulter's troubled, divided Ireland tended to shape themselves into more comfortable patterns of completion and closure in the relatively quiet, conservative Dominion of 1950 Canada. While several of Coulter's canonical characters, including John A. Macdonald, do suggest that it is possible to view Riel as a tragically flawed instrument of destiny necessarily sacrificed to "the larger purpose of Providence for *all* [Canadian] peoples" (3), there is little to indicate that Coulter himself intended either Riel or the considerable complexities and ironies surrounding him to be reduced to anything quite so simple or comforting.

To the contrary, in exploring the beginnings of massive European immigration on the prairies, and what it meant to the small, racially and linguistically mixed communities already in place, Coulter also considered the long-term as well as the immediate implications of nineteenth-century Canadian immigration policies, which were still resonating in the fractious cultural, social, and political dynamics of the Northwest of the mid-twentieth century.

Ultimately, O'Donohue suggests that Riel has to know in his heart of hearts that Wolseley's promise to "afford equal protection to the lives and property of all races and creeds" (54) is empty for the simple, devastating reason that the commander's real mission in Manitoba, whether Ottawa officially acknowledges it or not, is not to keep the peace but "to grab the land, and fight to keep it for Macdonald's immigrants" (53). O'Donohue implies that even now that "one little drop of Irish Limerick blood" (25) should be enough to remind Riel that massive immigration/colonization is a long-standing British strategy for dealing with intransigent native populations, including the Irish, who do not readily facilitate imperial commercial or political interests:

> If we tolerate them [surveyors] Canadians will swarm in after them in thousands. They'll grab both us and ours. [. . .] For what? To help them build great buildings and roads and railways and canals—but not here! Not for us in the North-West. No, but for themselves in Canada. To make their own big cities bigger and richer still! [. . .] We won't let Canada do to us what England did to Ireland. (3)

In his 1885 trial in Part Two, Riel argues instead for the creation of a "New World" of tolerance and diversity in the Northwest, as supported by a new religion based solely on "humanity and morality and charity" (91). To avoid repeating "those evils which exist in Europe" (115), the arrival of newcomers has to be regulated with respect for the customs and traditions of the older communities on the land and a willingness to build with them to meet the actual needs of a new Northwest nation:

Yet, now, we make a beginning. We invite to our new world Italians, Poles, Bavarians, Belgians, the Swedes, the Irish, the Jews—all, all are welcome here, provided only they will help us with their work and with their money. (115)

"In essence," suggests historian Lewis H. Thomas, commenting on the historical Riel's speech, "it was a not unreasonable programme for creating a multi-cultural society." It was also a view that resonated with the multicultural approach of many extension and educational drama practitioners and that Coulter himself felt was one of the main goals of drama production: the "blending of varied races, creeds and classes in the fellowship of a common enterprise, and mutual understanding, co-operation and friendliness" that could move a progressive new society toward "a new day" (Armstrong).

Nonetheless, if Coulter felt that his audience of 1950 was sufficiently distanced from Canada's nineteenth-century understanding of itself to appreciate the irony of a man being dismissed either as a madman or a traitor for having suggested something so sensible, he was to learn otherwise on opening night. It was true, Coulter observed, that the more enlightened members of his Toronto audience, including poet E.J. Pratt, were so swept up in the sublimity of the tragedy that they were jarred into "horrified protest" by "the harsh realism" of the "appalling moment" when the "hangman and scaffold are suddenly revealed awaiting Riel upstage" (Coulter, *In My Day* 262). Nonetheless, the playwright also noted that there was a select group of the audience that "were not in the least horrified [. . .] but on the contrary thought it the best thing in the play." This was "the little company of bemedaled veterans of the Second Riel Rebellion, with whom Mrs. [Dora Mavor] Moore had enterprisingly dressed the front row of the house. One of them said to me afterwards, 'Gosh, sir, I was all through that bloody rebellion; but tonight's the first time I ever knew a goddam thing about that bastard!'" (263). It had apparently never occurred to Coulter that at least some of his audience might assume that, as an Ulsterman himself, he had naturally written a morality play with the villain getting his just deserts.

It may have been that reaction, or even the tendency of the enlightened 1950s audience to simplistically read Riel as the flawed instrument of greater Canadian destiny, that motivated Coulter, seventeen years later, to write two further Riel plays that concentrated solely on Riel the revolutionary: *The Trial of Louis Riel*, which Coulter described as "strictly a documentary" (*Crime* i) that involved him editing down the transcripts of the actual five-day trial at Regina in 1885 "without loss of essentials to the two hours of playing-time on stage" (*In My Day* 271), and *The Crime of Louis Riel*, a condensed version of *Riel* that telescoped the two rebellions into one and reassigned many of O'Donohue's lines to Riel. What seems more likely, though, is that in Canada's centennial year Coulter felt there was a new parable to be read into Riel for a nation that was more turbulent—questioning of authority at home and abroad—and multicultural than it had been in 1950. In *The Crime of Louis Riel*, he made it clear that he read in the struggle against systemic oppression and injustice being waged "in Riel's remote corner of the North-West" a parable for the same battles being "as bitterly waged today" by "subject peoples" in Asia, Africa, and Cuba, who were just as intent as Riel's Métis on "profoundly changing our world" (*Crime* 1):

> I see the Metis leader and the rebellions which he led as precursors of later and present uprisings all over the world, particularly the so-called Third World—armed resistance by small nations against forcible take-over by some powerful neighbour, an impassioned rejection of even greatly enhanced material well-being in order to be free—free of the humiliation of paternalistic government by an outsider, free to develop in their own way from their own roots. (*Crime* i)

In this later play, the shrewd, genial John A. Macdonald of *Riel* has hardened into an imperialist capitalist who callously manipulates European immigrants and Northwest Métis alike to his own ends: "But if our geologists and engineers aren't wildly mistaken—the riches under the earth out there are of prodigiously more account than any quantity of buffalo-meat and furs. Besides we have a few thousands of overflow Europeans to find homes and occupation for" (*Crime* 21). By contrast, Riel now adds "Asians and Africans" (54) to the list of racial and ethnic diversity welcome to his New World. There is a suggestion that possibly those, "[n]o matter if the colour of their skin is white or brown or black," who have known the outrage of being "taken over and incorporated into some other country without their own consent" (11), or been "overrun. Driven out and destroyed" (40) by "some powerful neighbor" or white "paternalistic government" (*Crime* i) will be quicker to respect the desire of "Indians and half-breeds" to "go on living our own kind of life, [. . .] to respect, keep up, our own old customs and laws" (40). While some of the Irish substrata of the original play remains, *The Crime of Louis Riel* gives a stronger sense of the kind of contemporary multicultural society Coulter could see Canada evolving toward as it headed into its next century.

By 1968, the one-hundred-and-first anniversary of the Confederation of his adopted country, the one-hundredth anniversary of McGee's assassination, and the ninety-eighth anniversary of Riel's declaration of his provisional government, Coulter could take pride in having restored a curiously Irish hero permanently to the Canadian dramatic canon and public consciousness—and in doing so, in Geraldine Anthony's words, finally emerging from "forgotten playwright [. . .] to the dean of Canadian playwrights" (*John Coulter* 71). He lived to see a full production of his epic 1950 *Riel* at the National Arts Centre in 1975, though sadly not at his beloved Abbey Theatre.

COULTER AND THE DREAM OF THE NATIONAL THEATRE: DANCING WITH THE DEVIL

Clearly, the officially sanctioned drama structures and policies coming out of the early twentieth century immigration experience in Canada were as often as complex, diverse, fractious, and contradictory as the immigrants and the Canadians involved in them. In practice, some immigrants and their art were deemed as "more equal" than others, but all arguably wrestled with the experience of exile, displacement, and a restless desire for change and revolution that left them perpetually uncomfortable with the stable, British Canadian norm. Coulter, as an Irishman, certainly took his own turn at celebrating dangerous, subversive influences in Canada by making a tragic hero out of Louis

Riel, the Métis leader who resisted British colonialism and hegemony in pursuit of his own utopian vision of nationhood in Manitoba and Saskatchewan.

Still, phrased in the cadences of familiar British dramatic languages and
forms, and of Irish tropes, Coulter's *Riel* could easily have been designed for
the venerable Abbey Theatre, where Coulter hoped the play would finally
appear (Coulter, *In My Day* 356). He may have had even greater hopes that
it would be staged at the Stratford Festival of Canada, founded in 1952 with
similar nationalistic aspirations. By the mid-1970s, Coulter could simultaneously dismiss the latter as "the Shakespearean Museum Theatre of Stratford,
Ontario"(Anthony, *Stage Voices* 18) while remaining wistful that even the
fact that he had designed *Riel* "for presentation in the Elizabethan manner:
a continuous flow of scenes on a bare stage with the aid of no more than
indicative settings and properties and modern stage lighting" (Coulter, *Riel* v)
never seemed inducement enough to get it onto Stratford's neo-Shakespearean
Festival stage (Coulter, *In My Day*, 268).

Ironically, Coulter's dramatic vindication of Western Canada's most iconic
rebel cemented Coulter's own iconic status as one of the first mature playwrights
of an emerging national theatre of the Massey mode in Canada. Yet in its reliance on the Abbey (and to a lesser extent, the Globe Theatre) as a model, it was a
dream that again in Filewod's words, was "taken entirely from the cultural experience of another country" and in serving institutions like Stratford and the NAC
ended up reinforcing an existing "historical arrangement of wealth and power"
("National Theatre" 414–15). In fact, it may have been the neo-Shakespearean
elements of the play, intended to give epic size, dignity, and gravitas to Riel and
his tragedy, that encouraged even sympathetic audiences to read the character
more conservatively than Coulter intended, and to ultimately return to a steady
diet of "real" Shakespearean tragic heroes at Stratford and its ilk.

It is also not the least of the many ironies of the play's success that
Coulter's scathing critique of British Canada's nineteenth-century imperialist
assault on Indigenous and Métis sovereignty—which included his condem-
nation of federal policies designed to forcibly clear the land to make way for
massive waves of European immigration—exists in uneasy conjunction with
the terms of Coulter's own success in Canada as a "preferred" immigrant. In

this regard, he shared the dilemma of a number of the Western drama extension specialists, many of them immigrants themselves, who struggled to use drama to serve and preserve ethnic diversity at the grassroots level while being complicit in systems aimed at assimilating "dangerous" aliens in the interests of national unity. However, in Coulter's case, the discomfort may have been sharpened by his awareness that in Ireland, rebellion, despite its high human cost—a cost that Coulter himself pointedly acknowledged in a number of his Irish plays—ultimately led to the achievement of Irish nationhood and self-determination. In Canada, rebellion had to be crushed as a necessary prerequisite to allowing the subsequent waves of immigration—Ukrainian and Irish alike—to roll into the West and create Canada as a unique "nation of immigrants," drawing its cultural, artistic, and theatrical strengths from its growing mosaic. That Coulter continued to struggle with that paradox, especially as it related to Riel and to audiences' responses to the character, can be seen in the fact that he revisited Riel and reinterpreted him for contemporary Canadians in no less than three different, full-length dramas.

CONCLUSION

Coulter's death at the age of ninety-one in 1980 marked the end of a unique life of perpetual movement and change across years and borders—one that had come within three years of overlapping with Riel's second uprising. One suspects that the Irish ex-patriate who wrote to a friend in 1949 that "emigrants who leave their own country after they reach, say, twenty, are likely to remain exiles rather than immigrants to the end of their days" (Anthony, *John Coulter* 20) likely felt a strong affinity with Riel, the fellow pilgrim constantly shifting between differing worlds and nations, while remaining in a perpetual state of exile, rootlessness, and transition between vision and memory, dream and reality. Describing his native Ulster in 1971 as an increasingly "demented world" (Coulter, *Drums* 3) spiralling ever more deeply into sectarian violence, Coulter likely also felt that "a New World" that would avoid "those evils which exist in Europe" would be the work not of "some days or years but [...] hundreds of years" (*Riel* 115).

It is also the final irony, in a life and career marked by so many, that the Coulter play that has ultimately endured as a stage piece is not his epic master-piece *Riel*, nor his more Brechtian *The Crime of Louis Riel*, but the documentary that he dismissed "frankly as a tourist attraction" for Saskatchewan and, as such, among the more artistically doubtful products of "the Canadian Riel Industry" he had initiated (*In My Day* 271, 268). On the one-hundred-and-twenty-fifth anniversary of the hanging of Louis Riel, on 16 November 2010, Coulter's *Trial of Louis Riel* played to a sold-out audience of 478 patrons (including me) in the historic Roxy Theatre in Saskatoon; eight hundred schoolchildren had to be turned away from the sold-out matinee performance earlier that day (Fuller, "Riel Play"); busloads of other young people were brought in from neighbour-ing reserves for the evening performance—an event attended, and in some instances acted out, by members of the Métis, Indigenous, francophone, and anglophone communities in the Saskatoon district, among them descendants of those involved in the original conflict and legal proceedings, including Riel's extended family and those whose ancestors participated in the original trial as witnesses and jurymen. In this context, Coulter's play, stripped down to a kind of verbatim theatre, using dialogue "strictly limited to and derived from transcripts of evidence at Louis Riel's trial, conviction, and sentence to death" (Coulter, *In My Day* 271), did indeed resonate powerfully as "parable, lovely and rich and lively dramatic parable" with its audience (Coulter, "The Canadian" 118), by allowing as many interpretations and conclusions about Riel as there were people and communities in the theatre.

Going into its fifty-first year of production in Saskatchewan in 2018, Coulter's *Trial* claims to be the second-longest continuously running pro-duction in Canada outside of the musical *Anne of Green Gables* (Fuller, "Riel Play"), and the "longest-running historical dramatic production in North America" ("Home"). As such, it remains Coulter's most enduring reminder of all those—immigrant, emigrant, exile, native-born—"of whatever colour or whatever country who are driven to reject, rebel, take arms and fight against what they regard as government by an encroaching alien power" (Coulter, *Crime* 1)—even when that power may be Canada itself.

TORONTO THEATRE, AMERICAN MIGRATION, AND THE VIETNAM WAR

DAVID DEGROW

(d) The Director of Selective Service shall establish a random selection sequence for induction. Such random selection sequence shall be determined as the President may direct, and shall be applied nationwide. [. . .]

(a) When a call is received [. . .] from the State Director of Selective Service for a specified number of men to be delivered for induction [. . .] the Executive Secretary or clerk [. . .] shall select and issue orders to report for induction to the number of men required to fill the call from among its registrants who have been classified in Class I-A or Class I-A-O and have been found acceptable for service in the Armed Forces.
—Richard Nixon, Executive Order 11497—Amending the Selective Service Regulations to Prescribe Random Selection

On 26 November 1969, President Richard Nixon issued executive order 11497 amending the Military Selective Service Act of 1967 to begin the process of inducting non-volunteers into the United States Armed Forces in order to supply troops for escalating American military operations in Vietnam. Five days later, the first lottery was conducted to determine the order of call for induction. In this process, men born between 1 January 1944 and 31 December 1950 were categorized into groups based on the calendar day of their birth. A piece of paper, inscribed with a number corresponding to each calendar day of the year, was inserted into one of 366 blue plastic capsules. These capsules were drawn at random in a televised ceremony, until every day of the year had been paired with a set of sequence numbers. Each eligible nineteen- to twenty-six-year-old American male designated Class I-A or I-A-O[1] was in this way assigned a sequence number that was a combination of the number associated with the calendar day of their birth and another number based on the first letters of their last, first, and middle names ("The Vietnam Lotteries"). Each eligible male would then be mailed their number on a draft card that they were legally required to carry with them at all times while eligible.

This formalization of the draft policy by the US government placed a choice in front of every American man of draft age as to how to respond. Some enlisted; some took advantage of a variety of loopholes by which combat service or even induction could be avoided; some declared themselves conscientious objectors; and some chose to be imprisoned rather than to serve. · Tens of thousands chose to leave the country, either legally or illegally, which resulted in a mass migration of nineteen- to twenty-six-year-old American men (and many others) to Canada between 1965 and 1974. Although the decision was in many cases very difficult personally, most of these migrants were able to create a relatively stable existence for themselves in Canada while they waited for a change in government policy, such as the Carter administration's amnesty in 1977,[2] or they remained permanently.

---

1   The Selective Service System is the organ of the United States government responsible for the registration and management of conscription and possible draftees, with which all American men must register within thirty days of their eighteenth birthday. Between 1948 and 1976, the SSS used a classification system that assigned a Roman numeral and a letter to each inductee based on their availability for military service. Class I-A denotes "Available for military service," while Class I-A-O denotes "Conscientious Objector— Conscientiously opposed to training and military service requiring the use of arms—fulfills his service obligation in a noncombatant position within the military" ("Classifications").

2   Through Proclamation 4483 and Executive Order 11967 issued 21 January 1974, President Jimmy Carter "grant[ed] full, complete and unconditional pardon to: (1) all

This American migration coincided with a significant moment of cultural change in Canada. 1967 marked Canada's centennial year, and the years that followed saw a significant boom for the arts. In Toronto, this boom included the appearance of several new experimental theatre companies, including Theatre Passe Muraille (1968), Factory Theatre Lab (1970), Tarragon Theatre (1970), and Toronto Free Theatre (1971), among others. The coincidence of the migration of young Americans—especially young men—who were able easily to gain access to Toronto professional theatre, and the appearance of these new theatre companies, meant that Vietnam War resisters were part of, worked with, or were connected to almost every new and experimental theatre company working in Toronto between 1968 and 1974.

My essay will examine this migration from two directions. First, it will describe the particular histories of a number of theatre artists and others who came to Toronto in response to the Vietnam War, with the goal of recording this migration and attempting to frame its impact on Toronto theatre at this important time in Canada's cultural history. The second goal of this article, necessary in the context of a book on immigration and theatre in Canada, is to discuss this group as an example of a "privileged migration." Migrating war resisters were able to access a prepared (if not necessarily "easy") route to Canada, in some cases even following a step-by-step road map to Toronto published by the Toronto Anti-Draft Programme (TADP). Having arrived in Toronto, these war resisters could access support from organizations like the TADP, or could become part of countercultural institutions like Rochdale College, all through pre-existing networks. Once connected with these organizations, these mens' privileges of class, gender, race, education, and English-fluency—the same privileges that had facilitated this group's migration to Canada—would then facilitate access to theatre in Toronto. My essay will explore this process by briefly describing the particular experiences and careers of actor Steven Bush, designer Frank Masi, actor Robert Nasmith, director Miles Potter, administrator Shain Jaffe, and critic Jon Kaplan. The

persons who may have committed any offence between August 4, 1964 and March 28, 1973 in violation of the Military Selective Service Act" (Carter).

result will add to the current histories of this important period in Canadian theatre history, while also demonstrating how a migration can meaningfully (if unquantifiably) influence and advance an art form *if* given meaningful access to the arts ecologies of that society.

TERMINOLOGY

One of the difficulties in engaging with this topic is how to name and discuss the group of immigrants in question, and their movement to Canada, as a whole. First, there is no way to statistically identify how many people came to Canada for reasons related to the Vietnam War, nor to what extent the war influenced their decisions.[3] Intention in regards to the war is in many ways the differentiating factor between the various American citizens who came to Canada during this period, as well as the key determinant of the terminology that applies to them. "Draft dodger" is perhaps the most commonly used term for a member of this group in popular culture, but this expression can really only be applied to those who chose to come to Canada to evade the draft, and some object to the implication of avoidance of duty that the term connotes. "Draft resister" similarly ascribes a political motivation to this group that applies to some but not to all of its members. The names "migrant," "asylum seeker," and "refugee" can only be applied to this group incompletely and problematically, as these terms have specific legal definitions under the United Nations's 1951 Convention Relating to the Status of Refugees and the

---

3   Joseph Jones's study *Contending Statistics* provides a comprehensive assessment of the various statistics and statements by which the numbers of Vietnam War resisters migrating to Canada have been assessed. Jones suggests that "this frequently asked question has no precise answer" (11), but demonstrates that the oft-cited approximation of sixty thousand is a mean estimate between the 15,968 American males aged nineteen to twenty-six who obtained official immigrant status in Canada between 1966 and 1972, and the possible 100,000+ total that would include "a greater span of ages, a broader period of immigration, associated women, other family, sojourners that left no record in immigration statistics, or assumed identities" (34).

1967 Protocol to the Convention.[4] Under these protocols, a draft evader can only be considered a refugee if the laws of the evader's nation do not provide alternative service options to conscientious objectors, and only if the evader can establish a "well-founded fear of persecution" (Nicholson and Kumin 133). In fact, theatremakers who came to Toronto because of the Vietnam War did so for a number of reasons. Some came specifically to avoid the draft ("draft evaders"). Others came after having protested the war, or as an act of protest itself, some while under investigation by law enforcement ("draft resisters"). A few deserted from basic training or active service ("deserters"). Each different situation had different possible consequences, ranging from social stigma and self-imposed exile, to prison time. In this essay, I will either use the term "war resister" or the specific legal term that would apply to an individual, but will describe the larger movement of the full group of people involved as a "migration."

---

4   The United Nations High Commissioner for Refugees's *Guide to International Refugee Protection* defines these terms as follows:

A **refugee** is someone who has left his or her country of origin and is unable or unwilling to return there because of a serious threat to his or her life or freedom. The international legal definition of the term is contained in the 1951 Convention. Refugees are entitled to protection from forcible return to their country of origin (the principle of *non-refoulement*) and have other rights and duties that are set out in the 1951 Convention.

"Asylum-seeker" is a general designation for someone who is seeking international protection. In some countries it is a legal term referring to a person who has applied for refugee status and has not yet received a final decision on his or her claim. Not every asylum-seeker will ultimately be recognized as a refugee. However, an asylum-seeker should not be sent back to his or her country of origin until the asylum claim has been examined in a fair procedure.

A **migrant** is best understood as someone who chooses to move, not because of a direct threat to life or freedom, but in order to find work, for education, family reunion, or other personal reasons. Unlike refugees, migrants do not have a fear of persecution or serious harm in their home countries. Migrants continue to enjoy the protection of their own governments even when abroad and can return home. (Nicholson and Kumin 17)

A PRIVILEGED MIGRATION

This study is perhaps valuable in the context of a book on (im)migration and theatre because this particular migration's traits and demographics made access to work in the professional Canadian theatre much easier for them than for most other migrant groups. Like many, this migration was produced by the threat of persecution to a particular group: in this case, the threat of social and judicial persecution/prosecution against Americans of draft age if they did not participate in the United States's war in Vietnam in some capacity. The result was a mass movement of young English-speaking people, the vast majority of whom "came from white, middle- to upper middle-class homes [and who] were college educated or were about to enter or graduate from university" (Kusch 69). This group's privileges of class, education, and English fluency gave them "access to networks of association, political action and cultural production" (Churchill 31) that stretched from the United States to Canada: networks that not only provided for draft evaders' basic needs upon arrival, but also made it possible for many to begin careers in all areas of Canadian society, which is exactly what enabled these individuals to have a significant effect on theatre in Toronto at this time and far into the future.

Ric Knowles's conception of the "intercultural performance ecology" at work in Toronto is valuable in this context. In *Performing the Intercultural City*, Knowles explains this "ecology" as a metaphor that describes "a city's shifting network of 'actors'—performers, performances, institutions, artists, administrators and audiences—organized variously into companies, caucuses, committees and communities" (5). Knowles likens it metaphorically to the "networks" of John Law's Actor Network theory, to Tim Ingold's "meshwork," and to Deleuze and Guattari's "rhizome" in order to represent the "shifting, de-centred, non-hierarchical and horizontal quality of the relationships" between the "actors" in intercultural performance in Toronto (7). This metaphor of ecologies can also be used to understand the overlapping networks of academia, anti-war organizations, countercultural institutions, and finally the small but growing theatre ecology that existed in Toronto in the late 1960s and early 1970s.

Within a few years of the expansion of United States's military involvement in Vietnam in 1966, and the corresponding increases in conscription levels to supply it, a route for draft evaders from the US to Toronto had been developed and documented, with instructions distributed across the country. By the late 1960s, American university campuses abounded with student groups providing support and counselling to those seeking to avoid military service. Through these groups, many potential draftees would have encountered the *Manual for Draft-Age Immigrants to Canada*, one of the primary informational documents available to Americans considering draft evasion by migration. The manual, edited by twenty-year-old draft evader Mark Satin, gave step-by-step instructions on how to immigrate to Canada, with information about a variety of aspects of the immigration process and a series of short articles describing various aspects of Canadian society by way of cultural introduction. Aside from the creation and dispersal of the manual, the Toronto Anti-Draft Programme also provided assistance for evaders at every step of their migration to Canada. In his book *Northern Passage*, John Hagan describes how the TADP helped evaders to enter the country legally by providing the necessary documentation and the "float," which consisted of a sum of $1,000 that was rotated from one resister to the next as they went for their interviews with immigration, because "the rules instructed immigration officers to assign points to those arriving in the country with some money to support themselves" (102). Once evaders had arrived in Toronto, the TADP also took on a role providing the essentials of life, giving "shelter and sustenance, [...] offering legal advice, lending money, providing room and board, and assisting in finding work" (76). This migration's privileges of education and English-fluency created direct access to the anti-war and anti-draft ecologies that had been coming into operation since the mid 1960s; they could then follow these networks across the US and into Canada.

Once arrived, this group's privileges and the cultural similarities between the US and Canada facilitated easy integration into Canadian society, and particularly into the theatre ecology of Toronto. Barry Freeman's *Staging Strangers* is valuable in this context because its descriptions of the various kinds of "strangers" depicted in Canadian theatre outlines all of the things that these

American migrants were *not*. Freeman uses Chris Rumford's description of the stranger as the starting point for his argument: "to be a stranger [. . .] you have to be seen—and once seen you can be positioned as newcomers, wanderers, foreigners, outsiders" (qtd. in Freeman 23). One's "strangeness" is therefore tied to one's visibility as a migrant and an outsider. Due to the similarities of culture and language between Canada and the United States, as well as the similarities of age, race, and class between the migrants and the young Canadians working in both anti-war groups and in the arts, these Americans were not considered foreigners or outsiders in the same ways as other migrant groups, and so in many cases were able to enter Canadian society and the theatre ecology of Toronto on effectively the same footing as Canadians.

STEVEN BUSH AND THE TORONTO ANTI-DRAFT PROGRAMME

The experience of actor Steven Bush demonstrates a typical journey that a theatremaker could follow, and the networks a privileged migrant could traverse, in travelling from the United States to a career in Toronto theatre. In 1968 Bush was an actor working in Memphis, Tennessee, who had been part of demonstrations against the Vietnam War. In an act of protest with thousands of other draftees, Bush had mailed his draft card back to the Selective Service System. As a result, Bush was interviewed by agents of the Federal Bureau of Investigation, and so he began to examine his options. Bush describes this decision in his theatrical memoir *Beating the Bushes:*

> In Atlanta, the FBI shows up on my porch. Why? Along with thousands of other young American males, I'd turned in my draft card [. . .] This makes me arrestable.
>   Soooo: To go underground? Go to jail? Or . . . go to another country. Canada suddenly becomes very attractive: Lots of cool clean air, we're told . . . Leonard Cohen, Joni Mitchell, Ian & Sylvia . . . and

perhaps best of all: A Prime Minster rumoured to be a pot-head. I make plans to head North. (17)

In this passage Bush gives a sense of the limited options draft resisters saw available to them: either accept a prison term for their beliefs, attempt to hide from the authorities in the United States, or go to Canada. The passage also gives a sense that anti-war Americans were drawn to Canada because of a perception that the country was both politically and culturally more progressive than its American counterpart in a wide variety of areas, making it an infinitely preferable choice for some.

Bush came to Toronto by following the networks already in place. The idea was suggested to him through his work with the peace movement in Atlanta, where he encountered the Toronto Anti-Draft Programme's manual and other literature. The task of following the steps laid out in that text was facilitated for Bush by his personal connections in both Atlanta and Toronto. When he arrived, people from the theatre and the peace movement who had already moved to Toronto provided him with places to stay in communes located around Baldwin Street. Meanwhile, the theatre and television industries in Toronto were still relatively small and the communities involved were tightly connected. For example, Bush and Theatre Passe Muraille founder Jim Garrard met at a dinner party hosted by a mutual friend, while at that time it was also possible "without an appointment or an agent, [to] just walk in and see the casting agent at the CBC" (Bush, Personal interview). Thanks to these networks, Bush quickly connected with a number of theatre companies, including Toronto Workshop Productions (TWP) under George Luscombe. Founded in 1958 after Luscombe's return from working with Joan Littlewood's Theatre Workshop in England, TWP was one of the first experimental theatre companies in Canada, noted for its progressive socialist politics and for employing actors of similar leanings. Hence, draft evaders gravitated to the company, and their influence was quickly visible in plays like *Chicago '70*, about the trial of the Chicago Seven, created in almost real time from news being sent to them daily from Chicago. Bush would decide to remain in

Canada after the Vietnam War ended, and would go on to a lengthy career in Canadian theatre as an actor, director, and educator that continues today.

Bush's example demonstrates two things. First, his career demonstrates the visible but somehow unquantifiable nature of the impact these artists made on theatre in this city. Bush has been acting and directing in Toronto for some fifty years, has taught at the University of Toronto regularly since 1993, and continues to be a part of independent theatre productions, most recently as part of the Dora Award–nominated ensemble of Modern Times Stage Company's *Blood Weddings* (staged in 2015 and 2017). He is also effectively the primary historian of the work of Toronto Workshop Productions and the methods of George Luscombe—and he would not have come to Canada had it not been for the draft. At the same time, Bush's experience also demonstrates how at this time access to war-resister networks—and to the privileges of not being a "stranger"—could facilitate a quick transition into full-time work in the Canadian theatre.

JUDITH AND FRANK MASI, ROBERT NASMITH, AND ROCHDALE COLLEGE

Other American theatremakers gained similar access to Toronto's theatre ecology through the countercultural networks that had been developing in the city, which by the late 1960s had manifested into larger "institutions" like Rochdale College, the experimental housing co-operative and free university on Bloor Street. The college had been built to house the expected influx of "baby boomer" students arriving at the University of Toronto, and framed as an experimental educational institution in order to take advantage of a number of federal tax breaks. However, the building's construction had been delayed several months due to a labour strike, with the result that Rochdale's intended student residents were forced to find other accommodation in advance of the 1968–69 school year. As the college approached opening with no tenants, the college's administration decided to make admission to the college and the residence available to anyone (Bradbeer). As a result, the building quickly became home to the hippies and countercultural elements that had been recently displaced from Yorkville by an apocryphal hepatitis outbreak that had led to an official and unofficial quarantine of the area (Henderson 110). The combination of hippies, students, draft evaders, and others that took up residence at Rochdale quickly made the college building a headquarters for the countercultural scene in Toronto.

Once living at Rochdale, residents could engage with the various experimental education programs the college had supported. These included a theatre project conceived by Jim Garrard, a recent graduate of the University of Toronto's theatre program who had been involved with Rochdale since its inception, and who wished to integrate his theatrical ideas into the college's "curriculum." This program was intended to "make theatre relevant for society" (*the rochdale drama project*); the resultant company planned to operate using the building as its stage and the college's residents as its performers. This company was to be named Theatre Passe Muraille (TPM), and it was to consist of three units: a permanent, resident performance unit; a community theatre unit; and an education unit, all of which would operate in the Rochdale College building. The professional performing unit would present experimental theatre productions developed through ensemble research and development, and would offer public performances at a low price. This professional company came to be comprised of some dozen people; about a quarter of whom were there in some way as a response to the Vietnam War, including war-resisters Frank and Judith Masi.

The Masis had come to Toronto to resist the draft and had taken up residence at Rochdale. As professional theatremakers in the US before coming to Toronto, the couple was drawn to the work of Theatre Passe Muraille, which began as readings and play development sessions in Garrard's apartment. As one of the few members of this group with professional training and experience, Frank Masi quickly became TPM's first set designer and technical director, while Judith acted in the company's first productions (Johnston 38). Frank Masi's work would include the design for Passe Muraille's first public performance of *Tom Paine* in the parking garage of Rochdale College (in which the white lines painted on the floor became the set), as well as for the company's second production, *Futz* at the Central Library Theatre in 1969.

Masi's experience with these productions made him the favoured candidate to act as the technical director for the Festival of Underground Theatre in 1970 (Johnston 70). Historians of this period in Canadian theatre have generally recognized this festival as the event that brought TPM, Factory, Tarragon, and Toronto Free Theatre and their artistic directors (self-named the "New Directors Group") into the public eye, and perhaps more importantly as the moment when these directors were able to get provincial arts granting bodies to engage with their work. After contributing to the festival, Frank Masi continued designing productions in Toronto and mentored future designers like Jim Plaxton, who would himself go on to design several productions for Theatre Passe Muraille.

Robert Nasmith, a veteran of the Vietnam conflict, and a Canadian who had returned to Canada after finishing his deployment in 1966, also connected with independent theatre in Toronto through Rochdale College. Nasmith had moved from Ontario to California in 1962 to make his career as an actor, but while there had gotten into a domestic altercation with his mother that resulted in his working with a court-mandated psychiatrist. This psychiatrist in turn recommended the military—"Together Dr. Campbell and I decided that I needed discipline and that I needed adventure"—and so he enlisted (Albino). Nasmith joined the 173rd Airborne Brigade Combat Team, one of the first major US ground combat units to serve in Vietnam, eventually becoming its combat photographer. Nasmith had planned to stay in Vietnam and become a photo journalist, until surviving a helicopter crash in 1966 changed his mind. He returned to Toronto in 1967 and started working as a medical photographer at Mount Sinai Hospital. Nasmith soon heard about the opening of Rochdale College and quickly moved into the residence, where he soon took on a lead role in the operations of the co-operative, first as its executive secretary and then as its president (Albino). There, he connected with Jim Garrard, performing in Garrard's final project at the University of Toronto and joining Theatre Passe Muraille. Rochdale was also where Nasmith met Michael Hollingsworth and Deanne Taylor, founders of VideoCabaret, the Toronto-based experimental theatre company; he went on to perform in several of their plays, including a number in

The History of the Village of the Small Huts series, Hollingsworth's theatrical history of Canada. Thanks to his involvement with these two companies, Nasmith was part of several significant productions through the 1970s; he has gone on to an extensive career in theatre across Canada, whose highlights include co-founding Theatre by the Sea in Vancouver and serving on the board of directors for Theatre Passe Muraille. As in the case of the Masis, it is difficult to assess the specific impact Nasmith had on these various companies, or on theatre in Toronto more generally. What is certain, however, is that the Vietnam War created the circumstances that brought him back to Toronto at this pivotal moment, making it possible for him to access the developing independent theatre scene in Toronto through Rochdale College, and to build a career based on the connections he made there. The Masis' and Robert Nasmith's experiences demonstrate how the overlapping ecologies of Vietnam War resistance, counterculture, and the theatre operating at this time in Toronto, and in Rochdale College in particular, made possible a situation in which war resisters and Canadian theatremakers came to form interlocking, mutually influential communities, which in turn made possible an easy transition from one to the other.

HOMEMADE THEATRE AND MILES POTTER

Personal connections made through larger organizations were not the only way for American theatremakers to gain access to professional theatre in Toronto. Many, like the performers of Homemade Theatre and actor Miles Potter, were able to gain access to theatre ecologies in Toronto directly through the time-honoured tradition of starting a theatre company and getting their work seen. American comedians and improvisers Larry and Fred Mollins and Phil Savath, who had all left the US to evade the draft, formed Homemade Theatre after arriving in Toronto (F. MacDonnell). This company brought the concept of the Improv Olympics from Chicago to Canada, and premiered it in Toronto in 1974, creating an event that would eventually become the Canadian Improv Games, while the company would also have a television program on CBC called *Homemade TV*. Though all the company's members eventually returned to the

US, the Improv Games continues to connect Canadian students with theatre arts: one abiding legacy of the Vietnam-era migration to Canada.

Actor Miles Potter followed a similar path into the full-time company of Theatre Passe Muraille. Potter arrived in Toronto in the late 1960s after vowing to run to Canada should he be drafted. He received a sequence number that made him unlikely to be called up for service; however, like many anti-war Americans, Potter saw the draft lottery as a ploy by the government to split opposition to the war by convincing the American people of the fairness of the conscription system, and so decided to leave the US anyway in protest (Potter). In Toronto, Potter shared a one-bedroom apartment with his friend Ed Fisher, who had also come from the United States, and with him started a small children's theatre company and began performing at the Poor Alex Theatre off Bloor Street in Toronto. Director Louis Del Grande (another American expatriate) saw Potter in one of these performances and offered him a role in his production of Lope de Vega's *The Dog in the Manger*, which was staged in Theatre Passe Muraille's new facility at 11 Trinity Square. Paul Thompson, the new artistic director of Theatre Passe Muraille, in turn saw Potter in Del Grande's production and asked him if he wanted to join a new company of actors that would be travelling to Southern Ontario to develop a piece of theatre based on the experiences of a rural farming community. Potter agreed, and so along with actors like David Fox, Janet Amos, and Anne Anglin spent two months in Clinton, Ontario, and produced the now-iconic *Farm Show*. Like many of his compatriots, Potter went on to an extensive and continuing career in Canadian theatre, and now regularly directs at the Stratford Festival and elsewhere.

The experiences of Potter and Homemade Theatre again demonstrate how the privileges of education and cultural similarity facilitated access to Canadian theatre. These artists' ability to create theatre that gained the attention of their Canadian peers was in many ways the result of their American theatre training and their experience in the US, as was their ability to capitalize on the opportunities offered to them. Moreover, they encountered no barriers of difference that might have limited access to those opportunities, and as a result were part of foundational Canadian theatre institutions like the Improv Games and Theatre Passe Muraille.

SHAIN JAFFE AND JON KAPLAN

Some American migrants, by contrast, arrived in Canada with limited direct personal or professional connection to the theatre. Even so, they were able to gain access to this ecology through theatre classes and theatre reviewing. Two migrants who came to careers in Toronto theatre in this way had outsized individual impacts in the areas of administration and criticism: Shain Jaffe and Jon Kaplan. Jaffe, a businessman and administrator from Ohio, arrived in Toronto in early 1970 after having deserted from basic training at Fort Gordon, Georgia. While seeking refuge and support from local deserter support organizations, Jaffe, like Bush, was informed of the possibilities that migration to Canada could offer, and was connected with the Toronto Anti-Draft Programme. Unlike the Masis and Nasmith, when Jaffe arrived in Toronto he was told not to connect with Rochdale College because of the police surveillance that had become directed at it. Jaffe and Nasmith described the situation in a 2017 interview:

> **JAFFE:** Some of us were very much afraid of Rochdale because of the heat. We were told by the folks on Madison Avenue and a few other places that Rochdale was constantly under observation, and all the information went directly to the FBI.
>
> **NASMITH:** There was a lot of heat. [. . .] It was a hard place for draft dodgers to be. (Jaffe et al.)

Jaffe connected with theatre in Toronto through acting classes at the Garret Theatre on Yonge Street. There he met local actor Ken Gass, who would soon begin Factory Theatre Lab. Jaffe and Gass hit it off, and began work on a theatrical periodical to be published from Theatre Passe Muraille's new venue in Trinity Square. This in turn brought Jaffe into the orbit of Passe Muraille just as it was entering its first financial crisis. Without the space and funding provided by residency at Rochdale College, Theatre Passe Muraille was no longer able to sustain its operations and expenditures in the way it had been operating. Paul Thompson described the situation at Passe Muraille when he joined the company in 1969 as follows:

> Garrard was a huge idealist and wanted a company of twelve people that he wanted to pay real money every week, [...] and the cheques started to bounce [so] it seemed like the most sensible thing to do was to grab the cheque book. (Theatre Museum Canada)

Realizing Jaffe's experience, Thompson quickly enlisted him to create and maintain accurate records for the company (establishing TPM's actual financial position for the first time), and to create a structurally sound budgeting model, which Jaffe did while acting in a few of TPM's productions. Jaffe was then hired on as General Manager of the newly formed Toronto Free Theatre. In this capacity he suggested the former Berkeley Street Gas Works, slated for demolition in 1971, as a possible venue for the company to construct a theatre. This would shortly become the Berkeley Street Theatre, which continues to operate today as the home of the Canadian Stage Company. Jaffe would would eventually move into film representation, representing playwright George F. Walker among others, and would later move into film representation. Again, there is no way to estimate exactly what Jaffe's impact was on Toronto theatre, but his presence certainly helped guarantee the continued existence of both Theatre Passe Muraille and Factory Theatre Lab, and was integral in the development of Toronto Free Theatre and the Berkeley Street Theatre, all of which have had a significant impact on theatre in Toronto.

Jon Kaplan arrived in Toronto in 1969 to begin his master's degree at York University after finishing his undergraduate degree at Brandeis University in Boston. Kaplan was firmly within the age brackets set for the draft, and so rather than take his chances, he decided to continue his education in Toronto. After graduating from York, Kaplan began writing theatre reviews for the *Body Politic*, Toronto's first queer magazine, and then used those articles to land a job as the part-time theatre critic for the new weekly publication *NOW Magazine*. This job soon turned into a full-time position that lasted until Kaplan's death in 2017. Viewing himself as a reviewer and supporter of theatre in the city rather than as a critic, Kaplan endeavoured to "present his thoughts to the potential viewer in hope that they'll want to go out and see the show" (Fulton). This way of viewing theatre, and Kaplan's resulting constructive criticism, presented a significant alternative to the work of other theatre critics in Toronto for almost forty years. Kaplan's approach endeared him significantly to the theatre community, which in turn allowed him access to the artists in ways that few theatre critics enjoy, and thus provided his readership with great insight into the work on Toronto stages. As one of the primary theatre critics in Toronto for some three decades, Kaplan's influence cannot be doubted. At the same time, his access to the theatre community was entirely facilitated by his access to post-secondary education in Canada.

CONCLUSION

The temporal coincidence in 1968–73 of the Vietnam War–resister migration with a significant period in the development of the arts in Canada created an ideal situation for the theatremakers among this migration to become part of the Toronto theatre ecology quickly and easily. There is no way to quantify each individual's contribution, but it is possible to develop a sense of their larger impact. This group of white, middle-class, and educated men swelled the ranks of the theatre ecology in Toronto, making it a more significant cultural force in the city, and helping some theatre companies through their "growing pains." At the same time, by being present in the early stages of these companies' development, war-resister theatremakers gained access to significant creative and leadership roles in the institutions those companies generated or became. Members of this migration also brought their artistic concerns and political perspectives, which through their leadership roles shaped the plays that were written and staged by these companies for years to come. Similarly, the support of members of this migration gave the theatre companies they connected with an advantage in both numbers and expertise, which almost certainly helped these companies thrive, potentially at the expense of others.

Given the cumulative influence of these theatremakers, it is not unreasonable to suggest that the history of not-for-profit theatre in Toronto was

significantly changed by this migration, and so this moment in Canadian theatre history demonstrates the influence and impact that a migrant group can
have if they are given meaningful access to a cultural ecology. The question
then becomes, what did this migration's access mean for the access of others?
What happened to the theatremakers and companies that were not able to
access members of this migration at this time? Were other companies able to
negotiate their own growing pains in the same way? And once members of
this migration became established in the Toronto theatre ecology, how did
their experience, priorities, and training affect who would be granted access
in the future? What would theatre in Toronto look like if every group, migrant
or otherwise, was given equitable access?

MONTRÉAL YIDDISH THEATRE AS YOUTH CULTURAL IMPERATIVE[1]

REBECCA MARGOLIS

Montréal became home to a new, dynamic, and lasting Yiddish theatre in the 1950s, even as the language began a steep decline within much of the Jewish world. Scholarly and popular studies of this theatre point to the role of Dora Wasserman (1919–2003), the energetic and visionary founder and director of a project that would become an enduring Yiddish amateur theatre soon after her arrival to Montréal in 1950 as a survivor of the Holocaust. This study suggests an additional contributor to this Yiddish theatre's success: its intersection with a youth-driven Yiddish cultural imperative, which expressed itself most strongly in the period of the 1960s and 1970s.

As a Soviet-trained actress, Wasserman founded a Yiddish activity group for young children that expanded into a popular afternoon drama activity for graduates of a local Yiddish high-school program. Over the next fifty years, Wasserman expanded the group into a flourishing community theatre that produced classics of the Yiddish stage alongside innovative translations of world theatre for local as well as international audiences to wide acclaim. Today, the Dora Wasserman Yiddish Theatre (DWYT) continues Wasserman's legacy by presenting annual Yiddish-language productions as well as drama activities for children and young adults. Although it emerged

---

1   This research was completed with the support of a grant from the Social Sciences and Humanities Research Council of Canada. Unless otherwise indicated, all translations from the Yiddish are my own.

within a distinctly post-Holocaust context, the theatre has offered a site for innovation as well as a space where the language could be spoken and heard, rather than a locus of memory and memorialization.

The DWYT emerged within shifting perceptions of Yiddish in the post-Holocaust era. In conjunction with pervasive tropes of Yiddish as "dead" or "dying," popular and scholarly discourse speaks of a Yiddish "revival," in particular in the evolution of klezmer music since the 1970s. Jeffrey Shandler's influential study, *Adventures in Yiddishland: Postvernacular Language and Culture*, suggests that Yiddish has entered its "postvernacular" phase, where "the language's secondary, symbolic level of meaning is always privileged over its primary level" (22). This shift from Yiddish as a communicative language to one that functions in symbolic ways forms an integral part of a fundamental post-Holocaust reorientation of the map of a "Yiddishland" that was historically rooted in Europe to newer immigrant centres, in particular in America. In addition to the locus of Yiddish increasingly existing within a performative sphere, this reorientation has been coupled with a fundamental shift in popular perceptions of the language; as Shandler suggests, "The trope of Yiddish as a dying or dead language has therefore proved something other than a sociolinguistic assessment both before and after the Holocaust. It has served, instead, as a discursive frame for addressing the shifting stature and significance of Yiddish in modern Jewish life" (179). In her study "Yiddish Endangerment as Phenomenological Reality and Discursive Strategy," Netta Avineri situates this trope at the very core of post-Holocaust Yiddish culture, arguing that proponents of secular Yiddish form a "metalinguistic community" for whom the language is key to group identity even if it is not necessarily spoken or being learned. With fewer and fewer audience members as well as cast members relating to the language as a vernacular, post-Holocaust Yiddish theatre can neatly be situated within this "postvernacular" sphere where utterances are relegated to the symbolic.

This study aims to complicate this dominant discourse surrounding Yiddish by examining the DWYT as a youth-driven cultural imperative to transmit Yiddish within a post-Holocaust world. With a focus on the transitional period of the 1960s and 1970s, when the children of the last generation of European-born Yiddish speakers were coming of age and embarking on their own activism on behalf of the language, the study examines what role community theatre can play not only in enacting the transmission of a language in jeopardy but also in harnessing that language as an expression of forward-looking youth culture. Using media reviews as well as interviews with participants in the theatre, the study will examine the youth Yiddish cultural imperative within the DWYT and beyond.

YIDDISH AS CULTURAL IMPERATIVE

The Holocaust marks rupture in the history of Yiddish civilization. After a thousand years of Yiddish vitality on European soil, the Nazi decimation of Jewish life annihilated half of the world's Yiddish speakers as well as the Ashkenazi heartland. A centuries-old bilingual Hebrew–Yiddish heritage—family lineages, communal institutions, folkways, traditions of religious observance and study, literary production, theatre and musical performance—was brutally uprooted between 1939 and 1945. In the epicentre of Yiddish civilization in Poland, fewer than 10% of a previous Jewish population of over three million would survive, only to be dispersed to new homes worldwide. After the Holocaust, Yiddish would be transmitted wholly in new immigrant offshoots: New York, Montréal, Buenos Aires, Melbourne, Tel Aviv, and others. In all of these locations, Yiddish would gradually cede its place to competing and established lingua francas within Jewish life: English, Spanish, or Ivrit (Israeli Hebrew).

The period preceding this rupture had been one of an expanding and efflorescent Yiddish civilization with its locus in Eastern Europe. Traditionally serving as a vernacular in relation to Hebrew's role as holy tongue and language of sacred text, Yiddish found multiple new functions in modernity above and beyond being spoken in the home and on the street by a majority of the Jewish population of Eastern Europe. Within the foment of the Jewish Enlightenment (Haskalah) of the nineteenth century, the language served as the primary means of disseminating new ideas along a religious and ideological spectrum that ranged from staunchly traditionalist to radically secular, politically conservative to leftist revolutionary. Spurred by the violence and unrest in Tsarist Russia, some 2.5 million Jews—a majority of them Yiddish speakers—migrated to new immigrant centres between 1880 and 1920. The language and culture of Yiddish speakers now formed a transnational civilization spanning the "Old World" of Europe and a "New World" periphery of immigrant hubs. After the first works of modern Yiddish literature were met with disparagement by proponents of the Haskalah, the language rapidly evolved a multi-faceted literary tradition that integrated European and American trends. By the interwar period, the uses of published Yiddish ranged from utilitarian to art for art's sake and included popular newspapers that reached millions as well as ephemeral modernist literary journals. Within competing ideologies about what it was to be a Jew in the modern world, Yiddishism declared Yiddish to be at the core of Jewishness. This new language-centred ideology, in competition with Hebraism, was symbolically represented by the Czernowitz Conference of 1908, where Yiddish was proposed as "*the* language" of the Jewish people. A global network of Yiddish theatre encompassed the major hubs of Warsaw, Moscow, and New York alongside minor sites worldwide, and featured local community performances alongside touring troupes and major stars. This vibrant theatre was a point of dynamic cultural creation and exchange, "enriched by a perpetual interchange between local innovations and the international movement of Yiddish theatre personnel, critics, and audiences" (Berkowitz 5). Yiddish emerged as the state-backed basis for a new Jewish culture in the Soviet Union that included literary production as well as a highly successful Soviet State theatre, the GOSET (Moscow State Yiddish Theatre, 1919–48).

Speaking, writing, and otherwise engaging with the language after the Holocaust entailed a reconstitution of the remnants of European Yiddish culture. Alongside the survivors who initially worked to rebuild Yiddish culture in European centres such as Łódź, these efforts occurred increasingly within the context of the newer Jewish immigrant centres. In cities such as Montréal, Yiddish retained a strong hold within the Eastern European Jewish community as a vernacular and language of education and culture. The language was bolstered by the arrival of thousands of Holocaust survivors to augment a Jewish community of some eighty thousand in the early 1950s, many of them Yiddish-speaking. The arrival of professionally trained actors and teachers as well as a sizable group of writers revitalized the cultural community and actively promoted Yiddish within systems of Jewish full-day and supplementary schools where the language was taught, as well as in a flourishing literary milieu. This group dedicated itself to implementing a new cultural imperative that emerged out of the destruction of the European Yiddish heartland in the Holocaust.

This expression of the Yiddish cultural imperative lay at the core of the profound conceptual reorientation of the post-Holocaust years. It expressed itself, for example, in the introductory essay to a new Yiddish-language journal of art and literature titled *Yidish* (Yiddish) published in Paris in 1946, where the author calls upon the survivors of the Holocaust to fulfill their duty to recreate Jewish culture as part of a wider revival (Kuper Margalioth 20–29). While Jewish cultural activity in the aftermath of the Holocaust took place in a variety of languages, David G. Roskies and Anita Diamant's study of Holocaust literature identifies Yiddish as its natural conduit in the 1950s: "Yiddish was still the universal Jewish language, and the Yiddish press was to remain for decades the main disseminator of Holocaust memory" (94–95). The response to the transnational post-Holocaust cultural imperative forms the subject of Jan Schwartz's study, *Survivors and Exiles: Yiddish Culture After the Holocaust,* which examines what he terms a "last blossoming of secular Yiddish culture" and the post-Holocaust generation of cultural activists' deliberate creation of a "virtual Ashkenaz" (3, 8). These individuals, who marked the last generation to experience Yiddish civilization on European soil, concentrated their efforts on the "ingathering of Yiddish cultural treasures" as well as seeking to create innovative works in the language (Schwartz 14). While the transnational Yiddish theatre was drastically reduced in scope, in some circles it assumed new significance: for example, according to a study of Yiddish in postwar Communist Poland, attending Yiddish theatre performances was akin to religious observance for members of the Jewish community (Nalewajko-Kulikov 37).

The multifaceted post-Holocaust Yiddish cultural imperative is embodied by Wasserman in multiple ways. She emerged out of the Soviet theatre tradition as a student of drama with the GOSET under legendary director Solomon Mikhoels, completing a four-year program in 1939. Having survived the Holocaust in Kazakhstan, she connected with an extensive local Yiddish cultural community soon after settling in Montréal. She engaged in a variety of Yiddish-language activities through local cultural organizations: recitations in the Yiddish schools, song performances at local events, and children's drama workshops at the local Jewish Public Library. She organized theatre groups for young people and directed ambitious Yiddish-language productions drawing on Yiddish as well as world literature. Members would meet once a week at her home to sing Yiddish songs, discuss cultural issues, and socialize in the language; Wasserman recalled, "Finding Yiddish-speaking children then was not a problem" (Larrue 149). However, Yiddish pedagogues and cultural activists engaged in proactive programming to support the ongoing use of the language among the younger generation in response to the inroads of English as a daily spoken language and Ivrit as Jewish lingua franca after the creation of the State of Israel. In 1957, under the aegis of one of the local schools where Yiddish coexisted with Hebrew as a language of Jewish life, Wasserman founded the Drama Group with graduates of the Jewish People's Schools, where she remained active for the next ten years. The group employed theatre techniques including the Stanislavski method and improvisation to work on a variety of material in Yiddish. It staged a variety of performances, including challenging dramatic works such as a Yiddish-language production of *Andorra*, a provocative parable about anti-Semitic intolerance by Swiss author Max Frisch. This demanding play was staged in 1965 in a Yiddish translation by the Jewish Public Library's Jacob Grossman, who was also a local Yiddish writer (Thalenberg). These early theatre activities formed the basis for Wasserman's lifelong career as a director of local Yiddish amateur theatre within the context of post-Holocaust Yiddish and the increasing hegemony of both English and Ivrit in Jewish life. Wasserman's activities would form the locus of a new Yiddish cultural imperative in the wake of the near-annihilation of the language and culture in its European homeland, and its attrition in its newer immigrant centres such as Montréal.

During this immediate postwar era, Montréal's vibrant Yiddish milieu was buoyed by the arrival of Holocaust survivors. The commitment to Yiddish by the new arrivals is exemplified in the experiences of Anna Fishman Gonshor and her husband, Aron Gonshor, both of whom have been closely involved with the Yiddish Theatre since childhood and maintained a lifelong connection to the language and culture. According to their respective oral histories, conducted in 2011 as part of the Yiddish Book Center's Wexler Oral History Project (a collection of over seven hundred interviews on the legacy of Yiddish culture), both were born into Yiddish-speaking immigrant families who settled in Montréal after the Holocaust and not only raised them in the language but imbued them with a strong sense of connection with the intellectual, literary, musical, ideological, and political legacies of Jewish Eastern Europe. Anna Fishman Gonshor recounts growing up steeped in a leftist Jewish tradition where culture supplanted religious observance and being exposed to Yiddish literature and performance by a circle of Jewish intellectuals and cultural figures. In the rich and variegated Yiddish milieu of Montréal's Jewish immigrant neighbourhood that encompassed home, school, summer camp, and cultural life, a focal point for her was the Jewish Public Library, where she participated in Dora Wasserman's children's group and subsequently as a young adult in her theatre group. Aron Gonshor, who has maintained a lifelong connection with the theatre as a performer and more recently as chair of the Dora Wasserman Yiddish Theatre, describes the basis for the milieu that generated the new Yiddish cultural imperative: "The Survivors came with a very great need to be able live out their lives in the way they were used to. And that life revolved around Yiddish as a language, but much more than a language. It was the whole socio-cultural context, and that ethos played itself out in Yiddish." He identifies Dora Wasserman's keen understanding of performance as a door to Yiddish language and culture for young people. As a youth member of Dora Wasserman's theatre group, Aron Gonshor recalls, "This is how we began to live our lives out culturally in Yiddish. And what an exciting time it was!" (Aron Gonshor 20:48–20:57). He characterizes the particular role that Wasserman played: "Dora was a life force. She had a tremendous shrewdness and understood what you needed to do to motivate people" (Aron Gonshor 25:38–25:55). The result was the involvement of cadres of young people who brought in their children, in some cases continuing to do so today into the third and fourth generations.

The trajectory of Wasserman's Yiddish theatre differed from the post-Holocaust Yiddish cultural imperative of her generation that spearheaded activities to gather, anthologize, and memorialize, or to create new works for an existing audience of Yiddish speakers. Instead, Wasserman's theatre created a new locus for creativity in Yiddish among both Yiddish speakers and non-Yiddish speakers. The theatre offered a site for the revitalization of Yiddish as a living language among future generations that potentially extended beyond rehearsals and performances. However, no expression of the post-Holocaust Yiddish cultural imperative was completely able to stem the tides of mass linguistic attrition, as a majority of the Canadian-raised children would go on to express themselves in the lingua francas of their adopted homes rather than in Yiddish.

It would ultimately be up the children of the generation of Holocaust survivors to generate a cultural imperative to maintain Yiddish as part of their identities as they came of age within the youth-oriented culture of the 1960s and 1970s. They evolved their own cultural imperative as distinct from the generation of their parents, with performance—notably music and theatre—occupying a prominent role. Dora Wasserman represents an exceptional figure in her deliberate efforts to transmit Yiddish as a living language to Canadian-born participants. Her theatre formed a fertile site for the expression of the youth-driven Yiddish cultural imperative.

THE 1960S AND 1970S

The 1960s and 1970s marked a period of transition in Canada. A century after Confederation, Canada was characterized by cultural upheaval and creativity, with theatre occupying a prominent place in the development of the country's emerging national identities. Theatre moved to the fore against the backdrop of Québec's rapid process of secularization during the Quiet Revolution and the emergence of a new Québécois identity with the French language at the core. In addition, the country as a whole was engaged in new discourse about the contributions of Canada's ethnic groups that would ultimately lead to Canada's policies of official multilingualism and to new creative outputs.

Within the Canadian Jewish community, English was unquestionably displacing Yiddish as lingua franca in the 1960s. This shift took place within broader patterns of linguistic acculturation common to Canadian immigrant populations; however, it was significantly heightened by the wartime eradication of the Yiddish motherland and the end of ongoing immigration of native speakers of the language. These oft-cited census statistics of Yiddish mother tongue (YMT) in Canada, tabulated every decade, reflect the steep decline of the language within a steadily growing Jewish population:

1931: 149,520/155,351 (96% of the Canadian Jewish population by religion)
1941: 129,806/168,585 (77%)
1951: 103,593/204,836 (51%)
1961: 82,448/254,368 (32%)
1971: 49,890/276,000 (18%) (Yam 28).

Nineteen seventy-one introduced a new statistic, Yiddish language home (YLH), with the census indicating that 9.5% of Canadian Jews spoke Yiddish at home on a regular basis. Demographer Joseph Yam's exhaustive 1973 study of this census identified the Yiddish group as "sizeable, albeit declining" (27), with virtually no population replenishment over the previous four decades (32). That same year, a monograph titled *Yiddish in Canada: The Death of a Language* was published by Canadian scholar Jack Thiessen. Sentiments of dismay about the future of Yiddish, in particular among the younger generation, were echoed in a multitude of contemporaneous articles that appeared in the Jewish community press.

The Dora Wasserman Yiddish Theatre entered its heyday against this decline. By the 1960s, a formerly flourishing commercial theatre scene had virtually disappeared, not only in Canada but worldwide. According to Jean-Marc Larrue's history of Yiddish theatre in Montréal, only a handful of amateur theatres remained, and Yiddish performances became increasingly sporadic due to the "limitations of the market" after a series of "disappointing" visits of an aging cadre of international Yiddish stars of the stage (121–22). By

1967, Dora Wasserman's Yiddish Theatre Group remained the last local theatre to perform in Yiddish, and it was flourishing as audiences continued to grow along with the number of annual performances. That year, the group left the Jewish People's Schools to seek out a larger venue and Wasserman arranged for the group's tenth anniversary celebration to be staged at the thousand-seat Monument-National Theatre, where the company mounted sold-out performances of *Tevye*, the classic Yiddish play based on the beloved stories of Sholem Aleichem. Wasserman found a permanent home at the newly erected Saidye Bronfman Centre, which also provided a budget for the theatre's operations as well as professional theatre staff to assist with choreography, design, sets, and lighting (Larrue 123).

The move allowed Wasserman to implement her vision and methods in a more sustained manner. Wasserman's Soviet theatre training favoured a collective approach where each role was of equal importance; leading and secondary roles were redistributed and works were specifically chosen to facilitate this system of performance. Larrue suggests that "joining the group was a little like joining a religious order" in the absolute commitment expressed by all participants, including Wasserman herself (127). All cast members were expected to attend all rehearsals, which entailed rigorous practise and repetition of all dialogue, music, movement, and dance. In 1968, Rumanian-born composer Eli Rubenstein joined the company; he would collaborate with Wasserman to compose and arrange songs for the theatre for the next twenty-five years. Whereas previously music had appeared in an incidental manner, with occasional songs or background accompaniment, music would now assume centre stage in ambitious large-scale performances. The first of Rubenstein's performances, *A Shtetl Wedding* (1969), featured fourteen songs composed for the play, including solos, duets, and choral pieces for a cast of over fifty members, and carefully choreographed crowd scenes. After popular success and rave reviews from critics, Wasserman and Rubinstein created other large-scale musical comedies based on works of Yiddish literature: *The Sages of Chelm* (1970), *Benjamin III* (1971), and *The Little Shoemakers* (1976). These productions and their new musical repertoire were staged to great acclaim, revived, and toured internationally, enhancing the theatre's reputation locally and abroad

(Larrue 128–29). In addition, Wasserman adapted works by *di klassikers* (the "classic Yiddish writers," Sholem Aleichem, I.L. Peretz, and others) and collaborated with living Yiddish writers, including Montréalers Shimshon Dunsky, Mordecai Husid, Moishe Shaffir, and others, as well as Nobel Prize laureate Isaac Bashevis Singer, and remained committed to addressing contemporary social themes such as immigration and family relationships. After the period under discussion, the theatre would go on to stage acclaimed Yiddish translations of world theatre, including Québécois playwright Michel Tremblay's classic work *Les Belles Soeurs* (see Margolis, "*Les belles-sœurs*").

The existence of an ethnic theatre in Yiddish was not unique among Canadian immigrant groups in its post–World War II revival, but it stands out in its abiding involvement of the younger generation. Alexandra Pritz's study of Ukrainian theatre in Canada reveals a number of parallels: the postwar period brought an influx of theatre professionals, including performers and directors, who turned their attention to amateur theatre in the absence of a professional one in a postwar flourishing of innovative foreign-language performance. Pritz describes several amateur Ukrainian groups that coexisted in Toronto, Winnipeg, and Edmonton in the 1950s and shared actors and resources, with repertoires including works written in the Ukraine and in Canada as well as new works translated into Ukrainian (71–93). One significant difference, however, lies in the relationship of this community theatre to the Ukrainian youth raised in Canada, who lacked enough knowledge of the language for Ukrainian drama to be accessible to them while a postwar migration from rural to urban settings further estranged many young people from their Ukrainian heritage. As Pritz states, "The loss of Ukrainian language was reflected more strongly on Ukrainian theatre than any other form of cultural expression" (95); an aging immigrant population and a lack of younger speakers caused an inevitable decline in all forms of Ukrainian-language theatre, with a resulting emphasis on dance and song.

By contrast, the Yiddish cultural imperative placed Wasserman's theatre in a unique position to attract young people during the transitional period of the 1960s and 1970s even as the language was facing a decline, in particular among those raised in Canada. This can be explained through several intertwining factors. First and foremost was Wasserman's energetic dedication to her vision and her enthusiasm for the project. Muriel Gold's 1972 M.A. thesis, "A Study of Three Montreal Children's Theatres," discusses Wasserman's enduring philosophy and lists the main goals of the group, based on an interview: "(a) to preserve the Yiddish language in Montreal, (b) to build an audience for Yiddish theatre, (c) to develop the imagination 'on a wide scale' through freeing the body through a variety of exercises, (d) to develop the child's inner resources which will lead him to an understanding and love of theatre" (44). These goals seamlessly combined a commitment to the creative continuity of Yiddish among the younger generation with a dedication to developing the potential of all of her students on an individual as well as collective level through drama. Wasserman deliberately conducted her drama sessions within an inclusive and informal atmosphere with a focus on the actors rather than the product. Second, due to Wasserman's energy and vision, the project, which called for voluntary participation, drew a cadre of self-selected youth who had been exposed to Yiddish at home as well as through the local cultural milieu. Third, the theatre performed a broad repertoire that included works by living Yiddish writers, thus exposing the participants to contemporary Yiddish culture in a participatory and meaningful way. Fourth, the theatre was supported on multiple levels by the broader community and its institutions. In addition to the Jewish schools, where the theatre had originated, the Dora Wasserman Yiddish Theatre emerged as a project of the Jewish Public Library (founded in 1914), Montréal's non-partisan lending library and cultural institution whose mandate stated an ongoing commitment to Yiddish literature and culture. The Jewish Public Library had previously provided support to an earlier wartime Yiddish theatre studio called Di Yidishe Teater Grupe (The Yiddish Theatre Group, or YTEG) directed by Soviet Yiddish actress Chayele Grober (Margolis, "Holocaust"). Moreover, the theatre was enthusiastically embraced by both Yiddish and non-Yiddish local theatre audiences. In 1972, Wasserman was awarded the Jewish Community's Performing Arts Award in recognition of two decades of dedication to the Yiddish theatre with the following words: "Dora Wasserman and her Yiddish Drama Group productions have possibly done more to revive interest in Yiddish and the Yiddish theatre, than almost any other single individual or group in Montreal" (qtd. in Gold 43).

A further significant factor is the new Yiddish cultural imperative of the 1960s, which expressed itself in a self-motivated commitment of youth to both speak Yiddish and engage with it on multiple levels as a living language. It was not enough to preserve the treasures of Yiddish; Yiddish had to be at the root of new creativity among young people. This same cultural imperative resulted in the emergence of an additional symbiotic relationship between the Yiddish theatre and wider youth activism for Yiddish. The theatre served as a springboard for a new youth-driven incarnation of the Yiddish cultural imperative in a new organization called Yugntruf (Youth for Yiddish).

Yugntruf was the brainchild of David Roskies, who would become a renowned scholar of Yiddish literature: a child of Yiddish-speaking immigrant activists whose childhood home hosted virtually every Yiddish cultural figure to visit Montréal. At the age of sixteen, he was an active member of Wasserman's Yiddish Youth Theatre and dreamed of making Yiddish films. Educated in the Yiddish schools and a participant in diverse community initiatives, he proposed a radically new approach to members of the local Jewish community who were promoting the use of English to attract young people to cultural activities: "Make Yiddish young again. Put Yiddish back where it belonged, into the mouths of people who could stand up and fight" (*Yiddishlands* 125–26). After Roskies proposed the founding of a new Yiddish magazine for youth, first to a friend and then to the broader international Yiddish community, the idea burgeoned into a youth-run organization made up of high-school and college students under the name Yugntruf. Founded in 1964, Yugntruf was a non-partisan organization dedicated to promoting Yiddish among young people as a vibrant, living language within a framework of 1960s youth activism. According to a subsequent report in the journal, delegates in their teens and twenties who converged at the founding conference held in New York arrived to find banners in the hall stating, "First Commandment—To Speak Yiddish," "Jews speak Yiddish," and "Yiddish is beautiful," while Roskies delivered an opening address on the theme "Youth is the Vanguard of Change." The delegates debated at great length the organization's principles, which included provisions for the members—all of whom were multilingual—deliberately to speak, read, and write Yiddish at every opportunity as a connection with their heritage and the global Jewish community. Members would fight for the honour of a language that had historically been maligned and bring new vitality to Yiddish ("Diskusye" 7–8). The first issue of the printed journal, which appeared just three months after the founding, featured an array of materials authored by the members, including the proceedings of the conference as well as editorials, reports about Yiddish activities worldwide, essays, games, and original works of literature and art. The journal would be published on a regular basis in New York with international contributors and an array of Yiddish-language content.

The relationship between Yugntruf and the Yiddish theatre expressed itself on multiple occasions. The organization's second annual gathering featured provisions for the expansion of performance groups for young people in music as well as theatre. The journal also included articles about the subject, with the Dora Wasserman Yiddish Theatre most prominently and enthusiastically represented.

For instance, the second issue of the *Yugntruf* journal (1965) contains a passionate article about the activities of the Montreal Youth Theatre program by one of its active members, Chayele (Eileen) Thalenberg. Thalenberg recounts how the program was founded a decade earlier as a Saturday-morning activity of Yiddish stories and song for young children led by Dora Wasserman at the Jewish Public Library. Since that time, the original members had grown into teenagers and newcomers had joined. The group split into two (ages eight to twelve and thirteen to fifteen) to perform adaptations of Yiddish plays as well as translations from world literature: Abraham Goldfaden's operetta, *Shumalis*; the folktales of Hershel Ostropol; the works of classic Yiddish writers I.L. Peretz and Sholem Aleichem; Oscar Wilde's children's story, *The Happy Prince*; and Max Frisch's drama, *Andorra*. In 1964, the older group had performed its first full production, an adaptation of Abraham Goldfaden's classic play originally written in 1880: *Two Kuni Lemels*. Thalenberg recounts that the group met weekly on Friday evenings with Wasserman at the Jewish Public

Library for rehearsals. They read the play over several times, Wasserman pointed out the characteristics of the characters, they discussed the plot and its conflicts, and they distributed parts. The members then meet with David Rome, director of the library, to discuss the play's meaning and the difficulties of staging the work. The library covered the costs for sets, props, and costumes and provided a stage, as a result of which "we [had] far fewer problems than other theatre groups" (12). Sometimes the sessions were given over to literary evenings featuring contemporary Yiddish writers such as Abraham Sutzkever, Melech Ravitch, and Itzik Manger; at other times, the group worked on dance or theatre exercises (*études*) or went to see plays in English, French, or Yiddish. Thalenberg discusses at length the group's most challenging project: Frisch's *Andorra*, which until that point had only been staged once in North America, in 1961. While the play poses challenges in terms of staging, she declares that "for young people, nothing is hard, especially when they buckle down" (12). Thalenberg's passion for the theatre group as a project for and by a community of Yiddish-oriented youth is palpable.

The DWYT also features prominently in the special 1971 issue of *Yugntruf* dedicated to "the Yiddish Theatre in America." This issue opens with an article by Dinele (Diane) Roskies discussing her experiences founding a student Yiddish theatre group at Brandeis University. Roskies points to the lack of models for contemporary Yiddish drama in America, where all that remains are television shows about Sholem Aleichem and "'Oy-vey' Vaudeville leftovers from a Second Avenue our generation has no memory of" (5). After discussing the challenges in staging two student productions—a sold-out musical adaptation of Aleichem and an original children's play set in Nazi-occupied Warsaw—she calls for renewed efforts in education and financial support for new initiatives within the wider Jewish community. Yiddish, she concludes, can potentially be a tool for real social change.

Roskies's article is followed by an article about the DWYT by the above-mentioned Anna Fishman Gonshor that takes a much different tone. Gonshor describes how the group had been formed fifteen years earlier under the auspices of the Jewish People's Schools and the direction of Dora Wasserman, when only graduates took part and they performed with costumes sewn out of old clothing. She recounts that the group included over forty members, not all of them graduates of the school, but all united by a love of Yiddish and the Yiddish theatre. The group performed to packed houses, both in Montréal and on tour in other cities across Canada, with professionally designed costumes, sets, and lighting. Gonshor attributes the success of the group to multiple factors: 1) Dora Wasserman's complete dedication to the group and her strong character; 2) the cast, which largely comprised young professionals (lawyers, teachers, engineers, architects), and its dedication to the theatre; 3) the school activists who supported the group morally as well as financially. Gonshor also points to Wasserman's unique ability to be tremendously innovative in providing appropriate material—sometimes in translation from other languages—in response to the challenge of finding a suitable repertoire. She notes that their recent performances, with original music composed by Rubinstein, played to packed houses in front of an estimated total eight thousand spectators. These included new audiences of university students interested in Yiddish. According to Gonshor, "It is not only an institution where young Jews can experience the Yiddish theatre. It grows out of, and influences, the renaissance of Yiddish cultural consciousness in North America" ("Di yidishe" 10).

Gonshor's article is followed by an editorial article signed "A Montrealer" (David Roskies, editor of the journal) titled "Der amerikaner yiddisher teater: vos tut men?" ("The American Yiddish Theatre: What Can Be Done?"). It opens: "Let's not fool ourselves. The Yiddish theatre could give up the ghost at any time" (Roskies, "Der amerikaner" 11). Speaking to the case of New York, at one time the world centre of Yiddish theatre, the author points out that of the once fourteen Yiddish theatres there remained only the Folksbiene and a few amateur theatre groups. When groups attempted professional Yiddish productions, they complained about a lack of audiences, while audiences complained about the low level of professionalism. The funds were there; what was missing was the spark to ignite the interest of the American Jewish world. The author blames assimilation and a lack of identity among American youth and called for a Yiddish theatre troupe with sufficient funds, an artistic repertoire, and a capable director: specifically, Polish-born director and Yiddish theatre devotee Ida Kamińska (1899–1980), who had most recently visited Montréal twice for two memorable performances in 1969 and 1970 as the last internationally renowned Yiddish artist to visit the city (Larrue 120). Roskies concludes: "The fate of the new Yiddish theatre now lies in our hands!" ("Der amerikaner" 12). One can assume that the model the author is thinking of is the DWYT. If Montréal can sustain a dynamic, youth-driven Yiddish theatre, why can't the much larger Jewish centre of New York?

The *Yugntruf* journal indicates that Yiddish theatre in Montréal evolved along a very different trajectory from other centres. It emerged in a symbiotic relationship with existing Jewish community organizations and propelled Yiddish into the public eye with highly successful performances. Most significantly, the theatre served as a hub for youth seeking to connect with the Yiddish language, culture, and heritage. This success can be attributed to the role of Dora Wasserman as well as to the particular dynamics of Yiddish life in Montréal, where the language remained an agent of creative as well as political expression in a community of writers, artists, and activists.

CONCLUSION

The Dora Wasserman Yiddish Theatre recently celebrated its sixtieth anniversary and continues with a third and fourth generation of actors. Yugntruf likewise celebrated its golden anniversary with an intergenerational reunion and with the journal continuing to be published. Both initiatives tapped into a particular Yiddish cultural imperative of the 1960s and 1970s to bring new youth-oriented vitality to Yiddish by successfully employing variants of Roskies's founding formula: "Make Yiddish Young Again." Both were based on the premise that continuity with prewar Yiddish culture was no longer possible; rather, new initiatives and dynamism were required to reach youth raised in the particular context of postwar North America. The Yiddish cultural imperative of the 1960s and 1970s was an enduring one. The alumnae of Wasserman's youth theatre—Anna and Aron Gonshor, Eileen Thalenberg, and countless others—have remained actively involved in Yiddish cultural life to the present day. They have involved their own children in the theatre and in other expressions of Yiddish culture. The imperative endures even as it changes with time. Aron Gonshor verbalizes the Yiddish cultural imperative that his generation first expressed some sixty years ago:

> Yiddish transcends the specific needs of an individual. That Yiddish is a legacy of the Jewish people. It is a legacy which is very poignant because so many of its speakers were killed. But the language, the culture, the ethos of Yiddish is much more important than any one of us. And so for those of us who have become involved with Yiddish theatre, we can recognize the gift we were given: the gift of Yiddish language, the gift of people like Dora and [her daughter and successor] Bryna, the gift of being able to convey the beauty of that language and all that it contains to the coming generation, let alone the people who are with us. But with that gift comes a responsibility: that you don't take what you have and squander it . . . The responsibility is: in whichever way you can, in whichever talent you have—whether it is knowledge of the language, the ability to act, to write, to speak, to teach, whatever that is, and in whatever small way you can do that—you are obliged to further that so that you don't come to your maker and he asks, "What did you not do?" . . . It is important for us to recognize that this a dynamic issue and that there is an imperative, and it is a time imperative: those of us who are native speakers are less and less and we have the responsibility to be able to lay such a strong foundation, that notwithstanding that time has its inexorable move, that we will at least be able to know that it is being left in decently good hands. (37:42–40:38)

PERFORMING HOMELAND AND MULTICULTURAL IMAGINARIES IN TORONTO'S CARAVAN FESTIVAL

JACQUELINE TAUCAR

Canadians encounter each other's multicultural mosaic tiles mainly at festivals, which are reduced to "simple theatre" at the level of
"a folkloric Disneyland."
—Darja Zorc-Maver and Igor Maver, "Guillermo Verdecchia and the
Frontera in Contemporary Canadian Diasporic Writing" 120

Now that we have Caravan, I won't have to think of
changing my name anymore.
—Letter from little girl to Caravan co-founder, Zena Kossar

Darja Zorc-Maver and Igor Maver's piercing critique above reflects the extant vein of ethnocultural festival scholarship, which includes work by Neil Bissoondath, Cynthia Thoroski, Sneja Gunew, Himani Bannerji, and others, that focuses on the reductive and trivializing aspects of such festivals. Evoking the underlying capitalist imperatives of Disney theme parks or McDonald's fast-food restaurants in reference to multicultural festivals, these authors' critiques envision a homogenization process in which ethnocultural differences are stripped of their complex or difficult aspects and are "safely" produced for mass consumption. These criticisms explore important problems inherent in multiculturalism as manifested in festival and spectacle, and are certainly valuable perspectives to consider in this article. However, I would argue that the criticisms of multicultural festivals as "Disneyfication" or "McMulticulturalism" are, ironically, just as susceptible to being described as reductive and myopic, characteristics ethnocultural festivals are often criticized for. This line of multicultural festival criticism is predominantly focused on the seeming superficiality and trivialization of the vehicle itself, but inevitably overlooks the broader system in which that vehicle operates and excludes other potential outcomes. The second quotation at the beginning of this section offers a contrasting perspective of *how* an ethnocultural festival, like the Toronto International Caravan Festival (hereafter Caravan), operates and what it means for different participants, both insiders and outsiders. For a girl living in Toronto ashamed of her "ethnic" last name, Caravan provided a stage for communities to represent their "Otherness," and, in doing so, created space for recognizing subjectivities outside the dominant Anglo British culture of post–World War II Toronto, although never in ideologically neutral conditions.

As the above examples demonstrate, on the one hand ethnocultural festivals homogenize and neutralize difference through capitalist production and commercialization, and on the other hand they open inclusive spaces for the representation of "Otherness" and resistant performances of the multicultural "script." At the Caravan Festival, I am consciously aware of the complex and ambivalent performances that produce multiple and contradictory understandings of multiculturalism. I see ethnocultural festivals in terms of what Homi K. Bhabha calls a third space, a hybrid space in which a number of competing discourses circulate, come into contact with one another, at times clash with one another, allowing for a new space of cultural negotiation and representation (211). Although some scholars have critiqued such forms of multicultural spectacle as reductive (Bissoondath, *Selling Illusions*; Thoroski; and Thoroski and Greenhill), I argue that the Caravan Festival produced, performed, and negotiated a plurality of contrasting and contested meanings of what I call the Canadian multicultural "script," which was developed in stages after World War II, and institutionalized in the Charter of Rights and Freedoms (1982) and the Canadian Multiculturalism Act (1988).

(EN)ACTING THE CANADIAN MULTICULTURAL "SCRIPT"

Drawing upon Richard Schechner's argument that a script may be written, oral, or embodied and outline a prescription for action ("Drama" 6), dramaturgically I see "multiculturalism" as a "script," and as a way of conceptualizing the Caravan Festival's performances. The legal documents and laws creating multiculturalism in Canada are "dramatic texts" or "scripts," which set guidelines, or directions, as to how to perform multiculturalism. By "script" I do not only refer to the textual record of multiculturalism such as the Royal Commission on Bilingualism and Biculturalism report in 1969 (hereafter the Bi and Bi Report) or the formalization of legislative texts of the Canadian Multiculturalism Policy (1971) or the Canadian Multiculturalism Act, but also to the physically performed normative understandings and assumptions of multiculturalism in everyday life that play off these "official" scripts. We perform scripts, but we also have the ability to adapt, interpret, and enact scripts so that they take on many different meanings. In a similar manner as the theatrical script changes to reflect the different physical environments, contexts, directors, actors, designers, and materials used to bring it to life on the stage, so too does multiculturalism, reflecting the conditions in which it is produced, the participants who produce it, and those that share in its performance.

Although many ethnocultural festivals take place in Toronto annually, I have experienced Caravan as a participant and as a second-generation Canadian whose parents immigrated to Canada from Eastern European countries. Like many other individuals growing up in the city or the Greater Toronto Area, I have distinct memories of attending ethnocultural festivals, especially Caravan, with my family, and specifically what it felt like to me to understand my "Ukrainianness" at this event and within the nation. Caravan is a particularly interesting case study thanks to the ways in which its performances claimed space and recognition for difference in the presumed monocultural Toronto of the 1970s, and in which the festival's development coincided with the emergence, growth, and institutionalization of Canada's multicultural "script." Canadian theatre history scholar Alan Filewod suggests that theatre is "not simply a matter of staged representation: it is an event both physical and symbolic; it transforms experience into a community narrative; and it materially constructs in the audience the community it addresses in its texts" (*Performing Canada* xvii). I would argue that the same is also true of ethnocultural festivals such as Caravan. As such, I consider the Caravan Festival a metaperformance that variously enacts Canadian multicultural nationhood, community, and be/longing for the immigrant diasporic communities settled in Toronto and Canada.

Canada is a nation of immigrants, informed by its settler-colonial histories and Indigenous exclusions, which are only now beginning to be acknowledged through the difficult processes of Truth and Reconciliation. Established as a colony in the seventeenth century, the territory now known as Canada was settled by both the French and the British on lands expropriated from Indigenous Peoples. In the twentieth century, with mass immigration occurring after World War II, the Canadian government began to rethink the evolving dynamic of Canadian society in the 1960s and move toward policies reflective of cultural heterogeneity. In 1969, book four of the Bi and Bi Report was published, recognizing the contributions of other ethnic groups beyond the English and the French to Canada's cultural enrichment, yet still excluding Indigenous Peoples. The report acknowledges that immigrants contribute "experience" and "energies" to Canadian institutions and society, and that "newcomers have their own traditions. Their distinct characteristics may be difficult to measure but are nonetheless valid cultural influences" (*Report* 12).

The assertions in the political arena that a new, more inclusive model of citizen participation in the larger society had to be adopted were being mirrored by the active celebration and affirmation of ethnocultural groups in Toronto's public spaces. In the same year that fourth book of the report was published, the Caravan Festival originated as an initiative by the husband-and-wife team of Leon and Zena Kossar, who were both children of Ukrainian immigrants, grew up in the Canadian Prairies, and moved to Toronto in the 1950s. Both Leon and Zena were writers for the *Toronto Telegram* newspaper. Covering community events, they were inspired to open the cultural happenings occurring in church basements and community centres across Toronto to a larger audience. The festival brought different people into contact, as Leon Kossar argued: "Caravan helped break down barriers by making everyone feel welcome in each other's homes. It's been a tremendous vehicle for building understanding among Canadians" (qtd. in McCabe).

The festival's beginnings can be read as a radical challenge to the cultural hegemony of Toronto in the late 1960s and 1970s. I would argue that Caravan originated out of a political imperative to create spaces of belonging in a city that was predominantly white. *Toronto Star* reporter Nora McCabe humorously quips that Caravan, as a showcase of diversity, "set up the pavilions, [opened] the doors and WASP Torontonians, who, back in 1969, couldn't buy rye bread at their local supermarket let alone Thai spring rolls, Mexican burritos, or Ukrainian perogies, would flock in." In 1974, *Toronto Star* reporter Trent Frayne wrote, "Toronto was once a mausoleum where nothing moved on Sunday but clergymen's lips," but with the waves of immigrants, "all of a sudden the town's drab monotone was overlaid by a merge of color and tone and style and language that produced a whole new ambiance." The Caravan Festival claimed space in the city and recognized the contributions of particular ethnic communities to the rich diversity of Toronto. At the same time, however, I see the Caravan Festival as the beginning of a "safe" and "tame" event through which the dominant centre (mostly white and of Anglo British heritage) could encounter difference—and their own neighbours—for the first time, but never quite on equal terms.

(PER)FORMING THE "HOMELAND IMAGINARY"

Toronto's ethnocultural festivals create a space of visibility and presence for the contributions and recognition of the diverse communities that make up the city, and they are often appropriated by the municipality to promote its image of multiculturalism. The Caravan Festival (1969–2002/03) became one of Toronto's largest spectacles of multiculturalism that drew millions of people to the city to partake in its events and the ways in which it performatively enacted the city's multicultural identity. Caravan's performance locations, called "pavilions," presented visitors with national cuisine and drink, song and dance, and folk-art displays through which cultural groups performed their social and cultural re-memberings of "home," or what I call traces of the "homeland imaginary," an ambivalent place that is always shifting and elusive, located in the dialectical tension between "home" and "away." The first Caravan Festival had twenty-nine pavilions representing the cultural capitals of some of the many different countries, or "homelands," from which people immigrated to Toronto, and yet to which they still remain affectively linked.

Through performance and spectacle, Caravan fomented community by creating "homeland imaginaries": symbolic worlds that sit in the in-between space between the new country, Canada, and the "old countries," the places of origin. For Benedict Anderson, the nation is an "imagined community" "because the members of even the smallest nation will never know most of their fellow members, meet them, or even hear of them, yet in the minds of each lives the image of their communion" (49). Branching off of Anderson's notion of a nation as an imagined political community, a socially constructed idea of a perceived affiliation between members of a group, the "homeland imaginary" exists for diasporic communities in the ways they maintain and perform social and cultural re-memberings of the places that they left. Such national identities and communities are constructed through the assembly of symbols and rituals—symbolic capital—in relation to territorial categories. Many immigrants left their places of origins to settle and create homes in Toronto, perhaps visiting the homeland and families they left, but encountering a lived reality very different from living "back home." With them they bring practices, languages, beliefs, and affiliations that are reflections, "traces," of the homeland: traces that are enacted in ethnocultural festivals. Such enactments function as "symbolic or iconographic capital," which Michel Bruneau describes as the processes and monuments that preserve and consolidate the links between the community and their territory despite the temporal and spatial distances that separate them (35).

The Caravan Festival not only functioned as one form of iconographic capital through which the community transmitted its identity, memory, and history from one generation to the next, but also created a space signifying an incomplete relationship or communion with the "new country" as well as the "old country." Such ambivalence manifests itself in the fact that the folkloric practices and costumes, and "traditional" foods and music, offered at the festival bear little resemblance to contemporary cultural practices and everyday life in the so-called "old country," yet are performed as markers of difference in the "new country." As such, the "homeland imaginary" is fundamentally framed by the temporal and historical boundaries of the then and there places of migration, as well as the acts of imagination that produce cultural identity in the here and now. Moreover, the traces of the homeland performed in one-hour Caravan performances need to be closely examined for providing an audience with a very selective and simplified depiction of the complex realities of the homeland. Performing these traces opens up an in-between space, a "third space" that is not reducible to one or another, a "here" or a "there," but rather holds the potential for both/and. The image of the homeland has been shaped and conditioned by living in the "new country" (with the effects of time, space, and nostalgia), and the places in which the performers now live are shaped by the places from which they have come.

Supporting and building community was as important to the Caravan Festival as providing opportunities for sharing and celebrating the ethno-cultural heritages and traditions of various groups in Toronto. All proceeds taken in by each pavilion would go right back into supporting the community by subsidizing cultural programming and maintaining buildings that had become the centres and "spiritual homes" of community life in the diaspora. For example, the proceeds from selling food at Caravan's "Krakow" pavilion in 1987 helped to provide the Polish community with language and arts programming, youth clubs, and help for newly arriving immigrants (Kates). These community centres and programs, funded in part through Caravan, acted as social supports for individuals who were displaced from their homelands after the Second World War. For the women volunteering to make food for Caravan's Russian "Volga" pavilion in 1990, Stasia Evasuk writes, "It's happy work as the women babble to each other in their native tongue of old Mother Russia. And it's obvious they enjoy each other's company. You can tell by their laughter." The volunteers were able to speak their first language and share stories and jokes together, drawing links between individuals and creating social capital. Such a joviality and common work brought about a sense of nostalgia, which I would argue is the product of loss of home and the marginalization experienced within the host country. Caravan afforded an opportunity for individuals from various diasporic groups to come together, building a valuable social network and therefore social capital, through the practice of making material culture.

Caravan developed and grew during a phase in which multiculturalism was formalized in Canada (1971 to 1981) through legislative acts with the federal adoption of Pierre Elliott Trudeau's Multicultural Policy in 1971 and the continued work toward developing formal relations between ethnocultural groups and government. These steps toward institutionalization are significant, constituting a uniquely Canadian form of nation-building that fomented multiculturalism as part of the Canadian identity.[1] Canada's multicultural policies are the foundational myths of Canadian social cohesion, or what Anderson calls an "imagined political community" (6), insomuch as "nationness, as well as nationalism, are cultural artefacts of a particular kind" (4). As Rainer Bauböck has argued, "No other Western country has gone as far as Canada in adopting multiculturalism not only as a policy towards minorities but also as a basic feature of shared identity" (93). Although there are other countries around the world in which multiculturalism is a sociological and lived reality, only Canada has institutionalized and enshrined the values of multiculturalism in its Constitution. In the institutionalization period (1981 to the present) multiculturalism became entrenched in the 1982 Charter of Rights and Freedoms, whose section twenty-seven states, "This Charter shall be interpreted in a manner consistent with the preservation and enhancement of the multicultural heritage of Canadians." In 1988 the Canadian government enacted the Canadian Multiculturalism Act, which retains the Charter's emphasis on the recognition of, and support for, the right to maintain one's cultural heritage.

---

1   See the work of Emma Ambrose and Cas Mudde, Will Kymlicka, and Andrew Parkin and Matthew Mendelsohn.

While introduced to "preserve, enhance and share" Canada's multicultural heritage, the policy develops a "script" of symbolic multiculturalism in simplistic celebrations and spectacles of ethnic diversity and cultural tolerance. Toronto's ethnocultural festivals, appropriated by officials to promote ideas of Canadian multiculturalism, illustrate the notion that multicultural policy and logic "depends on the existence of a multiplicity of historically grown 'imagined communities' on the Canadian soil that are reproduced in unequal power relations" (Winter 51). Although Caravan has been used by the city to "sell" an image of diversity and tolerance to the world, most especially for its 1996 Olympic bid (Noor), very little has been achieved in terms of dismantling barriers to full participation and inclusion, or breaking down the hegemony of dominant (white, anglophone) society. As racialized and ethnic minorities are continually constructed as "exotic" or for show, or as being from "elsewhere" or "Othered," the presence, histories, and contributions of minoritized Canadians to the nation are not only often absent from—or at best a footnote or sidebar in—the official "record," but are also constructed as being outside the nation.[2]

The institutionalized notion of preserving cultural heritage forms the basis for the multicultural "script" that the Caravan Festival enacted. Caravan evoked the image of being "back home" through carefully curated representations of national identities and heritages in the selective assemblage of song and dance, food and drink, and folk-art crafts. In doing so, Caravan recreated the feeling of a time and place beyond Canada's borders. It is important to note, however, that Caravan produced *selective* portraits of ethnocultural heritages and experiences that were unable to reflect the incredible diversity of the lived experiences within, and amongst, both individuals and groups in the diaspora. Moreover, the performances at the festival never rendered transparent the exercise of power by particular stakeholders within the ethnocultural communities, who made the decisions of what aspects of ethnocultural heritages were

---

2   See the work of Rinaldo Walcott on Toronto's Caribana festival that discusses the ways in which Canada's Caribbean community is simultaneously included and excluded from belonging to the nation.

included and excluded from the representation. For example, each country's pavilion was organized by a specific ethnic community or church group that would delegate responsibilities, such as food, entertainment, and material culture displays for education and souvenirs into separate smaller committees. As a result, it was only a small group of individuals who then became the primary stakeholders in making decisions regarding the definition, selection, preparation, and presentation of folk arts, entertainment, and a "national food culture" for each pavilion. The curation of ethnic identity was not self-reflexive or transparent as to who selected which diverse characteristics of identity that were used to represent the whole, or why some elements were eliminated, and who benefited from such representations. What is also not rendered visible is the way (dominant) white culture and privilege influences curation through the official multicultural "script," which tracks toward palatability and boutique forms for bourgeois consumption. Any representation of ethnocultural communities was filtered through the perception of a small group of stakeholders who made decisions on what aspects of their culture are presented, choosing on behalf of a majority whose experiences were far more diverse than what could be communicated in a one-hour song-and-dance show. As such, an underlying power imbalance existed when only a privileged group of individuals had an opportunity to articulate and present their vision of the community to the public, and as a result they may have benefited the most from the attention and accolades gained by the dominant (white) mainstream for participating in multiculturalism.

THE "BOUTIQUE" OF DIFFERENCE

The changing temporal and spatial conditions in the City of Toronto's social, political, and economic environment, I would argue, exposed the seams of the Canadian multicultural "script" enacted by Caravan over the course of the festival's history. During the time of institutionalization, the Caravan Festival was troubled by insufficient financial support and radical restructuring, which could be read as indicative of growing pains as the event was entering its second decade of operations during the recession of the 1980s and early 1990s. However, I perceive another aspect at play, in which the economic pressures during this time coupled with the fact that multiculturalism was "officially" recognized in the Charter and in federal policies to set the stage for shifting priorities. Although minorities were becoming more visible and actively asserting their differences at this time, Merrijoy Kelner emphasized that the power structure had not really changed: "few newcomers have cracked the WASP establishment, the White Anglo Saxon Protestant domination of banking, insurance, the stock exchange and the social ladder" (qtd. in Frayne). The dominant culture was tolerant of Toronto's colourful glow of multiculturalism because its position had never been threatened by immigration. Simply having the right to display one's ethnocultural heritage was not enough to guarantee full participation in society. Rather, substantive issues like persistent racism and lack of full access to economic resources were emerging within the discourses of multicultural relations. Shifting from the recognition of difference to creating economic opportunities marks a noted difference in the ways in which the multicultural "script" was performed at ethnocultural festivals and gestures to the underlying unequal power dynamics that were playing out. For instance, the festival was used as an opportunity for political performance to promote the official multicultural brand and generate social and economic capital by federal, provincial, and civic bodies. As such, they were able to reap, by association or proximity, the rewards of "performing" cultural acceptance, while often being financially absent or distant in their support for these events and/or the bodies of "others" who laboured to produce this image of diversity.

Although she is speaking from an Australian context,[3] Joanne Tompkins's critiques of the superficial ways in which official multiculturalism plays out in society are relevant in the Canadian context. Tompkins argues that:

---

3   Although they are very different nations with separate histories, Australian and Canada share a relationship in being settler-colonies of the British Commonwealth. Similarly, both countries experienced significant post-Second World War immigration and developed policies that are more inclusive of ethnocultural differences. The term multiculturalism was introduced in Australia in 1973, modelled after Canadian ideas.

> In many circles, [multiculturalism] has been reduced to a "food and
> folkdance" model of cultural diversity, fostering cultural display that
> provides suitable photograph opportunities for politicians. It has
> become, in practice, a convenient location for "them," effectively
> removed from the "us" of the general Australian imaginary, how-
> ever each category might be described. It does not have the cultural
> weight to generate an actual engagement with the real issue of, for
> instance, racial vilification. (142)

Tompkins gestures to the ways in which ethnocultural festivals are co-opted
by political players and governments, undermining or occluding attempts to
articulate oppositional positions. Through the repetition of cultural spectacle, ethnocultural festivals performatively inscribe or, as Judith Butler would
suggest, "re-iterate" (*Psychic Life* 16) the multicultural identity of the city,
from which municipal, provincial, and federal bodies profit by association
and proximity. Caravan thus became a popular campaign stop with federal
and provincial politicians, with visits from Prime Minister Pierre Trudeau and
Progressive Conservative leader Robert Stanfield in 1972 (an election year),
and Ontario Premier David Peterson in 1987. The city, however, maintained an
ambivalent relationship with festivals like Caravan and their discursive markers of difference. Each year, the city issued a City of Toronto Proclamation
celebrating Caravan as a cultural event and as a fundamental element of the
city's multicultural character. The city's multicultural masquerade is Janus-
faced in nature, celebrating "symbolic," or what Stanley Fish calls "boutique,"
forms of multiculturalism that often overlook and gloss over the difficult realities of racism, prejudice, and the lack of substantive gains in creating equal
opportunities or removing barriers to full participation in society.

Boutique multiculturalism, Fish contends, is characterized by a superficial
engagement with the ornamental elements of the "Other" in which boutique
multiculturalists can "admire or appreciate or enjoy or sympathize with or
(at the very least) 'recognize the legitimacy of' the traditions of cultures other
than their own" (378). This tolerance of other cultures, Fish argues, does
not come without limitations and prescriptions such as when certain values,

beliefs, or actions "[offend] against the canons of *civilized* decency as they have been either declared or assumed" (378, emphasis added). A prime example of boutique multiculturalism in action occurred in 2002, when then mayor Mel Lastman signed a City of Toronto Proclamation promoting Caravan as "a celebration of Toronto's exceptional quality of life, energy, creativity and unique diversity" and as "a remarkable portrait of our City's and our country's heritage" ("Festival Caravan Week"). Ironically, Lastman's celebratory proclamation of cultural diversity followed derogatory comments made the year before, alluding to his concerns about cannibals before a trip to Mombasa, Kenya ("Lastman Apologizes").

Caravan depicted "boutique," dehistoricized images of ethnicity, the conditions of which are prescribed by Canada's policy of multiculturalism that valorizes displays of "heritage." As previously described, Caravan's pavilions carefully staged displays of ethnic identity out of selectively assembled material culture and practices for a paying audience. For two dollars,[4] a "passport" could be purchased to gain entrance to all pavilions, where participants could step into the role of a "cultural tourist," visit places in the city to which they would not otherwise have reason to go, and be treated to displays of folk arts and crafts, performances of traditional songs and dances, and samples of the national cuisine. For example, the Polish pavilion "Krakow," located on Beverly Street in the Polish Cultural Centre (Polish Combatants' Hall), welcomed passport holders at the door with the "city's" "mayor" and "princess," who was specifically dressed in traditional garb (a peasant blouse with an elaborately embroidered corset-vest, a lace apron over a full skirt with bright floral motifs, and a floral headdress with flowing ribbons).[5] Tourists were then ushered into a hall—past displays selling souvenirs including traditional embroidery, folk-art crafts, and musical

---

4   In successive years, the costs of the passport would increase to fifteen dollars, which was the price of the last passport I purchased in 2002.

5   Mayors of pavilions were not always be dressed in full folkloric costume, but could wear select elements of clothing that would signify his heritage, for example a belt with traditional embroidery or characteristic hat. For the most part, mayors typically wore a suit or tuxedo with a name tag or sash indicating their role as the representative of the pavilion.

recordings—with multiple tables set up around a main stage and a buffet area, the delectable aromas of which enveloped the entire space and everyone in it. After "souvenir" shopping or selecting "national" delicacies to sample, tourists could sit and enjoy an hour-long entertainment featuring mostly local folk-dance ensembles performing iconic choreographies and musical groups playing "traditional" melodies.

In many ways, I believe the guise of entertainment and spectacle allowed for an opening to create a point of contact between people in Toronto who previously had no grounds for developing relationships and understandings. It is also, perhaps, this mingling of ethnocultural representation with entertainment or "spectacle" that has spurred the most vocal opposition to multiculturalism as a policy, which is often seen in terms of funding of ethnocultural festivals (Ryan 76). In a closer examination of multicultural arts funding, Peter Li found disparities in support for minoritized heritage and arts, which emphasized dehistoricized and static representations, while maintaining the cultural hegemony of the dominant (white, European) centre ("A World Apart" 369).[6] While unbalanced funding structures certainly shape the conditions of performance, Will Kymlicka has argued that funding cultural programming, especially that which focused on inter-ethnic communication, only constituted a small portion of the multicultural budget and not the majority, which went to other programs that worked toward greater inclusion and recognition of ethnocultural groups in Canada (45). Indeed, the conflation of ethnocultural festivals with the commodification of cultures certainly occurs and is appropriately criticized by Bissoondath and others. However, I would suggest that this overlooks the broader effects of capitalist forms of production, in particular, the opportunities for negotiation occurring between cultural producers and cultural consumers, which I will more closely examine later. The failure to move away from "entertainment," I contend, has particular

---

6   For a broader discussion regarding the effects of multicultural arts funding, including theatre, see the work of Ric Knowles; Knowles and Ingrid Mündel; Peter Li, "A World Apart"; Mayte Gómez; and others.

reverberations for how an ethnocultural festival like Caravan intersects with the multicultural "script."

Lillian Petroff, senior coordinator of educational programs for the Multicultural History Society of Ontario, says that the annual event "presents the danger that it commercializes and trivializes ethnicity" by perpetuating "the perception of ethnic groups as merely people who don costumes and dance" (qtd. in Freed). Cultural beliefs and practices are rarely static entities packed away in luggage and transported in total to be recreated in the new home, but are often changed and adapted to suit the new context. As such, performances at Caravan can reveal

> a disjuncture between the lived experience of the people residing in the countries and cultures being represented on the one hand, and the lived experiences of those given the official job of representing the cultures on the other hand . . . for some singers and dancers, the festival is the only context in which they participate in "ethnic" dancing or singing. (Bramadat 4)

Certainly, at festivals many identities that are being performed are nostalgic, symbolic, and reflective of the dominant consumerist milieu pervading the lifestyles of the majority of people in North America and the West.

Such a pervasive capitalist-consumer society evokes the spectre of cultural homogenization, as Bissoondath argues in *Selling Illusions: The Cult of Multiculturalism in Canada*. Bissoondath argues that the pavilions of Caravan and other ethnic festivals depict differences in a synthetic manner that reflects the processes of a Disney theme park, which removes any and all troubling or difficult elements (83). The threat of such commodified depictions contributes to perceptions of multiculturalism as static and non-threatening to the dominant status quo. Thoroski similarly argues that ethnocultural festivals are "like living museums, Disney's Epcot Centre [. . .] or the fast-food services of McDonalds's" and that "this homogenised brand of multiculturalism provides visitors with the illusion of cross-cultural close encounter along with the security of imagining the 'other' from a safe distance" (106).

Before accepting the position that ethnocultural representations are largely shaped by dominant consumer imperatives, threatening pre-existing more "authentic" identities, I contend that cultural identities and traditions are far more fluid, emerging dialogically, in an endless process of becoming, out of dynamic interactions with Canadian contexts and institutions. Moreover, I would argue what constitutes "authenticity" is also a performance that is not immutable or fixed, but rather contingent and contextually determined. Rather than placing authenticity on a true/false continuum, I turn to a model Ning Wang proposes, which is critically aware of the social, economic, and political forces underscoring authenticity. Wang asserts that "[t]hings appear authentic not because they are inherently authentic but because they are constructed in terms of point of view, beliefs, perspectives, or powers" and, as such they are negotiable and contextually determined (356). This complex negotiation occurs in performances of the "homeland imaginary" that not only exists in the specific cultural community's memories, idealizations, and imaginations of the homeland and that can be deemed inauthentic for its selective exclusions or inclusions of the actual homeland, but that also relates to "touristic" imaginations of that community that, as I mentioned earlier, can fixate on highly reductive elements of ethnicity. As such, interpreting ethnocultural festivals only as a form of entertainment commodity potentially undervalues the cultural practices—and their transformative, social, or spiritual affects—for the communities and performers who embody them, which, as I have argued earlier, are not insignificant. In other words, overdetermining the effects of capitalist-consumer culture on the performance of authenticity overlooks the embodied experiences and contributions of cultural producers in negotiating that performative process. These acts are no longer seen in terms of their performative effects and affects, but rather reduced to representation, in which culture and ethnicity are manufactured and oversimplified to fit, and be contained, within a socially ordered and systematized tourist gaze (Urry 1).

Detractors of Caravan also neglect to examine the ways in which the festival can subversively operate to question its own performances of multicultural identities. While for the most part Caravan carefully depicted experiences of an ethnocultural community's heritage for cultural tourists, I am particularly interested in the performative potential of inadvertent slippages occurring in their sight that disrupt or resist the multicultural "script." After completing their performance at the Krakow pavilion's matinee show, Daniel Girard reports that the youth dance troupe wanted to eat pizza much to the consternation of the pavilion's "princess" Christine Kwiatkowski: "We tried to wait as late as possible, but there were still visitors here when delivery guys started arriving. I think [audiences] found it weird to see pizza in a Polish pavilion." I am particularly drawn to Kwiatkowski's description of this incident as being "weird" and read it as a Brechtian *gestus* that renders strange the naturalized images of "Polishness" constructed and performed by individuals at the pavilion. The disruptive pizza illustrates that this generation of young "Polish" dancers have varied tastes extending beyond "Polish" foods, creating a performance that exceeds the festival's definition of "Polishness." Somehow, Kwiatkowski, and the cultural tourists who found it "weird to see pizza in a Polish pavilion," expected the depiction of a "pure" or "authentic" identity. Drawing attention to the very illusion of the staging, the pizza delivery fragments the appearance of "authenticity" at the pavilion, illustrating that the physical style of "ethnicity" is more complex and not safely contained within the curated boundaries of the festival, or even within the limits of the multicultural "script." The *gestic* pizza object draws uncomfortable attention (for the pavilion princess and tourist witnesses) that folkloric, "ethnic" identities are performed for audiences—and not an actual condition of their everyday life—shattering the veneer of difference and exoticism enacted by the multicultural "script."

PERFORMING THE "CULTURAL MOSAIC"

As critics have argued, the Canadian Multiculturalism Act is a method of diversity management that perpetuates limited and bounded ethnic representations via its focus on the preservation of ethnic heritages. While Caravan opened up space for the participation and recognition of minorities, I will explore how Caravan's spatial replication of the "cultural mosaic" reflects the staticity of ethnic representations and the limitations of the multicultural "script's" emphasis on the preservation of ethnic heritage. The spatial

Fig. 1. A Caravan "passport," June 2002.

dramaturgy of the Caravan Festival becomes an interesting case for examin-ing the literal and figurative construction of the metaphor used for Canadian multiculturalism, the cultural mosaic. The metaphor of the cultural mosaic performs the anxiety of mixing by setting up pieces of heritage in their places, separately from one another. The festival creates mini homelands, spatially separated from one another in particular "ethnic" neighbourhoods around the city, or—in the terminology of the festival—in "pavilions," which are named after capital cities of the home countries and can only be accessed by the pur-chase of "passports." Although Torontonians visited "Other" neighbourhoods during the Caravan Festival, the spatialization of pavilions as mini home-lands that required "passports" for entrance reinforces the mosaic metaphor of barriers and separation between cultures. The passport enacts the tropes of geographic borders between nations, or, in the case of Caravan, between the cultures that live side by side within the City of Toronto.

I interpret the "passport," through Brechtian dramaturgy, as a *gestic* prop that reveals the dynamics of inclusion in and exclusion from the nation. The

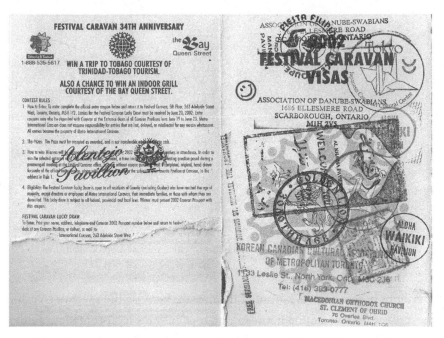

Fig. 2. A Caravan passport stamped with "entry visas" from different pavilions.

passport encourages a process of exoticization of "ethnic" Canadians that alienates them from belonging in the nation. While symbolic and used as a souvenir object, the passport performs the notion of border control and cultural tourism as individuals must present their "travel document" to be stamped at the entry of each pavilion visited. After "being approved" for entry, visitors are welcomed by the city's "Mayor" and "Princess," a performance of diplomacy that extends the border-crossing metaphor upon which the festival is premised. Each pavilion is situated locally within Toronto; however, the use of passports to enter each performance venue suggests that these "places" were exotic and "Othered."

The common travel trope of exoticization is often emphasized in articles in the daily newspapers, as Torontonians are implored to "forget your inhibitions about strange-sounding cuisines and prepare to become an explorer" (Rasky). The language of exploration and discovery serves to heighten the notions of difference and "Otherness" of ethnocultural groups in Toronto, which sets them apart from the nation. The spaces of the city between the

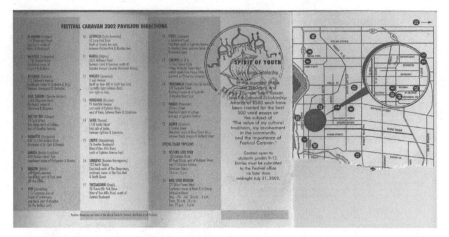

Fig. 3. A Caravan passport list of pavilions with a partial map of locations.

pavilions become like the grout of the mosaic, because the spectator/visitor
never sees the interaction between different cultures in Toronto, but rather
self-contained performances located in community halls or church basements.

Yet, for those individuals not part of the pavilion's ethnic community,
Caravan became a place to encounter the "Other" and learn about the traditions and heritages of people living in Toronto, albeit not entirely in conditions
of the ethnocultural group's choosing. Upon entrance to the pavilion, visitors
would be treated to entertainment by folkloric dance groups and bands that
would perform traces of the homeland through a standard structure. Each
pavilion was uniformly subject to a tripartite configuration of three elements,
circumscribed in their presentation: music and dance, food and drinks, displays and sale of folk arts and crafts. As Pauline Greenhill argues with regards
to Winnipeg's Folklorama Festival, which mimics Caravan's pavilion and
presentation of culture, the "similarities and differences within and between
groups are presented in discrete, separate locations, preventing actual encounters between different perspectives" (39). As such, any real differences between
groups were effectively erased by the emphasis on common elements that
structured pavilion displays. Moreover, Caravan is often minimized and "glo-
calized" in newspapers, as Esther Fisher writes, "How can you travel around
the world and never leave Toronto? It's possible at Caravan, Metro Toronto's

annual cultural festival." The presentation structure imposed on the pavilions in addition to the publicity focusing on exoticism and reductionism constrains ethnocultural representation and reception, which in turn constructs barriers to developing a deeper understanding of cultural difference in Toronto.

Performances at Caravan's pavilions could thus only showcase a very limited or static folkloric picture that circumscribed any complicated or problematic representations of dynamic lived culture. Furthermore, there is a risk of "McMulticulturalism," as Greenhill argues with regards to Winnipeg's Folklorama, using the term to describe ethnocultural events that tend to "mask difference as multicultural display" (40). Greenhill's definition of "McMulticulturalism" with regards to Folklorama is relevant to Caravan as their praxis is similar: "touristic orientation, pavilion formats, merging of international and local acts, prescribed audience roles—promotes similarity (usually that of a hegemonic order), just as McDonald's superficially different layout and décor from restaurant to restaurant never really fails to conceal a uniformity of service and product" (40). Caravan can similarly fall into such limiting and limited representations of "cultural others," as Bissoondath has also argued, in its format of entertaining multicultural spectacle. Bissoondath criticizes Toronto's Caravan Festival for being a "Canadian-mosaic version of the Jungle Cruise at Walt Disney World" (82). Similar to Greenhill's notion of "McMulticulturalism," Bissoondath's main criticism of multiculturalism is that it devalues "that which it claims to wish to protect and promote. Culture becomes an object for display rather than the heart and soul of the individuals formed by it" (88). In doing so, ethnocultural identity is both staged to promote Toronto's multiculturalism and stage-managed to fall within limited and "safe" boundaries of entertainment that eschews cross-cultural conflict or differences.

The cultural mosaic is a powerful metaphor to describe the Canadian style—or brand—of cultural diversity management. Nonetheless, I see potential implications and limitations of using this metaphor. The cultural mosaic is often associated with strategic essentialism, which allows for collective pooling of resources—economic, political, and social—for an articulation and defence of interests that individuals cannot accomplish on their own.

However, this can lead to divisive battles between groups for scant resources. Regarding Caravan, Norman Mohamid, executive director of the Ontario Council of Agencies Serving Immigrants, notes, "There are dangers to emphasizing differences, it can represent a hiving off and a separateness. And yet this notion of differentiation underlies the festival itself, even though the backdrop against which Caravan was first staged has changed" (qtd. in Thompson A2). Mohamid's concerns arising from multiculturalism's emphasis on celebrating and maintaining diversity as performed at Caravan gestures to the way that encouraging dehistoricized and static ethnocultural representations of "otherness" acts as a barrier to inclusion in society.

Bissoondath takes official multiculturalism to task for encouraging ethnic differentiation and a "psychology of separation" from mainstream culture, which results in separation into ethnic enclaves (42). Unity and cohesion are sacrificed in the struggle and competition between groups for resources. Bissoondath's assertion strikes at the cultural mosaic for its lack of unity and cohesion, arguing that "[m]ulticulturalism has failed us. In eradicating the centre, in evoking uncertainty as to *what* and *who* is Canadian, it has diminished all sense of Canadian values, of what is Canadian" (71, emphasis added). In my reading of Bissoondath's critique, significant questions arise. First, we must ask who defines what is *Canadian*. Whose history and narrative do we privilege in that definition, British or French? Whose do we exclude— for instance, those of the Indigenous Peoples of Canada? Second, who gets to define the terms of being Canadian, and to what end? Concepts such as "national unity" and "national identity" are complex and problematic ones that can maintain hegemonic and suppressive powers over those who fall outside of the accepted boundaries. As evidenced by ongoing debates regarding reasonable accommodation in Québec and the recent banning of the *niqab* in citizenship ceremonies, Canada's multicultural policy is not as inclusive or as ideal as we may imagine, for questions about which cultural practices fit within official policy frequently occur.

The way Toronto's Caravan Festival operated reflected the metaphor of the "cultural mosaic" in which cultures are performed side by side in discrete pavilions, foreclosing the potential for mixing and conflict. The anxiety of mixing is made physically manifest in the *gestic* object of the festival "passport," which gestures to notions of border control and access. The passport reframed the representation of cultures within Toronto as "exotic" and different, discursively producing "ethnic" Canadians as "Others" within the nation. The bounded nature of Caravan spaces and the mosaic metaphor of Canadian multiculturalism equally suffer from a sense of freezing ethnic identities in particular times and spaces, failing to recognize the lived realities of interactions between cultures in everyday life. Although audience members at Caravan took pride in the city's diversity and showed tolerance by travelling to diverse neighbourhoods, taking an interest in other cultures, their participation and crossing boundaries into different neighbourhoods did not necessitate any further engagement with the political and social issues that underlie multiculturalism. Caravan's oversimplified conceptions of cultural minorities and audiences' reception of them potentially sustained barriers to full participation and equality by not challenging the public's complicity in their creation or their passivity with regards to issues like racism.

While these are significant issues to consider when analyzing Toronto's ethnocultural festivals such as Caravan, it remains important to note that Caravan also contributed to a community's sense of belonging. The crude characterization of festival performances as "Disneyfication" or "McMulticulturalism" by Bissoondath and Greenhill respectively, ignores the significant investments in time and talent that volunteers dedicated to representing their cultures by producing and selling food, performances, and folk art, which in turn generated material benefits for their communities. As such, Caravan generated significant productive outcomes for its communities, in particular contributing to community-building and providing social supports in, and for, diasporic communities that may elude them in the host country's dominant culture. Moreover, volunteering produced both communal and affective alliances most visible in Caravan's Russian and Polish pavilions. Furthermore, there was a pleasure associated with participating in Caravan; as Daria Olynyk of the "Caravan" pavilion argued, volunteers "donate their time and talents because it's good for the community and they *enjoy* doing it" (qtd. in Serge, emphasis added). Caravan provided an opportunity for ethnocultural communities to claim visual space in the city and at the very least allowed for the beginnings of cross-cultural understanding, although in a limited and restrictive way. In addition, existing scholarship of the Caravan Festival ignores the ways in which the festival can and does subversively perform outside the carefully curated depictions of ethnocultural heritages that can complicate understandings of the multicultural "script." My analysis of the Caravan Festival begins to acknowledge the surfeit of contradictory and ambiguous multicultural "scripts" that exist, co-mingle, and clash with one another, and in doing so engages with the discursive marks of hegemonic culture as well as the transformative potential of this event.

TEESRI DUNIYA THEATRE: RESISTING INEQUITIES AND ETHNOCENTRIC NATIONALISM THROUGH POLITICALLY ENGAGED THEATRE

SHEETAL LODHIA, RAHUL VARMA, AND JASWANT GUZDER

Canada's cultural policies have been described as "multiculturalism within a bilingual framework,"[1] which implies an inclusive framework for all Canadians (Trudeau, Statement). Cultural diversity and equity in the arts have emerged as the country's national policy. However, the operational realities of these policies reveal a political process that has divided the theatre world along racial and cultural lines: a bicultural theatre of white English and French Canadians versus a theatre of cultural Others clustered as "multicultural," racialized minorities, ethnically diverse, or immigrant communities. Indigenous Peoples, problematically, remain invisible within this model. These two constituencies of the Canadian theatre world differ not only in their social organization, the patronage they receive, and the rules they are governed by, but also in the artistic standards by which they are judged: standards determined by dominant French and English colonial antecedents. Such biases diminish access for cultural minorities both by judging their creative work within the aesthetic standards of the dominant groups, and by (both silently and explicitly)

---

1 The Royal Commission on Bilingualism and Biculturalism was established in 1963 by Prime Minister Lester B. Pearson. The phrase, "multiculturalism within a bilingual framework," is also the title of scholar Eve Haque's 2012 work.

forcing cultural Others to attune their artistic expressions to comply with dominant group expectations.

For over three decades, Teesri Duniya Theatre in Québec has resisted cultural domination, assimilation, and ethnocultural centricity in favour of choosing the path of politically engaged theatre.[2] This essay focuses on plays staged by Teesri Duniya that reflect the lived cultural experiences of diverse communities, and offers a commentary on this body of artistic work as one that conveys politically engaged voices. Teesri has produced a discourse and a range of creative offerings that are dissonant with the prevailing policy of promoting Québécois nationalism, according to which assimilation remains the singular path for engagement with the cultural Other. The essay engages with the implications of, and the artistic predicament created by, this acculturation framework for minorities, demonstrating how a company can create counternarratives and alternative spaces for theatre that reflect a diverse landscape and integrate a truly heterogeneous and dynamic social process.

IMMIGRATION AND MULTICULTURALISM

To appreciate the ways in which Teesri Duniya Theatre has been socio-politically embedded in Canada and Québec, and to understand how Teesri has created alternative spaces for a diversity of voices, we shall briefly review relevant aspects of Canadian history and arts policies that have influenced cultural production within this nation. We must first acknowledge that Canada is a settler-colonial state, in which French colonizers, followed by English colonizers, assimilated, eradicated, or pushed to the margins Indigenous Peoples in Canada through both actual and cultural genocide. After World War I, new immigrants to Canada, who were defined as a "Third Force" (*Report*), were comprised of white settlers originating from European nations (Italy, Portugal, Germany, Poland, Hungary, etc.). Their presence rose to 22.6% by 1961 (Li, *Cultural Diversity* 2). These waves of allophone Europeans shifted and defined an ethnic diversification of Canada, albeit one still dominated by

---

2   A previous version of this article was published in *alt.theatre* (Varma, "Staging Peace").

white populations. In several reports written between 1967 and 1970 by the Royal Commission, Canada was reconfigured as a multicultural society, with three major constituencies and demographics: the two founding colonizing nations of the British and the French and the Third Force, which reflected the expansion of European ethnic diversity.

Multiculturalism,[3] as we know it today, did not begin to take shape until the Trudeau era, when the prime minister famously argued that "uniformity is neither desirable nor possible in a country the size of Canada" (Remarks). His multicultural policy saw growing numbers of immigrants from Asia, Africa, Latin America, and what is now known as the "Muslim world" who had previously been present as virtually irrelevant and unseen minorities. The visible minority population has grown progressively from 11.3% in 1996 to 22.3% in 2016, creating the new reality of a profoundly multicultural, multiracial, and multiethnic Canada, concentrated especially in major urban centres (Li, *Cultural Diversity* 2).

INTERCULTURAL VERSUS MULTICULTURAL

Thanks to the influence of historical antecedents and French nationalism, Québec's view of multiculturalism and immigration is notably distinct from that of the rest of Canada. Québec defines itself as a nation,[4] and while French is the dominant language in the province, "the francophone majority is a

---

3   The Canadian Multiculturalism Act was established in 1988 by Prime Minister Brian Mulroney and asserts that every Canadian has the right to equal treatment, including minorities' rights to practise and enjoy their cultures and religions. See Canadian Multiculturalism Act.

4   Gérard Bouchard notes that Québec defines itself as a "nation" of more than six million inhabitants based on "distinct characteristics: a large land-base, a strong historical consciousness, a francophone identity and culture (four fifths of Quebecers have French as their mother tongue), a long Christian tradition, and specific political, educational, legal, and other institutions" (10). Québec's status was recognized by parliament in 2006 and is "therefore a sociological nation with the status of a province within the Canadian Confederation" (10).

minority nation within Canada and a cultural minority on the continent"
(Bouchard 11). During the Trudeau era, multiculturalism as a concept was
seen by many in Québec as an opportunistic political ploy designed to diminish the primacy of Canada's French roots and to defuse the strong popular
nationalist and separatist movements, which included the iteration of a revolutionary antireligious, and anticolonial (against the English) movement in the
1960s known as the Quiet Revolution.[5] Christian Dufour in *Le Défi Québécois*
argues that multiculturalism was a "way of refusing to recognize the bicultural
nature of the country and the political consequences of Quebecois specificity"
(77). Dufour sets up a clear hierarchy between white cultures and racialized
ones, stating, "Multiculturalism, in principle, reduces the Quebecois fact to
an ethnic phenomenon" (77). These sentiments have been embraced widely
and were echoed by late Québec Premier René Lévesque, who declared that
"multiculturalism really is folklore ... [the] notion was devised to obscure 'the
Quebec business,' to give an impression that we are all ethnics and do not have
to worry about special status for Quebec" (Bissoondath 40). Characterizing
multiculturalism as folklore both reinforced antagonism and resistance to
integration of visible minorities and diminished their cultural presence in
Québec to a status of marginal mythologies and exoticism. By emphasizing
a binary of "us" Québécois versus "them" ethnics, this discourse created a
new kind of cultural divide between separatists and visible minority groups:
one that was arguably more discordant than the divide between the English
and French Quebecers.[6]

---

5   On 7 March 2011, Justin Trudeau, then a Liberal MP, stated to the *Globe and Mail*,
"The word multiculturalism has become synonymous in the mind of many Quebecers
as being something that is imposed by English Canada," an irony considering his father
adopted multiculturalism as a federal policy in 1971 (qtd. in Monpetit).

6   The division between racialized people and white Francophones was evident in the
30 October 1995 referendum on sovereignty when visible minorities and the Assembly of
First Nations Chiefs in Québec, alongside anglophone communities, voted against Québec
sovereignty, cementing ire against these groups by the dominant French culture. Jaques
Parizeau famously blamed "money and the ethnic vote" for the loss of the referendum.
Parizeau has gone on to suggest that "ethnic" was not a racial designation but, rather, a

"Interculturalism,"[7] rather than multiculturalism, is the policy adopted by Québec to define the specificity of their cultural predicament. Gérard Bouchard, in *Interculturalism: A View from Quebec*,[8] argues that interculturalism, unlike multiculturalism, relies on the centrality of a dominant culture—in Québec's case, a francophone one.[9] Moreover, the desired outcome of Interculturalism is

> promotion of the French language, emphasis on rights, respect for diversity, the fight against discrimination, the special attention given to the francophone majority culture, the recognition of ethnocultural minorities in a spirit of pluralism, the protection of fundamental values (including democracy, equality between men and women, non-discrimination, and secularism), the value of integration, the quest for a middle-course between assimilation and fragmentation (or the "mosaic"), the need for intercommunity interactions and exchanges, the development of a shared (public) culture and a Quebec sense of identity, the participation of all citizens in civic and political life, and the principle of reciprocity in the process of

language one, encompassing all non-francophone voters, though his clarification has been widely disputed (Haque 4).

7   Teesri Duniya has in fact adopted this term in our mandate in order to comply with Québec's funding regulations and to signal that we are willing to engage in intercultural dialogue and exchange. In this dissonant predicament, it is not surprising that we have had to adopt the language of the colonizer in order to be eligible for funding.

8   Sociologist and co-chair of the Québec Bouchard-Taylor Commission into the accommodation of minorities. The commission has come under attack in Québec for accommodating the needs and desires of religious and cultural others. In 2008 Bouchard and Charles Taylor released a three-hundred-page report and, speaking to CBC news, stated, "The foundations of collective life in Quebec are not in a critical situation . . . What we are facing, instead, is the need to adapt" ("Let's Move On").

9   We would argue that Bouchard highlights one of the implicit failures/biases of multiculturalism in that it does not acknowledge its dependence on a dominant culture, which, in the case of English Canada, is white (Christian/secular Christian) supremacy.

integrating immigrants (and in particular in the practice of accommodations). (29)

We quote liberally here, since the list is long and comprehensive. In particular, we wish to draw attention to two points that continue to challenge any
smooth "integration" of immigrants in Québec: the call for secularism and
the hope for a middle ground between assimilation and the "mosaic."[10]

The desire for and the tenets of secularism in Québec stem from a long
and "difficult relationship with the Catholic religion" (Bouchard 13). Coupled
with its colonial history, "Quebec . . . experienced more than two centuries of
domination both from the outside (the British Empire) and from the inside
(the clergy and its allies in the elites of business and the liberal professions)"
(12). Bouchard describes a lingering "desire for emancipation" and for "restoration" that manifests largely in fierce language protection attitudes (12).
The Catholic Church imposed oppressive rules, particularly against women
and, according to Bouchard, the Québécois reaction against such regulation is
"expressed today by an intense sensitivity to anything religious—a sensitivity
that entails a great deal of suspicion and even hostility" (13). These sensitivities
manifest in Québec as Eurocentric and Christocentric notions of religious
neutrality (from the French philosophy of laïcité)[11] that respond to displays
of purported religious symbology (except crosses)[12] as public displays of non-
secularism. There has been and continues to be a failure to recognize both the

---

10   Mosaic was the term used in the '80s and '90s (though coined early in Canada's
immigration history circa 1920) to describe the outcomes of multicultural policy in
English Canada. It refers to the (peaceful) coexistence of various cultures of people living
together in the same shared space (neighbourhood, city, province, country). In contrast
the American view was the "melting pot," a desire for relinquishment of origins, truly
assimilationist, to become "American." See Richard Day.

11   On laïcité, see Le Blanc.

12   In 2008 the province's general assembly voted unanimously to keep a crucifix mounted
over the platform speaker's chair. See "Let's Move On." The new provincial government
(as of 18 October 2018) has argued that the cross is not religious but "historical heritage"
("Le crucifix").

double standard involved in permitting some symbologies and not others and the fact that secularism looks different across cultures: what may be deemed cultural identity is not always already religious identity.[13] Therefore, debates persist about what "religiously" or culturally informed items people are and are not permitted to wear in public in Québec.[14]

Regarding the desire for a middle ground between assimilation and the multicultural mosaic, Bouchard himself cannot satisfactorily describe what that may look like:

---

13 This is a vast topic, and we are not experts except inasmuch as we ourselves have been subjected to double standards about what constitutes secularism and what we can and cannot enforce in our classrooms (both post-secondary and higher-education). The report "Secular Schools in Québec: A Necessary Change in Institutional Culture" may be a good place to start. The Government of Canada website on this topic describes a school system that was initially divided between Catholic and Protestant lines in Québec (where Protestant schools were also anglophone schools). After 1997 Québec adopted a policy of secularism that would divide schools along language and not religious lines. In 2005 confessional classes were replaced by mandatory ethics and religious culture programs. Clothing restrictions in the classroom were challenged in 2006 through a civil case involving a young Sikh boy who was finally allowed to wear his kirpan in public schools. Public opinion was centred on the ways in which the "majority had taken religion out of schools and [. . .] minority groups were bringing it back in" (Milot and Tremblay). Bill 60, popularly known as the Québec Charter of Values, in the name of secularism, neutrality, and equality proposed banning all "conspicuous" and visible religious symbols, namely the hijab, turban, and kippah worn by Muslim women and Sikh and Jewish men. The Charter proposed barring wearers of these items from holding positions as judges, doctors, daycare workers, or any other public officers. At present McGill and Concordia have banned discrimination for clothing and religious symbology and provide prayer rooms, whereas not all public schools provide the same. Premier François Legault is attempting to enforce Bill 60 again.

14 Bouchard is against banning face coverings and the prohibition of head scarves, turbans, etc., as reported by the *Globe and Mail*. He believes "the project [is one] that will divide us, that will lead us into a battle that will be an unpleasant debate and one in the long term that will hurt us" (Peritz and Perreaux).

> The spirit of Interculturalism, as I envisage it, is to overcome this antinomy and propose an integrated vision of the components of Quebec culture that respects the prerogatives of everyone. But it is still both inevitable and legitimate that the francophone majority, if only because of its demographic and historical weight, be recognized as the de facto main vector for integration. (12)

Indeed, Bouchard's vision still favours—through sheer population size, he says—something that looks more like assimilation than the mosaic. This leads to the popular view of the immigrant in Québec as a French-speaking citizen divested of religious symbols who brings acceptable portions of his/her culture to the forefront (including food, music—not too loud, of course—and an exotic body). Bouchard himself believes that people should be allowed to wear what they choose, including kippahs, turbans, and hijabs (Peritz and Perreaux), but this is not yet a popular viewpoint among the francophone majority. Other critics have categorized the reality of interculturalism as a public-private division where there is only a private acceptance of culture: in public, one must speak French and "look secular," while in private one can do whatever one likes.[15]

Part of this call for a clear, public Québécois identity relates to a prevailing perception of Quebecers as a society in danger of losing their language and culture. Bouchard and his co-author of the commission on accommodation, Charles Taylor, argue that the ire against "reasonable accommodation" in Québécois contexts stems from a "crisis of perception" where francophones perceive their culture to be constantly under threat. Bouchard cites a poll conducted in the province in June 2009 by Léger Marketing in which 90% of francophones felt that, "for various reasons, the French language is threatened in the Montreal region" (11). The promoters of interculturalism are sympathetic to the immigrant's difficulties, as Taylor expressed in a news conference releasing the commission's report:

---

15   See, for example, Joseph Rosen's "Among the Hasidim," which presents the public-private predicament nicely.

> Immigrants are called upon to share, to join the fundamental values
> of Quebec Society . . . They're called upon to learn French, and they're
> called up on to participate in the day-to-day life and to integrate . . .
> into Quebec society . . . In exchange, the whole society must give
> them the tools to do all this. ("Let's Move On")

Here is a kinder, gentler version of assimilation that includes a recognition of
what it takes to "participate" in Québec society, and a call to action to provide
better tools for doing so.

Although the Bouchard-Taylor Commission advocates for a forward-
thinking and seemingly inclusive[16] view of racialized persons and immigrants
to Québec—including the encouragement of francophone Quebecers to
learn English and other languages—the reality of life in Québec has yet
to align with this vision. Even today, the provincial immigration website,
www.quebecinterculturel.gouv.qc.ca, clearly declares Québec's main policy
as "favoriser l'intégration" (to favor or promote integration), which translates to many minorities as an unambiguous assertion of assimilation as
the priority.[17] Racialized and religious minorities in Québec continue to

---

16   The Bouchard-Taylor Commission included some progressive recommendations,
such as, for example, assisting newcomers in finding jobs, adopting a multilingual attitude
that includes more willingness to learn English and other languages (not at the expense
of French), assisting in language integration, recognizing foreign professional credentials
to assist in job acquisition, etc. Of course, there are some less-progressive recommendations, such as the request for gender accommodation in health-care settings to be denied
if those accommodations "compromise equality" (Bouchard and Taylor).

17   The *Montreal Gazette* reported the findings of a recent survey conducted in light
of Canadian Multiculturalism Day (www.canada.ca/en/canadian-heritage/campaigns/
celebrate-canada-days/multiculturalism-day.html) as to the differing attitudes of French
Canadians versus English Canadians in relation to immigration. Although both groups
look favourably upon immigration to Canada, francophones were more likely to support
assimilation, that is, the giving up of customs and non-Christian religions, and the adoption of French. See Bruemmer.

be marginalized,[18] with legitimate concerns about systemic oppression and racism foregrounded and clearly foreclosed by the primacy of a defined policy of French nationalism.[19] Indeed, one of the primary ways in which minority voices continue to be silenced is by a failure of governmental organizations to include marginal voices in policy-making. Bouchard's version of interculturalism succinctly sums up such systemic problems. While Bouchard seemed to be an ally in promoting a more inclusive vision of Québec, he still failed to include cultural Others in the decision-making process.

ARTS COUNCILS AND THEIR POLICIES

Prior to the adoption of official multicultural and equity policies by the Canada Council for the Arts and provincial arts councils, and often still in our current context, visible and ethnic minorities practised their arts activities largely in private homes, and during weekends at schools, community centres, and places of worship. When and if they got organized enough as a community, they received support from the federal departments of multiculturalism

---

18   Not just marginalized but openly attacked and, in some cases, murdered. The 29 January 2017 mosque shooting is one of many examples of open hostility toward nondominant religions and peoples.

19   Québec's trajectory of interculturalism includes the

creation of a ministry of immigration (1968), rejection of Canadian multiculturalism (1971), adoption of a charter of human rights and freedoms (1975), establishment of French as the official language of Québec (1974, '77), development of a "cultural convergence" policy (1978, '81), the Chancy report on intercultural education (1985), declaration of the government on interethnic and interracial relations (1986), enactment of a "moral contract" policy (1990–91), Québec-Ottawa agreement on the responsibility for immigration (1991), orientation focusing on citizenship (late 1990s, early 2000s), a multidimensional approach that fully reintroduced the cultural dimension into government policies (2004), the Bouchard-Taylor Commission (2007–2008), and struggle against racism. (Bouchard 28–29)

and certain provincial and municipal bodies.[20] This support came in the form of grants and free rehearsal space, usually provided once a week, usually on weekends, and usually at a school or city sports centre. Artists in these groups frequently did not qualify for the eligibility criteria of arts-funding bodies due to Eurocentric standards (Varma, "Teesri Duniya" 181).

As a result of mounting protest by scores of culturally diverse artists from across the country, the Advisory Committee to the Canada Council for Racial Equality in the Arts was established in 1990, which identified "cultural diversity as one of the principle challenges" in its mandate (Creighton-Kelly). For the first time, there was a recognition that "Canada's artists must reflect an increasing diversity of cultural and racial backgrounds and work within a broad range of art forms" (Creighton-Kelly). The two-pronged policies of official bilingualism and official multiculturalism were supposed to sustain the arts of Canadians inclusive of all cultural, linguistic, and racial backgrounds, and were to operate in "close co-operation with federal, provincial/territorial and municipal cultural agencies and departments" ("Equity"). In 1992, the Equity Office was established at the Canada Council, and a range of initiatives—including recruitment, staff-sensitization, reformation of eligibility criteria, and representation of diverse artists on juries—were subsequently undertaken to address equity issues.

DISPARITY IN FUNDING

Although official multicultural and now equity policies have been adopted by arts councils, the funding reality has yet to match their intent. There is also a disparity between federal regulations and provincial ones, especially in Québec. In the early '90s, for example, Rahul Varma (co-author of this paper), received his first Canada Council grant but was rejected by the Conseil des Arts et des Lettres du Québec (CALQ) for the same project, one which had

---

20   Teesri received funding in 1996 from the Department of Canadian Heritage. More on this later.

to do with race and violence against women of colour.[21] Whereas the jury at
the Canada Council included visible minorities, the council at CALQ was
comprised solely of white francophones.

Several decades later, at the time of this paper's writing in 2018, inclusivity and cultural difference dominate discussions at arts councils. With the
recent federal government focus on Indigenous reconciliation, arts councils
have finally made diversity a priority ("Government of Canada"). But funding
for visible minorities and Indigenous groups is still proportionally less than
that granted to white anglophone and francophone projects.[22] This disparity
becomes even clearer in Québec. In the fiscal year 2016–2017, a clear marker
of this inequity was the superior patronage afforded to francophone organizations compared to English-speaking and visible minority groups (Varma,
"Opinion: Systemic"). For example, in 2017, Les Grands Ballets Canadiens
received $2.5 million, Compagnie Marie Chouinard received $664,100, and
Usine C received $400,000. All of these companies are white francophone
groups. By contrast, Nyata Nyata and Sinha Danse each received $41,000,
Black Theatre Workshop received $54,000, and Teesri Duniya Theatre $25,000,
all of which are racialized groups ("Programme").[23] Since the definition of

---

21   Varma received $8,000 from the Canada Council in 1992 through the Research
Creation program to write *Counter Offence*, a proposal that was appraised highly for artistic merit, socio-political complexity, and mature treatment of the subject matter. CALQ
rejected the proposal for further funding two years later, stating "[the] theme is of some
interest but it lacks originality . . . [the] writing is not mature, very young . . . [the] project
is still naïve and needs to mature. The socio-political thinking is not very strong" (Jacob).

22   It should also be noted that the current CEO of the Canada Council, Simon Brault,
who is famous for his work *No Culture, No Future* (2009), a passionate and powerful plea
for the arts, fails to acknowledge a diverse art world in Québec and Canada. Rather the
work is focused on a white francocentric notion of art production, omitting the valuable
contributions of racialized and Indigenous Peoples to Québec and Canada.

23   Awards granted to (white) francophone groups:

Les Grands Ballets, $2.5 million
Compagnie Marie Chouinard, $664,100
Les Ballets Jazz De Montréal, $632,100

diversity has been framed entirely by francocentric notions, a curious phenomenon has even emerged in Québec where white anglophone companies are permitted to check off a "diversity" box in their applications to CALQ (Varma, "Opinion: Systemic").

ADVERSITY OF DIVERSITY IN QUÉBEC: ETHNOCENTRIC NATIONALISM AND THE ART WORLD OF VISIBLE MINORITIES

For most dominant cultures (in Canada both anglophone and francophone), ideas of inclusion and diversity frequently mirror an embedded Eurocentric emphasis and serve larger national narratives. Such acts in fact constitute oppression for marginalized people, since, as Taylor himself argues, "Non-recognition or misrecognition can inflict harm; it can be a form of oppression, imprisoning someone in a false, distorted, and reduced mode of being . . . . [D]ue recognition is not just a courtesy we owe people, it is a vital human need" (25). Purportedly diverse theatre that has received both funding and success in Canada has included, for example, productions of Shakespeare featuring a single racialized person, in which that one person must represent a whole race or even a whole body of diverse racialized people. A more overt racist occurrence is the appropriation by white actors of other cultures,

---

Maison Théâtre, $585,000
Usine C, $400,000
Théâtre aux Écuries, $225,000
Théâtre du Nouveau Monde, $1.5 million

Awards granted to racialized groups:

Nyata Nyata $41,000
Sinha Danse, $41,000
Black Theatre Workshop, $54,000
Teesri Duniya Theatre, $25,000

All of these numbers come from the CALQ website, where funding results are publicly available ("Programme").

including the widely endorsed tradition of blackface theatre in Québec, where white francophone actors artificially darken their skin to represent blackness, usually for comedic effect.[24] Given how rare appearances by racialized people are in contemporary theatre, television, and other cultural expressions, tactics such as the casting of isolated racialized actors or the representation of racialized characters by white actors often have the opposite effect to an ostensible intent of inclusivity, underlining the uncertain and dissonant status of visible minorities as "counting" as Canadian or Québécois. In short, representation matters in both mirroring and shaping collective policies.

To illustrate the challenges of representation and funding difficulties, we highlight the production of the same play by two different companies. Philippe Ducros's *L'affiche* (2009) depicts the occupation of Palestine.[25] Ducros's play, mounted in 2011, featured an all-white francophone cast, won multiple awards, and received rave reviews. Ducros went on to receive further funding from CALQ for his company Productions Hotel Motel. By contrast, Teesri mounted the same play in English under the title *The Poster* in 2011, featuring Arab actors playing the Arab roles. Teesri applied for funding in the same round of applications at CALQ and received nothing. Several factors were certainly at play, including the language barrier of English for many francophones (which speaks to larger nationalist ideologies), but also the politics of colour-conscious casting, which did not employ the expected actors and for which the French have not typically seen a need, since accusations of cultural appropriation (by racialized persons and other minorities) are only beginning to be taken seriously. We use "French" here, because similar politics have been in operation in France, where it has been perfectly acceptable for white actors to play non-white roles (or to play non-white music, or wear ethnic clothes, or dance non-white dances, or cook and sell for profit non-white food, etc.). The practice of appropriation

---

24   Much has been written about blackface in Québec. See Varma, "Opinion: Use," and scholar of Black history Philip S.S. Howard. Among numerous examples, the most recent is the portrayal of Black hockey player P.K. Subban in the Théâtre du Rideau Vert's year-end production in December 2014 ("P.K. Subban").

25   Ducros, a Québécois playwright and author, was the winner of a prestigious writer-in-residency program, Écritures Vagabondes, and went to Syria three times to write the play.

was so pervasive that up until July 2018 a Wikipedia entry for "l'appropriation culturelle" defined the term as "American" and "Canadian," and not a French value. Recently the page has been updated, but still maintains that appropriation is more of an "object of debate" in Québec than in France. Exemplary of such attitudes are recent controversies surrounding Robert Lepage's *Kanata* and *SLĀV*,[26] the former about seventeenth-century French settlers' encounters of Indigenous Peoples in Canada, and the latter about Black slavery in North America. *Kanata* was shut down in Québec due to protests and an open letter by Indigenous leaders about the lack of Indigenous consultation or people in the production. The play went on to tour France in December 2018, however, and Lepage has argued that, under protections of artistic freedoms, the play should speak for itself as to whether it is appropriative.

TEESRI DUNIYA, COUNTERNARRATIVES AND NARRATIVES THAT COUNT

Teesri Duniya Theatre believes that true diversity and equity equalizes various cultural strands and communities while building a more congenial and less hierarchical society. While the Québécois are invested in language, identity, and culture preservation due to their historical legacies, the implicit societal quandary is an absence of space within their nationalistic project for hybridized identities that are part of an increasingly globalized world where racialized, marginalized, and immigrant identities manifest in dynamic

---

26   On *Kanata*, see Maga. The production of *SLĀV* in Montréal brought cultural appropriation to the forefront again and preceded the mounting of *Kanata* by mere weeks, with most Francophones failing to comprehend why a play about Black slavery that does not feature Black actors, or did not adequately consult with Black communities and scholars, and which uses Black spirituals as the soundtrack, but sung by white people, is a problem. See Brunet, which is emblematic of a kind of French Canadian journalistic neutrality, in that it presents both supporting arguments for producing such a play and opposing viewpoints citing cultural appropriation. One of the Black artists, Aly (Webster) Ndiaye, who was "consulted" before the production of the play has spoken out against it, and people of colour and white allies have been protesting the play. One Black protester was slapped in the face by a white theatregoer, but the police did not intervene (Dunlevy).

pluralities. Multiculturalism has become the alternate Canadian premise endorsing cultural fluidity and supporting the growth of a heterogeneous democratic society with an international repositioning. And we say this, even while we note that one of the implicit failures/biases of multiculturalism is that it, unlike interculturalism, does not acknowledge its establishment based on a dominant culture, which, in the case of English Canada, is white, Christian/ secular Christian supremacy. And while the tensions of federal and provincial gestalts have shaped the emerging works of Teesri Duniya Theatre and many other culturally diverse companies, we demonstrate that racialized dual or hybrid identities represented in these works contribute a possible vision, offering inclusive, invaluable social capital that promotes both diversity and social cohesion among Canadian citizens.

Teesri Duniya's plays, as well as its unique publication *alt.theatre* (more on this later), highlight the important roles of theatre in challenging cultural stratification and political, social, and economic oppression. Teesri contests the bicultural hierarchy of Canadian identity politics, and brings the marginalized—the invisible—from the margins to the centre.[27] As we will explain, there has been a kind of push-and-pull effect for Teesri which is directly related to funding and the success of our plays. What we hope to show is that better funding leads to better commercial success and that the success of productions in spite of little funding is directly related to our vision of Canada (and art) as reflecting a critically engaged, dynamic, pluralistic, and inclusive society.

BEGINNINGS OF TEESRI DUNIYA THEATRE

Teesri Duniya Theatre, which means "Third World" theatre, was established in Montréal in 1981 by immigrant artists and activists from India, Rana Bose and Rahul Varma. The company's mandate is

---

27   Jerry Wasserman, in his introduction to the fifth edition of *Modern Canadian Plays, Vol. 2*, writes that *Counter Offence* and Teesri's work present "overlapping personal, social, and political agendas in a contemporary Montreal defined and divided by more than just English and French language" (135).

. . . dedicated to producing socially and politically relevant theatre that supports a multicultural vision of society, promoting
Interculturalism through works of theatre, and creating theatrical
styles based on the cultural experiences of visible minorities living in
Canada. Multicultural diversity, intercultural relations, relevance and
compelling stories are defining features of our work. The company is
committed to multiethnic casting and stories. ("Teesri")

Teesri's production trajectory expresses its two main objectives. First, we focus
on local stories about Canadians from diverse backgrounds, including newcomers, racialized minorities, Indigenous people, and those marginalized or
stereotyped by the mainstream (e.g., *Counter Offence, Land Where the Trees
Talk, No Man's Land*). Second, we emphasize international themes of human
rights, war, and women's rights figuring Canada as an international actor in
these agendas (e.g., *Bhopal, Truth and Treason,* and *State of Denial*).[28]
    Beginning with plays in Hindi and English, Teesri expanded its focus to
include many common immigrant realities, such as accusations of stealing
Canadian jobs, low-wage job realities, and violence at the hands of police. For
example, in *Equal Wages* we highlight the plight of immigrant women who
are blamed for stealing Canadian jobs but who end up in Canadian sweat-
shops. *Isolated Incident* is about the 1987 fatal shooting of an unarmed Black
youth by Montréal police. These local plays were written and developed within
six months by Rahul Varma and his co-authors, who received no salaries or
fees. Teesri spent roughly $1,000 to produce each play. The initial produc-
tions ran for one week, followed by multiple productions at different venues
across Montréal. *Isolated Incident* premiered at McGill's Morrice Hall, with a
showing at the Quebec Drama Festival at the Centaur Theatre. *Equal Wages*
first showed at the Atwater Library Auditorium, followed by runs at community centres and schools. Early plays were thus produced in record time and
showed moderate success in spite of financial barriers.

---

28   See appendix for a complete list of plays developed within the company.

Motivated by the lack of collective support for Indigenous art production and in order to bridge relationships across visible minority settlers and Indigenous Peoples, in 1990 Teesri produced *Land Where the Trees Talk*, written by Rahul Varma. Directed by Jack Langedijk, and in collaboration with the Native Friendship Centre and the Grand Council of the Crees, the play examines the James Bay hydro megaproject in northern Québec. The play was inspired by the Oka Crisis, in which Mohawk activists created a human barricade against Canadian armed forces for weeks, blockading the road to prevent confiscation of ancestral land for use as a commercial golf course. The play addresses environmental racism and the denial of social justice for Indigenous Peoples. Teesri's mandate is to showcase diverse actors; however, because the Oka crisis was in process, no Indigenous actors were available to participate in the play, since they were fully engaged in protests that unleashed overt racist attacks and a political crisis that reverberated across the country. Romeo Saganash, then vice-chairman of the Grand Council of the Crees of Québec and current NDP Member of Parliament, saw the play and was impressed with how effectively the human aspect of the political struggle was portrayed. In particular, a moment of the play that depicted the dangers of eating fish echoed his personal experience: "I remember when I first told my mother that she had to stop eating fish because of the mercury poisoning . . . and how she started crying" (qtd. in Donnelly, "Land"). Due to demand, the play was extended for a week. In the end, it had a zero net profit, because all the actors donated their salaries to the Cree protest.

The production of some of Teesri's plays has come with controversy, especially on the subject of Québec nationalism, which has manifested itself even in the availability of venues. In the '90s, Québec suffered from an absence of cultural spaces for minoritized groups, while there were (and are) a number of quality spaces for white anglo- and francophone arts. Teesri's *No Man's Land* (1992), about the exploitation of immigrant labour and the insecurities of Muslim refugees from India who suffer a double burden of dislocation when confronted with the social upheaval of Québec's possible separation from Canada, was to be performed at the Strathearn Intercultural Centre (now Montréal, arts interculturels (MAI)). However, the centre's board—a monocultural, almost entirely francophone group that included Parti Québécois cabinet minister Denise

Leblanc-Bantey—refused Teesri its venue to produce the play at the last minute, on the grounds that it failed to promote interculturalism (Donnelly, "Tempest"). Denied the venue, the play was produced in a garage, a kind of underground theatre, to enthusiastic reception by the public. Since 2000, after a change of board (and name) at the Strathearn, Teesri has been welcomed into the space, especially since our works have drawn ticket buyers to the centre.

PRODUCTIONS AND FUNDING SUCCESSES

Funding success also leads to commercial success, a trajectory demonstrated by Teesri's history. For its first fifteen years, Teesri received no support from arts-funding bodies. In fact, while Rahul Varma received his first grant from an arts council in 1992, the company, Teesri, received its first arts grant from the Canada Council only in 1995. This grant of $8,500 launched Teesri onto the national and global stage with the play *Counter Offence*, which opened to excellent reviews, and which was remounted the following year at the Monument-National in a co-production with Montréal's Black Theatre Workshop.[29] Reviewers emphasized the dynamism of the play and its roles in tackling political issues. On *Counter Offence*, the *Montreal Mirror* reported,

> You don't see theatre of this kind of merit, in French or in English, very often in this city or any other. It's gusty theatre that crawls under your skin and blisters the psyche ... [*Counter Offence*] may prove to be the most important play to have come down the chute all year ... Varma tackles all the hot button issues here, and together with his director, he does it with no little amount of imagination, intellectual brilliance and beauty. (Charlebois)

---

29 In fact, in 1996, Teesri Duniya received $15,000 from the Secretary of State, Multiculturalism and Status of Women of the Minister of Canadian Heritage, a federal body not explicitly dedicated to arts. That money was for actors in the company to gain professional certification and to be able to act professionally throughout Canada and abroad. Such a large sum of money was instrumental in providing the space and means for Teesri and its company to professionalize.

Fig. 1. Mark Walker as Officer Prugolt, Cas Anwar as Shapoor, and Stephen Orlov as
Galliard in *Counter Offence*, arts interculturels, Montréal, 1996.
Photo provided courtesy of Teesri Duniya Theatre.

Further reviews echo these sentiments. In *Place Public*, Stanley Asher wrote that
Counter Offence is a "play that makes a difference"; in *The Montreal Gazette*,
Pat Donnelly writes, "*Counter Offence* recalls [the] good old days of theatre . . .
when theatre sought nothing less than to change the world" ("*Counter Offence*").
The play was translated into French by Pierre Legris with a new title, *L'Affaire
Farhadi*, which was produced in 1999 and co-directed by Jack Langedijk and
Paul Lefebvre. *Counter Offence* subsequently played at Vancouver's Firehall Arts
Centre in 2000, and in Venice in Italian translation (*Il Caso Farhadi*), directed
by Bill Glassco. In 2014 it was included in the collection *Modern Canadian
Plays, Vol. 2*, edited by Jerry Wasserman for Talonbooks.

   Counter Offence depicts conjugal violence, where the struggle to end violence against women intersects with struggles to end racism. In the complexity
of these themes, the play demonstrates that for every social offence there is
a counter offence, for every cultural "truth" there is a competing or alternate narrative. The play's characters come from diverse cultural backgrounds

reflecting the heterogeneity of Québec and Canada. Shapoor, an Iranian man on a temporary visa, is accused of hitting his non-practising Muslim wife Shazia. When Sgt. Galliard, a white police officer, arrests him, Moolchand Misra, an Indo-Canadian activist, launches a "counter offensive" accusing Galliard of racism. On Shazia's side is Clarinda Keith, a Black female activist who takes the position of zero tolerance against wife battery, and who defends Galliard, in spite of the indefensible racial profiling and violence inflicted by white police officers against persons of colour. Other characters in the play are Shazia's South Asian parents and the police brotherhood's francophone boss. With the French-language production of *L'Affaire Farhadi*, Teesri earned the distinction of being the only culturally diverse company producing work in Québec's official language, despite a noticeable opposition to multicultural-ism within Québec. Montréal's *Gazette* declared, "*L'Affaire Farhadi* could be the vanguard of the revolution in French-language theatre" ("La nouvelle"). The play was well received and did well financially.

On the international front, the company's success with *Counter Offence* was followed by a global achieve-ment with *Bhopal* (2001). Varma received a writing grant from the Canada Council for this play, but not from the CALQ. However, CALQ awarded Teesri a pro-ject grant to produce the play in Montréal in 2001, alongside the Canada Council, Canadian Heritage, Conseil des arts de Montréal, and the City of Montréal. The play was a great success. *Bhopal* is about the 1984 Union Carbide pesticide factory explosion that affected tens of thousands of people in the Indian city of Bhopal. The play was remounted in 2003 with

Fig. 2. Michelin Dahlander as Shazia and Cas Anwar as Shapoor in *L'affaire Farhadi*, Theatre La Licorne, Montréal, 1999. Photo provided courtesy of Teesri Duniya Theatre.

Toronto's Cahoots Theatre, directed by Guillermo Verdecchia, then produced in 2005–06 in Montréal and Québec City in French translation by Théâtre Sortie de Secours and directed by Philippe Soldevila with translation funding by the Canada Council. The play was also translated into Hindi as *Zahreeli Hawa* (funded by the Canada Council) and toured six Indian cities in a production by acclaimed Indian director Habib Tanvir in 2003–04. The play was also translated into Punjabi as *Khamosh Chiragan di Daastan* by director Kewal Dhaliwal and produced by his company Manch Rangmanch in 2013. The French productions of *Bhopal* in Québec City and Montréal in 2005–06 were supported by both the CALQ and the Canada Council, and did well financially; however, subsequent to that Teesri did not receive funding from CALQ for many years.

Fig. 3. Aparna Sindoor as a dancer and Tova Roy as Madiha in *Bhopal*, Escpace Libre, Montréal, 2005. Photo provided courtesy of Teesri Duniya Theatre.

TEESRI'S MAGAZINE—*ALT.THEATRE*

Similar to its vision for theatrical production that presents minoritized people in dynamic pluralities, Teesri wanted to create space for emerging writing about marginalized theatre. Teesri thus founded a hybrid journal/magazine, *alt.theatre: cultural diversity and the stage*, filling the void that existed in the field of theatre research.[30] The publication focuses on productions by and for minoritized people in dialogue with the rest of the world, examining the intersection of politics, social activism, plurality, and the stage. *alt.theatre* was co-founded by Rahul Varma and Kapil Bawa in 1998 as a forum for discussion and analysis of non-mainstream theatre. *alt.theatre* gained international fame under former Editor-in-chief Edward (Ted) Little, with a culturally diverse board that included Denis Salter, and its readership continues to grow under Editor-in-chief Aaron Franks.

alt.theatre's mandate is not to showcase Teesri (even though we benefit from its growing readership), but rather to promote dialogue about non-mainstream theatre in general. The magazine publishes articles on new and alternative directions in the performing arts and dramaturgy; profiles of artists and companies; critical reviews of books, plays, and productions; creative work including excerpts of plays and photo essays; and comparative analyses of national and international approaches to cultural diversity and the arts. *alt.theatre* engages an average of forty contributors annually, its print run is five hundred copies, and its combined distribution (subscription and single sale) is about 75% of the print run. We are making efforts to gain traction in academic spheres by getting *alt.theatre* on JSTOR and other university search engines, efforts that we hope will be supported by university policies of inclusivity. The board of directors for both the magazine and the company are separate, as are all the funding streams. The readership outside Québec is higher than within, which is attributable to its largely English-language content and its focus on non-mainstream theatre.

PROMOTING DISCOURSE AND PUBLIC DIALOGUES

alt.theatre and Teesri have long nurtured and depended on their ties to local community. Certainly, we exist as community members ourselves, but we also value the voice and role of our spectators. Therefore, every Teesri production is supplemented by a panel discussion, consisting of panellists from

---

30   The magazine's online home is alttheatre.ca/.

a diverse array of classes, races, genders, abilities, etc., whose ideas reflect different cultural and ideological viewpoints. These dialogues following the plays help to redefine the role of audiences, shifting them from passive to active. Teesri's panel discussions are not question and answer, not top-down, but are instead constructed to generate dialogue, encourage sharing of differing points of views, and broadening the discussion to invite unspoken viewpoints and related issues.

We believe that our direct engagement with diverse communities and divergent voices has contributed to the success of plays that did not receive initial funding or backing. Our discussions have a kind of ripple effect, where individuals through word of mouth draw audience members to our productions. Panel discussions are free and are not linked to ticket costs; therefore, people can come to the panels without coming to the play. We have also observed higher ticket sales on the nights subsequent to panel discussions. We withhold any modesty in suggesting that the current trend of post-play panel discussions in Montréal stems from a practice originated by Teesri.

FIREWORKS PLAY DEVELOPMENT

To remedy some of the systemic issues related to funding non-traditional theatre and theatre that does not conform to dominant ideologies or national agendae, Teesri has a dramaturgical incubation program called Fireworks to develop new plays concerned with cultural diversity authored by diverse writers. The program emphasizes a multi- and intercultural aesthetic and supports works by playwrights from a range of cultural backgrounds. For Teesri, multiculturalism and interculturalism are inseparable and imbricated in marginalized artists' experiences. We create the space for their stories to flourish and for artists to receive creative training and mentorship from other artists who have had similar experiences. We recruit playwrights through open calls, personal invitations, and sponsored internships. Each year we select around five playwrights who are coached by Teesri's dramaturge over a period of six months. All of the selected playwrights come with existing commissions through arts councils or foundations, ranging from $3,000 to $10,000. The playwrights meet twice a month as a group to share, receive coaching, feedback, and further exercises for working on their plays. They are encouraged to write a complete draft of their play in these six months. Those who are at higher stages of readiness workshop with actors and present their plays to the public as table reads after a further six months. Fireworks takes a two-pronged approach to authorship, asking playwrights to first take a measured distance from their cultures of ancestry and, second, to resist homogenization by the dominant culture. Since Teesri is a production company and not a development one, it does not qualify for development funds for plays and playwrights. However, we continue to make incubation a part of our actions. Playwrights are not paid during the training period but are offered unionized fees for their public table reads. Teesri allocates approximately $10,000 to this program each year. To date, Fireworks has developed and showcased the work of over twenty playwrights, all from diverse backgrounds. Some of the authors who have come through Fireworks include Silvija Jestrovic (*Noah's Ark 747*), Jody Essery (*A Leaf in the Whirlwind*), James Forsythe (*To Stand Again*), Gabe Maharajan (*Eve in Rio*), and Stephen Orlov (*Birthmark*).

CONCLUSION

The challenge for a country diverse in people, cultures, languages, and histories is to build a nation of shared values. To achieve this goal, Teesri tells the stories of peoples, cultures, communities, languages, forms, and audiences eclipsed by dominant national theatres. Teesri has explored the complexities of social hybridity, multiculturalism, and diversity while also recognizing that Indigenous people and minorities have been integral to the fabric of Canada. We have seen how policies that seek to be more inclusive have a direct impact on success, as funding success has led to commercial success. As a company with local, national, and international content, Teesri has maintained its pride of place as one of the first truly diverse theatre production companies in Canada, and hopes to continue its work for years to come.

APPENDIX—PLAYS WRITTEN AND DEVELOPED
BY TEESRI DUNIYA THEATRE

Dawazey Khol Dou by Azra Naqvi (1981)

Bojha by Rahul Varma (1981)

Bhanumati Ka Pitara by Rahul Varma (1983)

Nazme-e-Faiz by Azra Naqvi (1983)

On the Double by Rana Bose (1986)

Job Stealer by Rahul Varma, Ian Lloyd George, and Helen Vlachos (1987)

Isolated Incident by Rahul Varma and Stephen Orlov (1988)

Equal Wages by Rahul Varma and Helen Vlachos (1989)

Land Where the Trees Talk by Rahul Varma (1990)

No Man's Land by Rahul Varma and Ken McDonough (1992)

Trading Injuries by Rahul Varma (1993 radio production)

Counter Offence by Rahul Varma (1996)

L'Affaire Farhadi, French translation of *Counter Offence* by Pierre Legris (1999)

Il Caso Farhadi, Italian translation of *Counter Offence* by Giulio Mara (2000)

Bhopal by Rahul Varma (2001)

Zahreeli Hawa, Hindi translation of *Bhopal* by Habib Tanvir (2004)

Bhopal, French translation of *Bhopal* by Paul Lefebvre (2005)

Khamosh Chiragan di Daastan, Punjabi translation of *Bhopal* by Kewal Dhaliwal (2013)

Truth and Treason by Rahul Varma (2009)

Dhokha, Hindi translation of *Truth and Treason* by Uma Jhunjhunwala (2016)

Soldier Up by James Forsythe (2010)

State of Denial by Rahul Varma (2012)

Standing Again by James Forsythe (2018)

STAGING THE ORDINARY / CONSTRUCTING HISTORY IN OLIVIER KEMEID'S THEATRE OF MEMORY, HISTORY, AND FORGETTING[1]

YANA MEERZON

In his study *Memory, History, Forgetting*, Paul Ricoeur proposes to rethink the methodologies of understanding historical condition by focusing on "history of life" as it is experienced by an ordinary person, someone who acts as "the measure of utility for life" (289). As a written account of the events and actions that took place in the past, history is the product of a narrative effort of a historian, whereas the act of writing—characterized by playfulness and invention—is a form of remembering and forgetting. The intermediate position of the act of writing turns a historian—the chronicler of the past, the writer of the living memory—into a philosopher, the maker of a performative narrative in which "the opposition between living memory and dead deposit becomes secondary" (Ricoeur 144). In this process of writing, a historical account is transformed into the narrative of philosophy or the act of performative recontextualization, in which "history remains a hindrance to memory" (145). To Ricoeur, the act of philosophical elevation remains a problem, since we, the readers, do not know whether such an account of history or memory acts as its remedy, poison, or both at once. Opened to an anonymous reading subject, Ricoeur argues, "[A] history book [. . .] has cut its ties to its speaker" (143). "The semantic autonomy of the text" emerges

---

1   All translations from French to English are mine, unless indicated otherwise.

as a "situation of distress" that can be helped only through "the interminable work of contextualization and recontextualization that makes up reading," i.e., the act of remembering and forgetting (143).

Ricoeur's philosophical inquiry, I propose, is reflected in the dramaturgical work of Olivier Kemeid, a Québécois writer, director, and public speaker. Kemeid's trilogy of exile—*L'Énéide* (2008); *Moi, dans les ruines rouges du siècle* (2012); and *Furieux et désespérés* (2014)—presents an example of theatre writing oscillating between the act of historiography and the act of philosophy. Reflecting upon the themes of history, memory, migration, and new nationalisms, Kemeid contextualizes his thoughts in similar terms to Ricoeur's: he recognizes the subjectivity of the narrating agent formed as the experiential act of history and as the act of interpretative utterance, the speech act of a philosophical inquiry. Explaining how his trilogy came to life, Kemeid says, "Passing through Virgil [in *L'Énéide*] via Sasha Samar [in *Moi, dans les ruines rouges du siècle*], [. . .] I arrived to this new play [*Furieux et désespérés*], in which I talk about myself, my memories, my photographs. This itinerary is without doubt the path of exile: a long detour on the road to the meeting with my own self, because exile is the act of return to oneself" (qtd. in Pepin, "Olivier Kemeid"). In his work, I contend, Kemeid constructs a dramatic narrative of history as interpretation, which draws upon the processes of making history and its representation, Ricoeur's "second-order reflection" (333). The trilogy engages with Kemeid's personal commitment to history and presents the condition of migration in three temporal dimensions: 1) the act of flight or making history, 2) the act of memory and constructing of narrative, and 3) the act of return or the gesture of forgetting and forgiving.

Kemeid's project is also unmistakably political. The trilogy reflects the new political climate in Québec, in which individuals and institutions are forced to negotiate the province's traditional cultural and linguistic values under the pressure of the growing economic and political presence of new immigrants. Kemeid selects events from the past in order to comment upon the political issues of the present, asking difficult questions about the new discourses of nationalism arising in Québec and worldwide, now less focused on the issues of language acquisition and identity-building and more upon those of cultural heritage, religious practices, and humanistic values. Kemeid aspires to speak on behalf of a new generation of Québec writers, engaged with the ethical questions of globalization, writing "their plays in dialogue with the state of today's world" (Marie-Christine Lesage, qtd. in De la Chenelière and Lefebvre 51). These plays often "take place elsewhere, deal with war, difficulties of politics" and "offer reflection on human destruction"; they feature a new tragic character "unable to function in a system, where intense productivity and profit are used in lieu of moral criteria"; and they construct a fictional world, where "economics invaded everything, so the relationships between human beings are mainly based on bargaining" (51).

To convey his concerns, Kemeid chooses Brechtian epic theatre, whose job "is not so much to develop actions as to represent conditions" (Benjamin, *Understanding Brecht* 4): a gesture approximating in its intentions the work of a philosopher. Kemeid's dramaturgy, similarly to Brecht's, presents the mundane reality of today's world shown through the gaze of a stranger (an asylum seeker, an immigrant storyteller), emphasizing the notion that "the more far reaching the devastations of our social order (the more these devastations undermine ourselves and our capacity to remain aware of them), the more marked must be the distance between the stranger and the events portrayed" (Benjamin, *Understanding Brecht* 5). This technique allows Kemeid to juxtapose and layer up different temporal frames of one story, in which the action acquires a sense of temporal incongruence; it grows remote both to the events in the fictional past and to those unfolding in the present. Such a technique permits Kemeid to locate the characters' past and present actions within the so-called "mythological" time of an epic or philosophical narrative, characterized by the act of interpretation, the process of making a hypothesis, and the gesture of contemplation. As Ricoeur explains, the act of contemplation reveals the subjectivity of a historian: seen as "a complex of language acts—of utterances—[it is] incorporated in the objectifying statements of historical discourse" (337). The act of interpretation takes a form of reflection, which "progresses from utterance as an act of language to the utterer as the who of the acts of interpretation. It is this operating complex that can constitute the subjective side correlative to the objective side of historical knowledge" (337).

The art of a historian resembles the art of an interpreter who transposes the chosen source material into a new set of cultural, artistic, and personal circumstances, in which a new speech act of the writer/adaptor takes place. Kemeid's exilic trilogy is an example of this process: *L'Énéide* is a revisioning of Virgil's epic that acts as homage to the author's family and his grandfather's escape from Egypt (Kemeid and Meerzon 95). It depicts Virgil's Aeneas as a contemplating anti-hero, forced by the external conditions of war and exile into the role of a tragic protagonist. Here the logic of history is thought through in phenomenological terms: as the characters' lived experience of the flight enforced upon them and of its consequences, and as an act of constructing subjectivity—the process of remodelling one's consciousness, self, and memory in historical terms (Ricoeur 105). Kemeid's character speaks of his destiny in the present continuous of his enforced flight. Based on Sasha Samar's personal story, *Moi, dans les ruines rouges du siècle* turns Kemeid's Aeneas into a Soviet Ukrainian boy, Sasha, who spends his youth searching for his biological mother. This play also focuses on the questions of constructing subjectivity, now posed within what Ricoeur calls a historical condition of one nation (329–32). Here the temporal dimensions of narrative are shifted: the story of the young Sasha Samar takes place in the past, whereas the act of its narrating/interpreting takes place in the present, the narrative time of storytelling. This multilevelled dramatic temporality finds its reflection in the act of autobiographical performance, with Sasha Samar playing his younger self and his narrating self at the same time. In this performative gesture, the act of constructing historical utterance turns into Ricoeur's act of healing or the moment of truth (334). Finally, *Furieux et désespérés* presents Kemeid's semi-autobiographical account of his first visit to Egypt in 2008. Kemeid positions the action of the play within the clearly recognizable historical framework of the 2011 Arab Spring, but elevates the theme of "impossibility of return," the issue that marks "the history and the essence of the drama of exile" (Pepin, "Olivier Kemeid"), to the mythological dimensions of reconciliation, or the act of forgiving as envisaged by Ricoeur (284–85).

At the same time, as Kemeid tells us, it is not the atrocities of history but the intimate stories of ordinary people, "the family tragedy unfolding on the background of this History, the odyssey of a lonely man lost in the ruins of his home country," that make up his theatre (*Dossier*). Kemeid's writing, much like Ricoeur's act of philosophy, originates between the act of historiography and the act of performance. Kemeid never experienced the condition of exile himself and speaks about it in historical and metaphorical terms, allying himself with many twentieth-century authors, from Albert Camus to Jean-Paul Sartre, to whom exile was a literary tradition: "Metaphorically, I consider any artist as an exile. [. . .] The role of the artist/intellectual is to leave the society, in order to make a better return, or return as other. This is the story of Ulysses" (Kemeid, qtd. in Pepin, "Olivier Kemeid"). At the same time, Kemeid also speaks from his own experience of cultural and linguistic simultaneities: to him, the story of Canada and of Québec "has to do with the Métis people and how they are accepted in Canada" (Kemeid and Meerzon 98). "My father is Egyptian and my mother is 'une Québécoise de souche,'" he explains; while "I myself am the product of this mix" (Kemeid and Meerzon 98). Hence, "as children of immigrants, we must think about this story. It is not just about our parents; it is more about us, the children, who will be building the country together" (Kemeid and Meerzon 98). This clear and in-depth recognition of this internal divide that makes the post-exilic subject defines Kemeid's artistic position; it also dictates his estranged and differed look at monumental history, as it emerges in Kemeid's theatre both as the product of the narrative of a historian and that of a philosopher. The three plays that make up his trilogy of exile approximate the time of fiction to the mythological, the historical, and the personal time of migration as experienced by a post-exilic subject, and thus they exemplify how the act of history, memory, and forgiving can be staged.

ON BANISHMENT, ESCAPE, AND MAKING NEW HISTORY

The paradigm of exile—both in its proverbial forms of banishment, enforced escape, and seeking a new home and in its newer incarnations as mass migration—can serve as the framework to discuss the logic of subjectivity constructed by history. Ricoeur ascribes the birth of a modern subject to the end of the eighteenth century, suggesting that the phrase "someone makes history" was unthinkable before the French Revolution (297). He defines the "makeability of history" as the act of "making history" by one individual and the act of "making histories" by many. This vision is unilateral because it is formed by "the very concept of history as a collective singular. This is the master category, the condition under which the time of history can be thought" (298). Often, in the theatre of exile, an exilic subject is defined similarly to Ricoeur's views, at the intersection of two axes: the axis of history and the axis of phenomenology. Olivier Kemeid constructs his exilic trilogy along these two axes as well: they are the axis of personal flight and the axis of *a collective singular* of history, Ricoeur's umbrella term, "under which the collection of particular histories is placed" (299). A *collective singular* "marks the bridging of the greatest gap imaginable between unitary history and the unlimited multiplicity of individual memories [as well as] the plurality of collective memories" (299). To Ricoeur, in other words, history is always an experiential category. A form of enactment, "it links together the past that has occurred, the anticipated future, and the present as it is being lived and acted." It takes on an omnitemporal dimension and anthropological meaning, and it appears as "the world history of peoples" (Ricoeur 300).

In his retelling of Virgil's myth, Kemeid reveals this exact reading of history. In Virgil's tale, constructed under the influence of Homer's *Iliad* and *Odyssey*, Aeneas, the protagonist, is forced to flee the ruins of his native city, Troy. The city has been destroyed by the war and its surviving citizens are forced to seek home in new lands. The historical function of Virgil's *Aeneid* is difficult to overestimate: often seen as a propaganda piece, this text became the defining narrative of the Roman Empire, in which the vision of a prosperous economic, cultural, political, and military regime was put forward. The poem recognized the primacy of the organized rule, the state's authority over its people, as the only social order that could provide a nourishing environment for its citizens and their happiness. It also became Virgil's philosophical, political, and artistic statement. Although the world of this poem was driven by cosmic *fatum und ratio*, it could not run without the "unexplainable suffering and sacrifice" of ordinary people, and hence it got Virgil caught within the dual dramatic causality, between "a public voice that celebrates in Rome the finest human achievement of nature's processes, and a private voice that regrets the cost of this in human lives" (M. Lee 159).

Kemeid's adaptation is driven by similar objectives. The play is not simply a transposition of Virgil's original into the new historical context, it is "a contemporary re-writing marked by the author's personal history" (Olivier 31). Here, Aeneas is thrown into Ricoeur's *collective singular* of history by chance, against his will. Similarly to Virgil's character, Kemeid's Aeneas is also an instrument of fate: an ordinary man put into the extraordinary circumstances of war and exile, looking for motivation to act. Neither the death of his wife and father, nor the rejection of his people by the immigration authorities, nor a trip to the underworld (represented by the labyrinth of the city's sewers) forces Aeneas into the role of a leader. In this gesture of Aeneas's inaction, Kemeid epitomizes both the Brechtian tragic character and the trauma of migration, when the present continuous of the flight takes over one's past and future:

AENEAS

The days go by and I stay glued here waiting by the door hoping
Achates will return
But he doesn't
The days go by and I disappear
I lose myself more and more in the flow of time
The man who once survived every storm
Has never been closer to drowning
[...]
For once in my life
I'm trying to live entirely in the present
[...]
I battle with images of the past every single day of my life
My house burning
My father drowning in the sea
Achates insulting me and running away from me

And images of you
the wife I couldn't bury
[. . .]
My life was taken away from me (61–62)

Kemeid's play (and specifically this dialogue) invites us to rethink the modern subject at the intersection of exile and history, similarly to Ricoeur's definition of the logic of modern subjectivity as the act of "inwardness," found in the phenomenological triad of identity, consciousness, and self (103). As defined by John Locke, identity is formed by the work of the mind as the act of comparison and rationalization: "identity is opposed to diversity, difference," it is a relational category, and "it equals sameness with self" (Ricoeur 104). Locke further differentiates between the identity of a man, as a living subject, and one's personal identity, as a break between "man and self." Echoing René Descartes, he defines consciousness as man's capacity for thinking and contemplation: the postulate that leads Ricoeur to introduce memory as part of this forming triad. Personal identity, he explains, is formed as temporal and corporeal consciousness, the embodied representation of self as memory (105). The question becomes, if Kemeid chooses Aeneas as his modern hero, who seems to be suspended in his act of inaction between history and time, between self and memory, what lesson does this play teach us about the state of today's world, being continuously reshaped by the tension between migration and nationalism?

In its style, Kemeid's theatre can be read through Walter Benjamin's views of storytelling as positioned between the act of historiography and the act of philosophy, and so is itself "an artisan form of communication. [. . .] It does not aim to convey the pure essence of the thing, like information or a report. It sinks the thing into the life of the storyteller, in order to bring it out of him again" ("The Storyteller" 91). To Benjamin, storytelling is defined by time as its structural variant. In Brecht's epic theatre, time takes on a leading function. Much like the novel, Brechtian drama recognizes "the whole inner action [. . .] [as] nothing else but a struggle against the power of time," so in his theatre we see how "the genuinely epic experiences of time: hope and memory" are created. As in the novel, so too in Brechtian plays "a creative memory [...] transfixes the object and transforms it" (György Lukács qtd. in Benjamin, "The Storyteller" 99). In the centre is a new tragic hero, contemplating his/her historical and ethical position. The hero is a thinking or wise man, "an empty stage on which the contradictions of our society are acted out" (Benjamin, *Understanding Brecht* 17–18).

Kemeid resolves this Brechtian dilemma of a wise sage through the Ghost of Creusa, who refuses to accept Aeneas's lamentation and his state of inaction. Self-pity is the state that no exilic subject can afford, because, as Creusa says:

> You will carry your past in you forever
> But you also have an enormous duty to your future
> Memories
> And hope
> You're nothing more than a hyphen
> A little hyphen
> Between the two
> You have to accept that
> [...]
> Don't try to get [your old life] back
> Don't try to go back to what you were before (61–62)

Aeneas's future is associated with his son's chance for happiness:

> CREUSA
> Your old life is lying beside me in my grave
> You have to give yourself a new one
> You have a chance to
> And you have our son (62)

This chance will eventually drive Aeneas out of his emotional stupor so that he can take his people to new shores, and attempt building a model city. To understand what sort of new nation he will build, Aeneas travels to the underworld, the place of the "happy dead" (78). Among those who "used their intelligence to make life better" and those who employed "their art in order to advance civilization," Kemeid places those who "have never committed a single crime / But despite that they are weighed down by sorrow / They are exiles / In search of a new land" (62, 79).

The picture Anchises (Aeneas's father), and after him Kemeid, draws of these peoples is unmistakably modern. It includes

Jews from Russia looking for their New Odessa
Algerians
Bengalis walking toward India
Cypriots
Vietnamese fleeing Hanoi and Saigon
Khmers
Hazaras from Afghanistan
Guatemalans
Indians
Miskits from Nicaragua
Native people of Mozambique
Namibians fleeing Lubango
Kurds from Iraq
Somalis trying to make it to Ethiopia and Ethiopians fleeing their
own country
Rohingyas from Burma in the marshes of Bangladesh
Liberians in Sierra Leone
Tutsis and Hutus their blood mixed
Tadjiks Ossetians Kosovars
People from Mali drowned in the Strait of Gibraltar
Mexicans shot down in Tijuana
The mutilated of Angola
Sudanese fleeing to Kenya
Congolese from Goma
Palestinians from Gaza

Iraqis Azeris Colombians Sri Lankans Georgians Haitians Dominicans Togolese Central Africans Chinese Indonisians Syrians (79–80)

Aeneas and his people complete this long list of the displaced and humiliated. His mission, as Anchises articulates it, is to "carry the rich seeds of your civilizations," "to found nations / Or destroy them" (80). He outlines the strategies to bring Aeneas's mission to life in the following lines:

Aeneas my son
Your search will be over soon
You will find the land you're looking for when you've laid down your
hatred at the foot of a barbed wire fence
Don't forget to establish rules for peace
Respect those who have been repressed
Disarm the conquerors
Marry a woman from the new country
A woman who has settled the land before you
A woman you will love and cherish
Mix your blood with hers
Don't wait for war to do it for you (80)

On one hand, in this monologue one can recognize the strategy of adaptation, something that many exilic subjects resort to in the new land. On the other, we can also see Kemeid's personal political program for today's Québec and its position on immigration: a program in which the foundations of the nation-state are to be reconsidered along the lines of linguistic tolerance and religious coexistence. This idealistic picture, however, is never brought to life. On the route to this utopian New World—"a truly universal empire / The empire of the displaced the defeated the fugitive the runaway the immigrant / The diaspora of wanderers and exiles / The empire of those who have something broken inside them / The largest empire in the world" (92)—Aeneas loses friends, loved ones, and political supporters. He does cross the "barb-wire fence," but he carries blood on his hands. He wishes peace, because together with other displaced people he has "left all [his] hatred at the foot of a barbed wire fence":

> All I ask for is peace
> That's what all of us ask for
> We've seen enough death
> We've crossed enough lands emptied by exile
> We don't want to cover these plains with our bodies (94)

The Old Farmer (perhaps a character from Voltaire's *Candide*, a type of philosopher who believes in the healing power of physical labour) welcomes Aeneas in this new world, Aeneas's new land and new home (94) and also asks how many people he brings along:

> Probably millions [Aeneas responds]
> But today there's only me Aeneas
> My son
> And a woman (94)

Kemeid leaves the ending open, as he implies that the New Rome—the centre of a new twenty-first-century empire based on the principles of cosmopolitanism and tolerance—is yet to be built. The ending also suggests these questions: Is it truly possible that the cosmopolitan condition of migration in today's globalized world can become the basis for these new democratic states? Or will the new city of exiles and outcasts turn into the mechanism of making new dictatorships? Does Kemeid propose to rethink our modern subject in terms of our own views of history? Or does he write his play as a warning sign, a paradox, in which the subject of migration might turn into the subject of totalitarianism?

ON HISTORY, MEMORY, AND ITS THEATRICAL REPRESENTATION

Freddie Rokem once wrote that a theatrical performance of history allows the testimony of an artist-survivor to be heard. Building on Benjamin's statement that storytelling is a type of performance and a form of time travelling, Rokem recognizes theatre performers as *hyper-historians* (*Performing History* 202–06). They enact the palimpsest of history on stage, when acting itself becomes the embodiment of history: a transposition of the historical past on stage, and also the story of the production process. The theatrical energy of performed history provides the space where the real and the metaphorical meet (202). The spectators "create the meanings of a performance, by activating different psychological and social energies" (192). Through such performance, in other words, historical consciousness is shaped and nurtured.

Kemeid's *Moi, dans les ruines rouges du siècle* brings Rokem's theory of the actor hyper-historian into practice. It enacts the biographical tale of Sasha Samar, his journey into the West, and his search for his biological mother, by casting Samar as the protagonist and the major player of this theatrical re-enatcment.

A Québécois actor of Ukrainian origin, Samar obtained his acting degree at the Kiev National University of Theater, Cinema and Television in 1993. A recipient of the National Academy of Arts of Ukraine prize, he worked for theatre and television in Ukraine until he landed in Montréal in 1996. *Moi, dans les ruines rouges du siècle* revolves around Samar's autobiographical character and his life journey: it "encompasses his story, his struggle, his hopes; truly a trip out of the ordinary" that is reflected through the monumental historical fiasco that was the collapse of the Soviet Union, its economy, political power, and culture ("Sasha Samar"). The play depicts its protagonist as a subject of historical memory and discourse. Inspired by Samar's recollections of his childhood, Kemeid contextualizes for his Québécois audiences what Ricoeur calls an exemplary history of a nation (290). Using signifiers of history or of Ricoeur's calendar time (393–95) that are familiar to his spectators—including the Canada/Russia Summit Series of 1973, the 1986 Chernobyl catastrophe, the 1980s war in Afghanistan, and perestroika—Kemeid drives the story of the Ukrainian boy home. At the same time, he creates the venue for Ricoeur's critical history, which constitutes the moment of judgment or "deserved forgetting" to take place (290).

Following Friedrich Nietzsche, Ricoeur recognizes three types of history: monumental or exemplary history, which is defined by "the usefulness of models to 'emulate and improve'"; antiquarian history, which serves to conserve and venerate customs and traditions "useful to life," history as an act of conservation not creation; and critical history, which constitutes the moment of judgment or "deserved forgetting," when "the danger of life coincides with its usefulness" (290). Merging these three historical modes, Kemeid demonstrates that in rewriting, restaging, and re-enacting the past, theatre not only makes it *visible* in the present, but it also *makes* the past in the present, opening it up for negotiation. The dramatic question Kemeid asks is similar to that of Ricoeur. He interprets Samar's personal journey as an example of constructing one's subjectivity as a historical condition and an act of memory, characterized by two ideological settings: as "a situation in which each person is [. . .] implicated [or] 'enclosed'" and as the phenomenon of "conditionality," "a condition of possibility," critical hermeneutics (Ricoeur 284). This duality of a historical subject can also be seen as a form of action, with each individual implicated in making the monumental history of the state and in creating plural histories of people. In this way, the play endorses Ricoeur's view of a historical condition, when certain historical knowledge is enacted in the present moment of the life of an individual, and when the historical truth is confirmed through the act of its enactment.

Telling Samar's story theatrically, however, presented a number of ethical difficulties both for the performer and for the writer, including the question of whether Samar's parents would have consented to appear on stage, in the fictionalized spotlight, exposed to the judgment of people from a different culture and forced to defend their position (Lehoux). In this ethical dilemma, one can find a reflection of the problem of representation as experienced by a historian: when a historical narrative finds its own "literary expression," when "the historian's discourse declares its ambition, its claim to represent the past *in truth*" (Ricoeur 228). In theatre, this ambition of "the historiographical operation, the operation of representing" (228), acquires a second degree of estrangement or "fictionality" when the power of poetic expression, the form as such, becomes the guarantor of the story's authenticity. The play insists on the unique authenticity of a theatrical representation, the authenticity originating not in a form of historical truth (the truth of the document) but in the form of the emotional change of a receiver.

In documentary and (auto)biographical performances, often it is the power of dramaturgical editing and directorial intervention that takes over the truth of the document, so that Aristotelian poetic licence allows an artist to re-enforce the feelings of compassion in his/her audiences. As Jean-Philippe Lehoux, the dramaturge for *Moi, dans les ruines rouges du siècle*, recollects, after some period of doubting the ethical dimensions of the project, Sasha Samar felt relief. "The quality of [Kemeid's] text seemed to reassure him. [. . .] Even if the story remained strictly biographical, it acquired a level of theatricality filtered through the work of Kemeid, who was forced to forgo many episodes of Sasha's life for Samar to keep the dramatic course of its history" (Lehoux). In this gesture, I argue, Kemeid's theatrical writing approximates the writing of a historian and turns into the work of philosophy, as understood by Ricoeur, who claims that in the act of representation, in his/her narrative effort, a historian turns into the agent of historical events, not just their chronicler (228–29). An act of interpretation turns the historian, a chronicler of the past, into an agent of the present, a historical subject him/herself actively involved in making the new history. Under the historian's creative gaze, the past can acquire a new dramatic meaning that the reader of history, a new agent of the new historical present, will be able to project onto his/her own historical condition and perhaps take on the necessary action to change it.

In *Moi, dans les ruines rouges du siècle* the character "Sasha Samar" is seen both as the subject of biographical narrative and as a new cosmopolitan of the Western world, similar in its historical functions to Kemeid's other protagonist, Aeneas. Both of them contribute to the remodelling of today's world. The difference, however, lies in the act of autobiographical performance itself: Samar's personal experience of life under totalitarianism, his accent and looks, guarantee the authenticity of Ricoeur's "historie de vie." Watching Kemeid's play, the audience becomes witness to multiple histories: those of the historical past and those of the actor enacting it. The character's suffering on stage provides us with the emotional space for "identification and involvement as well as distance," and in this ontological collision of energies, theatre turns into a "dialectical antidote to the destructive energies of history and its painful failures" (Rokem, *Performing History* 204). The actor's performance of personal biography, a document of personal history, becomes testimony to the historical events depicted on stage and to this actor/creator's own performative experience of enacting it. The questions this play raises are: What new history does Kemeid construct in staging the story of the Soviet Ukrainian boy searching for his mother for the Québécois audiences? What image of a new Québec does this play aspire to project? And how is this image similar or different to the official discourse of the province's self-affirmation, the way it wants to present itself for its own citizens and others? The response Kemeid provides is somewhat similar to one he offered when adapting Virgil's tale: Samar's story is important and educational because it presents the story of an ordinary man unfolding in the background of the ruins of monumental history. Written by a Québécois writer for Québécois audiences, it aims to engage them to think together about political and social prospects of their own country as a modern nation facing the challenges of globalization and immigration. It asks them to consider these questions, not at the level of civic institutions and their operating systems, but at the level of interpersonal relationships, as the destiny of a nation made of everyday people: the ordinary beings.

Kemeid's belief in the power of theatre to construct the narrative of the Other without any "cheap exoticism" or objectification deserves a special mention. Although it may sound somewhat naive, it reveals Kemeid's political position as a new cosmopolitan. It also explains the author's continuous desire to discuss monumental history as a compilation of individual narratives. Samar's story was intended to make Kemeid's audiences confront an underinvestigated period of world history and to remind them that history always has two sides. It aimed to challenge what North American people think about their Cold War enemy, the Soviet Union, as behind the Iron Curtain "there was also Vietnam and May 1968" (Kemeid, qtd. in Pepin, "Sasha Samar"). Kemeid expressed similar ideas in his program for the renewal of Québécois national theatre and dramaturgy. In his 2008 article, "Le théâtre contre la culture," he insisted that the artist's political agenda must be the only driving force of making theatre. A true Québécois artist must "not only take the role of the public platform, the mouth speaker for Québec culture, but to be its first critic, its first offender. The theatre must occupy such a position so it will not be afraid to assume the role of disruptive political force" (Kemeid, "Le théâtre" 84). Rethinking global historical processes, both in terms of peoples' personal biographies and in terms of collective mythology and historiography, constitutes a significant part of Kemeid's artistic program.

The act of performance is at the heart of such political and historical representation. It signifies the process of negotiating historical and present time: the durational time of theatrical presentation and its reception, and the simultaneity of past and present that characterizes performing history on stage. In Kemeid's play, Samar's autobiographical body appears in the multitude of meaning-forming functions: as a container of personal and national histories, a vehicle of the artist's personal testimony, a character in this autobiographical performance, and a witness to the trauma of the Other. The materiality of the exilic actor's body and behaviour often takes different forms than the actor and his/her director intended. It often functions as the distancing tool: Samar's stage presence—his "difference from within"—raises the question of how testimony compels ethical action, attentiveness, or participation on the part of his spectator, the witness of history being made and performed. The act of performance reveals the distance between what happened in the past and its later representations as a matter of negotiation. These negotiations are complex because our knowledge of the past is necessarily fragmentary, partial, and hence incomplete; so theatre performance has the power not merely to re-speak the past but to mark a historical moment in its very process of becoming. It can reinforce and evoke how the continuity of history is formed in the communal experience of nations and in the personal histories of individuals. In this performative gesture, the work of a historian turns into the work of a philosopher: from the chronicler of Québec's history, the history of new nationalisms, Kemeid turns into its contemplator.

ON THE IMPOSSIBILITY OF RETURN OR FORGETTING AND FORGIVING AS HISTORICAL IMPERATIVES

Furieux et désespérés (the third part of Kemeid's trilogy) engages with the question of returns. It dramatizes the processes of *historical forgetting* as "the problematic of memory and faithfulness to the past" and *forgiving* as "guilt and reconciliation with the past" (Ricoeur 412). Although Egypt is never mentioned—"it could be Tunisia, Turkey, [. . .] Sarajevo or Kigali" (Kemeid, qtd. in Pepin "Sasha Samar")—the play deals with no other objective but "to investigate" the author's own self. It focuses on the mechanisms of rupture and reconciliation as experienced by those who left and those who stayed behind. Those who left and those who stayed feel threatened by the contrivances of forgetting and search for the ways to forgive.

To Ricoeur, *the act of forgetting* "remains the disturbing threat that lurks in the background of the phenomenology of memory and the epistemology of history" (412). It can be experienced as "an attack on the reliability of memory," and thus can be seen as historical escapism, one's desire to avoid responsibility (413). Memory, of course, is a much deeper phenomenon: defined by one's personal and collective experience, it leaves emotional and psychological traces through which it creates our collective and individual selves.

Ricoeur recognizes three types of traces that the lived experience prints upon our psyche: the written or documentary trace found on the plane of "the historiographical operation"; the physical trace, "an affection left in us by a marking [or] striking event"; and the cerebral or cortical trace, "which the neurosciences deal with" (415). These traces constitute the processes of forming memories, but also of forgetting that in turn can lead to the erasure of the document(s). These complicated processes of remembering and forgetting can also guide the hand of a historian called to make new narratives of the past.

The act of forgiveness—Ricoeur further offers—constitutes the gesture of true historical consciousness: it indicates our ability to separate the guilty person from his/her unscrupulous deed; it stages our wish to forgive "the guilty person while condemning his action" (490) and to recognize that the guilty person can also be considered "capable of something other than his offenses and his faults" (493). Often, in the story of an exilic flight, the one who escaped is cast as a guilty person. Those who stayed behind, consciously or not, keep an exilic subject responsible for his/her well-being and safety in a new land. They often see those who went away in the aura of cowardice and even punishment, speaking of those who left in the language of betrayal and death. Those who return are held accountable for their deeds; they are expected to provide a reasonable explanation for their flight and even, some-times, scolded for their (non)success in the new land. Those who escaped experience the sense of guilt too; they often project it onto their children.

In Kemeid's *Furieux et désespérés*, it is the exilic guilt that keeps the protag-onist's father away from the old country and it is the same guilt of survival, the guilt of not knowing, that sends the young Mathieu on his journey back there. The play stages the post-exilic return as the act of reconciliation and *postmemory* (Hirsch). Family stories, photographs, objects, and other memorabilia of the parents' traumatic experience evoke vivid, memory-like visions in the imagina-tion of their children, almost as if the children had experienced these traumas themselves. For them, researching history turns into haunting experience.

At the centre of the play is the young Québécois, Mathieu, visiting the land of his father and trying to negotiate his own place in its modern hist-ory. Prompted by the guidebooks his father gave him, Mathieu sets out to compare the image of the land he carries in his mind with its reality. In the play, Mathieu—a grown-up version of Ascanius, the son of Aeneas from the first play of the trilogy—visits the land of his ancestors. The journey takes on a surreal dimension characteristic of the tales of migrant returns. As in a typical fairy tale, the dramatic action is brought to life through the gesture of the protagonist's arrival. Upon his landing, Mathieu is confronted with the enigma of the world he is to discover. Before he meets his extended family and becomes involved in the revolutionary events spreading over the country, he is taken on a journey along his father's memory lane.

The play opens with a monologue of a taxi driver, setting up the histor-ical context of the Arab Spring and the atmosphere of mistrust that awaits the post-exilic subject on his/her journey home, as well as a mythological background to his voyage. As the action unfolds, Mathieu gradually realizes how the old world works. Here, time takes over space, mythology over history. Between the two, he must make a choice. If he allies with Beatrice, his aunt, he will fall into the time of mythology, the world resting on the rules of ancient hospitality and religious beliefs. If he joins Nora, his cousin, he will step into the time of the present. Both choices involve forgiveness: those who stayed will have to accept Mathieu as one of their own; Mathieu, a returned migrant, will have to willingly step into the present, the time of history. Before Mathieu has a chance to choose, Nora puts his loyalty to the test by coercing him to take part in the upheaval. He joins the rebels, kills a prison guard, participates in manifestations, and loses Nora to the bombings. The ghost of Jean-François Champollion, the father of Egyptology and the most credited nineteenth-century decipherer of Egyptian hieroglyphics, comes to his aid: "you will find what you're looking for as soon as you stop being afraid of this country" (98). As the outsider to this war, however, Mathieu is granted forgiveness: he finds Nora and establishes his own view of the Old World. The play ends with Mathieu realizing his mission: he returns his father's memories to his native land and makes his own. As a token of forgiveness, Beatrice presents Mathieu with an old family photo that depicts the day of his father's departure to Canada: the mother is on the left, the father is a step behind; the cousins, the uncles, the aunts all smile—all but the grandmother, who is wearing black. What is left—many years, losses, new impressions, and encounters afterward—is the memory of the moment. The materiality of the photo brings back the effects of temporizing; it takes Mathieu out of the spell of the present time. A bridge between the past and the present, the photograph reveals the mechanisms of making memory so that history can come full circle. The experiential act of flight is echoed in the stillness of the photograph that depicts the rupture of the departure to come and the promise of an impossible return. The past and the present are collapsed in the enactment of the event, something that in the new circumstances of return turns into a gesture of erasure. The play ends with another *mise en scène* of separation, now staged for Mathieu's own departure. The same family, forty years after, is out on the balcony: "Beatrice is wearing black standing to the left; Nora is behind her; Nadia is on the right; Florence is in the center, at the back" (112). With this new photograph coming to life as reconciliation, the power of a theatrical performance to negotiate the past and the present, and to insist on the act of becoming, comes to the fore. A moment later, the image turns into a new object of memory: the world on the photograph will remain, as before, only a fantasy, an object of desire, immersed in the atmosphere of distant pain.

The author of epic narratives, Kemeid likes to stir emotions and controversy. Dealing with history and terror requires mixing genres and theatrical languages, a process that advances Kemeid's historical project further. The play speaks of the true historical consciousness that allows one to forget and forgive—because forgiveness, as Ricoeur proposes, is the only act of history that is capable of bringing the perpetrators and their victims to reconciliation (457–58). Forgiveness, however, is a difficult gift to give or receive; it is bound to the sense of guilt, but, if granted, it is capable of lifting this guilt, which paralyzes our power to act. Engaging with the temporal and ethical dimensions of myth seen and retold through the discourses of modern history, Kemeid adds one more "Ricoeurian" quality to his play: he imagines the family reunion unfolding between the surrealist reality of the dream and the clichéd collapse of cultural tastes and expectations. The world of Beatrice, Mathieu's aunt, is measured by ancient hospitality and generosity, whereas Mathieu's world is measured by progress and intellectualism, the rejection of spirituality and religion in which churches are destroyed by time, not wars.

In its desire to reflect the dangerous interdependency between the sentiments of globalization and nationalism, the tension between the East and the West, Kemeid's dramaturgy serves as a warning sign, made by the writer-citizen who is himself the product of immigration. In this position of the chronicler of history, Kemeid occupies the place between "the historian and the judge," to use Ricoeur's terms; he emerges "as a third party in the order of time: with a gaze that is structured on the basis of personal experience, variously instructed by penal judgment and by published historical inquiry" (333). A citizen, Ricoeur explains, is always found in search of "the assured judgment," but his/her quest is never complete, "placing him more on the side of the historian." Such a citizen remains an observer of history and its "ulti-mate arbiter"; he is the one who "carries the 'liberal' values of constitutional democracy" (333). By staging the tale of homecoming, as it is experienced by the second generation, Kemeid engages with this idea of a citizen as a detached spectator of history, "who pronounces retrospectively the conclu-sion of a book devoted to the limits of historical objectivity" (Ricoeur 335). At the same time, as Ricoeur reminds us, this citizen—the narrator of hist-ory—is him/herself a subject of history. The citizen/narrator's knowledge of the past oscillates between "subjectivity and objectivity to the extent that it places in relation, through the initiative of the historian, the past of people who lived before and the present of those who live today" (335). The art of the historian, as Ricoeur insists, is that of hermeneutics: through the process of questioning the authenticity and the truth of the document, a historian offers his/her understanding of the past and proposes a new narrative, based on his/her own act of interpretation of the chosen signs (335).

CONCLUSION

As Freddie Rokem reminds us, the lives of individuals consist of the moments of "micro-history" ("Discursive" 19). These events might seem insignificant to those who immediately experience them, like the characters of Brecht's *Mother Courage and Her Children*, but they become instrumental to those who study them as historians and philosophers, think about them artistically as theatremakers, and look at them as spectators. To us—readers of hist-ory—the events of this "micro-history" can reveal the profound patterns of larger historical designs and provide lessons in our own existential and moral struggles. Rokem raises the questions of our moral responsibility and per-sonal ethics when we are confronted with the impersonal events presented on stage, larger than any individual's life. In this context, the personal actions of individuals can take the form of *in*action. The question Brecht would ask is to what extent can one individual's decision of *in*action, as non-participation or conformism, influence the unfolding of history? Putting this question of historical consciousness forward—either in the form of philosophical inquiry (as Ricoeur does) or in the form of a theatrical play (as Brecht and after him Kemeid do)—is already one step onward, because, as Benjamin reminds us, the art of storytelling is already the "co-ordination of the soul, the eye, and the hand" of the artist ("The Storyteller" 108). This deeply personal connection that the storyteller experiences with his/her material makes his/her craft "solid, useful, and unique"; "seen in this way, the storyteller joins the ranks of the teachers and sages. He has counsel—not for a few situations [...] but for many, like the sage. For it is granted to him to reach back to a whole life-time." The artist as a chronicler of history is "the man who could let the wick of his life be consumed completely by the gentle flame of his story. [...] The storyteller is the figure in which the righteous man encounters himself" (Benjamin, "The Storyteller" 108).

With this view of the art of storytelling as the art of philosophy, Benjamin brings this article back to its point of departure, to the question Ricoeur would ask: To what extent can the act of philosophical writing be rightly seen as synonymous with the act of historical inquiry and the act of performance? To what extent is philosophical inquiry performative, and how similar or different is it to the act of storytelling or writing a play, of putting one's personal historical experience into poetic form? How can this process of translating history constitute a road back to oneself: the characterizing point of the exilic writing in general? Kemeid's trilogy is an example of such processes. It stages the author's personal pledge to history and presents the condition of exile in three temporal dimensions: as the act of flight or making history; as the act of memory or creating narratives; and as the act of return or the gesture of forgetting and forgiving, in which the new project of resistance begins. Kemeid's position always remains political. In his project of staging history, he is driven by the necessity of the artist-citizen to start new social battles in contemporary Québec. He reads the present moment in the history of Québec as a time of dissidence and resistance: after the decade of the 1990s that saw the implementation and the failure of the ideals of the 1960–1968 *révolution tranquille*, it is time for Québec to come up with a new ideological program. The liberal left, with which Kemeid identifies, proposes to recognize the figure and the voice of the Other—be it an Indigenous subject, a Canadian anglophone, or a new immigrant—as an integral force of today's Québec, now actively implemented in making this new Québec. Kemeid's trilogy serves as an example of how a theatre artist can participate in such movement; in his plays Kemeid the playwright supplies Kemeid the polemicist and the public speaker with the devices of storytelling, which allow Kemeid the historian to think about his country's past and future as a philosopher.

PART TWO.
CANADIAN IMMIGRATION
AND THE PARADIGMS OF
PERFORMANCE

HARVESTING THE BODY: DEVISING ACROSS DIFFERENCE AT MT SPACE

RIC KNOWLES

When Majdi Bou-Matar came to Canada from his native Lebanon in 2003, Kitchener, Ontario, was not known for risky, innovative, or physical theatre, or for theatre that either probed or sutured the interstices between the city's multiply diverse cultures. Bou-Matar, however, arrived having trained as a director in Lebanon and worked as an actor at the Afro-Arab Centre for Theatrical Research (CAAFRT) in Tunis, and he brought with him an interest in cutting-edge theatrical interculturalism that reversed the power dynamics of what Daphne Lei has called "HIT" (hegemonic intercultural theatre) as practised by charismatic western directors such as Peter Brook, Ariane Mnouchkine, and Robert Wilson. As he says,

> Being on stage with African actors with whom I did not share the same language strengthened my belief in a culturally diverse, physically-oriented inter-cultural theatre based on improvisations where spoken language is never a barrier.
>
> I found in Canada, with its official cultural policy, an ideal place to advance my knowledge and practice my art along with artists who share the same passion. ("Artistic Director")

Shortly after his arrival in Kitchener-Waterloo on 5 January 2004, he began to follow that passion by starting his first workshop with actors in the Theatre of the Arts at the University of Waterloo. That workshop resulted in a public

performance of *Nijinsky Through a Window* on 28 August 2004 that marked
the beginning of his theatre company, named the MT [multicultural theatre]
Space after Peter Brook's celebrated book, *The Empty Space*. The company was
incorporated on 7 February 2005:

> I have founded the MT Space to be a conduit for professional artists
> from diverse cultural backgrounds to share ideas, integrate in the
> community, and create new and innovative art, while at the same
> time build Canadian experience to be able to join the Canadian the-
> atre industry. I believe that immigrant artists, and those from diverse
> cultural backgrounds could play a much larger role in the shaping
> the future of Canadian theatre. ("Artistic Director")

This chapter considers Bou-Matar's creation process and argues that the intercultural work performed by MT Space's productions is a direct result of the
intercultural creation process that he has developed and practises with the
company: one that involves cross-cultural casting, devised creation based
on the diverse bodies assembled within the creation space, community
involvement and feedback, and the purposeful privileging of immigrant and
Indigenous voices.

The MT Space is one of a small group of companies within Canada's inter-
cultural theatre landscape—among them Teesri Duniya Theatre (founded
in Montréal in 1981 by Rana Bose and Rahul Varma), Modern Times Stage
Company (founded in Toronto in 1989 by Soheil Parsa and Peter Farbridge),
Aluna Theatre (founded in Toronto in 2001 by Beatriz Pizano and Trevor
Schwellnus), and Onelight Theatre (founded in Halifax in 2002 by Shahin
Sayadi)—that were founded by non-European immigrants who came to
Canada as adults, bringing with them influences beyond the Euro-American
canon and beyond the politics and pieties of Canadian multiculturalism. Each
of these companies has also engaged in the creation of new work, sometimes
devised creations; each has worked broadly across cultures rather than in only
culturally specific ways; each has taken on the relationship between immigrant and Indigenous communities in the land now called Canada; each has

explored issues surrounding the use of minority or multiple languages, translation, and accents; each has toured outside Canada; and each has mounted intersectional festivals and/or conferences addressing intercultural theatrical encounters. Taken together, these companies have opened the door for a reconsideration of theatrical interculturalism that focuses on the rehearsal hall as a space for intercultural negotiation and exchange, and on the stage as a dynamic space of cultural encounter that eschews the types of appropriative representational practice that have dominated western-based intercultural theatre since the beginnings of theatrical modernism.

The mandate of MT Space is to bring together culturally diverse artists to constitute and serve a culturally diverse community in the city of Kitchener, in the Kitchener-Waterloo region, in Ontario, in Canada, and in other parts of the world. Since its founding, the company has established deep roots in its own community, and has had a significant impact nationally and internationally through its devised mainstage shows, its "theatre for social change" creations in collaboration with schools and community groups, its We Are Culture and MT Space Presents presentation series, its workshops and classes, and its biennial international IMPACT Festival and Conference. Its mainstage shows have toured Canada, Jordan, Syria, Lebanon, Tunisia, Egypt, Bahrain, and the Côte d'Ivoire. Bou-Matar and Pam Patel, his successor as artistic director since July 2016 (Bou-Matar remains the company's resident director and artistic director of IMPACT), have significant national profiles as artists, advocates, and agitators, and the company's work has been particularly notable in bringing together immigrant and Indigenous artists and communities working purposefully across their differences. "MT Space believes in theatre that builds communities, changes policies and instigates social change," says Bou-Matar.[1] "Our theatre creations are political, relevant, and challenging. The first question I ask myself when confronted with an idea for a new show is: 'who cares?' I look for topics that are urgent and dangerous" ("Artistic Director). To date, those topics have included such things, in their

---

1 For a discussion of how MT Space and Bou-Matar understand and relate to community, see Houston and Bou-Matar.

mainstage shows, as the immigrant experience (*Seasons of Immigration*)[2]; the refugee experience (*Exit Strategy/Pinteresque, The Occupy Spring Project, The Raft*); the politics of freedom, home, sexuality, culture, and nationalism (*Yes and No*); terrorism (*The Last 15 Seconds*); love and sex across differences in gender, sexuality, "race,"[3] age, class, and culture (*Body 13*)[4]; human rights, mental health, addiction, and the war on terror (*Paradise*)[5]; the Occupy, Idle No More, and Arab Spring movements (*Occupy Spring, The Occupy Spring Project*); and the lives (and deaths) of dancer Vaslav Nijinsky (*The Nijinsky Plays*) and filmmaker Moustapha Akkad (*The Last 15 Seconds*).

But Bou-Matar's productions are not simply "about" these things, nor is their significance limited to their subject matter. The work also models a process of cross-cultural communication, collaboration, community consul- tation, and exchange while developing out of that process new and resilient company- and context-specific intercultural dramaturgies. This process has evolved since the company's early show, *Seasons of Immigration* (2005), which was provocative, charming, and instrumental early on in building an audience for the company. It suffered, however, from a tendency to look primarily at those things all immigrants have in common, constructing a single "multi- cultural community," and risking suggesting that all immigrant experiences are the same.[6] Since then Bou-Matar has worked at focusing on difference as much as similarity, and on the "firstness" of Indigenous cultures on Turtle

---

2   The title of this has also appeared as *The Seasons of Immigration to the West*. For accounts of the show, see Houston, and Knowles, "Collective."

3   I put "race" in quotation marks to acknowledge that, while the concept and the use of the term have real, material consequences, biological races do not, in fact, exist.

4   For an account of *Body 13*, see Knowles, *Performing* 58–60.

5   Although MT Space often involves playwrights in their creation process, *Paradise*, a collaboration with Patti Flather and Nakai Theatre, is the company's only production to date "of" a pre-existing script.

6   Part of what was missing from the show was a sense of different generations and peri- ods of immigration, and the fact that many encounters between new immigrants and "Canadians" were in fact encounters *between* immigrants. See Knowles, "Collective" 11.

Island that makes them significantly different from immigrant communities in terms of their relationship to the land (broadly understood), even though they share some elements of their relationship to the colonizing culture. These shifts have resulted in work that is at once *inter*cultural *and* culturally specific. The company also has come to articulate its mission explicitly as "working with different communities to build a community of difference" ("Mission and Vision"), avoiding the problematic rhetorics of official multiculturalism. This involves the company that is working on any given show in long, complex, and sometimes difficult daily discussions. Each day's rehearsal begins with reports from everyone about current news and developments effecting their own and their families' diverse circumstances, usually but not always in relation to the subject matter of the show, and each rehearsal exercise is followed by discussions that are about much more than theatrical effectiveness or impact.

* * *

The remainder of this essay will focus primarily on a Spring 2017 workshop of an ongoing work that is currently mistitled *The Occupy Spring Project*. Mistitled because it was first conceived as a development out of two earlier projects, *Exit Strategy/Pinteresque*, about the refugee experience, and *Occupy Spring*, inspired by the intersections among the Occupy, Idle No More, and Arab Spring movements. The revisiting of this work was premised on the feeling that some of it had been effective, remained relevant, and was worth extending, but that the world had changed significantly since the previous explorations, and that the process for them had in some ways been flawed. On the one hand, for example, excitement over the Occupy, Idle No More, and especially Arab Spring movements had in various ways not been sustained or had soured, and the world refugee crisis had catastrophically worsened. On the other hand, in the *Occupy Spring* workshops in September 2013, individual company members had been implicitly read as "representative" of their cultures in ways that proved to be problematic. The new project attempted at once to address new and urgent local and global circumstances and these difficult issues of representation, and it took as its focus the stories of two families—one Syrian, one Kanien'kehá:ka (Mohawk)—over many centuries, including the impact on both of global western imperialism and colonization. The reach of the show was considerable, but I will focus for the purposes of this chapter and book primarily on the emergence and development of one key "immigrant" scene.

Like most "mainstage" projects at MT Space, *The Occupy Spring Project* began with Bou-Matar in conversation with many of his regular collaborators about the topic under exploration and proceeded to the assembling of a company. Remaining from the earlier shows and workshops, but exacerbated by the refugee crisis in Syria and North Africa and by Indigenous activism in the wake of the Truth and Reconciliation Commission, was an interest in the historical and contemporary intersections and relationships among refugee, Indigenous, and white-settler cultures within Canada. Because the work is built from the bodies and (hi)stories of the group itself, assembling the team for such a project is crucial, requiring a large and diverse company with a significant number of Indigenous artists in both the cast and creative team, including, crucially, at least one from the territories—the Haldimand Tract[7]—on which we would be working. In the end, with the unavailability of the MT Space's Syrian-born star Nada Humsi, the company consisted of eight actors—Ashley Bomberry (Kanien'kehá:ka, from Six Nations), Trevor Copp (white settler), Nicholas Cumming (white settler), Nigel Irwin (Cree), Julia Krauss (German), Pam Patel (Gujarati Canadian), Ahmad Meree (Syrian, sponsored by MT Space as a recent refugee), and Gülce Oral (Turkish)—plus director Majdi Bou-Matar (Lebanese Canadian), Assistant Director Heather

---

7   The Haldimand Tract is a parcel of land six miles (ten kilometres) on either side of the Grand River from its mouth to its source that was granted to the Six Nations Confederacy in 1784 in recognition of their loyalty to the British Crown during the American Revolution, to be under their sole ownership in perpetuity. The land includes what are now Kitchener and Waterloo. The current Six Nations Reserve consists of 5% of the land originally granted; none of the Haldimand Tract was yielded at any time by the Haudenosaunee. The Kanien'kehá:ka, or Mohawk, are one of the six nations of the Haudenosaunee, or Iroquois, Confederacy.

Majaury (Anishinaabeg), writers Tara Beagan (Ntlaka'pamux and Irish) and Gary Kirkham (white settler), scenographer and videographer Andy Moro (Euro Cree), musician Nick Storring (white settler), and myself (white settler) as dramaturge. Everyone—including Moro as scenographer—was present throughout the process, and the distinctions between roles was loose: virtually everyone in the room served as a writer/creator, a dramaturge, and an assistant director, and there was little sense of disciplinary "turf." The workshop took place in Spring 2017 in the courtyard at Bonnie Stuart on Whitney Place, just a few blocks from Kitchener's radically multi-ethnic downtown, and issued in a workshop production at the nearby Registry Theatre in April.

Once the team is complete, in every project Bou-Matar undertakes, "We immerse ourselves in the locality of our topics, themes and stories. We dig deep into the histories, the traditions and the memories of our actors and characters alike. We harvest the body and its cultural baggage." Crucially, as he says, "We work together based on a strong recognition and acknowledgement of our differences. We use such differences to create friction and spark actions that are thoroughly shaped and negotiated with much research, talent and artistry." ("Artistic Director"). "The process I use in performance-making," he says, "is based on constructing each project as a creation in progress, consisting of daily improvisations, discussions and basic physical and dance training" (Bou-Matar 105).

> This approach combines different performing disciplines and styles, while at the same time allowing the personal story of each performer to be told through his/her own rhythm. Furthermore, it enhances each individual's own culturally embedded movement and expression. Some aspects of this process will involve musicians, designers, and writers. This ensures that the director has no definite expectations of the final overall form of the performance—a broader spectrum of creativity should lead to a more stimulating relationship between the performers and their audience. (Bou-Matar 105)

Rehearsals for all MT Space shows begin in much the same way. After land acknowledgement and smudging, introductions, a brief outline of "the rules of the game"—don't break the exercise by asking questions, don't leave the exercise unless you're injured, don't just stand there and do nothing—the actors get on their feet and walk in the space. The first step is to talk the actors through familiar ensemble relaxation exercises, with occasional theme-specific suggestions, in this case that they are preparing to "walk the globe," to "walk long distances, from Africa to Europe," for example, planting in the actors' minds and bodies the idea of the refugee experience.[8] As part of the

---

8   All quotations from Bou-Matar in rehearsal are from the May 2017 creation workshop for *The Occupy Spring Project* as recorded by the author. For those not familiar with the kinds of relaxation exercises I'm referring to, this is a transcription of the one that Bou-Matar used to talk the cast of *The Occupy Spring Project* through the exercise before going directly into show-specific work:

Walk in the space. Understand its balance, and its rhythm. Observe the point of contact between your body and the ground. Feel how your feet are connected to the floor. How is the weight of your body distributed across your feet, on the ground? The act of walking, nothing else. Your body weight drops vertically down and hits the ground through points of contact: pay attention to those points. Now starting from the top of your head, do a very slow scan downwards, like the MRI machines. Think of your body in horizontal places, starting from the top of your head and going down very slowly. Observe the tension. Is there any tension in the forehead? Let the weight of your skin, your tissue, your muscle go down with the natural force of gravity. When you observe the tension, release it. Let each muscle sit, gently, under the force of gravity, in its right spot. Forehead, slowly down to eyebrows. I see a few of you frowning: that's tension that you're applying to your forehead and eyebrows. Try to let it go, let the muscles just sit in their proper, natural spot. With your eyes open, keep going down to your eyes, and the area around your eyes. Down to your cheeks. Notice if you're twitching, or tensing up, or putting on a mask. Try to release it, to get rid of it, so you become. You just become. You be. Slowly down to the jaw, lots of tension in the jaw. Observe those muscles and release any tension. Keep going down to the neck, to the shoulders. Shoulder blades. If you feel there's any tension around your shoulders, try to release it. Continue your scan down, to your chest, your arms dropping down by the force of gravity: no pressure exerted, no force applied. Observe how this exercise of relaxation is affecting your weight, your feet, your walk. Always

exercise Bou-Matar asks the actors to pay particular attention, initially, to the distribution of the body's weight:

> Observe how that **weight** is being distributed through the act of walk-ing. How do you walk? Are you distributing that weight smoothly and evenly? Are you walking more on your tiptoes or on the back of your heels? Notice if you're putting more weight on one side of your feet or the other. How do you walk naturally, organically, with the least amount of effort? Just observe, and if you feel that your walk is awkward, or not comfortable, or forced, what do you do about it? How do you just simply carry this relaxed, balanced body, how do you balance this weight, as you move across the floor, using your feet? When you feel comfortable, when you feel you've found your most natural, basic, balanced walk, stick to it.

The next focus is on listening:

> Once you feel confident that you're relaxed, you're ready, you're bal-anced, start **listening**. Listen to the room. Listen to the pace of the room. Engage in the collective rhythm of the room. [. . .] Listen. Let your ears scan the space. You hear the squeaking of the wood beneath your feet, beneath one another's feet. Try to engage in the collective rhythm as if we are all one creature. As if we're all walking on only two feet. Listen better. Your body is ready, attentive, relaxed,

---

breathe—don't hold your breath. Keep going down towards your abdomen, your stomach muscles. Imagine your insides. Is there any tension there in your intestines? Hips, butt, butt cheeks. When you walk are you tensing your butt? Try to relax. Down to your thighs. Every muscle sits in its proper position. The knees. The knees carry a lot of weight, a lot of tension, a lot of pain. Down to your calves. All the way down to your feet, that are carrying your entire body weight, and distributing that on the ground, and they do it very wisely through the soles of your feet. [. . .] At this point your body is fully relaxed—no twitching, no scratching, no smiling, no frowning, no fingers rubbing against each other.

and you're aware of the whole space, starting with the sound. Can you hear the rhythm of the room? Can you hear eight bodies pacing like one? Hear your heart beat. Hear your partners' heartbeats. Can we all engage in a collective heartbeat? The heartbeat of the space, of the ensemble. You listen, not only with your ears: your knees listen, your chest listens. Listen to the space with your entire body.

Then sight and balance in the space:

Let's activate our **sight**. See. See 360 degrees around you. See with your back, with your knees, with your butt. You know who's behind you, who's to your right, who's to your left. You know like an animal how far the wall is, how far the door is. I know how far Nick is from me, I see it, I feel it. I know the space. I can measure. And keep that space **balanced**, at all times. How do we instinctively know that the space is balanced? How do I move instinctively to balance the space? Without losing our control on the listening. Now we're relaxed, our feet are distributing the weight in a balanced way. We are all of one heartbeat, one rhythm, and the space is balanced at all times.

"Those are your tasks," he says. "Achieve them," as the exercise subtly moves from body and space to story, to body and space as the sources of story.

Listen well. See how organically the rhythm changes. We collectively speed up, we collectively slow down. No twitching, no fixing your nose, fixing your shirt. We are performative bodies. Every gesture, every twitch, every look, carries a meaning, is a sign. There is already a tremendous weight of our stories that exist in our bodies. Try to carry them, not to crash under that weight. There is no room for losing balance, for fixing your hair, for fixing your shirt. You can't afford it. There is a huge weight, the weight of the story you're carrying. It requires all your attention. It requires all your relaxed body, your balanced body. Collectively you sped up, right. I don't know who speeded up first and I don't care. The space speeds up. Don't lag behind. Be ready. Listen. Listen better. [. . .] Keep the space balanced, keep the body relaxed. Don't go in circles, move to balance the space. Full control over the space, over your body, over the story you're carrying inside that body.

And stop. Put your feet together. When you stop come to a complete, grounded, and relaxed halt, so when you stop, you're rooted, you're grounded, nothing will shake you. You can take the wind in your face, you can take the storm because you're grounded. There's roots. And when you stop you see—with your back, with your shoulders, with your eyes—that the room is balanced. You're aware. You know where the wall is, where the others are. You're not in a trance. You're here. You're aware of every sound, every distance. You're aware of how the space feels and looks. And then we walk again. Go.

Bou-Matar reiterates the principles, the tasks: relaxed body, awareness of space, and balanced space. "And we stop and go as you please, organically together. And as you stop and go, the rhythm changes. You start playing music with your bodies and the space. You become like music, harmony, together. When you stop, listen. Listen to the heartbeat of the room, of the story, of the space."

Much of this work is effective in building the ensemble and instilling a sense of joint responsibility for what happens, but Bou-Matar has no truck with the concept of universality and is as much focused on difference, and on tension, as he is on the group as a unit. "There is tension," he says, "but not in the body. The tension is in the space. Between the bodies."

The story is high stakes, is tense, the air is tense. The stakes are very high. It's life and death. [. . .] Don't let it become boring. Music changes, grows, speeds up, slows down. You have a responsibility to the story in your body, for your people, your ancestors, your history. You cannot fuck this up.

The stories begin to build through relationships as they develop between the actors:

> As we continue to play the game, a look, a simple look in someone else's face, or eyes. You don't need to look at everyone at the same time. One look that will come organically. Either stop or walk. Don't be hesitant, not knowing. It's "walk, stop, look." That's the exercise. Don't play a character yet. Don't start acting. There's no acting in this: we look to know: who is this person? Black, tall, short, has a beard. Now you're playing. Now make that game more exciting. More unexpected. That's how the game gets more exciting. When it's pulsing. Unexpected. Changing all the time. You don't get stuck in patterns that are expected. Action, reaction. See how relations start forming, organically. Stay in the game. After you look to know, then what? What do you want from that look? There's a relation. How do you relate? Do you like that person, are you afraid of them, are you suspicious? Do you want to talk to them? Do you want them to look away? How do you relate? You want to build something with that look. It's important that we all start from the basics, that we don't start acting, representing, pretending. We're not going the make the story up. The story is here, in your blood memory, in your muscle. We don't impose a story.

After a break, Bou-Matar reiterated the principles of what he calls "the game":

> No muscles, no acting, no tension. 1. **Walk:** Balance. You're always grounded. You know exactly how the weight of your body is working. You have roots. Nothing will shift you. You'll bounce back. You feel that your feet go deep in history. 2. **Space:** The space is always balanced, but balance takes different forms. Seven people on one side of the space looking at the other side can produce balance. People arrive, waiting for a train, distribute themselves in space organically, shifting as new people arrive. 3. **Heartbeat:** It speeds up, slows down,

changes rhythms, but it doesn't stop. Heartbeat doesn't mean boring, it means alive, pumping blood all the time, and changing based on the physical or emotional state of the body. Your heartbeat is in sync all the time as an ensemble. When the heart stops, it stops only enough not to be dead. It kicks in at the right time when it needs to. It can't be a second before or a second after. Everyone tenses up, and then it kicks in. 4. **Look:** first to know, next to relate (create a relationship), third, to negotiate power.

The process will not be entirely new, apart from its nuances, to actors and directors anywhere—except perhaps in its acute attention to the ways in which actors themselves balance the playing space, and in its focus on ancestral bodies. But its nuance when working across significant differences in the casting and training of the actors allows Bou-Matar to build stories from specifically enculturated differences that feed the kinds of intercultural explorations that he is known for. The exercise builds, too, on an idea that Bou-Matar derives from his master and mentor, Fadhel Jaïbi, director of the Théâtre National Tunisien. Jaïbi introduced Bou-Matar to the idea that the body is physically attached to an elastic that connects us to our origins—in Bou-Matar's case, for example, to the mountains of Lebanon—and that goes back generations. The elasticity of this attachment varies, and does so in surprising ways and at surprising moments, but it is always there as something that draws us but against which we also struggle. Indeed, "the elastic *is* the body, and the baggage, you bring with you." All of Bou-Matar's movement exercises are informed by this simple physical imperative, which pulls his diverse actors in different ways, to different degrees, and at different times, and it ensures that his rehearsal hall's intercultural negotiations take place in embodied and often surprising ways.

Bou-Matar's opening exercises are foundational to all his creation work, but they sometimes issue directly in actual scenes. For *The Occupy Spring Project*, one of these was what we came to call the "Walking Hordes" scene, in which the actors devised a loop of movement from stage right to stage left at different paces on different horizontal planes and in different groupings, each actor circling backstage to begin again after crossing so that the stage was never empty. The curiously compelling scene, which directly evoked images of refugee and migrant treks the world over, lasted a full four and a half minutes and introduced several key elements of the show, including a Syrian family grouping that would prove to be central to the play's narrative. A little over three minutes into the scene, Ashley Bomberry, who would eventually emerge as the centre of the play's Kanien'kehá:ka family story, stopped, turned, and engaged in a brief encounter with Nicholas Cumming, economically representing first contact between the resident Indigenous population of Turtle Island and the arriving, abjectly helpless colonizers (the play's opening land and place acknowledgement and representation of the Haudenosaunee creation story having literally "addressed" the location at Kitchener's Registry Theatre on Turtle Island). At this point the walking hordes morphed, with a simple hand gesture and chest extension, into the arrival on this continent of settler-bearing sailing ships, and the narrative of colonization was firmly underway, established almost exclusively through movement that was firmly grounded in and by Bou-Matar's opening exercises and the bodies it made present in the space.

A variation on that exercise led early on to another key scene, the development of which is worth tracing in some detail. In the afternoon of the first day of rehearsals, Bou-Matar introduced an exercise on entering the space, building from how one person enters and positions herself with no preconceived scenario ("I'm running from the police," "I'm looking for someone") in mind, and then exploring how each subsequent entrance alters the space and changes spatial relationships. Actors were asked, first, to focus on their relationship to the space, and second on their relationship to the other or others in the space, all the while keeping in mind the morning's exercises and their personal "elastics"—the pulls and pressures of "the body that you bring with you," which is in a state of relaxed readiness, but is in no sense neutral.

The first to enter the space in the afternoon of 20 March 2017 was Gülce Oral, a talented young actor from Turkey who was new to Kitchener, Canada, and the unfamiliar MT Space rehearsal room. She entered slowly, tentatively, from stage left, her body tense, her eyes focused on the blank space before

Fig. 1. The first to enter the space in the afternoon of 20 March 2017 was Gülce Oral.
Photo by Ric Knowles.

her, eventually dropping to the floor, supported by her wrists, knees, and toes, a portrait of tension.

Ahmad Meree entered next, a recent refugee from Syria who would end up the centre of the play's Syrian family and its story. He crossed to Oral, concerned, kneeling behind her, at which point she recoiled, unable to look at him. As other actors entered what seemed to be a subway station—Trevor Copp, Julia Krauss, Nicholas Cumming, all somatically white—they exchanged looks, held their positions, and a story began to emerge as Meree tried unobtrusively to extricate Oral from the space.

Exactly what that story was varied throughout the creation process without ever changing the fundamental physical shape of the scene, which was oddly compelling. It is Bou-Matar's practice whenever a scene or scenario is improvised, re-improvised, recontextualized, and revisited, to open it up for discussion among the full company together with any visitors from the larger community who come by to watch and comment. In its initial form, for the onstage observers—and, we worried, for audience members—this was clearly a scene about an abused Middle Eastern woman trying to escape from her abusive Middle Eastern male partner or family member. It was a familiar story about "them." All agreed that the scene was powerful, but what

Fig. 2. Ahmad Meree tries to usher Gülce Oral out of the space. Photo by Ric Knowles.

were its gender, racial, and cultural politics? This discussion was one of many lengthy and difficult debates over the course of the creation process as news came out of Syria, Turkey, various Indigenous nations on Turtle Island, and Donald Trump's America. One full morning was spent discussing gender politics after a community member had attended rehearsals and sent an email about the gendered, "us-looking-at-them" organization of the rehearsal space. (The discussion resulted in some small reconfigurations of the hall, but not a wholescale respatialization.) Another morning Bou-Matar invited everyone to critique the process in front of another visiting community member. There were frequent discussions of how and why Indigenous characters, stories, and practices were, could, and should be represented, and by whom. And we confronted and analyzed many then-very-current media representations of "the refugee crisis" as well as the fallout from Canada's Truth and Reconciliation Commission. In light of these discussions and the development of the show's overarching stories of two families over the long arc of history, the scene between Oral, Meree, and the rest of the cast evolved and grew.

One of the major story exercises throughout the process that shaped the shifting meanings of this scene began on March 21, the second day of rehearsals. Bou-Matar invited each cast member to sit at the centre of a family portrait—composed around a bench as the actors entered one by one and took up a semiotically resonant position in tableau. The key cast member for the scene was then invited to introduce the family and tell its stories and that of the making of the portrait itself, stories that subsequent improvisations then animated: "This is my brother, Saeed. He dropped out of high school to join the Syrian army when he was sixteen." "This is my sister, Dunia. She has always been a rebel." "This is my brother Joseph. He had a warrior heart." And so on. The exercise was designed to generate story, of course, but one of its functions was also to make clear the different sizes, constitutions, and meanings of "family" and family relationships in different generational and cultural contexts, broadly defined. Discussions of the portraits revolved around patrilineal, matrilineal, and other lineages and slippages, the purpose and meaning of such portraiture, memory, naming, and misnaming, in always provocative ways. Needless to say, the families portrayed were by no means limited to, reifying of, or normalizing the heteropatriarchal, stereotypical, or culturally dominant in any of the represented cultures.

One of these portraits, of a Syrian family, had Meree at its centre: "This picture was taken at the beginning of the 2011 revolution in Syria," he began. From that beginning, the story as it evolved stretched backward to the 1917 partitioning of the Ottoman empire and to the role that the first Earl Kitchener played in surveying and mapping the Middle East as a technology of colonization that had its parallels in the show's representation of surveying, drawing grids, imposing borders, and stealing land on Turtle Island. Projected historical maps of both regions formed a key part of Andy Moro's evolving scenography.[9] The Syrian family story also stretched forward to the conscripting of one family member to fight for the regime against his own people, and

---

9   The show also made as much of the renaming during WWI of the city in which we were working from Berlin to Kitchener after the colonialist's death in 1916, as it elsewhere made of acknowledging the Haldimand Tract and the Haudenosaunee custodianship of the same land (see note six, above).

to the ultimate escape to Canada as refugees of four present-day family members: the father (played by Meree), his wife and their baby (played by Pam Patel and a bundle), and his sister (played by Oral). Among other things, as the show's stories and the company's work developed across the storylines of the Indigenous and Syrian families, it included the death during the Arab Spring revolution of the sister's lover (Nigel Irwin, who also played the child lost to the 1960s "scoops" in the show's Kanien'kehá:ka family); the group's escape on foot (among the Walking Hordes), by train, and by raft; the drowning of the wife and baby at the Turkish coast as their raft was intercepted; the rape of the sister by a border guard; and the arrival of the brother and sister at the train station in Kitchener where they met their white settler sponsors.

And it included, as one of the final scenes in the show, a revisiting of the scene between Meree and Oral that we have been following. In its final configuration the scene was very powerful. Oral entered as she had in the first improvisation, now lowering herself to the ground to make a snow angel in Kitchener's Victoria Park in winter. Meree entered to her, now understood to be the brother with whom she had escaped to Canada, and the others—white settler Canadians—watched uncomfortably, as they had before. But as the creation process evolves it comes to rely somewhat less on the improvisations of the actors alone, and by this time the scene had developed over several iterations and through shapings, sequencings, insertions, and editing contributed by the directing, writing, and dramaturgy team. As Meree approached her, Oral curled up and turned away, as she had before. "What are you doing?" he asked. "I'm letting my baby feel the snow." He became agitated, as he had before, interrogating her about "what baby," "who," and "when," expressing the anticipated pain and humiliation of a recent Syrian immigrant at a family situation he found shameful and struggling with the pulls and pushes of his cultural elastic as well as the exposure of feelings "on display" in a public park. To his repeated questions about whose baby "he" was, as her would-be protectors hovered, she finally told the observers, "It's ok, he's my brother," and told him, "He's a she." "A girl," he replied? Yes, she nodded, "She's *my* girl"—all anyone needed to know about whose baby it was (her Syrian lover's? the border guard's?). At this point, her brother unexpectedly laid back in the snow and began himself to make a snow angel, as his sister curled up by his side.

The show then returned briefly to the Sky Woman creation story with which it had started—"creation story begins again"[10]—and as Julia Krauss delivered an anguished monologue upstage centre, beginning with rage at the mapping, renaming, partitioning, and stealing of land but moving toward a visionary prophecy—"our daughters, our sons, our children are coming back"—new portraits of the Kanien'kehá:ka and Syrian families emerged downstage left and right. "This is my son, Joe," said the Kanien'kehá:ka mother played by Bomberry, having been reunited with the now-adult child who was stolen from her in the scoops depicted earlier in the show. "This," said Meree, holding a new bundle, "is my niece, Amal," as the lights began to fade. Amal (أمل) is a woman's name in Arabic; it also means hope.

* * *

Intercultural theatre has not always or notably had great success as cross-cultural negotiation when creative control has rested in the hands of individual playwrights or directors, particularly western men or other members of the dominant culture. Indeed, the stages of Europe and the international festival circuit have been littered with the problematic and appropriative intercultural work of charismatic white men. Might Bou-Matar's devising process at MT Space provide a model for the creation of a more productive intercultural theatre, particularly when authorship and authority are dispersed, and attempts are made to work across immigrant, arrivist, white settler, and Indigenous cultures on Turtle Island from non-dominant perspectives? It's not perfect. One of the issues that *The Occupy Spring Project* has wrestled with throughout

10   This phrase is the title and refrain of a talk and essay that Monique Mojica and I collaborated on for a conference celebrating Native American women's theatre at Miami University, Oxford, Ohio, in 2007. It is meant to signal the ways in which creation stories serve as models for regeneration, renewal, and transformation as they are played out over and over again in the lives of Indigenous peoples. See Mojica and Knowles.

is the representation—even improvisatory creation—of characters from one background by actors of other cultures. What does it mean for, say, Gujarati Canadian Pam Patel to create and perform, as she did in *The Occupy Spring Project*, the character of an Indigenous grandmother during the Caledonia resistance of 2006? Is it enough that she is a woman of colour? Is it enough that there were five Indigenous artists in the room, one of them from the community and another who had participated in the resistance? Is it made better or worse by the fact that the Indigenous (and other) actors and writers in the room were also creating and performing settler, immigrant, and refugee characters? How does a collective guard against distortion and appropriation, even with the best of intentions? Indeed, is *all* acting appropriative, and if so, what does this mean? And what about gender? Although creative authority was dispersed in the room and constantly revisited in discussion, the majority of team members "behind the table" were male, and final responsibility for decisions rested with a male director, albeit not one from the dominant culture. This has been a concern for every MT Space production I have participated in, though it is perhaps less so now that Pam Patel—a vocal intersectionalist feminist—has been installed as the company's artistic director.

No, the process isn't perfect—and indeed the concept of perfection (and completion) is anathema to work that needs to respond to current and ongoing conditions. But many of its elements are worthy of exploration beyond the MT Space. Chief among these are: 1) casting that is neither "colour blind," culturally specific, nor strictly thematic, but that disperses authority among a collective, problematizes concepts like "authenticity" and the ownership and responsibility for culturally specific choices, and includes people with lived experience of the cultures and histories represented; 2) the combination of working from fully embodied individual positions that acknowledge different histories and corporealities with the constant analytical revisiting and revisioning of scenes, scenarios, and representations within both the company and the larger community, who are invited to attend and respond to rehearsals at any time; 3) privileging difference over sameness (or universality); and 4) acknowledging that all such work is always "in progress," responding daily to shifting social and historical moments, power dynamics, and cultural imperatives.

   The Occupy Spring Project returned to the studio to continue the creation process in the Summer/Fall of 2018 and it premiered in Toronto in a different form and under the new title of *Amal* at Aluna Theatre's RUTAS festival in October. As *Amal*, it will tour nationally and internationally beginning in the spring of 2019, when it is scheduled as part of the Théâtre National Tunisien's regular season in Tunis, followed by performances at festivals in North Africa and the Middle East. At each restaging, the team hopes, as always, to "fail better."

MOMENTS OF ENCOUNTER: IRANIAN-CANADIAN IMMIGRANT AND DIASPORIC THEATRE

ART BABAYANTS AND MARJAN MOOSAVI

Dedicated to the memory of Levon Haftvan

لوون هفتوان / Լևոն Հաֆտվան /

(1966–2018).

INTRODUCTION: "LEAST THEATRICALLY REPRESENTED"

According to the *Canadian Encyclopedia*, in 2011 there were 163,290 Iranians[1] in Canada, with the largest proportion of them residing in the Greater Toronto Area (GTA) (Rahnema). Yet Ric Knowles identifies Iranian-Canadians as one of "Canada's least theatrically represented communities" (*Performing* 132). In his recent volume *Performing the Intercultural City* (2017), he also explains why certain communities (for instance, Iranians) have been largely excluded from the mainstream art scene of the multicultural Toronto (25). He links this exclusion to the problematic conflation of the official multiculturalism and the English-French bilingualism that Canada inscribed in its nation-building

---

1 *The Canadian Encyclopedia* also indicates that "[i]n 2016, according to Census data, 225,155 people in Canada had [Persian] as their mother tongue. In fact, [Persian] was the 11th-ranked immigrant language in the country" (Rahnema).

agenda back in the Pierre Elliott Trudeau era, which, amongst other factors, had implications for Toronto: "Within Toronto's arts, education, and theater communities, [official multiculturalism and bilingualism] meant availability of targeted arts funding for francophone or bilingual (English-French) work, but not for work from 'othered' cultures" (25). Iranian-Canadian art falls under the category of "othered" cultures, which explains why the work of Iranian-Canadian artists generally stays outside of the theatrical mainstream and remains largely unknown to Toronto audiences, theatre artists, critics, and scholars. This chapter is a modest attempt to rectify that situation; its specific focus is the Iranian-Canadian artists residing and working in the GTA.

In this chapter, the terms "Iranian" and "Persian" are used interchangeably to refer to people that officially hold an Iranian nationality; however, we would like to recognize that "Persian" denotes a much broader concept encompassing a large body of cultural output created by other Persian-speaking countries, including Afghanistan, Tajikistan, and their diaspora. While focusing on Iranian-Canadian artists only, the following discussion makes a special effort not to gloss over the extreme richness and complexity of Persia, a culture with one of the longest recorded histories in the world and a population that is ethnically, linguistically, and religiously diverse.

Keeping in mind the importance of the diversity we position ourselves not as impartial viewers but rather as individuals steeped in our own perspectives, histories, and biases. We are Marjan Moosavi, a theatre researcher, originally from Iran and a native speaker of Persian, who is currently an active participant in and scholar of Iranian diasporic cultural activities in Toronto, and Art Babayants, an Armenian-Canadian artist-scholar, who has previously collaborated with Iranian-Canadian artists and who represents a linguistic and cultural outsider's view on the material in question.

Our chapter first presents a brief overview of major Iranian-Canadian theatre artists' activities,[2] which ultimately provides a context for the case

---

2   As we mention above, our focus is Iranian-Canadian artists working in the GTA; however, it is important to recognize that Iranian-Canadian artists also live and work in other parts of Canada. For instance, Shahin Sayadi and his Onelight Theatre in Halifax (Shahin very recently moved to Toronto); Mohammad Rahmanian, Mahtab Nasirpour,

study at the centre of the second part of our chapter—a close-up analysis of the production of *Yek Daqiqeh Sokout* (*A Moment of Silence*)[3] written by one of Iran's most prominent contemporary playwrights, Mohammad Yaghoubi, and presented at Toronto's SummerWorks Performance Festival in 2016. We have chosen to focus specifically on this production for two reasons. The first is its unique position in the Iranian-Canadian repertoire—to date, it remains the only play from the contemporary Iranian canon that has been staged by its author in the capacity of director in both Persian and English. *A Moment of Silence* is a contemporary classic of Iranian theatre and the significance of its staging in the English language in Canada by its author—who had also premiered it in Iran—cannot be underestimated. Second, we were both involved in the Canadian production of this play as assistants to the director-playwright, which gave us direct access to the process of *domestication/ foreignization* of the original Persian play.

We use the term *domestication* as it has often been applied to the study of diasporic and immigrant theatre as well as theatre in translation. Following geographer Ash Amin and philosopher Sara Ahmed, Barry Freeman explains domestication along with ejection as "two equally undesirable possibilities for strangers: that they be either ejected from a community or else marked for domestication" (60). In relation to theatre, Freeman indicates that domestication implies a process of making a stranger (or a stranger culture) "safe" while also "avoiding the difficult material realities bearing down on strangers" (61). Following Freeman, we use the word *stranger* "simply as a guiding metaphor for an analysis of cultural difference in Canada" (xx). However, in our

---

Jubin Ghaziani, and Amir Naeem Hosseini in Vancouver; and Mani Soleymanlou, Naeem Jebeli, and Goussan Theatre Company in Montréal. Due to lack of documentation, this list is not comprehensive.

3   For the transliteration of Persian words, we have followed the Iranian Studies scheme with minor modifications and with the exception of terms, names, and titles that already have established anglicized forms (e.g. Ta'ziyeh). Based on Marjan's experience as an instructor of Persian, the distinction between /a/ and long /a/ is very important in pronouncing words with a natural Iranian accent, so the long /a/ (as in "father") is transliterated as /ā/ throughout the text.

writing we resist any attempts to look at immigrant artists from a majoritarian (anglophone) perspective. Our interest is to also turn the gaze on Canada's mainstream anglophone theatre and audiences and consider them as *strangers* to immigrant artists such as Yaghoubi. Indeed, domestication may appear to some Iranian-Canadian artists (such as Yaghoubi) as *foreignization*—in the end, it depends on whose perspective we adopt and who we see as a *stranger*. In other words, no one, including those who think of themselves as typically Canadian, can be seen as *domestic* or *foreign* a priori—everything depends on the perspective of a particular linguistic, cultural, or ethnic community existing in Canada. Therefore, in our chapter we will be repeatedly switching perspectives, often talking about *foreignization* or *domestication* simultaneously. In our case, it helps that each of us represents the *insider* and *outsider* perspective on the production at the centre of our chapter, which also allows us to switch perspectives and to treat the issue of *domestication* as synonymous with that of *foreignization*.

A BIRD'S-EYE VIEW OF IRANIAN-CANADIAN THEATRE ACTIVITY IN TORONTO

Before tackling the issue of domestication, we would like to introduce the broader historical context in which Persian-Canadian theatre activity emerged and developed. The first large wave of immigration from Iran happened in the early 1980s, when many Iranian artists came to Canada following the revolution of 1979. These self-exiled representatives of the Iranian intelligentsia were well-educated, seasoned theatre practitioners, such as Mahmoud Ostad Mohammad (1950–2013), Abbas Javanmard (b. 1929), Nosrat Partovi (b. 1937), and Jafar Vali (1933–2016). They eventually began to produce plays from the Iranian dramatic repertoire and from Persian literary canons and folklore on Toronto stages. Their productions were in Persian and were meant for the small but growing population of Iranian immigrants in Toronto. For this first generation of theatre artists, theatre was a site to share their nostalgia for their past, celebrate their historical identity, and maintain some connection with their homeland.[4]

With the emergence of another wave of immigration during the 1990s (after the Iran–Iraq War), several artistic centres, cultural organizations—namely the Vājeh Literary Club—and events came into existence in the GTA. These diasporic cultural entities played a crucial role in presenting various aspects of Persian poetry, drama, cinema, and visual arts to the Persian community in and around Toronto. The largest and most prestigious of these events is the biannual Tirgan Festival that, according to its official website, is the "world's largest celebration of Iranian arts and culture," taking place at the Harbourfront Centre for four days and attracting "150,000 visitors from Canada and around the world, 200+ artists, and 100+ performances, talks, presentations, and workshops" ("About"). Since 2006, Tirgan has featured many diasporic Iranian artists living in Europe and North America, including Bahram Beyzai, Levon Haftvan, and Soheil Parsa, to name a few.[5]

The majority of Iranian diasporic artists left Iran in response to the political and economic conditions of post-revolutionary and postwar Iran and the recurrent international economic sanctions; however, some of them have still had the possibility of travelling back and forth between Canada and Iran. In Canada, they have staged plays by distinguished Iranian dramatists like Bahram Beyzai (b. 1938) and Gholamhossein Saedi (1936–1985). For instance, in 2007, a two-hander by Saedi, *Mājaray-e Nāmous Parastān yā In beh Ān Dar* (*The Adventure of Honour Worshipers, or Tit for Tat*), was produced by ReeRaa

---

4   We would like to thank Sasan Ghahreman for sharing his comprehensive list of Toronto-based Iranian artists and performances in Persian. We are also grateful to Pooyan Tabatabaei for the detailed information he shared with us about Iranian immigrant artists during the last two decades. All translations from Persian are by Marjan Moosavi.

5   Tirgan depends on various grants from the federal, provincial, and municipal tiers of the Canadian government, donations from the community, and corporate sponsorships. Over three hundred Persian-speaking volunteers work for each edition of the festival and most of the festival events are free.

Theatre Company and directed by Vahid Rahbani. It is a social play with dark humour that criticizes bigotry, narrow-mindedness, and moral decay.[6]

One of the performers of *Tit for Tat* was Sasan Ghahreman (b. 1961), a director, actor, novelist, and photographer, and an active figure in this generation of artists consistently making theatre in Persian since the 1990s. His *Majles-e Sohrāb Koshi* (*The Ceremony of Killing Sohrāb*), which was first created in 1989 and based on Ferdowsi's mythical *Shahnemeh* (*The Book of Kings*), has been revived several times on various occasions during the 1990s and 2000s. Another tendency among Iranian-Canadian artists of that generation is to adapt European plays for Persian audiences. Ghahreman has recently begun to adapt the European dramatic repertoire into Persian for Persian-speaking audiences in Toronto. For instance, in 2013 he staged Brian Friel's *The Yalta Game* in Persian for five nights and kept the title of the play's source, Anton Chekhov's *The Lady with the Lapdog*, to generate a larger audience. In 2015 he staged Éric-Emmanuel Schmitt's *Partners in Crime*, which he both directed and performed in. Ghahreman has maintained his passion and tenacity for staging plays in Persian. His recent productions, like the previously mentioned performances by other artists, have relied on private funding, a semi-professional cast, and a minimal crew.

As this generation continued to stage plays from the Iranian and European repertoires, newer, distinct voices began to appear. Soheil Parsa (a co-founder of Modern Times Stage Company), Levon Haftvan (Lemaz Productions), and Vahid Rahbani (ReeRaa Theatre Company) are three renowned practitioners who were financially and professionally capable of producing their productions in English for a broader Canadian audience, presenting them at various Toronto theatre festivals.

Parsa, whose transnationalist vision and formally experimental works have gone far beyond his ethnicity, community, and Canadian citizenship, is a graduate of two theatre programs: the University of Tehran and York

---

6 Despite the gloominess of the play's content, the group created a comic poster representing caricatures of the characters and emphasizing live music—perhaps in an effort to generate a larger audience. The production of the play was funded by Levon Haftvan, one of its two performers.

University. He co-founded the Modern Times Stage Company (with Peter
Farbridge) in the late 1980s; since its inception, the company has staged
more than fifteen original plays, adaptations, and tradaptations[7] of modernist Iranian literature, including Beyzai and Abban Na'lbandian (1947–1987),
as well as European modernist classics.[8] What makes Parsa's work unique
for Toronto audiences and practitioners is the fact that he incorporates certain traditional conventions of Persian aesthetics and cultural narratives. In
Macbeth (1995), he employed the Ta'ziyeh stylistic conventions,[9] and in the
1998 production of *Aurash* (written by Beyzai) the original narrative of a
Persian hero is dramatized.[10]

---

7   As a commonly used term in adaptation and translation studies, the term "tradapta-
tion" refers to the cultural turns, interrogations, and transformations that occur during
and even after any adaptation, particularly in relation to the temporal and local specificity
of the adaptation process. Its usage dates to Michel Garneau's translation of *Macbeth* into
Québécois in 1978. For more detail, see Gentzler 69.

8   Both Beyzai and Parsa belong to the Bahá'í religious community, who are often harshly
marginalized by the Iranian clerics and state. Although they have both had a chance to
travel back to Iran in recent decades, due to the precarity of their situation and the arbi-
trariness of the Iranian state's regulations with regard to self-exiled artists, they choose
not to travel to Iran anymore. Since 2010, Beyzai has been living in California, and has
since held the position of Bita Daryabari Visiting Professor of Iranian Studies at Stanford
University. According to Modern Times Stage Company's website, "The company has been
honoured with 16 Toronto 'DORA AWARDS' and has been nominated for sixty. Director
Soheil Parsa has received several national and international distinctions" ("People").

9   As the most important commemorative drama in the Islamic world, Ta'ziyeh plays
are epic narratives of war, loss, and the martyrdom of a prominent Shi'i figure, presented
through stylized body movements and *mise en scène* with minimal iconic stage props, lots of
dirge singing, and extensive use of percussion instruments before a faithful audience sitting
around a bare, circular stage. For more information on Ta'ziyeh, see Moosavi, "Ta'ziyeh."

10   Parsa's theatrical practice and perspective have been extensively examined in various scholarly sources and interviews. See Knowles, *Performing*; Simonsen; and Rudakoff.

Parsa is not the only artist who sees theatre as a forum for staging stories that stretch beyond the local and the national. Haftvan (1966–2018),[11] the Armenian-Iranian-Canadian artist, and his Lemaz Productions also staged transnationally tuned plays in English. Haftvan's life and artistic career encompassed a long, adventurous journey, from Iran to the former Soviet Union (Armenia, Russia, and Ukraine) and Scandinavia before settling in Toronto. The diasporic experience was not new to him. Referring to his Armenian origin and minoritarian status in Iran, he described himself as follows: "I was born diasporic. I didn't become diasporic. I've been the 'other' from the beginning" (Babayants). Like Parsa, Haftvan gravitated toward European classics of the twentieth century. His most remembered works include productions of Harold Pinter's tense and erotic play *The Lover*, performed by Lara Kelly at SummerWorks in 2003, and the previously mentioned *Yalta Game* (2017). As the artistic director of Lemaz Productions, Haftvan was the sole producer of his works. To produce *The Lover* with a professional cast and crew—a rare case for diasporic artists, who often have to rely on volunteers and non-professionals—he spent $30,000 of his own money, but failed to recoup the expenses (Crew).[12]

Haftvan would have never been able to stage *The Lover* in Iran, as Iranian state theatre regulations prohibit plays with erotic themes and images. And while the Canadian theatre context allowed him to mount shows of this type, the Canadian reception of *The Lover* was tainted by certain orientalist expectations that sought to reaffirm stereotypes of Middle Easterners as sexually

---

11   As we were preparing the first draft of this article, we received the sad news of Levon Haftvan's passing. Levon died in Tehran in March 2018 on the set of a TV series and was buried at the Armenian cemetery in Tehran. He had lived in Canada for many years—first as a refugee, then as a permanent resident. While he did apply for a Canadian citizenship in 2017, he did not live long enough to receive it.

12   In his letter of support for Haftvan, his collaborator Vladimir Milman writes, "The performance attracted a diverse audience including Canadians from all different communities, Jews, Russians, Ukrainians, Persians, Armenians, as well as English-speaking Canadians, who settled in Canada long ago."

charged figures.[13] The festival reviewers Jon Kaplan and Glenn Sumi wrote, "Since much of the production team is Iranian, why not cast Iranians as Pinter's starchy Brit leads? That would be something to watch" (Kaplan and Sumi). They do not go on to explain why casting a play about the "sexual fantasies" and "extramarital affairs" of a "starchy" married couple in this way would be "something to watch." One cannot help but ask if it would have added more exoticism to see a Middle Eastern couple engaged in sexual games—perhaps even better if the couple were Muslim.[14]

Haftvan's friend and collaborator Vahid Rahbani was a young graduate from Montréal's National Theatre School who, after a short and vibrant career in Canada, returned to Iran in 2009. His adaptation of Pinter's *Ashes to Ashes*, produced by Lemaz and performed at the Tarragon Theatre as part of the 2007 SummerWorks Festival, was both a critical and popular success. In this production, Rahbani took a post-dramatic approach to the staging of global trauma and our ethical responsibility for it. The play included references to the death of the Iranian-Canadian photojournalist Zahra Kazemi. He used several innovative aesthetic choices to engage and provoke his audience. The crew marshalled the audience into the auditorium, then two soldiers aggressively imposed silence. Later, the actors built an isolating wall on the stage, and finally they expelled the audience. There was no closing blackout or curtain call (Fitzpatrick 61). In the beginning, Rebecca, one of the characters, walked on stage and took a collective photograph of the audience, a reference to Kazemi, who was taking a photo when she was arrested in Iran. In the

---

13   Many still remember the monumental book *The Thousand and One Nights* (also known as *Arabian Nights*) and its erotic imagery and stories.

14   Lemaz Productions's other works include an adaptation of *Hello Out There!* (2006) by Armenian-American William Saroyan, and a short adaptation of Chekhov's *The Seagull*, again in English and performed at SummerWorks in 2004. In 2016, Haftvan staged the Persian version of *The Yalta Game* in Tehran, and in 2017 he staged it for a Persian audience at the Fairview Library Theatre in Toronto. The recent *In Case of Nothing*, a collaboration with Sina Gilani (born and educated in Canada) and directed by Tatiana Jennings, was presented at the Box for SummerWorks in 2015. Haftvan also directed work in Armenian with the Armenian community of Toronto.

end, this photograph was projected onto the wall like a mirror reflection of the audience. According to Lisa Fitzpatrick, "response-ability," "addressability," and "witnessing" in presentation and reception of global injustice and violence were the constitutive elements that formulated Rahbani's ambition for facilitating ethical spectatorship in Toronto as his work dramatized "the ethical demands of human relationships with others" (64). As Fitzpatrick and Milija Gluhovic also confirm in their examinations of Rahbani's *Ashes to Ashes*, this adaptation functioned as a theatrical invitation for Canadian audiences to witness the trauma of an immigrant/stranger on a global stage (Fitzpatrick 63; Gluhovic 192).

In producing this adaptation, Lemaz's creative team indeed situated itself between the specificity of Kazemi and her fate in Tehran and of the Persian diaspora community in Toronto on the one hand, and the global significance of ethical questions about state persecution of dissident artists on the other. Such transcultural movements in between these sources of support are not new to diasporic theatrical productions and will be discussed later in this chapter.

While Parsa continues his work in Toronto, both Rahbani and Haftvan decided to go to Iran to create their work. In an interview, Haftvan explained this decision as due to the lack of material resources that the Canadian theatre context could provide and, in contrast, the wealth of professional resources with which Iran's state-funded theatre system supplied him (Babayants).[15] Those who immigrated to Canada in the 1990s seem to be leaving the country to produce professional work, with Parsa being a sole exception, at least among stage directors. Interestingly, Soheil Parsa seems to be the only Iranian-Canadian theatremaker from Toronto whose work gets consistent recognition by English-speaking scholars and critics. For instance, Parsa is the only Iranian-Canadian theatremaker mentioned in Knowles's list of diverse artists who "have had a major impact on the intercultural performance ecology of the city" (*Performing* 205).

---

15   Although the Iranian state has limited its financial support for theatrical groups since 2009, high-profile artists like Haftvan, Rahbani, and Yaghoubi still enjoy their well-established network of professional collaborators and private investors while working in Iran.

Over the last decade, a new generation of Iranian-Canadian theatre practitioners emerged in Toronto. Sina Gilani, Kevin Kashani, Bahareh Yaraghi, Tara
Grammy, and Parmida Kakavand (1.5 and second-generation Canadians)[16]
are among this group. This generation of theatre artists tend to be better
integrated into mainstream Toronto theatre than their forebears, and prefer
to collaborate with various English-speaking (non-Persian) theatre groups
rather than dedicate their time to the Persian community exclusively. For
instance, Grammy has worked with the culturally diverse collective Pandemic
Theatre, with whom she developed her one-woman show *Mahmoud* (2012,
written by Tara Grammy and Tom Arthur Davis). *Mahmoud* won the Best
of Fringe Award, enjoyed a North American tour, and was eventually published by Playwrights Canada Press. Another Persian name, perhaps better
known to a mainstream anglophone audience, is Ramin Karimloo: also a
1.5 generation Iranian-Canadian, a Tehran-born star of the West End and
Broadway famous for his performances in large-scale musicals such as *Les
Misérables* and *The Phantom of the Opera*. Karimloo, however, resides outside
of Canada and is not engaged in the production of Iranian-Canadian work.
At the same time, Iranian indie theatre artists, who are perhaps not willing
to completely detach themselves from the Persian community, remain very
much on the fringes of the Toronto theatre scene.[17] In this regard, the situation that we are observing in 2018 is not radically different from the situation

---

16   In diaspora and migration studies, the term *1.5 generation* refers to those immigrants
who moved to a new country as children and who, as a result, share a "split" cultural identity. See, for instance, Danico.

17   One such artist is Siavash Shabanpour (b. 1981), a graduate of the York University
theatre department, and an active poet as well as an educator, actor, and producer in the
Persian theatre community. Shabanpour often chooses his cast from the participants of
his acting workshops. The most recent work produced by his company, 2000 Feet Up,
is *The Body of a Woman as a Battlefield in The Bosnian War*, performed in English at
Capital Fringe in Washington DC and at the Chicago Fringe. His works, performed in
Persian, include directing *What's in a Name* by Alexandre de La Patellière and Matthieu
Delaporte, Neil Simon's *The Good Doctor* (2015), *Thirty Roubles for Delicacy* (2016), Martin
McDonagh's *The Cripple of Inishmaan* (2017), and *Chekhofnāmeh* (*The Book of Chekhov*),
based on Anton Chekhov's stories (2018).

of the 1980s, which we introduced at the beginning of the chapter. Overall, Iranian-Canadian artists continue to be seen as representatives of an "othered" and often exoticized culture.

A recent and perhaps distinct figure in Toronto's Iranian theatre scene is Mohammad Yaghoubi (b. 1967). It is his process of staging his own play, *A Moment of Silence*, a contemporary Persian classic, at Toronto's SummerWorks Performance Festival that we will focus on below.

MOHAMMAD YAGHOUBI AND NOWADAYS THEATRE

Ever since the well-known Iranian artists Mohammad Yaghoubi and Aida Keykhaii moved to Toronto, the Persian community in the GTA has been exposed to significantly more professional theatrical productions whose themes and aesthetics address contemporary socio-political issues. Despite the absence of their Iranian network, support, and funding, Yaghoubi and Keykhaii established Nowadays Theatre Company in 2015. One of the most acclaimed contemporary Iranian playwrights, Yaghoubi left his home country for Canada in 2014, learned English, and moved on to producing theatre work in Toronto in Persian and in English. *A Moment of Silence* became Yaghoubi's first English production in Toronto.[18] After this, the company switched to reviving various plays that had been previously staged in Iran and offering workshops to the Persian community—work that connects Nowadays to many other similar companies organized by recent immigrant artists.[19]

Keykhaii (b. 1974), a professional theatre, film, and TV actor, has had a prolific artistic career and enjoyed a vast professional network in her homeland. In Toronto, Keykhaii shifted her focus from acting to directing for a

---

18   In 2013, Yaghoubi directed a stage reading of *A Moment of Silence* for the Persian community that was performed in one of the music halls at the University of Toronto's Hart House.

19   For a detailed discussion of Toronto-based immigrant artists creating work for their own communities, see Chapter Two of Barry Freeman's *Staging Strangers* (31–57).

Persian audience. In 2017, she directed two plays: *Iceland* by Canadian Nicolas Billon in June 2017, and *Khāb dar Fenjān-e Khāli* (*Sleeping in an Empty Cup*) by the renowned Iranian female dramatist Naghmeh Samini for the Persian community.[20]

When selecting plays, both Yaghoubi and Keykhaii often choose scripts that offer a critical response to the current socio-political context, while knowing that their diasporic audience might prefer lighter, comic plays. For both Yaghoubi and Keykhaii, the aim of educating an Iranian diasporic audience is not only important but also urgent. The result is that most often their staged plays present poignant socio-cultural criticism and are tonally serious, even sad. For instance, Yaghoubi remounted *Hayoulā Khāni* (*Demon Reading*) in Toronto's Fairview Library Theatre in August 2017 in Persian. The play is a surrealistic critique of religious fanaticism and tyranny of censorship. In an interview, however, Yaghoubi notes that staging the play in Toronto was a response to dogmatic statements by the US president (Yaghoubi, *Iceland*).[21]

Nowadays has recently begun functioning as a theatrical home that connects Iranian-Canadian theatre practitioners to each other and to their communities. Before the emergence of Nowadays, many of these artists (including Siavash Shabanpour and Sasan Ghahreman) had been working independently, or only on occasion with Soheil Parsa. Not only are they now working collaboratively, but they are also providing peer critique of each other's work and publishing their responses and reviews in the widely read Persian magazines *Titr*, *Tehranto*, and *Shahrvand*.

---

20   The cast of *Iceland* consisted of professional Iranian actors residing in Iran. They had to apply for Canadian visas to be able to travel to Toronto for this performance. At the time that we are writing the final draft of this chapter, Keykhaii is directing *Swim Team*, written by Jāber Ramazāni, to be performed in English in Toronto at SummerWorks 2018.

21   Between the Toronto productions of *A Moment of Silence* and *Demon Reading* the company also restaged Persian adaptations of Martin McDonagh's *The Pillowman* (performed in Tehran in 2013) and David Auburn's *Proof* (performed in Tehran in 2012), both in Toronto's Fairview Library Theatre. *Demon Reading* was first performed in 2014 in Tehran City Theatre Complex with a different cast, with the exception of Keykhaii playing the female lead.

Fig. 1. From left to right, Melanie Pyne, Sarah Marchand, Parmida Kakavand, and Maxime Robin in the English premiere of *A Moment of Silence*, directed by Mohammad Yaghoubi, produced by Nowadays Theatre. Photo by Bahar Ahmadi provided courtesy of Abr Media.

A MOMENT OF SILENCE: MOMENTS OF ENCOUNTER, LIBERATION, AND SELF-REFLECTION

The Canadian premiere *of A Moment of Silence* was Yaghoubi's first experience directing in English. It was performed for eight nights at Factory Theatre for the 2016 SummerWorks Festival. *A Moment of Silence* is a contemporary classic and has a unique—and to some extent tragic—position within the contemporary Iranian repertoire. It has been continuously attacked by censors, and was most recently prohibited from being performed in Iran altogether (Yaghoubi, "Independent Art"). It is also the first Iranian play presented in Canada in English to be directed by the playwright himself.[22]

---

22 *A Moment of Silence* has been revived many times since its Tehran premiere. It was staged in Iran (May 2001 and December 2010); Prague, Czech Republic (June and

A Moment of Silence presents a story within a story. It begins with the story of a woman (Shiva) who periodically falls asleep for an unusually long period of time and then wakes up to find out that the world around her has drastically changed. She first sleeps through the Islamic Revolution, then through the war with Iraq, then through a series of murders of dissident artists as well as irreversible transformations in her own family. The second storyline reveals the struggles of a Tehran-based playwright who keeps receiving threatening phone calls from government agents and nationalistic bullies—all while conceiving of the story of Shiva and her family. On the one hand, *A Moment of Silence* is an audacious response to the brutal and unjust murders of intellectuals by agents of the Iranian government that occurred between 1988 and 1998. On the other hand, it comments on the quotidian socio-cultural issues that contemporary Iranians are grappling with: the mandatory hijab, a lack of civil rights for children born out of wedlock, and the overall absence of freedom of expression.

The surreal portrayal of Shiva's unusual condition of falling asleep for extended periods of time is interwoven with the playwright's writing process as she and her husband review and comment on political events in the recent history of Iran, or on the insecure status of dissident writers. Like Rahbani's *Ashes to Ashes, A Moment of Silence* shows varied and complex reactions to terror and surveillance. This is a feature that certainly speaks to international audiences to various degrees; however, it is perhaps lost on those Toronto audience members who have not experienced high levels of political and artistic surveillance and oppression. The play's metatheatrical qualities, fragmented structure, and lifelike characterization present a surreal, poetic, yet earthly and at times comic meditation on Iran's turbulent history and Iranians' experience of unexpected "change" and its aftermath. On a more universal level, it is also the playwright's manifesto about intellectuals' loss of freedom of expression and how this leads to losing joy and hope in one's personal life.

November 2015 and January 2016); Richmond, California, USA (March 2015); and Washington DC, USA (September 2015). It received stage readings in France, Canada, Belgium, and the USA. It has also been translated into English, French, Czech, Turkish, and Kurdish.

The final moment of the play is "a moment of silence" where the character of the playwright asks the audience to rise in commemoration of all artists and intellectuals murdered by the government. Based on the testimony of witnesses of its Tehran performance, this collective "moment of silence" created a genuinely strong moment of political activism for both the creative team and the audience members; according to Yaghoubi and critics, it even made some audience members sob. The same effect was mostly lost when *A Moment of Silence* was performed in Toronto, although we cannot assume, of course, that the strong emotional response did not happen only because of the general disconnection of Toronto audiences from the events in Iran.

DOMESTICATING/FOREIGNIZING
A MOMENT OF SILENCE

According to Yaghoubi, the foreignization of his play started even before it was submitted to SummerWorks. In a conversation with assistant director Art Babayants, he revealed that Parsa had advised him to add stage directions to the play, since Parsa was worried that the potentially conservative (that is, theatrically conservative) jury readers might see the absence of stage directions as a sign of Yaghoubi's lack of playwriting proficiency. Yaghoubi added numerous stage directions and, once the play was accepted, he continued redeveloping— sometimes radically rewriting—the original script. From the very start of the process, Yaghoubi faced linguistic and cultural challenges mostly caused by his difficulties with the English language, his unfamiliarity with Toronto anglophone theatre practitioners and audiences, and his lack of experience of directing and producing work outside of a state-owned theatre system.

First, we will address the linguistic challenges, which were at the forefront of his battles, as he had to deal with the inevitability of verbal and literary loss and the linguistic and semantic changes that the process of Canadianizing his play generated. The play had been translated into English by an Iranian-Armenian-American theatre artist (Torange Yeghiazarian), and later, in Canada, its text was once again edited by Matt Jones after a private session of play reading by native speakers of Canadian English. To Canadianize the script, Yaghoubi and

Jones had to make sure the language read and sounded less like a simple rendering into English and more like an approximation of the Persian text in terms of both its cultural spirit and transliterations. For instance, certain names that were likely to cause pronunciation difficulties were changed: Jamsheed was changed to Jimmy, Iraj was changed to Keyvān, and many book titles, historical references, and proper names were also either shortened or omitted. Other changes included lessening the loud and unpleasant sounds of explosions and adding live Persian drum music during some of the scene transitions.

Yaghoubi admits this loss and notes:

> The most important part that is lost is the play's puns and figurative language, and by this, I don't mean archaic or literary language. I believe the contemporary language used by common Iranians can also be replete with word play, witticism, and irony. For instance, in a scene called "Urashima," which is based on [the character] Sheida's stream of consciousness, I play with the words Urashima and Shiva, and through this alliteration,[23] I let the character move between reality and the abstract state of her mind. I am skeptical about whether the English translation can communicate what is going on at the level of word choice. (Moosavi, "Interview")

However, Yaghoubi was generally content with the overall outcome of the foreignization of his play. He believes the play's "distinctive dramatic structure" was preserved, a fact that gave him the confidence to introduce himself to Toronto audiences with this play (Moosavi, "Interview"). Moreover, relying on the English readers' feedback on the play in its North American staged reading, he concludes, perhaps hastily and nonchalantly, that "the audience was able to understand some of the witty nuances in the text" (Moosavi, "Interview"). Several questions transpire from these remarks. First, how sufficient and valid is the criterion of communicating "some of the witty nuances" in the transcultural restaging of a play? Second, to what extent can translation

---

23   Here, he refers to the phonetic similarities between the names of Urashima and Shiva.

become a dramaturgical mediator, particularly when a production is to be read in a different sign system?

The second obvious problem requiring domestication was the complex socio-cultural and historical context underpinning *A Moment of Silence*. The play is deeply connected to its Iranian local and historical context, and when performed in Iran (2000 and 2010), relying on its audience's collective memory and shared history, it engaged its local audience affectively and intellectually to great effect. In restaging his play for an English-speaking audience in Toronto, Marjan Moosavi, one of Yaghoubi's assistants/interpreters, prepared several lectures, handouts, and images to familiarize the Canadian cast with the socio-political context and history of Iran since 1979.

The most important dramaturgical alteration, however, happened when Yaghoubi changed the gender of one of the play's key characters—the playwright—from male to female. This shift, which disembedded the character

SHIVA is reading from
FOROUGH FAROKHZAD's
poetry book.

Fig. 2. Sara Marchand in the English premiere of *A Moment of Silence*, directed by Mohammad Yaghoubi, produced by Nowadays Theatre. Photo by Bahar Ahmadi provided courtesy of Abr Media.

from the play's previous stagings and overall dramaturgical constellation, clearly shows his openness and courage for exposing his authorial practice to change and self-reflection, as he also emphasized in one of his interviews: "I have an obsession with changing my own work, so this change was a pleasant response to that urge" (Moosavi, "Interview").

Nonetheless, this gesture bears certain complex implications in a Canadian cultural context. In the Toronto production, unlike in the Iranian one, the playwright who receives threatening calls is a woman. Explaining this change, Yaghoubi says, "I believe choosing a woman as a dissident play-wright is more applicable to the current reality of Iran and even of the world. Women's rights are the most political issue these days" (Moosavi, "Interview"). Like Rahbani's post-dramatic aesthetics, Yaghoubi's dramaturgical decision in changing the gender of the dissident playwright is, understandably, an attempt to facilitate ethical spectatorship by highlighting the global issue of women's rights. However, this decision runs the risk of exoticizing his Iranian character and dramatic narrative. In a scene presenting the final moments of her life, the female playwright is video-recording a prophetic speech because, by this point, she has realized that she will be the next victim of the political chain murders. Following a spontaneous decision, she takes off her head scarf and throws it away as her ultimate and extreme act of defiance. None of the other versions of the play, whether on stage or in print (even the English printed version), contain this scene. Obviously, Yaghoubi considered the Torontonian festival stage (and the theatrical ephemerality it provided) safe enough to include such a radical scene. But the idea and icon of hijab in the Western imagination and art has long been understood mistakenly as an instrument of women's subjugation and thus has been a means of orientalizing Muslim Middle Eastern women. Yaghoubi's decision to have his defiant playwright symbolically throw her scarf away might lead to the reinforcement of such a sustained orientalist gaze and set of misconceptions.

Some critics and audiences, particularly the Iranian-Canadian ones, believed that the Canadian restaging of the play in English ran the risk of turning it to a decontextualized, exoticized, and commodified play.[24] Others, including Yaghoubi himself, insisted on the universal quality of his story and dramaturgy. In these terms, Yaghoubi notes:

> Undoubtedly the play will resonate less with a Canadian audience, regarding both language and content. But it will change shape, and this is a quality of every artistic work. It transforms by encountering a new audience but it still contains its basic shape, and that's what matters most. Seeing a Canadian audience understand it so well is very enjoyable to me . . . And there is the privilege of writing without censorship, which is motivating me to write more. (Moosavi, "Interview")

This indicates that, to Yaghoubi, making his play amenable to a different aesthetic vision (Canadianization) and different involvement with a foreign audience is artistically valuable and a pleasure. Furthermore, for him, imparting a universal message matters most:

> The responses to the play that I have received have proven that regardless of its specific political content, it is raising universal issues about human relationships and experiences. Staging a play in a free country that criticizes an established order is not a defiant act but what matters most here is that *A Moment of Silence* is telling its story well enough to be understood by Canadians. (Moosavi, "Interview")

---

24 Most of these responses came to us through informal conversations with audiences, some of whom are well-seasoned Iranian theatre critics living in Toronto. Having watched the original Iranian production, one of them believed that since the play is a deeply context-bound piece, its performance in Canada simply flattens it. An American-Canadian English-French speaking friend who is also quite familiar with Iranian culture wrote, "Seeing blonde people was distracting. And I didn't feel they got the right sense of how Iranian men and women would relate to each other. Since the piece is set in Iran, it distracted. There is something ineffable about how people relate to each other. This afternoon, the actors didn't convince me that they were Iranians." Although we find this response strikingly problematic, we have to leave a deeper scholarly engagement with such comments for another paper.

Like *Ashes to Ashes*, *A Moment of Silence* provides another example of immigrant artists adjusting their own ethical vision and their audience's responses in encountering global issues.

Finally, the third aspect of domestication during the Toronto production of *A Moment of Silence* was Yaghoubi's own encounter with the Canadian theatre context, specifically with SummerWorks and their rehearsal and production process. Yaghoubi had to learn to cope with a shoestring budget (atypical for his Iranian productions) and the unusually short production and pre-performance period. These two major limitations seriously affected Yaghoubi's casting, stage design, and managerial choices. For instance, he had to limit his stage props to only a few elements and use exactly the same set design that Keykhaii had previously used in Iran when she directed *A Moment of Silence* in 2010. As Yaghoubi asserts, "Choosing a minimal set design is no longer an aesthetic choice but an obligation!" (Moosavi, "Interview"). Besides, coming from a different tradition of theatremaking, Yaghoubi was barely familiar with the position and duties of a stage manager. He also found the short four-week rehearsal period insufficient for the complex directorial and acting work that the play requires. As members of his production team, we both sensed the serious challenges Yaghoubi faced in such technical encounters.

THE FUTURE

For the new generation of Iranian theatre artists in diaspora, it is becoming increasingly urgent to dramatize contemporary ethical encounters with issues of global concern such as political disappearances, injustice, and gender inequality. Apart from global and ethical motivations, material limitations also cause these artists to move transculturally between their specific homeland or diasporic community and the broader societal context in which they live. On the one hand, Iranian immigrant artists rely on the funding organizations for whom cultural diversity is a key criterion as well as the linguistic and cultural communities they belong to. On the other hand, these artists are interested in reaching out to a wider audience, both for aesthetic experimentation and spectatorial engagement. Up to now, finding the middle ground has proven to be very challenging. Another major challenge for immigrant artists is the overall shortage of funding and professional networks that they experience in Canadian contexts. Access to funding is often impeded by various communication barriers, which can result from a lack of linguistic and cultural competencies that newcomer artists may experience, but also from the complicated bureaucratic procedures related to writing government grant applications.[25]

Although the thriving theatre scene targeting the Persian community has admittedly been a result of mainly incoherent and short-term endeavours, overall its very presence seems beneficial for Iranian-Canadians. First, it offers them a space, however liminal or ephemeral, that makes their invisible processes of cultural and ethical encounter spectacularly visible through performance at the festivals. Second, as in the case of other immigrant theatremaking, the theatrical output of Iranian immigrants often helps Canada's culturally, linguistically, and ethnically diverse audiences negotiate their similarities and differences (Meerzon, "Theatre" 183). Moreover, introducing plays from the Iranian dramatic repertoire familiarizes non-Persian Canadian audiences, even if on a small scale, with the vibrant and growing cultural capital of Iran and disentangles the prevailing image of Iran from the marginalizing web of orientalist gazes.[26] Yaghoubi highlights this objective in his interview with Marjan Moosavi:

> I believe in the vitality of performing art for uniting cultures. The fact that a group of Canadians is spending a month working and living with an Iranian text for performance is a fantastic opportunity. This could never happen when watching an Iranian film. Moreover, this event introduces Iran and Iranians to Canadians who may have acquired a

---

25   In interviews with Persian artist-immigrants, all of them mentioned the hardship of English grant writing as well as English formal correspondence, whether written or oral, with Canadian theatre officials. Therefore, the accessibility of Canadian resources is a big issue for them.

26   In this sense, we can claim that Iranian diasporic theatre, when done for a non-Persian audience, pursues an educational agenda whether it is intentional or not: it often simply proves to North Americans that Iran/Persia has fine arts and culture steeped in rich history and politics.

distorted image about them from the media. And lastly, performing *A Moment of Silence* introduces theatre audiences and artists in Canada to what's happening in contemporary Iranian theatre.[27] ("Interview")

Finally, like many other artists, Iranian theatre practitioners in Toronto enjoy the process of theatremaking as a self-reflexive, redemptive, and liberating process that allows them to embed and disembed their aesthetic perceptions and potentials, and to exercise their ethical responsibilities free from the state censorial intervention they face in Iran. For instance, Yaghoubi's recent play, *The Persimmons*, which he wrote in English, has been commissioned and will be produced by Toronto's Tarragon Theatre. This play dramatizes the lives of four immigrants who encounter each other in Toronto. As actors in the "theatre" of their migration, Iranian theatre artists' autonomy over their art and selves is in constant interplay between liberation and limitation.[28]

---

27   Yaghoubi's most recent attempt to deghettoize Iranian-Canadian theatre is worth mentioning here too. On 12–13 June 2018, he presented one of his plays, *Tanhā Rāh-e Momken* (*The Only Possible Way*, which was renamed for the Toronto staging as *Angels in Iran*), with the Persian students of his theatre workshop in Persian and with English surtitles. He made a decision to shift his performance venue from Fairview Library Theatre in North York to the George Ignatieff Theatre located in the heart of downton Toronto. Sadly, the anglophone theatre community of Toronto by and large ignored the event.

28   As we were finalizing this chapter, we learned that Yaghoubi and Keykaii's Nowadays Theatre became the company in residence at Canadian Stage (Toronto) as part of the RBC Emerging Artists Program. They received the Newcomer and Refugee Arts Engagement grant from the Toronto Arts Council and were able to stage *The Only Possible Way* in English by casting Iranian newcomers. This can be seen as a radical attempt at diversification, since previously those selected to partake in the RBC Emerging Artists Program had been mostly native speakers of English born and trained in Canada. While we welcome this radical move forward, we also have to acknowledge the irony of the situation where two very established Iranian artists, who had previously taught theatre in one of the most prestigious theatre schools and produced work internationally, were named "emerging" in the Canadian cultural context.

ASIAN CANADIAN IMMIGRANT DRAMA: TACTICAL INTERVENTIONS IN *ACQUIESCE* AND *KIM'S CONVENIENCE*

ELEANOR TY

David Yee's *acquiesce* and Ins Choi's *Kim's Convenience* are both plays that deal in part with the immigrant family's struggle to survive in its adopted land and with conflicts between the older and younger generations: issues common to other recent Asian Canadian works, such as Sunil Kuruvilla's *Rice Boy* and Catherine Hernandez's *Singkil*. Yee and Choi's plays have both received critical and popular acclaim, even though, according to the ex-artistic director of Soulpepper, "There is nothing original about the form of [*Kim's Convenience*] (it does not stray from the neoclassical unities of time, place, and action), and its subject matter is extremely familiar (literally)" (Schultz). Even so, I argue that these contemporary Asian Canadian plays present subtle resistance and innovation in their own ways, refining the traditional form of immigrant drama. Their power and magic come from the way they stay within and, at the same time, go beyond the confines of the genre. They depict the ways second-generation immigrants come to terms with their place in society, but are innovative in their use of such techniques as magic realism and humour. They also confront issues that are not usually dealt with by visible minorities, such as domestic violence and intra-ethnic conflicts.

Asian Canadian theatre is relatively young, but is becoming more recognized in Canada and internationally thanks to playwrights like Yee, Choi, and others. The first play in Nina Lee Aquino's edited collection (2009) of

Asian Canadian drama is Rick Shiomi's *Yellow Fever*, which dates back to 1982 and was first produced in San Francisco, and then in New York (Shiomi iii). Today, fu-GEN Theatre and Carlos Bulosan Theatre in Toronto, along with the Vancouver Asian Canadian Theatre, encourage, help develop, and produce plays that tour various parts of Canada. In her introduction to her second volume of Asian Canadian plays, Nina Aquino observes the changes in the themes of Asian Canadian drama over the last thirty years:

> I noticed that in the earlier plays (Volume 1), the hot topics were displacement, immigration, homesickness and questing to Gold Mountain . . . Then, somewhere in the middle (Volume 2), the writing started to go more inward. There's an acceptance of Canada as "home" and dealing with all the baggage of what that means . . . defining one's new identity, striding the hyphen that made up where you supposedly came from "originally" and your country of residence. The most recent plays, from the last decade, cover a much broader and explorative range of subject matter. (Vol. I, x)

Yee and Choi fit in this last category; they are still exploring the themes of identity and sense of belonging, but are also probing other issues like domestic violence, intergenerational conflict, and their relationships with other minority groups in Canada.

Reviews of both *acquiesce* and *Kim's Convenience* have been positive to laudatory. Yee's play was described as "meditative" and "lyrical" (Nestruck). It played in November 2016 and has been published by Playwrights Canada Press. Though Choi struggled with writing his play for five years, it won the New Play Contest held by the Toronto Fringe Festival in 2010; was remounted by Soulpepper in 2012; toured across Canada in 2013 and 2014; was revived and toured again to Halifax (January to February 2017), Toronto (February 2017), and Montréal (March 2017); and finally went to New York City in July 2017. The television series based on the play, which premiered on CBC in October 2016, has been highly successful and has now aired for two seasons. In this paper, I argue that this success is due in part to certain key tactics Yee and Choi both employ, such as tactical deviations and intersectionality, which allow them to produce highly entertaining, critically challenging, and con- sciousness-raising material. In both plays, while first-generation migration occurred a number of years ago, we continue to see the effects of the family's displacement on second-generation immigrant children.

In the analysis that follows, I use the term "immigrant" with some trep- idation, conscious that the term "unwittingly reinforce[s] certain historical fallacies and dangerously limiting notions of culture, ethnicity, and race," as Josephine Lee notes in her essay "Between Immigrant and Hyphenation." Referring to theatre in the US, Lee reminds us that immigration should be envisioned as "continuing an already-existing dynamic process of hybridity" and argues against the view that theatre is the "demonstration and continued fortification of a coherent, continuous, recognizable culture, and examined only in terms of how it helps a community preserve that culture" (48). While certain tropes are common to immigrant plays, such as the representation of ethnocultural differences, the sense of non-belonging, and nostalgia for one's original country, there are also historical differences between immi- grant groups. Asian Canadians, unlike European Canadians, were historically excluded from full citizenship and voting rights, with anti-immigration laws prohibiting land ownership and miscegenation. These "immigrant acts" (Lowe) changed the nature of Asian communities in Canada and affected their participation in the arts. As Lee observes about the term "Asian American," the term "Asian Canadian" "applies more readily to later generations who have already been 'partially assimilated' rather than immigrants" (51). Hence, cele- brated Asian Canadian plays like *Miss Orient(ed)* and *Banana Boys* are about 1.5- or second-generation immigrants and their struggles to find themselves between cultures.

David Yee is himself a second-generation biracial actor and playwright, and his drama *acquiesce* offers another example of the second-generation immigrant play. Nevertheless, it uses conventional tropes of immigrant drama in innovative ways. His play uses the familiar plot of the trip to the immi- grant family's homeland, but gives it an unfamiliar twist by adding magic, mystery, and comedy to the protagonist's journey of self-discovery. He plays with notions of time and space by using lighting, strange objects, and shallow and deep staging. The result is a dreamscape, a "beautiful mix of complex and evocative visual metaphors, strong, strange stage moments, startlingly simple movement transitions," reviewer Thea Fitz-James notes. Not only does Yee incorporate ghosts, folklore, and the fantastic, but he also reworks conventional thinking about the conflict between West versus East, the contrast of new and old worlds, the notion of the Asian family as model minority, and normative heterosexual relationships.

A death in the family is a common reason to journey to the country of one's ancestors, and David Yee begins his play with the death of the protagonist's father, who he has not seen in fifteen years. Sin Hwang has to travel from his home in Toronto to Hong Kong to attend the funeral. However, mysteries and impossible challenges face Sin as soon as he lands. When he arrives in Hong Kong, he is surprised to find that his "luggage" includes his father's cadaver, which has travelled as cargo on the plane unbeknownst to him. His cousin Kai, the executor of Hwang's father's will, gives him a list of tasks to complete while he is in Hong Kong. One of these tasks, as dictated by his father's will, is to write and deliver the father's eulogy, to be spoken in Cantonese, which the Asian Canadian protagonist cannot speak. Cousin Kai also expects Sin to learn about filial piety and gives Sin a book on *The 24 Paragons of Filial Piety* in order to make Sin understand his father's life. The need to learn the language of his father leads Sin to speak to and seek help from unusual figures: a stuffed Paddington Bear toy, a Buddhist monk, his gay cousin Kai, and his sometime girlfriend, Nine.

Yee employs literalization (making metaphors literal), puns, and jokes to show the ways in which language both obfuscates and reveals the past. Sin carries baggage around and within him, literally and metaphorically, without realizing the implications of its contents. His father's body has been weighing him down without his realizing it. The play contains several scenes where an ordinary object such as a suitcase turns out to hold unexpected things, and then metamorphoses into something else. In the opening scene, one suitcase seems to be filling with sand, falling from a shaft of light. But soon after, it becomes an "altar full of incense sticks burning in honour of the dead"

(Nestruck). In another scene, the suitcase becomes a sink filled with water for Sin to wash his face. Kelly Nestruck observes that "*Acquiesce* is about the strange, bottomless baggage given to us by our parents—and learning how to carry it." More than that, it is also about the magic, mystery, and inexplicable elements in our lives that we do not or refuse to see.

While immigrant narratives often use stories and folktales from the immigrant's land of origin to teach second-generation children, what is most interesting in Yee's play is the way in which it combines these stories and teachings with magic realism. Elements of magic enchant and create wonder in the play, but they are also suggestive of the spiritual aspect of our lives that is missing in the everyday modern world. As Sin starts to learn about Chinese customs, pearls begin to come out of his mouth: "*Sin opens his suitcase, lights incense sticks, and places them inside . . . He coughs . . . raising his hand to his mouth, and spits out a pearl . . . He begins to cough again. More pearls spill out of his mouth and into the suitcase. The inside of the suitcase begins to glow, and SIN takes a lantern out. It becomes the only light on Earth*" (Act I, Scene 12). The stage directions and the scene with the pearls suggest the illumination and "pearls of wisdom" that Sin expels. These pearls shed light and are contrasted with the technology of the West. In a flashback set in Toronto in the next scene, Sin and his girlfriend Nine are in the dark and Sin spills coffee on the only source of light in the room, his laptop computer, which then becomes damaged. The illumination of the East is contrasted with the darkness of the West, but the pearls or gems of the homeland are not well-absorbed by the protagonist. Thus, instead of figuring the West as light and the East as primitive or dark, Yee shows light to be within the protagonist, who has to learn to use it properly.

Lee's use of non-realist elements echoes that of other Asian Canadian playwrights, who have used similarly innovative stagings in their plays to signal changes in time or geographical location. For example, Factory Theatre's 2001 production of Betty Quan's *Mother Tongue* in Toronto featured a split stage, with the realist scenes of "present-day Vancouver in front and to the left of the audience and the dreamlike flashback scenes toward the right side and back of the audience" (Ty, *Unfastened* 51). In Quan's play, there was an obvious split between domestic, interior scenes in the present and dream-like sequences in the past, which were set against a backdrop painted in blue, suggesting water and waves. In Yee's play, the staging is much simpler and less binary, using the suitcase to "carry" us from reality to fantasy, from Hong Kong to Toronto, and from the earthly to the spiritual.

By creating such images, Yee both uses and resists the normative tropes of the immigrant play. My term for such strategies, "tactical deviations," is inspired by Michel de Certeau's analyses of the everyday practices of consumers as tactics, reading them as ways of resistance (de Certeau, Giard, and Mayol xxxiii). By using this term, I aim to suggest that authors like Yee (and, as we shall see, Choi) resist normative plots, ideologies, and genres by seeming to follow—yet also deviating from—them. They follow many of the conventions of the immigrant story of migration and the search for a new and better life in Canada, but use their plays to make subtle commentaries about contemporary Canadian society. For example, they challenge the myth of the Asian North American family as model minority. The term "model minority" was first used in the US in an article in *U.S. News and World Report* in 1966, which praised Asian Americans for their discipline, "low crime rates, a willingness to work hard, and strong family values" (qtd. in Ty, *Asianfail* 2). The article perpetuated the myth of America as the land of opportunity for those who worked hard, and helped to create stereotypes of Asians as self-sacrificing, model workers for the next couple of decades. Critics have noted that Asian Americans were often pitted against other minority groups, such as Blacks and Latinos, in order to diffuse the notion that America was a racist society (Ty, *Asianfail* 2–3). In the twenty-first century, Asian Americans and Asian Canadians are still expected to be successful professionals, doctors, engineers, and computer geeks who tend to value economic success and familial life. While the model minority discourse is more prevalent in the US, in Canada, as Gordon Pon notes, "presses like the *Toronto Star, Fortune Magazine, Globe and Mail, Montreal Gazette*, and *Toronto Life* have [also] championed the Chinese as the 'model minority'" (283). Dovetailing neatly "with Canadian discourses of multiculturalism," the model minority discourse "reinforce[s] the liberal belief that Canada and its institutions such as schools are accommodating, fair, and accessible to all those who work hard enough" (Pon 286). Consequently, Asian Canadians who do not succeed economically and professionally are seen as failures.

In one example of tactical deviation, Yee's *acquiesce* challenges some of these preconceptions about Asian Canadians. Firstly, the protagonist is a writer, instead of a mathematician, engineer, or scientist. He is not a mild-mannered Oriental, but a rather grumpy novelist. On the plane, when a passenger tries to engage him in conversation, he refuses to humour him. He does not exhibit the positive qualities associated with the model minority, but is full of self-loathing and anger. With his cousin Kai, he is unappreciative and petulant. The cousin encourages Sin to fulfill his role as eldest son of the family, but he is reluctant, does not quite know what he is supposed to do, and is not eager to learn. When his cousin takes him to the library, he plays *Pokémon GO* instead of studying his duties (Act I, Sc. 14). Kai says, "Everything is a game to you. Or a joke. We don't have time for this, you must complete the tasks at hand before the funeral" (Act I, Sc. 14). From his cousin, Sin learns that his father had left a brother behind when he went to Canada, and that this brother (Kai's father) and his family suffered in poverty. As he learns about his family history, he also learns about Chinese and Buddhist beliefs about the afterlife. Sin meets a monk who tells him that in the Buddhist tradition, people pray for the dead for forty-nine days to ensure that the dead will be led back to the human realm (Act I, Sc. 15).

Another way in which Yee practises tactical deviation is in his approach to genre. The seriousness of Sin's journey is juxtaposed with scenes of comedy. One of the funniest scenes in the play occurs in a funeral home in Hong Kong where the funeral assistant recites platitudes about the loss of a loved one to Sin and Kai: "Losing a loved one is hard *(sad face)*, and we want you to know that we understand *(open arms)* the empty space they have left in your heart *(makes a heart with her hands over her chest)*" (Act II, Sc. 19). The exaggerated gestures of sympathy are peppered with reminders about the commercialism of the funeral business. The assistant reminds them that the funeral home offers the "Deluxe Piety Package" (Act II, Sc. 19). Yet this is also the scene in which Sin discovers the dark secret of his family. For Sin Hwang, this mystery arises from his past and his relationship with his estranged father. Earlier, he had told his girlfriend that he didn't know his father, just that "he was a guy. He had glasses, wore a size-ten shoe, stood six foot. He drank Molson Canadian and Wiser's Whiskey" (Act I, Sc. 5). Only after his father's death does he find out that his father had a type of brain tumour that gave him hallucinations, mainly about his son. That son, Sin, also begins to experience these hallucinations after his father's death, seeing visions of his ex-girlfriend who had tried to help him. Through these ghosts or hallucinatory presences, we learn about Sin's father and uncle and their difficult lives they had. In this way, Yee shows us the unresolved anger and guilt between the brothers of the first generation.

The significance of having the father's physical body present is also revealed in the funeral parlour. Kai tells Sin that the son is expected to perform a ritual of washing his father's body three times so that there are "no impurities that might impede the departure from the physical world" (Act II, Sc. 19). As Sin starts to wash his father's body, he discovers that it is covered with scars, "*deep ones, caused by canings, and smaller ones from more precise instruments. Some ribs never healed properly from being broken and the underlying scar tissue creates an uneven topography over one side*" (Act II, Sc. 19). Kai recognizes the scars because his father had them too, and Sin shows Kai that his body is also full of the same kind of scars. The three of them—his father, his uncle, and he himself—share the same marks on their backs. These scars speak to a history of domestic violence that has been passed on in the family, which Sin believes he has inherited. The hallucinatory figures, Sin and Sin's girlfriend Nine, are the victims or potential victims of violence. The inclusion of this sensitive topic in a play about Asian Canadians, who are often depicted as model minorities, is another example of the way Yee's play pushes the boundaries of the immigrant play.

In the moment of epiphany, Nine appears to accuse Sin of being unable to acknowledge or see that he was been abused as a child. This, we discover, was the reason why he could not continue his relationship with Nine. He felt that he would continue the cycle of abuse at home with her and their children. Nine denounces him, "You men. You use cruelty as currency, pain as providence. You mythologize yourselves as warriors to dignify what should only ever be known as monstrousness. You . . . *revisionists*. You cowards" (Act II, Sc. 19). Although the past cannot be changed, the play ends with Kai acknowledging that "identifying the cycles that we're a part of . . . that's the first step" (Act II, Sc. 25). In a letter to his son, Sin's father Tien reveals that he, too, was thwarted and abused as a child. When he was young, he had a "natural capacity for painting" but was discouraged from pursuing art. His father "broke all the fingers" in his hand when he discovered that he had spent his money on expensive canvas and paint (Act II, Sc. 21). Instead of continuing to paint, during one harsh winter Tien decides to burn his canvases in order to keep the family warm. While he never had a chance to fulfill his dream, he wants his son to honour his death with his son's chosen craft, writing. In essence, the father breaks from the immigrant tradition of valuing self-sacrifice, hard work, and pragmatism to accept his son's interest in art. Ultimately, Sin learns the meaning of acquiescence. He explains, "Acquiesce means 'to accept something you don't want to, but without protest'" (Act II, Sc. 23). In his eulogy, Sin talks about the difficult life his father had: "But he made the best of what he was given, and told me to always do the same" (Act II, Sc. 24).

Yee's play hinges upon the kind of intergenerational conflicts typically found in Asian American literature of the '80s and '90s. However, its feminist stance; its attempts to explore the complex intersection of race, masculinity, violence, and failure; its innovative use of stage space and visual imagery; and its inclusion of magic and the spiritual place it as a text that goes beyond the traditional ethnic immigrant story. Thematically and technically, the play suggests a depth and darkness beyond that of everyday depictions of model minority immigrants.

Like Yee's play, Choi's *Kim's Convenience* shows conflicts between generations and questions the model minority myth of Asians in North America. Though much lighter in tone, it nevertheless presents a poignant depiction of the disjunction between the aspirations and desires of first- and second-generation immigrants. Choi, too, uses tactical deviations as his play not only looks at the struggles of an immigrant family, but explores the ways in which different visible minority groups negotiate space and perform their ethnic identities, and uses comedy to represent the interactions between the ethnic and gendered communities in a working-class, multiracial neighbourhood in Toronto. Based on the play, the CBC TV show *Kim's Convenience* won two prizes at the ACTRA Awards in February 2017: the Members' Choice Series Ensemble Award and Outstanding Performance by a Female for Jean Yoon. Both the play and TV series have been highly successful with general audiences, suggesting that *Kim's Convenience* is more than a strong comedy with great punchlines. It makes Asian Canadians, who have long been an absent presence in Canada, visible in the media, and its themes resonate with many other immigrant groups.

Choi's *Kim's Convenience* depicts a Korean Canadian family that runs a convenience store in a diverse, mainly Black community in Regent Park. It employs comedy and humour, which are particularly good ways to engage audiences as laughter diffuses tension and fears. *Kim's Convenience*, for example, bravely tackles foreignness through the exaggeration of Appa's (father's) and Umma's (mother's) Korean accents, gender differences through the mention of "the gay" and Toronto's Pride Parade, racial prejudice through its representation of Black customers and Janet's Black boyfriend, and familial estrangement through the son Jung. Stereotypes of Asians as kung-fu fighters, gays and lesbians as afficianados of fashion, and Blacks as criminals are alluded to and playfully redeployed. Through its witty repartee, focus on a small group of characters, and juxtaposition of the sentimental with the comedic, *Kim's Convenience* illuminates some of the crucial issues for twenty-first century immigrants. As Adrian Lee, reviewer for *Maclean's*, says, "What makes *Kim's Convenience* work . . . goes beyond the Korean heritage that the show refuses to leave behind—it's because of the universality of its spirit."

Like Yee, Choi evokes and then challenges the model minority myth to show the changing nature of diasporic communities. Appa, who was a teacher in Korea and immigrated to Canada for a better life, exemplifies an archetypal member of the Asian model minority. As the mother, Umma tells her son, Jung,

> Your appa was teacher in Korea. He was very good teacher. Student all love him . . . We have very good life in Korea. Then we coming

to Canada. But he can't be teacher here. His English is very . . . no good. We get store. And he work every day. No weekend, no time off, no vacation, always have to be open, no retirement. Why? Why he doing like that? For you. For you and Janet. He is choosing like that for you. (Sc. 15, 71)

Appa and Umma defer their pleasures and work long hours for the sake of their children. Appa says, "My whole life is this store. Everybody know this store, they know me" (Sc. 14, 61). However, neither Jung nor Janet has the same work ethic and attitude of self-sacrifice as their parents. When Appa asks Janet to take over the store, she tells him that she has no interest in running it. Like Sin who chooses to be a writer, she chooses to be a "photographer," to follow an artistic career, rather than pursue what is safe and economically successful (Sc. 7, 37).

Instead of becoming the stereotypical successful professional Asian Canadians, the second-generation children Janet and Jung are in their thirties and still trying to establish themselves. Janet and Jung are examples of what I have termed "Asianfail" because they fail to live up to the high achievements expected of model minority Asians (see Ty, *Asianfail* Introduction). They have not achieved high professional and economic status and do not excel at math or playing the violin. Jung ran away from home at sixteen, got into trouble with the law, and now works at a car-rental agency as a clerk. In high school, he had a lot of potential and was captain of the soccer team. He is unhappy and feels like a failure in his thirties. He compares himself to his friends from high school, who are now all successful. He says that on Facebook, all his friends have photos of big houses, expensive cars, and "vacations all around the world" (Sc. 15, 70). He tells his mother that he still lives "in a shithole in Parkdale. Apartment's a constant mess," and that his girlfriend thinks he's a loser (Sc. 15, 71). He feels like leaving and just going somewhere to start over. Jesse Green, a reviewer of the play for *The New York Times*, says that it was at this point that the play no longer felt like a cliché for him. He writes that Jung's sadness was very powerful, and caused him to remember his own family, who emigrated from Eastern Europe: "The play's questions of gratitude and ingratitude, and its exploration of the equivocal meanings of starting over, no longer felt rote at all." Jung's story of "Asianfail" is not an ordinary kind of "failure," but exemplifies the process through which children of immigrants have to work through and find their own desires and needs. Though their parents often have high hopes for their children, those children are not able to always fulfill the American or Canadian dream that their parents wished for them.

Choi's depiction of the failures of Janet and Jung constitute an example of tactical deviation, a way of questioning the norm. Success in contemporary society is often equated with financial and professional accomplishments, which neither Janet nor Jung pursue. Such failure is sometimes a way to escape what Judith Halberstam calls the "punishing norms" of capitalist society (2). In the play, Appa is not happy with Janet's choice of career. He would rather she pursue an economically lucrative career, or else take over the management of the store. He tells her: "Me and Umma is struggle whole life make life for you. We do what we have to do, hope you can be doctor, lawyer, big success, but what you do? Take picture. We don't have to come to Canada for you take picture" (Sc. 14, 61). For many immigrants, success equals professional and economic success, not achievements in arts, culture, or politics because these are realms from which they are typically excluded. In the play, Janet is allowed to continue her career as a photographer because Jung returns, and Appa eventually invites Jung to take over the store. There is a happy reconciliation of dreams and family members at the end of the play.

One important issue raised by the play in a humorous way is the cost of success for many immigrants. Asian North American immigrants have been praised as a successful minority group, but such praise ignores the difficult working conditions of many immigrants and their families. Sociologist Angie Chung argues for the need to look at the "emotion work" of second-generation Asian Americans, a point that also applies to Asian Canadians, commenting that "despite an environment of pervasive commercialism and utilitarianism, emotions based on nonquantifiable feelings of attachment, intimacy, gratitude and empathy alongside feelings of neglect, loneliness, envy, and resentment still play a central role in structuring the relationship between

Asian immigrant parents and their American-born children" (15). Chung stresses that "the willingness of children to help their parents is driven not only by pragmatic need, obligation, and guilt, but also by the affective bonds of intimacy, respect, and empathy in line with their shared emotional circumstances as an Asian family" (15). Like Mr. Kim, many Asian immigrants who run restaurants, dry cleaners, and convenience stores in Canada and the US are successful only because of the combined efforts of husbands, wives, and children who work long hours and are mostly underpaid or unpaid. When Appa insists on showing Janet his way of correctly tying a garbage bag, Janet gets mad and says, "If it were my job, then I would've gotten paid . . . For my whole life, I've worked at least four hours a day covering for you guys, and I've never asked you for anything in return. I've never complained about it and never bitched about not getting paid" (Sc. 14, 63). Appa counters with all the things that he has paid for, including "piano lessons, golf lessons, summer art camp, church camp, Blue Mountain ski pass, semi-formal, diet program, orthodontist, computer, camera, etc." (Sc. 14, 64–65). The argument is funny because it becomes absurd. It is impossible to actually tally up the cost of bringing up a child, but the play reveals the physical and emotional conditions of Asian North American small-business owners whose successes as model minorities are predicated on the "pooled labor contributions of husbands, wives, and children" who "contribute to the viability and success of these enterprises" (Kibria). While other children watch TV and have sleepovers, many immigrant children of parents with restaurants, takeouts, and convenience stores have to mind the store from an early age.

Another example of Choi's use of tactical deviation occurs when a lighthearted scene between two characters is revealed to have darker roots. A painful historical event alluded to in the play is Japan's colonization of Korea from 1910 to 1945. At the beginning of the play, Appa argues with a customer about the kind of energy beverage he sells. Appa tells him that it is made from "insam," but the customer says it looks like "ginseng" (Sc. 2, 22). Appa tries to explain his resistance to using the Japanese name: "Japan attack Korea 1904, make slave of Korean. I am Korean. Ginseng is Japanese name. Insam is Korean name" (Sc. 2, 24). The scene seems inconsequential and funny, but Appa has a deep-seated resentment of all things Japanese, including Japanese-made cars and everyone who buys these cars. He tells Janet to call the police when he sees a Japanese car parked illegally outside, even though Janet tells him, "Japanese people aren't the only ones driving Japanese cars" (Sc. 3, 26). What is ironic is that Appa has all sorts of ways to justify who is guilty of Japanese "associationship" (Sc. 3, 26). When Janet challenges him about his dislike of all things Japanese because he owns a Canon camera, he says that he only paid "half-price," so he has ripped off Japan (Sc. 3, 26). His muddled way of thinking creates humour, but these scenes also reveal the way historical memory plays into the identity of first-generation people in the Korean diaspora. Along with nostalgia, immigrants carry political and historical memories from their home countries that are not easily forgotten or elided by the discourse of Canadian multiculturalism and/or pan-ethnic Asian solidarity.

Conversations that show Appa's patriotism surface again at the end of the play when his son Jung returns. Appa and Jung recall a moment in the past when Jung passed Appa's "Korean history test," which consists of knowing important dates and their significance. Jung has to recite the significance of dates in relation to Korea, such as the invention of the turtle ship by a Korean admiral, the winning of World Cup soccer in 1966 by North Koreans, the arrival of the Hundai Pony in 1984, and so on (Sc. 20, 88). Appa's history quiz is a jumble of sports events, innovations, and popular-culture trivia. They range from the sublime to the ridiculous, but they show his pride and ethnocentrism. These scenes are engaging because they explore the day-to-day interactions of diasporic communities: their passions, cares, interests, and, yes, their prejudices. One reviewer notes, "And unlike the majority of comedies featuring minorities, it feels like the audience is laughing *with* the Kims, not *at* them, which is refreshing" (Floyd). Choi uses humour both to poke fun at and also to represent Korean nationalism and ethnic pride. These scenes are important tactical interventions because discussions of "Asian Canadian" diasporic experiences tend to focus mainly on the Chinese and Japanese. We tend to view Asian Canadians as a homogenous group, but Appa's catalogue of Korean global achievements shows the importance of ethnic particularities to Korean diasporic communities.

A crucial innovative element of *Kim's Convenience* is the representation of the local community of Regent Park, located in the east side of Old Toronto, and known as a working-class neighbourhood. In the 1960s and 1970s, many immigrants from the Caribbean, China, and Southeast Asia settled in the area, creating a racially diverse community. Many residents lived in public-housing units and were on social assistance. In Choi's play, the scene called "Steal or no steal" reflects some of the realities of this rough neighbourhood. Appa teaches Janet about customers, classifying them in his own racist, body-image based, and gendered stereotypes of who is most likely to steal. For example, he predicts that "a black guy, jean jacket" combo is "steal combo" while "fat black girl is no steal" (Sc. 9, 39, 40). But his classification system gets more complicated and hence hilarious: "brown guy, that's steal. Brown girl, that's no steal. Asian guy, that's no steal. Asian girl, that's steal. If you is the gay, that's no steal . . . But two lesbian, that's no steal, cancel-out combo" (Sc. 9, 51). While the silliness and confusion of logic create humour here, Appa's lesson also reveals years of experience behind the convenience-store counter and the fact that shoplifting is a recurring phenomenon in the neighbour-hood. His solution does not fix the structural inequities of the community, but it is an empathetic and personal one. When he catches a shoplifter with goods that the Jamaican customer hid in his clothing, Appa confronts him and tells him, "I know hapkido . . . It's Korean fighting style . . . You can pay cash or you can pay I kick you ass" (Sc. 8, 43). Appa grabs the customer and puts him on the floor in a submission hold and forces him to repeat: "I am steal from you store, Mr. Kim. Please forgive me" (Sc. 8, 43) and also, "Dear Jesus . . . Please forgive me I am steal from Mr. Kim" (Sc. 8, 44). The customer leaves, abashed, and thanks Appa. This thoroughly unorthodox treatment of a shoplifter is funny, and also dangerous; at the same time, however, the scene calls attention to the realities of this low-income neighbourhood, the survival strategies of people in it, and the way they negotiate relationships between minority groups. It reveals some of the interethnic struggles between marginalized newcomers who are all jostling for more economic power and cultural recognition in Canadian society.

In a later scene, Appa tells Janet that he is not against Blacks, and he encourages Janet to date Alex, the Black policeman, if she likes him. He tells her about a Korean friend of his in South Central LA, and how the Korean store owner there had cultivated good relations with his customers by giving them small loans. The customers repay him during the LA riot by forming a human chain around his store, guarding it from thieves, looters, and fire (Sc. 18, 76). In this way, Choi's play foregrounds the intra-ethnic and intersectional relations between different racial groups in Regent Park, representing the complexities of these encounters. Significantly, the play does not feature any white Canadian characters. Asian and Black people, who too often are sidekicks, villains, or short-term romantic partners of white leads in films and shows in North America, are given centre stage. Media scholar Lori Kido Lopez has pointed out the lack of Asian Americans in the media: "the limited number of representations serves to fix a particular image within the public imagination and restrict possibilities—both aesthetically within the world of imagery and within society, where racism has clearly material consequences" (7). Choi's play and its subsequent adaptation on TV works to counter this gap, making an important tactical intervention in media representations of Asian North Americans. Such work can render the strange into the familiar, making the Other non-threatening and ordinary. Though *Kim's Convenience* is a comedy, there are a number of serious issues raised in the TV show and in the play. These kinds of scenes provide insights into the lives of immigrant families at the same time as they offer visible-minority actors a chance to play "fully rounded character[s]," as actress Jean Yoon (Mrs. Kim) says (Hunt).

Both Yee and Choi's works are immigrant plays that entertain while also representing stories of racial and ethnic others in unstereotypical ways. They raise awareness about social issues that are not usually depicted in Asian Canadian works, such as domestic violence, familial estrangement, and the failure to follow the model minority stereotype. They are part of a growing group of playwrights who are using different theatrical conventions to tell the Asian Canadian immigrant story. Following them, a number of other Asian

Canadian playwrights are continuing to explore distinctive and uncommon ways to tell their stories. For example, in his one-man show called *Trace*, Jeff Ho uses not one but two pianos to tell and musically "play" his grandmother's and his mother's immigration stories, as well as his own "Asianfail" story (see Ty, *Asianfail*). Julie Tamiko Manning and Adrienne Wong's *Mixie and the Halfbreeds* uses vaudeville, dance movement, stand-up comedy, and satire to tackle issues of mixed-race identity in Canada. The success of these plays in Toronto and elsewhere signals the willingness of theatregoers to listen to the voices and stories from traditionally "invisible" visible-minority groups.

FROM *O NOSSO BAILE (OUR DANCE)* TO *O NOSSO FADO (OUR SONG)*: PORTUGUESE-CANADIAN SEX-ROLE STEREOTYPES AND THEATRE

AIDA JORDÃO

INTRODUCTION

The 1999 documentary play *O Nosso Baile (Our Dance)* by teatrOVAL pre-sented a chronological narrative of Portuguese immigration to Canada via dynamic scenes without dialogue, set mainly in a neighbourhood tavern that boasted a dance floor.[1] The play showed the Portuguese community of Toronto images of itself from the 1950s to the 1970s, beginning with the first wave of male-only immigrants and ending with the unveiling of the High Park monument celebrating our twenty-five years in Canada. The early scenes, which showed men living together without the female members of the family, manifested an exaggerated performance of masculinity, but this changed when mothers and daughters also immigrated. These women eventu-ally became leaders of the community themselves, challenging the traditional

---

1   The theatrical form was inspired by Ettore Scola's 1983 film, *Le Bal*, in turn based on Théatre du Campagnol's 1981 eponymous play about the history of Paris. Set in a dance hall, *Le Bal* is presented without dialogue in the manner of early English drama "dumb" shows.

binary conceits of male/female, masculine/feminine, and active/passive.[2] The play showed that after immigrating as dependants, the women soon became workers, and at times the economic heads of their families, thus subverting female sex-role models of women as dependent on men. This phenomenon of female empowerment, introduced in *O Nosso Baile,* was the subject of *O Nosso Fado (Our Song),* performed at the 2017 Sears Ontario Drama Festival and SummerWorks Performance Festival by the all-girls Loretto College School. The young female thespians of diverse ethnic backgrounds chose a 1974 cleaners' strike at the Toronto Dominion Centre as a story that celebrated Portuguese-Canadian women as workers and union organizers, showcasing their famed victory in the fight for better working conditions.[3] This recent play about the Portuguese-Canadian community represented its women as strong, dominant role models, also subverting binary sex and gender types. The play's title, denoting the story as one of "*nosso*" ("our") experiences, hearkened back to *O Nosso Baile.* The link between these two titles, and the performances they describe, has prompted me to further research how Portuguese-Canadian males and females are represented on "our" Toronto stages.

In this paper, I examine the sex-role stereotypes that are reflected, challenged, and revisioned in selected plays about Portuguese immigrants in order to better understand the gendered construction of an "imagined community" of Portuguese-Canadians. In using this term, I am inspired by Benedict

---

2   Since Aristotle, the hierarchical dualisms of male/female and masculine/feminine associated with mind/body, man/woman, reason/passion, and active/passive have influenced the discussion of sex/gender differences and are central to feminist concerns. Famously, Mary Anne Case examined stereotypical masculine and feminine characteristics of a binary nature used by psychologists in the 1990s, listing the masculine as "aggressive," "ambitious," and "analytical," and the feminine as "gentle," "yielding," and "emotional" (12–13). Current feminist scholarship strives to promote a non-binary view of male/female and masculine/feminine, engaging with a fluid conception of sex and gender (see Rich; Butler, *Gender* and *Bodies*; and Moi).

3   The specific strike is not mentioned in the play but cross-referencing an interview in Giles (75–76) and Marques and Medeiro's account in *Imigrantes Portugueses* (132), this is the strike that demanded clean garbage bags be supplied by management.

Anderson's theorization of a nation as "an imagined political community" whose members imagine themselves to be in "communion," albeit without knowing each other (6). Further to this, I follow Wenona Giles's notion that immigrant stereotypes situated within the host nation tend to satisfy or propose a cultural imaginary of sex and gender in accordance with that of the settler society. In *Portuguese Women in Toronto*, a study that probes the construction of identity of the title group, Giles argues that the Immigration Act of 1976 confirmed "the Canadian government's labour-market orientation and revealed its androcentric underpinnings. Sexist definitions of 'skill' and 'work' have delimited and defined immigrant women as dependants in subordinate positions" (21). It is all the more significant, therefore, that representations of Toronto's Portuguese immigrant women in community theatre have included wives and mothers who transition to new roles as women workers, showing a progressive construction of identity. That is, these women are not constrained by the "sexist definitions" imposed by the dominant society, but rather progressively (both in the temporal and political meanings of the word) reconstruct their identities and occupy societal positions that defy gender norms. It is my intention to examine how roles created for the stage relate to the sociological gendered condition of Portuguese immigrants and to the creation of Canadian theatre that mythologizes a community (Filewod, *Collective* 24–25). In addition to the community plays introduced above that deal specifically with historical events, I consider two Portuguese-identified male and female characters in alternative theatre works that contest and negotiate gender constructs and are also closely tied to historically specific experiences. One of these works is Mário Lourenço's subversive portrayal of a Portuguese UEFA Euro 2016 soccer commentator in Toronto Laboratory Theatre's *"In Sundry Languages,"* and the second is my own *On the Death of Inês de Castro*, about a Canadian actor's representation of a Portuguese medieval queen.

Most of the work analyzed here (apart from a brief mention of Portuguese-Canadian characters I created with Nightwood Theatre and the Company of

Sirens, and my embodiment of Inês de Castro)[4] lies outside the parameters of self-identified Canadian feminist theatre. There is no indication that teatrOVAL, the Loretto College schoolgirls or actor Mário Lourenço engaged in "performance practices that take gender difference, and gendered experience, as their primary social and political focus" (Solga 1). Nonetheless, I argue that the case studies in this paper can be read as feminist, and I employ a feminist lens to interrogate the stereotypes and revisionist creations in the plays. With the overarching objective of identifying the agency of female characters, I rest my analyses on the feminist theatre "poetics" of Sue-Ellen Case that purport to "deconstruct the traditional systems of representation and perception of women and posit women in the position of the subject" (114–15). To this end, I interrogate feminine and masculine tropes that may limit the social activities or material possibilities of female and male characters. This methodology is especially relevant when analyzing characters of the first generation of immigrants from Portugal, who were steeped in the patriarchal lore of the male as head of the household who is active in public life, and of the female as the subaltern relegated to the domestic sphere. The Portuguese Constitution of 1933 declared everyone equal under the law "except as regards women, the differences resulting from their nature and from the interest of the family" (qtd. in Sadlier 121). In this context, the association of the male with masculinity and the female with femininity was *de rigueur.* One popular Portuguese 1950s women's magazine, *Querida*, advised, "A woman's place is in the home. Work outside makes a woman masculine" (qtd. in Hatton 121). Moreover, under Portugal's fascist regime only women with post-secondary degrees or who were heads of households (e.g., widows) had the right to vote until 1968.[5] After this, all literate citizens could vote but universal suffrage was

---

4   I have previously written about my feminist plays and performance in, for example, "Women and Tradition: *Funeral em Branco* and *My Aunt's Neighbours*," "Performing the Portuguese Cleaning Lady: Subverting Gender, Class and Ethnic Typecasting on the Canadian Stage," and "(Re)Presenting Inês de Castro: Two Audiences, Two Languages, One Feminism."

5   The military dictatorship of 1926 was succeeded by the Estado Novo (New State) and held power until 1974. During this time several changes in suffrage were implemented.

only achieved in 1974 when the April 25 Revolution of the Carnations implemented a democratic state. Since most immigrants to Canada came from the
working class or the farming sector, it is unlikely that the Portuguese women
who landed in Toronto had ever voted or held a job that may have provided
independent means. This historical context gives us cause to interrogate "traditional systems of representation and perception of [Portuguese-Canadian]
women" from a feminist perspective.

   With few specific studies of Portuguese-Canadian theatre available,[6] I
draw on related fields to contextualize my chosen plays and provide possible theoretical frameworks for their analysis. The first field I draw from is
sociology, via the studies that document the lives of Portuguese-Canadian
immigrants and their descendants in Canada. Giles's analysis of gender relations, noted above, engages a "critique of essentialist frameworks or discursive
practices that construct a depoliticized notion of a homogeneous group of
Portuguese immigrants in ways that mesh class, gender, and other characteristics around which people mobilize" (11). My reading of the history and
theatre of Portuguese-Canadians, and of how sex and gender is represented
in each, prioritizes this viewpoint as well as Giles's consideration of nationalism and gender:

   It is an at least illusory and often invisible sense of home that defines
   and/or identifies a people. This identity is linked to a group's gender
   politics, as well as the potential for, and the limitations to, its political
   action. Nationalism is usually associated with a discourse about the

---

Women with post-secondary degrees who were married, widowed, or divorced were first
given the vote in 1931; in 1933 this was extended to independent single women with
degrees; in 1946 married women who were literate and paid property tax could also vote.
It was only in 1968 that sex-based discrimination was abolished but suffrage was still
limited to literate persons.

6   Apart from my own research, I am not aware of other scholarly work on Portuguese-
Canadian theatre in Ontario. Canadian-American playwright Elaine Avila, of
Azorean-Portuguese heritage, has published criticism of her plays in Western Canada
and the United States.

family or homes of the nation, women as "mothers of the nation,"
family values and the role of women in ensuring that these values
and morals are upheld. Women in particular stand to lose in this
kind of nationalist discourse, as their dependency on men becomes
either assumed or imposed. (14)

With this perspective in mind, I engage in a deconstruction of sex-role stereotypes in the dramatic case studies of this paper, reflecting in the process on
other scholarship on Portuguese-Canadians. For example, Fernando Nunes's
early monograph *Problems and Adjustments of the Portuguese Immigrant
Family in Canada*, for all its bold revelation of troubles in the· Portuguese
community and recommendations for overcoming the cultural conflicts of
immigration, now appears quaint in its categorization of immigrants as "The
Father," "The Mother," and "The Children" (19; 25; 29).[7] Moreover, Nunes
is uncritical of nationalist strategies that subordinate the immigrant to the
dominant class and suggests (after Aires Gameiro) that "[t]he development
of a feeling of patriotism towards Canada should be nurtured and allowed
to develop" (40), presumably to encourage a break with Portugal as *"pátria"*
(fatherland). Likewise, Edite Noivo's *Inside Ethnic Families: Three Generations
of Portuguese-Canadians*, focuses on the family to the exclusion of any other
identity marker. The issues of work and class are glossed over in less than a
dozen pages and always under broad headings such as, "Immigrant Projects
and Family Lifestyles," and "From the Workplace to the Home: Wounds that
Work Overtime" (54; 128). Nonetheless, Nunes's and Noivo's views on gender
relations are at times reflected in Portuguese-Canadian theatre, and thus
merit inclusion here.

The second area of study that is relevant to this analysis is the historiography
of Canadian theatre as theorized by Alan Filewod, both in his "deregimented"
notion of theatre history that encompasses peripheral histories independent
of evolutionary developments in mainstream theatre ("Named") and in his

---

7   Nunes's study rests squarely on interviews conducted by Grace M. Anderson and
David Higgs in their pioneering history of Portuguese-Canadians, *A Future to Inherit*.

breakthrough study of documentary and collective theatre in Canada (*Collective Encounters*). Filewod suggests not only severing "Canadian theatre history" from the nationalist project,[8] but also "examin[ing] historical formations of the theatrical on the same plane as popular culture" ("Introduction" xi).[9] Avoiding a linear, nationalistic genealogy is, simply put, the *only* way to include Portuguese-Canadian theatre projects—ranging from a few performances in a restaurant basement, to a high-school play presented at a summer festival, to one-time readings and workshops with professional artists and community members—in a broader history of "Canadian" theatre. In tandem, Filewod's analysis of "the collectively created documentary play" in Canadian alternative theatre can be applied to the Portuguese-Canadian cultural production examined here, since the plays in question document historical events and are created by insiders who research, improvise, and write dramatic scenarios (*Collective* viii). Furthermore, in the absence of literary texts (a point especially relevant for *O Nosso Baile*'s scenarios without dialogue), the performance becomes "a way of using the-atre to transform actuality into a performance of findings that is both ongoing process and created text" (x). Filewod's methodology adapts itself readily to an examination of how sex-role stereotypes are created by ensuring that the plays analyzed here are contextualized within their historical moment of creation. Thus, Giles's challenge to nationalist objectives that constrain the progress of Portuguese women in Toronto at a specific point in their history of immigration, for example, can be linked to female characterization on the Toronto stage at that same moment.

By examining Portuguese-Canadian performances that revision the representation of women in theatre and probe sex-role stereotypes, this study aims to further explore the gendered construction of identity in the community via its theatrical enactments. In so doing, I locate female agency and cite subversive male/female performance in "our" cultural production.

---

8   Filewod's thesis of deregimenting Canadian theatre stresses that "the national genea-logical project has on the whole denied the porousness of theatre culture" ("Named" 109).

9   In this way, playwrights like Myroslav Irchan, widely produced in the 1930s in Ukrainian, would have a place in "Canadian theatre" (Filewod, "Introduction" xi).

IT BEGAN WITH A DANCE

The first performance I will explore here, *O Nosso Baile (Our Dance)*, was created in 1999 by director Helder Ramos and a group of Portuguese-Canadian theatre aficionados to tell the story of the first twenty-five years of Portuguese immigration to Toronto from 1953 to 1978. As he explained in an interview, Ramos happened upon the empty restaurant basement of Tasca on Augusta Avenue and, recognizing its historical significance as the former Tivoli Billiards—the meeting place for Portuguese men when they first arrived from the home country—used it for a site-specific performance about these men and those who followed. The chosen location immediately gendered the project, as the Tivoli was a male-only domain and remained so even after the wives of the first male immigrants joined them. Moreover, by choosing a chronological order to tell this story—beginning with eight slides of all-male arrivals in Halifax and of men in bars in the 1950s and early 1960s, accompanied by the voice-over of a husband writing to his wife in Portugal— the performance clearly showed that it was only the men who were initially accepted as landed immigrants. The wives and children who joined them once they had set up house were their dependants. Ramos's layout of scenes thus immediately illustrated Giles's critique of Canada's Immigration Act that "delimited and defined immigrant women as dependants in subordinate positions" (21).

Nonetheless, in the opening scenes of *O Nosso Baile*, the male-only environment was presented ambiguously. In the absence of women, the men engaged in masculinist roughhousing, but also undertook activities traditionally performed by their wives or mothers. First, the men jostled for sleeping space in a cramped room,[10] in an absurdist ballet of trading places between day and night shifts. The potential homoerotic intimacy generated by sharing beds was dispelled by exaggeratedly masculine posturing. Each man proved himself physically stronger than the next in a card game played on a rickety

---

10   Nunes describes the "distressing conditions" of crowded living where, according to an interview by Anderson and Higgs, seventy-three men lived in one house (20).

table, accentuated by aggressive card slamming and congratulatory back slapping. The competitive card game then turned into a competition over who
had the widest back, literally, as Ramos noted, the male body fittest for hard
labour on Canadian soil. At the same time, in the absence of the women these
men were also required to perform tasks conventionally associated with the
female body, as illustrated in *O Nosso Baile*'s program cover photograph of
three men sewing and ironing. Nunes suggests that the long period spent
in the new country without their wives prepared Portuguese men to help
the women with housework when they joined the workforce shortly after
immigrating (27). The husbands who had done housework during their sol-
itary, bachelor-like existence could assist in housekeeping and child-raising.
However, once their wives joined them in Canada, few men welcomed such
blurring of the lines between the feminine/masculine roles. As evidenced
in Noivo's study of marital relations in a Portuguese-Canadian family, some
immigrant husbands dug in their heels on what they considered appropriate gender behaviour. One asserted that, "When I return from [shift] work, I
like to see the woman at home, the house clean, and the kids taken care of"
(97). Significantly, the women had also been alone during the long wait to
immigrate and had taken on the responsibilities of the traditional "male" of
the household. Once the wife arrived in Canada, she was often unwilling to
give up control over family matters and this resulted in "friction between her
and her husband" (Nunes 20). Giles notes, also, that the men relied on the
paycheques the women brought home when they were laid off at construction jobs or suffered work-related injuries (44–45). The family's relocation
to Canadian soil thus caused confusion in traditional working-class gender
roles, and *O Nosso Baile* reflected these changes in conventional male/female
domestic and social behaviour. This point was clearly demonstrated in a later
scene in the play when a male character threw his jacket on the floor and
waited for his wife to pick it up, which she refused to do (Ramos).

The play made much of the arrival of the first Portuguese women in
Canada, most of whom were sponsored by their husbands and fathers. In an
early workshop outline, a male character whose wife had recently arrived,
prepared the others for her entrance:

He "slaps" the rest of the men into shape, adjusts their clothing, kicks their feet off the table, wipes their faces & smooths their hair and exits. All are stunned

[image] *family reunification, first emigrant [sic] woman.*

He re-enters followed cautiously by his wife. She looks around in awe, & disgust. She runs her finger on the table, then decides it needs a good scrubbing and uses her scarf. When she finally sits down, then smiles, the men are relieved, they laugh, the couple embrace. (scene 1)

The slides that accompanied this scene in performance showed women on the deck of a ship in Halifax in 1954 and the Pereira sisters on Lisgar Street. Carlos Pereira, the father of the young women who were among the first to

Fig. 1. Maria Teresa and Maria Leonor Pereira pose in front of their new house at 110 Lisgar Street in Kensington Market, Toronto. Photo by Carlos Pereira. Photo provided courtesy of Domingos Marques.

immigrate to Toronto, recalls, "When my family arrived, there were no girls here. So when there were parties, their success depended on whether or not we would come. It would be me and my four daughters . . . I must be one of the most popular guys in the community" (Fernandes 3). The story of Pereira's daughters' popularity was suggested in *O Nosso Baile* when one young woman went to a party and the many men there all strove to dance with her. The men's earlier competitiveness over who had the strongest back transitioned to the dance floor, where one woman was passed from male partner to male partner. At first, the male characters exerted their dominance in possessing the female character, but eventually she ended up mothering all the men. The female character transitioned from a romantic object to a maternal symbol who gave succour to the males around her (Ramos). Giles's observation about women as "mothers of the nation," who uphold the values and morals of the populace is illustrated in both of these scenes (14).

In addition, Ramos stressed that *O Nosso Baile* was created with community members who told the story of "*o nosso*" / "our" experience in Toronto with wordless scenes built around iconic photographs and music of the time. As Filewod notes in his analysis of *The Farm Show*, Paul Thompson's celebrated collective creations for Theatre Passe Muraille used theatre to "locate and define the motifs and images which identify a culture" and to "point to the formative myths of a society" (*Collective* 24–25). Likewise, teatrOVAL chose to stage events that marked significant moments in the development of the Portuguese community (such as the opening of the first store, the first restaurant, the first folklore dance group, the first newspaper, and the first club, as well as the opening of the consulate, religious processions, Portugal Day festivities, soccer games, and the protests and strikes that drew the attention of the Canadian press) in order to mythologize the people and places of "our" community. The play was "written" as the actors improvised, mostly to record what had been created from day to day, finding "a way of using theatre to transform actuality into a performance of findings" (Filewod, *Collective* x).

Commenting on the gender division in the cast and character lists, Ramos explained that there were more female actors than female "players" in the early Portuguese community, so a few male characters were played by the women in the group. This was as true for the role of the consul general as it was for the soccer players in a scene celebrating the First Portuguese Canadian Club's soccer team victory of 1969. But where the women in the cast truly took the stage by storm was in their representation of the cleaners' strike of 1974. The soccer players of the previous scene—bona fide figures of masculinity worldwide— were replaced by unionized women workers who chanted slogans to demand their rights. *O Nosso Baile* stressed the roles of both male *and* female members of the Portuguese-Canadian community, ultimately showing how the women progressed to leadership roles. The story that began with a male-dominated workforce, showing women as their dependants, ended with the women in the spotlight as workers protesting labour oppression. As Giles observes, "The significance of the resistance by Portuguese first-generation women to exploitative working conditions cannot be underestimated, since these struggles are also a critique of immigration policy in Canada, which has oppressed women in quite specific and harsh ways" (74). *O Nosso Baile* documented the changes in male–female relationships in the early years of Portuguese immigration, interrogated the gendered aspect of the community, and gave exploited women a leading voice. The play added to Canadian theatre history and its progressive politics provided a much-needed representation of the "imagined community" of Portuguese-Canadians.[11] The women union activists, in particular, would reappear as representatives of the community in future arts projects.

THEN WE SANG

The mid-seventies cleaners' strikes would be followed by others into the early eighties, and these established a performative presence for Portuguese women on the streets of Toronto and on its stages. My own work in popular theatre

---

11   It should be mentioned, though, that teatrOVAL was criticized in a community newspaper for challenging the masculinist genealogical formation of the nation of Little Portugal. According to the reviewer, a slide showing the First Portuguese Canadian Club's 2009 "For Sale" sign mocked the Portuguese-Canadian (male) "pioneers" by emphasizing the loss of an iconic building that housed the social club they had founded (Coelho). Clearly, the play did not represent the "imagined community" of all Portuguese-Canadians.

(notably in the Company of Sirens's *The Working People's Picture Show*) included the role of a striking cleaner "negotiating" with Cadillac Fairview. The scene in question was based on the 1984 strike by the women who worked for the Federated Building Maintenance Company, represented by the Canadian Textile and Chemical Union; my picket-line speech was performed in schools and union halls throughout Ontario. It was also adapted for a special presentation at the Portuguese-Canadian Democratic Association, where we worked with community theatre members who wrote and performed with us. The 1989 CBC Radio drama by Tom MacDonnell, *Making It Up As We Go Along*—on which I worked as consultant and principal actor—focused on the same strike but from the perspective of the English-Canadian union steward. More recently, the cleaners' strike was also the subject of the Department of Public Memory's workshop/installation at Toronto's Nuit Blanche 2017, where I performed the cleaner's speech from *The Working People's Picture Show*. In this case, the ongoing process of representation resulted in the mythologizing not only of the cleaners' actions, but also of the performance of the event in Toronto theatre.

One of the most significant performative incarnations of Portuguese women's labour organizing in the 1970s, however, was the recent play created and performed by students of Loretto College School at the 2017 Sears and SummerWorks festivals, *O Nosso Fado (Our Song)*. It told the story of a second-generation Portuguese girl whose mother got involved in a strike action demanding gloves to protect the workers' hands from harsh cleaning products. As noted on the play's website,

> *O Nosso Fado* was inspired by Wenona Giles' real life account of Portuguese office [cleaners] in Toronto who staged their own wildcat strike in 1974. The company found the account of the women, and specifically the real-life reluctant organizer, Lurdes, to be a compelling and heart wrenching place to begin their own story. ("O Nosso Fado")

Indeed, Giles's interview with one of the women workers who had the courage to push the union to defend them is echoed in the play (75–76). As a case study for this paper, the play is intriguing on several fronts.

First, though it was penned by a student of Portuguese background and directed by a Portuguese-Canadian teacher, the play was performed by young women of diverse ethnicities.[12] Part of the monocultural history presented in *O Nosso Baile* was revisioned as an intercultural project where only the subject matter is strictly Portuguese-Canadian. In 2017, it was logical that the story was of interest to students from cultural groups whose members worked as cleaners in Toronto office buildings and who could thus apply their own experiences to the specifically Portuguese-Canadian historical situation. Some of the students, like the playwright Kathy Martinez,[13] had the after-school experience of accompanying their parents to their cleaning jobs. As teacher Sara Pedrosa confirms, the cast had four Portuguese-Canadians, one Pakistani-Canadian, and the rest were Filipino-Canadians; all of these performers related to the immigrant experience (Vicente 14). This is a fascinating development in theatre about Portuguese-Canadians: the play was performed outside of the community and defied a historicization of movements as simply "marked in generational waves" (Filewod, "Introduction" ix). Instead, *O Nosso Fado* moved laterally to embrace the demographic development of both the workers' roles and the ethnic cultures of the Loretto College student body.

Second, the play stressed the needs of daughters of Portuguese immigrant women and their aversion to occupying the class-determined positions of their mothers. As Giles notes of the work opportunities for the daughters of first-generation immigrants, "Their fluency in English, and their high school, college or university education have enabled many to move into white collar jobs, or, in their mothers' words, 'clean jobs'" (37). In *O Nosso Fado*, young Lucy showed disdain for her mother's work:

---

12   Cast of *O Nosso Fado*: Kathy Martinez: Maria; Angela Rosete: Lucy; Emily Pacheco: Fatima; Areeba Tabassum: Lourdes; Journey To: Manager, Radio Host; Angelina Avrampolous: Christopher, 1st Radio Caller; Paulyn Radam: Worker 5; Genesis Calliste: Worker 3, Marta; Trish Petilos: Worker 2, Bernadette; Linda Teixeira: Worker 4, Gabriella; Jessica Domingues: Worker 1, Regina; Veronica Borges: the Fadista.

13   Martinez's Spanish-sounding name is from her Portuguese father who first immigrated to Venezuela; there, his surname suffered a spelling change (Pedrosa).

MARIA: You wanna help? Pick up the pail and start cleaning.

LUCY: No.

MARIA: Excuse me?

LUCY: No.

MARIA: Why no?

LUCY: I don't want to.

MARIA: This is not a democracy. You have no choice. When I tell you to do something, you do it.

LUCY: This is YOUR job not mine.

MARIA: Why not your job? Don't you like your TV? Don't you like your clothes? Tell me, why not your job?

LUCY: Because I don't want to be like you.

MARIA: Like me . . . Like their slave . . . like the girl who can no longer go to school so that the family can have food to eat. Like the woman who came here with nothing. Like the mother who cleans toilets so her daughter can have opportunities. You don't want to be like me but without me, there is no you.

Lucy looks down, picks up the sponge and starts cleaning. (Martinez 14).

As Nunes observes, the question of identification is crucial to the relationship between the immigrant parent and child. Often there is a period where the child rejects her parents' "Portuguese ways" and "begins to view [her]self as

Fig. 2. In *O Nosso Fado*, Lourdes asks Lucy to help the cleaners send an email to the union rep. Areeba Tabassum (left) as Lourdes and Angela Rosete (right) as Lucy. Photo by Jessica Domingues.

the most capable one in the family to deal with the outside world" (42). This is certainly true of the play's Lucy, who was asked by the office workers to act as interpreter for the non-English-speaking cleaners, and by the cleaners, like Lourdes, to email the union and translate the steward's complicated instructions. Lucy resented her mother's and the other cleaners' lack of English and their consequent dependence on her. She and her mother argued bitterly about it throughout the play. A breakthrough occurred only when the mother cried that she wanted better working conditions for her daughter:

> **MARIA:** But you don't understand that you're blessed . . . All you do is complain. This job is a blessing. Having this job gives us enough for rent, for food, to save for your precious school. So that you don't have to be like me, like them. I don't care about my hands because I

know yours will never look like this. You don't want to be like me? I
don't want you to be like me either. (19–20)

Here, Maria was fully cognizant that giving her child an opportunity for a
better life, the objective of many immigrant families, meant supporting Lucy
in her academic endeavours instead of forcing her to do manual labour.

Third, the play deepened the representation of the Portuguese-Canadian
women cleaners of the 1970s shown in *O Nosso Baile*. Martinez and the company created situations and characters that complicated the relationship of
work and gendered family roles, while also exposing gendered class issues that
pointed up the inequitable situation of blue-collar working women and the
white-collar "suits" for whom they cleaned. A comical scene repeated at the
start of each work shift showed a female cleaner wiping and sweeping around
the male body of the office worker who was working late and prevented her
from doing her work. The ineffectual male union steward, who was presented
as a mere paper pusher with soft hands, was also a foil for the strong women
who did not desist in their requests for a contract to ensure management
would provide gloves to protect their hands from harmful chemicals.[14]

Finally, the play, as a "collective documentary" with the title *O Nosso Fado
(Our Song)*, hearkened back not only to *O Nosso Baile (Our Dance)*, but to the
Canadian alternative theatre tradition of mythologizing local culture with an
identifying motif. Like the speech patterns of the Ontario farmer in *The Farm
Show* that are unique to that rural milieu (Paul Thompson, cited in Filewod,
Collective 25), here the *fado* song is solely "ours" as no other Toronto commu-
nity performs it. Via its title, the Loretto College play claimed the Portuguese
national song *fado* (literally fate) as the lament that voices the troubles of
the Portuguese and transposed it to the more local community of Toronto.
In this production, *fado* singer Veronica Borges evoked the working life of
Portuguese women with her passionate rendition of *"Povo que lavas no rio"*

---

14   This detail differs from Giles's testimonial from a striker who complains of the health
risks of reusing dirty garbage bags (75–76), the issue of the Toronto Dominion Centre
wildcat strike in 1974.

("People Washing at the River"), a song that is keenly felt by all who work with their hands. When Maria reprised the song at the end of the play after a work stoppage and successful negotiation with management, she foregrounded the struggles of the blue-collar Portuguese immigrant who toils for the white-collar anglophone. As Giles notes, "These stories demonstrate the attitude of Portuguese women toward their employers, whom they fear, but also recognize as exploiting their labour and the labour of other immigrant women" (79). Especially in the face of such obstacles, the women cleaners' active role in overcoming their employment woes was exemplary and gave the young women of Loretto College prototypes through whom they could perform female agency. It is no wonder that they chose "our" *fado* to end the play. The song was performed as a hymn to working women, owning the situation of hard work but reacting against managerial exploitation. Rather than presenting a stereotype of the Portuguese cleaner as subaltern or servile, the students, in the tradition of feminist theatre and prior dramatizations like mine in the *Working People's Picture Show* and those in *O Nosso Baile*, celebrated the agency of the female protagonists of the labour struggle. Furthermore, by including second-generation characters who anachronistically read from iPads, they spoke directly to their twenty-first century classmates about the possibility of creating formative identities based on the motifs, like *fado*, "which identify a culture" (Filewod, *Collective* 24–25).

When it was first presented at the Sears Ontario Drama Festival, the play, which purported to "giv[e] voice to the voiceless" (@DramaLoretto, "@LCSMadness"), received at least one review in a community newspaper (Vicente) and was awarded the Toronto Regional Award of Excellence. Politician Cristina Martins wept as she told *Sol Português* reporter João Vicente that, unfortunately, the situations depicted in the play are still relevant today (14). With its subsequent performance at SummerWorks, *O Nosso Fado* spread the message of resistance to immigrant exploitation even further afield. The success of the play was evidenced in the numerous Twitter messages that praised the students for telling a story that is "everyone's song" (poster copy; @DramaLoretto, "Matt White"; @CMartinsTo), and in a theatre blog that declared, "The story packs a punch and makes us look and pay attention to those we take for granted" (Slotkin).

THEN WE PLAYED WITH SUBVERSIVE IDENTITIES: THE SOCCER PLAYER AND . . .

While *O Nosso Fado* deepens and complicates *O Nosso Baile*'s depiction of gender relations within the Portuguese community, recent shows by other Portuguese-Canadian theatremakers further problematize the issue. Portuguese-language community theatre is produced frequently in regional clubs and community centres in Toronto, but professionals of Portuguese background are few. I count myself among the latter, with my bilingual plays and portrayal of Portuguese characters in alternative Toronto theatre. The Company of Sirens and Nightwood Theatre have facilitated the workshops and staged readings of two of my plays, *Funeral in White* and *My Aunt's Neighbours* respectively, both of which featured Portuguese-Canadian female characters who transitioned from immigrant to worker and/or student (see Jordão, "Women" and "The Alt Stage"). While the first play unequivocally attacked patriarchal traditions that oppress women, the second upheld traditions that create a cohesive and supportive women's community across generations. In both, the woman's quest for independence, emotional and economic, was prioritized. Other Portuguese-Canadian theatre colleagues are teatrOVAL's director, Helder Ramos, who is a York University theatre graduate, and Mário Lourenço, a Portuguese actor who immigrated to Toronto in 2004. I have followed the career of Lourenço and have been glad to spectate and dramaturge a clown turn that he has performed with Toronto Laboratory Theatre's *"In Sundry Languages"* since 2015.[15] Lourenço's clown soccer player is the boldest subversion of a Portuguese-gendered stereotype that I have recently seen in Toronto theatre.

---

15   First presented at the Centre for Drama, Theatre & Performance Studies, University of Toronto, in 2015 and 2016; in 2017 the play was performed at the Toronto Fringe Festival and the Caminos festival.

The piece started as an exploration of Canadian identity and gender, with two actor-characters[16] discussing in Portuguese and Russian how they felt about immigration while passing a soccer ball between them. The character of Mário was happy with the openness, both physical and metaphorical, in Canadian society:

> **MARIO:** *(while playing)* Here in Canada, I found more space; as if I could be more of myself, more at ease . . . For example, as a man I was able to make more room for myself; to my sensibility and vulnerability as a man. *(Passes the ball to Yuri.)* (qtd. in Samur 239).

In our phone interview, Lourenço stressed that Canadian society allowed for a broader expression of masculinity than he had found in Portugal, and this led him to explore nationality and identity in *"In Sundry Languages."* He found that he was internalizing Canadian nationality and questioning what he had left behind in terms of stereotyped Portuguese male behaviour, which he associated with that of a soccer player or fan. He thus developed a soccer player character, first expressed in a clown turn where a soccer sports reporter/fan both sexualizes and brutalizes the euphoria of a winning goal. In the latest rendition of the character for the 2017 Caminos festival,[17] Lourenço's clown reported on the 2016 UEFA Euro Finals in Paris when Portugal took home the Euro Cup for the first time in forty-one years.

The importance of soccer in Toronto's Portuguese community cannot be understated. In the 1960s and '70s, several sport/social clubs were founded to support their namesakes in Portugal: for example, A Casa do Benfica, Vitória de Setúbal, the Azorean Sport Clube Angrense, and the Sport Clube Lusitania (Marques and Medeiros 134, 139, 140). In addition, other social clubs had

---

16   For more on autobiographical performance where actor/character identity is interrogated, see Yana Meerzon's "Between Je and Moi."

17   Lourenço's performance can be viewed here at 8:46 to 12:33 minutes: www.youtube.com/watch?v=CkQoavwoIIs&feature=youtu.be.

soccer teams that won Canadian championships and were celebrated in the community, as shown in *O Nosso Baile*. As Gilberto Fernandes reminds us,

> Soccer has always been a popular and important pastime and an important site of community organization for Portuguese-Canadians. Residents of Kensington Market remember the crowds of Portuguese immigrants hanging around the sidewalk in front of the Portuguese bookstore on the corner of Nassau St. and Bellevue Ave. listening to the weekend broadcast of Portuguese soccer matches. (7)

Today, at least two Portuguese-language community newspapers dedicate half of their pages to soccer coverage; the dentist in my neighbourhood has a larger-than-life-size photo of the Euro 2016 winning team plastered on his windows, making giants of the team players; and people around the world who may not know the names of Portuguese writers or politicians know Ronaldo, Figo, and Eusébio.[18]

Lourenço's soccer clown did not, however, glorify or paint a pretty picture of the sport and its fans. Lourenço argues that soccer breeds violence, that it upholds the values of a patriarchal society and encourages heteronormativity and homophobia. As the national game of Portugal, therefore, it represents the dominant masculinist values of the nation, which largely exclude and sometimes harm women.[19] Lourenço's piece started with the clown/reporter/fan dressed in a soccer uniform sporting a red nose and a microphone. He crossed himself before the game started, welcomed spectators to the Parisian stadium, passed

---

18   Cristiano Ronaldo currently plays for Real Madrid and Portugal's national team; retired in 2009, Luís Figo played for Sporting Clube Portugal, Barcelona, Real Madrid, Internazionale, and Portugal's national team; retired in 1979, Eusébio was Sport Lisboa & Benfica's famed player and also played on the national team.

19   Not limited to Portugal, domestic violence associated with soccer game results happens worldwide as incidents of wife assault increase on soccer weekends. The 2017 Day for the Elimination of Violence Against Women in Portugal counted on the support of the Liga Portuguesa de Futebol Profissional; at soccer games scheduled between 24 and 28 November, one minute of silence was observed to mark the occasion (Costa).

gas loudly as he settled in to watch the game, and physically reacted to goals missed and made. Simulated slapping and boxing moves foreshadowed the dark and violent ending following the winning goal. After hip gyrations and sexual humping moves, Lourenço's clown made a finger gun, shot into the air in a celebratory fashion and then shot the audience. Here, the violence incited by soccer pointed up the *machismo* that leads to male physical domination.

In his subversive characterization of a soccer fan, Lourenço decried the violent actions of Portuguese men even as he presented a familiar *macho* type that, while performed for audiences of the host nation, satisfied the cultural imaginary of gender prescribed by the "androcentric underpinnings" of Canadian institutions (Giles 21). As Yana Meerzon posits, building on Filewod's arguments, immigrant theatre needs new dramaturgies to develop "a theatrical imagined community" that stages its image of itself ("Theatre and Immigration" 184).[20] Ethnic-identified theatre artists contribute to the "imagined community" of nation that is in part created by theatre; however, as Lourenço's example shows, they clearly do not limit themselves to the types condoned by the dominant society. This immigrant theatre both reflects and affects the cultural imaginary of gender in our communities and aims to negotiate established gender constructs. With this point in mind, I conclude with a comment on my own creation of the actor/character Aida and her embodiment of a Portuguese medieval queen.[21]

. . . THE DEAD QUEEN

My feminist theatre work and scholarship converged when I decided to stage one of the literary texts analyzed in my Ph.D. dissertation. I performed a medieval ballad about Portugal's famed Dead Queen, Inês de Castro, through a character, Aida, who represented a Portuguese-Canadian feminist on holiday

---

20 Filewod paraphrases Anderson's conceptualization of nation as imagined "to suggest that theatre as it is imagined . . . is a legitimizing performance of the imagined community that is the nation" (*Performing* 1).

21 For a comprehensive analysis, see Jordão, "(Re)Presenting Inês de Castro."

Fig. 3. Aida Jordão as the Poet in *On the Death of Inês de Castro*. She would later give
voice to Inês and the Knight by standing behind their respective paper doll
cut-out costumes. Photo by Gabrielle Houle.

in Portugal. Like Mário Lourenço, who played a Canadian Mário commenting
on a Portuguese-identified Mário, I performed a Canadian Aida satirizing her
pseudo-tourist self and outsider perspective's take on a Portuguese historical
icon widely known for her femininity and feminine wiles. Indeed, I set up
the convention that Inês de Castro herself had written to the Canadian feminist actress Aida asking her to represent her (Inês) as an active agent of her
fate. Since Inês de Castro was the victim of men's games of war and peace—
assassinated in 1355 for reasons of state, she was arguably a woman acted
upon rather than acting herself—it was no easy task to give her that agency.
Nonetheless, I set out to do so in a twenty-minute dramatization entitled *On
the Death of Inês de Castro*.[22] Briefly, Inês de Castro was the mistress of Pedro,

22   Adapted from Garcia de Resende's *Trovas à morte de D. Inês de Castro* (1516) and
performed in 2008 at the Festival of Original Theatre (FOOT); Drama Centre; University

the heir to the throne, and was killed by Pedro's father, Afonso IV, because her powerful Galician family threatened peace between Portugal and Spain. Castro is known as the Dead Queen because Pedro, once he became king, exhumed her remains and, insisting they were married, made her queen by law and legitimized their three children.

In my telling, Inês voiced both herself and the males who determined her fate by moving from one role to another behind life-size paper doll cut-out "costumes" of Inês de Castro, the Poet, and the Knight. In the original medieval ballad, Inês only appeared to plead for her innocence, but in my representation she spoke for all the males who controlled her and thus blurred the lines of authorship and authority. As the subject of her own story, with agency in the feminist sense, this representation suggested a new Inês for the "theatrical imagined community" of Portuguese-Canadians in place of the Dead Queen known for her beauty and passivity (Sousa 11). In effect, I recast the feminine mythology of Inês with a fluid gender approach. Engaging with the scholarship of feminist medieval scholars, I considered this male-authored text as a cultural site where the female voice "defie[d] absolute categorization as either masculine or feminine" and suggested a "*mouvance* of gender identity" (Burns, qtd. in Jordão, "(Re)Presenting" 242). *On the Death of Inês de Castro* was a departure from my previous work about Portuguese-Canadian women dealing with the challenges of immigration and especially with stereotypical notions of what they could achieve as female immigrants. Nonetheless, as *O Nosso Baile* and *O Nosso Fado* aimed to give agency to Portuguese immigrant women, my performances of Inês at the University of Toronto and the Portuguese Consulate interrogated the representation of the "passive" medieval queen and mirrored the gendered roles in the other plays considered here by suggesting that female/male and feminine/masculine binaries could be overcome to challenge sex-role stereotypes.

---

of Toronto (in English); and Consulate General of Portugal, Toronto (in Portuguese).

As Filewod astutely observes,

> Theatre is not simply a matter of staged representation: it is an event
> both physical and symbolic; it transforms experience into a com-
> munity narrative; and it materially constructs in the audience the
> community it addresses . . . the theatre as a process models deep
> social structures. In this sense, theatre models the society in the
> process of enactment. (*Performing* xvii)

The Portuguese-Canadian communities of Toronto have grown and developed
since the early years of immigration in the 1950s, and the theatrical performances that have endeavoured to represent their members have grown with
them. The creation of male and female characters has (per)formed a part of
this "process of enactment" on stage and in society. The case studies examined in this paper, in addition to documenting some Portuguese-Canadian
theatre in Ontario, optimistically engage a revisionist analysis of male and
female characters to suggest that contemporary Portuguese-Canadian theatremakers are moving toward a gender-conscious dramaturgical project.
From "our" dance to "our" song, and with "our" subversive interpretations in
the mix, a new dramaturgy of gendered Portugueseness continues to emerge.

"NO ME INVENTES [DON'T INVENT ME]": PERFORMING THE LATINX IMMIGRANT STORY IN CANADA[1]

MARTHA HERRERA-LASSO GONZÁLEZ

"Fritta Caro" es el resultado de un estereotipo, de una ficción. Todos los que me ven a través de lo poco o mucho que conocen de Frida Kahlo me están inventando, yo soy una ilusión habitada por el espectro de la artista mexicana. Soy el cuestionamiento a un cliché que impide un conocimiento profundo, auténtico de otras mujeres, de otras artistas latinoamericanas."

["Fritta Caro" is the result of a stereotype, of a fiction. People who see me through what they know about Frida Kahlo are inventing me, and I am an illusion that is inhabited by the spectre of the Mexican artist. I am the questioning of a cliché that impedes a profound knowledge, authentic of other women, of other Latin American artists.][2]
—Helena Martin Franco, "Biografie"

In the "biography" of her self-fiction Fritta Caro, performance artist Helena Martin Franco expresses a recurring frustration for Latina artists who have migrated north—a feeling that their bodies, their voices, and their art are nothing more than a blank screen upon which stereotypes are constantly

1 With appreciation to Kimberly Skye Richards and Juan Manuel Aldape Muñóz for their thoughtful feedback on earlier drafts. The chapter also benefited greatly from conversations at the Theatre and Immigration Seminar (2018 ACRT/CATR) and the TDPS ABD Writing Group at UC Berkeley.

2 All translations from Spanish and French are mine, unless indicated otherwise.

being projected. In Canada, the work of immigrant artists has proven essential in exposing and undoing the prevalence of these reductive narratives as the predominant markers of *latinidad*. This chapter explores a history of immigration and theatre from the perspective of the Latinx Canadian experience, placing particular attention on Québec. It reimagines identity as performed through immigrant narratives in a way that makes explicit the complexity of Canada's cultural diversity, the complicated tensions of its nation-building exercise, and the importance of generating intercultural solidarities. By thinking through Latinx cultural production in Québec, this chapter adds to the work of decolonial scholars of exposing the logics that have shaped hemispheric imaginings to serve a range of colonial and neo-colonial agendas.[3] It therefore considers not only the cultural production of Latinx Canadian artists, but also the role of federal and Québécois immigration policies in determining the possibilities and circulation of these artists and their works.

Despite the profoundly colonial origins of the term Latin America, the term Latinx claims a different history. "Latin America" was first coined in the nineteenth century by Napoleon III of France in an attempt to create an image of the region that united Latin Roman Catholic cultures. By creating a cultural identity that excluded countries of British heritage, Napoleon III hoped to strengthen his colonial project in the Americas.[4] Yet Latino/a as an identifier

---

3   I understand a decolonial approach as concerned with exposing and undoing colonial logics. Puerto Rican philosopher Nelson Maldonado-Torres describes decolonial projects as "dedicated to the incessant task of elucidating the perverse forms in which the logic of coloniality operates, as a death-logic which is constitutive of modernity, and to opening up a horizon in which human life might be possible in all its abundance" (18). He argues that decolonial approaches are as old as coloniality itself, and that each decolonial project will be specific to the histories and politics of each place.

4   The Second Empire in Mexico, led by Emperor Maximilian and Empress Carlota, lasted only four years (1864–1867), but the term Latin America continues to operate as an important cultural identifier of the region. I urge us to keep in mind, as Natalie Alvarez has argued, that invoking the term Latin America involves invoking the colonial projects that have all but erased the Indigenous and Afro cultures of these territories in the aggrandizement of the European (Alvarez, "Latina/o Canadian Theatre and Performance: Living Archives" iv). For more on this history, see Rouquié.

was reclaimed in the US during the Civil Rights Movement in the 1960s, most visibly through the farmworkers' movement in California,[5] to unify the voice and needs of millions of peoples of Latin American descent. The term Latinx emerged in the mid-2000s in left-leaning, queer communities as a gender-neutral label for Latino/a and Latin@, "an inclusive term that recognizes the intersectionality of sexuality, language, immigration, ethnicity, culture, and phenotype" (Salinas and Lozano 9). It is rooted in Indigenous gender systems (such as the Zapoteco and the Mexica) that allow for more flexible models of sexual identity, and it refers to cultural and ethnic groups, not to a race. Unlike the word "Hispanic," which refers only to a Spanish-speaking popu-lation, the term Latinx does not necessitate the use of a specific language, so it is inclusive of the many languages spoken across the hemisphere. Although many of the artists discussed in this chapter worked long before the term Latinx emerged, I use it to refer to the larger collection of works I consider here, since the word is inclusive of Latino, Latina, and non-binary artists.[6]

When speaking of the Latinx Canadian, I refer both to immigrants to Canada born in Latin America and to people of Latin American descent living in Canada. The term does not privilege one culture or national origin over another, although, as we will see, it can fall into the trap of homogeniz-ing profound diversities under a single label. The concept of *latinidad* and the different terms used to denote it (Latina/o, Hispanic, Latinx) has carried its own sets of expectations specific to Canada since the implementation of Pierre Trudeau's official multiculturalism policies in the 1970s,[7] and many art-ists mentioned here have done important work to make the different agendas behind these terms visible. As a category of identity, *latinidad*[8] accounts for

---

5   The Farmworker's Movement led by César Chávez was primarily made up of agricul-tural workers of Mexican origins, many who identified as Chicano/a.

6   Only when the people discussed in this chapter self-identify as Latina or Latino will these identifiers be used.

7   These policies are discussed further later in the chapter.

8   For a thorough discussion on the history of *latinidad*, see Caminero-Santangelo. For more on the use of the term Latinx, see Salinas and Lozano.

cultural, political, and historical convergences that might be present amongst peoples of Latin American origins without losing sight of the specific ways in which these same peoples diverge. Without attempting to demarcate fixed boundaries, a notion of multiple *latinidades* speaks to the alliances and coalitions often generated amongst Latinxs in countries like Canada or the United States. As Marta Caminero-Santangelo argues, the hyphenated identity must be understood not only between a sense of the Latinx and the American (or Canadian), "but in the sense that 'Latino' is found in the boundaries between one so-called Latino group and another" (219).

The chapter begins with an overview of the history of immigration flows from Latin America into Canada, considering both federal and Québec immigration policies. Although the federal government has primary authority over final admissions and the granting of citizenship, the responsibility for immigration matters is shared between federal and provincial governments. Québec is a particularly interesting case in this respect, given its special status within Canada, as it is "recognized as a distinct society with jurisdiction over its migratory affairs and a specific vision of the processes of integration of immigrants" (Ricaño-Alcalá et al. 46).[9] The chapter continues with an overview of the key players in the history of Latinx Canadian theatre and performance since the 1970s, highlighting recurring themes, aesthetics, and production methods explored by these artists. The final section examines the work of Helena Martin Franco, a trilingual Colombian Canadian performance artist who has been working in Montréal since 1998. As part of her extensive work across genres (collage, video art, performance art), Martin Franco has created a series of *auto-ficciones* or self-fictions,[10] characters—such as Une

---

9   In 1968 Québec created its own department of immigration, and in 1991 it signed the most complete immigration treaty between the federal government and a province (Ricaño-Alcalá et al. 57). It is also the only Canadian province with representation abroad.

10   The term *auto-ficciones* translates into English as self-fictions, and in the case of Martin Franco's work, refers to fictional characters based on her own experiences as an immigrant in Québec. All characters are performed by Martin Franco, who creates a biography for each of these self-fictions and uploads it to her webpage, where she documents the life and work of these characters.

Femme Éléphant, Fritta Caro, and Corazón Desfasado—that accentuate an aspect of herself as an immigrant.[11] Martin Franco's work is a rich example of the recurring tendency of Latinx Canadian artists to focus their performance art on combating stereotypes of *latinidad*. The chapter focuses on her performances as Fritta Caro between 2007 and 2012 in a series of public interventions around different sites in Québec. These interventions allude to aspects of Canadian multiculturalism under which the immigrant is expected to use their culture as productive commodity. A stereotype of the Latina artist and a fictional presentation of a high-performance Canadian athlete, Fritta Caro "represents adaptation into a forced identity: a new Canadian citizen, she carries a memory, a logic and *raisons d'être* unknown to the host society" ("Biographie"). This final section considers how, in her performances of Fritta Caro, Martin Franco addresses the tensions between performing a successful immigrant story and the realities of migrating to Canada, exposing ways in which Latinx artists are so often reduced to legible commodities based on stereotypes as part of their integration process.

LATIN AMERICAN IMMIGRATION TO CANADA

Historically, Canadian immigration policies have juggled a constant tension between promoting and restricting immigration, "facing profound contradictions between demographic and economic objectives" (Ricaño-Alcalá et al. 14). Alexandre Beaudoin-Duquette argues that this history does not read as a linear evolution toward more progressive values:

> Canada seems to have maintained a kind of bipolar attitude towards immigration [. . .]. We're looking at a cold country that needs the Other in order to develop, and hence, at times promotes and at times represses immigration; at times it exalts its cultural diversity and at times it exalts its British heritage to the degree that it looks to

---

11   For more on Martin Franco's work, see frittacaro.helenamartinfranco.com/fr/.

assimilate its minorities or execute discriminatory policies. At times,
it does all these things simultaneously. (90)

In looking at how Latin American immigration into Canada has evolved in
the last fifty years, we see this ambivalence operate. Latin American immigration to Canada was minimal before the 1970s; in 1970, it made up only 3.2%
of Canada's foreign-born population.[12] By 1991, however, this number had
increased to 10.4%, and by 2016 it stood at 11.3% ("Distribution of Foreign-
Born Population"). This significant change in the inflow of Latin American
immigrants was the result of a variety of factors. Perhaps most significantly,
Latin American immigration to Canada has been prompted by violent domestic conflicts across the hemisphere. In many cases, as Alan B. Simmons argues,
people fleeing America-backed military governments had to look to other
countries for refuge, and Canada presented an ideal alternative since it combined "a safe haven and economic opportunity" (286). These immigration
waves can roughly be mapped as follows. A first wave, beginning in the 1970s,
resulted from military dictatorships in the Southern Cone (Chile [1973–
1989], Uruguay [1973–1983], and Argentina [1976–1983]); this first wave
also aligned itself with significant migration from French Caribbean countries to Québec, most significantly Haiti. A second wave of Central American
civil-war asylum seekers landed in the 1980s and 1990s (Guatemala [1960–
1996], Nicaragua [1979–1990], and El Salvador [1980–1992]), while a third
wave was prompted by drug-related and guerilla violence through the 2000s
in Colombia and Mexico. Immigration from the region has been historically
diverse, including different types of forced migration, both of refugees and
those yet to hold official refugee status,[13] economic immigrants, immigrants
who have decided to relocate to Canada voluntarily, and temporary workers.

---

12   This 3.2% consisted primarily of immigrants of European descent from the industri-
alized countries of Latin America (Mexico, Uruguay, Venezuela, Brazil, and Argentina)
who came to Canada during the 1950s and 1960s. See Simmons.

13   It wasn't until the 1976 Immigration Act that "refugee" became an official category,
and only after 1979 were forced migrants able to apply for refugee status. See Del Pozo.

The steady increase in a Latin American born population in Canada between 1970 and 1991 (from 3.2% to 10.4%) hit a wall in the new century primarily as a result of the post-9/11 emphasis on security and the more conservative immigration policies implemented by Stephen Harper's government.[14] In December 2004, the Safe Third Country Agreement was signed between the US and Canada, under which refugees are required to claim refugee status in the first country in which they land. As a consequence, the influx of refugee claimants from Latin American countries (in particular Colombia) decreased considerably given the lack of direct flights to Canada ("Canada-U.S. Safe Third Country Agreement"). On 13 July 2009, Canada imposed a tourist visa requirement on Mexican citizens, claiming that this measure was necessary in order to control the increase of refugee claims (Muñoz). Imposing a visa requirement overnight read as an aggressive diplomatic move and left many Mexican citizens who were due to fly into or through Canada stranded at airports around the world. Beginning on 30 December 2016, Justin Trudeau's government lifted the requirement, although Mexican citizens still require Electronic Travel Authorization to enter Canada (an eTA has a cost of $7 CAD with a five-year validity, and can be processed online). These two initiatives made it considerably harder for immigrants from Colombia and Mexico, the two most significant Latin American source countries of the first decade of the twenty-first century, to relocate in Canada.

Internally, the increase in immigration flows from Latin America into Canada also coincided with changes in federal immigration policies that in the 1960s shifted focus toward Canada's global competitiveness, emphasizing class rather than race as determining factors in official approaches to

---

14   Although the Harper government initiated programs to better Canada's relationship with the Americas, starting in 2007 and increasing these efforts in 2012, these economic interests clashed with conservative immigration policies, making for a "schizoid relationship" between Canada and many Latin American nationals (Alvarez, "Latina/o Canadian Theatre and Performance: Hemispheric" 4). For more on the Americas Strategy program initiated in 2007, see "Canada's Strategy for Engagement in the Americas."

immigration.[15] In 1962, the new Immigration Regulations began to eradicate overtly racial discriminatory policies and prioritized instead the economic immigrant. As Liette Gilbert argues, "Canada reaffirmed its commitment to attracting and admitting economic immigrants with its points established in 1967, reaffirmed in 1994, and made more stringent in 2001" (19). The point system evaluates and selects candidates who wish to immigrate into Canada based on education, language skills, work experience, age, arranged employment in Canada, and adaptability ("Six Selection Factors"). Through the sixties and seventies, Canada would adapt these principles into its multiculturalism initiative[16] and produce an immigration policy that recognized the ways in which immigrant allegiances to countries of origin represented an important economic advantage for Canada. The notion of "Multiculturalism as 'productive' diversity rather than a coexistence framework" would permeate these policies even more into "the 1990s global and neoliberal climate of global competitiveness, markets and trade" (L. Gilbert 19), although security concerns would take priority over these economic advantages after 9/11.

Internally, another factor that produced immigration from Latin America into Canada after the 1960s, specifically into Québec, had to do with the same forces that prompted the 1963 Royal Commission on Bilingualism and Biculturalism: Québec's *revolution tranquille*. As the Québécois reclaimed

---

15   Canada's first immigration campaigns were aimed at white immigrants, and immigration policy was designed to allow discrimination based on race. Article 83 of the 1910 Immigration Act states that the Government Council could "prohibit for a stated period, or permanently, the landing in Canada, of immigrants belonging to any race deemed unsuited to the climate or requirements of Canada, or of immigrants of any specified class, occupation or character" ("Immigration Act" 218). Unsurprisingly, according to the Canadian census, in 1961 85% of immigrants came from Europe ("150 Years").

16   Canadian Multiculturalism Policy was implemented in 1971 by Prime Minister Pierre Trudeau, and was "intended to preserve the cultural freedom of all individuals and provide recognition of the cultural contributions of diverse ethnic groups to Canadian society." Prompted by the 1963 Royal Commission on Bilingualism and Biculturalism, it consisted of social participation assistance for diverse cultural groups, support in creative exchanges between groups, and English and French language learning programs. See "Canadian Multiculturalism Policy."

cultural and economic agency in the province, these transformations created a need for agricultural workers[17] as well as for francophone professionals in other areas.[18] At the time of this inflow into the province Québec implemented an interculturalism policy that would determine official integration of other cultures. This interculturalism policy was a direct response to Prime Minister Pierre Trudeau's multiculturalism initiative in the 1970s, which had met considerable resistance both from Québec and from First Nations Peoples. Liette Gilbert describes the difference between Trudeau's multiculturalism and Québec interculturalism as follows:

> The ideological assumption of interculturalism is that diversity is not only something that should be recognized by a host society but instead it is something that will transform both newcomers and their new society. This position implies the reciprocal recognition of various cultural contributions (as in multiculturalism) but also seeks the social convergence of these groups toward the development of a shared civic identity. (17)

Interculturalism, in this sense, stresses how diversity produces change in both the newcomers *and* the host society, highlighting the effects that these changes have on the host culture. This policy responded to a sense within Québec that the francophone majority was at the same time a fragile minority that needed to protect its culture and its language (Bouchard). By creating its own intercultural policy, Québec garnered governance over the administration of its own cultural diversity.

---

17   The first Seasonal Agricultural Worker Program was officially established in 1966, between Canada and Jamaica, and has come to include Mexico and eleven Caribbean countries. See "Hire."

18   Many of these francophone professionals would be exiled from Haiti during the Duvalier regimes (1957–1986). This wave of francophone and Catholic Haitians that settled in Québec between 1967 and 1977 consisted primarily of highly trained professionals such as doctors and university professors, and is often referred to as the Haitian brain drain. See Icart.

Although the federal government has final say on entry, the 1991 Canada–Québec Accord grants the province relative control over its integration services, which have a particular focus on integration into francophone Québec society, under a "moral contract" combined with the concept of a "common public culture" that is specific to Québec (Ricaño-Alcalá et al. 59). The challenges that this moral contract represents for immigrants are often underestimated by these policies, especially since what is understood as moral or contractual can vary so much from one culture to another. In an interview for Radio Canada International, Helena Martin Franco suggests—after having lived as an immigrant in Québec for eighteen years—that this notion of social integration is not possible for foreign-born immigrants: "I say more than integration, one doesn't integrate, one adapts. [. . .] The issue of *integration* I think is a very comfortable term for government policies. But to me the first generation adapts, but it is always haunted by ghosts and is in a permanent state of conflict" (Interview). Before analyzing how the histories and policies discussed in this section are contested and embodied in Martin Franco's performances of immigration, however, it is important to understand the cultural production that has resulted from these immigration flows in the work of other Latinx Canadian artists since the 1970s.

LATINX THEATRE AND PERFORMANCE IN CANADA

The presence of Latinx Canadian theatre and performance in Canada aligns itself with the immigration waves that began in the 1970s, and can be seen primarily in large urban centres. At that time in Toronto, for example, there were a range of artistic manifestations, from the work done by Puerto Rican Canadian sound artist Rafael Barreto-Rivera, best known as a member of the Four Horsemen (a sound poetry group active from 1972 to 1988), to the work of Southern Cone émigrés such as Argentinian theatre artist Arturo Fresolone (founder of the experimental company Theatre of Change), and El Galpón, a Spanish-language theatre company run by Uruguayan and Argentinian theatre artists. Alberto Kurapel, perhaps the best known Latin American performance artist to be based in Montréal during the eighties and nineties, relocated from Chile after the *coup d'état* in 1973, and created the Compagnie des Arts Exilio, where he developed and explored his multimedia "teatro-performance" or "post-teatro" (Hazelton, "Kurapel's *Prometheus*" 2). At the same time, Chilean director Rodrigo González and his Théâtre du Chaos produced children's theatre and other collective works in Montréal, and Chilean playwright Jaime Silva founded La Barranca (inspired by Federico García Lorca's company), making for a rich Chilean Québécois theatre scene during those decades.[19] Most of these artists (with the exception of Barreto-Rivera) were trained in Latin America and arrived in Canada as established professionals. This explains their emphasis on producing Spanish-language plays as well as their interest in collective processes and experimental theatre. Many of them were exiled from violent military regimes, and their work combined their Latin American training with themes of exile as well as solidarity and activism. These methodologies of theatremaking probed a particular form of intercultural aesthetics that contemplated diverse Latin American backgrounds as well as the particular experience of migrating to Canada that often required working against damagining stereotypes of *latinidad*.

On the other side of the country, Lina de Guevara, a Chilean exile based in Victoria, founded the longest-running Latinx theatre company in Canada. Trained at the School of Dramatic Arts of the University of Chile in the sixties and relocated to Victoria in 1976, de Guevara created Puente Theatre in 1988 "with the mandate to express through theatre the experiences of immigrants and diverse minorities" (de Guevara, "Welcome"). Lina de Guevara ran the company until 2011, succeeded by Mercedes Bátiz-Benét, and for the last thirty years Puente has generated important spaces for First Nations as well as immigrant communities in Canada to explore civic participation through their participation in the arts.

---

19   Alvarez, "Latina/o Canadian Theatre and Performance: Living Archives" xi–xiii. For further context on Latin American artists in Canada during this period, see Hazelton, *Latinocanadá*.

In the 1990s a new generation of Latinx artists gained visibility: artists who were children of exiles or had relocated at a young age, and so trained in Canada. Such is the case of both Guillermo Verdecchia and Carmen Aguirre. When Verdecchia gained notoriety with his one-man show *Fronteras Americanas* (winner of the 1993 Governor General's Literary Award for Drama), a Latinx Canadian theatre artist was positioned at the centre of English Canadian mainstream theatre for the first time. This personal monologue showcased the duality of the author's experience—on the one hand, he played the stereotyped Latino, and on the other, an immigrant working hard to deconstruct these same stereotypes. Verdecchia has since continued to contribute as a scholar and an artist to the field of Canadian theatre, pushing against the homogeneity of the mainstream. Carmen Aguirre, based in Vancouver, was trained at Studio 58, and formed the Latino Theatre Group in 1999.[20] In addition to her work as an actor, Aguirre has written two memoirs and over twenty plays, including *Chile con Carne, The Trigger, The Refugee Hotel*, and *Blue Box*, in which she has experimented extensively with the ways in which autobiography can be dramatized and performed. Through her on- and offstage activism Aguirre has become an essential force in the creation of spaces for Latinx art and in the training of young artists in Canada.

Beyond the consolidation of the reputations of individual artists, the turn of the century saw a move toward the institutionalization of Latinx Canadian theatre and performance, evidenced in the creation of theatre companies and festivals that prioritize and cultivate Latinx content, most visibly in Toronto.[21] This includes both grassroots, community-driven companies such as Casa Maíz (2002), Teatro Crisalda (2006–2011), MataDanze (2006), Grupo Teatro Libre (2008), Double Double Performing Arts (2010), and Apus Coop (2012),

---

20   For more on Latino theatre in Vancouver, see Habell-Pallán.

21   Many of the artists included in Alvarez's collections, such as Rosa Labordé, Martha Chaves (key in creating queer spaces amidst growing efforts to establish diverse forms of latinidad), Beatriz Pizano, and Marilo Nuñez, have been important actors in the creation of professional pathways for Latinx Canadian artists such as Amaranta Leyva, Augusto Bitter, Mónica Garrido, Irma Villafuerte, Lilia Leon, and many more Canadian-born as well as newly immigrated Latinxs.

as well as professional companies like Aluna Theatre (2001), founded and run by Beatriz Pizano, and Alameda Theatre (2006–2015) founded and run by Marilo Nuñez. Given the dire need for visibility and conversation, theatre festivals that have come out of these efforts have been essential. Some of these include Aluna Theatre's Panamerican Routes/Rutas Panamericanas (held every two years since 2012) and their more recent Caminos festival, Alameda Theatre's play development De Colores Festival of New Works, and other theatre festivals and cultural initiatives with a Latin American focus.[22]

In the works of Latinx Canadian theatre and performance artists since the 1970s, the geopolitical and the personal are in constant conversation. These recurring stories of migration and exile tell the history of our hemispheric interdependence at the same time that they speak to and against the damaging stereotypes that so often substitute for complex personal stories in mainstream narratives. Both the themes of many of these works and the values that have gestated these companies and festivals show a focus on solidarity and alliances across immigrant communities and First Nations groups, working through collaborative techniques and across cultural and linguistic borders as they forge spaces of inclusion.

These efforts inevitably bring up notions of shared Latinx identity, a concept that reveals its own sets of complications. The work of performance artist Helena Martin Franco, most specifically in her performance project Fritta Caro, is an effective example of how all-encompassing notions of pan-*latinidad* can lead to the repetition of damaging stereotypes, and how art can work to nuance these complex alliances. Martin Franco moved to Montréal in 1998. Originally from Cartagena de Indias in the Colombian Caribbean, she holds an undergraduate degree in Fine Arts from the National School of Fine Arts in Cartagena (1988), began an M.F.A. in Painting from the National University of Colombia in Bogotá (1994), gained the M.F.A. degree in Visual Arts from UQAM in Montréal (2009), and has worked as an artist and an activist across the hemisphere since the 1980s, principally in Colombia and Québec (Martin

---

22   For more on these festivals and companies, see Alvarez, "Latina/o Canadian Theatre and Performance: Living Archives" xiii–xx.

Franco "cv-bio"). Although it coincided with a late 1990s wave of Colombian nationals fleeing guerrilla and drug violence, Martin Franco's move to Canada was prompted by her marriage to a Lebanese Québécois man. After her move in 1998 Martin Franco quickly discovered the challenges of being a Latina artist in Canada:

> As an artist, ever since I show my work in Montreal, the frequent associations made to the work of Frida Kahlo brought about the expression: "Frida me tiene Frita" [Frida has me fried/exasperated]. [. . .] Frida Kahlo appears as the only reference and it becomes a filter that impedes going further in the understanding and appreciation of my work. My proposals get drowned before they arrive. ("Biografie")

These experiences provoked in Martin Franco a simultaneous desire on the one hand to denounce and clarify, and on the other to assimilate and become legible to others. The tension produced by this struggle is one of Fritta Caro's driving explorations, as can be seen in the performances of this self-fiction between 2007 and 2012 around different sites in Québec.

FRITTA CARO: PERFORMING THE SUCCESSFUL IMMIGRANT

The name Fritta Caro is a play on words. It modifies the name of the famous Mexican painter, Frida Kahlo (1907–1954), to express Martin Franco's experience as a Latina artist in Montréal. The word "Fritta" translates as *fried*, and is used colloquially to mean being burned out or exasperated. Martin Franco adopts it to comment on being fed up with the constant Frida Kahlo references she has encountered. "Caro" translates into English as *expensive*, and references the high costs paid by immigrants in the process of migration.

> [The character] was born in Côtes-des-Neiges. She is created in the image and likeness of this Montreal neighbourhood where diverse foreign cultures live side by side. Out of the entire province of

> Québec, Côtes-des-Neiges and Parc-Extension are the neighbour-
> hoods where the majority of new immigrants arrive. Like many of
> them, Fritta Caro must deal with new laws, habituate to an unknown
> lifestyle and redefine her expectations of the life she begins. (Martin
> Franco, "Biografie")

The character combines the image of Frida Kahlo with the idea of a high-performance Canadian athlete. Kahlo is referenced in the name as well as in her
famous hairstyle—braided hair made to crown the head and decorated with
colourful flowers, which in Fritta Caro's case are red and white. The notion
of a high-performance athlete is legible in her dress, which consists of red-
and-white tracksuit pants, white running shoes, a long-sleeved red cotton
shirt, and over this a white T-shirt that shows a large maple leaf decorated
in gold, red, and white. Fritta Caro also carries two large, identical red tote
bags, one in each hand, with large white squares on each side showing the
word CANADA in red under a red maple leaf. During some interventions,
Fritta Caro also wears a red Mexican-style shawl around her shoulders: an
element distinctive of Frida Kahlo's dress. When she walks, Fritta Caro keeps
a solemn demeanour, quiet and observant, maintaining the symmetry in her
stride as the identical tote bags hang from each hand.[23]

Ever since Fritta Caro's first interventions, a question has prevailed for the
artist: Why does Fritta Caro feel more like she's in Canada than in Québec?
("La coupe canadienne"). Her choice of dress—as opposed to the use of the
Québec colours and flag—shows her desire to accurately perform the country, not the province. She has been granted entry by the federal Canadian
government and must integrate into the national narratives required of a
Latina in this new country. Yet she has landed in the neighbourhood of Côtes-
des-Neiges in Montréal, a city where these national narratives are often as
unwelcome as are many immigrants—after all, to many in Québec, performing a Québécois identity is performing a nation, not a province. Fritta Caro

---

23   For images, videos, and further descriptions of the character see frittacaro.helena-
martinfranco.com.

Fig. 1. Fritta Caro at the mall. Helena Martin Franco as Fritta Caro during the 2010 performance *Mes noms* at the Promenades Cathédrale and Les Cours Mont-Royal malls in Montréal. Photo by Sylvie Moisan.

wears a uniform that is not her own: a combination of Canadian national imaginary and a Latina stereotype, together a provocation in many of the sites where she intervenes.

In 2007, Martin Franco set out to make a video of Fritta Caro's birth. She did not intend the making of this video to be a performance intervention; rather, the video would be uploaded to her webpage as part of Fritta Caro's fictional biography. Yet she made the video in the Hochelaga-Maisonneuve neighbourhood, one of the whitest and most separatist neighbourhoods in Québec. She had selected the Telegraph gallery located in this neighbourhood, outside which she would film the birth of Fritta Caro by wrapping herself in a Canadian flag and styling her Frida-like hair (Martin Franco, "Incarnation/Conjugation"). As she performed for the camera, wrapped in a Canadian flag, she received hostile reactions from cars and passersby. This provocation was not premeditated; Martin Franco did not know the full context of this particular neighbourhood, and thus, unknowingly, she made of the filming process a performance intervention in itself. In his analysis of this

Fig. 2. Fritta Caro is born. Helena Martin Franco as Fritta Caro, seen from inside the Montréal Télégraphe gallery during the creation of the *Incarnation/Encarnación* video performance in 2007. Photo by Sylvie Moisan.

misunderstanding, Beaudoin-Duquette argues that Martin Franco's outsider's ignorance produced an unintentional performance, one much more daring and dangerous than the artist was aware of at the time (175). In this example we see how both the character of Fritta Caro and Helena Martin Franco herself are profoundly vulnerable in their context. Because they are expected to embody the nationalist sentiments both of Québec and of Canada, their immigrant performances are set up for failure as these provincial and federal expectations oppose each other.

One of the guiding principles in Caro's performances is symmetry: symmetry as a necessary part of her forced identity where she must constantly mould herself to fit her surroundings. On her webpage, Caro's 2010 intervention at a mall in the town of Sainte-Thérèse, Québec, is described as follows:

Fritta Caro walks shyly from the hallway between the bathrooms and the cafeteria towards the "waiting room." She walks looking to align herself with the walls, the furniture, the flowerpots, the telephone booths, in line with the silent manner of the objects in this place. She desires symmetry and wants to be in harmony with her surroundings. Her uniform inspires a type of solemnity. She walks amidst things, amidst people. Some people feel uncomfortable, others move to another table. Others follow her with their eyes. Excited, a couple asks if this is an art action like the living statues in tourist European cities. ("La coupe canadienne")

This performance suggests, on the one hand, a deep and concentrated effort on Caro's part to assimilate into her surroundings, to fit in perfectly. At the same time, her uniform and her directed movements are precisely what make her stand out, what bring both positive and negative attention to her. The performance reveals the awkwardness and the exhaustive effort made by immigrants to accomplish assimilation. At some point during this same intervention, as she waited for a "Canadian haircut" (she would ask the stylist explicitly for a Canadian haircut), mall security approached her:

MALL SECURITY: What are you doing?

FRITTA: Waiting.

MALL SECURITY: What are you waiting for?

FRITTA: I'm getting my hair cut.

MALL SECURITY: Do you have an appointment?

FRITTA: Yes.

MALL SECURITY: But you are coming up to people, you are bothering them.

FRITTA: No, people are coming up to me.

MALL SECURITY: Move the tote bags, they disturb the clients' circulation. ("La coupe canadienne")

Fritta Caro, hard as she may try to fit in, makes everyone uncomfortable. Mall security can't quite pin down what she is doing wrong, but her immigrant performance and her difference certainly seem like they require regulation and supervision, or, at the very least, the other customers must be sheltered from its nuisance. Something is off. Caro retains her marker of difference, the Latina reference to Kahlo, but aside from this she is nothing more than her efforts to perform Canadian. Hence, Beaudoin-Duquette describes the character of Fritta Caro as a "payaso melancólico" (219) or melancholic clown, dressed in clown-like garb, trying her best to please, never able to achieve the symmetry she strives for, and left exhausted and underpaid despite her immense efforts.

Fritta Caro's persona as a high-performance athlete speaks to Martin Franco's commentary on the unrealistic expectations of the immigrant, who must perform at the highest level in order to achieve the desired prize: Canadian citizenship (performing Canadian) and a place in Montréal (performing Québécois). According to Citizenship and Immigration Canada, successful integration is defined as "the ability to contribute, *free of barriers*, to all aspects of Canadian life, that is, economic, social, cultural and political" (Citizenship and Immigration Canada 16, emphasis added). Although integration services are available to all immigrants, most of these don't extend beyond twelve months, so most of the labour required in meeting these goals is left to the immigrant. The immigrant cannot let down their guard or take a break from the arduous task of belonging—learning a new language, studying for citizenship exams, learning new social codes, struggling to have foreign accreditation recognized, justifying their presence in this new place, educating others about their home country. Additionally, in Canada the work of belonging means adapting to a French or English culture, thus negating the deeper histories of the land as well as present-day Indigenous cultures. In fact, for an immigrant to become a Canadian citizen she is required to take an oath bearing allegiance to the Queen of England. In order to fulfill her immigrant performance successfully, she is required to negate the same Indigenous groups with whom Latinx art communities have created such important alliances.

Essentially, such policies are not designed to generate solidarity or intercultural alliances. We see clearly how Fritta Caro's mall interventions allude to the idea of the immigrant using the stereotypes of their culture as a productive commodity within a multiculturalist scheme. As both Gilbert and Beaudoin-Duquette have argued, ideas of multiculturalism "ended up constructing a stereotype of the ideal immigrant who contributes without asking anything in return" (Beaudoin-Duquette 147). This ideal immigrant not only speaks English or French, but is able to integrate at all levels described by Immigration, Refugees, and Citizenship Canada—economic, social, cultural, and political—without generating conflict. Martin Franco, for example, as an artist, is expected to merge her identity and her art into a Kahloesque product that is legible as Latina in this economy in such a way that her contributions reinforce the values of multiculturalism without questioning the Canadian stereotypes of *latinidad* or asking its publics to expand their own conceptions of what may constitute art. As she states, the art world seems less interested in what the Latinx artist wants to explore than in what it expects the Latinx artist should produce (Martin Franco, Interview). When looking at the work Martin Franco continues to do in Colombia, we find that her artistic interests go much beyond working against Latinx stereotypes.[24] Like so many other artists in Canada, however, in order to begin to explore anything beyond her *latinidad* here she must first work toward generating creative spaces that are not dictated by these stereotypes.

---

24   Martin Franco is co-founder of CAVCA (Comunidad de Artistas Visuales de Cartagena y Bolívar), an art collective in Cartagena de Indias focused on the decolonization of art in the Colombian Caribbean. Alongside Muriel Angulo and Alexa Cuesta, Martin Franco created the Meninas Emputás!, a performance group that stages interventions against elitist curatorial practices in mainstream art spaces and festivals in Colombia. She most recently presented a series of video-art pieces by women artists on the politics of the body, presented at Bogotá's 2018 Experimental Film Festival.

Latinx Canadian theatre and performance is not only Latinx, it is also Canadian, and requires the active participation of many non-Latinx artists and publics. Since the 1970s, much Latinx Canadian theatre and performance has been focused on the work of undoing stereotypes, of educating Canadian publics on the histories of the Americas, and of exposing the hemispheric interdependence of these histories, producing an invaluably rich repertoire to Canadian culture. Yet as Latinx art continues to grow, it is key to acknowledge that this work requires non-Latinx publics that cultivate their own efforts in interacting with and amongst immigrant cultures, as successful alliances in the theatre communities have shown.[25] "It is not only the work that the immigrant must do," reflects Martin Franco, "but also how on the other side an effort must be made to understand those who arrive with their language, their customs, their traditions. It's really a collective effort" (Interview). These types of alliances also necessitate that Latinxs look beyond Canada's "official" cultures and acknowledge in turn its complicated diversity, even when our own colonial histories in Latin American have predisposed us to think of the North as primarily white European. As the histories of theatre in Canada continue to show, the arts are key to this project, and have proven to be a ripe arena for the creation of diverse alliances where new ways of embodying, enacting, and experiencing immigration are imagined into being. As Martin Franco writes in her descriptions of Fritta Caro's journey, "looking to undo and dodge the traps that lie in wait for her, she questions institutional approaches to alterity and the 'us' that defines 'them'" ("Altéro(s)philie").

---

25   Puente Theatre and the Rutas Panamericanas Festival are clear examples of this.

QUÉBEC THEATRE AND ITS LANGUAGES IN THREE SNAPSHOTS, LOOSELY FRAMED

NICOLE NOLETTE

SPRING 2013: A FEW EXITS FROM THE FRAME

In a 2013 article in the cultural magazine *Spirale*, theatre critic Hervé Guay discusses two solo shows by actor-playwrights that found success on the stages of Montréal's Théâtre La Chapelle and Théâtre d'Aujourd'hui between November 2012 and February 2013. The first is *Un*, by Mani Soleymanlou, an artist of Iranian descent who migrated with his family to Toronto after a short stay in France. The other show is *Les trois exils de Christian E.*, by Christian Essiambre, an Acadian actor, and Philippe Soldevila, a director from Québec City whose early career featured collaborations with Robert Lepage. Both Soleymanlou and Essiambre are immigrants to Montréal and, more generally, to Québec. According to Guay, their two shows should be understood in the context of the popularity of autobiographical performance amongst actors active in the English Canadian theatre scene. Alan Filewod, for example, notes that in the 1990s, autobiographical solo performances or "auto-performances" offered "the quickest, most accessible and cheapest route to theatrical celebrity" ("Actors" 55). For actors, they were inexpensive to rehearse; for theatres, they were inexpensive to host. Following Filewod's hypothesis, Guay proposes that we consider *Un* to be a critique of Québec's performance as a nation by its solo actor, and *Les trois exils* to be a play for visibility by an actor who is, in a sense, using the

dramaturgy of the play to showcase himself in a "constant process of audi-
tioning to ensure future work." In both cases, self-representation is a space of
divergence, "a means of emancipation for those who feel excluded from the
narrow frame of the 'beau milieu'" (Guay, "Sorties du cadre" 87). In this sense,
we might equally consider that these same plays have something to say about
the "narrow frame of the 'beau milieu'"—or about Québec theatre more generally. Both plays are worth examining not only for their means of *emancipation*
from Québec theatre, but also for their ambivalent *integration* into this context.
How does one insert oneself into a milieu where/when one is an outsider? How
does one write oneself into the history of Québec theatre in order to make a
career there, given that the history of Québec theatre, to cite Yves Jubinville's
observation of 2001, is still written "in bits, in scraps, in crumbs," that "rather
than producing a singular model of comprehension, [multiply] its points of
entry into the past" ("Une mémoire" 37)?

In 1988, facing what she called the lack of a history of Québec drama and
sketching out what the writing of such a history would entail, Lucie Robert
named the first challenge: "the language." As she wrote, "Quebec drama obses-
sively poses questions of language in all their possible forms. It never stops
asking how to speak? In what circumstances? For whom? With what effects?
In what language?" ("Pour une histoire" 167) Persistent attempts to organize this history later multiplied around these questions, including one by
Robert herself in the article, "The Language of Theatre" (1995). Dominique
Lafon nevertheless declared in 2003 that "language remains the blind spot of
theatre scholarship in Quebec," where (often socio-political) readings have
focused on *joual* to the exclusion of other languages (182). For this reason,
"the language" of Québec theatre is often linked to the affirmation of collective francophone identity in the 1960s and 1970s, and, more precisely, to the
event (or advent) of Michel Tremblay's *Les Belles Soeurs* in 1968. Jeanne Bovet
sought to remedy the blind spot identified by Lafon by editing, in 2007, an
issue of *Études françaises* on the languages of Québec drama, stressing several
factors that henceforth allowed for the consideration of a plurality of languages, including "historical distance": "Rather than *the* language, it would be
better to speak of *languages* of Quebec drama, given the multiple expressions

that the play of authors' accents, idiolects, translations, linguistic *métissage*, styles, and poetics allow us to read and to hear" ("Présentation" 6). Historical distance would allow Bovet and her collaborators also to "reaffirm the role of the playwright when confronted with the sociopolitical referent" in their approach to the languages of Québec theatre (7). An equal task remains in relation to the *history* of the linguistic practices of Québec theatre, whether or not they fit within the "narrow frame of the '*beau milieu.*'"

In the pages that follow, I propose to return to the thorny intersection of language, history, and Québec theatre as it relates to the theme of this volume on theatre and (im)migration. I will begin by offering an overview of several historical points of departure for the question of language in literary and theatrical studies, focusing in particular on two moments that, according to specialists, marked this history. I will advance the hypothesis that if it is now possible to discuss the poetics of the languages of Québec theatre while excluding the socio-political referent, or at least bracketing it, language continues to raise issues of identity in certain cases that go beyond the "narrow frame of the '*beau milieu.*'" In shows like *Un* and *Les trois exils de Christian E.*, francophone artists with backgrounds outside the borders of Québec but who chose to work and make work in the province combine linguistic themes and discourses on identity. Paradoxically, this strategy is a means for integration in a "beau milieu" that excludes as historically inflected these themes and discourses. In other words, these two solo works allow the artists to present a position of geographic and national marginality in relation to Québec theatre while meeting audience expectations that outsiders must perform an earlier moment in Québec's theatre history. In this way, both Christian Essiambre and Mani Soleymanlou ensure their current and future success in Québec's theatre scene.

1968: *JOUAL* AND ITS EFFECTS

Joual is generally considered to have presided at the birth of Québec theatre with the public reading, followed by the staging, of *Les Belles Soeurs* at the Rideau Vert in 1968. Michel Biron, François Dumont, and Élisabeth

Nardout-Lafarge write in *Histoire de la littérature québécoise* that at the time, "we were witnessing a spectacular transformation of dramatic language and of theatre as an institution. If there is a rupture in the history of Québec theatre, it is [. . .] in 1968 that it occurs" (446).[1] The rupture took place on many levels. A work of *"joual-reflet,"*[2] the play, performed entirely in *joual*, pushed, according to some, the conceit of a mirror held up to a working-class Montréal neighbourhood to an unprecedented extreme. Furthermore, the rupture, operating in relation to French linguistic norms, turned *joual* into a linguistic weapon. On the level of political intervention, Michel Bélair claims *Les Belles Soeurs* for the nationalist project of the *nouveau théâtre québécois*, an "attempt to affirm a Quebecois way of being" (56). If Tremblay's theatre is not explicitly nationalist, Bélair explains that the playwright's use of *joual* constitutes a cultural affirmation that is well aligned with Québec society's stated contemporaneous desire to welcome a political and cultural break with Canada and then French Canada. In this context, the play becomes an incarnation of the moment after which "as a matter 'of course' *joual* is the official language of Quebec theatre" (Bélair 112): the language present in the subsequent theatre of Michel Tremblay, but also in that of other writers, such as Jean-Claude Germain, Jacqueline Barrette, Sauvageau, Jean Barbeau, Michel Garneau, and Françoise Loranger, to name only those mentioned in *Histoire de la littérature québécoise* (Biron et al. 469).

---

1   It is equally possible to say that Québec theatre's birth through language owes a debt to an act of translation: in 1969 Éloi de Grandmont adapted George Bernard Shaw's *Pygmalion* in the popular language of Québec rather than Parisian slang, a move that would be largely repeated over the following decade. For an analysis of this "iconoclastic," "perlocutionary," and "identitarian" gesture, see Annie Brisset's important work, *Sociocritique de la traduction: théâtre et altérité au Québec (1968–1988)*. For a nuanced critique of Brisset's analysis, in particular in relation to translations of Michel Tremblay, see Sathya Rao, "L'actualité de Michel Tremblay traducteur et adaptateur."

2   Lise Gauvin offers five rhetorical moves associated with *joual* at different times by Michel Tremblay: *"joual-reflet," "joual-politique," "joual universel," "joual exportable,"* and *"joual: ni écran ni refuge" (Langagement* 125–126).

From the moment that Québec theatre defined itself through its use of *joual* as a dramatic language, and as a consequence of the fragmentation of French Canada, the theatre produced in this ill-defined and divided territory also found linguistic expressions that reflected its diverse francophone communities. The 1970s saw the appearance of André Paiement's *"joual franco-ontarien"*[3] in Sudbury, Roger Auger's assertive bilingualism in Saint-Boniface, and the *empremier* speech of a bygone era belonging to the universe of Antonine Maillet in Acadie. These varieties of French were brought to the stage as mimetic representations of the way French is or was spoken in Canada, enabling a constant identification for local spectators. As François Paré states, however, Québec literature quickly "transform[ed] its own creolized language into a structuring exercise of literary writing," thus relegating the historic moment of "its 'act of speech' to its North American diaspora" (*Exiguity* 36). The extraordinary connection between the *joual* of Montréal's eastern neighbourhoods and its stage representations were quickly reconfigured as playwrights appropriated the work of literature, of forming new drama for the page or visual languages for the stage. This expulsive gesture explains, for Paré, that what we saw in Maillet was a confirmation of "the structuring act of orality in Acadian literary discourse" (36).[4] For Québec literature, by contrast, to become Québécois was to lay claim to literature at the same time as it laid claim to Québécois as an adjective; it was to relinquish orality at the same time as it relinquished the adjective "French Canadian." In this sense, the rise of *joual*, which assured a place for Québec literature among world literatures, is "an absolutely extraordinary ideological reversal which has affected a profound change not only in the relationship between France and Quebec,

---

3   The author of *Lavalléville* made clear that the "language used in the production was that of the region: Franco-Ontarian *joual*. It is very important that the play's text be adapted to the inflection of the language (whatever it may be) of the place where the play is performed" (Paiement 4).

4   Recalling the rhetoric of *joual* in Québec, Annette Boudreau and Raoul Boudreau, of the Université de Moncton, later argued that *La Sagouine* represented the "transposition of a rich oral literature into a written literature, which had the effect not only of fixing an oral language but of rehabilitating it by making it into a literary language" (170–71).

but also and above all in that which Quebec held, and still holds, with other literatures of exiguity" (36).

Lise Gauvin identifies in her writing the transcoding of orality, and moreover, the "*literarization* of *joual*," a way of transforming a colloquial register into readable drama, as the primary contribution of *Les Belles Soeurs*: "Tremblay's effect is a complex effect, relying strongly on a system of written representations of the orality of social languages, but a system closer to a poetic approach than a realist imitation" (*Langagement* 141; see also Gauvin, "Le théâtre de la langue"). On the one hand, Alvina Ruprecht speaks of the "phonic texture" of *Les Belles Soeurs's joual* (439), and Mathilde Dargnat meticulously details the stylistic work (lexical, phonetic, and syntactic) Tremblay deploys in the literary transcription of *joual* (*Michel Tremblay*; "L'oral comme fiction"; "L'oral au pied de la lettre"). On the other hand, Gauvin, like Dargnat, maintains that literarization occurs through the rhythm, the prosody, and the theatrical figures chosen by Tremblay. Monologues and choruses, poetic litanies and a tragic mode: these are noble codes meant to interrupt the realist reading of *joual* and its speakers, however vulgar the words may be, however similar they sound to the language of Montréal's eastern neighbourhoods.

As much as researchers have dug deep into the poetic and linguistic attributes of *Les Belles Soeurs* to emphasize the literary exercise to which Michel Tremblay lends himself, Jubinville has insisted, based on sociocritique and a close analysis of the play's manuscripts in the French style of *critique génétique*, on the onstage fate of his *joual*. For the Québec actor, the advent of *Les Belles Soeurs* is "the chance to re-appropriate a terrain that is at once the stage and the actor's own body" in order to access pure emotion (Jubinville, "Frontières du théâtre" 136). An examination of the play's drafts reveals that the concept of the "*effet joual*," introduced by Gauvin to distinguish between the linguistic referent and its literary manifestations, can just as easily describe an effort to reconstruct the affective experience of *joual* in a stage representation. It is an effort demonstrated in rapid-fire retorts, multiplying of points of view, digressions from the plot, and the equivocality of colloquial speech. In this respect, the "*effet joual*" is also "the *dialogic* mechanism of its transcription, which determines the manner in which the actors inhabit their roles" (Jubinville, "Le partage des voix" 108). In short, it offers a way to emphasize the Québec actor's acting.

1980 OR THE FORMALIST PHASE DISPERSED

After its moment of glory in the 1970s, the use of *joual* dwindled away with little fanfare, becoming, according to Gilbert David, "simply the guarantee of a seamless reflection of the world" (64).[5] Clearly, the theatre world's attention shifted elsewhere: a transition asserted itself in relation to earlier realist (or neorealist) and explicitly socio-political preoccupations. Jane Moss speaks of a displacement of the linguistic question as a "drama of language" that mines the psychology of its characters in long poetic monologues ("Larry Tremblay").[6] Lucie Robert evokes a decentring of "*la langue*" in favour of language (*langage*) and its concomitant issues of power ("The Language of Theatre" 126).[7] In this historical narrative, following in the footsteps of Normand Chaurette, René-Daniel Dubois, and Michel Marc Bouchard—who, in the 1980s, laid the foundations for a theatre with renewed interest in the literary text while renewing, as well, the dramatic forms of that text—a generation of writers including Normand Canac-Marquis, Hélène Pedneault, Claude Poissant, Daniel Danis, and Larry Tremblay turned to a diversity of poetic languages. Instead of insisting on a break, Dominique Lafon suggests that this transformation could be considered as a new "*effet joual*" (192): a stylistic and

---

5   The author offers the plays of Marie Laberge (*L'homme gris*) and of Serge Boucher (*24 poses [portraits]* and *Avec Norm*) as examples of a "populist complacency" toward colloquial Québécois language among naturalist playwrights following the track laid by Michel Tremblay.

6   Moss herself takes the term "drama of language" from Sylvie Bérard's review of *Celle-là* by Daniel Danis, where she maintains that "the materiality of the verb is palpable" (49).

7   For a perspective on the changes in the scope of Québec drama that arose throughout the 1980s, among which figures the question of language, see also Jean-Cléo Godin and Dominique Lafon, *Dramaturgies québécoises des années quatre-vingt*.

ideological heritage bequeathed by the linguistic liberation of *joual* and its transcoding into literary signifiers.

A second approach to this transition begins with other signifiers, in particular with the theatre of the object and of the image (for example, that of Ex Machina and Carbone 14). As Jubinville states, "The stage writing of a Gilles Maheu [. . .] fifteen years after *Les Belles Soeurs* will use the body to exploit, at the same time, its expressive power and its unsettling opacity" ("Frontières du théâtre" 146): its acoustic image as well as its ideology of resistance. In this sense, another, unexpected, aspect of *joual* that carries through is the engaged body (the contemporary location of the real in theatre) in the work of, for example, Stéphane Crête and Dave St-Pierre. Louis Patrick Leroux argues that "Quebec's new realism isn't necessarily linguistic: it is corporeal and, as always, existential" ("From *langue* to Body" 122; see also "De la langue au corps" 72). Whether this constitutes a transition, a turn, a rupture, or a strange continuity, it is linked to the establishment of the many institutions that would make French the public language of Québec after the election of the Parti Québécois in 1976, or to the loss of the 1980 referendum, that marked the beginning of a post-nationalist era.

In considering the larger context of emergent literatures, however, Gilbert David (64–65) recalls that the course taken in Québec corresponds to the two phases described by Pascale Casanova in *World Republic of Letters*:

> Formal preoccupations, which is to say specifically literary concerns, appear in small literatures only in a second phase, when an initial stock of literary resources has been accumulated and the first international artists find themselves in a position to challenge the aesthetic assumptions associated with realism and to exploit the revolutionary advances achieved at the Greenwich meridian. (200)

In this second phase, writers can choose between two major strategies: on the one hand, *assimilation*, not in the pejorative, Québécois definition of the term, but in the sense of an "integration within a dominant literary space through a dilution or erasing of original differences"; on the other, *differentiation*, or "the assertion of difference, typically on the basis of a claim to national identity" (179). In a quick classification, David groups Jovette Marchessault, Normand Chaurette, Carole Fréchette, and Larry Tremblay[8] as well as "immigrant authors, like Marco Micone, Abla Farhoud, Wajdi Mouawad or Pan Bouyoucas, whose language of education was so-called standard French" on the side of *assimilation*, while Michel Tremblay, Réjean Ducharme, René-Daniel Dubois, Jean-François Caron, Alexis Martin, and Olivier Choinière lean more toward the side of *differentiation* (64–65). Between the two poles is a continuum of practices, including the "deliberate oscillation" of Jean-Pierre Ronfard's *Vie et mort du roi boiteux* and Daniel Danis's "splitting" between orality and literariness. In francophone Canada, where Casanova's two phases have been more widely employed, Moss shows a similar passage from identity to post-identity theatre in Ontario, where the literary rupture would have been the cleanest ("Les théâtres francophones post-identitaires"; "Le théâtre francophone en Ontario"). Though we can find the two writing strategies in contemporary practice, the two phases are, however, far from assumed in minority literatures, to the extent that it is not clear that the history told by these phases is itself universal.

In a similar manner, in Québec the desire to stage language and its implications for identity has perhaps not so much disappeared as it has been pushed toward linguistic heterogeneity, charged throughout the 1980s with "signalling the presence of elsewhere in local ideas, and the resulting processes of cultural confrontation and accommodation" (Simon, *Le trafic des langues* 152; see also L'Hérault).[9] For Sherry Simon, two projects best illustrate this tendency to

---

8 This is without including the play *The Dragonfly of Chicoutimi* (1995), famous for the fact that it was written in English, but, as Robert Dion notes, under the influence of French: "here it is French that corrupts English, that subjects it to a beginning of creolization in the same line as a *'joualization'* of English" (88).

9 Apart from Marco Micone, one could also name Abla Farhoud, Bernard Antoun, Alberto Kurapel, and Yves Sioui Durand, whose work displays a marked multilingualism and postmodernism: "In the 1980s and 1990s, when the Québec public seemed to have turned its back on political theatre, playwrights like Durand, Kurapel, Antoun, Farhoud and Micone renewed the stage with their spectacles of Otherness, thus demonstrating

combine the internal and the external, the here and the there: Marco Micone's theatrical trilogy, committed to representing the immigrant experience of the Italo Québécois community, and Robert Lepage's *La Trilogie des dragons*, which explores renewed crossings between the local and the intercontinental, reproducing its thematic gesture in its circulation. The question of Micone's trilogy, seen through Erin Hurley's analysis, can be found in the creation, outside of French, of a theatrical language conducive to the emergence of the Italo Québécois, a dramatic subject until recently little represented on Montréal stages. Hurley astutely notes that such a gesture did not appear yesterday; in fact, it is the same gesture that made *joual* famous in the 1960s and 1970s, namely the theatrical valorization of a contact language that retains the scars left behind by contact and that produces a previously unknown subjectivity on stage ("Devenir Autre" 8–11). In the absence of a contemporary Italo Québécois language in which French would take precedence, however, one cannot say that Micone simply imitates reality. His creative work in making a hybrid theatrical language is, rather, a double intervention that brings into being a language intended both for the future of the Italian community and for a present integration into Québec's public sphere. As Simon explains, the polyglot theatre staged by Robert Lepage is as doubly composed as Micone's: on the one hand, a code of complicity ensures its success in Québec and, on the other, another code connects it to international networks (*Le trafic des langues* 152–53). On this level, the forms adopted by Lepage also recall the approaches to bilingual (French-English) theatre commonly proposed by anglophone artists in Montréal like David Fennario or Marianne Ackermann of Theatre 1774, of which Simon has said, "In the same way as a play in *joual* can mobilize the feeling of community and of history shared by its public, a bilingual play also creates a community. Only, this community is defined by its capacity to live on both sides of the linguistic divide" (*Le trafic des langues* 163).[10]

---

the contribution that theater can make to our understanding and engagement with social realities" (J. Moss, "Cendres de cailloux" 95).

10   Simon references Fennario's *Balconville* and Ackermann's *L'Affaire Tartuffe*. For Lepage's theatre, see also Simon, "Robert Lepage and the Languages of Spectacle"; and

2012 OR A CALL FOR AND EXPECTATION OF MULTILINGUALISM

It is just such a "community still to come" (Simon, *Le trafic des langues* 163) in the Montréal theatre scene that Philippe Couture and Christian Saint-Pierre invoke in a thematic issue of *Jeu: Revue de théâtre* in 2012, forcefully returning to Québec's linguistic question and, from there, to the capacity to represent a less conflicted multilingual reality. They note the participation of institutions (Talisman Theatre, Imago Theatre, Teesri Duniya Theatre) and artists (Marie Brassard, Catherine Bourgeois, Annabel Soutar, Alexandre Marine, Jacob Wren, and Stacey Christodoulou) as well as actors (Éloi ArchamBaudoin, Delphine Bienvenu, Romy Daniel, Catherine De Sève, and Emmanuel Schwartz) in the development of a theatre scene where this openness to multilingualism might continue to grow, all the while noting the road that remains ahead:

> We dream of seeing in the Quebec theatre scene better-fostered dialogues, proofs of hybridization, of intersection, of entanglements, references, cultures, and languages that bump into each other to create new materials—to produce rare, unpredictable results, that will be more than the sum of their parts. Will we manage one day to defeat all the fears, once and for all, which remain legion and often irrational? Will we succeed in transforming our rivalries, turning them into a way of thinking about our society according to new paradigms, with less conflict in the relationship between languages and cultures? This is our dearest wish. (Couture and Saint-Pierre, 8)

Paradoxically, this project, so tied to Montréal in its references, opens the door to the territory abandoned by the *nouveau théâtre québécois*. In the issue that follows this appeal, Louise Ladouceur and I present articles on the theatrical heterolingualism of francophone Canada, while the brief history of Québec

---

Bovet "Identity and Universality" and "Présentation."

theatre proposed by Hervé Guay in light of onstage multilingualism takes him to the docks of Port-Royal, in Acadie, to describe Marc Lescarbot's *Théâtre de Neptune en la Nouvelle-France* (1606) before invoking the nineteenth-century comedies of Joseph Quesnel and Pierre Petitclair, burlesque and *revues* in the beginning of the twentieth century, the Jeune Théâtre of the end of the 1960s and the 1970s, *Balconville*, *The Dragonfly of Chicoutimi*, and the "linguistic pluralism" of migrant writers from the 1980s and 1990s.[11]

It is perhaps not surprising that in the same year as the publication of this issue of *Jeu*, Mani Soleymanlou appeared on stage at the Théâtre La Chapelle in *Un* and Christian Essiambre, a few months later, in *Les trois exils de Christian E.* at Théâtre d'Aujourd'hui. The two actors bear witness to their exclusion from the labour market of Montréal theatre, both creating, through their plays, new work (in both the theatrical and economic sense) in a renewed national discourse. "Profession: Immigrant," quips Soleymanlou in a later manifesto:

> I am part of a cultural scene that little represents me. When I write "represents me," I wear the mantle of the immigrant, I endorse the statute of the stranger. Why not, when I'm reminded of it every day? How can I ignore the fact that my talent as an actor has been, for a long time, reduced to my ability to do accents that come from a fictive, Hollywood version of the Arab world? ("Rajoutons des souches" 21)

Christian Essiambre also displays a willingness to play the role that the theatre world gives him. If Soleymanlou agrees to play the taxi driver with the Arab accent, the character of Christian E. buys a case of lobsters for his agent:

---

11   The issue also includes articles on circus, dance, Eugenio Barba, Jan Lauwers, Harry Standjofski, Denis Bernard, the writing of multilingualism in Montréal theatre, as well as the plays *The Medea Effect* and *En français comme en anglais, it's easy to criticize* and *My Pregnant Brother/Mon frère est enceinte*.

I moved to Montreal two years ago and I haven't gotten a single
contract as an actor! The only thing I've gotten since I've been here,
after getting hung up on by all the agents, is getting to talk—talk!
to an agent to get told "Hey! You're Acadian? Well then bring me a
crate of lobster and I'll get you an audition." [. . .] Do you know how
much a crate of lobster costs? Well that's what it cost me to get ONE
audition! For FIDO! You know what? The first and only audition I
got since getting to Montreal, I got it 'cause I look like a Bouvier des
Flandres! A Bouvier des Flandres, Christ! . . . *(He sits down, calm.)*
If I didn't get it, it's because of my Acadian accent.[12] (Soldevila and
Essiambre 30–31)

The two actors, in order to integrate themselves into the Québec theatre scene,
take from it its most marked code: language.

The Acadian actor thus stages his efforts to learn the diction of Québécois
speech, removing Acadian traits such as the conjugation of the first person with
the third ("*j'étions*") and adding the typical Québec affrication ("*acadzien*"), diph-
thongized long vowels ("*souviyens*") and closing of the vowel "oi" (*québécois*):

« J'étions pas acadien. Chus acadzien. »
[. . .]
« Acadziyen. » « Acadzian. »
[. . .]

---

12   "Ça fait deux ans que chus déménagé icitte à Montréal, pis que j'pogne pas un maudit
contrat comme comédien ! La seule affaire qu'j'ai réussi à pogner depuis qu'chus icitte là,
après m'faire raccrocher l'téléphone au nez par toués agents, c'est d'finalement réussi à
parler; parler ! à un agent pour m'faire dire « Heille ! t'es Acadien ? Ben, amène-moi une
caisse de homards, m'a t'en faire passer des auditions. » [. . .] Savez vous comment ça
coûte une caisse de homards ? Ben c'est ça que ça m'a coûté pour finir par passer UNE . . .
UNE audition ! Pour FIDO !! Savez-vous quoi ? La première, pis la seule audition que j'ai eue
depuis que chus à Montréal, là, je l'ai eue parce que j'orsemblais à un Bouvier des Flandres !
UN BOUVIER DES FLANDRES, CRISSE ! . . . [. . .] *(Il se ressaisit, calme.)* Si j'l'ai pas eu là, c'à
cause de mon accent acadien."

« Je me souviyens que je suis acadzien. »

[...]

« Mais je parle / »

[...]

Je jase? OK.

« Mais je jase québécoâ. »

[...]

En québécois? « Je jase en québécois. » (31)

Then, he situates his Québécois spectators' expectations between the *par-lure* of Antonine Maillet's *La Sagouine* and the *chiac* associated with Acadian Montréal musical productions before raising them by voicing a repertoire of accents that he turns into an auto-ethnographic tour of the villages of the Acadian peninsula, from Bas-Caraquet to Saint-Simon by way of Tracadie. In the end, he turns his gaze on his Québec spectators, precisely those who are waiting to see an Acadian take the stage to give a speech about Acadie, by repeating this ethnographic tour through the regions of Québec. He goes on to imitate a *Montréalais*, a *Beauceron*, an *Outremontais*, a *Jeannoise*, and a teenager from Ville-Vanier. After his obvious hesitation in his early Québécois diction lessons, Christian E. goes on to master a whole series of regional accents. He is thus able to ascend to the Montréal stage to recount his own journey, as well as the marvellous and tragic history of his family, those "four cousins born of four sisters, in seven days" (81).[13]

As for Soleymanlou, he takes the stage thanks to the initiative of Théâtre de Quat'Sous's Lundi découvertes (Discovery Mondays), where the goal is to "discover a Québécois artist hailing from a cultural community. That's where I started writing this magnificient story. Discover an artist hailing from a cultural community: Mani Soleymanlou and his country of origin ... IRAN"[14] (*Trois* 190). Enthusiastic in the beginning, this identity-based writing

---

13 « 'Quat' cousins, nés de quat' sœurs, en sept jours."

14 "Découvrir un artiste québécois issu d'un milieu culturel. C'est là que l'écriture de cette magnifique histoire a commencé. Découvrir un artiste québécois issu d'un milieu

soon runs into obstacles, one of the most important being the absence of the
Persian language: "How can I dare to speak about Persian poetry and literature
when I can't even write or read in the language" (20).[15] In these conditions,
the material of the self is not enough to satisfy the expectations of the Lundi
découvertes, and it is fiction that picks up the baton in the second part of the
play, where "il" and "elle," a young man and a young woman who could have
lived the Iranian events unknown by someone who emigrated, take over. The
move into fiction here is a critical gesture, marking the failure of the autobiographical enterprise of the Lundi découvertes lectures when confronted
with a subject who refuses to assume his expected subjectivity:

> Québécois artist . . . Am I Québécois?
> Are all those who have the opportunity to be here—Iranian,
> Lebanese, Haitian, Peruvian, Ukrainian—because they don't want
> to or can't live in their birth country, necessarily Québécois?
> In the same way as the Québécois who is seeking his own iden-
> tity, his own recognition, his own nation, his own language, his own
> independance?[16] (38)

Yet, instead of confirming this refusal, in the play's denouement the character
embraces the mandate of his identity in a trilingual logorrhea:

Je me définis et me décris sur mon clavier. J'écris :

Partir, toujours, boroh. Aller vivre ailleurs, ba maman o baba. Ses parents le lui ont permis. Ils ont laissé battre ses deux ailes d'origine iranienne qui n'ont, pendant toute leur jeunesse, jamais cessé de battre, az yek chahr be yek chahr, d'un pays à un autre, d'un continent à un autre, d'une langue à une autre. Être pendant quelque temps Français, ensuite Canadien who became Canadian, ensuite Québécois, mais toujours Iranien. Eye vay goftam digé, be farsi assountaré !

Donc voilà, c'est dit, devant vous, vous êtes témoins : Iranien. I am Persian.

Ché djour irouni ? Irounié moderne ? A new breed of Persan comme ses amis à Toronto, là où il ne se questionnait never. Irounié moderne, un Iranien contemporain, comme des millions d'Autres, enfant de parents errants apeurés par la vie que leur enfant pourrait avoir. Maman babaiké batchahashoono var midarano mirane, ces parents qui décident que leur enfant ne devrait pas grandir dans un tel environnement. Farar mikonane, vaseye batchahashoon. Fuir le nid et s'envoler vers un lieu, Paaris, Toronto, Otava, Montreal, un lieu, anywhere, but he will always dream to go back à son premier lieu, là d'où coule le sang, là où présentement coule le sang, tooyé khiabounbha, il coule le sang, the same blood qui coule dans ses veines iraniennes, in khooni ké inja, fuit le contact de l'asphalte. Ce sang iranien dans ses veines iraniennes tantôt déguisées en Farançavi, tantôt Canadaï, dorénavant Québéki, vali hamishé Irouni, Négahé toé qui fait naître ce vide. Ké madjbouram mikoné que befahman that this emptiness khoobé. Ké hitch eibi nadaré que man natoonam bégam kojaihastam, hich eibe nadaré que man sétaa zaboune harfimizaname, doesn't matter, bé darak, etefaghan khéli khoobé. Karé man, az ine rooz bébad, iné ké be tamamé donya begam qué aré, man Irouniam, agah, hich eibi nadaré, tazé fahmidam ké bad nist, ce vide. (47–48)

In this monologue, the character's self-proclaimed void is filled with writing, with definitions and descriptions, with words and languages. There is a striking similarity here to Marco Micone's *"gens du silence,"* whose silence does not hinder the effusive abundance of words when the playwright composes a language for them.

From linguistic correction to the emancipation of an actor through his onstage use of a language that belongs to him, the historical event of *joual* creates the analogous plots of the solo shows *Un* and *Les trois exils de Christian E.* The spectacle of the acquisition of a theatrical language is for both actors "the chance to reappropriate a terrain that is at once the stage and the actor's own body" in order to access pure emotion, a way of being in a role that represents him (Jubinville, "Frontières du théâtre" 136). Language again becomes the place of truth, of the *real* in theatre. The work of transcoding orality begins again in the memory of writing for the stage. The version of *Trois exils de Christian E.* published by Dramaturges Éditeurs contains a note to the reader on the transcription; the character in *Un* states, "I define myself and I describe myself on my keyboard. I write"[17] (Soleymanlou, *Trois* 47). Thus, plays and actors that are products of the world outside the "narrow frame of the *'beau milieu'*" take up the historical moment that defined that milieu in order to be better recognized within it. In this sense, even if this statement seems paradoxical, the linguistic differentiation enacted within these two plays is a *literary* assimilation in the sense defined by Pascale Casanova, revealing the artists' and their work's *integration* into Québec's dominant literary system. If *joual* was a place of resistance possessed of an "unsettling opacity," or even a political weapon, we can say the same thing in regard to Soleymanlou's statement, which confirms, through a trope that is perhaps too comforting, the place of artists from outside the national frame in a preliminary phase of theatre history. We should not be surprised to learn the reaction of the Québec public, as reported by Soleymanlou:

---

17   "Je me définis et me décris sur mon clavier. J'écris."

Almost no one, publicly, seemed shocked by what I thought was a direct criticism of the rapport maintained between Quebec and the other, the newcomer, the one who, from now on, would also people this land. Of my words, what lingered was essentially a kind of exoticism, almost reassuring in the eyes of those who had heard me, and surprise at my quest for an identity. What I tried to erase, whether a connection with a particular culture or, moreover, any connection with my Iranian cultural heritage, made me the on-call Iranian. What a coincidence. I played my part. ("Rajoutons des souches" 22)

We should not be surprised, either, that the strategy of integration continues, for Soleymanlou as for Essiambre, as well as for Micone and Lepage elsewhere, in the form of the theatrical trilogy, which is able to integrate new voices and new subjectivities absent from contemporary stage representations with every play. *Un* is succeeded by *Deux* and *Trois*; *Les trois exils de Christian E.* by further episodes in *Le long voyage de Pierre-Guy B.* and *L'incroyable légèreté de Luc L.*; much as *Gens du silence*, *Addolorata*, and *Déjà l'agonie* or *Le dragon vert*, *Le dragon rouge*, and *Le dragon blanc* link together. Here is a way of accepting the expectations of the "narrow frame of the '*beau milieu*,'" as well as a way of responding to these expectations.

My argument here is not so much that the new multilingualism used by (im)migrant subjects on the Québec stage can be seen as equal to *joual* in its power to reshape national theatre for a new Québec, though that argument could also be made. Rather, I have sought to render visible the script *joual* has written for the history of Québec theatre, starting with the *nouveau théâtre québécois*, to highlight how each moment has connected language, form, and identity to different constituencies: in the first phase, to francophone performers outside Québec, in the second, to immigrant performers within Québec. And while I see Essiambre and Soleymanlou speaking to these concerns in their respective solo performances, I question whether, when, and/or how (im)migrant subjects might be as well-received when they produce multilingual performances that do not have to speak to matters of national theatre, identity, or the ability of outsiders to work in such an environment. Will (im)migrant subjects always be loquacious "people of silence," inventors of new languages and discourses of identity, or might they too one day experiment with other forms and other contents?

VIRTUAL MIGRATION: NEW CANADIAN DIGITAL PERFORMANCE EXPERIENCES

PETER KULING

The territory no longer precedes the map, nor does it survive it.
—Jean Baudrillard, *Simulacra and Simulation*

Active virtual hashtags allow people involved in migration around the globe, as well as those following them on social media, to access unprecedented networks of real-time updates and political reactions, as well as empathetic posts about their respective journeys. For example, #ReuniteFamilies gained huge popularity on Twitter and Instagram in 2018 for posts about children being separated from their parents crossing the US border. The question of how often actual migrants check these social-media platforms—especially in languages they may not typically use—pales in comparison to the vocal outcry from non-migrants responding, often very emotionally, to such issues as President Donald Trump's border-control policies. Digital posts about troubled migration illustrate how smart phones allow current virtual publics to spread their opinions and reactions to real-time issues of migration and immigration as they happen. During the process, these publics often create avenues of misguided empathy and misunderstanding about the specifics of actual refugee experiences in current border conflicts. As new virtual borders appear across different forms of social media, the experiences of actual migrants often become lost or distorted by the collective "virtual audience" mapping out their versions of reality within politically charged digital spaces of communication.

Such digital strategies also play out as dramaturgy. To understand that process, this paper examines how several recent theatre productions in

Toronto use technology in performance to generate positive and negative audience responses from narratives and experiences focused on questions of immigration to Canada. By telling stories of absent migrants deported as a result of Canadian immigration laws or by transforming Toronto audience participants into imagined individual migrants themselves, these theatrical experiences pin their entire success on attendees' virtual empathy and real-world engagement in order to provoke further thinking about problematic immigration trends. My work specifically focuses on four different shows by three theatre companies over the last four years, which have been chosen to offer specific examples of dangerous tendencies within performances of migration. These include museumification[1] and semiotic stereotypes used to clarify narrative progression, as well as the gamification of immigration narratives created through durational experiences, checkpoint-based narratives, and heavy technological mediation.

In August 2017, the SummerWorks Performance Festival in Toronto focused on narratives and stories of immigrants, likely as a result of populist elections and leadership around the globe following the election of President Donald Trump. Two of the four plays I will discuss here—Dustin Harvey and Adrienne Wong's *Landline* and DopoLavoro Teatrale's *The Invisible City*—appeared in the SummerWorks 2017 lineup, while *The Apartment* was developed by DopoLavoro Teatrale to test out technology in performance before the festival started. Ken Cameron's *How iRan*, meanwhile, originally premiered at the IMPACT 13 Festival in Kitchener, Ontario, and went on to further productions at the Calgary Public Library in 2014 and most recently at the Ottawa Fringe in 2016. *The Apartment* was DopoLavoro Teatrale or DLT's shorter "test" play, produced with the Theatre Centre and Instituto Italiano di Cultura in Toronto, to prepare for longer durational experimental work during *The Invisible City*, which premiered in Toronto in August 2017 at SummerWorks. *Landline* premiered simultaneously in Vancouver and Halifax

---

1   I use museumification, as per Michael Di Giovine's definition, to connote a situation "wherein everything is considered not for its use but for its value as a potential museum artifact" (261). Both migrants and audience members are museumified within these performance experiences.

in 2013 and has since run in cities across Canada and around the world; it was remounted between Toronto and Hamilton, Ontario, at SummerWorks 2017. Of all the performances discussed in this piece, only *Landline* continues to run consistently, while *How iRan* remains open to being remounted. DLT has closed both *The Apartment* and *The Invisible City* to focus on new immersive production efforts in early stages of development.

All these productions share the common characteristic of requiring audiences to use technology to listen, read, interact, and move through performance spaces rife with motifs and narratives concerning displacement, strangeness, and migration. I have chosen them for the apparent similarities in the aesthetics and motifs generated by their use of technology as the principal narrator or device for telling stories of migration. Like Emma Cox in her analysis of the "mythopoetics of migration" (10), I question here the pros and cons of creating "encounters with foreignness—with foreign people, with foreign places" (4), especially when it comes to actively constructing audience experiences through specific technologies. Using smart phones and other digital devices in performances, these productions aim to create new virtual zones of audience interaction with migration issues, allowing audiences to confront their own empathy for absent migrants at different stages in their actual journeys. However, actual immigrants do not appear in any of these shows. Instead, we encounter their collective personal effects, voices, emails, tweets, and other personal communications, in place of real actors on site providing testimonials through dialogue. Site-specific, immersive, and devised strategies are employed to tell migrants' stories differently and to force audience members, to different extents, to participate in journeys around Toronto as virtual migrants themselves. In these experiments, technology allows each company to manipulate the prevalent social desire to connect and empathize with others online—sometimes even with complete strangers—as audience members journey in real time through unscripted, virtual, and often displacing performance experiences.

Shows like *How iRan*, *Landline*, *The Apartment*, and *The Invisible City* map out new territories of performance engaged with issues of migration and displacement. Intended for single or individual audience members (sometimes paired with other audience members), they cannot be recreated the same way twice. These pop-up productions have little to no script—those with a playscript use it mostly as an encounter guide—and require active audience participation through designed and real urban spaces in order to exist. Smart phones and iPods become stage managers, addressing spectators through virtual cues and signs to guide them into new environments and unexpected encounters.

All of these productions share stories about peoples displaced forcefully by governments or willingly by choice. Instead of scrolling past tweets or Instagram posts concerning refugees and immigration experiences, willing participants are asked to investigate and experience others' migratory choices or results. In an era of extensive smart-phone obsession, these plays literally require spectators to become "consumed" by their phones in order to journey and find each play's ending. By encouraging audiences to re-evaluate their own personal relationships to urban spaces, these device-driven shows ulti-mately comment on the privileged nature of Canadian social-media-engaged audiences' responses to politically enforced migration.

SYNCHRONIC DRAMATURGY

Ric Knowles describes reliance on semiotic virtualization as an assent to the power of synchronic signs: "Not only is the value in a sign stable only in the synchronic present, it is also stable only insofar as its community assents to, enacts, and evokes the system through each utterance that participates in the system" (*How Theatre Means* 23). In all of the shows I discuss here, digital synchronic signs become dramaturgical keys used by audiences to unlock new paths. Simulated realities and performance experiences dominate these works, forcing audiences to play along and perform as themselves in tandem with the cultural or theatrical situations encountered. They position specta-tors as "virtual migrants" within the confined boundaries of a performance and invite them to act, react, or remain silent as desired. While some of these shows do contain fairly conventional narratives, they all harness the divide between the artificiality of performance and the lived reality of spectator experience. By merging real and simulated elements together, they become living palimpsests of the hyper real.

As Jean Baudrillard explains, the hyper real generates performative experiences "sheltered from the imaginary, and from any distinction between the real and the imaginary, leaving room only for the orbital recurrence of models and for the simulated generation of differences" (2–3). When experiencing the plays I consider in this essay, audience members are constantly torn between the actual reality of objects, places, people, and (especially) the technology they use to interact with and complete their experiences and the highly simulated elements of narrative development, performers, and memories evoked via audio track or in-person in real urban spaces, homes, and galleries. They also confront simulated differentiation between themselves, other audience members, and/or characters, both real and imaginary. Added into this exciting mix are new virtual possibilities of "play" and "ritual" emerging from the unique and unexpected interactions occurring within these and other recent Canadian technology-driven shows.[2]

Richard Schechner describes how we experience ritual and play differently than other kinds of sports, entertainments, and even theatre itself: "Ritual and play are alike in many ways—periods of playful license are often followed by or interdigitated with periods of ritual control" (*Performance* 15). In Schechner's model of performance experiences, play functions as a completely free activity—almost childlike due to its lack of consequences—while ritual emerges as "the individual's submission to forces 'larger' or at least 'other' than oneself" (15). Plays using digital devices and technology generate Schechnerian forms of play and ritual by moving audiences into environments where they absolutely must resort to using technology to facilitate their lack of understanding. They can resist, but then the play will simply end and not emerge as an experience. How will we respond to an actor texting us in real time or a live call-centre

---

2 Recent Canadian theatre relying entirely on technology in performance includes Jordan Tannahill's *rihannaboi95* (2013), Les Petites Cellules Chaude's *Le iShow* (2013–15), SpiderWebShow's *The Revolutions* (2017), Zuppa Theatre's *The Archive of Missing Things* (2017), Laurence Dauphinais and Maxime Carbonneau's *Siri* (2017), and Theatre Replacement's *Mine* (2018).

operator asking us questions or an audio track guiding us to the next designed encounter space? Can we remain free or even playful? What happens if we do not respond, if we alter the structure of the experience, or if we interact with the real and digital environments in ways counterintuitive to the environments created by their artists? Movement choices in all these shows function like video-game decisions, where players chart individual paths based on evaluations of risk and reward prior to acting. Aiming to accentuate new feelings of discomfort, awkwardness, and alienation surrounding motifs of migration, production companies use technology to force us into unexpected theatrical experiences despite our assumed freedom as audience members. Using synchronic cues delivered by specialized devices within a ritualistic framework, audiences are both free and restrained as they wander, listen, react, and interact with performance content during their own individual journey through each play.

In the sections that follow, I consider each of these unique performance experiences separately by exploring how the use of specific digitally mediated performance devices—iPods, smart phones, digital maps, SMS texting—provides different performance results for each play's specific focus on ideas and narratives of migration. I describe each of these works as I myself experienced them, referring to published scripts whenever available. Moving from the production deemed least immersive to the one most completely open to the audience's free will and choice, my research identifies how digital media and synchronic dramaturgy actively change audience experiences in plays focused on issues of contemporary migration. While it may seem somewhat gimmicky to create plays entirely on smart devices, these productions use technology strategically to force spectators into atypical situations that generate affective reactions to material objects and reconfigured urban environments. By tracing out commonalities within these plays, I demonstrate technology's ability to provide audiences with a unique connection to the plights of real-world migrants, while also encouraging them to remain self-critical about the genuine and realistic qualities of these connections. Through their use of technology, these theatrical experiments transform the experiences of everyday Canadians into hyper real performances about failing migration systems, virtual empathy, and our dangerous reliance on digital smart devices.

KEN CAMERON'S *HOW IRAN*

Ken Cameron's *How iRan* has appeared throughout Canada in different installation environments and theatre festivals since 2013. This play's hybridized
performance layout functions as a museum-like experience, taking the form
of a "site-specific piece inspired by incarcerated Iranian Canadian blogger
Hossein Derakhshan, designed to be shuffled at random on an iPod" (Kuling
and Levin 7). Extensive properties and designed artifacts fill checkpoints
within the performance space at which audience members can stop and listen
to Hossein's story. There are no physical actors present, only several voice
actors on iPod audio tracks, and each audience member proceeds on their
own "unique" path with free but guided exploration of the space. Cameron's
performance experience relies on the shuffle gimmick of the least expensive
version of the Apple iPod; random sequencing actively stimulates an individual experience. Audience members also pre-select one of three iPods, coloured
red, green, or white like the Iranian flag, which contain all the audio tracks
of a particular character. The sequence of the tracks gets shuffled as they tour
the museum checkpoints of the installation.[3]

Claiming that Canadian theatre has always been focused on and created
by immigrants, Patrick Finn argues, "*How iRan* stages stories by people who
are not yet able to speak" (61). Finn correctly identifies how speech acts, for
these characters come with threats of incarceration, but reminds us that it
was Hossein's online blogging—as opposed to this audio performance—that
got him into trouble with the Iranian government. Fear of speaking freely
without some form of larger consequence—something many new immigrants
like Hossein face, literally or figuratively, during their own self-establishment
in Canada—pervades this play's narrative. Cameron's piece also assumes that
Canadian audiences are interested in a kind of passive, guided experience—
technological or not—with narratives of cultural difference and immigration

---

3   Ken Cameron recreated an online shuffled version of his playscript for *Canadian
Theatre Review* 159, "Digital Performance," by using HTML to randomize scene sequences
for online readers after they selected a coloured iPod.

challenges. As a result, aspects of museumification abound. At the performance checkpoints, audience members interact with physical items left by characters currently speaking over their iPod headphones. The small and portable nature of the iPod Shuffle lends itself well to this kind of audio-only guided museum experience, but ultimately takes away from spectators' ability to assume direct agency by manipulating tracks, searching them, and actively restructuring or even repeating parts of their journey. Although such "free" agency is definitely not a required element of effective technologically mediated performance, its absence renders Cameron's audience more passive than those of the other shows considered here. Because audiences are unable actively to play with the performance elements in front of them, they experience *How iRan* more as a ritual walkthrough than as a playful game that they control.

Cameron's play also relies heavily on the marketing gimmick of the iPod shuffle itself, which provides a sense of randomization despite the limited playlist of tracks offered by Hossein's narrative of immigration and deportation. Moreover, no single audience member can ever access the entire story during the show, as it's divided amongst three different iPods. Like most contemporary museums, this production encourages audiences to fill in gaps in their experience via different forms of engagement, whether those be auditory, physical, spatial, or more. All the objects in the show—even the iPods themselves—hint at a possible completeness, yet problematize the assumption that one has to completely "experience" everything to understand the key problem of forced deportation back to Iran. Arguably the most important aspect of this story, Hossein's expulsion from Canada, remains the only fixed constant throughout any version of the show; it is included as an audio track on all iPods, even if the sequences are themselves individually randomized.

Do we, as listeners, fall victim to assumptions and misappropriations due to our lack of a complete understanding of Hossein's story? Are there benefits to encountering Hossein's story randomly, or might there be more to gain by going through Hossein's story in a linear fashion, or by at least having the option to access all of the possible performance tracks in Cameron's show? It may strike some audience members as odd that there are zero computer stations to sit down, read, and comment on any of Hossein's actual blog posts throughout the experience. Instead, like many contemporary video games or even Punchdrunk's *Sleep No More*, *How iRan*'s narrative forcibly ushers audience members toward a common final scene, thereby removing any agency to return to and spend more time in its designed environments. The price of common cultural experience here may be a passive engagement with this guided-tour performance.

Audiences do encounter Hossein's personal challenges with both migration and deportation, but are not given any material means to interact with them or resolve their problems. The only interactive and synchronically varied elements of Cameron's piece are the aforementioned checkpoint stations filled with physical objects. As in a guided tour in a museum, participants have no choice but to continue on from these stations once they are finished with an audio track and eventually move on to the end of their personal pathway. Many of Cameron's designed artifacts also appear as stereotypical representations of Iranian culture and of forcible displacement more broadly: shoes, suitcases, fabrics, books, photographs, and so on. Do these pieces add anything to this performance experience beyond filling an otherwise empty space with visuals complicit in further stereotyping Canadian impressions of immigrants? Are audiences interested in unpacking different levels of meaning within these assorted items, much as they are required to do when listening to different versions of Hossein's own story? While the important narrative of the blogger trapped in Iran generates a unique form of connection between spectator and immigrant, the virtual migrants in this piece—that is, the audience members themselves—remain distant and ineffective in changing the outcome of the material or developing solutions to the recorded elements of this performance experience.

Ken Cameron's work merits more inquiry from autobiographical and biographical theatre perspectives due to the intense real-world connections between blogger Hossein Derakhshan and the playwright. In performance, however, this play's synchronic dramaturgy and innovative use of technology encourage audiences to see it multiple times to have different experiences similar to other popular immersive performances containing multiple narratives like *Sleep No More*. Anecdotally, audience members have often said that they are returning to complete their show experience by selecting a different coloured iPod during second and third viewings. The randomization feature of each Apple iPod, whose metonymical name "shuffle" echoes the process of narrative progression within this play, provides a passive entry point into a hybrid experience of radio drama coupled within curated museum pieces that elicits audience affect via stories of immigration, deportation, and detainment. Cameron's play combines these elements to generate powerful motifs that leave audiences hungry to shuffle through his technologically mediated performance experience more than once.

DOPOLAVORO TEATRALE'S *THE APARTMENT* AND *THE INVISIBLE CITY*

Mediated by a discovered iPhone instead of a shuffled iPod like *How iRan*, DLT's *The Apartment* is a short thirty-minute experimental piece developed to test interactive dramaturgy and audience choices for use in larger immersive experiences. *The Apartment* transforms its solo Toronto audience member into a prospective tenant seeing an apartment recently vacated by a Canadian immigrant. Spectators meet with the show's creator, Daniele Bartolini, in a local park—my experience took place north of Bloor Street off Huron Street near the University of Toronto—and are asked to wait for a rental agent to arrive to begin their journey. Learning that a rental agent will walk you to an available unit causes quick assessment of all the possible "apartments" one might be about to visit.[4]

As the show begins, an actor posing as a rental agent ends her phone call, asks for me by name, and invites me to see the place. During our short walk to the unit, the rental agent apologizes for the fact that the former tenant's belongings are still all over the apartment. This brief performance intro offers

---

4   I found myself wondering, due to the show's promotional image of a shadowy dark-skinned immigrant, which apartment in the Annex—a high-end Toronto neighbourhood—would be genuinely affordable for either a new immigrant or even most people in the GTA.

a refreshing example of performing within a virtual reality, as there is little about this brief exchange that does not feel completely real. As I do not feel compelled to lie about my name, profession, or where I live, I can ask a few specific questions about the apartment like a prospective tenant. For the five minutes it takes to reach the performance space, the actor ensures that our "forced" small talk feels like a genuine conversation; her question, "Are you from Toronto?" is quickly followed up by, "Who is actually from Toronto, right?" This query becomes a leitmotif of this short performance experience. Reminding solo audience members, however briefly, about where they actually come from encourages them to feel somewhat unfamiliar in a place they likely already call home.

This strange feeling persists throughout the entire play: one person's forced entry and exploration of a lived-in apartment filled with its former tenant's personal objects, all connected to motifs of migration, deportation, and personal identity. In *Staging Strangers*, Barry Freeman cites DLT's work as an example of the experience of performing oneself within different patterns of intercultural exchange. He explains how new types of site-specific and audience-driven performances force us to confront moments where we must choose to either play ourselves or not. Using "the stranger as a guiding metaphor for an analysis of cultural difference in theatre in Canada" (xx), Freeman considers what happens to audience members when the choices, people, and places they encounter during performances either connect or collide with their real lives. Freeman's model of performance as mitigating a public experience of strangeness serves as a useful means of considering the private choices made within *The Apartment* concerning migration and immigration.

The Apartment does not place audiences in visible public spaces like DLT's *The Stranger*; even the real estate agent "leaves" to take another call and only returns when the audience leaves the show. However, within the private setting of *The Apartment*, audiences are forced to critically watch themselves as they encounter and make different strange personal choices in someone else's living space. Like players in an escape room replete with puzzles and items relevant to escaping, audience members are encouraged to gamify material objects in their surroundings. They are made to feel out of place when they literally touch and use a stranger's personal technology: iPhone, VCR, CD player. Audiences also take part in some simple household actions, such as reading mail and turning lights on and off. No unexpected human stranger emerges in *The Apartment*; instead, strangeness gets displaced onto these routine everyday experiences audiences must enact to complete the show.

After the audience member lies down on the resident's bed and watches several scenes from an Italian film played on an old tube television, an iPhone placed in a dresser drawer buzzes and beeps with an SMS text message. This continues over and over until the audience member—hesitant or not—responds to it. The tenant's partner, who lives in another country, asks the spectator to help her find her lover. In yet another level of gamification, symbolic elements throughout the space cue us to imagine and recreate the final moments of the missing tenant's residence in the apartment. Books, pictures, mail, food, and clothing all synchronically hint at troubling outcomes as the narrative of the missing resident gets pieced back together. DLT's synchronic production design, filled with multiple levels of semiotic meaning, attempts to transform audience members into strangers themselves; we are forced to encounter this immigrant's personal effects as privileged non-deported citizens of Canada, regardless of our backgrounds. As if to respond to Freeman's larger query about audience members emerging as strangers, *The Apartment* distinctly assumes that its audience members, despite their unique and diverse backgrounds, can easily assume the role of a Canadian citizen. Forcing us to adopt privileged positions compared to those of immigrants, DLT uses interactive technology to encourage us to reflect on our own socio-cultural status while empathizing via SMS with a woman who has lost her partner due to Canadian immigration laws and foreign policy.

DLT also makes strangeness a key facet of interacting with objects and spaces rather than other people. It becomes even stranger to have to justify why you have picked up someone else's iPhone and replied to their texts than to be reminded of your own position as a stranger by the person on the other end of the line. In fact, once you explain that you simply found the phone, the person texting on the other end never questions your intentions; rather, they immediately ask you to help figure out what happened to their lost love interest. Perhaps they assume you are a "helpful" Canadian who can solve their problems.

The iPhone and other objects call out to us and encourage interaction as we move through the designed space. Much like opening a supposedly locked door, these kinds of jarring moments of interactivity are things I usually attempt to avoid in such immersive or site-specific kinds of plays. Here I began to fear an outcome worse than deportation; I genuinely expected to find a corpse or something hinting at foul play or suicide somewhere in the abandoned apartment. *The Apartment* centres its experiential approaches on the complete absence of the immigrant, leading to an objectification of the migrant as a kind of solvable puzzle solely needed to be completed rather than engaged with. Through these ideas, DLT manages to encourage and generate a kind of synchronic disconnection from the immigrant, perhaps hinting at Canadians' general disconnection from genuine concern or action on issues of immigration. The production's technological and paratextual materials confirm this sense of disconnect. The deported migrant in *The Apartment*—a show co-produced by the Instituto Italiano di Cultura—has a clear Italian background, as evidenced in the extensive books, posters, music, and items all in Italian throughout the apartment. However, DLT created a promotional image for the show of a heavily shadowed man in an abstract small living space, dressed to resemble a Middle Eastern immigrant more than the Italian character of the show. While this early image may have just been promotional, the disconnection between the synchronic cues in the marketing campaign compared to those within the experience was noticeable and dramaturgically confusing.

As *The Apartment* unfolds, spectators must converse via text message with a virtual character in another country—most likely played by Bartolini—that clearly knows the apartment and asks us to search for the missing resident and other specific things. Multiple clues point to the narrative solution, such as an airplane ticket itinerary, a dog-eared book on Canadian citizenship, and opened government mail—on actual letterhead—from Global Affairs Canada. However, despite the unlikely premise that audience members are holding the smart phone of the former tenant and texting with their life partner in Italy about their whereabouts, this experimental performance requires audiences to experience uncovering the undesired results of Canadian immigration policy within a home. The person on the other end of the phone asks you to look through the apartment for clues as to where their loved one may have gone; immediately or not, audience members are eventually guided to collect enough evidence to substantiate a conclusion of forced deportation. Following this, we have to tell the person on the phone this news ourselves, however we choose to phrase it with words or capture it with images.

One thing not accounted for in *The Apartment* is the potential for unique and overwhelmingly powerful affective results for those audience members who have undergone similar experiences of deportation and immigration themselves. Like military games and media that prove too challenging for people who've lived through war, *The Apartment*'s assumptions run the risk of generating real-world affective responses within their immersive environment. The complete absence of the deported tenant in *The Apartment* becomes a situation of constant concern. At one point, spectators are asked to feed the tenant's goldfish. The character texting on the smart phone states that their partner used to love his fish and would not have wanted it to go hungry. On a table in the kitchen, there is a goldfish in a bowl, a banana, fish food, and an iPod: spectators are asked to feed the fish, listen to the music on the iPod, and snack on the banana themselves. In this special moment of the performance, metonymical and synchronic connections merge, as one embodies the deported tenant by tending to things that mattered to him—the fish, his music, and his hunger—within his last living space in Canada.

Leaving the apartment and returning to the real-yet-staged encounter of saying goodbye to the rental agent, spectators may be aware the space will be immediately reset by production assistants for the next participant, causing us to think about ourselves as another version of the vacated resident. Will the ways we have altered or interacted with the space persist into the next participant's experience? In this way, the apartment itself becomes a metonym for the audience's impact upon theatre performances. Bartolini, who is also DLT's artistic director, greets audience members when they first arrive to the space and alters the performative experience based on his assessment of each audience member and what worked during previous performances. An overall post-performance question emerges: Does Daniele himself learn from his "digital" conversations and further improve new experiences with each performance? Audience members are themselves forcibly removed from the space—like the tenant—after being given a final moment to write a message on a single Post-it Note they can leave behind. As we leave *The Apartment*, a few questions related to enforced deportation from Canada persist: What other clues—besides the final note—have we inadvertently left behind that could not be truly reset? Does each audience member's presence persist into the next experience of this experimental performance—through physical item misplacement and undeleted digital traces—within DLT's *The Apartment*?

* * *

Similar feelings of displacement and estrangement abound in DLT's follow-up performance, *The Invisible City*, which transforms groups of Canadian audience members into virtual migrants asked to explore new and often unknown places in the Greater Toronto Area. A durational and immersive performance, this show takes place over roughly twenty-four hours, from one evening to the following night. Audience members are required to use a fully charged cellular phone that allows them to call, text, and interact with the wider city as per directions they receive via email from the show's creators. *The Invisible City*, like many immersive and site-specific experiences, requires participants to also sign a waiver related to any unexpected circumstances that could arise from their experiences during the performance. Taking on a tone of general indemnity, the waiver ultimately echoes many statements of theme parks as well as transportation contracts for airplanes, ships, and trains: "I understand that I may be required to walk, run, cross streets and potentially use other means of transportation during the performance" (DopoLavoro Teatrale). *The Invisible City* unfolds throughout the entire city of Toronto, leaving audience members with uneasy feelings surrounding the total required travel time to visit all locations to complete their experience. The audience also anticipates eventually meeting all other five participants in each of their groups, which can lead to distracting virtual speculation based entirely on the words and ideas those groups share with one another.

The first email correspondence from the creators of *The Invisible City* instructs participants to be ready the night before their experience:

Here are a few instructions for tonight:

At 11:00 PM go to your bedroom or a place that is comfortable and where you can be on your own.

We recommend you use a pair of headphones, lie down, relax and have a listen to the audio track attached below.

Once the track is over, at **11:05 PM** call [**Phone Number Redacted**] and enter the conference code: [**Code Redacted**].

Make sure that your phone is fully charged.

A few suggestions about how to experience the first episode:

- Brush your teeth

- Put on your pyjamas

- Dim the lights.

And very important, tonight you will be **Number Four.** (R. Turner)

At eleven p.m. I turn off the lights and shut the blinds in my bedroom, asking my partner to leave me to quietly start the play. I brush my teeth before getting into bed while wearing headphones with a microphone connected to my iPhone. I open the attached file labelled as the audio track and listen to a five-minute soundscape, after which I dial the local phone number and enter my code to join the group call.

In Baudrillard's sense of the term, my conversation with four other strangers and the call-centre operator becomes an embodiment of something absolutely and truly "virtual." An audibly rich non-space—a virtual zone where I try to make sense of all the sounds I can hear—transforms my bedroom by transporting me into an abstract and virtual environment. No one speaks for a few minutes until the typical sounds of joining the call—beeps, dings—subside and all we hear is soft breathing. The voice on the other end of the call, with a heavy and discernable Indian accent, explains that he is running the call from Mumbai. (It remains unknown to date if DLT hired an actual Indian call-centre employee or whether they simply cast a local actor to play this role.) The call-centre leader starts out by explicitly requesting us not to use our names or to say anything about our identities (such as addresses, racial backgrounds, or ages); he explains that we will only be referred to by number, a means of further virtualizing our experience. Then he asks us to describe what we see out a nearby window, to explain what we ate for dinner that evening, and, most notably, to discuss why we choose to live in a city like Toronto, which he says he has never visited. In these moments, the anonymity created via conference-calling technology allows participants to be somewhat vulnerable to each other, inviting us to selectively lie or reveal truths through conversation. After the conference call ends, an email immediately arrives with a follow-up audio track to listen to as we fall asleep.

The following morning, *The Invisible City* production team contacts audience members with new instructions for completing their performance experience. These instructions provide audience members with optional possibilities for the experience that include visiting places around the GTA. For example, if the audience member finds herself in downtown Toronto, she can go to a specific address for a blindfolded experience enacted by the actors from the show. During these side quests, another narrative progression idea from contemporary video gaming emerges, in which some audience members occasionally encounter other spectators.[5] These side quests help this full-day

---

5   Audience members are encouraged to go somewhere completely new and to speak at length with people to whom they would not typically talk. One person I sat down beside asked me whether I was an actor from the play and what my number was during the previous evening's phone call. DLT previously produced similar moments of audience members awkwardly coming into unexpected contact during a previous immersive experience called *The Off Limits Zone* produced at the Hearn Generating Station during the 2016 Luminato Festival in Toronto.

theatre experience create different real-world interactions that inform the concluding parts of the performance event.

The final scenes of *The Invisible City* take place in a condominium development model suite near the Centre for Addiction and Mental Health at Queen West and Ossington Avenue in downtown Toronto. Audience members enter this performative space together; they are now invited to share stories about their experiences during the past twenty-four hours. Everyone is also asked to bring an item to share with the group. When I reveal a physical photograph of my one-year-old son, the other spectators get visibly excited about the materiality of the object as well as my openness in leaving the image behind. The performance ends with the audience members witnessing several short scenes focused on people feeling lost—as we ourselves had been—in the sheer vastness of Toronto's urban environments. This portion of the experience— featuring diverse actors and situations—has a less clear narrative path than what happened over the previous full day. It offers participants a traditional theatre experience with real performers. As we leave the performance space through a back door, one of the actors suggests we continue experiencing Toronto in new ways. After the show, I remember feeling a stronger urge to talk to random people than I usually do in the downtown core. Reconnecting with people, whom we often forget due to our largely interior focus on smart phones or other digital devices, emerges as a main motif persisting beyond the experience of *The Invisible City*.

The Invisible City builds upon ideas developed in *The Apartment*, but transforms them on an immense scale throughout the entire city of Toronto as well as through a large durational amount of time, which allows more freedom for audience members to live with all of their experiences. In effect, *The Invisible City* transitions the feeling of alienation and deportation embodied by the absent immigrant in *The Apartment* to the spectator (and their subsequent tiny group at the end). The name of the play also suggests a necessity to observe and think about the people—initially absent and anonymous—who journey with you toward the performance's final conclusions. While not directly using deportation or immediate digital interactions—emails are the only communication you have with Bartolini's team—spectators become agents of engagement with actors, citizens, public spaces, and their own thoughts about displacement throughout the show. *The Invisible City* also teaches us to try and focus beyond the digital device guiding us, ending with entirely interpersonal discussions and performances without phones. The final items everyone interacts with in the last scene are pieces of Lego, which they use to create their vision of Toronto's skyline. Through genuine interpersonal and intercultural communication, something that we all need to practise better in everyday situations, DLT reminds audiences to use technology to find human interactions instead of replacing them. In a durational performance that serves as an incredibly slow reveal of Brechtian gestus, *The Invisible City* finds unique and atypical ways to help showcase the problems of virtual interaction over genuine face-to-face time. Audiences are pushed to stop relying on stereotypes during their interactions with their other group members, to move past gamification of other individuals and the museumification of urban places, ultimately re-emerging after twenty-four hours within the performance as self-aware people stepping back out into Queen Street West as the play ends.

DUSTIN HARVEY AND ADRIENNE WONG'S *LANDLINE*

Encouraging spectators to perform as themselves instead of as a random sequential number, *Landline*, by Dustin Harvey and Adrienne Wong, connects two different people across Canada—or sometimes across the world—via the synchronization of iPods, SMS texting, and a Skype call. In the process, it creates a synchronic co-migratory experience of walking around different urban centres. Each audience member begins in a different city as the artists synchronize iPods with other participants and trade spectators' phone numbers. From there, solo audience members are asked to walk around their local streets and respond to audio cues that invite them to reflect upon different city spaces they have visited in the past while following their gut down streets they may have never walked, and also to keep a co-journeyer updated in real time about their thoughts via texts. While the experience has a distinct and linear process, it also aims to open urban spaces to anything participants want to pursue. Even though people can be performing together from as far away as Halifax and Vancouver, they need to offer a virtually mutual experience capable of harnessing part of each city's realness. As this performative event is happening live in two disparate parts of Canada at the same time, *Landline* may be one of the few theatrical experiments capable of virtually transcending the time and space of audience experience.

Landline alters spectators' usual patterns of movement by encouraging them to make quick and responsive choices to the world around them, not unlike migrants' experiences with unknown terrain or personal encounters. While the space of the performance will likely be a part of a city with which spectators are vaguely familiar—since they are probably residents of the city where they experience the show—participants still have to conceptualize another person in a different place mirroring their choices as well as their personal journey. The audio cues force participants into odd situations: "Is there someone you can walk behind? Not too close. Not close enough to cause them discomfort. Accompany them for one block" (72). Here the play's co-creators ask us to observe someone and to tail them, encouraging participants to walk like residents of the community they are walking through. Audience members in both cities may feel uncomfortable with some of the things Harvey and Wong ask them to think about or discuss with their co-spectator. At the same time, the total anonymity of a synchronic participant—a co-audience member who like the other one becomes a product of the spaces they move through—may in fact help them be more open about their experiences and feelings. This affective performance resonance is shared between both performers as they migrate and share each other's experiences virtually. In fact, they amalgamate two cities, like a palimpsest, into one common experience.

Landline attempts to mark specific urban locations with the personal memories of their participations. It also aspires to synchronize revelations about feelings between the two participants, ultimately drawing out genuine and immediate responses from audiences. Audience members have to explain exactly what they are seeing to their show partners, with only words to help each other through the experience. For example, one audio direction asks the participants to "[d]escribe the location you are standing in, and your motivation for choosing this place" (74). All sorts of different semiotic and symbolic factors form part of the participants' choices; the creators ask spectators to think about why they might be drawn to certain urban spaces, places, and communities. The participants are also asked to find ways to explain their rationale to someone with no visual or virtual understanding of where they are and why they feel this might be the "best" route for their urban journey. In such moments, paired spectators in *Landline* become necessary strangers, people who do not know each other yet must share intimate and personal details to successfully move through this show's urban and distant checkpoints.

Before the beginning of the performance, *Landline* also offers its participants a handout printed map of the regions they are allowed to visit, effectively using the map to represent the boundaries of the performance space but not control the experience. This is largely due to the need to return audience members to the concluding point as the play ends, but it also helps them to avoid veering too far off course from the spaces and environments within the zone selected by Harvey and Wong. The show ends with a Skype call connecting each participant with their co-participant, allowing spectators to talk and see one another's faces after a full hour of wandering and texting. These calls are often done with a group of pairings all together that leads to the guessing game of figuring out if one's visualization of their virtual "friend" fits any of the people they see on the screen.

Landline creates a new kind of unity between urban experience and digital communication only achievable by manipulating a wide variety of digital technologies coupled with willing participants capable of exploring their memories and experiences within Canadian urban spaces. In doing so, Harvey and Wong create one of the most stirring examples of virtual yet real experience designed to dispel feelings of strangeness between Canadians and their communities. *Landline* encourages participants to think critically and genuinely about the public spaces they inhabit while reflecting on the power of their own experiences in tandem with a stranger who cannot share their own perspective, no matter how well they communicate with the outsider. Wong and Harvey remind us of theatre's potential to educate audiences about their position in shared urban and cultural spaces, emphasizing the diversity of lives present in many layers—real time, technological, memory driven—as all walk the same streets together. This vision represents the ground we all walk on in post-multicultural Canada, as current inhabitants of a shared land with its own established and recovered histories as well as divergent and virtual futures.

Thanks to the distance between performers, *Landline* helps audiences share their exact personal experiences with complete strangers. Smart phones obviously cannot communicate emotion, memory, and strangeness as well as real experiences, but through the digital device carried by each participant a virtual avatar of another cultural and cosmopolitan background shares their reality with a simulated Other, literally engaging with atypical yet necessary empathy and understanding of a completely strange or alternate view of the world. Harvey and Wong remind us of the ground we stand on through their title, which certainly speaks to the archaic technology of vanishing home phones, but also allows us to draw a virtual line between ourselves and a distant person who mirrors our own experiences in real time. Through common experiences, audiences participate in a very educational way of moving beyond multiculturalism through technology to new methods of affective relationships with one another.

#REUNITEAUDIENCES

New plays mediating audience actions through portable technology offer a unique type of performance: one that is somewhat immersive, yet that is more focused on celebrating the ways in which virtual experiences synchronically affect audiences differently than real ones. The idea of virtual synchronicity, shared by all these performance texts, exemplifies what Baudrillard describes as "the proof of theater through antitheater" (19). By using antitheatrical technology, these plays cause audience actions and reactions connected to contemporary narratives of displacement, migration, and strangeness. Sometimes these playwrights and companies ask people to focus on themselves (as in *Landline* and *The Invisible City*), while in other cases they invite them to emote with unseen immigrants in the story (as in *How iRan* and *The Apartment*). These "new" kinds of virtual interactions are themselves heavily mediated and focused on the Canadian middle class, but also are potentially powerful as they encourage spectators to move beyond misplaced empathy and ineffective multiculturalism to consider current political issues of non-citizenry, self-migration, and estrangement in Canada. It's not fair to claim that these are site-specific performances, since all of them coexist between real places (apartments, streets, museums) and conceptual ones (digital mapping, texts, audio tracks), ultimately guiding our movement and our emotions toward common goals. Each example discussed here has succeeded and failed in different capacities with audiences and critics, but they all represent positive steps toward overcoming stereotypes and providing new educational experiences through Canada theatre mediated by digital technology that addresses issues of migration and immigration. As audiences connect and reunite—both virtually and in real life—these creative shows invite us to do the same after the performance throughout our post-multicultural Canadian communities.

PART THREE.
CANADIAN IMMIGRATION
IN THE FIRST PERSON
SINGULAR AND PLURAL

BUILDING INTERCULTURAL BRIDGES: AN INTERVIEW WITH PUENTE THEATRE FOUNDER LINA DE GUEVARA

MONICA PRENDERGAST WITH LINA DE GUEVARA

INTRODUCTION

Fig. 1. Lina de Guevara.
Photo by David Lowes.

Lina de Guevara is a professional Chilean actress and theatre educator who fled her native country after the government of Salvador Allende was overthrown in a military coup led by General Augusto Pinochet. She and her family came to Canada in 1976 and settled in Victoria, British Columbia. There, de Guevara founded Puente (Bridge) Theatre. Over the next thirty years, until her retirement in 2011, she led the company in producing and directing a large body of community-based and other plays about the immigrant experience. A number of Puente's plays were solo ones, devised between immigrant or Indigenous women and de Guevara. These storytelling performances were generated in a unique collaborative process developed by de Guevara over time. She also brought plays from many countries to Victoria audiences in an annual playreading series called WorldPlay, hosted by the Belfry Theatre (the city's regional theatre). De Guevara is an expert Theatre of the Oppressed facilitator, trained by Augusto Boal, and continues to teach and lead work-shops in her mid-eighties.

This chapter is based on an oral history interview held in Lina's home in Oak Bay, Victoria, on 15 March 2018 that captures the highlights of her long and distinguished career. The interview was transcribed by doctoral research assistant Claire Burgoyne and has been edited and condensed.

* * *

M: You've had a lifelong relationship with theatre so I'm interested to begin with your first memories. When do you remember first going to the theatre or learning about theatre in your life?

L: You know, what happened to me really was more like the relationship with the arts because my father was an artist. That was always present in my life. I started with dance. I loved dance. I was going to be a dancer. That was my main interest.

M: Ballet dance?

L: Yes. Well, actually it was modern dance because in Chile that was the main type of dance that existed at that point, was dance based on the expressionis-tic German school of dance. That was the Chilean National Ballet. That was the type of dance that they presented. I really loved it and I wanted to be a dancer. But also, because I had a Danish mother [who] was very practical-oriented, [I wanted] to do something practical; when I was choosing a career, I chose to go to teachers' college and I studied history and geography. But at the same time I did that I was taking dance classes. It was an environment that was really very supportive of the idea that art should be in your life. So I had those two things.

M: Do you have a memory of seeing a play in your early years [that had an impact on you], because obviously there was a shift there from an interest in dance to an interest in theatre. Can you recall how that came about?

L: You know when I was in the theatre school, I went to evening classes and then I took part in *Fuenteovejuna*. Do you know that play?

M: Yes, I do.

L: Which was quite spectacular, and I had a really good time taking part in that because it's a huge show and very emotional and so on. So I would say maybe that was one of the [first plays that impressed me]; also I saw *Carmina Burana*. And *Carmina Burana* was presented as a ballet, but it had also very theatrical characters. *Carmina Burana* was actually quite an event for me.

M: How old would you have been when you saw that?

L: About fifteen. There was a lot going on [in the arts] and we were all part of it.

M: This was in Santiago?

L: Yes. For instance, as a teenager, the main thing that people would do would be to go to the orchestra concerts. We all went to the cheaper seats. That's where you met everybody who was anybody. It was like the social thing. Everybody went there. It really wasn't expensive. I have to say that one of the best things that I had in Chile was university education that was practically free.

M: Yes, and supportive parents?

L: Supportive parents.

M: What about your theatre training? Do you remember if there was a moment when you decided you were more interested in acting than dancing?

L: It wasn't so much that I decided. My body decided. I did not really have a very flexible body. You know I could dance prettily. I could move my arms, but I couldn't do, like—the dance was very demanding. It was very acrobatic and I just couldn't do that. I've never been a very flexible person. I made that decision that I had to take acting classes; that was because I realized that I was more of an actor than a dancer.

M: Did you have an acting teacher who was an influence on you?

L: We had the Chilean theatre scene, [which] was also quite interesting in terms of the way that it appeared. There were several theatre companies that were star-oriented. These companies were named after the main actor and all the plays that they performed had this one actor or actress as leads. Then there was a group of teachers from the teachers' college that got together and they decided they were going to do a different kind of theatre. Most of them were socialists. Chile was a very political country, always, so the idea of socialism and creating a better society and fighting politically was very ingrained, because Chile was a country where there were lots of very poor people. There was a middle class that was fairly well educated because we had free education. We [middle-class people] went to public schools where you didn't have to pay. Rich people went to private schools.

M: When you were doing your actor training, it sounds like you were also working with professionals from the theatre community.

L: Yes, definitely. Those people that I was talking about, had decided . . . [to create] something that [they] called Teatro Experimental de la Universidad de Chile, so experimental theatre from the University of Chile. They were the ones that started to create a theatre that had a different thing, not stars. They were very based on Stanislavski.

M: So this was in the '40s.

L: Well, I would say '40s, yes, '40s and '50s.

M: When you were in university?

L: Yes. They also did a lot of Chilean theatre. They supported Chilean writers but not exclusively. We saw lots of theatre from all over the world. And again, you could go to the theatre and not ruin yourself, in terms of money. It was affordable. So I went to theatre school twice. I did three years of night school or evening school, which was very good. We presented different kinds of plays and it was a good background. Then after that I took one full year of the university day school, which was very strict. Then I got married and then when I was starting my second year we went to Cuba and lived there for two years, and then when I came back I finished theatre school . . . In a way, that break in Cuba was very good for me because I worked there with a theatre company called Teatro Estudio in Havana, which was a very experimental theatre group. I taught movement and I worked also on the committee that selected plays and did analysis of plays and on the relationship of plays with the revolution. For example, we did a whole series of American plays because one of the main influences in Cuban theatre had always been the United States of America.

M: Of course, at that time Americans were still holidaying in Cuba.

L: Well no, the revolution had already happened.

M: At this point.

L: Yes, at this point it was 1962.

M: So it was just after the revolution.

L: It was after the revolution. Yes, I think it was 1962.

M: It's interesting they were doing American plays.

L: Well, we chose to do that.

M: So then you went back to Chile and then you were working in the professional theatre?

L: I finished my training, and then we lived in Santiago and I was working in the company of the university. I was already working in a professional capacity after I graduated from the theatre school, then I worked in the university.

M: But the [company was] funded by the university.

L: Funded by the university. It was a completely professional company. Maybe students could come for small roles, but it really was a completely professional company. That was a good experience for me, but it wasn't very good. It was a mix. I felt that they cut my wings in that experience. There was something in the atmosphere that was not very healthy for me. I had been feeling very free and so on. When I started working there, there was a hierarchy. There was some kind of thing that wasn't healthy. That I hadn't encountered before. It's interesting, I've always thought that for a young person those types of things can really damage you, so in my own career I've always been very careful not to damage people because I realized that I really did have some kind of psychological trauma. I was doing okay but I did not feel okay.

M: When you say hierarchy, it's that thing with the director being . . .

L: We had a German director that directed me in Brecht's *Mr. Puntila and his Man Matti*. I played the daughter of Puntila and [the director] was horrendous . . . he didn't speak Spanish, he was from the Berliner Ensemble. He really was horrible. He wanted to direct me in German; he gave me emphasis in my lines, and I got completely confused.

M: Now we're sort of heading toward the coup.

L: When we went back to Chile we did not want to stay in Santiago because we did not want to stay in a big city. We wanted to live closer to nature. Then we got this fantastic opening in the University Austral that was starting their theatre school and their arts program and so on.

M: You took a position.

L: Yes, because the first theatre school director was a friend of mine, a writer [Jaime Silva]. I had worked on some plays he had written. He was a wonderful writer full of ideas. He wanted us to go there. There was another university in that city that was a technical university where [my husband] could also get a job.

M: The city is?

L: Valdivia.

M: Valdivia.

L: It's in the south of Chile. Valdivia is like living here in Victoria, really, the climate, the landscape, everything. It was a new university.

M: You're starting up the theatre program.

L: Starting up the theatre program.

M: And you were teaching acting?

L: I was teaching acting. The man that was teaching acting before, Jaime Silva, became the dean of the faculty and so I became the director of the theatre school. It was a very good moment. We felt that we could do lots of experiments. Then the military coup happened. I really want to sort of convey these ideas about my theatre school and the theatre that I worked with, the theatre of the university, as very important influences. Especially the theatre school [in Santiago] because first of all I had these wonderful teachers that had been trained by the man called Kurt Jooss. You know that story?[1]

M: I don't think so.

L: No? So that story is an interesting story. Before the war [Jooss] had been told by the Nazis that he had to fire all the Jews in his school, or his group. Instead of doing that he, together with a group of adult dancers, went to Chile. He was the founder of the Chilean National Ballet. All those dances that I'm telling you about, you know the one with the choir, *Carmina Burana* . . . and all those different dances, [including] *The Green Table*. I think it was the first expressionistic piece of ballet that was staged in Chile. What it shows is this green table, a long table with all these characters with masks, they are talking and discussing and so on. While they're doing that you get all the scenes [of catastrophe] of what's going on in the world at that time. It was representing the League of Nations and what a failure it had been. There was a character called Death, there was another called the Speculator, there were people in the villages, and so on. It was a totally new way.

M: So he brought this German expressionist dance.

L: Three of my main teachers had been trained by Jooss. I checked him in the *Encyclopedia of Dance* the other day and there was a beautiful article about him, and it talks about his experience. I had that influence and that is what I like so much about dance and so on because it was that type of dance that meant something. Another one of the ideas was that theatre had to have meaning.

---

1   At this point we are reminded of how German artists such as Jooss fled to Chile before the war and had a huge influence on Chilean culture. The irony is that Chile itself fell into fascism at this time. For Lina, the belief in theatre as a progressive tool was endangered by the military dictatorship.

M: Socially engaged.

L: Socially engaged theatre. It could not just be theatre for you to look pretty.

M: Okay, let's move ahead to the military coup and your journey to Canada and Victoria, or actually your return journey.

L: That is a return journey because we had the first experience [in Toronto] when [my husband] Celso was studying.

M: How did that come about? During the coup and afterward.

L: During the coup was a total shock for us. We knew that we wanted to leave. One of the main reasons was because we'd been in Cuba and we knew that people who had exactly the same history that we had, had disappeared or were in jail or whatever. We were lucky because we were not in Santiago. We were in Valdivia where it was less dangerous than Santiago would have been. We knew that at any moment anything could happen. So then we applied to come back to Canada almost immediately and we were rejected even though we all spoke English and my husband had a Canadian master's degree.

M: Did they give a reason for the rejection?

L: No.

M: Were you applying as refugees?

L: No, we applied as immigrants, which was better than refugees. We had people here in Canada, friends, that wrote letters of support. The way that those things work is very uneven. Then what happened is that we kept on staying there [in Chile] for about two and a half years or three years under the military regime. We had to be very careful. We did lots of really interesting work in the theatre school. But everything was always scary. What happened

[then] was that they brought an exhibition of Inuit art to the university. I met the man in charge of the exhibition and I talked to him and said we really want to go to Canada. He said apply again. So I did. He had talked to the person in charge, and we were accepted.

M: So was he a government person?

L: Yes. His name was Michael Kergin. We know that afterward he worked with Joe Clark, so he must have been a conservative, but he was a good conservative. After a few years here I phoned him once. I went to Ottawa for something and then I phoned him and I said, "Michael, I want you to know that we both have work, that our children are going to school, and you made a good choice in accepting us to come to Canada."

M: So you came straight to Victoria? Did you come straight here?

L: No, we came to Toronto. What we knew about Victoria was what everybody knows about Victoria: the newly dead and the . . .

M: The newly wed and the nearly dead.

L: Yes.

M: And the best weather in Canada.

L: We didn't even know that. We just knew that it was a little village. I thought I had to live in Toronto.

M: The big city.

L: Yes, I wanted to live in a big city and not a small city because I would have less opportunity. By chance there was an ad requiring a professor of engineering for Camosun College [in Victoria]. [Celso] applied and got the job. So then we came here . . .

M: What year was that?

L: We arrived in 1976. I think it was all the same year. We would have had six months in Toronto and then we came here. We had no idea that we had arrived in paradise. We could see it, that it was wonderful, the landscape, and so similar to the south of Chile, which is the other thing that I always say. I don't know if I could have remained in Canada if I'd have been in the east. That's a very hard climate. This is so similar to Valdivia.

M: So you arrived here in 1976 and you had a young family at that time. So now you move into the beginnings of Puente. Tell me how Puente began.

L: I was very confused at the beginning because I tried to get jobs as an actor. I had an accent. Again, I was into this insecurity of not knowing how you can be an actor in this kind of environment that you don't know anything about. I taught at the Bastion Theatre. Bastion Theatre had a school and I ran a children's theatre company. All that was really good. It was really interesting for me to work with children because I hadn't done that before and I learned a lot from the children. But it wasn't exactly what I wanted to do. I could not get any work here either in the Belfry or Bastion or any of the other [theatres]. I did play a character in *Dracula* at Langham Court [community theatre]. I played a German doctor so I had to have a German accent. That was easy. I did some things with Kaleidoscope. For me Kaleidoscope was a very interesting theatre company.

M: They [co-artistic directors Elizabeth and Colin Gorrie] were doing experimental work.

L: I felt very at home in that environment. Whereas I did not feel at home in the other type of environment, which was very English. I couldn't do English accents, I did not feel that I could fit in there. I was more into something experimental. I was very confused. I didn't know exactly what I was going to do. I felt that I had had a very good career in Chile. We didn't do anything political [because of the dictatorship], but we did good theatre. I played Amanda in *The Glass Menagerie* and I played Winnie in *Happy Days*. So I got those chances that were like the chance of a lifetime.

M: This is quite typical for an immigrant coming from another country and coming up against those types of cultural challenges.

L: Cultural challenges.

M: Barriers . . .

L: Barriers. Like real barriers, which forced me to go back to my own resources. Like what can I do here? I got this idea that I should tell the story of myself, what happened to me. Your life becomes all upside down. In those days the one-woman show or the one-person show was barely starting. That wasn't the usual thing and I remember seeing *Billy Bishop Goes to War* and being, "Wow, one person does everything!" But that wasn't what I wanted to do. That was when I went to New York to the Festival of Theatre of the Americas. That's where I met Augusto Boal. That's where I heard Honor Ford-Smith speak. She was from Jamaica and had created the Sistren Theatre company. Sistren was a theatre company made by Jamaican women who lived incredibly oppressed lives and who had a lot to say about it. She was a theatre person who decided she was going to help.

M: Quite an inspiration for you.

L: So I thought, wow, I can do this.

M: Did you see one of their shows?

L: No, I heard her and then I read some of her material about Sistren. I think it was 1977 that I went to that conference. When I got back I started trying to see how I was going to do it. That was a time when there was a ministry called Employment and Immigration and they had grants for people who had been declared to be unemployable. So I had to find those women that were going to tell their story and who had also been declared unemployable because they couldn't speak English. By following the example of Honor Ford-Smith, I said, "That's how I can do it." Then I got help in creating my grant. And then also [at] the Belfry it was Glynis that had just started [as artisitic director] and she also . . .

M: Glynis Leyshon? She was the artistic director.

L: Glynis and also Mary [Desprez, General Manager] . . . Because I couldn't get a grant on my own. I needed to have help. I got good help [from] the people who gave me some very practical ideas on what to write in the grant and how to write it and so on. Then we got Pat O'Brien who was our financial advisor. So the Belfry administered the money.

M: But you got the grant.

L: I got the grant. I started looking for the women I was going to work with. I interviewed these women. I just thought that they were fine. They were women who had suffered a lot; who had gone through huge struggles to come here.

M: From what countries?

L: There were two Chilean ones and three Central American, one was from Nicaragua, and the others were from El Salvador. They wanted to tell their story. They wanted to be somebody. They wanted not to disappear and be nothing.

M: They were all Spanish-speaking.

Fig. 2. Yolanda Huerta, Ana Strauss, Aura Alberto, Emperatriz Toledo, and Magdalena Diaz in *I Wasn't Born Here*, a collective creation. Directed by Lina de Guevara in July 1988, at Puente Theatre, Victoria. Photo by Robin J. Hood.

Fig. 3. Emperatriz Toledo, Magdalena Diaz, Ana Strauss, and Yolanda Huerta in *I Wasn't Born Here*, a collective creation. Directed by Lina de Guevara in July 1988, at Puente Theatre, Victoria. Photo by Robin J. Hood.

L: Yes, that was the main thing for me. I wanted to tell the story of women from Latin America. I thought that at that point these women needed jobs. They had been declared to be unemployable. They did not speak English. Well, there was one who spoke English but not the others. They were traumatized by their experiences. They were depressed. There were not many that applied. Theatre is not something that everybody will come and try.

M: What was the show called?

L: It was called *I Wasn't Born Here.*

M: And where were the performances?

L: The first performance was at the Belfry.

M: On the mainstage?

L: Oh yes.

M: So the Belfry really did sponsor you.

L: Oh yes. The Belfry, they were very supportive.

M: Was it successful? The show?

L: Yes, because we got invitations to go to lots of places. In those days there was something called the Canadian Popular Theatre Alliance and they invited us to go to Guelph, so we took the show to Guelph and we did really well. The work was compared to . . . what's the name of the genius from Québec?

M: Oh, [Robert] Lepage.

ʟ: Robert Lepage. Another company that was equally experimental, which was interesting because [our] play had a lot of truth, the women were really immigrants. They spoke very little English. We all the time had to ask, how do we solve it, how do we play it, how do we tell the story, not to other Latin Americans? We want to tell the story to the Canadian public. How do we do that if the actors don't know how to speak English? We had a lot of visual things. We had signs, you know—like using signs. We had scenes that were set in English and in Spanish and then in English, like a mirror. There was one woman spoke a little bit more English so she got to be the one that did the [scenes] where you had to speak more. They learned.

ᴍ: Were you in it?

ʟ: No, I directed.

ᴍ: Did you have some Canadian actors in it?

ʟ: No. We had a stage manager that was Canadian, but it was all done by the immigrant women.

ᴍ: This the beginning of Puente.

ʟ: We sat one day and said, "What would we like to call this?" We tried different names and so on and the group, we chose Puente.

ᴍ: Bridge Theatre.

ʟ: Yes. The idea of being a bridge.

ᴍ: So that was the beginning of the company and of course there's a thirty-year history of Puente following that first production. It would take us many days or weeks to cover everything so I'm going to ask you to touch on two or three of what you think are the most significant accomplishments.

Fig. 4. Edgar Acevedo and Manuel Alberto, masks by Maureen Mackintosh, in *Crossing Borders*, a collective creation. Directed by Lina de Guevara in February 1990, at Puente Theatre, Victoria. Photo by Robin J. Hood.

Fig. 5. Julio Cabrera, Oscar Cruz, Edgar Acevedo, Enrique Rivas, and Manuel Alberto in *Crossing Borders*, a collective creation. Directed by Lina de Guevara in February 1990, at Puente Theatre, Victoria. Photo by Robin J. Hood.

L: You know, the interesting thing about the company was that we first did theatre about Latin America. All the plays that we did had to do with the reality of Latin American immigrants. Then there came a moment at which I thought, we're prepared to do theatre about the reality of all immigrants. And then we did the first community play, which was the first community play done in BC. It was [a] play that we did about immigrant women from all over the world.

M: And that was? The title of that play was?

L: That was *Sisters/Strangers*. In that play we included professional actors. When we did *Canadian Tango*, which was a play about an immigrant couple, I realized I could not work with people who were not actors to deal with topics as delicate as couples. The mode, the form, of the community play is that you can have core groups of professional actors and large groups of people who are not professionals. That's the way that worked. We did several plays following that pattern. There was a play called *Storytelling Our Lives*, which had three different versions.

M: Have you always kept your focus on women?

L: No, the second play that we did was about men. It was called *Crossing Borders*. The men's stories and the women's stories were very different, and that's what led me as a side project into the work on wife assault. Prevention of wife assault. Well, together with all this connection with immigrants. They came with social problems. The issue that immigrants face. I had met—in that same festival [where I heard Honor Ford-Smith] I had met Augusto Boal; I was very impressed by him. Then I attended a workshop with him. There was a three-week workshop in Manitoulin Island and again [I was] very impressed. I said, here we have a tool to solve this problem or to find a solution to these very serious problems. I couldn't just wash my hands of someone else's problems. It was my community. So we started doing that, it was like a sideline from the other plays.

M: Doing Forum Theatre . . .

L: Doing Forum Theatre and similar projects of that kind. We did several big projects like that, that had to do with including more people. One thing that has always bothered me a lot was the ignorance [in Canada] of the theatrical culture in Latin America. Something that wasn't present as if it didn't exist. There was very little knowledge . . .

M: In Canada.

L: In Canada, very little knowledge of our cultural values. Everything that people knew about Latin America was mostly bad: about hunger, about strikes, about upheaval, everything was bad. It's very depressing to be in that kind of environment. That was when I started with the play-reading [series]. I said, we have wonderful theatre and there is wonderful theatre everywhere that immigrants come from so I wanted to show it.

M: The WorldPlay series.

L: We could not mount those plays because we didn't have the actors to do them. We didn't have the translations. That was very expensive. There was not enough money. Basically the problem was the actors. For a long time, there were no professional actors in Victoria that were also from Latin America. There were some in Vancouver but that's also a lot of money to transport those people over here.

M: So you were inviting local actors to read.

L: To read those plays. We did not pay the actors. That's the only time we haven't paid the actors, because otherwise we couldn't do it. That's why I was always careful not to demand a lot of time of the person participating. It was usually done in one or two rehearsals.

M: So the community-play model of bringing local actors together with immigrant actors, who were also local, was happening in the play series and in other productions moving forward?

L: It made Puente bigger, to have more scope. Then we got that grant that we would get every year.

M: The operating grant.

L: There was a special grant, I don't remember the name of it, but there was a special grant for companies such as Puente. It was a way of trying to promote diversity. So that worked really well.

M: Now we're kind of getting to [the] point where I was arriving in Victoria [in 1998] and my first encounter with Puente was the series of solo woman plays that you created in partnership with women from different countries. Could you tell us a little bit about that?

L: There was one funny thing that happened with Puente. Lots of people said to me, "How come you don't have any First Nations people in your company?" and I would say, "Well, First Nations people are not immigrants. This is a company for immigrant people." People were completely astonished. I thought, there's something wrong here. You cannot imagine how many people said that to me over and over again. They saw that I was using people who were "different" and so of course they immediately had the idea that you had to have First Nations people. I did a reading of one First Nations play in WorldPlay. Everyone [was] telling me I have to have First Nations people reading a First Nations play. In that reading, when I went to the rehearsal [there] was a beautiful woman seated there and I started talking to her. It was Krystal. The moment I saw her I thought, I want to do a play with this woman.

M: Krystal Cook.

L: We started also with the idea of doing one-woman shows. I had been doing [it] with all those community plays. You know, usually they say people love community plays. The directors and actors, everybody loves them, but the directors usually only do one. It's true. It's a humongous amount of work. It's not really understood properly. People still think that when you're talking about the community play that you're talking about a community theatre, or an activity of the community, but it's not that. It has a very specific philosophy that's not understood yet. It hasn't grown because it has never gotten the support that it should have because it's such [an] important activity. It's too much work for one person or for one small theatre company to take it on.

M: Yes, there could be dozens or even hundreds of people.

L: And it lasts a long time. The whole project. It's a long-term project. But what comes out of such a project is so fantastic for the community.

M: So you got quite exhausted from doing that kind work and decided to do one-woman plays.

L: Yes, I think that the first play that I did was the play with Raji [Bassi] about her story of being a woman from India [*Uthe/Athe*]. I came into this idea of doing a series of one-woman shows. Which were quite successful.

M: You had Indo Canadian, Indigenous, Asian . . .

L: There was a Chinese/Filipino one [*Patriot in Search of a Country*], and then there was *Chile Con Carne*. That was a play written by Carmen [Aguirre]. Usually all the plays that we did were created by us. Working with Krystal was extraordinary for me as a discovery of her reality. Also, I realized there were connections between the fact that many immigrants from Latin America were mistaken for Indigenous people here. You start realizing that there is a connection. There is a physical connection that's very, very strong. There's a connection in ways of life. That was a big inspiration for me.[2] I felt very connected with all the one-woman plays that we did. I felt that I was discovering something new. Also I tried to do more plays from Latin America. So I did *The Woman Who Fell From the Sky*, which is a Mexican play, and I did *The Pilgrimage of the Nuns of Concepción*, which is a Chilean play. These were the first times that Aboriginal people from Latin America were portrayed in principal roles on stage in Victoria.

M: Let's move into your more recent work. Your more recent work since leaving Puente, [which] was in . . .

L: 2011.

M: You have continued to work with the Inter-Cultural Association [ICA] and worked on other projects.

L: You know, what happened with me with leaving Puente [was], at the end, I was tired of the complications of running a theatre company. And also, I had become a director all the time and that wasn't why I went into theatre. I wanted to be an actor, to be more free of the responsibility of the financial [aspects]. So then because Paulina [Grainger, Puente's general manager,] went to work for [ICA], in charge of art and outreach, I started working there.

M: Paulina Grainger was the general manager [of Puente] for ten years and then moved over to the ICA and you kept your close working relationship with her by taking up projects there.

L: Yes. We had worked together with the ICA before. The same thing happened with the [Victoria Immigrant and Refugee Centre]. They appreciated the work of Puente, so they supported us. The arts had become a very important

---

2   This realization led to Lina's play *The Journey to Mapu* and its publication in the anthology *Fronteras Vivientes: Eight Latina/o Canadian Plays* (2013).

tool for the Inter-Cultural Association. They wanted to use that fully. I think that the first play that we did was the one you saw based on [faith-based intercultural] stories, *Interlaced*.³ To do this project we used sort of the same methodology that you would use to do any play. Starting with the warm-ups, a physical game, then easing people into the story so that each can tell their story. People started getting over the shyness of telling, first getting over the fact of saying, "We can't tell stories, we don't have stories." People always put themselves down. So you have to convince them that it will work and so on. Then after they started telling their first stories, we brought in some professional storytellers so that they could tell a story and then we would say to the group: What did you like about the story? What do you think that you could learn from this person? And they would say, "Well, they speak loudly and they talk to everybody, not with just one person." We tried different things and so they were learning.

M: The storytellers were from the Victoria Storytellers' Guild?

L: Yes, and then at the end we decided to do a presentation. We did have a choice of stories that lent themselves best to be presented. We had music, we had a background, we trained the actors, we were using all the theatrical tools that we had for the show, so the show would be good. People wouldn't feel pity for us. They would enjoy the show. So that's how we started and then from that we went into doing other shows. I've always wanted to do stories with the police and never have been able to do them because it's very difficult for the police to feel that they need to do this. I think that they've become convinced more now after they've seen the success of the project. We did a project in 2015 with the Saanich Police. Again, using the same methodology, you know, the Theatre of the Oppressed idea; working with the image, working with the story, personal stories, creating our own play always. I think that's very important.

---

3   The participants were from the Ismaili Muslim, Hindu, and Jewish communities. The stories told were prompted by the question: How do I live my religion?

M: So in that project there were immigrant actors working with Saanich Police.

L: Yes. First we worked with the two groups separately. We asked the police to tell stories about when they had been in interactions with immigrants and felt unhappy about the result. Then we worked with the immigrants and asked them the same question. We have our technique now of how to tell stories and so on in small groups, etc. Then we put the problem together with actors from the police and immigrant actors who had been trained specially to do Forum. So the project was very successful. When we showed it to other police organizations, they were really impressed. We did also a very good project with people with disabilities because there are many immigrants working with handicapped people. It's the kind of job that they get.

M: Right, caregiving.

L: Caregiving. That also was really quite wonderful because we had the people with disabilities performing and being really convincing. There were many discoveries in this new field in which we were working, in which the purpose is not necessarily to do a big presentation on a stage but it is to do presentations for the specific community by using all the tools of theatre, the different tools of theatre; some of them are discovered in rehearsal, others are based mostly in Forum Theatre.

M: So storytelling would be at the heart of the practice and then sometimes the stories are turned into scenes . . .

L: Yes, exactly.

M: . . . and intervene . . .

L: The intervention of the audience is also important, making it possible for the audience to take that step of going from sitting down to moving and taking part. And people do, and they really care about it. If you're really and truly presenting something that they know because it happened in their own lives, they will participate. It has not happened to me that people don't participate. Even when you're going sometimes, "Oh, it's going to be hard," but it's not. It all depends on how you warm up the audience.

M: Well, that's your job as the Joker?

L: Yes.

M: So you talked a little bit about what you feel has been really helpful in terms of working with immigrants. Can you say more about that?

L: You know, for the longest time, because we're dealing with what it means to be an immigrant, I have started all these public presentations by doing a timeline. The timeline [of arrival in Canada] is a very powerful image. It makes people come on stage, take the step from sitting down in the audience [to] coming on stage and, not only that, to making a statement. The statement is easy to do, because you say, "I am from the country you're from and I have been here since . . . "

M: It's about taking a stand.

L: They have to take that position and then it keeps going until you get to people who say, "Well I'm here from I don't know how many generations." "And where did your great-great-great-grandparents come from?" "Oh they came from France." Until you get to First Nations. Which . . . at the beginning it was a big surprise. You know sometimes people did not expect that First Nations people were going to be included in the timeline because they were not immigrants. Since the very beginning when we started doing this, there has been a big change in awareness. Now it's become an homage to the identity of First Nations.

M: Do you have some projects coming with ICA?

L: We just finished two projects that were very successful. They were for the 150th anniversary of Canada. There was one project called *I Wasn't Always a Canadian*, which was a mixture of theatre and photography. We went through people telling their own stories and the world map [of where the storytellers came from], and then a photographer attended all the sessions with people. Then those people got their picture taken and portraits made of them. Those portraits were presented in some banners. These are now banners that ICA uses when they have public presentations. So you've got the picture and then the story. There was an exhibition at the Cedar Hill Recreation Centre and another one at the [Royal BC] Museum for two weeks. We got an amazing amount of written feedback about how meaningful it had been, how much the participants and visitors had learned and so on. It was very good. And then, at the same time we were doing that, we did another play called *Bridging Conversations*. That was conversations between youth and old people.

M: Intergenerational.

L: Intergenerational conversations about many different topics and very related, of course, to the immigrant experience. Those were the last projects that we did. What is interesting is that the Inter-Cultural Association is the only one, it's the only association of this kind in BC that has taken the arts as seriously as they have.

M: Right. Using the arts as a methodology.

L: Using the arts as a methodology and a constant. Well, Paulina, of course, she's an expert in applying for grants and so on. The plays are always successful and they're very well documented. We have a scribe in every project, so we have written down everything that has happened in every project. So there's an amazing documentation there of all the details of how we did this. It really does bring amazing inspiration.

M: Let's move toward finishing here, Lina, just in terms of reflecting back on this body of work covering dozens of years of your life. So this question is a little bit broader, maybe a bit more philosophical in terms of the meaning that theatre has for people in general and in your life in particular. You've been touching on this throughout our conversation about the power of theatre, the empowerment of theatre as a place where people can tell their stories. When you think about the future, do you see the energy of the work that you've done continuing forward?

L: I think that it can continue. I really think that art, and this is something I've always said, art is part of our heritage as human beings. You know, we're human beings and then we do art as one form of expression. We need to express ourselves. Everybody needs that. When we don't have that we get sick. We get emotionally ill. Especially we get emotionally ill because [of] this promotion that art is only for some very privileged people who have special qualities and so on. Of course there's that, there are special people who have amazing qualities and they are an inspiration. Everybody has something to say in their lives and something to express. I think that the fact that art has become a business is killing the possibility for every human being to express themselves. I find it's very dangerous. I really abhor that idea that only a few can do it. I have seen so many times the happiness, or the feeling of pride, or the wellness that happens when people can express themselves even with a gesture. Even just a gesture—they really show who they are. I think that it's difficult work, it's not simple. I was very lucky because I got a lot of background and a lot of movement and inspiration that came from different places. Doing applied theatre is harder. When you're working with people who at first don't know that they can speak loud, to be heard. When you have to go through those first things and they have absolutely no trust in themselves, that's work.

M: I've had that experience working at William Head [on Stage, an inmate-run prison theatre company]. So many of those men have never been on a stage. That way of mentoring over a period of weeks and months, and then they are in the spotlight.

L: It's hard and it's amazing.

M: Yes, it is.

L: That's exactly the same process. I would really like to say to people who think that applied theatre is a minor art, "Beware, because you can really mess up if you don't do a good job." As I was saying, [there were] those moments in my life where I felt that I was being messed up even though I had so much going for me. It took just a few misguided directors or people that I was working with to make me feel completely rejected and insecure. That's not a good feeling. That's a moment when I could say, "Well, I'm not doing this anymore because I'm not good enough."

M: That's a nice bridge to my last question, Lina, which is, if you were sitting with a young theatre artist . . . what kind of advice would you offer a young artist?

L: I would say, "Respect your art and respect yourself." Work with what is life-giving, or whatever activity can be life-giving, as opposed to the opposite or what tends to squash things or looking down on people. The results of work well done are amazing. They're extraordinary. They can be miraculous. It's worth taking care of it. And study a lot. The more resources you have the better job you'll do. More than anything, respect the human spirit. Also it's important to know that you have to have discipline. You have to make them see that theatre is a hard master. The kids really learn that. I remember saying to them, "You know I'm so happy when the audience forgets that you are children and they just enjoy the play because it's such a good play." The kids say, "Oh, that's a wonderful thing." I think that's it. Forget that they are poor immigrants coming from nowhere. You can have the emotion and enjoyment of seeing something that is alive.

M: That's lovely. Thank you, Lina. It's great. We could talk on and on for hours but I think this is probably enough for one chapter.

DISPLACED—THREE CULTURES, THREE TIME PERIODS, THREE REASONS TO FLEE: RECOUNTING THE DEVISED CREATIVE PROCESS

NATASHA MARTINA KOECHL

Soma is the Greek word for body and somatics pertains to the practice of perceiving one's self through the body. As a somatic practitioner and artist, it is my perception that the universal language resides in the use of physical expression rather than words. Through how we gesture and posture, another individual can be impacted by our meaning, whether they share the same language or not. Therefore, physical expression can become a medium in which several cultures can come together in order to experience, as members of the audience, issues that resonate across a broad spectrum of perspectives. In my involvement of writing, producing, and directing a piece of theatre that incorporated music, movement, and text, I found the piece allowed for diverse cultures to come together and freely discuss their own stories and experiences in reflection to the stories told on stage. Some of the most impactive theatre I have been a witness to is when the movement can say so much more than the dialogue and I am left to interpret its meaning.

In this article, I discuss how, through the lens of the body and the female perspective, my collaborator Sue Mythen and I explored themes surrounding immigration to create a piece entitled *Displaced*. Our aim was to explore how each newcomer's body "remembers" the "memory" of their past experiences, and how that process sheds light on their reasons for etching out a new life for themselves in Canada. We also considered how the memory of the past, whether consciously or unconsciously, could evoke an empathetic response from those who witness the struggles that face every newcomer at some point in their journey. Other than the Indigenous Peoples of this land, we are all immigrants, but as Canadians we tend to forget how the decisions of our ancestors sowed the seeds for us in this lifetime. This is what Elizabeth Renzetti writes about it:

> I've spent much of this week thinking about what Canada would look
> like without its generations of desperately poor people who huddled
> onto crowded ships and made the journey to a country that did not
> welcome them with open arms. I wouldn't be here writing this story
> if some of those people hadn't attempted the crossing; perhaps you
> wouldn't be here reading it.[1]

I tend to agree with this position, as when you look at the trajectory of Canadian immigration little has changed in the last one hundred and fifty years with respect to the newcomer experience in relation to day-to-day hardships. Newcomers, particularly from different ethnicities, still cope with isolation, prejudice, and the balancing act between holding onto their cultural identity, while trying to assimilate to Canadian customs.

Displaced looks at the challenges three female immigrants faced moving to Canada.[2]

In our production, Mary, an Irish emigrant, flees her country due to the Great Hunger of 1847, leaving behind her three surviving children and the graves of her husband and her three deceased children. She sails for the British province of Canada with her youngest child Roísín—a mere two months.

---

1   But as Alan Filewod's paper notes in this volume, perhaps the decisions our ancestors made were themselves insensible to the Indigenous People's right to their land, which the settlers later came to claim as their own.

2   The cast included Jacqueline Block as Mary, Emma Laishram as Dara, and Anna Mazurik as Sofia. Costume and Set Design by Carla Orosz and Lighting Design by Amberlin Hsu. Direction by Natasha Martina.

Fig. 1. From left, Anna Mazurik as Sofia, Emma Laishram as Dara
and Jacqueline Block as Mary. Photo by JL Photo.

old—and with the dream of soon earning enough to send for the others. But
after two months on a "coffin ship," Mary embarks on British Canadian soil
alone, with no food or money, and nothing left of her daughter but the shawl
that held her. Sofia, a German emigrant, makes her way to Canada in 1947.
Haunted by the political and economic upheaval in her home country, and
the image of her Jewish husband, Julius, who took his own life shortly before
the end of the war, Sofia arrives on Canadian soil determined to sever all
ties with the past and begin a new life. Finally, Dara, a young Afghan refugee, flees a forced marriage and the inequity, despotism, and economic strife
caused by the Taliban invasion of her country. Making her way to Canada
illegally aboard a freighter ship in 2007, she nonetheless arrives on Canadian
soil with the aspiration to leave behind the silences imposed by fear, sexual
oppression, and violence, and to find her own voice. The use of movement and
music serves here as catalysts in unravelling the delicate issues of the human
experience that arose out of these three women's memories and shared spaces.

In June of 2015, my company, Ground Cover Theatre, premiered *Displaced* at the St. Ambroise Montréal Fringe Festival, followed by a run at the Saskatoon PotashCorp Fringe Festival in August of the same year.[3] The response was overwhelmingly positive (Fournier). The show was nominated for two awards in Montréal and received five stars in the Saskatoon *StarPhoenix*, and I was encouraged to remount the production in 2017 as part of the the Live Five Independent Theatre season in Saskatoon (26 January–5 February 2017) and the Shumiatcher Sandbox series at the Globe Theatre in Regina (9–18 February 2017).[4]

LAYING THE GROUNDWORK

From what roots did this successful piece grow? The creation of original work can be exhilarating and angst-ridden all at the same time. The canvas is completely blank, affording one the freedom to move in any direction, and yet the daunting task lies in conceiving the idea itself. In 2010, after reading *Alias Grace* by Margaret Atwood, I was riveted by the story of Grace Marks, and I was struck by the trials and tribulations she encountered upon her arrival in the British province of Canada as one of the onslaught of Irish immigrants fleeing the Great Famine. As I began to dig deeper into Canada's past, I was confounded by the atrocious conditions of Grosse Isle,

---

3   The cast included Katie Moore as Mary, Emma Laishram as Dara, and Anna Mazurik as Sofia. Costume and Lighting Design by Amberlin Hsu. Direction by Natasha Martina.

4   After its sold-out run in Saskatoon, the production was awarded four Saskatoon and Area Theatre Awards for Outstanding Direction, Ensemble, Original Script, and Music Composition. The following year, *Displaced* was invited to be a part of the M1 Singapore Fringe, a curated multidisciplinary festival "of theatre, dance, music, visual arts and mixed media created and presented by Singaporeans and international artists" ("About the Fringe"). In 2018, the festival was entitled Let's Walk, based on the Singaporean contemporary artist Amanda Heng's piece of the same name, which looks at the "lack of progress for women in society" (M. Martin). The cast included Jacqueline Block as Mary, Emma Laishram as Dara, and Anna Mazurik as Sofia. Costume and Set Design by Carla Orosz and Lighting Design by Amberlin Hsu. Direction by Natasha Martina.

the now-defunct quarantine station, which saw thousands of Irish immigrants who were lucky enough to survive pass through its gates, while others, riddled with pestilence, languished within the station and eventually died. Sue Mythen, my co-creator, suggested another book entitled *Gerard Keegan's Famine Diary: Journey to a New World* by James L. Mangan, which provided even starker first-hand accounts of Irish suffering in transit dating back to 1845. To this day, the journal entry of a young girl witnessing her father run off the end of the deck of a coffin ship, due to a state of hunger and lunacy, is imprinted on my brain. It was that sole image that sparked an idea to create a piece about the impact of the wave of Irish men and women who came to Canada during "an Gorta Mór" (the Great Hunger). In 2011 I travelled to Dublin, where I spent three days conducting research at Trinity College Library, in addition to visiting various historical sites, such as the Famine Memorial and the Jeanie Johnston Tall Ship Museum. It was on day three of sitting in the library that I began to question whether writing a piece about the Irish famine and its relationship to mass immigration to Canada during 1845–1847 was personal enough to allow me to create an original theatrical work. I realized that, unlike Sue, I had no personal connection to the Great Famine. Therefore, I felt my contribution would not be as fully embodied as Sue's experiences, since she grew up with a deeper historical understanding of that time.

Notwithstanding my lack of personal connection, however, what I could relate to was the theme of immigration; my entire family immigrated to Canada between 1952 and 1967. In 1952, with Germany still in disarray after the war, experiencing food rationing and scarce job opportunities, my godparents set out on a freighter ship, leaving their families behind in pursuit of a new life in Canada. With only nine dollars in their pocket—it was a prerequisite at the time that no one could enter Canada with more than that amount—they narrowly missed being subjected to quarantine outside Montréal after a gentleman travelling on to the United States lent them twenty-five dollars to pay for the privilege of skipping detention. They then proceeded on to Vancouver by rail. Within twenty-four hours of their arrival, my godfather found a job as a bricklayer, and my godmother began cleaning houses for some of the wealthiest people in the Lower Mainland. Every time they recount their journey to Canada, they proudly remind me that within months of their arrival they paid back their debt of twenty-five dollars to the kind gentleman who took a chance lending them money without any guarantee he would ever get it back. Thirteen years later, my late father journeyed to Canada from Austria, and two years after that my mother arrived from Switzerland, at the start of the 1967 Expo in Montréal.

Since I grew up with the Germanic culture profoundly impacting my identity as a second-generation Canadian I began to reflect on the course of Canadian immigration as a whole. My family encountered many obstacles in their quest to carve a new life for themselves, and reflecting on today's world, similar hardships continue to be experienced by newcomers. Often newcomers give up everything for the sake of their children, to start afresh in a new land. Therefore, I recognized that a third branch to this story needed to be created in order to bring this piece into the twenty-first century. I settled on Afghan immigration to Canada after I had the opportunity, in 2012, to work as Assistant Director and Movement Coach on Theatre Calgary and the Citadel Theatre's co-production of Khaled Hosseini's *The Kite Runner*. Part of my job was to immerse myself in the culture and history of Afghanistan, which played a pivotal role in shaping the character of Dara. Up until the outbreak of the Syrian crisis, the Afghan people were one of the largest displaced refugee communities in the world. I began to reach out to the refugee community in Saskatoon by volunteering at the Open Door Society, where I participated in many conversation circles that gave newcomers a chance to practise their English. Hearing their stories and struggles answered a lot of my questions concerning the process for present-day refugees in coming to Canada, as well as the struggles they endure day to day as they try and assimilate to a new culture. I am grateful to the Open Door Society, which put me in touch with two women who originated from Afghanistan and who gave Emma Laishram (who played Dara) and I advice regarding Afghan cultural practices and provided us with support in the verbal translation of the Dari text used in the script. With cultural appropriation at the forefront of today's conversation, particularly with regard to the arts, the company and I wanted to make sure we were being very respectful to the Afghan culture, in particular to the rituals surrounding prayer.

DEVISING PROCESS

With a theatrical idea now in mind, Sue and I proceeded with the first developmental stage (2011), utilizing ten days in a studio to brainstorm how these three stories could coalesce to form a piece that would inspire, provoke, and stir debate amongst audience members. Sue and I knew we would not approach this piece in the traditional sense of putting pen to paper, but rather our concepts would be first explored through the expression of gesture and posture. As movement practitioners, we are more comfortable in sprouting an idea from a phrase, an image, or a piece of music. Sue is Head of Movement at the Lir Academy in Ireland's National Academy of Dramatic Art at Trinity College, and throughout her twenty-year career she has collaborated on several new works. Together, we did a lot of word association, writing down themes all three of our imagined women would have experienced with regard to their struggles in assimilating to a new culture, while also trying to honour their respective cultural customs. Some of these themes included displacement, prejudice, survival, female friendship, cultural identity, and isolation. We then explored these themes in movement and came up with repeatable gestures that could be intertwined to create an overlap of the individual characters' emotional response. We discussed early on that we wanted the movement to serve as the characters' subtext, expressing the idea that the newcomers' words might be saying one thing, but what they are actually feeling and experiencing is another.

When you look at the trajectory of female newcomers coming to Canada from varying classes and educational backgrounds, many of them had to resort to some sort of job in domestic service. Thus, with regard to our theatrical narrative we began to address how these women's experiences interconnected through commonalities of location, including port of entry, workplace, and home. Our movement explorations started to explore the idea of "repetition" through the day-to-day monotony of their work life. We examined how the routine of scrubbing floors, washing laundry, and ironing deflates any sense of boundary between the past and the present when it comes to a newcomer's life. The tedium of manual labour can take a toll on anyone, but when compounded by the struggles of trying to adapt to a new country it can be further aggravated by the undue stress and trauma of the unknown: will the newcomers make enough money to pay their expenses, feed their family, and save for their future? We expanded upon these leitmotifs by exploring the women's homes through the daily ritual of prayer, bathing, eating, and sleeping to see if we could illuminate the degree of isolation and loneliness these women felt upon their arrival in a new land. And within that exploration we began to question and explore how these characters' individual cultures could be illuminated through their physical gestures.

The second developmental phase occurred in 2012. I invited one of my former students, Anna Seibel, to join the process, so we had the ability to shape all three roles. Over the course of five days, we revisited the images we had created the year before. We began to explore the arc of these three individual stories, and how they could potentially unite. We started by posing key questions in order to inform the developmental process with a view toward crafting dialogue. Some of these questions included: What became of these women upon their debarkation in Canada? What type of life did each endure? How did they have to alter their cultural customs to fit into the Canadian way of life? In my research, I came across a study that looked at women immigrants, particularly from African countries, and how they had to adapt their customs in order to assimilate to the Canadian culture. Certain observers who took part in the study remarked that it was an impediment to their progress toward assimilation if they chose to keep their respective customs, because it "provoked intolerant reactions and rejection by the mainstream population" (Epp et al. 267).

To tie in the theme of intolerance, we discussed what possible events could have triggered each character on the path toward fleeing to another land and asked how this "memory" impacted who they became and their future decisions regarding the maintenance of their cultural identity. In the aforementioned study, the question "How do people remember?" came up and they discovered "that when people tell of their past lives, in some cases decades after the actual events, their accounts are filtered through a complex memory process that is created through an interplay of who they were then and who they are now" (Epp et al. 399). Tying this into my practice as a Somatic Movement Educator in Body-Mind Centering,® I found myself pondering the notion of our cellular structure and how it is greatly influenced by our genetic makeup. It is a known fact that the makeup of a woman's eggs is determined by her grandmother, not her mother. Therefore, intergenerational trauma can implicate itself into the "memory" of not just one human being, but multiple human beings as it is carried down the generations. Body-Mind Centering® is an embodied movement practice that utilizes the awareness and application of the various body systems in order to harness inner perceptivity on a body level. One of the systems that is addressed is going back to one's embryological development in order to access awareness around the biomechanics of human movement. Hence, we explored embryological and developmental movement to illuminate the characters' past experiences in order to distill their inner subtext. We hoped through this process we could discover gestural scores that would highlight the emotional baggage from their past experiences and their need to either "unleash it" or "contain it," depending on the individual choices they made upon their arrival in Canada.

For example, Mary's path was triggered out of desperation to feed her family due to the loss of her husband from typhus. With three young children left back in Ireland and one newborn in tow, Mary made the voyage to Canada in the hopes of sending money back home, in order to reunite her family on the other side of the world.

> MARY: The tears in my eyes overwhelm me seeing the ravages of hunger on the bones of my children, all hollow and listless, fading away for the want of some food. Joseph, my eldest is the man now, and will stay with the young ones, and myself and Roísín, join the tide of human suffering walking step by step to the sea. (Martina and Mythen 4)

"Walking step by step to the sea" became a link toward a repeatable gesture among all three of the women walking or in some cases running in order to flee their old life. In Sofia's case it was fleeing a double life as a German Gentile woman who adopted the Jewish traditions of her late husband. Years prior I had directed a production of *All Through the Night* by Shirley Lauro, a story about the lives of German Gentile women prior to, during, and after World War II. Part of my research delved into "mixed" marriages during that time, and I was greatly affected by how German women became ostracized by their family and friends due to their marriage to a "*verboten*" Jewish man. Of course, coming from a Germanic background I still felt the "memory" of the actions of my people during that time, and I wanted to use that memory as a resource in creating the life of Sofia. I created some of Sofia's story from the life of "Charlotte Israel," who was married to a Jewish gentleman by the name of Julius Israel. Julius was a tailor by day and great musician by night, but it was all taken away by the hands of the Nazis. To further highlight Sofia's backstory, I intertwined the historical significance of events surrounding Rosenstrasse: a protest that occurred in Berlin from 27 February until 9 March 1943, where "*mischling*" children and Jewish men were rounded up and housed at a Jewish community centre on Rose Street (Rosenstrasse). This protest was so significant because German women put their lives on the line by verbally protesting in the hundreds for the release of their husbands and children ("Neither Black Nor White"). I sought to highlight this heart-rending moment in history through Sofia's outcry and plea to save her husband.

> **SOFIA:** District upon district all over Berlin the "privileged" men and children are rounded up. Head to Rosenstrasse! More and more of us women gather. "Give us our husbands back. We want our families back." I can see that one round of machine-gun fire could have us all wiped out. It takes all my courage to stay and protest. Eight days later, Julius is released. (Martina and Mythen 4)

In our story Julius was released, but just before the war ended, he took his own life:

SOFIA: Several weeks later there is a bang at the door. The men said they could only identify Julius by his violin case, which he left perched on the edge of the bridge railing. (5)

Haunted by Julius's broken promise never to leave her side, Sofia came to Canada with the goal of starting again.

SOFIA: My land is no longer my home. The only way forward is to never look back. (5)

Sofia's need to flee ultimately became about a choice to start again, while the audience discovers that Dara's decision to flee came out of a desperate attempt to survive. Dara, a young Afghan girl, arrived in Canada in 2007. We learn that she tried to flee a forced marriage, and was subsequently caught by the police and subjected to torture at the hands of her father (Baba) and the police.

DARA: I get about 10 miles outside of the city, but then I am picked up for not being escorted by a male. Baba grabs the opportunity to punish me for disobeying his wishes and happily he lets me sit in jail for days. My feet are bound and whipped until I can no longer walk but lie passively as my torture continues through the night. (4)

Shortly after, we learn Dara's mother sacrificed everything for her daughter by helping Dara to flee Afghanistan through the aid of her uncle:

DARA: Madar never takes me home. I remain at my Uncle's house until he feels I am strong enough to make the journey to Turkey. For the last time, I see my Madar. She places in my hand Ady's precious music box and enough money to hopefully pay for my journey. Then Madar gently nudges me into the night and I keep running. (5)

Upon Dara's arrival to Canada, we saw her struggle to keep her independence while also trying to "blend in" to the Canadian way of life. As a woman

Fig. 2. From left, Jacqueline Block as Mary, Anna Mazurik as Sofia, and Emma Laishram as Dara. Photo by JL Photo.

in Afghanistan, Dara had no rights. Therefore, over the course of the play she begins to negotiate her past with her present situation, and eventually she gains the courage to share her story and seal her independence.

The following year (2013), through the assistance of an Interdisciplinary Centre for Culture and Creativity fellowship and an Independent Artist grant through the Saskatchewan Arts Board, I was able to facilitate a third stage of this play's development. Jason Cullimore was brought in as the commissioned composer, along with three of my former students, Janessa Johnsrude, Jenna-Lee Hyde, and Emma Thorpe, who collaborated with Sue and I over twelve days. The goal of this phase of development was to begin to craft the textual score. The text was largely found through crafted improvisations based around previous discussions surrounding character, plot, themes, and images. We wanted to keep the exposition to a minimum and really focus more on these women's voyage to and arrival in Canada, and on what motivated them in their daily life. Also, the structure of the set started to evolve and become a significant component of the show's choreography, helping to unite the

Fig. 3. From left, Anna Mazurik as Sofia, Emma Laishram as Dara, and
Jacqueline Block as Mary. Photo by JL Photo.

women's stories. It was during the first developmental stage that Sue and I
had stumbled across a fantastic photograph of three men lying in separate
boxes, one stacked on top of the other. We immediately associated that image
with the three women, huddled in their bunks within the confines of a coffin
ship, a steamship, and a freighter. We recognized that if the boxes were put
on wheels, there could be endless opportunities leading to an assortment of
locations and uses. In one exploration we utilized the boxes as turnstiles to
give the impression of these three women being shoved through like cattle
as they are questioned, assessed, and in some cases berated for their reasons
in coming to Canada. We called this the "immigration sequence," and we
directed the actors to coordinate moving back and forth between playing
their individual characters alongside the depiction of an immigration officer confronted with a newcomer. The improvisations were crafted around
the historical trajectory of how each character, at their own disparate points
in time, would have been faced with specific challenges and expectations in
receiving approval to be accepted into Canada.

In addition, we also layered into the scene male voice-overs to depict the various Immigration Acts of the last one hundred and fifty years or so. During 1847, entering the British province of Canada, Mary's "health" was her ticket in, since the British wanted to vacate the Irish from Ireland. The "coffin ships" didn't shy away from their title; more than a third of the Irish perished during the two-month voyage to North America due to malnutrition, typhus, and dysentery. Subsequently, if an Irish immigrant could walk upon her debarkation onto Grosse Isle, she was considered "healthy," even though she was skin and bone. The actor playing Mary simply played with passivity of weight, while collapsing in her upper torso to depict her struggle to walk and remain erect after the near-death voyage. The audience then heard the following text yelled above the crowds while Mary was pushed and shoved by the boxes to depict the coarse and brutal behaviour of the British toward the Irish:

> **BRITISH MALE VOICE OVER:** Attention! Attention Please! Anyone who can still walk, move along to the healthy sheds! (Martina and Mythen 13)

By contrast, Sofia arrived under the aegis of opened borders for displaced persons after World War II (1945–1951), under which she was subjected to certain Canadian regulations in her first two years of entry ("The Arrival"). It has been noted that many women who fell under these regulations and originated from war-torn Europe came into Canada as domestic servants. Under the caveat of being "displaced persons," newcomers went through more extensive physical and medical testing to ensure they could hold a job and not be burdened with taking care of additional family members.

> Composed of immigration, medical, security, and labour officials, these teams went from one displaced persons' camp to another, interviewing large numbers of desperate people living out of suitcases, or where possible, the trunk of a car. In a sense they resembled itinerant "head hunters," only their mission was to select able-bodied

refugees "like good beef cattle, with a preference for strong young
men [and women] who could do manual labour and would not be
encumbered by aging relatives . . . (V. Knowles 165)

Sofia was a perfect candidate. She was widowed—hence single—strong, young,
and capable of performing the necessary domestic tasks. Even though Sofia
was an educated woman, she was relegated to serving her assigned "mistress" of the house for a minimum of two years, as stipulated by the amended
immigration policies. In the show, we saw Sofia's defiance toward the immigration officer as she tried to negotiate the officer's perception of her identity
and capabilities.

Dara, in turn, arrived in Canada sixty years later with no legal papers in
hand, and was processed as a temporary refugee until she could prove she
would be subjected to danger if she returned to Afghanistan. It was recently
reported on CBC that 15% of women seeking refugee status in Canada do so
due to gender persecution in their homeland. The report noted that "[c]laims
based on domestic violence are, like all refugee claims, assessed based on two
elements: the risk an individual faces and to what degree they can be protected
in their home country" (Carman and Elash). Over the course of the "immigration sequence," Dara was subjected to multiple questions regarding the
legitimacy of her story, and whether she could "prove" she would be in danger
if she returned to Afghanistan. Dara remained composed, saying very little.
In the past, when Dara spoke up in her home country, she was subjected to
torture, and hence, during the immigration sequence, Dara merely answered
the questions with a nod of her head.

These three characters' stories intersected not only at their ports of entry
and in the parallels offered by their work lives, but in their home lives as
well. As the director, I wanted to find, through the language of movement,
how I could distill the loneliness and isolation these women felt each time
they returned home to a place surrounded by silence. On three different
occasions, the audience was given a glimpse into their private lives, capturing the moments when they were most vulnerable and sought comfort
in the familiarity of their cultural customs. To underlie this depiction of

their home lives, the composer was directed to score the music with three different leitmotifs. He utilized the instruments of a wooden flute, a violin, and a tabla to create a thematic score that would embody the immigrants' histories. Additionally, objects were utilized for each character that symbolized something from their pasts. For Mary, the key object was her shawl, which initially gave warmth to her newborn baby and then quickly became a reminder of what she lost on the journey to Canada. Sofia's only link to her husband was through his violin, which she kept with her at all times; only later in the story did the audience discover that she used the violin case to house her sewing supplies, and her sketchbook. Dara revealed her grandmother's music box, which was given to her by her mother before she fled. Over the duration of the piece, three choreographic sequences were depicted and displayed each immigrant's home life and how the aforementioned objects became the women's only lifelines to their past. Furthermore, one's faith is often considered a private sanctum, and, therefore, the audience witnessed the women's desire to seek further guidance through the ritual of prayer, highlighting their shared need to find faith and hope in the present, while holding on to their respective pasts. The leitmotifs of the wooden flute, violin, and tabla were distinctly layered into each of these three choreographic progressions. The clarity of these three instruments helped me to create a sense of isolation within each of these women's lives, while at the same time the women found moments within the music where their individual gestures could be shared in order to unify their experiences. In one of several movement sequences, all of the following actions happened simultaneously:

> *All three women return to their individual tenement. Mary comes in worn suggesting she has been working late into the night. Slowly she takes off her boots, and displays money hidden inside. One by one she counts the coins and then restores the money to her secure hiding place. Mary is beside herself with the little money that she has to send back home. Then, she takes out her rosary, wraps her shawl around her, and begins to kneel down and pray. Sofia comes in and sets her*

*violin down and proceeds to take out her money and count it. We can
see she is earnestly frustrated over the lack of money she currently has
saved. Sofia then covers her head with a scarf and begins the ritual in
preparation for Sabbath. Dara comes in with a bucket in hand and
proceeds to set her belongings down before she counts the little money
she made that day. Frustrated and feeling deflated she places the money
in the music box. Then, she begins the ritual of washing her hands and
feet in preparation for prayer.*

We hear all three women end the sequence with:

> **DARA:** Assalamu alaikum wa rahmatullah.

> **MARY:** Siochana agus Beannachtai De ort Agas.

> **SOFIA:** Geh in Frieden mit Gottes Segen.

> **DARA, SOFIA & MARY:** Peace be upon you and God's Blessings.

> *Lights dim as all three women take in a deep inhale and let out a sigh
> and begin to transition into a new day.* (Martina and Mythen 32–33)

The three actors' movements synchronized beautifully as they managed to
capture their individual stories in conjunction with their shared need to be
heard by the one person that hadn't left their side—God.

The introduction of secondary characters became essential in providing each immigrant woman with something to root her to Canada through
the connection to a friend, neighbour, or employer. It was through these
secondary characters that the audience learned how Mary, Sofia, and Dara
dealt with the day-to-day adjustment of adapting to a new country and its
customs, while negotiating a new life for themselves. For Mary, this process
became about the desperate choices she made in order to secure the future
of her children, who were wasting away in Ireland. But those choices had

consequences, and jeopardized Mary's mental and physical health and her relationship with her neighbour Brigid. Mary gave in to the temptation of selling drink and ran a house of ill repute so she could speed up the process of bringing her children to Canada. This was potentially where some might have argued that we branched into more of a stereotypical storyline for the character of Mary as the Irish drunkard. But we were inspired by a fantastic quotation from Anne Bogart: "Stereotypes are containers for memory, history and assumption" (105). Bogart began to pursue the subject of "stereotypes" after a lengthy discussion with her collaborator Tadashi Suzuki, who feared his protege Kayoko Shiraishi would succumb to "clichéd" acting upon leaving his company to work on the North American stage. Bogart began to question what it meant to be original and innovative, and why the idea of cliché had/s a negative connotation surrounding it. She decided to pursue "stereotype" not as enemy but as ally, arguing that if you consciously look at the stereotype in "three-dimensional" form, then you are doing due diligence as a creator to interact with the subject from all sides: "When performing a stereotype as an ally, you do not embrace a stereotype in order to hold it rigid; rather, you burn through it, undefining it and allowing human experience to perform its alchemy" (104–05). For that reason, we didn't shy away from the concept of "stereotype" with regard to the three characters, because within the image itself a "memory" is planted that can often evoke an immediate response in an audience. And by broadening the idea of the "stereotype" to something that has emotional integrity, we wished to impact how the audience empathized with each character. So in Mary's case she wasn't being portrayed as a one-dimensional drunkard but as a woman with strong Catholic morals who decided to seek employment that could ultimately save her family. Survival was at the essence of Mary's enactment of the human experience. Eventually, Mary's activities were exposed by her friend Brigid, and she was subjected to a fine, which she couldn't pay, and was subsequently thrown in jail. Some time passes and Brigid goes to visit Mary in jail for the sole purpose of delivering a letter from Mary's son Joseph, who wrote that her children had received the money and were set to depart for British Canada. Mary was relieved to hear her efforts were not in vain, but she didn't have the strength to recover from the hardships she had endured over the last two years and died in Brigid's arms.

Sofia's new relationships in Canada were just as complicated as Mary's, but thankfully Sofia managed to harness a more positive outcome near the end of the play. Initially, Sofia's encounter with her employer was strained, due to Mrs. Brown's ignorance and prejudice toward a German woman. But over time, Mrs. Brown began to recognize Sofia's abilities and skills gained as a dressmaker in Germany—skills Mrs. Brown admired because they set Sofia apart from herself and other wealthy women who relied on their husbands' incomes. As a result, a relationship began to develop between the two women, and Mrs. Brown planted the idea in Sofia's head that she should consider going into her own business as a dressmaker. But the only way Sofia could have conceivably pursued such an expensive proposition was if she sold Julius's violin to Mrs. Brown.

Similar to Sofia, Dara was confronted with many challenges in the early days of her arrival, but upon meeting Leslie, a middle-class white girl studying sociology, things began to change. Leslie educated Dara about self-respect and not falling prey to those who wished to take advantage of her. But the conflict resided in Leslie's ignorance about the challenges newcomers faced in proving they were "good citizens." Over the course of the play the audience discovered that Dara was being subjected to harassment at the hands of her employer. Dara then confided in Leslie about the harassment and, subsequently, Leslie encouraged Dara to speak up for herself. However, what Leslie neglected to understand in this version of the story was that Dara feared jeopardizing her job security, which was a requirement in order to secure her permanent residency.

THE ART OF DRAMATURGY

At the end of the third developmental phase, Sue Mythen stepped away from the devising process, and between 2014 and 2015 I conducted two additional developmental phases: one through the support of the Saskatchewan Playwrights Centre under the dramaturgical mentorship of Gordon Portman and another on my own, working solely on refining the choreographic scores in order to solidify the musical compositions. Gordon's insights and input were invaluable to the process, assisting me in creating more conflict between the newcomers and the secondary characters as a means to raise the individual newcomers' stakes in needing to stay in Canada. He asked pointed questions:

Where is the opportunity for ironic and non-ironic parallels to occur? For example: Mary's success in selling booze to Sofia's dressmaking and Dara's language skills?

How could their successes be displayed through movement or reoccurring gestures?

How does Mary arrive at the position of selling drink and running a house of ill repute?

This resulted in adding in the additional character of Mrs. O'Neill, the neighbour that lives above Brigid and Mary, and is known for being up "all hours of the night, rising her skirts and letting anyone have a poke at her."

How does the absence of a male character serve or not serve the female experience?

Is there value in Sofia's dream of having her own dress shop come up as a result of what happens with Mrs. Brown, rather than having it in her mind to pursue right from the beginning of the play?

It was through Gordon's questions that I was able to refine the script further in preparation for its premier at the St. Ambroise Montréal Fringe Festival and the Saskatoon PotashCorp Fringe Theatre Festival in June and August 2015. The response was overwhelmingly positive; the only criticism we received had to do with the relationship between Dara and Leslie, as it seemed to lack a clear arc in regards to propelling Dara's story. So, with a new objective in mind, I set out, with further dramaturgical assistance from Gordon, to re-envision the role of Dara prior to the play's remount in 2017. Gordon helped me to refine my questions surrounding Dara's narrative:

What is Dara's motivation for staying in Canada?

How could the secondary character of Leslie be reshaped to create more impact and possible parallels alongside Dara's struggle to be accepted in society? Could the two characters share something in common?

Does an additional character need to be added, similar to the one-off scene with Mrs. O'Neill and Mary, that displays the bureaucracy of Dara's day-to-day struggle to "prove" she would be a good citizen of Canada?

The script was significantly altered to reflect more of Dara's day-to-day struggles in navigating the process toward establishing permanent residency. In the revised version, right near the beginning of the play, we saw an encounter between Dara and her settlement worker. The settlement worker clearly laid out for Dara the requirements she had to fulfill in order to prove her eligibility to stay in Canada. Those requirements included stability in her job, improving her English, and sharing her story in detail. In the previous script this scene didn't exist.

Additionally, in the earlier script, Leslie was written as a typical Canadian gal: young, fortunate, and somewhat naive about the harsh realities newcomers face moving to a new country. Leslie befriended Dara in a coffee shop and eventually convinced Dara to share her story with her sociology class. But this storyline was subsequently scrapped, and in the newest version Leslie was rewritten as a young homeless girl, creating a stronger bond between Dara and Leslie in their shared need to be accepted. Leslie became the motivating factor in encouraging Dara to "tell" her story at her refugee board hearing, and the story of so many women in Afghanistan who continue to be silenced.

AUDIENCE RESPONSE

On two different occasions, sponsored by the City of Saskatoon, we had the distinct pleasure of performing this piece for an invited audience that was made up of newcomers to that city. After the show, food and beverages were provided to the newcomers, who were encouraged to stay and participate in a talkback with the cast. So many of the newcomers that attended were overcome with emotion and commented on how it was rare to experience theatre where the immigrant/refugee experience was addressed in such a truthful way. Many of the newcomers shared their own individual stories and reiterated some of the themes highlighted in the play, most notably the degree of isolation and loneliness they felt in the first months and years of settling into a new city. At one point, the discussion centred around the newcomers' goal to provide for the future of their children; they stressed that they were willing to give up everything to see that their children could succeed in a safe and prosperous environment. Similarly, several theatre critiques from well-established newspapers across Saskatchewan, Québec, and Singapore commented on how the piece shed light into the immigrant experience. Cam Fuller from the Saskatoon *StarPhoenix* wrote,

> Aside from an appreciation of the talent involved, what you're also left with, after the 80-minute one-act, is a deeper understanding of the struggle involved in starting a new life, the heartbreak and uncertainty and the tragedy behind the stories of those who never made it. Not to mention the courage and innate optimism of the human spirit which builds communities and forges nations. ("*Displaced*")

To Olivia Ho from *The Straits Times*, *Displaced* was one of the timeliest plays programmed for this festival; it is a heartfelt illustration of the cyclical nature of migration and a call for openness. Frequently, I was asked "why I chose to write this play." As a second-generation Canadian, I witnessed first hand the trials and tribulations my parents and godparents experienced as first-generation Canadian immigrants to the country, and how most of their successes were achieved through the help of fellow Canadians. Not much has changed with respect to newcomers experiencing similar hardships. Therefore, my hope was to instill in those who attended the production an element of compassion and willingness to remain open and non-judgmental toward newcomers. I never imagined, back in 2011, that this piece would carry so much weight. However, the rise of xenophobia, islamophobia, and the Trump era, all contributing to cross-cultural intolerance, started to bubble in 2015 and sadly has reached a feverish pitch in 2018; the outlook seems bleak in the years to follow.

CONCLUSION

As Canadians, we are only in the early stages of creating stories with cross-cultural voices that evoke the changing landscape of Canadian theatre. As an academic and practitioner, part of my goal is to produce original work that stirs discussion and discourse amongst theatregoers. Of course, there is value in theatre providing entertainment for the sake of laughter and enjoyment, but when I look back at the productions that have continued to percolate in my mind, they were often memorable for two reasons: imagery and thought-provoking subject matter.

Just months before *Displaced* was remounted in 2017, my father passed away and I found that the resonance of the piece carried even more weight in my need to share the story of these three women. My father immigrated to Canada in 1965 with no English and very little family in Canada to lend support. In the space of fifty-one years my father held multiple blue-collar jobs as an iron worker, contractor, and plumber until he eventually built a prosperous mechanical company, alongside my mother, who was also a new immigrant to Canada. At one point in their career they provided jobs for over a hundred and fifty employees. Not a small feat for two individuals who didn't have two dimes to rub together. And though *Displaced* was told through the lens of the female experience, there is no denying that, in particular, economically impoverished newcomers face a very tough journey in assimilating to a country like Canada. But often we only hear in the news media the negative side effects of newcomers in terms of being an economic burden or not wishing to "change their ways" with regard to assimilation. But what about those newcomers—like my mother and father—who continue to provide more opportunity for the next generation of Canadians? *Displaced* became a vehicle for self-reflection—one from the perspective of the newcomer and one from the perspective of the witness ("About *Displaced*"). Some of the newcomers that sat in the audience felt heard. And some of those that participated as a witness found in themselves a greater willingness to lend compassion toward newcomers.

> *Displaced* is moving, powerful theatre that combats xenophobia with compassion—by putting these strangely familiar characters in an empathetic light, allowing the audience to find the most elemental points of connection in watching them, not as immigrants but as fellow humans. (bakchormeeboy)

IMMIGRANT THEATRE AND CELEBRATION: HOPE IN THE FACE OF ADVERSITY

YASMINE KANDIL

I arrived in Canada in August of 2003, alone. I left behind my immediate family and a huge extended family. I had so much hope that I would access a life that I was sorely missing in my native home of Egypt. It took some time to build the life I dreamed I would live, with many bumps along the way. But what was most remarkable about this journey is that I didn't quite understand what it meant to be an immigrant, and how that status and identity was perceived by my predominantly white Canadian hosts. It wasn't until I began my applied theatre practice with a group of immigrant and refugee women in Victoria, BC, that I started truly to understand the value of holding my culture, heritage, and traditions close to my heart. Without them, I would have been lost, trying so hard to please this academic supervisor, that relationship partner, and this employment manager. Holding sacred these values meant that I could negotiate, along with those in my Canadian life, this new space that I'm trying to call home. What follows is my account of how my practice of applied theatre has evolved since the start of my journey in Canada, and how I grew and changed with it. At the end of this section I offer my thesis and topics of exploration resulting from this research. But first, I begin with the context of where my research began.

Peter O'Connor and Michael Anderson write about the unique relationship that applied theatre researchers have with our research material because of the form of representation that we employ, working essentially through embodied theatrical representation. They write, "Arts-based research recognizes that we know the world through all our senses, through our bodies rather than through what comes from our mind alone" ("Research" 26). In my applied theatre endeavours I have enjoyed the collaborative relationships I have developed with the participants whose narratives we explore in our creative process. These participants engage with me (and the research team) in devising, creating, witnessing, shaping, and shifting our theatre explorations.

When I first came to Canada in 2003, I searched for ways where I could apply the skills I had practised in my native home, Egypt, to reach out to underprivileged communities through theatre. My first experience was with a group of immigrant and refugee women, who were part of a settlement program offered to them through the local settlement centre the Inter-Cultural Association of Greater Victoria. My theatre workshops saw them collaborating with each other to reflect on their new experiences in Canada. Some of the topics explored related to familial dynamics of alienation between parents and teenage children, where the children wanted the space to integrate into their new Canadian identities while the parents felt threatened that this new integration meant an erasure of their native heritage, values, and ways of life. Other explorations centred around the issue of identity and the power imbalance at home between the husband, who is able to find gainful employment, and the wife, who is expected to be a "housewife," thus limiting her potential and minimizing the sense of identity that she would have otherwise enjoyed in her native home.

Over the years, I have worked with a number of different groups in Canada (immigrant and refugee women; immigrant and refugee youth; Canadian youth at risk; actors, volunteers, and medical professionals taking part in the delivery of medical curriculums; police officers, police staff, and clinicians engaged in the delivery of training to help police better manage de-escalation strategies with people in mental crisis). In this paper, I will focus on the evolution of my practice with immigrant and refugee communities, and what I have learned about applied theatre through this work. I will draw on three separate projects in order to reflect on a) how to build community through staging narratives, b) how to best handle and stage participant stories of trauma and memories from home, c) ways in which autonomy and ethical representation can strengthen participant involvement, and d) finding connectivity with our research subjects by implicating ourselves and our audience in their narratives. By examining these different areas of learning and reflection through these three projects, I develop an applied-theatre approach to working with immigrant and refugee communities in Canada that is insightful, ethical, and takes into account the complexity of experiences that becomes part of our engagement with them. I begin with a definition of applied theatre in the Canadian context.

DEFINING APPLIED THEATRE
(IN THE CANADIAN CONTEXT)

Applied theatre emerged at a time when people were seeking alternative models of communication to engage with communities who lack access to mainstream theatre. Artists wanted to democratize the practice of theatre, and they wanted to use it to respond to local and global issues with the people whose lives were directly impacted by these events. Perhaps one of the most prolific practitioners at the time of applied theatre's emergence was Augusto Boal, who created Theatre of the Oppressed in Brazil in 1979. When he was exiled to France a few years later, the practice became a movement that spread to many parts of Europe, North America, and the Asian continent. Boal worked on the notion of changing audiences or "'spectators'—passive beings in the theatrical phenomenon—into subjects, into actors, transformers of the dramatic action" ("Theatre" 131). Boal believed that "[t]he theatre is a weapon, and it is the people who should wield it" (131).

According to Tim Prentki and Sheila Preston, "Applied theatre has emerged in recent years as a term describing a broad set of theatrical practices and creative processes that take participants and audiences beyond the scope of conventional, mainstream theatre into the realm of a theatre that is responsive to ordinary people and their stories, local settings and priorities" (9). In the 1990s and early 2000s in Canada, this practice was termed "Popular

Theatre" (Prentki and Selman), and its definition by these authors clearly outlines its difference from mainstream theatre. Prentki and Selman write,

> In the case of popular theatre, "popular" implies that the process of making and showing the theatre piece is owned and controlled by a specific community, that the issues and stories grow out of the community involved, that that community is a vital part of a process of identifying, examining and taking action on matters which that community believes need to change. The "popular" refers to "of the people," *belonging* to the people. (Prentki and Selman 9)

The drive to create theatre that was accessible to the people arose from the discontent with forms of mainstream theatre that are removed from the issues of the masses. For example, Prentki and Jan Selman criticize what was then called "populist theatre," or the "megamusical," calling it "imported culture, created and controlled by interests external to the local community" and "escapist, [. . .] of little relevance" (9). Attracted to a more accessible form of theatre, those working with or on topics related to immigrant and refugee experiences have gravitated toward community-based theatre models. One such theatre artist is Canadian Chilean Lina de Guevara, who describes immigrant theatre as

> [a practice] about people who are yearning for better times, who have had to leave their homelands, because of war, poverty, and turmoil. My work has been about the dispossessed: a theatre of denunciation, of renovation, of change. I believe that theatre for elites ends up being anemic, disconnected with reality, without energy. And even though sometimes there's exquisite expertise in it, it becomes pointless when the content is vacuous. ("Impact" 319)

De Guevara's use of the verb "yearning" is illuminating, as it draws our attention to a state of discontent, of never quite being able to "settle" until the past is reconciled with. Applied theatre that is created "with," "for," or "by" the immigrant and refugee communities tends to address issues of reconciling the alienation and shock involved in leaving home and making a new home in Canada.

As I myself learned about the practice of applied theatre with the immigrant and refugee community, I explored the use of theatre as a tool through which young participants could claim Canada as their new home and begin to feel a sense of belonging in the "here and now" of their lives. Through this experience, I became more aware of the importance of staging memories from home, as well as of acknowledging traumatic experiences and making space for them in the teller's narrative. I also gained a greater understanding of the value of theatre as a means of celebration, and of the importance of the witness, both for the teller and for the performer.

"HERE I STAND"

In 2009, the Victoria Immigrant and Refugee Centre Society (VIRCS) hired me to devise a series of workshops with immigrant and refugee youth, and to use the material generated from these workshops to stage a performance that depicted the youth's struggles with settlement. Involved in the project were a total of fifteen youth ranging from fourteen to eighteen years of age. We worked together for a total of twelve weeks, rehearsing three hours each week. Once we had enough material, we rehearsed for a series of five- to six-hour days for about two weeks to devise a performance featuring the youth as performers.

The organization had been given funding by the City of Victoria to explore the hardships of the youth involved through theatre workshops and to create a platform to share this material with the audience via a devised show. The implication was that the teens were ready and willing to begin conversations about such hardships. But when I began facilitating the workshops I found the group reticent to share their experiences. We had created a number of exercises to "break the ice" and to help them feel less shy about discussing what was on their minds, so this reservation came as a surprise both to me and to the settlement worker, who initiated the project.

Such resistance, it turns out, is not unusual in dynamics where participants are prompted to discuss their hardships. Erica Nagel describes how she met similar reluctance amongst community members to indulge in negative memories, noting that "many wanted to ignore the pain of the past and look boldly towards reconciliation with the past or the future of their family. Most interviewers were happy to relate intimate details of their personal and family history, but were reluctant to discuss the conflict [that was the impetus behind this project]" (155).

Through my own experience as an immigrant, and by observing these young participants, I have come to understand that immigrants arrive in a new country with a drive to create a new life and to make the best of their new Canadian experiences. In this "quest" to make Canada home, how much time is devoted along this path for the newcomer to look back, acknowledge the life they left behind, and the loss that comes with that? As one consultant's report argues, "[I]n the settlement process so much of the emphasis is on the newcomer looking forward, moving and settling, that they are not given permission to engage in another important aspect of settlement: looking back" ("Regional Consultations" 6). Hence, Jo-Anne Lee and Sandrina De Finney advocate for facilitators to take time to uncover the topics that are shared, and not take them at face value: "when dealing with sensitive and invisible topics such as racism and sexism, facilitators must be prepared to dig deeper and assess what the stories, whether silenced, untold, contested, or enthusiastically taken up, say and reflect about the participants' lived experiences" (111).

In this 2009 project in Victoria, the process had to make room for the youth to explore their positive memories from home, where, through image work, we would celebrate the events, people, and places that they held dear to their heart, but that had no place in Canada. As our musician played live music to these images from home, participants brought to life scenes that spoke of family get-togethers over food in Egypt and sunny afternoons enjoying birds, flowers, and the shade of large leafy trees in Ethiopia. Connections with grandparents, cousins, and aunts in the presence of dogs, other children, and olive trees were some of the memories by the participant from Uzbekistan;

and sitting at Mount Carmel, gazing down at the vibrant city of Tel Aviv, was the image created by our Israeli participant.

These scenes not only created for our audience a picture of what life was like for our participants, but they also helped to carve out a space in which the youth's memories could be acknowledged and celebrated. This simple step enabled these teenagers to claim the experience of immigration as their own; perhaps that is why they chose to call the performance *Here I Stand*, feeling as though they had finally claimed a space in which they could stand their ground, proud of who they were.

Here, a celebratory approach helped achieve a number of goals. First, through creating and embodying their memories the participants felt a sense of belonging; second, the sharing of these memories reconciled their past, which was a whole other life that involved their culture and their families, with their new Canadian future; and third, the process of the audience witnessing these memories validated their experiences and stories further and made possible the building of community between settler Canadians and newcomers. In the sections that follow, I will discuss each of these points in further detail to show how they worked in practice.

BELONGING THROUGH CREATING MEMORIES

The power of our approach of recreating memories from home was that these memories took on a new life and became part of the immigrant youth's new Canadian identity. This is not a new technique; it has been utilized in reminiscence theatre with the elderly, as first envisioned by Pam Schweitzer, who founded the Age Exchange project in the UK in 1983. Reminiscence theatre is defined as a practice that "uses the strategies and techniques of drama in education to generate the recall of memories and experiences of the elderly" (Prendergast and Saxton, *Applied Theatre* 215). Helen Nicholson explores memory, witnessing, and identity-forming in her work with the elderly; she writes, "One of the social functions of memory is to contribute to shaping the future by providing people with insights into the past and by offering symbolic frameworks through which to interpret contemporary experiences" (269).

In this context, the techniques of reminiscence theatre and the functions of recalling memories proved paramount in creating autonomy and a sense of belonging for our participants. I realized that immigrant youth invest much of their energy each day in trying to figure out their contemporary experiences as they navigate the difficult terrain of fitting in at school, making new friends, and negotiating a new Canadian identity that takes into account their past experiences. The past for this group of youth is incredibly significant as it forms their identity, but this aspect of their experience is hardly noticed or acknowledged in their new environment.

The process of sharing the past, whether the experiences involved are similar or different, provides a space for participants in applied theatre work to know that they are not alone in their encounters with difference. Thus, for instance, Jan Cohen-Cruz explores the implications of story circles where participants practise listening and sharing and discover what it means to move that story from the private to the public sphere. She comments, "Telling personal stories in [story circles] is a way to have a public conversation, to be in relationship with others. Such stories do not necessarily address oppression; they are as likely to be about cultural celebration and individual affirmation" (104). In the next section I will discuss the importance of facilitating a space where participants from the immigrant and refugee community can reconcile their past with their present.

RECONCILING PAST AND PRESENT

The Canadian Council on Social Development (CCSD) conducted a survey with forty-nine immigrant youth between the ages of fifteen and twenty-four living in Toronto, Vancouver, and Montréal. The participants of this study came from Africa, the Middle East, Europe, Asia, the United States, and South America. The purpose of the study was to find out how this demographic, which made up 37% of immigrants that arrived in Canada between the years 1996 and 1998, was adapting to their new country, what their needs were, and if they found adequate support from local organizations. The study revealed the following:

a. [The participants'] key challenges were learning the language and overcoming social isolation.

b. [The participants] were aware of their parents' struggles of finding gainful employment.

c. School was the center of their lives.

d. [The participants] experienced ostracism, bullying, and difficulties with schoolwork.

e. The schoolteachers and staff constituted part of the problem.

f. [The participants expressed an] inability to be totally accepted as Canadians due to their accents and physical features.

g. They felt overwhelmed and alienated by society's rampant consumerism and superficiality. This caused them to feel isolated at high school. ("Regional Consultations")

These findings were reflected in the lived experiences of the participants in the Victoria applied-theatre project. In our workshops, when I asked the group to transform the images of their memories from home into images of their life in Canada, the contrast couldn't have been any starker. Images of family connections and get-togethers quickly transformed into lonely encounters, or tense relations between siblings in a small apartment; sitting languidly under the African sun transformed into playing video games in solitude; and so on. Despite our knowledge that some of the youth escaped very difficult political situations in their home countries, the memories they carried with them were ones that held their home in a special place in their heart. It is very common for immigrants to romanticize their home countries and to carry with them their positive past experiences of community and belonging, because that is what they miss so much upon coming to Canada.

Our process had to take into account that the past was not the same as the present, and that in order to create a positive future participants would need to reconcile themselves to the loss of the life they used to have. As such, part of creating their new identity centred upon bringing the past into the present and forming identities that were shaped by the past. They no longer had to erase their native culture in order to become "Canadian." As Nicholson writes,

> Connecting to the past through recalling personal memories is also a process that invites people to make sense of the present, to locate their lives in relation to public events, and to share and re-evaluate their cultural beliefs, values and aspirations. In this way, memory is intimately connected with the complexity of personal and cultural identities. (273)

Besides reconciling the past with the present, immigrant and refugee youth also have to deal with the added layer of the intergenerational conflict with their parents, which is fuelled by the parents' anxiety that the Canadian culture is replacing and erasing the youth's native traditions and values. The CCSD study includes articles written by second-generation immigrants that further confirm the complexity of this population's experience in the process of settlement. "Don't ever forget where you're from" was common advice given to immigrant children by their parents, even when those children were born in Canada. In this same study, an adult immigrant reflected upon the experience of feeling "trapped, impelled to choose between embracing Canadian mainstream culture and my parents' values and traditions" (1). The study also included the participants' perception that "parents are 99% responsible for intergenerational conflict" (2), and relayed the participants' need for parents to be more understanding and trusting of their children's choices and abilities and to "learn to listen before giving into the impulse to say 'no'" (2). In this section I have discussed the value of creating a space where immigrant and refugee participants could celebrate their memories from home as part of creating their Canadian identity. Now I discuss how the intricate and careful process of witnessing can contribute to the validation of one's experience as a newcomer to Canada.

WITNESSING AS VALIDATION

The process of sharing a personal story in the context of a community-based theatre project involves many stages of reckoning. First, the teller grapples with bringing the story from the place in which they'd kept it private to a space where others could witness it. This process involves the teller making peace with this gesture of sharing, and it includes them learning that the applied-theatre space is a safe one for them to share their personal story. Second, once the teller has told their story, the participant group that is listening to it acts as witnesses. This means they now have the responsibility to hold the story sacred, and to treat it with the care and respect that matches the ethics of engagement established in this space of collective creation; as Cohen-Cruz notes, "Ultimately the role of the witness is to assure that the storytelling experience serves the teller" (105). This second step is one of the most crucial ones, as tellers can often revisit traumatic events in this telling, and the support of the group of collaborators will act as a holding space that can contain the experience and remind the teller that they are safe to share it. Without the support of this second step, the teller may never reach a point of truly feeling empowered enough to share their story with the theatrical audience, people who are strangers to the teller.

When the first two steps are carried out and their benefits reaped by the teller, the third step of the process is sharing the personal narrative with the audience. The audience in this context may or may not be allies of the teller and the group of participants involved in the creative endeavour, but the implication is that they are an integral audience, as opposed to an accidental audience. As defined by Richard Schechner, "An integral audience is one where people come because they have to or because the event is of special significance to them" (*Performance Theory* 220).

In the Victoria group's performances of *Here I Stand*, the audience was mostly comprised of settler Canadians (Canadians who come from earlier waves of colonial settlement), and this meant that the impact of the performance was even more significant for the participants. Although by Schechner's definition this audience does not fit the description of being "integral," I would argue that they are in fact very much integral in that the settler Canadians make up the fabric of society that has the potential to create an inclusive, welcoming, and understanding community for our immigrant and refugee youth. In this case, the settler Canadian audience stands in solidarity with the tellers, as Linda Park-Fuller explains: "[i]n asking audience members to 'bear witness' we are asking them to 'stand in with' the performer/narrator—to inhabit for a moment the narrator's world. [. . .] Witnessing means bringing that experience home to one's own world" (36).

There are, of course, complications when immigrants and refugees begin to unravel their histories and their experiences of hardships and (sometimes) of trauma, since "what the teller has lived with as an everyday occurrence may become unbearable when revealed to people for whom such acts are unacceptable" (Cohen-Cruz 103). Immigrants are often caught in the in-between space for some time, swaying between the past experiences that form their social references and the cultural norms and ways of life of their new home, which inform the way that this society views the immigrant, their past, and their histories. Until one is able to reconcile with the past, the present will be a mixture of hope for a better future and a reminder of the atrocities one has lived with in the past. The audience in this context can act as a reminder of the present, a place from which the immigrant or refugee can begin to formulate their understanding of their new identities and their future. The space where the teller and audience meet is the platform from which true dialogue can begin: one that includes the immigrant's notion of themselves, informed by their past experiences. This exchange is a rare one, where the immigrant for once is the one inviting the audience member into their space, their world, and their encounter. This gesture reverses, in a subtle way, the dominant power dynamic of the immigrant as the outsider, the guest, that has been invited into (or sometimes is viewed as having intruded upon) the world of settler Canadians.

As an exploration of the Victoria project with immigrant and refugee youth shows, the practice of applied theatre couldn't have been more fitting for this type of engagement. Applied theatre is malleable, able to absorb shifts and changes in its process and direction based on what is taking place in the moment. The practice also has imbedded in it processes (non-scripted rehears-als and performances, workshops of exploration that integrate participants' experiences, equal emphasis on process and product) that allow non-prac-titioners to pause, ponder, reflect, reassess, and re-envision the work based on their personal journeys. Scripted work does not lend itself to this sort of flexibility. Because applied theatre is more immediate, it facilitates a way for practitioners to meet participants where they are. This was made evident to me when I was able to shift my initial approach to using reminiscence tech-niques to make space for the participants' memories from home, rather than forging on with the predetermined agenda of exploring their hardships.

My next experience shows me stepping into the role of the performer of my immigrant story. This project teases out the tensions of being involved in work that ascribes to mainstream theatre practices when the process begs for practices rooted in applied theatre. In particular, I will discuss the ethical tensions of representation and collaboration between myself, an immigrant, and theatre practitioners who are non-immigrants.

"ARRIVAL"[1]

In 2013, I was involved in a project that showcased five stories of different people who had immigrated to Canada. I was one of the people whose story was chosen to be part of this initiative. I also was cast as one of the perform-ers in the show, where I played the character from Egypt. I encountered a number of ethical shortcomings in this project, but the ones I will discuss here are twofold: a) the issue of autonomy that participants should have over their stories in projects about their life experiences, and b) the subject of ownership of these stories and the life they take on once they are shared.

In the case of this project, I submitted a written narrative of my story in response to a call put out by a local not-for-profit organization that wanted

---

1   *Arrival* was the name of the performance in question. I have deliberately omitted the name of our director, as well as those of the collaborating team of performers and other artists owing to my critique of this work.

to create a devised performance about the immigrant experience. Since this organization had put together a number of applied theatre projects in the past, I inferred that this project would follow similar protocols of devising and including storytellers in the staging part of the process. When I arrived to the first day of rehearsals, I was surprised to find that the script had already been compiled by the director of the show, and that my story had been cut and pasted into the larger narrative of the piece. My experience, which included a traumatic incident, was there in the script, for all present to read through and witness.

This might not have been a deeply uncomfortable and emotionally difficult experience for me if the process had accounted for my journey as the teller. Unfortunately, those present in the room were dealing with the script as an entity removed from me as the teller. Amongst us in this first reading were designers, the musician, and other actors who were second- and third-generation immigrants. I was the only storyteller present, and I was the only performer who was an immigrant and who could speak personally about this experience. There were conversations about adding accents to signify the origin of those whose stories were being staged, and there were suggestions of wearing masks to represent the cultural origins of those storytellers; I was to wear the mask of Nefertiti, for example. The focus seemed to be on how to display the experiences of immigrants while exoticizing their cultures for what would be our predominantly white settler Canadian audience. Absent from the process was an appreciation of and curiosity about the immigrant experience and what the second- and third-generation Canadian actors could learn about the immigrant journey from people who might have had a similar experience to the actors' relatives and ancestors.

This process related directly to Dwight Conquergood's theorization of the "ethical pitfalls" of performance, which draws attention to what he calls "the curator's exhibitionism" and describes it as the "fascination with the exotic" (7). He goes on to say that these performances "resemble curio postcards, souvenirs, trophies brought back from the tour for display cases. Instead of bringing us into genuine contact (and risk) with the lives of strangers, performances in this mode bring back museum exhibits, mute and staring" (7).

Simply because words in a text have been written by immigrants does not mean that the process will not fall into the traps of appropriation and misrepresentation of people's cultures and experiences. In fact, the danger is even more prevalent in this case because these words are now in the hands of the creative team. If not handled with the care and respect that they deserve, they could end up alienating the very community this project is intended to serve.

The point emerges clearly from Julie Salverson's writing about her experience working as a playwright on a project in Toronto about refugee narratives; the work was called *Are the Birds in Canada the Same?* After the completion of the work, one of the participants described the experience as being "awful" and confessed that he'd had nightmares throughout the process, despite appearing to be happy and engaged during rehearsals (qtd. in Salverson, "Performing Emergency" 185). Salverson discusses the ethical implications of working with people whose life experiences have been traumatic, and acknowledges the complexity of trying to "contain" the pain of someone's experience within the theatrical space ("Performing Emergency" 186). As she puts it,

> Thoughtlessly soliciting autobiography may reproduce a form of cultural colonialism that is at the very least voyeuristic. This is particularly true when the voice of the artist or educator herself goes unexamined; or, when the choices students or project participants make for speech are privileged over choices made for silence, neglecting the highly complex negotiations that are involved in the politics of knowing and being known. ("Performing Emergency" 182)

Judith Ackroyd and John O'Toole discuss similar issues of ownership and power in relation to ethnodrama,[2] drawing out the complexities of using participant stories as performance material and the life that the "data" takes

---

2   Ethnography is the study of people, their culture, and their lives. Ethnodrama is the use of drama to perform the researcher's observations of their research subjects. Points of discussion around this practice have been on the ethics of involving people in the research so they have agency over how their actions and choices are seen, observed, and represented. See Conquergood; and Ackroyd and O'Toole.

once it is shared, staged, and performed; they attest that ethnodramatists enjoy "a lot of control. It is not only power in the presentation but power in the research process too. Decisions are made at every stage of the research and performance process" (52).

As immigrants, we welcome opportunities to share our experiences, not only as a means to celebrate our journey, but also as a means to educate and inform others about the struggles we have encountered. It is not the responsibility of the participant to ensure that ethical protocols are followed in these creative encounters. Rather, it is the responsibility of those facilitating the experience to become informed of the protocols of engagement in applied theatre contexts, where the teller's needs are accounted for in the planning, staging, and performance process.

Here are a number of ways that this process can account for participant autonomy:

1) Treat the stories shared with the respect and sacredness they deserve. Get permission from the teller before altering the story, morphing it, or integrating it into other stories of a similar nature.

2) If a story includes accounts of traumatic experiences, the director or facilitator, or project coordinator, must check with the teller about sharing aspects of this story with the rest of the participants and creative team. Perhaps the teller wants the story included in the performance, but they might wish their identity as the owner of the story not to be revealed to the rest of the team.

3) In cases where the teller is part of the performance, the creative team must check in with the teller that the staging is doing the story justice, and that the performed account neither trivializes the experience, nor sensationalizes it for the sake of including "the juicy bits" (Saldaña).

4) Often, performances that are based on participant experiences treat the experience as though once the story is staged it is set in

stone. This is a grave mistake, as people's lives change, and participants' stories and accounts of their experiences evolve. If this process is about celebrating participants and giving them power and autonomy over their stories, then the creative endeavour must stay true to their experiences and how the participants wish them to be represented.

Creating performances about people whose voices are not often heard can be incredibly fulfilling for both the practitioner working with the group and the participants involved in the telling of their narratives. As I've learned from my personal experience, when the stories are not handled with the sacredness they deserve the experience can paradoxically become disempowering, and sometimes traumatizing for those sharing their personal experience. The work of applied theatre offers us a golden opportunity to delve into this rich world of exploring and retelling these stories that would otherwise remain unexplored by the tellers and those witnessing the performances. The work also demands that we become familiar with the ethical practices of applied theatre, and to be vigilant in being attentive to the needs of the participants whose stories we are working with.

"RETURN TO THE NILE"

The final project I will discuss in this paper is one that took place in St. Catharines, Ontario, with a group of Brock University undergraduate students as my co-researchers in a devised theatre project about the experiences of six local newcomer immigrants and refugees. Here I explore the relationship between students who identify as "Canadian" and the material that they uncover about migrant journeys, which compels the students to explore their less obvious immigrant heritage.

I spoke earlier about collective creation as the method that I adopt when I engage with participants in community-based settings. I carry out a similar process when I work with my undergraduate students. We move from the dynamic of professor and students to that of researcher and co-researchers.

This enables us all to embrace the "foolish witness" status that Salverson offers as a possible solution to the traps of becoming a "tragic witness" or a "paralyzed witness"[3] ("Witnessing Subjects"). This process can be liberating for students as they begin to take ownership of their experiences and to recognize how they are implicated in the narratives they are witnessing. It can also be incredibly frustrating and frightening, as students awaken to the injustices committed toward people they believe they have no right to represent—in other words, toward "the Other."

This relationship with the Other is a contentious one, as explored by Conquergood in his delineation of another one of the "ethical pitfalls" mentioned earlier; this one he calls "the skeptic's cop-out" (8). Conquergood addresses this pitfall through describing how "we find ourselves separated by the whole density of our own culture from objects or cultures [. . .] initially defined as other from ourselves and thus as irremediably inaccessible" (Frederic Jameson, qtd. in Conquergood 43–44). What balance must an arts-based researcher strike between connecting with the narratives presented by our participants and creating the necessary distance to enable us to discover the contradictions that exist within these narratives? These societal, personal, or relational contradictions permit us to avoid depictions of narratives that are either black or white, of victims and heroes. Contradictions bring out the complexity of human encounters with life and reflect that richness in the applied theatre work that we do. Once we as facilitators and practitioners bring that distance in the work we do, we then can create spaces where our participants can enjoy this same process. In this context Prentki defines the "notion of distance" as

---

3   Salverson explores how at times we become paralyzed by the enormity of another's experience that we freeze and stop being able to engage with the material they present us with; on a similar note, audiences can find themselves trapped in becoming a "tragic witness," where they dwell in overdramatizing the tragedy of another's experience as a means of responding to the event. Salverson advocates for us to embrace our foolishness, in that we acknowledge how little we know about another's experience, and that we approach the work from that place of not knowing, and of acknowledging our vulnerability in the face of that; she calls this the "foolish witness" ("Witnessing Subjects").

the "detached eye," that enables learners of TfD [Theatre for Development] workshop participants to explore their lives with both the emotional integrity of lived experience and the critical analysis necessary for understanding that experience in relation to the governing forces of their society. ("Fool's Play" 69)

In my research-based practice, and with Prentki's "notion of distance" in mind, I have learned to involve participants in shaping the narratives of their lives early on in the process. This helps to provide them with a sense of autonomy over the stories they have shared with us, the research team.

In this particular research project with my students, our task was to create a performance based on the immigrant and refugee participants' narratives of immigration. By inviting these members to our rehearsals early on in the process, we discovered that they did not want our performance to depict their harsh life experiences. Instead, they wished for us to celebrate their heritage, their culture, their memories from home, and to depict their lives in Canada with hope of success and prosperity. The process took several months for us as the research team to uncover the participants' memories from home and their stories of settling in Canada, and to tease out what we knew to be the harshness of living in a foreign land without familiar people and cultural norms, and without a sense of true belonging.

In the midst of all this, I observed my students take inspiration from these narratives to research their own migrant backgrounds. Each of them was the son, daughter, or grandchild of someone who had immigrated to Canada. They each had stories to uncover about their family history. This process was unsettling at first, as some of them worked hard to mask this immigrant heritage from their school friends in an effort to "fit in." Others, conversely, grappled with pinning down one thread of ancestry that they could claim belonging to; one student's monologue included him owning his status as a "European mutt" who felt like he had lost something he never even had—a culture.

In this performance, my white "European mutt" student played a Sudanese man, and my Dutch student played his mother. The question of representation arose at some point in our rehearsals. Perhaps the fact that I too am of

Middle Eastern descent and an immigrant gave the students permission to venture into these narratives without fear of being accused of appropriation. But I believe that it was more truly the process that gave them this permission. It was the delicate act of engaging, listening, witnessing, and allowing themselves to be moved and "destabilized" (Levinas 185) by the participants' narratives that allowed the students to play people to whose race they do not belong. Conquergood has sharp criticism for assumptions that playing only your own race and gender is acceptable; he claims that this is "cowardice or imperialism of the most arrogant kind" (8). This was a lesson that my students had the opportunity to learn through experience.

Once we discover our own positionality toward the work we are creating, what then becomes the role of our audience members? Do they become implicated listeners (Salverson, "Witnessing Subjects"), or does our art require more of our audience? Adrian Jackson writes about the delicate process of "seduction and provocation" that occurs when Boalian Forum Theatre successfully draws in the audience so that they feel compelled to intervene in the action of the play in order to right injustice. Outside of the context of Forum Theatre, how can this same process of seduction and provocation enable us to acknowledge and make adequate use of the active role that our audience can play in effecting change in the lives of participants in our theatre experience? I return again to O'Connor and Anderson, who point to how our art transfers from our own bodies to those of our audience members: "[u]nderstanding is created both in and through the body of the actor, but is also understood and felt within the bodies of the audience. The ability of the body to know in ways that are as valid as any other form of knowing is what uniquely positions theatre as a form of research" ("Research" 27). When my students and I performed at the local settlement centre for immigrants and refugees, we noticed how moved our audience was. It is as though the process of embodiment went through two stages: the first was between the participants and our co-researcher/actors, and the second between the co-researcher/actors and our audience. The care and ethical response in each stage enabled the genuine telling of the story and the embodiment of that experience to transfer to our audience, who seemed to receive the narratives with the delicacy they were devised with.

AFTERTHOUGHT

In 2016, our drama department at Brock University hosted a number of world-renowned scholars and practitioners of applied theatre to carry out workshops with our students and regional drama educators on the topic of active citizenship. Dr. Jonothan Neelands, who is a Drama in Education practitioner based in the UK, created a workshop on the immigrant journey based on the illustrated book *The Arrival* by Shaun Tan. We explored issues of loss, separation, and alienation as part of playing out situations in the protagonist's journey. The workshop was engaging in nature and involved the use of a number of Drama in Education conventions. We had not located this migrant's country of origin, nor where he was migrating to, so the topic could be applied to any context. As a closing activity, Dr. Neelands asked half the group to use our smart phones to look up images from worn-torn Syria and he instructed us to hold them up and disperse ourselves in the space, while the other half of the group could walk through and take in these images. Part of concluding this activity was to reflect on how this made us feel. I recall feeling disturbed that this was what a North American participant was left with: images of Syria that were already plastered all over the news and social-media outlets. I had been to Syria in 2002 on a work assignment, and I remembered how magnificent the mosques of Damascus were, and the marketplace that had endless supplies of some of the rarest herbs and spices and merchandise from all over the region. If this were my country, this is how I would want those who might have never been to it to imagine it: as vibrant and thriving. Why is it difficult for some practitioners to envision that the immigrant journey could also be connected to a celebration of the positive aspects of their country and culture? Why must this treacherous journey be forever linked to the predominant impression that media outlets promote? And what picture does that paint of us to our white settler community? What are the ethical implications at play here? And could Dr. Neelands's approach, as well-intentioned as it was, be seen as a perpetuation of the sensationalized images we keep seeing of war-torn countries in media outlets?

CONCLUSION

As Ora Avni writes,

> Yes, we want to "heal." Society wants to heal; history wants to heal.
> But no, a simple "life goes on," "tell your story," "come to terms with
> your pain," or "sort out your ghost" will not do. It will not do, because
> the problem lies not in the individual—survivor or not—but it is
> his or her interaction with society, and more precisely, in his or her
> relationship to the narratives and values by which this community
> defines and represents itself. (216)

I've witnessed and been part of a number of initiatives that were focused on
the immigrant experience in Canada. I believe that there is room for us to
create encounters of genuine curiosity between our newcomer population
and our white settler Canadians. Avni's words remind us that the onus should
not be placed on the newcomer to make peace with their past and to "fit in."
As a society, we have a responsibility to raise awareness, to witness, and to
grapple with our implication in the stories and experiences of immigrants
and refugees.

In my work in Canada over the past decade and a half, I have evolved as
a practitioner, researcher, and participant using applied theatre not only to
engage with the immigrant and refugee community, but also as a way of bringing my own narrative as an immigrant woman of colour to light, and of using
this journey to create spaces for my students to arrive at new understandings
of identity, difference, and encounters with the Other. I have discovered that
the key to finding a balance between the creative vision of the practitioner
and meeting participants at a space where they feel visible and heard is to
bring a humble curiosity to the process. I do not know all the answers; I'm
here to learn; and the experience is one of dialogue and exchange between
my narrative and the narratives of those with whom I'm working. I resonate
with what Dustin Scott Harvey writes,

The principle underlying my work and guiding my curiosity is the beauty found in the connections between strangers. It is found in the way the theatre brings us together, creates a platform for sharing, draws attention to relationships, and humanizes a space. It proposes for a moment that beauty is something real, something to be encountered. (35)

We can never erase ourselves from the experiences of those we are working with. Our implication is already present; we just have to have the courage to unearth it, reconcile with it, and use it as fuel to create connection and motivation for our research to impart change. With art we can create beautiful spaces, and we can look past the atrocities that we know others have witnessed in their lives.

SHIFTING IDENTITIES IN NEW TERRITORIES: CREATING THEATRE WITH AND BY IMMIGRANTS

TAIWO AFOLABI, ANITA HALLEWAS, AND KIRSTEN SADEGHI-YEKTA

INTRODUCTION

In a community devising session one day, a community member asked one of the authors of this paper, "How would you describe yourself?" For all three authors this is a complex question. We are theatremakers, facilitators, and teachers who are also immigrants to Canada. We work with other immigrants, other applied theatre practitioners, as well as with students and community members, using theatre to share and tell the stories of these communities. In conducting this work we are required to explore the identities of others and ourselves and through our own reflections here we see a recurring theme: using fiction as a tool for sharing important social themes that are best related through the effect of distancing. This paper brings various examples of work into dialogue with one another in order to explore the linked discoveries we have made about the shifting nature not only of theatre praxis but of identities themselves.

SELF-POSITIONING OF WRITER/RESEARCHERS

TAIWO

Born in Ile-Ife, in the southwest of Nigeria, Taiwo had his pre-secondary schooling in Ile-Ife before he moved to Jos in north-central Nigeria for his post-secondary education. This internal migration positioned Taiwo to be in a constant state of "double-consciousness," as his identity was influenced by the perceptions of others (Du Bois 4). His experience influenced him to think around questions of border and identity. Nigeria has over two hundred and fifty tribes with diverse languages and Taiwo comes from the Yoruba tribe. Crossing cultural borders made him struggle with his identity because Jos is not considered a northern state, yet the Hausa language, which is generally associated with the northern part of Nigeria, is a major language spoken in Jos. Language, an aspect of culture, brings to the fore reactions around accents, underlining how accent defines identity and how it provokes certain responses from the other who is listening. For instance, when Taiwo was studying in Jos, each time he visited home in Ile-Ife, he was referred to as a Hausa person, even though he does not speak the Hausa language fluently and not everybody living in Jos is from the Hausa tribe. At times, as he perceived himself both in the reality of his birth and the perceptions of the Other, Taiwo felt that he was neither here nor there, but existed in a "liminal" state or "betwixt or between" (V. Turner 97).

Taiwo studied in Jos during a time when there were frequent attacks in the area (2007–2011). The causes of the bloody attacks included religion, tribalism, and politics. However, beyond these horrendous happenings exist long-standing socio-cultural injustices, as well as economic and political instability in the country. Taiwo's experience in Jos encouraged in him the vision to engage theatre as a platform to convey compelling ideas and spark engaging debates about social justice, education, and development. Theatre practice is people-driven, and it is connected to culture, history, and memory. Thus, theatre can be used as a strategy to engender learning, spark participation, and foster cohesive communal values during creative and devising processes.

Four years after leaving Jos, in 2015, he moved across internationally recognized state borders, not as a refugee but as an international student in quest for knowledge. Taiwo's exodus both internally (within Nigeria) and internationally (outside Nigeria) influenced his practice. As a teaching assistant in Introduction to Applied Theatre at the University of Victoria for three years, taught by Dr. Kirsten Sadeghi-Yekta, Taiwo provided guidance to students as they devised performances as part of their community engagements. The challenge of "shifting identities" in diverse sites became imperative as Taiwo performed this role (Bhavnani and Phoenix 4). Thus, in this essay Taiwo reflects on his community and classroom experiences to tease out the nuances involved in working within an applied theatre setting in Canada amongst immigrants and newly arrived youth, especially within the rhetoric of promoting diversity and inclusion in society.

ANITA

Anita was born into an immigrant family in the eastern suburbs of Melbourne, Australia. Her Italian and Dutch parents strove to give Anita and her five siblings a normal Australian upbringing. Their idea of normal meant a distinct absence of immigrant culture to avoid standing out. Both her parents had experienced racism within their new communities; they felt like strangers in their new home countries, not yet part of the community, and did not want the same fate for their children. Since the deaths of both her parents Anita has learnt more about their history, such as the shame her mother carried on arriving in Australia as a refugee. Anita too has brought her own children up as first-generation immigrants; Anita immigrated to Canada in 2008 in pursuit of a pleasure-seeking lifestyle. How much has changed in just two generations: the parent immigrates to flee persecution, the child to seek hedonism.

Having immigrated to Canada from another English-speaking country, Anita's experience of the shifting of cultures is different to that of her colleagues who also write here. The drama-in-education program she studied at university in Australia is very similar to that offered to Canadians; the popular culture she was exposed to as a child was not the same as theirs, but often similar. An immigrant to Canada who is a native English speaker has distinct advantages compared to other immigrants and Anita often felt that she did not have the right to complain about prejudices she experienced assimilating into Canadian culture. Anita, like her parents, was not a visible-minority migrant; however, in a small ski town with low employment opportunities, opening her mouth to speak meant she was often verbally attacked at being another Australian stealing someone else's job. In the ten years since arriving in Revelstoke, BC, her identity has constantly evolved, both with her own growth as a mother, teacher, and theatre practitioner, but also seasonally with the ebb and flow of the ski town she calls home. In the off-season, Anita is a local who contributes as a volunteer, feeling valued and acknowledged as a community member. In the winter, Australians become the loud and obnoxious skier arrivals, and she finds herself more so echoing her parents' behaviour in the hope of blending in.

Her parents' passion for music and theatre (they met in a choir) led to Anita's love for theatre, and in turn to her becoming a drama teacher. After graduating university, she taught drama in high schools in various countries before immigrating to Canada in 2008. In 2014 Anita established the theatre company Flying Arrow Productions (FAP) in Revelstoke. Soon after, she began her master's in Applied Theatre at the University of Victoria, where Anita experienced her own personal and more conscious shift toward social theatre. The most recent and largest project she has undertaken with FAP, *Welcome Home?*, was an intergenerational community-theatre project that Anita focuses on in the pages that follow.

KIRSTEN

Born and raised in the suburbs of Rotterdam, the Netherlands, Kirsten's mother took her to the theatre at a young age: she was around four years old when she saw her first short play. Fascinated by the detailed costumes and props and in love with all actors, she dates the beginning of her theatre career to this experience.

After her post-secondary education, Kirsten volunteered in different parts of Latin America, where she started working in the field of *teatro popular*, characterized by the slogan "democratization of theatre": *teatro del pueblo para el pueblo* (theatre for and by the people) (Rodriguez Silva in Pulido 60). Astonished by this aesthetic quality and the subtle use of social themes in the performances, Kirsten turned her focus toward social theatre.

Finally, she moved to England to commence her doctoral degree in applied theatre. During Kirsten's fieldwork in post-conflict and development settings in Asia and Latin America, her skills in flexibility, linguistics, and collaboration and many others were tested, and she struggled with questions such as: How do the countries' complicated histories—pre-colonial, colonial, and post-colonial—affect practice in these different contexts? What are the practitioners' and communities' histories, and how can a practitioner relate to these histories? Kirsten asked how she could position herself as an out-sider and still interact with cultural differences. Could she, as a practitioner, take sides, whilst simultaneously relating with participants? Even though she felt welcome in these environments and owes the people she shared these experiences a great deal, Kirsten finds the outsider's position a complex one.

The majority of Kirsten's work thus far has been shaped by people she met in these different countries, many of whom are now her inspirations. All of her academic work and practice has taken place outside the borders of her home country. In that sense, Kirsten has always been an immigrant to her field, silently observing the intricate nature of linguistic accents and unshared memories. This has also given her insight into belonging to more than one place. For a few years now, Kirsten has been residing permanently in British Columbia with her Canadian partner, and soon they will welcome their second child: two first-generation Canadians who will be learning English, Farsi, and Dutch at the same time.

Now, as the instructor of the second-year applied theatre class that Taiwo mentioned earlier, Kirsten introduces theatre students to the challenges and joys immigrant employees face in Canada. This work allows her to person-ally reflect on what it means to make theatre in her new home country as an immigrant for different audiences and across diverse languages and cultures.

CONCEPTUAL FRAMEWORK: SHIFTING IDENTITIES

The idea of shifting identities points to the multiplicity, transformation, and transmutation of identities depending on circumstances or experiences. Identity and race have a strong link. Engaging the same concept in their book, *Shifting Identities, Shifting Racisms*, Kum-Kum Bhavnani and Ann Phoenix suggest that this notion shows there can be multiple identities and multiple forms of racism. The idea of shifting indicates that "identities are constantly variable and renegotiable" (Bhavnani and Phoenix 5), hence it is an ongoing process as identities are not fixed. For instance, appearance, race, religion, and sexual orientation can all inform how one is identified. Such shifting of identities, whether intentional or not, may also shift the boundaries of racism, and vice versa. Furthermore, the term shifting connotes an unstable position or direction of identities because identities are formed and informed, exposed or hidden, performed and packaged in a manner that can be propelled by a range of events, ideas, geographical locations and political atmospheres, economic realities, and cultural beliefs.

The constant variability and renegotiation of identity's boundaries, the transformation and temporality of identities, form the critical lens with which we engage in thinking around our practice. An understanding of the shifting nature of identities is paramount because it plays a significant role as we work with diverse communities. For instance, histories, personal experiences, and cultural and socio-political nuances can influence how we identify ourselves and how we are identified.

The authors' community engagement relating to methodological, ontological, and epistemological standpoints share similarities that explore the commonalities and differences in immigrants working with immigrants and refugees in Canada. Our reflections situate ways in which "identities are multiple, relational, historically located and potentially contradictory" (Bhavnani and Phoenix 12). The temporality of identities constantly provides a platform to renegotiate ideas when striving for inclusion and diversity. Thus, the shifting identities of both practitioners and participants become a channel to facilitate agency and create new ways of making theatre in our new home countries. Taiwo, Anita, and Kirsten's experiences help them better understand how to negotiate their practice in ethical ways and to re/think applied theatre practice as immigrants and non-immigrants. They imagine the notion of identity as changing, not static, but constantly renegotiated through social interactions and relationships. Specifically, they ask: How did they conceive their practice before immigrating to Canada and how are their identities performed differently devising in new communities? How does their practice reflect their identities and vice versa? How is their identity conceived/perceived, especially among students and community members?

Finally, when identities shift, the idea of strangeness surfaces. In his book *Staging Strangers*, Barry Freeman considers how the idea of both near and distant strangers has been performed in immigrant theatre, multicultural theatre, and a theatre of global ethics (xxi). Freeman's notion of staging strangeness further reiterates how shifting identities can make one a stranger, especially when one is unfamiliar within new communities because the stranger is by nature no "owner of soil" (Simmel, *The Sociology* 402). Here Taiwo, Anita, and Kirsten are concerned with the socio-political and cultural ethos of shifting identities and of strangeness, especially when considering the treatment of people who are seen as strangers/foreigners/outsiders or immigrants. We are interested in how the notion of shifting identities shapes our practice, either reversing or dissolving our consciousness and perceptions. How does Benedict Anderson's idea of "imagined communities" (6) then affect their applied theatre practice socio-culturally, thematically, and linguistically, since the notion of immigration means that one has moved or, using his preferred term, shifted physically from one geographical location to another and across borders and boundaries (Afolabi, n.p). With such exodus come political implications in the constant struggle to belong and to become part of the new place. In this essay, Taiwo, Kirsten, and Anita therefore set out to find the connections between their practice, the communities of strangers in which they are engaged, and the complexities of their own strangeness.

CASE STUDY ONE—INTRODUCTION TO APPLIED THEATRE COURSE: PROJECT SUMMARY

A second-year applied theatre course at the University of Victoria, British Columbia, acts as a case study for Taiwo and Kirsten to explore the challenges and potential of creating theatre as immigrant facilitators with other immigrants. The course introduces students to applied-theatre practice and offers them the opportunity to develop community-based theatre projects. It also provides students an avenue to practise devising with the knowledge they have acquired. It is a three-unit course and students are engaged throughout the sessions. The particular class Taiwo and Kirsten will discuss in this paper consisted of twelve students: eleven Canadians (born and raised in Canada) and one international student. The class was divided into two groups working with two different communities: one with the Immigrant Employee Support Network (IESN) at the University of Victoria, and one with seniors on a reminiscence theatre project. The first group worked on a commissioned project from the IESN, a group that supports immigrant employees within the university. IESN members were interested in exploring ideas around support and work experiences. Students interviewed the IESN members to share their experiences and staged a performance inspired by the stories. Interviews became a research tool through which students collected stories that then inspired the devising process.

Working as an immigrant can be isolating, especially when the host society is not aware of or does not consider the workers' cultural and linguistic nuances and differences. Founded in 2011, IESN is a support group established by immigrant employees at the University of Victoria to create awareness and provide safe spaces for discussion while also creating opportunities for immigrant employees to gain workplace skills. The network now provides an array of educational workshops and meetings.

During the winters of 2016, 2017, and 2018, students interviewed IESN members who were interested in sharing their stories. They learned that many IESN members were not employed when they first entered Canada because their certificates were not recognized, even though they had degrees from their home countries. Others were at the apex of their careers before they moved here. However, when they entered Canada, many of them had to start all over again. Specifically, many group members were not employed because they did not have the appropriate work experience. Many of them were placed in menial jobs such as house cleaning and they were not even asked about their career/professional development plan. Others had to go to school in Canada in order to receive Canadian certificates. In short, there was a wide range of issues that IESN group members were hoping to discuss by using theatre as a dramatic tool. As this was a commissioned project, students had to work with a predetermined theme. During class meetings, Taiwo and Kirsten explained to the students the need to show openness and a willingness to work with different organizations, especially when the theme had been chosen in advance.

Taiwo and Kirsten were both responsible for providing guidance to students in their devising process. As a teaching assistant, Taiwo facilitated workshops and provided tools, games, and ideas that could assist students in their devising. Performing this task challenged his practice because some artistic/technical vocabulary they used was different than the one in which he had been trained. Language and accent were another challenge. Taiwo had to constantly improvise effective ways to close communication gaps. As the only Black person in the classroom, taking on a leadership role and, for most of the students, providing their first encounter with a teacher from a different culture than their own, Taiwo had to shift amongst multiple identities—imagined, perceived, and real. Prior to this class, he worked with artists and students who either had a similar artistic language for communication or were able to develop one over time, which made collaboration less painful. For this class, it was important to create ways to connect across cultural boundaries.

MATERIALS

For this second-year course, one of the students' first assignments is to study a range of mandatory articles on theatre, refugees and immigration. In the case-study class of 2015, the students read the special issue of *Theatre Research in Canada* on Theatre and Immigration[1] and discussed these in class (Meerzon, *Theatre*). After reading the articles on audible minorities, inequality in Canadian theatre based on linguistic accents, and the ways people connect language accents to IQ (Manole 257), the students were noticeably uncomfortable. The one international student in the group could easily relate to the material in the articles, while the other group members had clearly gained new knowledge on this topic. Even though this knowledge facilitated a shift in their thinking, the students were not entirely confident for the interviews,

---

1   More specifically, see Manole and Ashperger.

as they felt out of place with this client group. As the instructor and as an immigrant employee, Kirsten was on one hand surprised that the students were not aware of the majority of the immigrants' issues, and on the other hand felt that the students' lack of knowledge encouraged her to engage with them, and to teach them practical ways to work with the IESN.

METHOD

The devising process was divided into different parts. After reading and discussing the assigned literature on theatre and immigration, the students received a two-week workshop on interviewing. The main methodological literature Taiwo and Kirsten used on conducting interviews with immigrants was adapted from a range of research centres focused on refugees and disaster responses. Through this rather complete overview, Taiwo and Kirsten strove to steer the students away from formality through instruction in how to be an interviewer and a learner. In class, Taiwo and Kirsten mainly used the term "conversations" instead of "interviews," as one of the main goals was to learn how to have a genuine and open dialogue with the interviewee. Taiwo and Kirsten took the students through listening exercises, showing how they could actively listen to people around them and ways to express interest in what the interviewee told them. Taiwo and Kirsten talked about ways they could encourage the interviewees to expand on their answers with as many details as possible. One of the most prevalent topics Taiwo and Kirsten discussed was how important it is to use the interviewee's own language to ask new questions. It was in this moment Taiwo and Kirsten saw the growth in the students: in class discussions they explained that many of them were not privileged to speak more than one language, and that they did not know what it meant to belong to more than one place. This project gave the students the opportunity to explore how it felt to shift identities in a linguistic sense. It was at this phase that the students started to grasp the joys and challenges of immigrant life. At the final stage of these two weeks, Taiwo and Kirsten took the students through the Six Piece Story exercise through which they were offered the opportunity to dramatize and simultaneously imagine their interviewee

(Vettraino and Linds 73). The majority of the students who volunteered to share their drawings showed obvious stereotypical images of immigrants and refugees. The discussion that followed in the classroom offered the students a space to rethink their initial ideas and to shift these images.

The following stage was the interviews. The client groups were carefully selected. In most cases the groups had approached the university themselves after seeing or hearing about applied theatre. Participants were informed beforehand about the process and they were all aware that their stories would only be used as inspiration for a performance. The interviews with the IESN took place at the university, but at a different building than the theatre department, in order to offer the students a learning experience outside their known environment. As an instructor, Kirsten began the interviews with a short game called "Yes, let's . . . " to encourage relaxation in the room. During this simple game, the facilitator asks the participants to mimic an action by saying, "Let's . . . (massage our faces, for example)." The whole group enthusiastically responds with the words, "Yes, let's massage our faces," after which all participants do the specified action. The facilitator then encourages the participants to come up with other simple actions and to repeat this pattern. The exercise does not necessarily require the participants to get on their feet, so it can be used with a range of age groups and in a variety of spaces.

Two thousand and fifteen was the first time Kirsten worked with the IESN, and all the group members, including the students, seemed more relaxed after the game. The interviews were one on one and the room quickly filled with many stories. It was rare that Kirsten and Taiwo observed any silent or awkward moments. After an hour, the employees had to return to their offices, and the students explained how moved and surprised they were with the stories they had heard. Some of the stories were very hard to forget, some of them were beautiful, and other, more difficult stories were unfortunately part of the interviewee's daily lives. With utter discretion in handling the interviewee's stories, the students began their devising process when they returned the following week.

After the students had sufficient time to discuss their stories, Kirsten asked them a few provocative questions that she hoped would spark reoccurring themes and offer them a starting point for the creative process. Then, Kirsten invited Taiwo and/or upper-year students to mentor the other students with the first steps through a range of movement exercises and musical and rhythmic games, amongst other approaches.

In 2015, the students that were devising a play for the IESN—in comparison to the reminiscence group—struggled to start their process. The challenge was not necessarily the group dynamics, but the students found it difficult to work with the predetermined theme of immigrant employees as well as the sensitivity of the stories they had heard. The international student took a leadership role during this step. As they had been at the beginning of the process, the students were concerned with the socio-political and cultural ethos of strangeness considering that the interviewees' stories were unfamiliar, strange, and unknown to them. Critical then is the question: How can we shift identities to tell others' stories without lived experiences that relate to those identities and realities?

FICTION

Possibly the teaching teams' own experience as immigrants helped the students get over their fears, and once the students had outlined the key themes, they spent many hours editing and turning real stories into fictional ones. The fusion of fiction and fact was pivotal to this process because it provided an opportunity to distance performance from real-life experience. Taiwo and Kirsten specifically did not use verbatim theatre in order to protect the privacy of the employees' stories, to create a more general story that would be accessible to all audience members, and to forego the need of transferring a message rather than provoke audience awareness by reoccurring themes.

In the 2018 case, students used the central metaphor of a hospital workplace with its challenges and celebrations to fictionalize immigrant experiences. Beyond the challenge of trying to understand how things worked in the new "workplace," there were other issues that immigrants obviously experienced. The perceived individualistic and competitive attitudes of the Western world made it more challenging for the new employees because there were no people to talk to.

FINAL PRODUCT

In the end, the students created a performance that aimed to animate the joys and challenges of the lives of immigrant employees. Their stories captured the realities of working and living in a foreign environment where linguistic and intercultural differences can be a daily source of amusement and frustration. After the short performance, the audience delved deeper into this topic through a facilitated dialogue using "actor in role." Taiwo facilitated this exercise, and the audience members actively engaged with the actors on stage. The discussion between a few audience members and actors became quite heated when the topic of employment was raised. The actor who played an unfair employer was asked many critical questions and throughout the discussion the student not only remained "in role," but also managed to offer possible solutions for the issues at stake. Thus, the students used their research efforts and found a way to shift the identity of the role she had taken on.

FACILITATION: SHIFTING IDENTITIES AND STRANGENESS THROUGH LANGUAGE AND ACCENTS

Taiwo understood his responsibilities as a facilitator in animating the devising process as he constantly crosses borders and boundaries, translates experiences from the past into the present, and explores how these integrate into the machine of devising understood in the new culture in which he is presently located. Thus, the idea of shifting identities spoke to the ways he needed to move across an array of experiences and artistic expressions. For instance, he found it shocking and strange that the use of technology, especially YouTube, inspires artistic creation in the Canadian classroom. Some students even incorporated ideas from videos, shows, or movies they had seen in the past. In Taiwo's previous experience, the devising process was not inspired by such ideas. In fact, in his culture, he always wants to create an ensemble without any influence from previously created works. Thus, shifting between known ways, materials for devising, and methods of practice into a newly different landscape was strange yet imperative for his personal artistic growth. Taiwo constantly queries: How will Canadian artists shift gears if they find themselves devising and collaborating in an environment with little or no access to the digital world?

Secondly, language shifts create strangeness because language not only expresses identities but also constructs them in the same way that an accent creates assumptions about geographical and cultural identities. David Evans's book *Language and Identity: Discourse in the World* explores the interrelationship between language and identity and shows how accents consciously and unconsciously influence people's perception of the other. Language shapes social discourse and perception of minority ethnolinguistic communities because language serves as a tool in shifting identities. For instance, in this new devising environment, Taiwo's choice of words, especially when giving instructions, seemed unclear to some students. He found himself repeating instructions multiple times as well as giving paralinguistic clues and using a variety of synonyms in order to be understood, presumably because of his accent. In this scenario, language served two purposes: it both constructed and disrupted strangeness. Over time, Taiwo developed a working language with the students as they collaborated and learnt to understand each other.

Looking back on Kirsten's many encounters in the classroom as an immigrant instructor, she recalls the laughter that ensued after silly linguistic errors, her enormous expectations that were fulfilled by the students, and the creative and magnificent end results. Most importantly, she recalls the many ongoing questions she still has as an instructor, which will hopefully shape her practice more critically. After working in countries such as Brazil and Nicaragua where younger people do not avoid overtly political stances on stage and get on their feet immediately through music and songs, Kirsten noticed that in Canada it takes more time to start the creative process. At the beginning of each class Kirsten would be the instructor; quickly thereafter, she would become a facilitator, mentor, teacher, and co-deviser, leading students through warm-up games and improvisation exercises while illustrating the possibilities of fictionalization, movement, and music. The students handled the sensitive material of the interviews with great care, while at times Kirsten wondered how they would react if the situation had a greater urgency and they lacked the time to overthink the issues at stake. Would that create an immediate shift in their thinking and creative process?

ANITA'S CASE STUDY: WELCOME HOME?

In the same province, but almost a thousand kilometres away, Anita conducted an intergenerational theatre project with the community of Revelstoke between October 2016 and June 2017. More than a hundred and fifty residents participated in the project: an impressive figure in a town of 6,760 people. The project began with an interest in exploring the community's attitude to sponsoring a refugee family; Anita was surprised by a newspaper survey that stated 53% of respondents did not want the Syrian family to come. The survey might not have been scientific; however, it still suggested Revelstoke was unwelcoming and fearful of change. Anita's work began with a town-hall meeting to discuss the project; the project would be the first of its kind in the community where scripted productions in traditional performance spaces were the norm. The project was intended to be highly collaborative to allow for community ownership: an opportunity for applied theatre to transform the community. The transformations Anita sees in her community practice are varied: the joy of people collaborating, new friendships and camaraderie, engaged audience members, and children and youth learning during workshops. The project began with workshops designed as a means to collect data that would be used later to devise the play *Welcome Home?* which was performed as a site-specific performance at the Revelstoke Railway Museum.

APPLIED THEATRE WORKSHOPS FOR DATA COLLECTION

Twenty-two workshops were conducted with children, youth, adults, and seniors to engage a cross-section of the community. A workshop held for preschoolers explored the theme of judging others on their appearance and associated stereotypes, and was a modified version of a workshop designed by

John O'Toole and Julie Dunn, *The Giant Who Threw Tantrums* (O'Toole and Dunn 40–54). Children playing the roles of community members engaged with the giant (Anita in character). Both in and out of role, the children wanted to support the giant, offering friendship and solutions as to how she could better connect with the community. Anita noticed during this workshop how easily young participants engage with the content and the task of role-playing; it is a natural and innate act for children. In contrast, shifting Anita's position from one of authority (mother/teacher) to one of playfulness can be difficult; how do you stay in character and still answer the questions of the children (many of the children in the room knew Anita as the mother of their friend)? In addition to this, how do you encourage playfulness with parents whom you know from the supermarket aisle and the bank? Anita always enjoys the surprise experienced by parents when they observe the incredible empathy their children have in a simple situation of genuine acceptance, regardless of a person's size/shape/ethnicity.

Workshops with school-aged children occurred with two classes exploring themes of racism, displacement, and stereotyping. Anita had the advantage of knowing one group from previous drama workshops; they were familiar with her manner and the role she played as teacher-facilitator. Their positive association with Anita in this role meant they were excited for the classes and were supportive of her presence, which in turn allowed for faster capacity building. This greatly contrasted Anita's experience with the preschoolers: where the preschoolers saw their friend's mother, these children saw a drama teacher. Regardless of the setting, children meeting Anita for the first time comment on her accent; Anita's response is a playful one, "No, *you* have an accent!," at which they laugh, thinking Anita absurd. Her many roles— teacher, mother, immigrant—often clash in the classroom. With the shifting of how participants view her identity comes a different expectation for her own performance.

The school workshops required modifications after the first week, as Anita's initial plans had been too heavy in content (she had spent too much time thinking about the refugee crisis and not enough time thinking about the overarching themes of the work). She needed to add more fiction and playfulness to the drama. The idea of fictionalizing drama is not new, and is a concept supported by many practitioners,[2] including her colleagues writing with her here. It is a strategy Anita should have used from the outset. The use of fiction is something she studied during her time at the University of Victoria, and a strategy used globally and a skill Anita has worked to perfect since moving to Canada—a shift in her own practice inspired by those in her new geographical location. Although she was attempting to explore messages of racism and stereotypes, Anita was in a classroom with almost completely white Canadians. Their own experiences of racism (witnessing or experiencing) were minimal and so the lessons needed to explore the same themes in ways that were meaningful to the participants' personal experiences.

To cope with these challenges, Anita designed a workshop based on the children's picture book *Extra Yarn* by Mac Barnett and Jon Klassen to explore the themes of excluding others and love winning out over hate. The children identified with the themes of the workshop and afterward they were able to discuss how those themes might connect to their everyday lives. Anita was initially wary of using the *Extra Yarn* workshop with an older teenage group during the same project due to taking its inspiration from a children's book. Her prejudgment was ill-founded; the teens connected with the simple message of the story and Anita was once again reminded at the value of fiction in allowing participants to explore deeper and sometimes darker topics. The teen participants commented at how inspired they were by the theme of love winning over hate (there was a discovery of mutual passion for the topic), which led to discussions of recent events in the media (the election of Donald Trump and mass shootings in schools) where they found useful real-life connections to the theme. The continued success with the workshop encouraged Anita to modify it for an abstract-painting workshop held later that month. By extracting key theatrical moments from the workshop Anita discovered it was the simple message that provoked powerfully evocative abstract paintings with labels such as hater, cruel, redeemed, and forgiveness.

---

2   See O'Connor and Anderson; Balfour et al.; Clark et al.; and Prendergast and Saxton, "Seduction."

These canvas paintings were later hung at the opening of the devised performance to encourage further community conversation on the topic. When continuing with the teenage group, Anita created a workshop inspired by the myth of Pandora's box and John William Waterhouse's painting of the same title, which resulted in a powerfully written social poem created by the participants. This social poem would later be used verbatim as the final lines in the devised play *Welcome Home?* The workshop appealed to the teens (and again to the adults and seniors Anita worked with later), possibly because the story of Pandora strikes a universal chord; Greek myths are something many generations and nationalities are familiar with, and this worked in Anita's favour.

REFLECTION: HOW DO IDENTITIES SHIFT IN THE FACILITATION PROCESS?

Each youth and adult workshop ended with feedback and discussion. Two of the youth members were new immigrants from the Philippines. They were also the only new participants in the youth group; Anita had been working with the other teens in various theatrical capacities for many years and had grown to be their mentor (another identity). Anita initially found engaging those young women in discussions challenging; they appeared shy and reluctant to share their thoughts and feelings. Was it due to a lack of vocabulary? Or a cultural difference? These young women were grappling with their own identities in this new community. They were a visible minority, learning a new language and living in a town in which just over 4% of the population identified as a visible minority. Revelstoke is strikingly white. Although Anita could empathize with them as another newly arrived immigrant (something they were surprised to learn Anita was), there were other aspects of their newness that Anita did not share in: standing out in this town of white people and learning the language and its idiosyncrasies in order to try and fit in were never big issues for her. The whiteness of the town meant that workshops were often filled with Anglo Canadians, some of whom had never left town and others who had migrated from other communities, provinces, and colonial nations (Australia and Britain predominantly). A contrasting realization

occurred when Anita conducted an evening workshop with the adult participants. The goal of this workshop was to demonstrate the value of using
fiction versus real-life testimony to demonstrate useful strategies in planning
for future devising. Anita used a man's story who had escaped persecution
in Damascus; the testimony shared the moment he fled for his life, detail-
ing conversations, threats, and fears. The testimony was read as a "lure" for
the workshop participants, as a way to draw workshop participants in. The
workshop then compared this refugee's testimony to that of Douglas Adams's
fictitious refugee, Arthur Dent, from the *Hitchhiker's Guide to the Galaxy*.
The intention was to compare Arthur Dent to the "real" refugee in order to
demonstrate how fiction can distance an audience and allow them to better
see the themes and problems in a particular story. The irony and paradox were
that this workshop, specifically the testimony from the Syrian refugee, triggered a sense of despair in one workshop participant. This participant wrote
to Anita after the event stating that she was unsure if she could continue with
the process if the following workshops would be the same. This participant,
an Anglo Australian–born Canadian in her sixties, had never personally fled
war, but had worked as a medical doctor in war-torn and developing countries in the eighties and nineties. The story Anita had used in the workshop
reminded her of the many stories that had been shared with her by survivors
during those years. This reaction resonates with Julie Salverson's argument
that theatre based in naturalism can create an "aesthetic of injury . . . [and]
reinscribe a victim discourse that sustains the psychic residues of violent histories, codifying the very powerlessness they seek to address" ("Transgressive"
35). In this case, Anita had not taken her own advice of using fiction as a sensitive way to explore complicated topics. Another lesson this situation taught
her is that working with a very white and mostly non-immigrant audience
does not automatically equal no risk of previous trauma or emotional injury.
This learning required a shifting in Anita's own understanding of her fellow
community members and a reminder to not make presumptions based on
ethnicity, colour, or background.

The adult workshops were always a stark contrast to working with the
children and youth. There was an enduring reluctance for adult participants

to engage physically in the workshops, confirming Anita's previous thoughts relating to age and ease of participation in drama. Adults need to shed so many layers of labels to shift those identities and individual histories. Shaking off these layers in order to accept play as a genuine medium of reflection and discussion requires a strong commitment and confidence. When children are encouraged to role-play in workshops, they readily welcome the identity shift, playing different characters faultlessly and seamlessly. Canadian adults struggle with this identity shift. Working as an adult facilitator with others who do not always see you in this role has its own challenges, too. Anita's experience in Revelstoke stands in stark contrast to Kirsten's in Brazil, where play and getting up on your feet is more normal, even for adults. During the workshops, Anita often reflected on the presence of each adult sitting with her and their frequent unease with *physically* shifting. Did they feel their presence there was enough? Could they have been encouraged to share or participate more? Why was the snow play of skiing so easy for them and this so difficult? Each evening Anita consciously made decisions on how to set up the room: Would she be *acting for* the participants? Or was she hoping for a genuine participatory process? Anita was often plagued with fear that with the snow/rain/cold no one would come at all. Her own identity insecurities came into play, too: many of the adults sitting before her were highly educated, preachers, Ph.D. recipients, older and wiser community members. Workshop topics included hatred, scapegoating, abandonment, and the poor treatment of First Nations people, and these participants very often knew more on these topics than she did. How would she manage that? How could she ensure that each voice was heard? How could she facilitate valuable, respectful, and collaborative discussion? By slowing down the process and engaging in listening and hearing through a genuine dialogical approach participants were more evenly placed on an equal footing with the facilitator (and other participants, regardless of their own identity, education and background), reminding that every voice is important (Freire 87–92). Participants can feel more engaged in the process with the intention to encourage participants to share, speak out, and respond more openly. This process requires trust and safety and is built through strong relationships over time.

CONCLUSION

Both of these case studies reflect on the shifting identities of facilitators and participants. Anita, Taiwo, and Kirsten's community engagements, as examined here, constructed, deconstructed, and reconstructed realities, demonstrating how practice changes over time and how perceptions make identities shift, thus validating and at times disrupting assumptions. Through facilitation and devising the authors constantly create ways to invite our communities into the creative process. As facilitators and immigrants, shifting identities in their communities and in the classroom, especially engaging on issues such as diversity and identity, raises many questions. How did participants respond to moments of strangeness in the collaborative process? Did the participants' experiences in these theatre processes assist them in shifting toward building empathy? Finally, to what extent has their practice shifted due to new ways of engaging with people in the spaces in which they have found themselves? The very act of reflection allows the writers as practitioners to step back and view their practice from different angles and in new ways. The benefits, challenges, and limitations relating to their practice as immigrants and theatremakers will continue to change over time as their roles evolve and their understanding of their new homes also shift.

ON MOBILITY, RESONANCES, AND MAKING A LOVING

LISA NDEJURU

"Making a loving" was a funny typo. A lapse. I wanted to write that I have to make a living. It kept coming up, and I think it fits.

It is 4:33 a.m. in Kigali, Rwanda. It is still the day before, 10:33 p.m., in Montréal, Québec. Both places are home. Sitting here in Kigali, trying to engage with "the historical, artistic, educational and methodological influence immigrant theatre artists had, could have had, or did not have, on the development of Canadian theatre and performance stages, both in English and French, and/or other languages," I am trying to think and articulate my own experience as a theatre artist and scholar who works across space and time (Meerzon, "Call for Papers").

HISTORY

Most people know Rwanda because of the genocide perpetrated there against the Tutsi in 1994. Fewer people know about the previous three decades of persecution, imprisonment, and exile.

My paternal grandfather, like many others, was assassinated in Rwanda in 1962. My other grandfather was imprisoned, then he managed to flee to neighbouring Uganda, where he lived in a refugee camp with his wife and children until his death. My mother, too, was imprisoned when she was eighteen years

Fig. 1. Rwanda—"the land of a thousand hills"—is one of Africa's geographically smallest and most densely populated nations. Photo by David Ward.

old, shortly before she graduated from high school. Later, she and my father met on a dance floor while Salvatore Adamo sang "Inch Allah." Growing up, our family story only ever started on that dance floor, with that song. I was told nothing about what came before.

I was born in Rwanda but raised in Germany: my father had been allowed to leave the country on a six-month scholarship. I was a toddler when my mother and I joined him in Köln. He managed somehow to prolong his permit, worked three jobs to provide for us, and studied for ten years, eventually receiving a doctorate. We immigrated to Canada in 1982, when I was twelve years old. It wasn't until 1990, after a difficult adaptation to Canadian life and a troubled young adulthood that I went with my family to Africa, to Uganda, to visit my grandparents, and I saw the reality of the Rwandan Tutsi refugee camps. That was also the first time I met aunts, cousins, and uncles, kin, some who were soldiers, sometimes seasoned soldiers, who had fought in the Ugandan army, young warriors preparing to fight for the right of the refugees to return to Rwanda. I remember falling in love with these people I looked like, feeling a sense of belonging even when I could not agree with the war. Did I agree with the status quo of the refugee camps, my cousins would ask. And of course I could not do that either. My research and creative practice were born out of irreconcilable differences I did not know how to hold simultaneously. My comprehension broke down completely four years later, when the genocide took place. Watching the horror unfold on TV in Montréal, I could not understand how we could see it but not stop it. It was the end of reason. I had no words, only an incredible drive to find ways to make sense of it.

"We have to talk about this," I would tell anybody who would listen.

ART

Theatre, performance, and community art have given me tools to talk about the incomprehensible. They have afforded ways to channel the driving need to process these events, individually and as part of a community. And I have been able to continue and push both the reflection and dialogue through writing and performing my work.

I struggle with my position. On one hand, it makes sense to situate oneself and think about issues from a single perspective. If I were writing in Montréal, I could think of myself as an "immigrant theatre artist"—a person coming from "elsewhere" with a "different" experience and "different storytelling ways." I could explore how or whether my work and that of others like me might transform—or not—experiences and storytelling in ways and spaces called "Canadian." But sitting here in Kigali, knowing I am going back soon to Montréal, committed to coming back to Kigali and unsure how living and working in both spaces with my family will play out, that description feels too small and restrictive. It doesn't allow for the transnational back and forth, for the broadening resonance I feel when the themes I am working on or through reverberate in many places.

I keep thinking that this idea of mobility should not be new, since artists travel all the time—touring, for example. Festivals are also all about artists from everywhere gathering and showcasing their work. Or when the works of person X, created in place Y, are retold in place A by people B . . . like in the story I heard during a Postmarginal[1] symposium in Montréal this summer. A magrebine actor and director remembered how "back home" everybody (whole casts) played Molière or Shakespeare and no one thought they were being "diverse." He was saying this in response to often-disingenuous concerns about realism and representation served up to him to explain the lack of roles for diverse actors in the theatre. He smiled bitterly as he told the story. To me it raised interesting questions about the colonial legacy of culture (or the cultural legacy of colonialism). What does it mean to play Molière and Shakespeare in the francophonie or the commonwealth? Listening to him I felt as though he was suffering insult on top of injury: having trained extensively in the fine arts, in the canons of universal (or so presumed) high culture, to then be denied access to what he thought to be a common repertoire.[2]

EDUCATION

I do not come out of traditional theatre/performance training or practice, nor is my academic trajectory a purely theatre or performance-based one.

I fell in love with theatre at seventeen while studying in a French private school in Montréal that my immigrant mother was starving herself to pay for. When I told her I wanted to pursue a career in theatre, she cried and cried and begged me not to condemn my family to a life of poverty. It felt quite

---

1   Postmarginal is a series of symposia and reflections inspired by the work of Toronto's Modern Times Stage Company. The first three-day event, co-chaired at Brock University by Associate Professor Natalie Alvarez and Ric Knowles (professor emeritus at Guelph university), Beyond Representation: Cultural Diversity as Theatrical Practice, took place in Toronto in April 2017. Inspired by the tradition of interdisciplinary work of MT Space's artistic director Soheil Parsa, the event meant to bring together various scholars, critics, and practitioners to investigate whether and how the MT process of working with artists of every culture could in some way contribute to the debates concerning the diversification of Canada's stages.

2   Other professionals face similar devaluing of their skills and training when immigrating, but they often retain the possibility of qualifying through retraining. Retraining would not address the challenge he faces as an actor whose work by definition is to personify a character, i.e., someone else.

tragic at the time, as though something I needed to do, like breathing, was forbidden. And so theatre—writing; dance; performance; applied, community, and therapeutic theatre; work in new media—became something I did in creative, community, therapeutic, and educational spaces . . . and rarely, if ever, for money.

This summer, three decades later, I felt grateful to my mother for the very first time. Attending the Postmarginal symposium in Montréal and looking at diversity in the Québec theatre scene, I felt as though she had protected me: I have not had to face a dearth of roles or funding as an actor or theatre-maker because I am racialized. Nor have I had to confront any of the other vexing "diversity" issues Donna-Michelle St. Bernard so powerfully exposes in "What Did You Say About My Mama?"

Instead I resonate with St. Bernard when she writes, "[I]t feels like we are alternately saying 'stop treating us as alien to the mainstream' and at other times 'recognize us as different, and give us the resources to assert our (aesthetic, cultural, linguistic) difference'" (98). And when she asks, "Can we reconcile the coexistence of these stances?" (98) I believe not only that we can, but even more, that it is in everyone's best interest if we do.

NOT ONLY OURS

St. Bernard asks, "What are we supposed to do . . . if we don't want to conflate colour with culture, if we don't want to self identify as marginalized, or to disregard the shared experience of colonized peoples, or to become a generic mush called 'diverse people'?" (98) I believe we should not have to do any of those things. We could instead claim access to more and multiple registers. And what if doing so could afford a broader range for everyone?

MAKING MEANING

I have created and enjoyed rather open and welcoming spaces in my theatre "career." But then, I have never yet tried to make a living in those spaces. Mostly I have tried to make meaning. In 1996, for example, multidisciplinary artist

Armenian Canadian Lusnak Abdalian produced an event called *Genocides* at the Gesù in Montréal. Painters, musicians, and other performers from communities impacted by genocide all brought their works forward. Lusnak had invited me as a Rwandan, and I created a piece with two members of what would become Isangano, Montréal's cultural group of young Rwandans. In it I played with traditional Rwandan dances to highlight their vital role for my community.

During three decades of exile beginning in 1959, those steps and rhythms and songs were the same you would find everywhere Rwandans were in the world. In "I couldn't join in, but I understand" (2012) I wrote:

> I remember how during the late 80s and early 90s the mobilization of the Rwandan diaspora was in large part about political education. What grew into the Rwandan Patriotic Front (and later developed into an army) began as a political movement with a vision for the future. That's what Rwandans inside and outside of the country were attracted to: an inclusive, diverse, democratic society where all could live in dignity and work together.
>
> When I met members of the RPF/RPA in Kampala in 1990 as they were preparing for war, I could not imagine joining their armed struggle. But I understood it. I had just visited family members living for years in squalid refugee camps. That kind of life certainly was not viable.
>
> Many young Rwandans my age from Montréal, Ottawa, Québec City, Toronto—my friends and cousins—and others from the USA, Belgium, and France—joined exiles living in the countries bordering Rwanda to fight a four-year guerrilla war for the right to return.
>
> People I loved were changed forever. When I saw my cousin K in 1996, he was a different person, made distant—hardened, maybe— by war and by the experience of witnessing genocide. (from *Le petit coin intact*)

When the war for the right to return broke out in 1990, those drums and dances were the heartbeat of a worldwide diaspora mobilizing. The songs and the dances and the rhythms sustained us. Then came the songs of mourning. The genocide against the Tutsi in 1994 was more than anyone could comprehend. More than a million of our people were slaughtered in one hundred days. It was a rip in the fabric of our understanding.

I don't remember what we called that first public performance in 1996 at Le Gesù. I had written and performed a text reflecting on what it meant to dance those traditional Rwandan dances, which spoke of a golden, almost mythical Rwandan past, of beloved cows and kings in urban contemporary North American or diasporic spaces. I worked with members of my traditional Rwandan dance troupe. It was a very important event. The pianist Pierre Jasmin—who had just returned from playing in the Balkans with the Québécois organization Les Aartistes pour la Paix—stood up after the performance and told us how much he connected with the work, and it moved me because it meant we could touch people beyond our own community. Apart from a cassette tape with a recorded heartbeat, I did not document or keep anything of the performance. It was the first time I had been invited to work with a professional producer, who helped me translate my vision to the stage with sound and lighting. Our choice to shift from the sound of drumming to that of a heartbeat and back was one of our ways to evoke the many anachronisms and contradictions we navigated in dancing and playing with the *va-et-vient* between identities, traditions, the present and future.

During these years I wrote a lot, but did not leave any traces. My father challenged me: "If you want to be taken seriously, you have to publish your work." In 2002 I wrote *Je me souviens*.[3] I published it in *Montreal Cultures*[4] and then performed it with the Isangano troupe as invited artists at an open-door event at the National Theatre School in 2003. There were no pictures.

---

3   Even though my piece also references the motto of the province of Québec, I knew nothing of the late Lorena Gale's work of the same name.

4   *Montreal Cultures* was the now-defunct magazine published by Culture Montréal, a gathering of Montréal citizens, artists, and cultural institutions that came together in 2002 to co-shape the city's first-ever cultural policy. Please see culturemontreal.ca for more information on the *regroupement* and its current activities today.

Yana Meerzon writes, "Immigrant theatre, based on the principles of amalgamation and continuity, adapts to the new social, economic, and cultural structures of its projected audiences" ("Theatre and Immigration" 185). In writing *Je me souviens* I was speaking to my new reality, specifically to the Québec nationalists in my life. People I worked with and loved. During the referendum in the 1990s, a friend's father, exasperated, had ranted at me that immigrants should never have been allowed to vote because they could not possibly understand the issues or what was at stake. I responded with a ninety-minute piece of storytelling, traditional Rwandan dance, and performance. I wanted it to say, "As a newcomer I can appreciate your struggle for survival, for belonging, for recognition. As an African I support your struggle for emancipation. But I come from a place where the *vivre ensemble* failed completely, where purity was a pretext for segregation, and where for decades minorities were persecuted and killed. I need us all to get along. So if we cannot find a common horizon, I cannot take up your battle."

Je me souviens also came out of a reflection inspired by my role and service on the Culture Montréal steering committee, which aimed to

Ancrer la culture au cœur du développement de Montréal
par des activités de réflexion, de concertation et
des interventions structurées autour des citoyens,
des créateurs et du territoire.[5] ("Notre mission")

Culture Montréal was a "citizens" movement created in 2002 to accompany the launch of the city's first municipal cultural policy. Simon Brault, then head of the National Theatre School, who today heads the Canada Council for the Arts, was president, and around the table sat the heads of Montréal's biggest cultural institutions, like Cirque du Soleil, the museums, Héritage

---

5   "Anchor culture to the heart of Montréal's development through reflection, consultation, and structured interventions around the city's citizens, artists, and territory" (my own translation).

Montréal, Présence autochtone, as well as representatives of the Festival du Monde Arabe de Montréal, Les Filles électriques, and Journées de la culture.

I had not been elected to the steering committee. Rather, I was co-opted as a Black person representing a cultural minority and as a (relatively) young person representing emerging cultural workers. I had participated in Culture Montréal's first open round-table dialogues to mobilize Montréalers to organize for an inclusive and exciting cultural future. Not having been elected to the steering committee, I was conscious of not representing anyone and felt that I did not have a real mandate. I could have seized the opportunity to build a different constituency than the one I ended up choosing. I thought long and hard about to whom I would want to be accountable, of whom I believed I was actually a part. I could have chosen to go with the racialized, "Black," or immigrant communit(ies), the emergent generation of creators, but I chose to engage the Rwandan community I was more or less on the sidelines of, more or less involved with, more or less recognized by, constantly pushed and pulled into and out of.

I chose this community because of the questions I had always carried around with me as I was dancing cows and kings in modern urban diasporic spaces. Because of the pull I feel for the songs and the voices of my elders, even though I don't understand what they say. I chose that "us" because I had been obsessed with our community ever since 1990, when I went back to Africa for the first time since leaving in the 1970s and saw the massive global mobilization and exodus of young men enlisting in the war for the right of the Tutsi to return to Rwanda. Because obsessed was not enough of a word to qualify my preoccupation after 1994 and the genocide, due to my desire to contribute and help make sense of things.

Je me souviens was about the things we are left with, the ruptures in our fabrics. About the history that made it so I cannot speak to my grandmother because I don't speak the Rwandan language. I chose to work with the Isangano dancers again on this piece because dance is a language my grandmother and I have in common. Something I can do to make her smile. At the same time it was about how slowly a language—that is, a consensual common set of references—is created and how quickly the common ground can be destroyed. If I took the dances my grandmother knew and loved that spoke of cows and kings and a golden age of precolonial Rwanda and changed the music, changed the costumes, changed the movements, changed the story to speak of the urban contemporary spaces we inhabit today, I would be killing a vital relational, replenishing function the dance held for the entire community. Historian Mircea Eliade writes about the resacralizing role of ritual (23). I played a long time with that ambivalence of the traditional and the contemporary: dancing traditional movements to Bobby McFerrin's 1990 album *Medicine Music*, wearing both traditional costumes and jeans. And although my community is a very supportive one that attended my explorations as I was doing them, I didn't carry those ideas through to the end. They were a rupture I was not willing or able to fully assume.

Meerzon writes that immigrant theatre "is not binary; it presents cultural and cognitive synaesthesia and originates as a fusion of the artists' inherited cultural traditions and those of a new world, so it repeatedly stages the tension between continuity and difference" ("Between Je and Moi" 291). Ultimately *Je me souviens* was about my relationship with a memory that is and is not my own, about dislocation and the feeling of loss of continuity, of feeling Othered, of not understanding the origins of the challenges facing us as people of Rwandan descent, yet feeling responsible for them or somehow misshapen. It was about feelings of inadequacy, guilt, and powerlessness. I was claiming Rwandan symbols of the drum, the warrior, and the gentlewoman, characters in traditional dancing. They, the cows, and the king were my chosen symbols of an aspiration to authenticity. This choice, in turn, raised a whole other set of critical questions: What do authenticity or integrity even mean, when I know how destructive ideas of purity can be? I wanted to engage with colonialism, Christianity, war, and genocide. And ultimately I cared about generativity. What I mean is that I am more interested in the future than I am in pointing fingers or in laying blame.

In 2003 I went to Baghdad with Canada's Iraq solidarity team to join Voices in the Wilderness, an international activist organization formed to protest US-imposed sanctions and war. After Rwanda's war and the genocide, I had been very involved in peace work and non-violence, and what that might mean concretely, not after the fact, but before. Our roles as part of the team were to provide first-hand accounts to our home countries and networks of solidarity that were supporting us in our efforts and the larger struggle against the war. I wrote a lot in Baghdad. I wrote *La guerre est une danse lente* for the Iraq peace team and performed it on one of the last evenings we sat huddled in the Aldar Hotel, translating it into English as I went:

> La guerre est une lente danse, a slow dance with an unknown outcome. Nothing like uninterrupted news coverage on TV. Comme pour l'amour au cinéma, il manque les temps morts, les coups de coude, l'inélégance. Je ne sais pas pour vous mais pour moi c'est plus lent, plus terrible peut-être que ce que j'avais compris.[6]

I was thinking of Iraq as a proud daughter of an old and wealthy family and the US as a beau turned bully . . . there was a time they had gotten along, but then when he wanted to own her wealth and she declined, it got ugly.

> Aujourd'hui elle est toujours très belle. Ses mains portent la trace du temps. Elle reste très droite. Digne surtout. Moins insouciante. Elle a appris a faire plus avec moins. Elle n'en veut pas à ses frères mais aux dires de certains, elle est restée arrogante.[7] (*La guerre est une danse lente*)

The piece was an homage to the history, hospitality, civility, and sophistication of Baghdad, the city I encountered. Meeting people allowed such a

---

6 "Just as with lovemaking in the movies, you don't see the awkward parts, where it stops, where an elbow accidentally jabs you, the inelegant bits. I don't know how it is for you, but I have found it slower, more terrible maybe, than what I had previously understood" (my own translation).

7 "Today she is still very beautiful, her hands show the passage of time. She still stands straight and very dignified. She is less careless and has learned to do more with less. She does not resent her brothers, but some say she is still arrogant" (my own translation).

different appreciation than what we could understand from Western media accounts.

Back in Montréal, visual artist Eva Quintas, co-founder of the new media company Agence TOPO, invited me to participate in her collective web art and storytelling project *Civilités/Civilities*. In *Simultanéité* I was able to present some of the people I had met and interviewed and experiment with non-linear storytelling.[8] It was an opportunity to try and express the strangeness of holding small, mundane concerns in the midst of crisis. I tried to express the terrifying normalcy of entering and leaving a war zone. How much a "war zone" can actually accommodate. How race and privilege played out there. How many different people and organizations, and who are not those families primarily impacted, are active. How much agency and mobility there is when one is not part of those primarily impacted. And how little when one is. I remember how the street children would see me and call out, "Sudania, Sudania!" thinking that because I was Black, I had to be one of the many Sudanese refugees in the city.

During the Rwandan war and the genocide, I had been paralyzed. In Baghdad I learned about the power of non-violence and dissent. After returning from Baghdad, first in 2003 and again in 2004, I returned to my community and initiated *Tuganire*,[9] a community art and dialogue project looking to empower the community through finding/making beauty in our relationships and conversations. *Tuganire* was supported by the Levier Foundation's Engrenage Noir program. It was a lovely project where eleven different groups of Rwandans in the city of Montréal managed to come together and highlight commonalities. Conversations became a desire to create a cultural centre where everyone could belong. It was to be called *Umurage* (heritage).

Around that same time (2004 to 2006), I discovered Playback Theatre and trained with its founder, Jonathan Fox. Playback is a form of improvisational

---

8   The interviews from this project are available online at www.agencetopo.qc.ca/civi-lites/lisa_video.html.

9   In Kinyarwanda, the Rwandan language, *tuganire* means "let's talk/discuss and find solutions."

community theatre that Fox created with his partner, Jo Salas, in New England in 1975. I also trained in other applied theatre practices, like Brazilian popular educator Augusto Boal's Theatre of the Oppressed. I became certified in psychodrama, a form of therapeutic theatre developed by Jacob Levy Moreno.

With fellow artists Rodrigue Mugisha and the Kagabo brothers Hervé (Loulou) and Christian (Pompon), I also tried to re-establish SpektAfrica, a company that had been founded by Rwandan playwright Jean Marie Vianney Kayishema before he went back to Rwanda. In our community Kayishema was famous for the formal historical tragedies he wrote about precolonial Rwanda. The production of his piece *Pitie pour la reine* (the story of Queen Murorunkwere, mother of Rwabugiri, the last Rwandan king to reign before contact with the colonizers) at the Gesù was the first time I had seen a Rwandan story played on Rwandan bodies in a language I could understand. Kayishema cast young people and had them play in French. I remember my eyes leaking almost all the way through. The audience was made up of community members. Family and people I knew really well would laugh in places I could not understand. Even in French.

SpektAfrica was a collective effort toward voice, agency, and recognition. Working together gave us courage. We started writing original material. For Commemoration 2005 we wrote *Écriture à quatre mains*.[10] As much as the creative work was important, it also felt important to step out of the basements, become official, get our papers, and step into the fray. And so we registered and applied for grants. In parallel to his work with us, Mugisha kept working closely with Théâtre Parenthèse and was able to write, workshop, and stage *La malediction des nuages*,[11] a poetic, dreamlike play where the history of the slave passages resonates with that of refugees crossing the

---

10 The title does not translate well, but it speaks to the act of four people writing. My contribution was a text called "Grand-père" (Grandfather) in which I questioned/blamed my murdered grandfather and his generation for having allowed colonization to harm us to the extent that it did. My ideas shocked my parents so much that they invited an elder of my grandfather's generation to speak to me, another very important event and learning I write about in "Mutware" (Chief) in *Le petit coin intact*.

11 The curse of the clouds (my own translation).

Fig. 2. Rodrigue Mugisha's play, *La malediction des nuages* explored migrant and refugee issues in an imaginary underwater Mediterranean world of the dead. From left, Lisa Ndejuru and Christian Kagabo in the April 2010 production at Théâtre Parenthèse, Montréal. Photo by David Ward.

Mediterranean Sea. He, Pompon, and I performed it together the first time he presented it in March of 2010.

We wrote and performed. But we also all had to make a loving. We had school, family, and community responsibilities. When the Kagabo brothers left for Edmonton to make a living, those of us who remained did not sustain the effort of developing an organization. I have not thought about this in so long, and never usually even mention it because I feel that we all know creating is hard. So many artists are struggling, "diverse" or not, that it doesn't feel worth mentioning. It comes up now because, in exploring what a contribution of mine might look like, I'm excavating memories I usually don't access or recall, but that may be relevant here.

I have written elsewhere how *Tuganire* came to a brutal and tragic end in 2007, on opening night ("*Tuganire*" 224). Another of our own stabbed one of our beautiful young men. The community was divided once again. Traumatized and mourning.

Since then, these questions have been the focus of my work: How do we take up with the past in order to look to the future? What do I keep, what

Fig. 3. Catherine Dajczman and Lisa Ndejuru, with other members of the Living Histories Ensemble, in the group's first playback theatre performance for the Montréal community of Rwandan Genocide survivors. April 2011, Concordia University, Montréal. Photo by David Ward.

do I let go of, and what might that mean? Working with oral history, creative writing, and performance in a community/university setting, I have been fortunate to live in Concordia University's Centre for Oral History and Digital Storytelling since its inception in 2005. Until 2012 we worked on *Life Stories of Montrealers Displaced by Genocide, War, and Other Human Rights Violations* ("Montreal Life Stories").

Nisha Sajnani, Joliane Allaire, Paul Gareau, Lucy Lu, Alan Wong, Warren Linds, and I co-founded the Living Histories Ensemble (LHE). Coming together in 2007, LHE aimed to "to engage directly with survivors of mass violence and their stories for the purpose of individual and community healing" (Little and High 246). Edward Little and Steven High describe how Playback Theatre "emerged as a key theatrical space within the Montreal Life Stories project itself . . . [T]he aim was in playback, audience members share stories that are then played back by actors improvising under the direction of a 'conductor'" (246).

I am very proud of what LHE was able to accomplish in the Rwandan community. We were able to work in a range of situations that each needed

a specific sensitivity. Performing for survivors during genocide commemoration meant working with guilt, shame, incomprehension, cherished and
painful memories at risk of eroding over time. Performing to create an
inclusive space for all Rwandan stories to meaningfully engage with the
legacy of the genocide meant holding respectful, deep listening spaces to
welcome diverse perspectives and experiences. In a book chapter entitled "A
Modest Reconciliation," I wrote about the range of experiences and stories
we were able to elicit and serve, and how the work with the living histories
allowed Rwandans from every horizon to safely and bravely engage with
their own specific story.

In 2011, the project awarded me an artist residency and I wrote *Le petit coin
intact*, a bilingual (French and English) monologue in response to the Montreal
Life Stories project. The repertoire comprises twelve to nineteen vignettes that
I choose from to perform in a given context. I first performed *Le petit coin*
during our culminating event in March 2012 in the small La Balustrade theatre
of Montréal's Monument-National venue. *Rencontres*, the culmination, was a
"month-long series of 47 public events, including workshops, art installations,
audio walks, screenings, community assemblies, etc." (Little and High 242).

In discussing Iranian Canadian artist Mani Soleymanlou's work, Meerzon
writes about "the therapeutic function of immigrants' art that informs its
authorship and leads to the self-reflexivity of the form" ("Between Je and Moi"
305). I wonder whether reflecting on the battles I chose to wage and those I
didn't says something about the contexts and conditions of making immigrant
theatre? I don't come out of classical theatre training, but I care deeply about
the theatre and performance community. And in immigrant fashion, I want
to live in and contribute to this community, even though I am not entirely
"from there" and therefore cannot do so except from the spaces I am located
in: in-between places, outside of industry, more closely aligned with applied,
community, and political theatre, but moving back and forth into writing,
performance creation, and storytelling.

I do have strengths and fluencies. For example, I am somewhat francophone and very sensitive to the contexts and sensibilities of francophone
culture and ethos in Québec. Minority-majority, *vivre ensemble*, and

emancipation are themes I easily relate to. I also relate to notions of indigeneity, colonization, authenticity, tradition, modernity, and what comes next.

I want to further explore the literature on theatres of exile and of immigration. Writing about identities and migration, the French Lebanese writer
Amin Maalouf wrote, "Le pays d'acceuil n'est ni une page blanche, ni une page
achevée, c'est une page en train de s'écrire" (50).[12] I feel that is true of the host
country, just as it is of the country of origin, and even of the other countries
that may have been a part of the journey. Even (or especially) the travellers
themselves are constantly in the making.

Le petit coin intact was in many ways an *anstoss*: something to push
against. It laid open some big questions and emotions I held. With some of
these questions I have found answers and/or appeasement. I no longer rage
at my late grandfather, for example. Nor do I feel as though I am dealing with
the consequences of a history I had no hand in creating. I tell the story in *Le
petit coin intact.*With others the process is ongoing. Every day I learn about
history and culture. I also still want to learn the Rwandan language.

I have since had the opportunity to perform *Le petit coin intact* in several academic conferences and university classrooms in Canada. During the
2016 Association of Critical Heritage Studies conference held at Concordia
University in Montréal, I had the opportunity to re-curate and perform it in
response to the conference leitmotif: What does heritage change?

My piece started like this:

I am Lisa Ndejuru, daughter of Aimable Ndejuru
Son of Ndejuru, Claver
Son of Ngwije
Son of Karenzi
Son of Gitondo
Son of Karorero
Son of Kivunangoma

---

12   "The host country is neither a white page nor a finished one, it is being written" (my
own translation).

Son of Rwiru
Son of Murahire
Son of Nkongoli
Son of Makara

And on and on it goes, for thirty some generations.

Same story for my mother's side of the family. That's how we used
to introduce ourselves in Rwanda. By our location within a certain
lineage.

I am a daughter of the clan of the Abega of Makara,
of the branch of Nkongoli. And I am a product of an
unbroken Rwandan history that can be traced for
more than a thousand years.

Here on Turtle Island I am not a guest.
To call myself a guest would imply somebody invited me.
I showed up uninvited.

It was the first time I tried to speak any piece of my ancestry in public. Several
vignettes later I end with,

Like it or not, I'm on the settler team now.
It's complicated. Indigeneity. Colonizers. Victims.
Occupiers. Displacement. Oppressors. Genocide.
Truth? Reconciliation?
It's complicated for all of us.

Speaking of Soleymanlou's audience, Meerzon writes that "like the performer,
these spectators find themselves marching on the roads of utopia, searching
for places and communities to belong" ("Between Je and Moi" 307). I have
taken *Le petit coin intact* English- and French-speaking classes at CEGEP

and university levels. I have found it to be dialogic when I perform it, but my favourite thing is the conversations that follow after I distribute the texts and students read it out loud. Students share their own stories, and the pieces in their history that they grapple with. They are often children of immigrants, Indigenous youths, youths with multiple allegiances or identities that they struggle to hold simultaneously. They carry stories of loss, stories of political or family violence and how it has impacted their lives. Taking the work into classes and workshops, where there is more time to share and discuss than in a simple performance space, I have been moved by how many youth are touched by one aspect or another of my work. It seems to echo.

I could never have imagined or asked for all that I received and was a part of during the Montreal Life Stories project. My Ph.D. dissertation attempts to account for some of it, and to work through what we were able to do in a context of shared authority, community, university, the arts, and the stories.

Post-colonial writer Homi Bhabha asked:

> Must we always polarize in order to polemicize? Are we trapped in a politics of struggle where the representation of social antagonisms and historical contradictions can take no other form than a binarism of theory vs. politics? Can the aim of freedom or knowledge be the simple inversion of the relation of oppressor and oppressed, margin and periphery, negative image and positive image? Is our only way out of such dualism the espousal of an implacable oppositionality or the invention of an originary counter-myth of radical purity? Must the project of our liberationist aesthetics be forever part of a totaliz-ing, Utopian vision of Being and History that seeks to transcend the contradictions and ambivalences that constitute the very structure of human subjectivity and its systems of cultural representation? (5)

I don't think so. Bhabha was arguing against an opposition between militant action and theory in the film milieu. In Canada, the struggle for diversity and equity are very present, from the #CanStageSoWhite debate to the Postmarginal symposia. As an immigrant, my own position very much echoes St. Bernard's: "Let's save some time: diversity is good. We should have some. Next time we talk, can we continue the conversation from there instead of starting from scratch every time?" (99).

Our stories echo across difference, across time and space and race. We know that. So how do we live together now? How do we all make a living/ loving? How do we play together, knowing what came before, knowing we can never go back and erase the past? What do we keep? What do we let go of? How do we move forward? What does it mean? These questions echo every-where: here in Rwanda; next week in Montréal, Canada; in South Africa; in Australia, Europe, Central and South America, Asia . . . This coming summer will mark the twenty-fifth commemoration of the genocide. I will be creat-ing and performing with other hyphenated Canadian collaborators at the Ubumuntu Arts Festival in Rwanda. We want to meet Rwandan counterparts, to listen, reflect, and share stories and to seed possible futures.

Fig. 4. Members of the Living History Ensemble, in residence at the Art Gallery of Ontario. From left, Warren Linds, Lisa Ndejuru, Lucy Lu, and Alan Wong, May 2014, at the AGO, Toronto. Photo by David Ward.

WORKS CITED

@CMartinsTo. "You don't want to miss this. Starting Aug. 1 at Factory Theatre, 125 Bathurst St. #ONossoFado is everyone's song. #Davenport @SummerWorks." *Twitter*, 14 Jun. 2017, 7:17 a.m., twitter.com/CMartinsTO/status/874994234822152193.

@DramaLoretto. "@LCSMadness Tech rehearsal @harthouseuoft for the regional @SearsDramaFest. Looking forward to giving voice to the voiceless. #ONossoFado." *Twitter*, 8 Apr. 2017, 10:03 a.m., twitter.com/DramaLoretto /status/850755895063662592.

---. "Matt White sending #ONossoFado to regionals @harthouseuoft on Apr 8. @ LCSMadness @LorettoAlumnae #LorettoCS – 'Our song is everyone's song.'" *Twitter*, 1 Apr. 2017, 3:31 p.m., twitter.com/DramaLoretto/status/848301890362380288.

25ᵀᴴ Street Theatre. *Paper Wheat: The Book*. Western Producer Prairie Books, 1982.

"150 Years of Immigration to Canada." *Statistics Canada*, www.statcan.gc.ca/pub/11-630-x /11-630-x2016006-eng.htm.

"About." *Tirgan*, www.tirgan.ca/about/.

"About *Displaced*." *Ground Cover Theatre*, www.groundcovertheatre.com/displaced-2/.

"About the Fringe." *M1 Singapore Fringe Festival*, 2018. *The Internet Archive*, web.archive.org /web/20180522103807/www.singaporefringe.com/fringe2018/about.php.

Ackroyd, Judith, and John O'Toole. *Performing Research: Tensions, Triumphs and Trade-Offs of Ethnodrama*. Trentham Books, 2010.

Adams, Douglas. *The Hitchhiker's Guide to the Galaxy Omnibus: A Trilogy in Five Parts*. Pan Macmillan, 2017.

Afolabi, Taiwo. "Diversity Metrics? A Reflection on Themes From a Refugee Theatre Project in Canada." *Cultural Policy and Management Yearbook on Art and Heritage After Forced Migration*, edited by Nevra Erturk and Deniz Unsal, Istanbul Bilgi U and Letiim, 2019.

Ahmed, Sara. *The Promise of Happiness*. Duke UP, 2010.

---. *Strange Encounters: Embodied Others in Post-Coloniality*. Routledge, 2000.

Albino, Mary. "Finding a Home on Stage." *Toronto Star*, 12 May 2011, www.thestar.com /life/2011/05/12/finding_a_home_on_stage.html.

"Although it was Reported that 'B' Battery was to be Ordered East." *Qu'Appelle Progress*. 11 Jun. 1886, p. 6. Saskatchewan Archives Board, R-1.590.

Alvarez, Natalie. "Latina/o Canadian Theatre and Performance: Hemispheric Perspectives." *Latina/o Canadian Theatre and Performance*, edited by Alvarez, Playwrights Canada, 2013, pp. 1–16.

---. "Latina/o Canadian Theatre and Performance: Living Archives, Living Borders." *Fronteras Vivientes: Eight Latina/o Canadian Plays*, edited by Alvarez, Playwrights Canada, 2013, pp. iii–xxvii.

Ambrose, Emma, and Cas Mudde. "Canadian Multiculturalism and the Absence of the Far Right." *Nationalism and Ethnic Politics*, vol. 21, no. 2, 2015, pp. 213–36.

Amos, F. *History of Qu'Appelle & Pioneer Days*. Saskatchewan Archives Board, R-E698. Manuscript.

Anderson, Benedict. *Imagined Communities: Reflections on the Origin and Spread of Nationalism*. Revised ed., Verso, 2006.

Anderson, Grace M., and David Higgs. *A Future to Inherit: The Portuguese Communities of Canada*. McClelland and Stewart, 1976.

Anderson, Mark Cronlund, and Carmen L. Robertson. *Seeing Red: A History of Natives in Canadian Newspapers*. U of Manitoba P, 2011.

Anthony, Geraldine. *John Coulter*. Twayne, 1976.

---, editor. *Stage Voices: Twelve Canadian Playwrights Talk About Their Lives and Work*. Doubleday, 1978.

Aquino, Nina Lee, editor. *Love + RelAsianships: A Collection of Contemporary Asian-Canadian Drama*. Vol. 1, Playwrights Canada, 2009.

---, editor. *Love + RelAsianships: A Collection of Contemporary Asian-Canadian Drama*. Vol. 2, Playwrights Canada, 2009.

"Area Belle." *Qu'Appelle Progress*, 11 Dec. 1885. Saskatchewan Archives Board, R-1.590.

"The Arrival of Displaced Persons in Canada, 1945-1951." *Government of Canada*, 15 Feb. 2016, www.canada.ca/en/parks-canada/news/2016/02/the-arrival-of-displaced -persons-in-canada-1945-1951.html.

Armstrong, Rev. George D. "Through the Study Window." *Vegreville Observer*, 22 Feb. 1933, p 4.

"Artistic Director Spotlight: Majdi Bou-Matar, MT Space." *Centre in the Square*, 17 Mar. 2014, centreinthesquare.com/artistic-director-spotlight-majdi-bou-matar-mt-space/.

Asher, Stanley. "A Play That Makes a Difference." *Place Publique*, 25 Sep. 1995, p. 11.

Ashperger, Cynthia. "The Tongue Play: An Auto-Ethnography." *Theatre Research in Canada*, vol. 36, no. 2, 2015, pp. 320–28.

Atkinson, William Stabler. *So This Is Canada*. Mount Saint Vincent U, Canadian Drama Collection, C.D.Coll 19.13. Microfilm.

Atwood, Margaret. *Alias Grace*. Virago, 2009.

Avineri, Netta. "Yiddish Endangerment as Phenomenological Reality and Discursive Strategy: Crossing Into the Past and Crossing Out the Present." *Language and Communication*, vol. 38, 2014, pp. 18–32.

Avni, Ora. "Beyond Psychoanalysis: Elie Wiesel's *Night* in Historical Perspective." *Auschwitz and After: Race, Culture, and "the Jewish Question" in France*, edited by L. D. Kritzman, Routledge, 1995, pp. 203–18.

Babayants, Art. "I Was Born Diasporic: Interview with Levon Haftvan." Toronto, 1 Dec. 2017.

Backhouse, Constance. *Colour-Coded: A Legal History of Racism in Canada, 1900–1950*. U of Toronto P, 1999.

---. "Extended Endnotes." *Colour Coded: A Legal History of Racism in Canada, 1900– 1950*, Osgoode Society for Canadian Legal History, 1999. *Constance Backhouse*, www.constancebackhouse.ca/fileadmin/user_upload/endnotes.pdf.

bakchormeeboy. "M1 Singapore Fringe Festival 2018: Displaced by Ground Cover Theatre (Review)." *Bakchormeeboy*, 29 Jan. 2018, bakchormeeboy.com/2018/01/29 /m1-singapore-fringe-festival-2018-displaced-by-ground-cover-theatre-review/.

Bakhtin, Mikhail. "Forms of Time and of the Chronotope in the Novel." *The Dialogic Imagination: Four Essays*, edited by Michael Holquist, U of Texas P, 1982, pp.84–258.

Balan, Jars. "Salt and Braided Bread: Ukrainian Life in Canada." *Ukrainian Literature in Canada*, jrank.org/literature/pages/8826/Ukrainian-Canadian-literature.html.

Balfour, Michael, Penny Bundy, Bruce Burton, Julie Dunn, and Nina Woodrow. *Applied Theatre: Resettlement: Drama, Refugees and Resilience*. Bloomsbury Methuen Drama, 2015.

"A Band of Cree Treated Qu'Appellites." *Qu'Appelle Progress*, 27 May 1897, p. 4. Saskatchewan Archives Board, R-1.590.

Barnard, M. W., and A. S. Hickman, "The Battle of Imbembesi." *Rhodesiana*, no. 15, 1966, pp. 1–12. *Rhodesia and South Africa: Military History*, www.rhodesia.nl/rhodesiana /volume15.pdf.

Barnett, Mac, and Jon Klassen. *Extra Yarn*. Balzer & Bray, 2012.

Bartolini, Daniele, and DopoLavoro Teatrale. *The Apartment*. Jun. 2017, Toronto, Ontario.

---. *The Invisible City*. Aug. 2017, Toronto, Ontario.

Bauböck, Rainer. "If You Say Multiculturalism is the Wrong Answer, Then What Was the Question You Asked?" *Canadian Diversity/Diversité canadienne*, vol. 4, no. 1, 2005, pp. 90–94.

Baudrillard, Jean. *Simulacra and Simulation*. Translated by Sheila Faria Glaser, U of Michigan P, 1994.

Bauman, Zygmunt. *Collateral Damage: Social Inequalities in a Global Age*. Polity, 2011.

---. "Symptoms in Search of an Object and a Name." *The Great Regression*, edited by Heinrich Geiselberger, Polity, 2017, pp. 13–25.

"B. Battery Dramatic Club." *Qu'Appelle Progress*, March 1886. Saskatchewan Archives Board, R-1.590.

"B Battery Leaves." *Qu'Appelle Progress*, 16 Jul. 1886. Saskatchewan Archives Board, R-1.590.

Beaudoin-Duquette, Alexandre. "Propaganda Migratoria Canadiense y Arte Latinoamericano en Montreal: Un Contrapunteo Disonante." U Nacional Autónoma de México, 2015. Dissertation.

"Beaver Lake: The Ukrainian Problem." *Vegreville Observer*, 26 Mar. 1919, p 1.

Beck, Ulrich. "Cosmopolitanism as Imagined Communities of Global Risk." *American Behavioral Scientist*, vol. 55, no. 10, 2011, pp. 1346–61.

Beit Hatfutsot. "Winnipeg." *Beit Hatfutsot*, dbs.bh.org.il/place/winnipeg.

Bélair, Michel. *Le nouveau théâtre québécois*. Leméac, 1973.

Benjamin, Walter. "The Storyteller." *Illuminations, Essays and Reflections*, translated by Harry Zohn, edited by Hannah Arendt, Schocken, 1970 pp. 83–111.

---. *Understanding Brecht*. Translated by Anna Bostock, Verso, 1998.

Bérard, Sylvie. "L'appel du corps." *Lettres québécoises: la revue de l'actualité littéraire*, no. 71, 1993, pp. 49–50.

Berkowitz, Joel, editor. *Yiddish Theater: New Approaches*. Littman Library of Jewish Civilization, 2003.

Bhabha, Homi K. "The Commitment to Theory." *New Formations*, vol. 5, no. 1, 1988, pp. 5–23.

Bhavnani, Kum-Kum, and Ann Phoenix. *Shifting Identities, Shifting Racisms: A Feminism & Psychology Reader*. Sage, 1994.

Biron, Michel, et al. *Histoire de la littérature québécoise*. Boréal, 2007.

Bissoondath, Neil. *Selling Illusions: The Cult of Multiculturalism in Canada*. 2nd ed. Penguin, 2002.

Blad, Cory, and Philippe Couton. "The Rise of an Intercultural Nation: Immigration, Diversity and Nationhood in Quebec." *Journal of Ethnic and Migration Studies*, vol. 35, no. 4, 2009, pp. 645–67.

Boal, Augusto. "Theatre of the Oppressed." *The Applied Theatre Reader*, edited by Tim Prentki and Sheila Preston, Routledge, 2009, pp. 130–37.

---. *Theatre of the Oppressed*. Translated by Charles A. and Maria Odilia Leal McBride, Theatre Communications Group, 1979.

Bogart, Anne. *A Director Prepares: Seven Essays on Art and Theatre*. Routledge, 2010.

Booth, Michael. "Soldiers of the Queen: Drury Lane Imperialism." *Melodrama: The Cultural Emergence of a Genre*, edited by Michael Hays and Anastasia Nikolopoulou, St. Martin's, 1999, 3–20.

Bouchard, Gérard. *Interculturalism: A View From Quebec*. Translated by Howard Scott, U of Toronto P, 2015.

Bouchard, Gérard, and Charles Taylor. "Building the Future: A Time for Rconciliation." Commission de consultation sur les pratiques d'acommodement reliées aux differences Culturelle, 2008.

Boudreau, Annette, and Raoul Boudreau. "La littérature comme moyen de reconquête de la parole. L'exemple de l'Acadie." *Glottopol*, no. 3, 2004, pp. 166–80.

Bou-Matar, Majdi. "Creating an MT Space: Multicultural Performance Beyond Folklore." *Canadian Theatre Review*, vol. 125, 2006, pp. 105–07.

Bovet, Jeanne. "Identity and Universality: Multilingualism in Robert Lepage's Theater." *Theater sans frontières: Essays on the Dramatic Universe of Robert Lepage*, edited by Joseph I. Donohoe and Jane M. Koustas, Michigan State UP, 2000, pp. 3–19.

---. "Du plurilinguisme comme fiction identitaire: à la rencontre de l'intime." *Études françaises*, vol. 43, no. 1, 2007, pp. 43–62.

---. "Présentation." *Études françaises*, vol. 43, no. 1, 2007, pp. 5–7.

Bradbeer, Janice. "Once Upon A City: Rochdale College and the hippie dream." *Toronto Star*, 6 Apr. 2017, www.thestar.com/yourtoronto/once-upon-a-city-archives/2017/04/06/once-upon-a-city-rochdale-college-and-the-hippie-dream.html.

Bramadat, Paul. "Towards a New Politics of Authenticity: Ethno-Cultural Representation in Theory and Practice." *Canadian Ethnic Studies*, vol. 37, no.1, 2005, pp. 1–20.

Brault, Simon. *No Culture, No Future*. Translated by Jonathan Kaplansky, Cormorant, 2010.

Brisset, Annie. *Sociocritique de la traduction: théâtre et altérité au Québec (1968–1988)*. Le Préambule, 1990. L'Univers des discours.

Brodsky, Joseph. "The Condition We Call Exile." *On Grief and Reason: Essays*, Farrar, Straus, and Giroux, 1995, pp. 22–35.

Broughall, George. *The 90th on Active Service, or, Campaigning in the North-West*. George Bishop, 1885. CIHM Microfiche series 1985, archive.org/details/cihm_30039.

Bruemmer, René. "English, French Hold Differing Views on Integration of Newcomers: Poll." *Montreal Gazette*, 27 Jun. 2018, montrealgazette.com/news/local-news/english-french-hold-differing-views-on-integration-of-newcomers-poll.

Bruneau, Michel. "Diasporas, Transnational Spaces and Communities." *Diasporas and Transnationalism: Concepts, Theories and Methods*, edited by Rainer Bauböck and Thomas Faist, Amsterdam UP, 2010, pp. 35–50.

Brunet, Alain. "*SLĀV*, considérations sur la musique et . . . l'appropriation Culturelle." *La Presse*, 27 Jun. 2018, www.lapresse.ca/arts/festivals/festival-de-jazz/201806/28/01-5187484-slv-considerations-sur-la-musique-et-lappropriation-culturelle.php.

Bush, Steven. *Beating the Bushes: A Memoir in Many Voices in the Form of a Dramatic Monologue With Some Imaginative Improvements but Very Little Outright Lying*. Talon, 2010.

---. *Conversations with George Luscombe: Steven Bush in Conversation with the Canadian Theatre Visionary*. Mosaic, 2012.

---. Personal interview with David DeGrow. 31 Aug. 2017, Toronto, Ontario.

Butler, Judith. *Bodies that Matter: On the Discursive Limits of "Sex."* Routledge, 1993.

---. *Gender Trouble: Feminism and the Subversion of Identity.* Routledge, 1990.

---. *The Psychic Life of Power: Theories in Subjection.* Stanford UP, 1997.

Butts, Edward, and Michelle Filice. "Almighty Voice." *The Canadian Encyclopedia*, 19 Jul. 2016, www.thecanadianencyclopedia.ca/en/article/almighty-voice.

Cameron, Ken. "*How iRan*: Three Plays for iPod." *Canadian Theatre Review*, no. 159, pp. 62–67.

Caminero-Santangelo, Marta. *On Latinidad.* UP of Florida, 2007.

"Canada's Strategy for Engagement in the Americas." *Global Affairs Canada*, www.international.gc.ca/americas-ameriques/assets/pdfs/strategy-eng.PDF.

"Canada-U.S. Safe Third Country Agreement." *Government of Canada*, www.canada.ca/en /immigration-refugees-citizenship/corporate/mandate/policies-operational -instructions-agreements/agreements/safe-third-country-agreement.html.

Canadian Charter of Rights and Freedoms. *Constitution Act, 1982.* Government of Canada, 1982. *Justice Laws Website*, laws-lois.justice.gc.ca/eng/const/page-15.html.

Canadian Human Rights Commission. "The Plight of Immigrants." chrc-ccdp.gc.ca /historical-perspective/en/getBriefed/1900/immigrants.asp.

Canadian Multiculturalism Act. Government of Canada, 12 Jul. 1988. *Justice Laws Website*, laws-lois.justice.gc.ca/eng/acts/c-18.7/page-1.html.

"Canadian Multiculturalism Policy, 1971." *Canadian Museum of Immigration at Pier 21*, www.pier21.ca/research/immigration-history/canadian-multiculturalism-policy-1971.

Carman, Tara, and Anita Elash. "Gender Persecution the Top Reason Women Seek Asylum in Canada." *CBC News*. 7 Feb. 2018, www.cbc.ca/news/canada /asylum-seekers-data-gender-persecution-1.4506245.

Carter, Jimmy. "Proclamation 4483-Granting Pardon for Violations of the Selective Service Act, August 4, 1964 to March 28, 1973." 21 Jan. 1977. *The American Presidency Project*, www.presidency.ucsb.edu/ws/index.php?pid=7255.

Casanova, Pascale. *La république mondiale des lettres.* 2nd ed., Seuil, 2008.

---. *The World Republic of Letters.* Translated by M.B. DeBevoise, Harvard UP, 2004.

Case, Mary Anne. "Disaggregating Gender from Sex and Sexual Orientation: The Effeminate Man in the Law and Feminist Jurisprudence." *The Yale Law Journal*, vol. 105, no. 1, Oct. 1995, pp. 1–105.

Case, Sue-Ellen. *Feminism and Theatre*. 1988. Reissued edition, Palgrave Macmillan, 2008.

Charlebois, Gaetan. "Backlashing the Backlash." *Montreal Mirror*, 28 Mar. 1996.

Choi, Ins. *Kim's Convenience*. House of Anansi, 2012. Kindle Edition.

Chung, Angie Y. *Saving Face: The Emotional Costs of the Asian Immigrant Family Myth*. Rutgers UP, 2016.

Churchill, David S. "American Expatriates and the Building of Alternative Social Space in Toronto, 1965–1977." *Urban History Review*, vol. 39, no. 1, 2010, pp. 31–80.

Citizenship and Immigration Canada. *Immigrant Integration in Canada: Policy Objectives, Program Delivery, and Challenges*. 2001, atwork.settlement.org/downloads/atwork /Immigrant_Integration_in_Canada_discussion_paper_Hauck_May01.pdf.

"Civilités/Civilities." *Agence TOPO*, www.agencetopo.qc.ca/civilites.

Clark, Jim, Warwick Dobson, Tony Goode, Jonothan Neelands. *Lesson for the Living: Drama and the Integrated Curriculum*. Mayfair Cornerstone, 1994.

"Classifications." *Selective Service System*, www.sss.gov/Classifications.

"Classroom Hints." *Alberta Teacher's Association Magazine*, vol. 14, no. 4, Dec. 1933, pp. 26–29.

Cocking, George. *The Conquest of Canada*. London, 1766.

Coelho, José Mário. "TeatrOVAL apresenta 'O Nosso Baile.'" *O Milénio*, no. 32, 24 Jun. 1999, p. 25.

Cohen-Cruz, Jan. "Redefining the Private: From Personal Storytelling to Political Act." *A Boal Companion: Dialogues on Theatre and Cultural Politics*, edited by Cohen-Cruz and Mady Schutzman, Routledge, 2006, pp. 103–13.

Coleman, Daniel. *White Civility: The Literary Project of English Canada*. U of Toronto P, 2006.

Company of Sirens. *The Working People's Picture Show*. 1988. Unpublished manuscript.

Conquergood, Dwight. "Performing a Moral Act: Ethical Dimensions of the Ethnography of Performance." *Text and Performance Quarterly*, vol. 5, 1985, pp. 1–13.

Corbett, E.A. *We Have With Us Tonight*. Ryerson, 1957.

Costa, Rita Marques. "Um minuto de silêncio para acabar com a violência contra as mulheres." *Publico*, 24 Nov. 2017, www.publico.pt/2017/11/25/sociedade/noticia/um-minuto-de-silencio-para-acabar-com-a-violencia-contra-as-mulheres-1793835.

Coulter, John. "The Canadian Theatre and the Irish Exemplar." *Canadian Theatre History: Selected Readings*, edited by Don Rubin, Copp Clark, 1996, pp.119–24.

---. *The Crime of Louis Riel*. Playwrights Co-op, 1976.

---. *The Drums Are Out*. DePaul U, 1971. Irish Drama Series 6.

---. *In My Day: Memoirs*. Hounslow, 1980.

---. *Riel*. Cromlech, 1972.

---. *The Trial of Louis Riel*. Oberon, 1968.

Couture, Philippe, and Christian Saint-Pierre. "À quand un théâtre montréalais bilingue?" *Jeu: Revue de théâtre*, no. 145, 2012, pp. 6–8.

Cox, Emma. *Theatre and Migration*. Palgrave McMillan, 2014.

Creighton-Kelly, Chris. *Report on Racial Equality in the Arts at the Canada Council*. Canada Council for the Arts, 1990.

Creswicke, Louis. *South Africa and the Transvaal War, Vol. 1*. T.C. & E.C. Jack, 1900. *Project Gutenberg*, 3 Dec. 2007, www.gutenberg.org/files/23692/23692-h/23692-h.htm.

Crew, Robert. "Life Tales of the Unexpected." *Toronto Star*, 17 Feb. 2005, p. J8.

Cronin, Michael. *Translation and Identity*. Routledge, 2006.

Curtis, Liane, et al. *Culture and Identity: Ideas and Overviews*. Ethnocultural, Racial, Religious, and Linguistic Diversity and Identity Seminar, 1–2 Nov. 2001, Halifax, Nova Scotia, canada.metropolis.net/events/ethnocultural/publications/cult_ident_e.pdf.

Danico, Mary Yu. *The 1.5 Generation: Becoming Korean American in Hawaii*. U of Hawaii Press, 2004.

Dargnat, Mathilde. *Michel Tremblay: le « joual » dans Les belles-sœurs*. L'Harmattan, 2002. Collection Critiques littéraires.

---. "L'oral au pied de la lettre: raison et déraison graphiques." *Études françaises*, vol. 43, no. 1, 2007, pp. 83–100.

---. "L'oral comme fiction: stylistique de l'oralité populaire dans le théâtre de Michel Tremblay (1968–1998)." U de Montréal, 2006.

David, Gilbert. "Le langue-à-langue de Daniel Danis: une parole au corps à corps." *Études françaises*, vol. 43, no. 1, 2007, pp. 63–81.

Davies, Robertson, "A Dialogue on the State of Theatre in Canada." *Canadian Theatre History: Selected Readings*, edited by Don Rubin, Copp Clark, 1996, pp. 155–75.

Davin, Nicholas Flood. *Fair Grit or The Advantages of Coalition. Canada's Lost Plays, Volume One: The Nineteenth Century*, edited by Anton Wagner and Richard Plant, CTR, 1978, pp. 138–57.

---. *Report on Industrial schools for Indians and Half-breeds. Internet Archive*, archive.org/details/cihm_03651.

Davis-Fisch, Heather. "Lawless Lawyers: Indigeneity, Civility, and Violence." *Theatre Research in Canada*, vol. 35, no. 1, 2014, pp. 31–48, journals.lib.unb.ca/index.php /TRIC/article/view/21937.

Day, Moira. "Esther Thompson and Edith Bellamy Sinclair: The Forgotten First Ladies of English-Language Manitoba Extension Drama." Canadian Association for Theatre Research/ Association Canadienne de la Recherche Théâtrale Conference, 1 Jun. 2008, Vancouver, British Columbia.

Day, Richard. *Multiculturalism and the History of Canadian Diversity*. U of Toronto P, 2000.

de Certeau, Michel, Luce Giard, and Pierre Mayol. *The Practice of Everyday Life: Living and Cooking*. Vol. 2, translated by Timothy J. Tomasik, U of Minnesota P, 1998.

"A Deep-Freeze Lear in Eskimo Land." *Life*, 17 Nov. 1961, p. 198.

de Guevara, Lina. "Impact of the Immigrant Experience on My Theatre Career." *Theatre Research in Canada*, vol. 32, no. 6, 2015, pp. 312–19.

---. *Journey to Mapu. Fronteras Vivientes: Eight Latina/o Canadian Plays*, edited by Natalie Alvarez, 2013, pp. 347–400.

---. "Welcome." *Lina de Guevara*, linadeguevara.ca/.

De la Chenelière, Evelyne, and Pierre Lefebvre. "Entre la page et le plateau: dialogue avec Marie-Christine Lesage." *Liberté*, vol. 52, no. 3, 2011, pp. 40–53.

Del Pozo, José. *Les Chiliens au Québec: immigrants et réfugiés, de 1955 à nos jours*. Boréal, 2009.

Department of Agriculture. *Census of the Three Provisional Districts of the Northwest Territories, 1884–85*. Government of Canada, 1886.

Di Giovine, Michael. *The Heritage-scape: UNESCO, World-Heritage, and Tourism*. Lexington, 2009.

Dib, Kamal, et al. "Integration and Identity in Canada: The Importance of Multicultural Common Spaces." *Canadian Ethnic Studies*, vol. 40, no. 1, 2008, pp. 161–87.

Dion, Robert. "*The Dragonfly of Chicoutimi*: Un cas extrême d'hétérolinguisme?" Les Herbes rouges, 2005. Territoires.

"Disclosure of Grant and Prize Recipients." *Canada Council for the Arts*, canadacouncil.ca/about/public-accountability/proactive-disclosure /grant-recipients?form=submitted&page=2&year=2016&discipline=Theatre &program=all&recipient=&province=ON&city=&area=all&riding=all&Sort1 =Recipient&Sort2=Recipient&Sort3=Recipient.

"Diskusye arum di takones fun yugntruf" ("Discussion Around the Principles of Yugntruf"). *Yugntruf*, no. 2, 1965, pp. 5–6. *Yugntruf*, yugntruf.org/zhurnal /zhurnal.php?ui=embed&numer=2#page/5/mode/1up.

"Distribution of Foreign-Born Population, By Region of Birth, Canada, 1971 to 2036." *Statistics Canada*, www.statcan.gc.ca/eng/dai/btd/othervisuals/other009.

Dolan, Jill. "Performance, Utopia, and the 'Utopian Performative'" *Theatre Journal*, vol. 53, 2001, pp. 455–479.

Dominion Bureau of Statistics. *Fifth Census of Canada 1911, Vol. 2: Religions, Origins, Birthplace, Citizenship, Literacy and Infirmities, By Provinces, Districts, and Sub-Districts*. Government of Canada, 1913.

Donnelly, Pat. "*Counter Offence* Recalls Good Old Days of Theatre." *Montréal Gazette*, 3 Oct. 1997.

---. "Land has Echoes in Real Life Drama." *Montréal Gazette*, 28 Sep. 1990, p. C1.

---. "La nouvelle vague?: *L'Affaire Farhadi* Could be the Vanguard of the Revolution in French-Language Theatre." *Montréal Gazette*, 27 Feb. 1999, p. D1.

---. "Teesri Duniya's *The Poster* Leaves Imprint." *Montréal Gazette*, 25 Nov. 2011, montrealgazette.com/entertainment/theatre/teesri-duniyas-the-poster-leaves imprint.

---. "Tempest over *No Man's Land* has a familiar ring to it." *Montréal Gazette*, 12 Sep. 1992, p. E3.

DopoLavoro Teatrale and SummerWorks Performance Festival. "Audience Waiver: The Invisible City." 2017. Google Form.

Drummond, William Henry. *The Habitant: and Other French-Canadian Poems*. G. P. Putnam's Sons, 1897. *Project Gutenberg*, www.gutenberg.org/cache/epub/9801 /pg9801.html.

Du Bois, W.E.B. *The Souls of Black Folk*. Oxford UP, 2007.

Duchense, Scott. "The Impossible Theatre: Roy Mitchell and The Chester Mysteries: Experience, Initiation and Brotherhood." *Theatre Research in Canada*, vol. 27, no. 2, 2006, pp. 227–44.

Dufour, Christian. *Le Défi Québécois*. l'Hexagone, 1989.

Dunlevy, T'cha. "Jazz Fest Review: *SLĀV* Misses the Mark, and Precious Opportunity." *Montréal Gazette*, 4 Jul. 2018, montrealgazette.com/entertainment/music /jazz-fest-review-slav-misses-the-mark-and-precious-opportunity.

Eco, Umberto. "Migration, Tolerance, and the Intolerable." *Five Moral Pieces*, translated by Alastair McEwen, Harcourt, 2001, pp. 89–111.

Edwards, Justin D. *Gothic Canada: Reading the Spectre of a National Literature*. U of Alberta P, 2005.

Eliade, Mircea. *Myths, Dreams, and Mysteries: The Encounter Between Contemporary Faiths and Archaic Realities*. Harper & Row, 1957.

"Emmanuel College Band Concert." *Prince Albert Advocate*, 3 Feb. 1902, p. 1. Saskatchewan Archives Board, R-1.571.

"'Enemy Aliens'—The Internment of Ukrainian Canadians." *Life at Home During the War: Canada and the First World War*. Canadian War Museum, www.warmuseum.ca/firstworldwar/history/life-at-home-during-the-war /enemy-aliens/the-internment-of-ukrainian-canadians/.

"The Entertainment to be Given." *Prince Albert Advocate*, 13 Jan. 1901, "Town and Country." Saskatchewan Archives Board, R-1.571.

Epp, Marlene, Franca Iacovetta, and Frances Swyripa, editors. *Sisters or Strangers?: Immigrant, Ethnic and Racialized Women in Canadian History*. U of Toronto P, 2004.

"Equity." *Canada Council for the Arts*, canadacouncil.ca/commitments/equity.

Evans, David. *Language and Identity: Discourse in the World*. Bloomsbury, 2015.

Evasuk, Stasia. "Caravan Crew Assembling Piroshkis." *Toronto Star*, 26 May 1990, p. J4.

"Everybody Talks of Going to See Pauline Johnson Tonight." *Qu'Appelle Progress*, 8 Sep. 1898, p. 4. Saskatchewan Archives Board, R-1.590.

"The Famous Indian Poetess." *Prince Albert Times*, 2 Oct. 1907, p. 7. Saskatchewan Archives Board, R-1.586.

Farrow, Tina. "Jean-Baptiste Riel d'Ireland Born as Jack Reilly, 1649, Ireland." *Genealogy*, 19 Jul. 2010, www.genealogy.com/forum/surnames/topics/riel/433.

Fatona, Andrea Monike. *Where Outreach Meets Outrage: Racial Equity at The Canada Council for the Arts (1989–1999)*. U of Toronto, 2011. Thesis.

Fernandes, Gilberto. *The Portuguese in Toronto, 1953–2013: 60th Anniversary of Portuguese Immigration to Canada*. Exhibit Catalogue, 2013.

"Festival Caravan Week." City of Toronto Proclamation, Jun. 2002.

Filewod, Alan. "Actors Acting Not Acting: Auto-performance in Canadian Theatre." *La création biographique*, edited by Marta Dvorak, PU de Rennes / Association Française d'études canadiennes, 1997, pp. 51–57. Collection de l'AFEC 5.

---. *Collective Encounters: Documentary Theatre in English Canada*. U of Toronto P, 1987.

---. "Erasing Historical Difference: The Alternative Orthodoxy in Canadian Theatre." *Theatre Journal*, vol. 41, no. 2, 1989, pp. 201–10.

---. "Introduction: The Histories of Theatre History." *Theatre Histories*, edited by Filewod, Playwrights Canada, 2009, pp. vii–xi.

---. "Named in Passing: Deregimenting Canadian Theatre History." *Writing and Rewriting National Theatre*, edited by S.E. Wilner, U of Iowa P, 2004, pp. 106–26.

---. "National Theatre, National Obsession." *Canadian Theatre History: Selected Readings*, edited by Don Rubin, Copp Clark, 1996, pp. 408–15.

---. *Performing Canada: The Nation Enacted in the Imagined Theatre*. Textual Studies in Canada, 2002. Critical Performance/s in Canada.

---. "Playing on Indigenous Land: Settlers, Immigrants and Theatre in Fictive Canada." Page, Stage, Screen, Voice: A Canadian Studies Seminar, Croatian-Canadian Academic Society, 12 May 2018, Zagreb, Croatia.

Finn, Patrick. "Inside Information: Ken Cameron's *How iRan*." *Canadian Theatre Review*, no. 159, 2014, pp. 58–61.

Fischer-Lichte, Erika. "Interweaving Cultures in Performance: Different States of Being In-Between." *New Theatre Quarterly*, vol. 25, no. 4, 2009, pp. 391–401.

Fish, Stanley. "Boutique Multiculturalism, or Why Liberals are Incapable of Thinking about Hate Speech." *Critical Inquiry*, vol. 23, no. 2, 1997, pp. 378–95.

Fisher, Esther. "Tastebuds Can Travel at Caravan." *Globe and Mail*, 19 Jun. 1985, p. B11.

Fitz-James, Thea. Review of *acquiesce* by David Yee. *My Entertainment World: My Theatre*, 7 Nov. 2016, www.myentertainmentworld.ca/2016/11/acquiesce/.

Fitzpatrick, Lisa. "The Performance of Violence and the Ethics of Spectatorship." *Performance Research*, vol. 16, no. 1, 2011, pp. 59–67.

Floyd, Saiya. "Soulpepper on 42ND Street: *Kim's Convenience*." *My Entertainment World: My Theatre*, 5 Jul. 2017, www.myentertainmentworld.ca/2017/07/soulpepper-ny-kims/.

Foucault, Michel. "Nietzsche, Genealogy, History." *Language, Counter-Memory, Practice: Selected Essays and Interviews*, edited by Donald F. Bouchard, translated by Donald F. Bouchard and Sherry Simon, Cornell UP, 1977, pp. 139–165.

Fournier, Kat. "From the Montreal Fringe. Intersecting Plots and Immersive Storytelling in 'Displaced' by Ground Cover Theatre." *Capital Critics' Circle / Le Cercle Des Critiques De La Capitale*, 15 Jun. 2015, capitalcriticscircle.com/montreal-fringe-2015-intersecting -plots-immersive-storytelling-displaced-ground-cover-theatre/.

Francis, Daniel. *The Imaginary Indian: The Image of the Indian in Canadian Culture*. 2nd ed., Arsenal Pulp, 2011.

Frayne, Trent. "Caravan: It's a Concentrate of All That Makes Metro Toronto Hum." *Toronto Star*, 22 Jun. 1974, p. B1.

Freed, Dale Ann. "Caravan's Nine-Day Festival Brings the Exotic to Metro." *Toronto Star*, 16 Jun. 1994, p. A7.

Freeman, Barry. *Staging Strangers: Theatre and Global Ethics*. McGill-Queen's UP, 2017.

Freire, Paulo. *Pedagogy of the Oppressed*. Continuum, 2006.

Fuller, Cam. "*Displaced* Finds a Place at Live Five." *StarPhoenix* [Saskatoon], 1 Feb. 2017, thestarphoenix.com/entertainment/local-arts/displaced-finds-a-place-at-live-five.

---. "Riel Play Still Going Strong." *StarPhoenix* [Saskatoon], 15 Nov. 2010, B1.

Fulton, Allegra. "Spotlight: Jon Kaplan." *Intermission Magazine*, 17 Mar. 2017, www.intermissionmagazine.ca/spotlight/jon-kaplan/.

Garcea, Joseph, et al. "Introduction: Multiculturalism Discourses in Canada." *Canadian Ethnic Studies*, vol. 40, no. 1, 2008, pp. 1–10.

Gardner, David. "Canada's Eskimo 'Lear.'" *Theatre Research in Canada*, vol. 7, no. 1, Spring 1986, journals.lib.unb.ca/index.php/tric/article/view/7413/8472.

"Garrison Theatricals." *Qu'Appelle Progress*, March 1886. Saskatchewan Archives Board, R-1.590.

The Gaspé Manifesto. "A Strange Enterprise: The Dilemma of the Playwright in Canada." *Canadian Theatre History: Selected Readings*, edited by Don Rubin. Copp Clark, 1996, pp. 302–06.

Gauvin, Lise. *Langagement: l'écrivain et la langue au Québec*. Boréal, 2000.

---. "Le théâtre de la langue." *Le Monde de Michel Tremblay: des Belles-Soeurs à Marcel poursuivi par les chiens*, edited by Gilbert David and Pierre Lavoie, Cahiers de théâtre jeu, Editions Lansman, 1993, pp. 335–57.

Gentzler, Edwin. *Translation and Rewriting in the Age of Post-Translation Studies.* Routledge, 2017.

Gilbert, Helen, and Joanne Tompkins. *Post-Colonial Drama: Theory, Practice, Politics.* Routledge, 1996.

Gilbert, Liette. "Legitimizing Neoliberalism Rather than Equality: Canadian Multiculturalism in the Current Reality of North America." *Norteamérica. Revista Académica del CISAN-UNAM*, vol. 2, no. 1, 2007, pp. 11–35.

Giles, Wenona. *Portuguese Women in Toronto: Gender, Immigration and Nationalism.* U of Toronto P, 2002.

Girard, Daniel. "Caravan Calls '89 Fair a Success." *Toronto Star*, 25 Jun. 1989, p. A25.

"Glossary." *Immigration and Citizenship Canada*, www.cic.gc.ca/english/helpcentre /glossary.asp#self_employed_person/.

Gluhovic, Milija. *Performing European Memories: Trauma, Ethics, Politics.* Palgrave Macmillan, 2013.

Godin, Jean-Cléo, and Dominique Lafon. *Dramaturgies québécoises des années quatre-vingt: Michel Marc Bouchard, Normand Chaurette, René-Daniel Dubois, Marie Laberge.* Leméac, 1999. Théâtre/essai.

Gold, Muriel. "A Study of Three Montreal Children's Theatres." McGill, 1972. digitool.library.mcgill.ca/webclient/StreamGate?folder_id=0&dvs=1520881820442~90. M.A. thesis.

Gonshor, Anna. "Anna Gonshor's Oral History." Conducted by Sara Israel, Wexler Oral History Project, *Yiddish Book Center*, 13 Dec. 2011, www.yiddishbookcenter.org /collections/oral-histories/interviews/woh-fi-0000212/anna-gonshor-2011.

---. "Di yidishe dramatishe grupe in montreol" ("The Yiddish Drama Group in Montreal"). *Yugntruf*, no. 22, 1971, pp. 9–11. *Yugntruf*, yugntruf.org/zhurnal /zhurnal.php?ui=embed&numer=22#page/9/mode/1up.

Gonshor, Aron. "Anna Gonshor's Oral History." Conducted by Sara Israel, Wexler Oral History Project, *Yiddish Book Center*, 15 Dec. 2011, www.yiddishbookcenter.org /collections/oral-histories/interviews/woh-fi-0000213/aron-gonshor-2011.

"Government of Canada Sets a Principled Foundation for Advancing Renewed Relationships with Indigenous Peoples based on the Recognition of Rights." *Department of Justice Canada*, 14 Jun. 2017, www.canada.ca/en/department-justice/news/2017/07/government_of_canadasetsaprincipledfoundationforadvancingrenewed.html.

Graham, Karen. "It's OK to Use the Word 'Racist' or 'Racism' if it Fits." *Digital Journal*, 31 Mar. 2019, http://www.digitaljournal.com/news/world/it-s-ok-to-use-the-word-racist-or-racism-if-it-fits/article/546605.

Grammy, Tara, and Tom Arthur Davis. *Mahmoud.* Playwrights Canada, 2015.

"Great Iroquois Indian Poetess." *Times* (Prince Albert), 19 Sep. 1907, p. 3. Saskatchewan Archives Board, R-1.586.

Green, Jesse. "*Kim's Convenience* Shares Family Ties, for Better and Worse." *New York Times*, 6 Jul. 2017, www.nytimes.com/2017/07/06/theater/review-kims-convenience.html.

Greenhill, Pauline. "Backyard World/Canadian Culture: Looking at Festival Agendas." *Canadian University Music Review*, vol. 19, no. 2, 1999, pp. 37–46.

Guay, Hervé. "Bref historique du multilinguisme dans le théâtre québécois." *Jeu: Revue de théâtre*, no. 145, 2012, pp. 44–50.

---. "Sorties du cadre." *Spirale : arts • lettres • sciences humaines*, no. 244, 2013, pp. 85–87.

Habell-Pallán, Michelle. "'Don't Call Us Hispanic.' Popular Latino Theater in Vancouver." *Latino/a Popular Culture*, edited by Habell- Pallán and Mary Romero. New York UP, 2002, pp. 268–93.

Hagan, John. *Northern Passage: American Vietnam War Resisters in Canada.* Harvard UP, 2001.

Halberstam, Judith. *The Queer Art of Failure.* Duke UP, 2011.

Haque, Eve. *Multiculturalism Within a Bilingual Framework.* U of Toronto P, 2012.

Harvey, Dustin, and Adrienne Wong. *Landline. Canadian Theatre Review*, no. 159, 2014, pp. 68–80.

---. *Landline: Toronto and Hamilton.* August 2017, Toronto, Ontario.

Harvey, Dustin Scott. "Make What You Need." *In Defence of Theatre: Aesthetic Practices and Social Interventions*, edited by Kathleen Gallagher and Barry Freeman, U of Toronto P, 2016, pp. 35–48.

Hatton, Barry. *The Portuguese: A Modern History.* Signal, 2011.

Hazelton, Hugh. *Latinocanadá: A Critical Study of Ten Latin American Writers of Canada.* McGill-Queen's UP, 2007.

---. "Kurapel's *Prometheus*: Breaking the Bounds." *Fronteras Vivientes: Eight Latina/o Canadian Plays*, edited by Natalie Alvarez, Playwrights Canada, 2013, pp. 2–10.

Henderson, Stuart. "Off the Streets and into the Fortress: Experiments in Hip Separatism at Toronto's Rochdale College, 1968–1975." *The Canadian Historical Review*, vol. 92, no.1, March 2011, pp. 107–33.

L'Hérault, Pierre. "Pour une cartographie de l'hétérogène: dérives identitaires des années 1980." *Fictions de l'identitaire au Québec*, edited by Sherry Simon et al., XYZ, 1991, pp. 56–102. Etudes et documents.

Hernandez, Catherine. *Singkil.* Playwrights Canada, 2009.

Hewitt, Steven. "'Old Myths Die Hard': The Transformation of the Mounted Police in Alberta and Saskatchewan." U of Saskatchewan, 1997. Dissertation.

"Hire a Temporary Worker Through the Seasonal Agricultural Worker Program." *Government of Canada*, www.canada.ca/en/employment-social-development /services/foreign-workers/agricultural/seasonal-agricultural.html.

Hirsch, Marianne. *The Generation of Postmemory: Writing and Visual Culture After the Holocaust.* Columbia UP, 2012.

Historical Atlas of Canada Online Learning Project. "Immigrants to Canada 1891–1961." www.historicalatlas.ca/website/hacolp/national_perspectives/population/UNIT_22 /U22_Graph_Immigrants_to_Canada_9161.htm.

Ho, Olivia. "Timely, Heartfelt Look at Refugees Through the Ages." *The Straits Times*, 28 Jan. 2018, www.straitstimes.com/lifestyle/arts /timely-heartfelt-look-at-refugees-through-the-ages.

Hogan, Skylee-Storm, and Krista McCracken. "Doing the Work: The Historian's Place in Indigenization and Decolonization." *Active History*, 12 Dec. 2016, activehistory.ca/2016/12 /doing-the-work-the-historians-place-in-indigenization-and-decolonization/.

"Home." *RielCo Productions Inc.*, rielcoproductions.com.

Houston, Andrew. "Seasons of Immigration to . . . a Non-Place Near You." Rev. of *The Season of Immigration to the West*, prod. by MT Space, Kitchener, ON, 13–14 June 2005, *Canadian Theatre Review*, vol. 125, 2006, pp. 110–15.

Houston, Andrew, and Majdi Bou-Matar. "Building Community and Occupying Space: An Interview with Majdi Bou-Matar." *Canadian Theatre Review*, vol. 157, 2014, pp. 75–78.

Howard, Philip S.S. "On the Back of Blackness: Contemporary Canadian Blackface and the Consumptive Production of Post-Racialist, White Canadian Subjects." *Social Identities*, vol. 24, no. 1, 2008, pp. 87–103.

Hunt, Nigel. "Breaking New Ground: *Kim's Convenience* to be Canada's 1st Sitcom Led by Asians." *CBC News*, 1 Oct. 2016, www.cbc.ca/news/entertainment /kims-convenience-diversity-1.3783998.

Hurley, Erin. "Devenir Autre: Languages of Marco Micone's 'culture immigrée.'" *Theatre Research in Canada / Recherches théâtrales au Canada*, vol. 25, no. 1, 2004, pp. 1–23.

---. *National Performance: Representing Quebec from Expo 67 to Céline Dion*. U of Toronto P, 2011.

Icart, Jean-Claude. "La communauté haïtienne de Montréal." *Haïti Tribune*, vol. 18, 2004, p. 4.

Ignatieff, Michael. *Blood and Belonging: Journeys into the New Nationalism*. Viking, 1993.

Imre, Zoltán. "Staging the Nation: Changing Concepts of a National Theatre in Europe." *New Theatre Quarterly*, vol. 24, no. 1, 2008, pp. 75–95.

"Immigration Act, 1910." *Canadian Museum of Immigration at Pier 21*, www.pier21.ca /research/immigration-history/immigration-act-1910.

Jackson, Adrian. "Provoking Intervention." *The Applied Theatre Reader*, edited by Tim Prentki and Sheila Preston, Routledge, 2009, pp. 41–46.

Jacob, Marjolaine. "Jury's Comments." Letter to the Rahul Varma. 26 Aug. 1994.

Jaffe, Shain, Chris Clifford, Robert Nasmith, and Jim Plaxton. Personal interview with David DeGrow. 18 Apr. 2017.

Jameson, Fredric. "Marxism and Historicism." *New Literary History*, vol. 11, no. 1, 1979, pp. 41–73.

Jauvoish, Simon. *Dawn in Heaven*. Mount Saint Vincent U, Canadian Drama Collection, C.D.Coll 24.13. Microfilm.

Jennings, Sarah. *Art and Politics: The History of the National Arts Centre*. Dundurn, 2009.

Johnson, E. Pauline. *Canadian Born*. 1903. *Project Gutenberg Canada*, 31 Dec. 2010, www.gutenberg.ca/ebooks/johnsonpauline-canadianborn /johnsonpauline-canadianborn-00-h-dir/johnsonpauline-canadianborn-00-h.html.

---. *Flint and Feather: Collected Verse by E. Pauline Johnson*. Project Gutenberg, www.gutenberg.org/ebooks/5625.

---. "The Riders of the Plains." Johnson, *Canadian Born*, pp. 27–30.

---. "A Strong Race Opinion: On the Indian Girl in Modern Fiction." 1892. *Canadian Literature*, Apr. 2013, canlit.ca/wp-content/uploads/2016/02/a_strong_race_opinion.pdf.

---. "Wolverine." *Flint and Feather: Collected Verse.* 1917. *Project Gutenberg,* 24 Jun. 2004, www.gutenberg.org/ebooks/5625.

Johnston, Denis W. *Up the Mainstream: The Rise of Toronto's Alternative Theatres, 1968–1975.* U of Toronto P, 1991.

Jones, Joseph. *Contending Statistics: The Numbers for U.S. Vietnam War Resisters in Canada.* Quarter Sheaf, 2005.

Jordão, Aida. "The Alt Stage and the Po-mo Page: Canadian Spaces for an Anglo-Portuguese Dramaturgy." Special issue of *Theatre Research in Canada,* "Defying the Monolingual Stage," edited by Art Babayants and Nicole Nolette, vol. 38, no. 2, Fall 2017, pp. 186–200.

---. "Performing the Portuguese Cleaning Lady: Subverting Gender, Class and Ethnic Typecasting on the Canadian Stage." *The Voice and Choice of Women in Portugal and in the Diaspora,* edited by Deolinda M. Adão, Institute of Governmental Studies, 2011, pp. 249–57.

---. "(Re)Presenting Inês de Castro: Two Audiences, Two Languages, One Feminism." *Revista de Estudos Anglo-Portugueses (REAP),* no. 18, 2009, pp. 259–77.

---. "Women and Tradition: *Funeral em Branco* and *My Aunt's Neighbours.*" *The Voice and Choice of Portuguese Immigrant Women,* edited by M. Marujo, A. Baptista, and A. Barbosa, U of Toronto, Department of Spanish and Portuguese, 2005, pp. 62–67.

Jubinville, Yves. "Frontières du théâtre: Sociocritique du joual et vie théâtrale au Québec depuis *Les belles-soeurs.*" *Emblématiques de l'époque du joual: Jacques Renaud, Gérald Godin, Michel Tremblay, Yvon Deschamps,* edited by André Gervais, Lanctôt, 2000, pp. 135–46.

---. "Une mémoire en veilleuse : Bilan et défis de l'historiographie théâtrale au Québec." *Le théâtre québécois, 1975–1995,* edited by Dominique Lafon, Les Editions Fides, 2001, pp. 37–54.

---. "Le partage des voix: Approche génétique de la langue dans les dramaturgies québécoises contemporaines." *Études françaises,* vol. 43, no. 1, pp. 111–19.

Kandil, Yasmine. "Effective Methods of Theatre for Development: Understanding the Conditions That Provide Autonomy and Empowerment for Marginalized Communities." University of Victoria, 2012. Dissertation.

Kaplan, Jon, and Glenn Sumi. "Summerworks Reviews." *NOW Magazine,* 14 Aug. 2003. nowtoronto.com/stage/theatre/summerworks-reviews-2003-08-14/.

Kates, Joanna. "Potpourri Taste of Poland a Labor of Love." *Globe and Mail,* 24 Jun. 1987, p. C11.

Kemeid, Olivier. *The Aeneid: Inspired by Virgil's* The Aeneid. Translated by Maureen Labonté. *Scripting (Im)migration*, edited by Yana Meerzon, Playwrights Canada, 2019, pp. 9–94.

---. *Dossier Pédagogique. Théâtre la Seizième*, 10 Jan. 2012, web.archive.org /web/20180505191421/http://seizieme.ca/wp-content/uploads/2013/10 /Ruines-rouges-dossier-pedagogique.pdf.

---. *Furieux et désespérés*. Centre des auteurs dramatiques, 2014. Unpublished script.

---. *Moi, dans les ruines rouges du siècle*. Leméac, 2013.

---. "Le théâtre contre la culture." *Jeu*, vol. 126, no. 1, 2008, pp. 83–85.

Kemeid, Olivier, and Yana Meerzon. "A Dialogue Between Olivier Kemeid and Yana Meerzon." *Scripting (Im)migration*, edited by Meerzon, Playwrights Canada, 2019, 95–100.

Keyes, Daniel. "Whites Singing Red Face in British Columbia in the 1950s." *Theatre Research in Canada*, vol. 32, no. 1, 2011, www.journals.hil.unb.ca/index.php/tric /article/view/18572/20164.

Kibria, Nazli. "Immigrant Families." *Asian American Society: An Encyclopedia*, edited by Mary Yu Danico, Sage, 2014.

King, Robin Levinson. "A Brief History of Americans Moving to Canada." *Toronto Star*, 9 Mar. 2016, www.thestar.com/news/canada/2016/03/09/moving-to-canada -an-american-rite.html.

Knowles, Ric. "Collective Differences in MT Space." *alt.theatre*, vol. 4, no. 4, 2006, pp. 8–11.

---. General Editor's Preface. *Performing Indigeneity*, edited by Yvette Nolan and Knowles, Playwrights Canada, 2016, pp. v–vii.

---. *How Theatre Means*. Palgrave-McMillan, 2014.

---. *Performing the Intercultural City*. U of Michigan P, 2017.

Knowles, Ric, and Ingrid Mündel, editors. *"Ethnic," Multicultural, and Intercultural Theory*. Playwrights Canada, 2009. Critical Perspectives on Canadian Theatre in English 14.

Knowles, Valerie. *Strangers at Our Gates: Canadian Immigration and Immigration Policy, 1540–2006*. Revised ed, Dundurn, 2007.

"Di konstitutsye fun der Yugntruf bavegung" ("The Constitution of the Yugntruf Movement"). *Yugntruf*, no. 2, 1965, pp. 7–8. *Yugntruf*, yugntruf.org/zhurnal /zhurnal.php?ui=embed&numer=2#page/7/mode/1up.

Kordan, Bohdan. *Enemy Aliens, Prisoners of War: Internment in Canada During the Great War.* McGill-Queens UP, 2002.

Kovacs, Alexandra (Sasha). "Beyond Shame and Blame in Pauline Johnson's Performance Histories." *Canadian Theatre Histories and Historiographies,* edited by Heather Davis-Fisch, Playwrights Canada, 2017, pp. 31–51. New Essays on Canadian Theatre 7.

---. "Pauline Johnson: Poet and Performer." *Canadian Plays and Performance Documents, 1606–1967,* edited by Allana Lindgren, Glen Nichols, and Tony Vickery, U of Alberta P, forthcoming.

Kuling, Peter, and Laura Levin. "Editorial: Digital Performance in Canada." *Canadian Theatre Review,* no. 159, 2014, pp. 5–8.

Kuper Margaliot, Ayelet. "Yiddish Periodicals Published by Displaced Persons, 1946–1949." Oxford, 1997. *University of Oxford,* ora.ox.ac.uk/objects/uuid :82b97ea5-3b1e-4feb-b8af-e3f9f6ae7317. Ph.D. dissertation.

Kuruvilla, Sunil. *Rice Boy.* Playwrights Canada, 2000.

Kusch, Frank. *All American Boys: Draft Dodgers in Canada from the Vietnam War.* Praeger, 2001.

Kymlicka, Will. *Finding Our Way: Rethinking Ethnocultural Relations in Canada.* Oxford UP, 1998.

Ladouceur, Louise. "Bilinguisme et traduction ludique sur les scènes franco-canadiennes de l'Ouest." *Jeu: Revue de théâtre,* no. 145, 2012, pp. 90–95.

Lafon, Dominique. "La langue-à-dire du théâtre québécois." *Théâtres québécois et cana-diens-français au XXe siècle : trajectoires et territoires,* edited by Hélène Beauchamp and Gilbert David, PU du Québec, 2003, pp. 181–96.

Larin, Stephen. "Canada's Election Message to the World: Xenophobia Doesn't Play Here." *Globe and Mail,* 22 October, 2015, www.theglobeandmail.com /opinion/canadas-election-message-to-the-world-xenophobia-doesnt-play-here /article26915541/.

Larrue, Jean-Marc. *Le théâtre yiddish à Montréal/Yiddish Theatre in Montreal.* Bilingual ed., Éditions Jeu, 1996.

"Lastman Apologizes Over and Over for 'Off the Cuff' Remarks." *CBC,* 22 Jun. 2001, www.cbc.ca /news/canada/lastman-apologizes-over-and-over-for-off-the-cuff-remarks-1.254922.

Lauro, Shirley. *All Through the Night.* Samuel French, 2010.

Le Blanc, Charles. *Laïcité et Humanisme.* U of Ottawa P, 2015.

"Le crucifix de l'Assemblée nationale restera à sa place." *Radio-Canada*, 24 Oct. 2017, ici.radio-canada.ca/nouvelle/1063196/crucifix-assemblee-nationale-restera-place.

Lee, Adrian. *"Kim's Convenience*: A TV First That Doesn't Buckle Under Pressure." *Maclean's* 10 Oct. 2016, www.macleans.ca/culture/television/kims-convenience-a-tv-first-that-doesnt-buckle-under-the-pressure/.

Lee, Jo-Anne, and Sandrina De Finney. "Using Popular Theatre for Engaging Racialized Minority Girls in Exploring Questions of Identity and Belonging." *Child & Youth Services*, vol. 26, no. 2, 2004, pp. 95–118.

Lee, Josephine. "Between Immigration and Hyphenation: The Problems of Theorizing Asian American Theater." *Journal of Dramatic Theory and Criticism*, vol. 13, no. 1, Fall 1998, pp. 45–69.

Lee, M. Owen. *Fathers and Sons in Virgil's Aeneid: Tum Genitor Natum*. State U of New York P, 1979.

Lehoux, Jean-Philippe. "Le pari d'un mythe." *Dossier Pédagogique* by Olivier Kemeid, *Théâtre la Seizième*, 10 Jan. 2012, web.archive.org/web/20180505191421/http://seizieme.ca/wp-content/uploads/2013/10/Ruines-rouges-dossier-pedagogique.pdf.

Lei, Daphne. "Interruption, Intervention, Interculturalism: Robert Wilson's HIT Productions in Taiwan." *Theatre Journal*, vol. 63, no. 4, 2011, pp. 571–86.

Leroux, Louis Patrick. "From *langue* to Body: The Quest for the 'Real' in Québécois Theatre." *New Canadian Realisms*, edited by Roberta Barker and Kim Solga, Playwrights Canada, 2012, pp. 106–23.

---. "De la langue au corps. L'inscription et le discours du 'vrai' dans le corps performant, d'*Aurore, l'enfant martyre* à Dave St-Pierre." *Le jeu des positions: discours du théâtre québécois*, edited by Leroux and Hervé Guay, Nota Bene, 2014, pp. 31–73. Séminaires 23.

"Let's Move On, Says Quebec Accommodation Commission." CBC News, 22 May 2008, www.cbc.ca/news/canada/montreal/let-s-move-on-says-quebec-accommodation-commission-1.709976.

Levinas, Emmanuel. *Otherwise Than Being or Beyond Essence*. Translated by A. Lingis, Duquesne UP, 1998.

Li, Peter S. *Cultural Diversity in Canada: The Social Construction of Racial Differences*. Research and Statistics Division, Canadian Department of Justice, 2000. *Department of Justice*, www.justice.gc.ca/eng/rp-pr/csj-sjc/jsp-sjp/rp02_8-dr02_8/rp02_8.pdf.

---. "A World Apart: The Multicultural World of Visible Minorities and the Art World of Canada." *The Canadian Review of Sociology and Anthropology*, vol. 31, no. 4, 1994, pp. 365–91.

Lindberg, Darcy. "The Myth of the Wheat King and the Killing of Colten Boushie." *The Conversation*, 1 Mar. 2018, theconversation.com /the-myth-of-the-wheat-king-and-the-killing-of-colten-boushie-92398.

Little, Edward, and Steven High. "Partners in Conversation: Ethics and the Emergent Practice of Oral History Performance." *History, Memory, Performance*, Palgrave Macmillan, 2015, pp. 240–56.

Lopez, Lori Kido. *Asian American Media Activism: Fighting for Cultural Citizenship*. New York UP, 2016.

Lourenço, Mário. Personal interview with Aida Jordão, 15 Dec. 2017.

Lowe, Lisa. *Immigrant Acts: On Asian American Cultural Politics*. Duke UP, 2012.

Lowman, Emma Battell, and Adam J. Barker. *Settler: Identity and Colonialism in 21st Century Canada*. Fernwood, 2015.

Maalouf, Amin. *Les identités meurtrières*. Grasset, 1998.

MacDonnell, Fina. "Re. 1970's Toronto theatre." Email received by David DeGrow, 19 Jan. 2017.

MacDonnell, Tom. *Making It Up As We Go Along. CBC Radio*, 1 May 1989–5 May 1989.

Maga, Carly. "Robert Lepage's Controversial Kanata Misses the Mark in Paris." *Toronto Star*, 18 Dec. 2018, www.thestar.com/entertainment/stage/opinion/2018/12/18 /robert-lepages-kanata-pisode-1-la-controverse-misses-the-mark.html.

Maldonado-Torres, Nelson. "Enrique Dussel's Liberation Thought in the Decolonial Turn." *TRANSMODERNITY*, vol. 1, no. 1, 2011, pp. 1–30.

Mangan, James J. *Gerard Keegan's Famine Diary: Journey to a New World*. Wolfhound, 1991.

Manole, Diana. "Accented Actors: From Stage to Stages via a Convenience Store." *Theatre Research in Canada*, vol. 36, no. 2, 2015, pp. 255–74.

Manuel, Arthur. *Unsettling Canada: A National Wake-up Call*. Between the Lines, 2015.

Maracle, Lee. *My Conversations with Canadians*. BookThug, 2017.

Margolis, Rebecca. "*Les belles-sœurs* and *Di shvegerins*: Translating Québécois into Yiddish for the Montreal Stage in 1992." *Translation Effects: The Making of Modern Culture in Canada*, edited by Luise von Flotow and Sherry Simon, U of Ottawa P, 2013, pp. 461–78.

---. "Holocaust and Post-Holocaust Yiddish Theatre in Montreal: A Canadian Response to Catastrophe." *Leket. Jiddistik Heute / Yiddish Studies Today / yidishe shtudyes haynt*, edited by Marion Aptroot, Düsseldorf UP, 2012, pp. 525–40. *Düsseldorf University*, docserv.uni-duesseldorf.de/servlets/DerivateServlet/Derivate-23711/cuknya6h /Leket_ganz_A.pdf.

Marques, Domingos, and João Medeiros. *Imigrantes Portugueses: 25 Anos no Canadá.* Movimento Comunitário Português, Festival Português, Ministry of Culture and Recreation, 1978.

Martin, Mayo. "Pioneer Performance Artist Amanda Heng Inspires Next Year's Singapore Fringe Fest." *Channel News Asia*, 10 Oct. 2017, www.channelnewsasia.com/news /lifestyle/pioneer-performance-artist-amanda-heng-inspires-next-year-s-9270206.

Martina Koechl, Natasha, and Sue Mythen. *Displaced*. 2017. Manuscript.

Martinez, Kathy. *O Nosso Fado*. 2017. Manuscript.

Martin Franco, Helena. "Altéro(s)philie ou les jeux de force de Fritta Caro." *Fritta Caro*, frittacaro.helenamartinfranco.com/fr/.

---. "Biografie." *Fritta Caro*, frittacaro.helenamartinfranco.com/fr/bio/.

---. "La coupe canadienne." *Fritta Caro*, frittacaro.helenamartinfranco.com/fr /performances/31-mars/.

---. "cv-bio." *Helena Martin Franco / Corazón Desfasado / Fritta Caro / Une Femme Éléphant*, www.helenamartinfranco.com/cv-fr.html.

---. "Incarnation/Conjuration." *Fritta Caro*, frittacaro.helenamartinfranco.com/fr /performances/incarnationconjuration/.

---. Interview with Pablo Gómez Barrios. *Radio Canada Internacional*, 17 May 2017, www.rcinet.ca/es/2017/05/17/helena-martin-franco-la-mujer-de-multiples-identidades/.

Martynowych, Orest T. "Ukrainian Immigrant Theatre 1904–1923." umanitoba.ca /faculties/arts/departments/ukrainian_canadian_studies/media/13_ESAY _Ukrainian_Immigrant_Theatre.pdf.

Massey, Vincent. Introduction. *Canadian Plays from Hart House Theatre, Volume 1*, edited by Massey, Macmillan, 1926, pp. v–vii.

McCabe, Nora. "Caravan Still 'Their Baby' for Cultural Dynamos: Zena and Leon Kossar Say Caravan Broke Down Barriers." *Toronto Star*, 14 Jun. 1998, p. C3.

McConachie, Bruce. "Towards a History of National Theatres in Europe." *National Theatres in a Changing Europe*, edited by S.E. Wilmer, Palgrave, 2008, pp. 48–60.

McDougall, Robert L. "Duncan Campbell Scott." *The Canadian Encyclopedia*, 18 Jan. 2018, www.thecanadianencyclopedia.ca/en/article/duncan-campbell-scott/.

McLennan, David. "Qu'Appelle." *The Encyclopedia of Saskatchewan*, esask.uregina.ca /entry/quappelle.jsp.

Meerzon, Yana. "Between Je and Moi: Staging the Heteroglossia of Immigrant Autobiography." *Theatre Research in Canada*, vol. 36, no. 2, 2015, pp. 290–311.

---. "Call for Papers." 2017.

---. "Multiculturalism, (Im)Migration, Theatre: The National Arts Centre, Ottawa, a Case of Staging Canadian Nationalism." *Journal of Contemporary Drama in English*, vol. 6, no. 1, 2018, pp. 113–130.

---. "Theatre and Immigration: From the Multiculturalism Act to the Sites of Imagined Communities." *Theatre Research in Canada*, vol. 36, no. 2, 2015, pp. 181–96.

---, editor. *Theatre Research in Canada*. Vol. 36, no. 2, 2015. Theatre & Immigration.

Milman, Vladimir. "URGENT: Support Needed for Levon Haftvan." *Torontovka.com*, 9 Dec. 2006, www.torontovka.com/forum?key=life.forum.topic&id=57473.

Milot, Micheline, and Stéphanie Tremblay. "Religion in the Quebec Public School System: A Change for Equality and Diversity." Government of Canada, 29 Sep. 2017, web.archive.org/web/20180808061109/www.horizons.gc.ca/en/content /religion-quebec-public-school-system-change-equality-and-diversity.

"Miss E. Pauline Johnson, the Famous Indian Elocutionist." *Prince Albert Advocate*, 25 Jan. 1898, p. 8. Saskatchewan Archives Board, R-1.571.

"Miss E. Pauline Johnson." *Prince Albert Advocate*, 1 Feb. 1898, p. 2. Saskatchewan Archives Board, R-1.571.

"Miss E. Pauline Johnson." *Qu'Appelle Progress*, 10 Feb. 1898, p. 8. Saskatchewan Archives Board, R-1.590.

"Miss E. Pauline Johnson's." *Qu'Appelle Progress*, 8 Sep. 1898, p. 4. Saskatchewan Archives Board, R-1.590.

"Miss Johnson Concluded." *Prince Albert Advocate*, 22 Feb. 1898, p. 8. Saskatchewan Archives Board, R-1.571.

"Miss Johnson's Entertainment." *Qu'Appelle Progress*, 15 Sep. 1898, p. 4. Saskatchewan Archives Board, R-1.590.

"Miss Johnson's Entertainments." *Qu'Appelle Progress*, 17 Feb. 1898, p. 8. Saskatchewan Archives Board, R-1.590.

"Miss Pauline Johnson, the Famous Authoress and Elocutionist." *Prince Albert Advocate*, 8 Feb. 1904, p. 8. Saskatchewan Archives Board, R-1.571.

"Miss Pauline Johnson." *Prince Albert Advocate*, 15 Feb. 1898, p. 8. Saskatchewan Archives Board, R-1.571.

"Mission and Vision." *MT Space*, www.mtspace.ca/mission-vision.

Mitchell, Roy. *Creative Theatre*. John Day, 1929.

Mixie and the Halfbreeds. By Julie Tamiko Manning and Adrienne Wong, directed by Jenna Rodgers, performances by Zoe Doyle and Vanessa Trenton, Fu-Gen Theatre Company, 3–15 Apr. 2018, Pia Bouman School, Scotiabank Studio Theatre, Toronto.

Mohr, Thomas. "Law and the Foundation of the Free State on 6 December 1922." *The Irish Jurist*, vol. 59, 2018, pp. 31–58.

Moi, Toril. *What is a Woman?: And Other Essays*. Oxford UP, 1999.

Mojica, Monique, and Ric Knowles. "Creation Story Begins Again: Performing Transformation, Bridging Cosmologies." *Performing Worlds into Being: Native American Women's Theater*, edited by Ann Elizabeth Armstrong, Kelli Lyon Johnson, and William A. Wortman, Miami UP, 2009, pp. 2–6.

Monpetit, Jonathan. "Quebec Group Pushes 'Interculturalism' in Place of Multiculturalism." *Globe and Mail*, 7 March 2011, www.theglobeandmail.com/news/politics/quebec-group-pushes-interculturalism-in-place-of-multiculturalism/article5569581/.

Moosavi, Marjan. "Interview with Mohammad Yaghoubi, Acclaimed Iranian Playwright and Director." *The Theatre Times*, 15 Oct. 2016, thetheatretimes.com/interview-mohammad-yaghoubi-acclaimed-iranian-playwright/.

---. "Ta'ziyeh—Ritual Performance During Muharram." *The Theatre Times*, 16 Oct. 2016, thetheatretimes.com/taziyeh-ritual-performance-during-muharram/.

Moss, Laura, ed. *Is Canada Postcolonial? Unsettling Canadian Literature*. Wilfrid Laurier UP, 2003.

Moss, Jane. "Cendres de cailloux et le langage lapidaire de Daniel Danis." *Dalhousie French Studies*, vol. 42, Spring 1998, pp. 173–85.

---. "Larry Tremblay and the Drama of Language." *American Review of Canadian Studies*, vol. 25, no. 2–3, 1995, pp. 251–67.

---. "Multiculturalism and Postmodern Theater: Staging Quebec's Otherness." *Mosaic*, vol. 29, no. 3, 1996, pp. 75–96.

---. "Le théâtre francophone en Ontario." *Introduction à la littérature franco-ontarienne*, edited by Melançon and Lucie Hotte, Prise de parole, 2010, pp. 71–111.

---. "Les théâtres francophones post-identitaire : état des lieux." *Canadian Literature*, no. 187, 1998, pp. 57–71.

"The Mounted Police." *Qu'Appelle Progress*, 4 Nov. 1886, p. 6. Saskatchewan Archives Board, R-1.590.

"Mrs. E.S. Haynes Tells Toronto About Dramatics." *Edmonton Bulletin*, 13 Mar. 1935, p. 14.

Muñoz, Alma E. "Canadá exige visa a visitants mexicanos, frente al exceso de solicitudes de refugio." *La Jornada* [Mexico City], 14 Jul. 2009, p. 13.

Nagel, Erica. "Aesthetic of Neighborliness: Possibilities for Integrating Community-Based Practices into Documentary Theatre." *Research in Drama Education*, vol. 17, no. 2, 2007, pp. 153–68.

Nalewajko-Kulikov, Joanna. "Yiddish Form, Socialist Content: Yiddish in Postwar Poland, 1945–1968." *Yiddish After 1945*, edited by Miriam Aptroot, Amsterdam Yiddish Symposium 11, Menasseh Ben Israel Institute, 2018, pp. 26–46.

Ndejuru, Lisa. *Je me souviens. Montréal Cultures*, March 2002.

---. *La guerre est une danse lente*. Aldar Hotel, Baghdad, March 2003.

---. "A Modest Reconciliation: Coming to Terms with Conflicted Stories Through Oral History, Dialogue, and Playback Theatre in Montreal's Rwandan Canadian Community." *Forced Migration, Reconciliation, and Justice*, edited by Megan Bradley, McGill-Queen's, 2015, pp.123–44.

---. *Le petit coin intact*. Monument National, Montréal, March 2012.

---. *Simultaneité*. Montréal, 2003. *Agence TOPO*, www.agencetopo.qc.ca/civilites /lisa_table.html.

---. "*Tuganire*: parlons en, discutons!" *Affirming Collaboration: Community and Humanist Activist Art in Québec and Elsewhere*, edited by Devora Neumark and Johanne Chagnon, Brush Education, 2011, pp. 224–230.

Ndiaye, Aly (Webster). "The Problem with *SLĀV*: Why Black People Aren't Applauding a Tribute to Slave Songs." *CBC News*, 28 Jun. 2018, www.cbc.ca/news/canada/montreal /the-problem-with-sl%C4%81v-1.4727432.

"Neither Black Nor White: Intermarried Jews and Mischlinge During the Third Reich." *Nuremburg Laws*, www.owlnet.rice.edu/~rar4619/home.html.

Nestor, Rob. "Almighty Voice." *Encyclopedia of Saskatchewan. Internet Archive*, web.archive.org/web/20170611085512/http://esask.uregina.ca/entry /almighty_voice_1875-97.html.

Nestruck, J. Kelly. "David Yee Plumbs New Emotional Depths with Affecting Play *Acquiesce*." *Globe and Mail*, 4 Nov. 2016, www.theglobeandmail.com/arts/theatre-and-performance /theatre-reviews/david-yee-plumbs-new-emotional-depths-with-affecting-play -acquiesce/article32677079/.

Nicholson, Frances, and Judith Kumin. *A Guide to International Refugee Protection and Building State Asylum Systems: Handbook for Parliamentarians No. 27, 2017.* Inter-Parliamentary Union and the United Nations High Commissioner for Refugees, 2017. *United Nations High Commissioner for Refugees*, www.unhcr.org/publications /legal/3d4aba564/refugee-protection-guide-international-refugee-law-handbook -parliamentarians.html.

Nicholson, Helen. "Re-Locating Memory: Performance, Reminiscence and Communities of Diaspora." *The Applied Theatre Reader*, edited by Tim Prentki and Sheila Preston, Routledge, 2009, pp. 268–75.

Nixon, Richard. "Executive Order 11497-Amending the Selective Service Regulations to Prescribe Random Selection." 26 Nov. 1969. *The American Presidency Project*, www.presidency.ucsb.edu/ws/?pid=106002.

Noivo, Edite. *Inside Ethnic Families: Three Generations of Portuguese-Canadians.* McGill-Queen's UP, 1997.

Nolette, Nicole. "Du théâtre hétérolingue franco-canadien au Québec: sur le *Djibou/Dark Owl* et *Elephant Wake*." *Jeu: Revue de théâtre*, no. 145, 2012, pp. 83–89.

Noor, Javeed. "The Couple Who Put Toronto on the Map." *Toronto Star*, 4 Apr. 2009, www.thestar.com/news/gta/2009/04/04/the_couple_who_put_toronto_on_the_map.html.

"Notre mission." *Culture Montréal*, culturemontreal.ca/notre-mission/.

"The Novel Entertainment." *Prince Albert Advocate*, 15 Feb. 1898, p. 8. Saskatchewan Archives Board, R-1.571.

Nunes, Fernando. *Problems and Adjustments of the Portuguese Immigrant Family in Canada.* Secretaria de Estado das Comunidades Portuguesas, Centro de Estudos, 1986.

"The *Observer* Regards it as Most Regrettable." Editorial, *Vegreville Observer*, 2 Apr. 1919, p. 4.

O'Connor, Peter, and Michael Anderson, editors. *Applied Theatre: Research: Radical Departures.* Bloomsbury Methuen, 2015.

---. "Research in a Post-Normal World." *Applied Theatre Research: Radical Departures*, edited by O'Connor and Anderson, Bloomsbury, 2015, pp. 1–94.

Olivier, Aurélie. "Nous sommes tous des exilés: L'Énéide." *Jeu*, vol. 127, no. 2, 2008, pp. 31–34.

"O Nosso Fado." *O Nosso Fado*, www.onossofado.com. Inactive.

O'Toole, John, and Julie Dunn. *Pretending to Learn: Helping Children Learn Through Drama*. Longman, 2002.

Paiement, André. *Théâtre*. Vol. 3, Prise de parole, 1978.

Paquin, Elzéar. *Riel*. Translated by Eugene and Renate Benson, *Canada's Lost Plays, Volume Four: Colonial Quebec: French-Canadian Drama 1606–1906*, edited by Anton Wagner, CTR, 1982, pp. 203–69.

Parati, Graziella. *Migrant Writers and Urban Space in Italy: Proximities and Affect in Literature and Film*. Palgrave, 2017.

Paré, François. *Exiguity: Reflections on the Margins of Literature*. Translated by Lin Burman, Wilfred Laurier UP, 1997.

---. *Les littératures de l'exiguïté*. 2nd ed., Bibliothèque canadienne-française, Le Nordir, 2001.

Parizeau, Jacques. Public address, 30 Oct. 1995.

Park-Fuller, Linda M. "Performing Absence: The Staged Personal Narrative as Testimony." *Text and Performance Quarterly*, vol. 20, no. 1, 2009, pp. 20–42.

Parkin, Andrew, and Matthew Mendelsohn. "A New Canada: An Identity Shaped by Diversity." *The CRIC Papers*, Centre for Research and Information on Canada, Oct.2003, library.carleton.ca/sites/default/files/find/data/surveys/pdf_files/cric-gmnc-03-not_000.pdf.

Pedrosa, Sara. "Re: photos of O Nosso Fado." Email received by A. Jordão, 18 Jun. 2018.

"People." *Modern Times Stage Company*, moderntimesstage.com/people/.

Pepin, Elsa. "Olivier Kemeid / Furieux et désespérés. La grande histoire jusqu'à soi." *Voir*, 13 Feb. 2013, voir.ca/scene/2013/02/14/olivier-kemeid-furieux-et-desesperes-la-grande-histoire-jusqua-soi/.

---. "Sasha Samar et Olivier Kemeid. Le théâtre et la vie: fatale attraction." *Voir*, 5 Jan. 2012, voir.ca/scene/2012/01/05/sasha-samar-et-olivier-kemeid-le-theatre-et-la-vie-fatale-attraction/.

Peritz, Ingrid, and Les Perreaux. "Quebec Reveals Religious Symbols to be Banned From Public Sector." Globe and Mail, 10 Sep. 2013, www.theglobeandmail.com/news/politics/quebec-unveils-plan-for-controversial-charter-of-values/article14214307/.

"P.K. Subban Blackface in Théâtre du Rideau Vert Play Deemed Offensive by Some." *CBC News*, 21 Dec. 2014, www.cbc.ca/news/canada/montreal/p-k-subban-blackface-in-th%C3%A9%C3%A2tre-du-rideau-vert-play-deemed-offensive-by-some-1.2880720.

Pon, Gordon. "Importing the Asian Model Minority Discourse into Canada: Implications for Social Work and Education." *Canadian Social Work Review*, vol. 17, no. 2, 2000, pp. 277–91.

Portes, Alejandro, and Rubén G. Rumbaut. *Legacies: The Story of the Immigrant Second Generation*. U of California P, 2001.

"Position School District To Be Improved: Remarks of Insp. Gibson at Trustees' Meeting Draw Objections." *Lethbridge Herald*, 31 Jan. 1935, p. 3.

Potter, Miles. "Re: Interview About Early Days of Passe Muraille?" Email received by David DeGrow, 15 Jan. 2018.

Prendergast, Monica, and Juliana Saxton, editors. *Applied Theatre: International Case Studies and Challenges for Practice*, second ed., Intellect, 2016.

---. "Seduction of the Real: The Significance of Fiction in Applied Theatre." *Research in Drama Education: The Journal of Applied Theatre and Performance*, vol. 20, no. 3, 2015, pp. 280–84.

Prentki, Tim. "Fool's Play or Juggling with Neoliberalism." *Applied Theater: Development*, edited by Prentki, Bloomsbury Methuen, 2015, pp. 56–89.

Prentki, Tim, and Sheila Preston, editors. *The Applied Theatre Reader*. Routledge, 2009.

Prentki, Tim, and Jan Selman. *Popular Theatre in Political Culture*. Intellect, 2003.

"Programme de soutien aux organismes—annonce des résultats." *Conseil des arts et des lettres du Québec*, www.calq.gouv.qc.ca/en/grants/programmes-de-soutien-aux-organismes/.

"The Programmes for the Emmanuel College Boys' Entertainment." *Prince Albert Advocate*, 27 Jan. 1902, "Town and Country." Saskatchewan Archives Board, R-1.571.

Pritz, Alexandra. "Ukrainian Cultural Traditions in Canada: Theatre, Choral Music and Dance, 1891–1967." U of Ottawa, 1977. *University of Ottawa*, ruor.uottawa.ca /handle/10393/10564. Ph.D. dissertation.

Pulido, Daniel, editor. *Teatro Popular. Por los Derechos Sexuales y Reproductivos en Nicaragua. Movimiento de Teatro Popular Sin Fronteras (Movitep-SF)*, Managua Majagüe, 2008.

Qu'Appelle Historical Society. *Qu'Appelle Footprints to Progress: A History of Qu'Appelle and District*, Qu'Appelle Historical Society, 1980.

Quan, Betty. *Mother Tongue*. 1996. Scirocco, 1999.

Rahnema, Saeed. "Iranian Canadians." *The Canadian Encyclopedia*, 23 Jan. 2018, www.thecanadianencyclopedia.ca/en/article/iranians/.

Ramos, Helder. Personal interview with Aida Jordão, 7 Dec. 2017.

Rao, Sathya. "L'actualité de Michel Tremblay traducteur et adaptateur: derrière le miroir de l'idéologie." *Recherches sémiotiques*, vol. 29, no. 2–3, 2009, pp. 115–32.

Rasky, Frank. "Eat Your Way Around the World." *Toronto Star*, 20 Jun. 1979, p. D1.

Regan, Paulette. *Unsettling the Settler Within: Indian Residential Schools, Truth Telling, and Reconciliation in Canada.* UBC Press, 2011.

"Regional Consultations on Services to Newcomer & Ethno-Cultural Minority Children, Youth and Families. Consultation Summary." 2000. *Mothers Matter Centre*, www.mothersmattercentre.ca/wp-content/articles/Newcomer_Ethnocultural _minority_children_youth_families_AMSSA_%202011.pdf.

Renaud, Andrea. *The History of Theatre Passe Muraille from 1968–69 to 1996–*. Vol. 1–3, Toronto Reference Library, 792.09713 R249.

Renzetti, Elizabeth. "Those Weary, Huddled Masses Become the Fabric of Canada." *Globe and Mail*, 5 Sep. 2015, www.theglobeandmail.com/opinion /those-weary-huddled-massesbecome-the-fabric-of-canada/article26225470/.

Report of the Royal Commission on Bilingualism and Biculturalism. Government of Canada, 1967.

"Révolution tranquille." *L'Encyclopédie Canadienne*, www.encyclopediecanadienne.ca/fr /article/revolution-tranquille/.

Ricaño-Alcalá, Pilar, et al. *Forced Migrations of Colombians: Colombia, Ecuador, Canada.* Corporación Región, U of British Columbia and FLACSO Ecuador, 2008.

Rich, Adrienne. "Compulsory Heterosexuality and Lesbian Existence." *Signs: Journal of Women in Culture and Society*, vol. 5, no. 4, Summer 1980, pp. 631–660.

Ricoeur, Paul. *Memory, History, Forgetting.* Translated by Kathleen Blamey and David Pellauer, U of Chicago P, 2004.

Roach, Joseph. *Cities of the Dead: Circum-Atlantic Performance.* Columbia UP, 1996.

Robert, Lucie. "The Language of Theatre." *Essays on Modern Quebec Theater*, edited by Joseph I Donohoe and Jonathan M. Weiss, Michigan State UP, 1995, pp. 109–29.

---. "Pour une histoire de la dramaturgie québécoise." *L'Annuaire théâtral: Revue québécoise d'études théâtrales*, no. 5–6, 1988, pp. 163–69.

Rokem, Freddie. "Discursive Practices and Narrative Models: History, Poetry, Philosophy." *History, Memory, Performance*, edited by David Dean, Yana Meerzon, and Kathryn Prince, Palgrave McMillan, 2015, pp. 19–35.

---. *Performing History: Theatrical Representations of the Past in Contemporary Theatre.* U of Iowa P, 2000.

Rosen, Joseph. "Among the Hasidim." *The Walrus,* 22 Feb. 2017, thewalrus.ca /among-the-hasidim/.

Roskies, David G. (writing as "A Montrealer"). "Der amerikaner yiddisher teater: vos tut men?" ("The American Yiddish Theatre: What Should Be Done?"). *Yugntruf,* no. 22, 1971, pp. 11–13. *Yugntruf,* yugntruf.org/zhurnal/zhurnal .php?ui=embed&numer=22#page/10/mode/1up.

---. "A Personal History of Holocaust Remembrance." *Forward,* 25 Apr. 2017, forward.com/culture/369875/a-personal-history-of-holocaust-remembrance/.

---. *Yiddishlands: A Memoir.* Wayne State UP, 2008.

Roskies, David G., and Anita Diamant. *Holocaust Literature: A History and Guide.* Brandeis UP, 2012.

Roskies, Dinele. "Shafndik a yiddish teater" ("Creating a Yiddish Theatre"). *Yugntruf,* no. 22, 1971, pp. 5–8. *Yugntruf,* yugntruf.org/zhurnal /zhurnal.php?ui=embed&numer=22#page/5/mode/1up.

Roslin, Charles. "Canada's Bolshevist Drama—Miroslav Irchan, Playwright and Prophet of a Proletarian Revolution." *Prophets and Proletarians: Documents on the History of the Rise and Decline of Ukrainian Communism in Canada,* compiled, edited, and translated by John Kolasky, Canadian Institute of Ukrainian Studies, 1990, pp. 72–77.

Rouquié, Alain. *Extremo Occidente: Introducción a América Latina.* Translated by Daniel Zadunaisky, Emecé Editores, 1990.

"Royal Commission on Chinese Immigration, 1885." *Canadian Museum of Immigration at Pier 21,* pier21.ca/research/immigration-history /royal-commission-on-chinese-immigration-1885.

Rubin, Don, editor. *Canadian Theatre History: Selected Readings.* Copp Clark, 1996.

---. "Creeping Toward a Culture: The Theatre in English Canada Since 1945." *Canadian Theatre History: Selected Readings,* edited by Rubin, Copp Clark, 1996, pp. 307–20.

Rudakoff, Judith, editor. *Questionable Activities: The Best.* Playwrights Canada, 2000.

Ruprecht, Alvina. "Effets sonores et signification dans *Les Belles-soeurs* de Michel Tremblay." *Voix et Images,* vol. 12, no. 3, 1987, pp. 439–51.

Rutherford, Robert W. *The Surrender of Poundmaker to Major-General Middleton at Battleford, Saskatchewan, on May 26, 1885.* 1887. *Library and Archives Canada,* www.collectionscanada.gc.ca/pam_archives/index.php?fuseaction=genitem .displayItem&rec_nbr=2837188&lang=eng&rec_nbr_list=2837188.

Ryan, Phil. *Multicultiphobia*. U of Toronto P, 2010.

Sadlier, Darlene J. "Feminism in Portugal: A Brief History." *The Question of How: Women Writers and New Portuguese Literature*, Greenwood, 1989, pp. 113–29.

Saldaña, J. "Ethical Issues in an Ethnographic Performance Text: The 'Dramatic Impact of 'Juicy Stuff.'" *Research in Drama Education*, vol. 3, no. 2, 1998, pp. 181–96.

Salinas, Jr., Cristobal, and Adele Lozano. "Mapping and Recontextualizing the Evolution of the Term Latinx: An Environmental Scanning in Higher Education." *Journal of Latinos and Education*, vol. 16, 2017, DOI: 10.1080/15348431.2017.1390464.

Salverson, Julie. "Performing Emergency: Witnessing, Popular Theatre, and the Lie of the Literal." *Theatre Topics*, vol. 6, no. 2, 1996, pp. 181–91.

---. "Transgressive Storytelling or an Aesthetic of Injury: Performance, Pedagogy and Ethics." *Theatre Research in Canada*, vol. 20, no. 1, 1999, pp. 35–51.

---. "Witnessing Subjects: A Fool's Help." *A Boal Companion: Dialogues on Theatre and Cultural Politics*, edited by Jan Cohen-Cruz and Mady Schutzman, Routledge, 2006, pp. 146–57.

Samur, Sebastian. "'In Sundry Languages' Pleasure and Disorientation through Multilingual Melange." Special issue of *Theatre Research in Canada*, "Defying the Monolingual Stage," edited by Art Babayants and Nicole Nolette, vol. 38, no. 2, Fall 2017, pp. 236–41.

"Sasha Samar." *Agent Rebel*, www.agentrebel.com/en/actors-details/sasha-samar.

Satin, Mark, editor. *Manual for Draft-Age Immigrants to Canada*. Toronto Anti-Draft Programme, House of Anansi, 1968.

Saunders, Richard. "Canada as a Fiction in the Imperial Genre." *Fictive Canada: Indigenous Slaves and the Captivating Narratives of a Mythic Nation*, edited by Saunders. *Press for Conversion* 69, Fall 2017, pp. 2–3.

Schechner, Richard. "Drama, Theatre, Script, and Performance." *The Drama Review*, vol. 17, no. 3, 1973, pp. 5–36.

---. *Performance Theory*. Revised ed., Routledge, 2003.

Schultz, Albert. Foreword. *Kim's Convenience* by Ins Choi, House of Anansi, 2012. Kindle Edition.

Schwartz, Jan. *Survivors and Exiles: Yiddish Culture after the Holocaust*. Wayne State UP, 2015.

Schweitzer, Pam. *Reminiscence Theatre: Making Theatre from Memories*. Jessica Kingsley, 2007.

Scott, Duncan Campbell. *Pierre. Canadian Plays from Hart House Theatre, Volume 1*, edited by Vincent Massey, Macmillan, 1926, pp. 51–76.

"Secular Schools in Québec: A Necessary Change in Institutional Culture." Brief to the Minister of Education, Recreation and Sports, Gouvernement du Québec, Oct. 2006, www.education.gouv.qc.ca/fileadmin/site_web/documents/ministere/organismes /CAR_Avis_LaiciteScolaire_ang.pdf.

Serge, Joe. "Ukrainian Pavilion Ready to Cook, Dance up a Storm." *Toronto Star*, 5 Jun. 1989, p. C3.

Shandler, Jeffrey. *Adventures in Yiddishland: Postvernacular Language and Culture.* U of California P, 2006.

Shiomi, R.A. Preface. *Love + RelAsianships: A Collection of Contemporary Asian-Canadian Drama*. Vol. 1, edited by Nina Lee Aquino, Playwrights Canada, 2009, pp. iii–v

Sifton, Clifford. "The Immigrants Canada Wants." *Maclean's*, 1 Apr. 1922, archive.macleans.ca /search?QueryTerm=%22The+Immigrants+Canada+Wants%22&DocType =All&sort=.

Simmel, Georg. *The Sociology of Georg Simmel.* Translated and edited by Kurt Heinrich Wolff, Free Press, 1950.

---. "The Stranger." *The Sociology of Georg Simmel*, translated and edited by Kurt H. Wolff, Free Press, 1950, pp. 402–08.

Simmons, Alan B. "Latin American Migration to Canada: New Linkages in the Hemispheric Migration and Refugee Flow System." *International Journal*, vol. 48, no. 2, 1993, pp. 282–309.

Simon, Sherry. "Robert Lepage and the Languages of Spectacle." *Theater sans frontières: Essays on the Dramatic Universe of Robert Lepage*, edited by Joseph I. Donohoe and Jane M. Koustas, Michigan State UP, 2000, pp. 215–30.

---. *Le trafic des langues: traduction et culture dans la littérature québécoise.* Boréal, 1994.

Simonsen, Barbara, editor. *The Art of Rehearsal: Conversations with Contemporary Theatre Makers.* Bloomsbury, 2017.

"Six Selection Factors—Federal Skilled Workers (Express Entry)." *Government of Canada*, www.canada.ca/en/immigration-refugees-citizenship/services/immigrate-canada /express-entry/become-candidate/eligibility/federal-skilled-workers/six-selection -factors-federal-skilled-workers.html.

Slotkin, Lynn. "More from SummerWorks: *Almeida (The Glorious)* and *O Nosso Fado.*" *The Slotkin Letter*, 7 Aug. 2017, slotkinletter.com/2017/08 /more-from-summerworks-almeida-the-glorious-and-o-nosso-fado.

"A Small Rebellion." *Prince Albert Advocate*, 1 Jun. 1897. Saskatchewan Archives Board, R-1.571.

Soldevila, Philippe, and Christian Essiambre. *Les trois exils de Christian E.*, Dramaturges Éditeurs, 2013.

Soleymanlou, Mani. "Rajoutons des souches." *Liberté*, no. 300, 2013, pp. 21–22.

---. *Trois*. L'Instant même, 2014. Instant scène.

Solga, Kim. *Theatre and Feminism*. Palgrave Macmillan, 2016.

Sousa, Maria Leonor Machado de. *Inês de Castro: Um Tema Português na Europa*. 2nd ed., ACD Editores, 2004.

Speechly, H. M. *A Story of the Women's Institutes of Manitoba 1910–1934*. Manitoba Women's Institute, 1934.

Stanley, George F. G. "O'Donohue, William Bernard." *Dictionary of Canadian Biography*, vol. 10, U of Toronto/U Laval, 1972. *Dictionary of Canadian Biography*, www.biographi.ca/en/bio/o_donoghue_william_bernard_10E.html.

St. Bernard, Donna-Michelle. "What Did You Say About My Mama? On Being Productively Uppity." *Canadian Theatre Review*, vol. 146, no. 1, 2011, pp. 95–99.

Stewart, Allan. *"To the Memory of Brave Men": The Last Stand of Major Allan Wilson at the Shangani, Rhodesia, 4 December 1893*. *ArtUK.org*, www.artuk.org/discover/artworks /to-the-memory-of-brave-men-the-last-stand-of-major-allan-wilson-at-the -shangani-rhodesia-4-december-1893-58693.

Taylor, Charles. *Multiculturalism and the Politics of Recognition*. Princeton UP, 1992.

teatrOVAL. *O Nosso Baile*. Apr.–Jun. 1999. Workshop script and program.

"Teesri Duniya Theatre (Montreal)." *Alternatives*, www.alternatives.ca/en/allies /teesri-duniya-theatre-montreal.

Thalenberg, Chayele (Eileen). "Der montrealer yiddisher yugnt teater" ("The Montreal Yiddish Youth Theatre"). *Yugntruf*, no. 2, 1965, pp. 11–12. *Yugntruf*, yugntruf.org /zhurnal/zhurnal.php?ui=embed&numer=2#page/11/mode/1up.

Theatre Museum Canada. "Paul Thompson on involvement at Theatre Passe Muraille (Part 4 of 21)." *YouTube*, 30 Jul. 2009, youtu.be/uo-a16Mxxcs.

Theatre Passe Muraille. *the rochdale drama project*. 1969. *The History of Theatre Passe Muraille from 1968–69 to 1996*, vol. 1, by Andrea Renaud, 1996, pp. 1–17. Reference Library Collection, Toronto Public Library.

Thiessen, Jack. *Yiddish in Canada: The Death of a Language*. Verlag Schuster, 1973.

Thobani, Sunera. *Exalted Subjects: Studies in the Making of Race and Nation in Canada.* U of Toronto P, 2007.

Thomas, Lewis H. "Riel, Louis (1844–85)." *Dictionary of Canadian Biography*, vol. 11, U of Toronto/U Laval, 1982. *Dictionary of Canadian Biography*, www.biographi.ca/en /bio/riel_louis_1844_85_11E.html.

Thompson, Esther. "District Activities." *Institute News*, vol. 2, no. 2, May 1929, pp. 1, 3.

Thoroski, Cynthia. "Adventures in Ethnicity: Consuming Performances of Cultural Identity in Winnipeg's Folklorama." *Canadian Folklore*, vol. 19, no. 2, 1997, pp. 105–12.

Thoroski, Cynthia, and Pauline Greenhill. "Putting a Price on Culture: Ethnic Organisations, Volunteers, and the Marketing of Multiculturaly Festivals." *Ethnologies*, vol. 23, no. 1, 2001, pp. 189–209.

Tompkins, Joanne. *Unsettling Space: Contestations in Contemporary Australian Theatre.* Palgrave Macmillan, 2006.

Trace. By Jeff Ho, directed by Nina Aquino, performance by Jeff Ho, Factory Theatre, 16 Nov. to 3 Dec. 2017, Toronto.

Trudeau, Pierre Elliott. Remarks at the Ukrainian-Canadian Congress, 9 Oct. 1971.

---. Statement to the House of Commons. 8 Oct. 1971. *Canada History*, www.canadahistory.com /sections/documents/Primeministers/trudeau/docs-onmulticulturalism.htm.

Turner, Jane. *Eugenio Barba.* Routledge, 2004.

Turner, Raylene. "Number Four – The Invisible City." Email received by Peter Kuling, 3 Aug. 2017.

Turner, Victor. *Betwixt and Between: The Liminal Period in Rites De Passage. The Forest of Symbols: Aspects of Ndembu Ritual.* Cornell UP, 1967.

Ty, Eleanor. *Asianfail: Narratives of Disenchantment and the Model Minority.* U of Illinois P, 2017.

---. *Unfastened: Globality and Asian North American Narratives.* U of Minnesota P, 2010.

Urry, John. *The Tourist Gaze.* Sage, 2002.

Van Dyk, Lindsay. "Canadian Immigration Acts and Legislation." *Canadian Museum of Immigration at Pier 21*, pier21.ca/research/immigration-history /canadian-immigration-acts-and-legislation.

Varma, Rahul. "Opinion: Systemic Discrimination and Cultural Hegemony in Arts Funding" *Montréal Gazette*, 14 Nov. 2017, montrealgazette.com/opinion /opinion-systemic-discrimination-and-cultural-hegemony-in-arts-funding.

---. "Opinion: Use of Blackface is Unnecessary and Totally Demeaning." *Montréal Gazette*, 2 Jan. 2015, montrealgazette.com/entertainment/theatre /opinion-use-of-blackface-is-unnecessary-and-totally-demeaning.

---. "Staging Peace in Times of War: Celebrating Teesri Duniya Theatre's Twenty-Fifth Anniversary." *alt.theatre*, vol. 4, nos. 2 & 3, May 2006, pp. 4–7.

---. "Teesri Duniya Theatre: Diversifying Diversity with Relevant Works of Theatre." *South Asian Popular Culture*, vol. 7, no. 3, Oct 2009, pp. 179–94.

Vettraino, Elinor, and Warren Linds. *Playing in a House of Mirrors. Applied Theatre as Reflective Practice*. Sense, 2015.

Vicente, João. "Sears Ontario Drama Festival: Estudantes apresentam emocionante peça de teatro centrada em lutas laborais da comunidade portuguesa." *Sol Português*, no. 1682, 10 Mar. 2017, pp. 14–15.

"The Vietnam Lotteries." *Selective Service System*, www.sss.gov/About/History -And-Records/lotter1.

Wagner, Anton, editor. *Canada's Lost Plays, Volume Three: The Developing Mosaic*. CTR, 1980.

---, editor. *Canada's Lost Plays, Volume Four: Colonial Quebec: French-Canadian Drama 1606–1906*. CTR, 1982.

Wagner, Anton, and Richard Plant, editors. *Canada's Lost Plays, Volume One: The Nineteenth Century*. CTR, 1978.

Waiser, Bill, "Our Shared Destiny?" *The Heavy Hand of History: Interpreting Saskatchewan's Past*, edited by Gregory P. Marchildon, Canadian Plains Research Center, 2005, pp. 7–30.

Walcott, Rinaldo. "Caribbean Pop Culture in Canada; Or, the Impossibility of Belonging to the Nation." *Small Axe*, vol. 9, no. 1, 2001, pp. 123–39.

Wallace, Robert C. Letter to I. Goresky. 19 May 1933. Director of Extension: Correspondence, Robert Charles Wallace Papers, Papers of the Presidents, University of Alberta Archives, Edmonton, Alberta, Acc. 3/2/5/2-1.

Wang, Ning. "Rethinking Authenticity in Tourism Experience." *Annals of Tourism Research*, vol. 26, 1999, pp. 349–370.

"War Play at Auditorium Great Success." *Winnipeg Tribune*, 14 May 1934, www.newspapers.com/newspage/39311527/.

Wasserman, Jerry. Introduction to *Counter Offence. Modern Canadian Plays, Vol. 2*, 5th ed., edited by Wasserman, Talon, 2013, p. 135.

Watts-Dunton, Theodore. "In Memorium: Pauline Johnson." *Flint and Feather: Collected Verse*, by E. Pauline Johnson, Musson, 1917. *Project Gutenberg*, www.gutenberg.org /cache/epub/5625/pg5625.

"W.B. Yeats Tells of New School of Dramatic Arts." *Varsity* [University of Toronto student paper], 4 Feb. 1920, p. 1.

Wickenheiser, Carol. Interview with Ian McWilliams, 30 Aug. 2010.

Wilson, David. *Irish Nationalism in Canada*. McGill-Queens UP, 2014.

---. *Thomas D'Arcy McGee*. Vol. I, McGill-Queens UP, 2008.

---. *Thomas D'Arcy McGee*. Vol. II, McGill-Queens UP, 2011.

Winter, Elke. "Bridging Unequal Relations, Ethnic Diversity, and the Dream of Unified Nationhood: Multiculturalism in Canada." *Zeitschrift für Kanada-Studien*, vol. 1, 2007, pp. 38–57.

Writers and Players Club. "Brief to the Royal Commission on National Development in the Arts, Letters and Sciences." Royal Commission on National Development in the Arts, Letters and Sciences 1949–1951, Briefs. *Library and Archives Canada*, www.collectionscanada.gc.ca/massey/h5-319-e.html.

Yaghoubi, Mohammad. "*Iceland* in Toronto: Interview with *Sharvand*." *Sharvand*, 1 Jun. 2017, shahrvand.com/archives/84606.

---. "The Independent Art, the Only Possible Way: Interview with Ayat Mandergar." *Ayat Mandergar*, Mar. 2016, ayatmandergar.ir/fa/news/468.

Yam, J. *Selected Data on the Canadian Population Whose Mother Tongue is Yiddish. Canadian Jewish Population Studies*, vol. 3, no. 2, Dec. 1973. *Berman Jewish Policy Archive*, www.bjpa.org/search-results/publication/20116.

Yee, David. *acquiesce*. Playwrights Canada, 2017. Kindle edition.

Zorc-Maver, Darja, and Igor Maver. "Guillermo Verdecchia and the *Frontera* in Contemporary Canadian Diasporic Writing." *Acta Literaria*, vol. 43, no. 2, 2011, pp. 119–26.

ABOUT THE CONTRIBUTORS

Taiwo Afolabi is a theatre practitioner, educator, and researcher who has undertaken numerous projects in over fifteen countries across four continents. He is a Ph.D. candidate in the Department of Theatre, a Queen Elizabeth Scholar, a Research Associate at the University of Johannesburg, and a Graduate Fellow at the Centre for Global Studies, University of Victoria. Taiwo's doctoral research broadly focuses on forced migration, displacement, and the ethics of community-based research among vulnerable groups such as refugees and internally displaced persons for citizen participation. He founded Theatre Emissary International and co-coordinates the Network of Emerging Arts Professionals of the International Theatre Institute/UNESCO. He holds a B.A. (Hons.) in Theatre Arts and an M.A. in the Performing Arts at the University of Jos and the University of Ilorin, Nigeria, respectively.

Art Babayants is a theatre artist, educator, and researcher who has worked in Canada and abroad. His research looks at the phenomenology of multilingual acting and spectating as well as the concept of multilingual dramaturgy. He has published on the issues of stage multilingualism, diasporic theatre, queer dramaturgy, applied theatre, and contemporary musical theatre; he has also co-edited *Theatre and Learning* (2015) and the special bilingual issue of *Theatre Research in Canada / Recherches théâtrales au Canada* (Fall 2017) dedicated to multilingual theatre in Canada. As a theatre practitioner, Art has presented his work at various Toronto festivals, such as Fringe (2017), SummerWorks (2016), Nuit Blanche (2015), and Caminos (2017). Since 1997, Art has also been developing theatre projects integrating acting and second-language teaching—his most recent ESL/drama creation called Embodied English is a sought-after course for advanced ESL learners. Art holds a lecturer position at the Faculty of Media, Art, and Performance at the University of Regina, Saskatchewan.

Moira Day is a professor of Drama at the University of Saskatchewan, where she also serves as an adjunct member of Women's and Gender Studies, and the Classical, Medieval, and Renaissance Studies Unit. A former co-editor of *Theatre Research in Canada / Recherches théâtrales au Canada*, she has also edited a play anthology featuring the work of pioneering Western Canadian playwright, Elsie Park Gowan, as well as a collection of plays and an anthology of essays on the contemporary theatre in Manitoba, Saskatchewan, and Alberta. She has also co-edited special issues on Canadian Theatre in the Context of World Theatre, and on Religion and Theatre in Canada for *TRIC*, and a special issue, with Mary Blackstone, on contemporary Saskatchewan theatre for *Canadian Theatre Review*. She has published and lectured widely in the field of Canadian theatre, with a particular focus on women and prairie theatre prior to 1960.

David DeGrow is a lighting designer, teacher, and student living in Toronto. He has designed and managed over three hundred productions across Canada. He is a Ph.D. candidate at the University of Toronto's Centre for Drama, Theatre and Performance Studies, where his research focuses on the impact of theatre architecture on the creation and experience of theatre, and on the city around it.

Chilean-born **Lina de Guevara** is a director, actor, and specialist in Transformational Theatre and *commedia dell'arte* and the founder of Puente Theatre in Victoria, BC. She was the theatre's artistic director from its founding in 1988 until retiring in June 2011. Puente's mandate is to create and produce plays about diversity and the immigrant experience. Her directing credits include *Sisters/Strangers, Storytelling Our Lives, I Wasn't Born Here, Crossing Borders, Uthe/Athe, Emergence, Canadian Tango, Scene and Heard*, and many others. Some Canadian and Chilean acting credits include *Alice's Gift*, *From the Heart*, *The Life Inside*, *Happy Days*, *The Glass Menagerie*, and *Mr. Puntilla*. Currently Lina freelances as a director, facilitator, performer, and storyteller. With the Inter-Cultural Association of Greater Victoria (ICA) she continues creating and leading applied-theatre workshops with the objective of easing immigrants' transition into Canadian life.

Alan Filewod is a former Professor of Theatre Studies at the University of Guelph. His books include *Collective Encounters: Documentary Theatre in English Canada* (1987), *Performing "Canada": The Nation Enacted in the Imagined Theatre* (2002), *Workers' Playtime: Theatre and the Labour Movement since 1970* (with David Watt, 2001), *Committing Theatre: Theatre Radicalism and Political Intervention in Canada* (2011), and a critical edition of the banned communist play *Eight Men Speak* (2013). He is a past president of the Association for Canadian Theatre Research and of the Association for Canadian and Quebec Literatures / Association des littératures canadienne et québécoise, and is a former editor of *Canadian Theatre Review*.

Jaswant Guzder is a professor in McGill's Department of Psychiatry as a child psychiatrist, cultural psychiatrist (founding co-director and senior consultant of Cultural Consultation Service) at the Jewish General Hospital, and a visual artist. She has been working with the UWI Jamaica Carimensa team to develop the Dream a World Cultural Therapy project since 2005. Her other global health project work has been mainly in India, Sri Lanka, Turkey, and Nepal. Her teaching and research areas have been involved with high-risk children, cultural psychiatry, refugee health, and personality development. Her academic career includes research, teaching, and training in addition to her continued clinical practice. As an artist she has just completed an art residency and solo exhibit in Rome at the Museo Laboratoria della Mente.

Anita Hallewas is currently undertaking her Ph.D. at UNSW, Australia, with a research focus in refugee theatre, specifically how theatre might improve the quality of life for those living in refugee camps and the ethical implications related to that practice. She is an active applied-theatre practitioner and is the managing artistic director of a theatre company that specializes in applied-theatre programming with a special interest in encouraging intergenerational collaboration. Anita has an M.A. in Applied Theatre from the University of Victoria, Canada, and a B.A. BTech from Deakin Universty, Australia.

Martha Herrera-Lasso is a Ph.D. candidate in Performance Studies from UC Berkeley, has an M.A. in Theatre from the University of British Columbia and a B.A. in Playwriting from the National University in Mexico City (UNAM). She has worked as a playwright, a translator, and a dramaturge across North America, and is interested in reimagining the region as an artist and a scholar. Her current research is concerned with the practical and theoretical implications of international theatre collaborations between Mexico and Québec, read through the politics of linguistic, cultural, and aesthetic translation.

Aida Jordão is a theatre scholar and practitioner with a Ph.D. from the Centre for Drama, Theatre & Performance Studies at the University of Toronto. Her current research, teaching and theatremaking, build on her dissertation, "Inês de Castro in Theatre and Film: A Feminist Exhumation of the Dead Queen," and engage with women-centred plays and Portuguese-Canadian cultural interventions. Aida is also committed to workers' theatre and is the proud recipient of the 2019 Mayworks Artist Award for Excellence in Contribution to Labour Arts. Publications include "The Alt Stage and the Po-mo Page: Canadian Spaces for an Anglo-Portuguese Dramaturgy" in *Theatre Research in Canada* [*TRiC*] 38:2; "Inês de Castro and Saudade in Toronto: O Projecto's Community Play" in *Portuguese Studies Review* 22.2; and the play *Funeral in White* in *Memória: An Anthology of Portuguese Canadian Writers*. Aida teaches at York University and the University of Toronto.

Yasmine Kandil, a native of Egypt, came to Canada in 2003. She has worked with a number of organizations in Victoria, BC, and later in St. Catharines, Ontario, using the arts to collaborate with people who are marginalized. Her areas of research are in celebratory theatre, theatre for development, ethics of applied theatre practice, testimonial theatre, and most recently in curriculum development for police training. Her international interests are focused on the emergence of widespread use of applied theatre techniques in post-revolution Egypt. Yasmine is presently working on a four-year SSHRC project with Dr. Natalie Alvarez and Dr. Jennifer Lavoie looking at the efficacy of scenario-based training in helping police de-escalate people in mental crisis. Yasmine holds an M.F.A. in Theatre Directing and a Ph.D. in Applied Theatre and is presently Assistant Professor of Drama in Education and Applied Theatre at Brock University, Ontario.

Ric Knowles is former editor of *Theatre Journal, Modern Drama,* and *Canadian Theatre Review,* is the author or editor of twenty award-winning books on theatre and performance, and is a practising professional drama-turge. His scholarship and creative practice for the past fifteen years have focused on intercultural performance. In 2017 he was awarded a lifetime achievement award from the Canadian Association for Theatre Research.

Natasha Martina Koechl is Associate Professor in the Department of Drama at the University of Saskatchewan, specializing in movement for actors. She is a Somatic Movement Educator in Body-Mind Centering˚ and a certified Laban Movement Analyst. Her artistic research lies in the creation of orig-inal work through her theatre company Ground Cover Theatre, where it is her mandate to draw upon current issues of debate, because groundbreaking theatre is dependent upon stories that provoke questions and lead if not to new, then at least to deeper insights.

Peter Kuling is Assistant Professor in the Department of Theatre at the University of Ottawa. His research focuses on theatre history and theories of adaptation/intermedia experiences via traditional theatre—Shakespearean drama and Canadian theatre—and unconventional performance venues—YouTube, video games, and professional sports. Themes of sexuality/queerness and national identities emerge throughout his research in these diverse the-atre and performance areas. His work has appeared in different Canadian journals—*Theatre Research in Canada, Canadian Theatre Review*—as well as new collections by Playwrights Canada Press and the Arden Shakespeare series.

Sheetal Lodhia has been working to foster relationships between academic institutions and the world at large, championing interdisciplinarity, collaboration, and broad purchase for knowledge. Sheetal recently completed her term as Executive Director of the Institute for the Public Life of Arts and Ideas (IPLAI) at McGill University and is currently working in the private sector. She is also a board member of Teesri Duniya Theatre. A doctoral graduate in English Literature from Queen's University, she has researched, published, and taught in Renaissance poetry, prose, and drama; the history of medicine; colonialism; and cultural studies. She has produced articles, a video documentary short, art installations, and radio documentaries.

Rebecca Margolis is Associate Professor in the University of Ottawa's Vered Jewish Canadian Studies Program. Her research examines Yiddish as a language and the culture of immigration, ethnicity, and identity in Canadian life. She has published widely on Canadian Yiddish literature, theatre, and film. Her book, *Jewish Roots, Canadian Soil: Yiddish Culture in Montreal, 1905–1945*, deals with the immigrant period. Her forthcoming book, *A Dying Language Lives: Yiddish Transmission in Canada after the Holocaust*, examines publishing, activism, and performance as sites of engagement.

Ian McWilliams holds an Interdisciplinary Ph.D. in Canadian Plains Studies at the University of Regina and researches town hall opera houses and related performative events within late-nineteenth- and early-twentieth-century prairie communities as catalysts and means for placemaking and development of social cohesion in the Canadian West. Currently an Applied Research Facilitator at Saskatchewan Polytechnic, he has also been an instructor at the University of Saskatchewan Department of Drama as well as a researcher for both the Saskatchewan Partnership for Arts Research (SPAR) and the Saskatchewan Arts Alliance (SAA). For the past two decades, Ian has been variously employed as an actor, broadcaster, student, and educator. He earned both his B.F.A. and M.A. at the University of Saskatchewan.

Professor **Yana Meerzon** teaches at the Department of Theatre, University of Ottawa. Her research interests are in drama and performance theory, theatre of exile and migration, and cultural and interdisciplinary studies. Her publications include *A Path of the Character: Michael Chekhov's Inspired Acting and Theatre Semiotics* (2005) and *Performing Exile, Performing Self: Drama, Theatre, Film* (Palgrave 2012). She has also co-edited several collections, such as *Performance, Exile and "America"* (Palgrave 2009); *Adapting Chekhov: The Text and Its Mutations* (Routledge 2012); *History, Memory, Performance* (Palgrave 2015); *The Routledge Companion to Michael Chekhov* (2015); and a special issue of *Theatre Research in Canada* (Fall 2015) and *Modern Drama* (Fall 2018) on theatre and immigration. Currently, she is working on a new book project, provisionally entitled *Being Cosmopolitan: Staging Subjectivity in the Age of Migration and Rising Nationalism.*

Marjan Moosavi is an Iranian-Canadian theatre scholar currently completing her Ph.D. at the University of Toronto's Centre for Drama, Theatre and Performance Studies. Her professional work is rounded out with dramaturgy, dramatic translation, and teaching West Asian and Iranian Theatre. She has articles on Iranian dramaturgy and theatre published in *The Routledge Companion to Dramaturgy, Asian Theatre Journal, The Drama Review, New Theatre Quarterly*, and *Ecumenica*. She is Regional Managing Editor of Iran for *The Theatre Time*. In Spring 2018 she designed and taught the Middle Eastern Theatre course at the University of Toronto and will teach it again in fall 2019. Recently, she has curated the first Photo Exhibition on the Middle Eastern Theatre (1950–1970) and traditional performances from seven countries presented at the University of Toronto's Centre for Drama, Theatre and Performance Studies for three months.

Lisa Ndejuru is a psychotherapist, psychodramatist, and theatre practitioner. Her research-creation explores survival and life, stories and silence, persecution, genocide, war, and dislocation through deep listening, storytelling, and play. She seeks tools and techniques for individual and collective meaning-making and empowerment in the aftermath of large-scale political violence. She holds the 2018/2019 John F. Lemieux Fellowship in Genocide Studies and Human Rights.

Nicole Nolette is the Canada Research Chair in Minority Studies and Assistant Professor at the Department of French Studies at the University of Waterloo. Her book, *Jouer la traduction: Théâtre et hétérolinguisme au Canada francophone*, published with the University of Ottawa Press in 2015, received the Ann Saddlemyer Award from the Canadian Association for Theatre Research in 2016 and the award for the Best Work in Theatre (2014–2016) from the Société québécoise d'études théâtrales. She was a SSHRC Postdoctoral Fellow affiliated with the Cultural Agents Initiative at Harvard University from 2014 to 2016. Since July 2017, she has been French Associate Editor of *Theatre Research in Canada*.

Monica Prendergast is Professor of Drama/Theatre Education in the Department of Curriculum & Instruction at the University of Victoria. Her research interests are varied and include drama-based curriculum and pedagogy, drama/theatre in community contexts, and arts-based qualitative research methods. Dr. Prendergast's theatre and drama books include *Applied Theatre* and *Applied Drama* (both with Juliana Saxton); *Teaching Spectatorship*; *Staging the Not-yet*; and *Drama, Theatre and Performance Education in Canada*. Monica's most recent books are *Web of Performance: An Ensemble Workbook for Youth* (with Will Weigler) and *Portrayals of Teachers and Teaching on Stage and in Film: Dramatic Depictions* (with Diane Conrad). Her CV includes over fifty peer-reviewed journal contributions, numerous chapters, book reviews, and professional contributions. Monica also reviews theatre for CBC Radio Canada and writes a column on theatre for *Focus Magazine*.

Kirsten Sadeghi-Yekta holds a Ph.D. from the University of Manchester, England, and a B.A. and M.A. in Theatre Studies from Utrecht University, the Netherlands. She is a faculty member in the Theatre Department at the University of Victoria, BC. Currently, she is working on her SSHRC Partnership Development Grant and Insight Development Grant on Coast Salish language revitalization through theatre. Her theatre facilitation includes working with children in the Downtown Eastside in Vancouver, young people in Brazilian favelas, young women in rural areas of Cambodia, adolescents in Nicaragua, and students with special needs in the Netherlands.

Jacqueline Taucar received her Ph.D. at University of Toronto's Centre for Drama, Theatre and Performance Studies. Her dissertation, "Acting Out(side) the Multicultural Script in Ethnocultural Festivals," examines popular ethnocultural festivals, including Toronto International Caravan, Caribana/ Caribbean Carnival, and Taste of the Danforth. Jacqueline produces carnival costumes with Louis Saldenah Mas-K's Mas camp, and is currently working on her next project archiving costumes from the first fifty years of Toronto's Caribbean Carnival (Caribana).

Eleanor Ty is Professor of English at Wilfrid Laurier University and a Fulbright Canada Research Chair for 2018–2019. She has published on Asian North American and eighteenth-century British literature. Her book, *Asianfail: Narratives of Disenchantment and the Model Minority* (University of Illinois Press 2017), won the Asian/Pacific American Award for Literature in Adult Non-Fiction for 2017. Author of *Unfastened: Globality and Asian North American Narratives* (University of Minnesota Press 2010); *The Politics of the Visible in Asian North American Narratives* (University of Toronto Press 2004); *Empowering the Feminine: The Narratives of Mary Robinson, Jane West, and Amelia Opie, 1796–1812* (University of Toronto Press 1998); and *Unsex'd Revolutionaries: Five Women Novelists of the 1790s* (University of Toronto Press 1993), she has co-edited two volumes of essays on cultural memory, and two on Asian North American writing.

Rahul Varma is a playwright and artistic director of Teesri Duniya Theatre, which he co-founded in 1981. In 1998, he co-founded the theatre quarterly *alt. theatre: cultural diversity and the stage*. He writes both in Hindi and English, a language he acquired as an adult. Some of his recent plays are *Land Where the Trees Talk*, *No Man's Land*, *Trading Injuries*, *Counter Offence*, *Bhopal*, *Truth and Treason*, and *State of Denial*. Some of his plays have been translated into French, Italian, Hindi, and Punjabi. He is a recipient of the Juror's Award from the Quebec Drama Federation; an award for promoting interculturalism by the Montréal English Critic's Circle; the South Asian Theatre Festival Award; and the Montréal English Theatre Award for Equity, Inclusion, and Diversity. He was a finalist for the QWF Literary Award for Playwriting.

INDEX

First edition: June 2019
Printed and bound in Canada

Cover photo of Christophe Rapin from Orange Noyée's production of *3* by
Mani Soleymanlou. Photo © and provided courtesy of Valérie Remise.
Cover design by Leon Aureus.

**PLAYWRIGHTS
CANADA PRESS**
202-269 Richmond St. W.
Toronto, ON
M5V 1X1

416.703.0013
info@playwrightscanada.com
www.playwrightscanada.com
@playcanpress